THE

MICHAEL ERIC DYSON

READER

ALSO BY MICHAEL ERIC DYSON

Mercy, Mercy Me
Why I Love Black Women
Open Mike
Holler If You Hear Me
I May Not Get There With You
Race Rules
Between God and Gangsta Rap
Making Malcolm
Reflecting Black

THE

MICHAEL ERIC DYSON

READER

———————— *Michael Eric Dyson*

BASIC CIVITAS BOOKS
A MEMBER OF THE PERSEUS BOOKS GROUP
NEW YORK

Books published by Basic Civitas are available at special discounts for bulk purchases in the United States by corporations, institutions, and other organizations. For more information, please contact the Special Markets Department at the Perseus Books Group, 11 Cambridge Center, Cambridge MA 02142, or call (617) 252-5298, (800) 255-1514, or e-mail specialmarkets@perseusbooks.com.

Dyson, Michael Eric.

   [Selections. 2004]

   The Michael Eric Dyson reader / Michael Eric Dyson.

     p. cm.

   Includes bibliographical references.

   ISBN 0-465-01768-1 (alk. paper)

   1. African Americans–Race identity.   2. United States–Race relations. 3. African Americans–Intellectual life.   4. African American philosophy. 5. African Americans–Social conditions–1975- .   6. African Americans in popular culture.   7. Popular culture–United States.   I. Title.

E185.625.D969   2004

305.896'073–dc22

2003017294

04 05 06 / 10 9 8 7 6 5 4 3 2 1

TO TWO EXTRAORDINARY WOMEN

Rosa Elizabeth Smith
(1921-2002)
Beloved matriarch
Wise counselor
Soulful confidante
and
Fiesty Mother-in-law

AND

Judith Rodin
President, the University of Pennsylvania, 1994-2004
Visionary leader
Brilliant thinker
Beautiful woman
and
Dear Friend

THE PARADOX OF EDUCATION IS PRECISELY THIS—THAT AS ONE BEGINS TO BECOME CONSCIOUS ONE BEGINS TO EXAMINE THE SOCIETY IN WHICH HE IS BEING EDUCATED. THE PURPOSE OF EDUCATION, FINALLY, IS TO CREATE IN A PERSON THE ABILITY TO LOOK AT THE WORLD FOR HIMSELF, TO MAKE HIS OWN DECISIONS, TO SAY TO HIMSELF THIS IS BLACK OR THIS IS WHITE, TO DECIDE FOR HIMSELF WHETHER THERE IS A GOD IN HEAVEN OR NOT. TO ASK QUESTIONS OF THE UNIVERSE, AND THEN LEARN TO LIVE WITH THOSE QUESTIONS, IS THE WAY HE ACHIEVES HIS OWN IDENTITY. BUT NO SOCIETY IS REALLY ANXIOUS TO HAVE THAT KIND OF PERSON AROUND. WHAT SOCIETIES REALLY, IDEALLY, WANT IS A CITIZENRY WHICH WILL SIMPLY OBEY THE RULES OF SOCIETY. IF A SOCIETY SUCCEEDS IN THIS, THAT SOCIETY IS ABOUT TO PERISH. THE OBLIGATION OF ANYONE WHO THINKS OF HIMSELF AS RESPONSIBLE IS TO EXAMINE SOCIETY AND TRY TO CHANGE IT AND TO FIGHT IT—AT NO MATTER WHAT RISK.

—James Baldwin

AGAINST THE URGENCY OF PEOPLE DYING IN THE STREETS, WHAT IN GOD'S NAME IS THE POINT OF CULTURAL STUDIES? WHAT IS THE POINT OF THE STUDY OF REPRESENTATIONS, IF THERE IS NO RESPONSE TO THE QUESTION OF WHAT YOU SAY TO SOMEONE WHO WANTS TO KNOW IF THEY SHOULD TAKE A DRUG AND IF THAT MEANS THEY'LL DIE TWO DAYS LATER OR A FEW MONTHS EARLIER? AT THAT POINT, I THINK ANYBODY WHO IS INTO CULTURAL STUDIES SERIOUSLY AS AN INTELLECTUAL PRACTICE, MUST FEEL, ON THEIR PULSE, ITS EPHEMERALITY, ITS INSUBSTANTIALITY, HOW LITTLE IT REGISTERS, HOW LITTLE WE'VE BEEN ABLE TO CHANGE ANYTHING OR GET ANYBODY TO DO ANYTHING. IF YOU DON'T FEEL THAT AS ONE TENSION IN THE WORK THAT YOU ARE DOING, THEORY HAS LET YOU OFF THE HOOK.

—Stuart Hall

CONTENTS

FOREWORD

Robin D. G. Kelley

I first encountered Michael Eric Dyson on the page over ten years ago. I'd seen a few of his essays in *Z Magazine* sometime around 1989 or 1990, but at that time he was virtually unknown (to me, at least, but I was only two years out of graduate school and didn't get out much). Then, in 1993, a copy of his first book, *Reflecting Black: African-American Cultural Criticism,* crossed my desk, and the *Nation* magazine asked me to review it. Although it was a wide-ranging collection of essays, I found the book to be nicely organized, coherent, powerful, and critically relevant to the moment.

The old folks might remember that 1993 was a period when the so-called "black public intellectual" was coming into being, prompted largely by the publication of Cornel West's *Race Matters* that same year. West's collection of essays became a runaway bestseller, opening up critical black radical thought to a wider audience in an age when Los Angeles was still rebuilding from the rebellion of April 1992. But with West's mass appeal came a backlash, from the left and right, against *Race Matters* and everything Professor West stood for. Of course, there were legitimate debates and criticisms that shed light on crucial issues of race, class, gender, and power, but much of the backlash was motivated by jealousy or a confused notion that "real" radicals cannot attract a mass audience without selling out. Indeed, I remember multiple backlashes against black academics, as well as some horrible battles between folks on the page that did not enlighten me or my peers one bit. This was the context in which I read Dyson's first book. In my review in the *Nation* I mentioned the "nasty ad hominem reviews, petty jealousies, blanket condemnations of black scholarship, hateful and sinister commentaries." "As I kick it down here with the ordinary faculty folk," I complained, "writing grant proposals and reading sorry undergraduate essays—and witness the war of words—I have these perverse daydreams of Rodney King pleading with black intellectuals to get along while The Pharcyde, that funny, funky, Thelonious Monk–loving West Coast hip-hop group chant 'Who Is the Nigga in Charge?'"

Dyson's book was a welcome relief from the wars of blackademe. Of course, he had his own debates to wage and own axes to grind, but for the most part he wrote about black people, what we've created, what we've come to represent, and why we should not be too quick to make snap judgments about what is "authentically black." He warned against blind "race loyalty" and insisted that real liberation requires independent thinking and a willingness to criticize black leaders, intellectuals, and cultural heroes. His voice was fresh, his language vibrant, and to top it all off, he was a working-class kid from Detroit committed to activism and the social gospel. "Evident in every essay," I observed at the time, "is a belief that the Gospel is a lived struggle, not merely a popular compilation of writings, folklore, and pithy slogans separate from everyday life. Thus Dyson, like Cornel West, is concerned with what he sees as a spiritual crisis in America, especially among young people. But rather than follow the common trend nowadays of chastising African-American youth for relinquishing some golden-age spirituality and ethics of their parents' generation, he seeks signs of the spirit in various secular cultural forms. Spirituality, Dyson recognizes, may be in crisis, but it ain't gone. It looks different, and if we are going to locate it we must use different interpretive tools."

So before I even met the man, I knew there was something special about him. Given his writing style at the time, I imagined him to be a modern-day holy man, meditative, contemplative, deeply spiritual. He probably talked slow like the old preachers, but he was only thirty-four years old. When I finally did meet him, a few weeks after the review appeared in the *Nation*, I wasn't prepared for this tornado of a man who spoke faster than the speed of light and dropped more one-liners than Richard Pryor on a good night. He was as agile with Western philosophy as he was with soul, R&B, and hip-hop. It was as if W.E.B. DuBois and Fab Five Freddy had been merged together in some Frankensteinian experiment. And through it all, his lovely and brilliant wife, Marcia Dyson, kept him on the ground and balanced. Both kept us in stitches. I laughed so much and learned so much that night that the muscles in the back of my head cramped up.

The Michael Eric Dyson Reader will have some skeptics, to be sure. How could anyone who experienced such a meteoric rise—from pastor to Ph.D. candidate to Distinguished Professor in a little over a decade—claim to have produced enough for a "reader"? He has published eight books in that short period, and he has more in press soon to see the light of day. And if you put this book on the scale, you'll see that this carefully selected fraction of his output competes in the heavyweight division. Nevertheless, quantity isn't everything, and his detractors will continue to call him names like "race hustler" and "charlatan" and related adjectives that suggest that Dyson doesn't do his work and just slides by on his quick wit and glib tongue. (While I vehemently disagree with these assessments, I have thought of Michael at times as somewhat of a magician; he has an uncanny ability to pull lyrics and quotes and dictionary definitions out of his head, and the story of how he produced his dissertation, told in the first chapter of the *Reader*, is worthy of David Blaine.)

The truth is, Michael Eric Dyson is an incredibly hardworking intellectual, one who is on a mission to inspire the rest of us to remake the world. Most people, fans and critics alike, don't realize how hard he works because he makes it look easy and he writes a lot without footnotes. But dig deeper and one quickly realizes that beneath the surface of his wit and humor one finds intellectual depth, scholarly integrity, and a startling level of erudition. As the works included here reveal, Dyson is one of the few scholars in the country who can honestly be called multidisciplinary. His books and essays on black cultural production draw on the most sophisticated literary and cultural criticism, critical theory, sociology, ethnography, and history, and he brings to his work a rich and varied understanding of music and music criticism. What's more, Dyson has been able to write for a general audience without minimizing his scholarly tone and rigor.

His essays selected here examine a wide terrain of culture, politics, and social criticism, and nearly all of his work is policy-oriented, immediate, and, I might add, politically engaged. His essays should be read as efforts to understand the plight of aggrieved populations—notably black working people, youth, and women—and how their lives and cultures speak to the conditions they face. On the other hand, he insists that people take responsibility for their behavior and criticizes black institutions for failing black communities. His essays on the Black Church, for example, are bold challenges to the failure of black clerical leadership and the apparent moral hypocrisy running through contemporary institutionalized religion. He had nothing to gain by writing these pieces, and they are well-documented and well-argued, and have played a crucial role in placing behind-the-scenes debates into a wider realm. The same goes for his scintillating work on black public intellectuals. He takes no prisoners, on the one hand, and yet offers smart, concise commentary on the debate over black intellectuals that takes a long, historical view of the work they have done over the past century. The "Coda," in particular, is not a self-congratulatory essay but a call to arms, one that demands political engagement as a component of our intellectual work. Finally, for all the efforts to place music and other cultural forms within particular antiracist, class-conscious contexts, to see contemporary black culture as subaltern social struggles generated by racist backlash, poverty, and Reaganomics, Dyson refuses to over-interpret or romanticize. Nor does he accept the dualism of "nihilism" vs. "black radicalism" that has frozen too many writers.

As his work on Malcolm X and other political and cultural icons demonstrates, Dyson has a gift for grasping the politics of representation. Rather than quibble over the details of Malcolm's life or his self-representation, Dyson chooses wisely to pay more attention to the meaning of Malcolm X for our time, whether in the academy or the theater. He succinctly captures what Malcolm, the icon, has meant to a rising generation of black nationalists. Unlike other commentators who dismiss African-American youth wearing X-hats as suffering from an infantile disorder, Dyson tries to make sense of these young people within the context of their time. He does not try to speak for them but allows them to speak for themselves. As he makes abundantly clear, the rise of hip-hop culture, the resurgence of black nationalism, and the success of *New Jack* and ghettocentric filmmakers are largely responsible for the return of the fallen minister to the pantheon of black heroes.

Ironically, the work that is represented with only one excerpt here happens to be my personal favorite: *I May Not Get There With You: The True Martin Luther King, Jr.*

(2000). I urge all of you who hold this book in your hand to add Dyson's masterful study of Dr. King to your collection. He doesn't attempt to find the "real" King, but he does juxtapose the ways in which he's used politically (especially by right-wing anti–Civil Rights activists, black nationalists, hip-hop generation youths, corporate America, etc.) with King's own words, actions, and the movement histories on which we've come to rely. He delves deeply into primary and secondary sources and is not afraid to examine controversial issues such as King's sexual liaisons, patriarchal attitudes, and his left-wing turn. He succeeds in toppling the icon of King and puts in his place a human being replete with flaws, weaknesses, and youthful exuberance. In a world where Malcolm X is often promoted as the embodiment of postwar black radicalism and King regarded as a safe voice in the wilderness, Dyson demonstrates just how his socialist, class, and antiwar politics persuaded the Civil Rights establishment to more or less silence him. And it was that silence, that suppression of history, which allowed conservatives and corporate leaders to claim King's message as their own. While Dyson received a great deal of (unfair) criticism for his willingness to deal with King's sexual escapades and missteps, to me this is one of the strengths of the book and of all of Dyson's scholarship. Rather than suppress or ignore what we don't like or what we might think is not relevant to the "real" King, Dyson embraces it, dissects, and tries to understand in the time and place of his subject, not from a presentist standpoint.

This is what Dyson is all about; it is a quality of his writing and speaking that I recognized ten years ago, and it is as strong as ever. He is willing to take the criticisms, the ribbing, the ridicule, because in the end speaking truth to power and standing up for justice is far more important than garnering good reviews and friends in high places. Among black academics, the battle royale still rages, but Dyson doesn't jump into those three rings. Instead, he's working his ass off trying to give white supremacy—and patriarchy, and classism, and youth bashing—a black eye.

PREFACE

Over the last fifteen years, I have had the extraordinary privilege to be an academic and a public intellectual—an engaged and politically active scholar devoted to changing the world as best I can with the gifts at hand. I was the first person in my family to have the opportunity to pursue higher education and to live the life of the mind. For ten years now, I have had a Ph.D. I believe that obligates me, as a member of a historically oppressed group, to pursue social justice for those who have been closed away from school doors and the halls of economic opportunity for far too long. But my privilege also summons me to think sharply and substantively about a wide range of intellectual issues, and to address the social and moral crises of the culture. I have never, not for even a second, believed that one couldn't at the same time be smart and good, informed and involved, thoughtful and active. They are for me flip sides of the same vocational coin.

For the last twenty-five years, I have had the high honor to be called "Reverend Dyson." I found my calling in a black Baptist church in Detroit whose ministry prized intellectual preparation as the hallmark of faithful service. Although tough circumstances meant that I didn't enroll in college until I was twenty-one, I learned very early—from my mother, Addie Mae; from my Sunday School instructors at church; and from my public school teachers—that education is the doorway to life and liberty. In my case, it was as well a path to a sense of ministry that embraces the head and heart. Even though I haven't been a parish minister for twenty years now, I consider my role as an engaged intellectual the extension of my calling to "preach the gospel to the poor," and to "heal the broken-hearted, to preach deliverance to the captives, and recovering of sight to the blind, to set at liberty them that are bruised."

Since my second year of graduate school, I have written professionally for a wide range of academic and popular journals, magazines, and newspapers. During the last decade, I have also published eight books—some with scholars in mind, others aimed at a literate general public—all with the intent of reflecting on important and interesting topics in the life of the mind, the life of the soul, the life of the race, and the life of the nation. Because of my writing, I have lectured at universities and in union halls; held forth in junior colleges and in juvenile detention centers; preached in churches and in synagogues, temples, and mosques; addressed civil rights groups and professional gatherings; spoken to public and private grade schools, middle schools, and high schools; engaged adults and adolescents in jails and prisons across America; and traveled over water to deliver talks in Italy and Brazil, in Amsterdam and in Cuba, and in Jamaica and the Bahamas. It is also because of my writing that I have appeared across the mediascape on radio and television programs throughout the land—and in cyberspace—to debate current affairs and pressing social issues, and to hold up the banner of progressive politics. In my mind, writing is thinking, struggling, fighting, imagining, loving, hoping, preaching, crying, wishing, and inspiring, all at once.

This book charts the geography of my intellectual journey. It maps the regions of my intellectual interests—religion and philosophy, race theory and rap music, masculinity and multiculturalism, feminist thought and gender relations, black identity and popular culture, moral thought and sexuality, cultural criticism and critical theory, intellectual life and institutional racism, soul music and jazz history, black film and postmodernism, and a great deal besides. This reader is a diagram as well of the intellectual and rhetorical treasures I have mined over the years and a record of the struggles I have waged to understand better, to think deeper, and to write clearer about matters of life and death. What guides all of my thought and action is the belief that human beings who think creatively and act boldly can shape history and relieve suffering for the good of the neighborhood and the planet. I hope you, the reader, enjoy this reader, and journey with me through the intellectual and political wilderness of our international life in the hopes of finding a city of moral beauty and justice for all.

As a pledge of my citizenship in such a city, I would like to thank those who have helped me along the way. I would like to thank my wonderful editor Liz Maguire, my dear friend and intellectual compatriot who works with me to realize my vision in print. I would also like to thank Megan Hustad for all her concern and hard work. I would also like to thank Kay Mariea and her team who worked diligently and expertly to make this book appear. I would also like to thank my Penn family for their love and support, especially Tukufu Zuberi, Ann Matter, Sam Preston, Gale Garrison, Carol Davis, Onyx Finney, Marie Hudson—and, of course, Judith Rodin, our leader who we all love and miss already, and who is one-half of the dynamic duo to whom I dedicate this book. Finally, I would like to thank my family—Marcia (who, as usual, sacrificed greatly and put aside her own work to read mine; thanks so much), Michael, Maisha, and Mwata, and my mother, Addie Mae Dyson, and my brothers, Anthony, Gregory, and Brian—for their love and support. And to Everett Dyson-Bey, my brilliant and courageous brother who remains incarcerated after fifteen years, I pray for your imminent release and return to your family and to your work of enlightening and uplifting the world. And to Doc, Marcia, Beverly, Elaine, Geraldine, Jimmy, and Robert—with the memory of "Smally" and Michelle never far away—I hope the dedication of this book to your magnificent wife and beloved mother, Rosa Elizabeth Smith, acknowledges how much we all miss her big heart, her big smile, and her big spirit.

INTRODUCTION:
WHY I AM AN INTELLECTUAL

I can't remember when I decided I wanted to be an intellectual. I'm not even sure if that's the sort of thing one fully determines before it happens. For that matter, I can't remember when I *became* an intellectual–a person with a great passion to think and study and to distribute the fruits of his labor in useful form. There was no bolt of lightning for me; unlike St. Paul, I didn't have a dramatic conversion that saved me from ignorance and put me on a path of learning. It simply dawned on me in my various pursuits–as grade school spelling bee champ, as junior high school orator, as high school renegade who skipped class in search of better education, as factory laborer who preferred books to welding, and as a failed pastor who returned to college to complete my degree before heading to graduate school–that I had a calling to what Hannah Arendt gracefully termed "the life of the mind."

I do remember when I became an academic–a scholar who makes a living as an intellectual in higher education. Already I've used terms that some see as roughly equivalent, but one might quibble with such a view. Not to be catty, but there are differences in the terms used to describe what people do who operate in higher education. An *academic* toils in the vineyards of higher learning, usually as a teacher who may also focus on research. A *scholar* is an academic (only in this case, since I'm referring to those who function within the academy; of course, there are many scholars who work outside of its precincts) whose focus is on research. And an *intellectual* in higher education is an academic or scholar who swims beyond her specialty and embraces the surging waves of knowledge as they wash against entrenched disciplines. It should be obvious that my take on the distinctions between academics, intellectuals, and scholars is quite subjective and more anecdotal than analytical. Of course, there's no linguistic cop watching over these definitions to keep them from being mixed. No science lies behind my observation, except, of course, the science of observation.

There is no great advantage in admitting that one is, or wants to be, an intellectual. (For confirmation, one need only look at politics, where the current occupant of the White House got big campaign returns on depicting his opponent as an egghead elitist, even as he shrewdly played up his own bum-fumbling everydayness to identify with "the folk" and to preemptively strike against those who protested his lack of intellectual fitness for office.) Nevertheless, on a day-to-day basis, an intellectual is what I am–though, it must be noted, an intellectual whose baptism in black religion shows up decisively in my work. But since I've been booted out of the pastorate of a black church for attempting to ordain women, and given that my extremely liberal views on homosexuality run counter to the received wisdom of black theological lights, I must confess that my version of the faith might provoke as many cries of heresy as it may win converts. I've taken to pulpits around the nation for a quarter century to proclaim my vision of the gospel, one whose keystones are social revolution, racial and economic equality, intergenerational understanding, and gender and sexual justice.

Except it's nearly as tough these days being a preacher as it is being an intellectual, particularly with the ignorance that parades under the banner of religious belief. (Witness the attempt of a self-proclaimed God-fearing chief judge to plop down a two-ton replica of the Ten Commandments in a Montgomery, Alabama, courthouse, surrounded by a cloud of witnesses unified in their bitter opposition to secularists and errant believers like me who feel that God doesn't need the protection of the state. And all of this, mind you, at the time of the fortieth anniversary of the 1963 March on Washington, whose leader, the Rev. Martin Luther King, Jr., faced violent opposition to civil rights in Montgomery, *in the name of God*, from the ancestors of some of the same folk who now want to ram their view of God down the throats of their fellow citizens. Besides, many of the protesters—supporters, no doubt, of the death penalty—wouldn't wish officers of the court and justice system to obey at least one of the commandments, to wit, not to kill. Maybe that's why King, an ordained Baptist pastor, was adamantly opposed to school prayer: he knew that many of the same folk who claimed to love God would just as well send some of God's "other" children—those who don't share their faith or even their race or nationality or politics—straight to hell.)

My religious background has a lot to do with how I see the life of the mind: not as career but vocation, and not as a pursuit isolated from the joy and grief of ordinary folk, but as a calling to help hurting humanity. I suppose, in retrospect, it would be fair to say that one of the reasons I became an intellectual was to talk back to suffering—and if possible, to relieve it. I wanted to be as smart as I could be about the pain and heartache of people I knew were unjustly oppressed. First off, there were the poor, working poor, and working-class black folk I saw in my own tribe and in the ghetto neighborhoods I lived in. Later, as I matured and traveled around the country, there were the people who suffered because of the skin or class into which they were born, or the way they had sex, or the way they thought about it. And finally, as I have learned the world, there are the folk on whom brutality descends because of their color, their native tongue, their religion, or the region of land to which their lives are staked.

Of course, these might be good reasons for becoming a minister, that is, if you embrace a social gospel, one that cares about people's bodies and health and housing as much as it attends to their souls. But to many, these are poor grounds on which to base an intellectual life. For me they spring from the same soil. The intellectuals I admire most are just as eager to preach resistance to ignorance, pain, and yes, evil, as evangelists are to promulgate spiritual salvation. I haven't the slightest interest in using my academic perch to proselytize students or colleagues to my way of thinking about God. (Get me in a pulpit, and it's a different matter altogether, although I am now far less interested in saving men's souls from the hell to come as I am in inspiring my listeners to relieve the suffering of victims who live in hell in Detroit or Delhi.) In fact, some of the thinkers and activists I am in lockstep with about the way the world should go share nothing of my church or the Bible on which it rests. And, by turn, some of the same folk who share communion with me would just as soon see my way of thinking about race and politics perish in holy flames. (If I had to choose, I'd rather sink with atheists who say they don't believe in God, yet love God's children, and show it with the work they do and in their compassion for the vulnerable, than rise with believers whose view of God is shriveled and vicious, and who punish others, and themselves, ultimately, with hard-hearted moralizing, and a cruel indifference to the suffering of the unwashed that grows from the despotic ill-temperedness of the self-righteous.)

Intellectuals have an obligation to be as smart as we can possibly be, but we have an even greater obligation to be good with the smarts we possess. We don't have to apologize for not being factory laborers, sanitation workers, or even politicians. There's no shame in thinking well about the mathematics of black holes or the theory of social privilege, about the biology of evolution or the chemistry of genetic inheritance, about the philosophy of gender or the psychology of race, since they contribute to the knowledge of ourselves and the world we inhabit. But as for me and my house—those whose intellectual work takes a public bent, and whose knowledge can combat the plagues on our social and moral lives, and on our physical existence, too—we must consider the plight of factory laborers and sanitation workers. We've got to think about those who work under depressing and alienating conditions, and who suffer assaults on their worth in economies that ignore or exploit them. While a laundry list of oppressions, brutalities, and sufferings is hardly sufficient, it may be a necessary start to healing the ills of our fellow man and woman. Those who hurt because of race, class, sexuality, gender, age, health, environment, disability, religion, region, and the like must disturb intellectuals into action.

If the goal is to do more than recite such lists, then intellectuals must join the struggle to aid the vulnerable. I got the notion that struggle is key to the intellectual's vocation from the communities I grew up in. In the fifth grade, I was transformed by the teaching of Mrs. James, mostly because she helped her students see themselves in a fresh and powerful racial light. My birth certificate says I'm a Negro, like all birth certificates of colored children born as I was in the late fifties. But Mrs. James helped us to shed old definitions and to embrace a new grammar of self-respect tied to what soul singer Curtis Mayfield called "a choice of colors." She convinced us that we were black, not colored or Negro. Although what Malcolm X derisively called the "so-called Negro revolution" had altered the fate of millions of black bodies, it hadn't changed nearly as many minds. Black was still considered an epithet among many Negroes, especially those who resented the kinky hairstyles and African pendants and clothing adopted by the youth. On many a day I heard black folk repeat a saw they didn't realize cut their psyches and history in half: "Don't call me black; I ain't no African." To an outsider, and even to some of us on the inside, it was tricky trying to negotiate the terms that flocked to our identities. And there were quite a few choices, including colored, Negro, black, Afro-American, and later, of course, African-American. Which one you answered to depended a lot on how old you were, what part of the country you lived in, and how willing you were to examine yourself in the wake of a huge change in social status. Mrs. James took us on a whirlwind tour of black struggle. She took special delight in pointing out the exuberant champions of our survival: ministers and cowboys, lawyers and seamstresses, secretaries and inventors, railroad workers and politicians, folk who used their minds, pens, feet, mouths, and deeds to prove that we weren't savages or coons and that we deserved respect for our intelligence and morality. At the very least, their example showed that we were the equals of our condescending "saviors."

In unfolding her lesson plan, Mrs. James persuaded me that my skills and talents, like those of our leaders, must help the struggle for black freedom. As long as I have understood what an intellectual is—especially one who rises from a people for whom history is not a blackboard, like it is for those with power, but a skuzzy washrag with grime and stains—I have believed that she should combat half-truths about the people she loves. To skeptics, that smacks of provincialism, propaganda, and the hijacking of knowledge for ethnic therapy and consolation. To be sure, if that's what we end up with, we're mere replicas of the very forces we decry as inexorably biased. But such fear is relieved when we consider the context in which our intellectual lives play out. The life of the mind is tied to the public good, and unavoidably, at least initially, the promise of this good is defined by the well-being of *my* tribe and kin. If there are insuperable barriers to our getting a fair share of what everyone deserves, the public good is diminished. Under these circumstances, it is, at best, a disappointing abstraction of a social ideal that is placed unjustly beyond our reach. The identification of the public good with what's good for my group has limits and dangers, of course, since at times the public good may run counter to my group's benefit. In fact, in many instances— say, when the Voting Rights Act undercut the monopoly on political power for Southern whites, or when the Equal Rights Amendment gave women the chance to compete with men for jobs—the public good was served by cutting off an unjust group privilege. We have to be willing to wish for every other group what we wish for our own if we are to make the identification of the public good with the good of our group work. The public good is hampered when we idolize our slice of the social welfare and elevate our group above all others in the political order. Such a thing is bad enough if groups simply aspire to unjust social dominance, but if they've got the power to get it done, it greatly harms the commonweal.

If I say that as an intellectual I want to tell the truth about black culture and the folk I love, and thus contribute to the black freedom struggle, I'm not seeking to hog the social good for my group. I simply want to make society better by improving the plight of black and other oppressed people. Our plight affects the whole: if we prosper, society is better; if we go down, the larger culture suffers as well. It's just as harmful for our society to embrace misinformation and half-truth about black folk as it is for blacks to keep silent about it. On that misinformation and half-truth rests public policies and social theories that take a yeoman's intellectual effort to erode even a little. God knows what effort is needed to fight centuries of racial distortion and the fear of black identity fueled by stereotypes, myths, and outright lies. The struggle to specify the complex character of black life—how it is far more flexible, durable, and intricate, and contradictory and elusive too, than is usually acknowledged, even among some blacks—is part of the black freedom struggle too. Protest marches were crucial to our liberation; sit-ins and boycotts were fundamental to our freedom; and the court brief was decisive in striking down legal barriers to our social flourishing. But the will to clarify our aims and examine our identity is, in its own way, just as important to our freedom as the blows struck in our defense by revolutionary stalwarts. Neither does love cancel out criticism; nor should it prevent black intellectuals from publicly discussing hard truths about black life that might embarrass or anger us. The role of the black intellectual is to discover, uncover, and recover truth as best we can, and to subject our efforts to healthy debate and examination. I learned from Malcolm X in particular that the black freedom struggle is no good without self-criticism and holding each other morally accountable.

It must be admitted that the black intellectual is sometimes wary of being candid about our blemishes because the nation is in chronic denial about its flaws, even as it can't seem to get enough of cataloguing black failure. That's why the black intellectual's desire to tell the truth is seen by many blacks as naive and traitorous. To make matters worse, some mainstream critics argue that black intellectuals pollute the quest for truth and knowledge when they use it to fight oppression. But if we're honest, we'll admit that the quest for truth and knowledge is never free of social and cultural intrusions. Knowledge and truth are never divorced from the ends for which they exist. Even those drunk on a belief in objectivity must acknowledge that culture and custom are at war with the idea of an unchanging reality that transcends our means to know it. That doesn't mean that anything goes, that there are no moral landmarks to which we can point, that tradition must be jettisoned and history arbitrarily revised, that truth is up for grabs to the highest intellectual bidder, or that knowledge is hostage to emotion.

And neither am I trying to sidestep the paradox of the pursuit of knowledge for its own sake. It is important, however, to rigorously question such an ideal; it is much more difficult to achieve than we might imagine. Even when it looks as if someone has successfully pulled it off—for instance, when Einstein huddled in a Berne patent office to tackle Brownian motion and the theory of relativity—we must look deeper. Einstein had no idea that he would be called upon to follow the trail of his discovery to the killing grounds of Hiroshima and Nagasaki. And even if we say that Einstein simply wanted to figure out the relationship of space and time for knowledge's sake, that turns out not to be true either. He had bigger fish to fry: through knowing the relation of time to space, Einstein wanted to know how reason ordered the universe. That's why he famously disputed the view of indeterminacy put forth by Heisenberg in his uncertainty principle by declaring, "God does not play dice with the universe." What Einstein's example proves is that hardly anyone pursues knowledge for its own sake, not now at least, and not in our culture, even when they believe they do. We want to know things because we want to do better, be better, or get better—or to do awful, hateful things to our fellow citizens, to get back at traitors, to punish enemies, and to exact revenge on conquerors.

Of course, the sheer pleasure of knowledge, of engaging great ideas and wrestling with great thinkers, is not in dispute—Socrates's dialogues, Shakespeare's sonnets, Beethoven's concertos, Newton's calculus, Douglass's autobiographies, all have great intrinsic worth. I am not arguing for a crude instrumentalism to every bit of knowledge; nor am I saying that every fact has to fit in place and serve a concrete function. That sort of thinking suits a mechanical view of the world long since demolished by science and common sense. There is something ennobling about reading lovely sentences that hang together because of poetry and penetrating thought. There is, too, genuine joy in noting the elegance of a mathematical equation. All of these good things need no justification outside of the fact of their existence; their goodness is the reason for their existence, and vice versa. But the pursuit of knowledge for its own sake can only be a good thing when it is a possibility for everyone. Knowledge, after all, is not neutral, neither the getting of it nor the keeping of it, or even the uses of it.

Besides the pleasures it brings, knowledge can also be dangerous, subversive, and liberating. That's why slaves were legally prevented from reading; that's also why tyrants and their governments are afraid of literate dissenters. Under tyranny, and in many ostensibly free societies, reading and writing always mean so much more than reading and writing. Even though, despite widespread misquotation, Foucault never said it, and in fact meant quite the opposite, knowledge *is* power, at least a kind of power that is instantly recognized, even when it's in the hands of the dispossessed. Dictators and demagogues alike realize that knowledge for its own sake never manages to end there. When I get knowledge, I get desire: I get hungry for the same liberty I find in the books I read, the science I study, the music I hear. I want my society as eloquent as the poetry I memorize. I want my living conditions to match the beauty of the algebraic formula I work. I want my people as blissful and harmonious as the symphony I listen to. I may also want to stamp out the horrors I read about, put an end to the suffering I hear in the music of the desperate, or use what I know to help the subjugated. I might get inspired or enraged, mad or distraught, stumped or determined to act.

Try as we might to quarantine knowledge, it invariably sneezes on us far beyond its imposed limits. Knowledge exists for a lot more than its own sake. The proponents of social injustice, whether in America or Eastern Europe, understand this all too well, but so do their victims. It's where Langston Hughes reaches across space and time to embrace Vaclav Havel. It's also why Frederick Douglass said that "knowledge unfits a child to be a slave." Or, as George Clinton memorably phrased it, "free your mind, and your ass will follow." As an end in itself, knowledge has much to recommend to the eager pursuer of truth, but even the questions one wants answered—what is truth? does God exist? how should I treat my fellow man? am I my neighbor's keeper?—say as much about us as about the curiosity that drives us. We've got questions for reasons, and those reasons are often bigger than mere curiosity or knowledge for its own sake. What's often at stake is our identity, our sanity, our souls, our survival.

The pursuit of knowledge for its own sake can only make sense in a society where knowledge, at least the ownership of it, makes no moral difference, and where learning and thinking lack political value. I'm not saying that we live in an Orwellian nightmare where free thought is corrupted and suppressed. Neither am I saying that we live in a nation where thinking is only politically useful if it supports the interests of the state. But the liberty to think out loud as one wishes to, without qualification or permission, is pretty rare, even in our society, and where such freedom exists, it's the result of vigilant effort to unmask the official story, the enshrined truth. The freedom to pursue truth wherever it leads, at least in social and political terms, depends on where you stand in the culture and how much clout you have. A real freethinker can be shunned or silenced for straying too far from the nation's political consensus. If, for example, one runs afoul of the attorney general's pulverizing views of how terror should be defined and fought, he might be harassed, stigmatized, or arrested. Knowledge is never just knowledge, it can never simply be pursued without regard to context, and its results are just as likely to upset as to unify us. All of which is to say that the black intellectual, without even trying, is a threat to a society that subordinates his people. There is little choice as to whether the black intellectual is involved in the struggle of black folk; to be alive and black makes one a candidate for social animus, and thus, a player in the theater of race.

I learned this lesson in Mrs. James's classroom and in the factories where I worked before eventually going to college when I was twenty-one. My longest tenure came in the wheel brake and drum factory where my father labored for more than thirty years before being laid off and forced into maintenance work and odd jobs, from painting houses to cutting grass and laying sod, all of which his five sons joined him in. My father worked long, long hours. He got as much overtime as he could to feed seven mouths and to tamp down the criminal allure of the ghetto streets for his boys. Detroit was then known as the "murder capital of the world," and the grisly homicide rate rode largely on the decimation of black flesh in drug deals and acts motivated by severe privation. Both of these forces loomed in the lives of our neighbors, and eventually, struck our own house when, after our father's death, my younger brother got sent to prison for second-degree murder, accused of killing a fellow drug dealer. My father and mother waged soul-depleting war against the violence that surrounded us, holding out the prospect of hard work as the antidote to the devil's temptations.

Taking note of, but not completely understanding, and hence, not unqualifiedly supporting my intellectual bent, my father nevertheless brought home encouragement in the form of factory laborers he discovered were also attending college or liked books like me. They were usually young, black (sometimes African) male workers who saw the factory as a means to a larger end: enjoying upward mobility, bettering the lot of their family, financing college, and, in some cases, bringing the worker's revolution closer to fulfillment. These men were usually active in the same United Auto Workers (UAW) union where my father was a member. This was in the late sixties and early seventies, when the League of Revolutionary Black Workers (LRBW) and Dodge Revolutionary Union Movement (DRUM) were agitating for social change in the Detroit automobile factories that were the bloodline for the big three car companies: General Motors, Chrysler, and Ford. I picked up some of their fervor during impromptu political lessons taught by my father's co-workers on the lunch breaks they often spent at our house during the afternoon shift. At other times, I caught dramatic glimpses of the social agenda of black laborers when my father and his besieged co-workers walked the picket line outside their company to demand higher wages and better benefits.

Later, when I went to work in the factory as a teen father fending off welfare, and with the hope of saving money for college, I got provocative instruction from workers who drilled the point in my head: learning is for liberation, and knowledge must be turned to social benefit if we are to justify the faith placed in us by our forbears. In between unloading brake drums, and welding and balancing them, I got a strong dose of Marxism, but a homegrown version attuned to the gritty particularities of black working life. That didn't mean there wasn't high theory; there was theory aplenty, though it was tailored to our needs and driven by our aspirations as a degraded and oppressed people—but a people who resolved to rise up from their suffering through self-determining struggle. I was awed by these grassroots intellectuals who stood their ground and defended their lives with their brains and words. There wasn't even a hint of anti-intellectualism among them. They didn't pooh-pooh self-criticism like some do in the highest rungs of government, saloons, malls, some sidewalk streets—and in major parts of the media.

The factory wasn't the only place I got a sense of intellectual vocation. I absorbed it in the sanctuary as well. My pastor, Frederick G. Sampson, was an American original, a tall, commanding, impossibly literate dark-brown prince of the pulpit who lived up to that title when it still resonated in the world of homiletics. It was Sampson, more than any figure in my life, who convinced me of the service that intellectuals must render. Sampson believed that those who breathed the life of the mind must serve the people in whose womb they came to exist. His thinking made sense to me because of how faithfully he adhered to his own principle. He wasn't a preacher who festooned his pulpit oratory with violent grunts or theatrical posing, though he was a verbal master with dramatic flair. Sampson unabashedly laced his rhetoric with the theology and poetry and philosophy he ardently consumed. In the pulpit, he moved effortlessly from Bertrand Russell to W.E.B. Du Bois, from Shakespeare to Paul Laurence Dunbar, and from the King's English spoken to the Queen's taste to the wily black vernaculars that bathed the tongues of his Southern kinsmen. Outside the pulpit, Sampson's insatiable curiosity lead him to devour books and to traffic in ideas, wherever he could get good ones, whether from the mouth of a learned colleague or the neighborhood drunk. Critical encounter was nearly erotic to him, but the joy and passion he brought to intellectual life didn't obscure its necessary everydayness, its practical application, its edifying repetitiveness, and most of all, its usefulness to common folk.

Sampson believed that his preaching and thinking should open the minds and hearts of the people who listened to him. They should, he believed, find surer footing in their faith because of the words he carefully chose. At the same time, he challenged the dogmatisms of all true believers, whether they were pew dwellers or zealous ideologues. Sampson stirred things up by staring them down: he refused to blink away the encroaching doubts that made belief improbable to outsiders (and to more insiders than were willing to admit it), inviting his flock to wrestle with feelings of divine abandonment and the unanswerable tragedies that smear our existence. But none of this kept him from making the church a conduit of social justice for ordinary folk who might never darken the doors of his sanctuary. And above all, he believed that the black privileged should use their considerable economic and intellectual resources to help those who lag far behind.

It is because of Sampson that I believe that intellectuals must serve the communities we live and work in. We've got to look beyond a comfortable career, a safe niche behind academe's protective walls, and a serene existence removed from cultural and political battles that shape the nation's fate. But we must be willing to shirk the contemptuous pose of distant observer—undoubtedly, we still need observation, and it mustn't be fatally intertwined in the events or ideas we're called on to examine, but intellectuals must at some point get our hands dirty as we help our world become more just. We must even be willing to give up one of academe's most self-serving bombasts: that "serious" thinkers stand apart from the seductions of pop culture to dig into archives and render compelling histories of events long before our time. That's all good, but it's surely not all-knowing about what intellectuals are good for. In a show of remarkable adolescence, and obsolescence too, there are many academics who believe that speaking in the tongue of the common person betrays the profession. Well, perhaps that's so, but it's a betrayal we should be proud of, and one that should spur us to resist the tedius professionalism that has noisily ripped through the academy's upper ranks. (That's largely not the case for the thousands upon thousands of part-time teachers whose plight is barely distinguishable from any group of maligned workers, and the battalion of non-unionized graduate students who are depended on to teach vast numbers of American undergraduates.)

It was Jesse Jackson who once remarked to me, "If you say something I can't understand, that's a failure of *your* education, not mine," and he was right. No sloppy thinker or lazy rhetorician himself, Jackson knows the intellectual effort it takes to understand an idea so well that one can explain it to the learned and the layman alike. To paraphrase Ecclesiastes, there is a time and place for every academic language under the sun—and for the jargons, obscurantisms, esoterica, dialects, glosses, and inside meanings that attend their path. But there is also the need to write and speak clearly about important matters for the masses of folk who will never make it to class.

There is in the academy today something akin to hip-hop's vexing quest for the rapper who can "keep it real," that is, the rapper who best matches his lyrics with a life of crime or ghetto glory, depending on which version of reality wins the day. Many academics are caught up in trying to prove who's more authentic, who's more academically hard core, who's the realest smart person around. That usually ends up being the scholar who is most "rigorous," and in academic circles that's often the thinker who is least accessible or who eschews "public" scholarship. But these debates break down on their own logic: academics and scholars who are rigorous don't have to do work that panders to the mainstream in order to be effective (after all, devoted students can carry their former professors, or their work, with them to the State Department or to *Newsweek*). Work that can be widely understood or that is relevant to current affairs shouldn't be automatically suspect or seen as second rate. As Jackson understood, our failure to make our work accessible may be as much the fault of intellectuals as it is the problem of a dumbed-down society.

These are the beliefs that guide my vision of the intellectual—the American intellectual, the black intellectual, the engaged intellectual, the public intellectual (and in a way, aren't all of us intellecuals in the academy *public* intellectuals, since universities are among the biggest public spheres in the country?). Relieving suffering, reinforcing struggle, and rendering service are not bad ways to live the life of the mind.

PART ONE

DYSONOGRAPHY

Although I have yet to write a memoir, I have at times written about my life as it relates to my work. I do this, in part, because I believe that intellectuals and academics who have been poor or working class must testify to our experiences and struggles, and perhaps inspire others to emulate, even exceed, our efforts. I also find that the personal voice, when its tones rise above grating narcissism, can emphasize truths that sound needlessly abstract in the academic's mouth. When enough of these stories get out, perhaps folk who, on first blush, might seem unlikely to succeed in higher education will get a fair chance.

One

NOT FROM SOME ZEUS'S HEAD:
MY INTELLECTUAL DEVELOPMENT

Of all the books I have written, Open Mike, *a series of interviews conducted with me over the past decade, best captures the oral traditions that have nurtured me since birth. This interview sketches my intellectual evolution, personal odyssey, and vocational development. It charts my path from ghetto youth, teen welfare father, factory laborer, and street hustler to ordained Baptist pastor, Princeton graduate student, and Ivy League professor. I hoped in the interview to underscore not only the racial character of higher education, but to draw attention to the class dimensions that are often obscured, even in some black academic circles. This interview, conducted by the talented journalist and writer Lana Williams, also gave me the chance to explain my rather unusual route to academic success: writing my dissertation before I submitted my proposal, writing my first book before I completed my Ph.D. thesis, and garnering a doctorate and being promoted to full professor in the same year. I have provoked no small controversy for showing my class roots in the academy, and for bringing an unapologetically black masculine style into the classroom. Deep inside—as this interview shows—I take pride in trying to stay rooted in the streets and church sanctuaries that produced me, even as I stretch my mind and soul through encounters with the wider world.*

Michael, let's talk a little about your self-perception. I've seen articles describing you as an intellectual giant, a person who has created a rather unique niche, as having one foot in the scholarly world and the other "on the block," and somehow synthesizing the two. When I've seen you, you've been very vocal in your opinions on issues or themes outside of yourself. But the little I've heard about you as a man, a person ... how did you pull this off? That "raising up from the bootstraps" thing is cool, but where we're from, a lot of us have had to do that. Yet you are special and unique and obviously on a distinct path that, on the one hand, you're carving, but on the other, seems like it was laid out there for you. How did you have the good sense to follow it, to take that dive? How'd you do that?

There's no question that nobody is self-made in America. All this mythology of the rugged individual has to be deconstructed. We've got to get at the heart of the essential lie that America was founded on this ethic of personal and private individual achievement. That has to be scrapped because a form of American Protestant communalism is the basis of discourse about American democracy. Recent studies in American political history evince a strong philosophical disagreement with the underlying principles of this American mythology—that we came here as solo artists and that we developed as individuals articulating ourselves against the wilderness of the collective. That's really not the case. People are produced by cultures and communities, by larger networks of association, love, kin, affection, and so on. And the same is true for me. I was produced, first of all, in the womb of a family that loved me, with my mother and father in the house. My father adopted me when I was two years old. I called him daddy because I didn't know any other man in my life. He was my daddy and my father. I'm one of five boys who grew up together in our immediate family. There were four older brothers and sisters, all of whom now are deceased.

When were you born?

October 23, 1958. Being born in what we would call the ghetto of Detroit had a decisive influence on my life and an impact on how I understand the relationship between scholarship and the street, between the world of the mind and the world of concrete outside of the academy. I think being born in the ghetto and being reared there, and dealing with the inner-city black community, connected me to other African American people who were doing extraordinarily important things. Detroit was a vibrant, vital black world teeming with possibility beyond the ballyhooed violence that stalked poor and working-class blacks. It was a wonderfully rich experience seeing black folk who lived meaningful lives, who ran their own businesses, and who eventually ran the city. When I was still in my teens, Coleman Young was elected the first black mayor of Detroit. I encountered in the political landscape powerful figures like Kenneth Cockrel, a Marxist black lawyer who was very important in my own rhetorical development, especially the stylistic etiquette of joining black radical discourse to a powerful social criticism of the forces of oppression. My pastor, Dr. Frederick Sampson, came to my church when I was twelve years old. He was the decisive intellectual influence in my life, with his fusion in his rhetorical repertoire of metaphysical poetry, racial uplift, and classical learning. Another pastor, Dr. Charles Adams, also thrilled us with his brilliant preaching and his exploration of the radical social implications of the Bible and theology. My fifth-grade teacher, Mrs. James, was extraordinarily important in my understanding of black people. She taught us about black history when folks didn't want to hear that, even other black teachers at Wingert Elementary School, which I attended from kindergarten through sixth grade. My Sunday school teachers in church appreciated black history and black culture and exposed us to the broad outlines of our people's sojourn in America, which gave us a sense of somebodyness as black children. It wasn't done so much by my teachers deploying a formal didacticism or a pedagogy geared toward instilling pride, but as they took for granted that black folk could achieve and love each other. That had a huge influence on me. They gave us a sense of helping ourselves while not harming others. We could love ourselves without hating anyone else, including white brothers and sisters. It wasn't about them, it was about us. They taught us to take for granted the existence of a black universe rooted in a black psychic infrastructure that had no need to pay deference to white culture, embracing all folk while defending black humanity and interests in the face of inimical forces.

That was the kind of world in which I was reared. This framework of existential and spiritual nurture provided a rich background for me—Sampson with this attention to the spiritual needs of African American people, Cockrel with his black Marxist discourse, Adams with this attention to the social ramifications of the gospel, and Mrs. James with her attention to the need for black history and memory as a resource to stabilize the black present and to secure the black future. They were among the folk who gave me a sense of self, who helped to create Michael Eric Dyson, who helped me understand the different bricks that must be laid at the foundation of my head and heart in order to have a healthy identity. So, I didn't spring fully formed out of some racial Zeus's head; I was shaped and molded in an environment where black achievement was taken for granted, where black excellence was expected, where black aspiration was crucial, and where black intellectual engagement was the norm of the day—on every level. And I'm not primarily referring to formal education in school. I'm referring largely to everyday life with brothers and sisters who were playing the numbers and playing the dozens. They were trying to use their linguistic and rhetorical capacity to defend their interests and worldviews.

That's just what I was going to ask, if you had that duality even then, where on the one hand, you were already processing what you were being given, and exposed to from your elders, but I was thinking—what were you doing with the fellas on the street, your peers? That's what you're talking about.

Oh yeah. There was at least a duality going on. I felt I belonged to many worlds. I kicked it with the fellas on the street and spent a lot of time engaging the Motown curriculum: Smokey Robinson, Stevie Wonder, Marvin Gaye, and so on. And at the same time, I learned to engage Paul Laurence Dunbar, W.E.B. Du Bois, Paul Robeson, and other great figures. Those interests didn't develop automatically, but were encouraged by teachers like Mrs. James, who wanted to make sure we knew about Jan Metzeliger and the shoe-lacing machine; Deadwood Dick and Wild Bill Pickett and the hidden tradition of black cowboys; Garrett T. Morgan and the invention of the traffic signal; Daniel Hale Williams and open heart surgery; Charles Drew and blood plasma; and Elijah McCoy and the lubricating cup. Her interest in black life was contagious. At Webber Junior High School, I was fortunate to encounter teachers who were instrumental in my further development. My seventh-grade English teacher, Mr. Burdette, enhanced my speaking skills by encouraging me to become involved in oratorical contests sponsored by the Detroit Optimist Club. And Mrs. Click taught me to type quickly and accurately, and besides that, gave me tremendous affection as a growing young man who had a huge crush on her. To tell the truth, I had crushes on many of my female teachers, starting with Mrs. Jefferson in kindergarten, to Mrs. Stewart and Mrs. Williams at Webber, and Mrs. Ray and Mrs. Carter at Northwestern, almost all of them English teachers. In my mind, love, language, and learning were profoundly linked in what may be termed an erotics of epistemology.

When I got to Northwestern High School, I had a crush on yet another teacher, Madame Black, who taught me French and so much more. She gave me a sense of my burgeoning intellectual power and encouraged me to tutor other students in French. She also gave me a sense that I should use language as a doorway into further investigation of American and African American culture. So did her husband, Dr. Cordell Black, whom I perceived then as my friendly competition! Dr. Black was a professor at Oakland University who often came to pick up Madame Black after school, and I'd still be there, and he'd see me trying to read Jean-Paul Sartre's masterly philosophical tome, *L'etre et le neant,* in its original French, a book that, in English, translates to *Being and Nothingness.* He'd laugh a laugh of wonder and encouragement and say, "Look at him, look at his aspiration and ambition." But most important, he also encouraged me to read Du Bois and Fanon and other classics in black letters. These figures gave important direction to my scholarly inclinations.

But I can't romanticize things. At the same time, there was quite a bit of pain and conflict going on as well. There was the pain of being called by some of my peers "brainiac," "Poindexter," and "Professor." Of course, it was their way of slyly, sometimes harshly, complimenting what they thought of as my smarts. But recognition and resentment were, in that beautiful phrase of Ralph Bunche's, "inexorably concomitant." To be sure, there was also a hierarchy of virtues established, one that comedian Chris Rock refers to when he jokes in a routine that black folk who get out of prison get much more "dap," or respect, from other blacks than those who've just graduated with a master's degree from college. I faced a version of that phenomenon, something that is termed in pedagogical theory as "rival epistemologies," or competing schemes of understanding how the world operates and the place of knowledge and formal training in its orbit. Some blacks think you can't be simultaneously cool and smart, at least in the sense of formal education. But I also experienced strong support in my peer group. Some of my peers said, "This brother's destined for a different world than we are." Others said, "He's in the ghetto, he's with us, but he's got something different. We don't always understand it, we tease him about it, but we admire him too." Some of my male peers—I'm thinking especially of a young man named Michael Squirewell—sought to protect me from some of the worst elements in our neighborhood. Unfortunately, that doesn't happen as often today as it did then.

I grew up in Detroit during the restructuring of the automobile industry. My father worked at Kelsey-Hayes Wheelbrake, and Drum Company, which I call his alma mater, a place where I "matriculated" as well between the ages of nineteen and twenty. I didn't go to college until I was twenty-one years old. I had been a teen father, lived on welfare, and hustled several years before furthering my formal education. I had gotten off track from the enabling tradition and heritage handed on to me by my teachers. I had gone to Cranbrook, one of the most highly esteemed private schools in the country, located in Bloomfield Hills, a suburb of Detroit. I was dating a young lady from my church, whose father, Damon Keith, was a deacon there, as well as a federal judge and one of the city's most prominent citizens. Judge Keith arranged for me to take the IQ and entry exams, and when I scored well, I was admitted, even though I couldn't afford the $11,000 annual tuition, which was damned near my father's yearly salary. Judge Keith arranged for me to receive a partial scholarship from New Detroit, a local civic and leadership organization, and to work for the other part of my tuition by traveling the forty or so miles from what was then the second richest suburb in the country to one of the bleakest neighborhoods in America, on the East Side of Detroit, to fill bags with food items, and to do maintenance work, for a group that aided the poor, Operation Hope, run by Bernard Parker. Two of Judge Keith's daughters, including the young lady I dated, attended Kingswood, the female complement to the all-boys Cranbrook. The schools have since merged.

I went to Cranbrook—where I agreed to repeat the eleventh grade in order to get sufficient academic grounding and to get at least two years at this prestigious institution under my belt, with an eye to getting into a quality college or university—and in some ways, I had a tremendous experience, and in other ways, it was a very painful one. I was seventeen years old, and I had never gone to school with white kids before. Now here I was going to school with kids who were extremely rich, many of them the sons and daughters of some of the wealthiest parents in the country. I remember, for instance, doing a report with Bill Taubman, the son of Alfred Taubman, one of the richest men in the nation. I was also the classmate of an heir apparent to Rockwell International, and the half-brother, Robert Zimmerman, of director Steven Spielberg. And at Kingswood, where we sometimes took classes, things were no different, and I remember Ford Motor Company head Lee Iaccoca's daughter, Kathy, was a student at the time. When I got out to Cranbrook, which rested on over three hundred acres of verdant, prosperous geography, nestled in a city of extraordinary material blessing, I felt like the Jimmy Stewart character in Hitchcock's *Vertigo*. My head began to spin.

As if that wasn't enough, there were strains of overt racism poisoning the common good. This was during the time that *Roots* was being televised. I came home to my dorm room one evening to find a newspaper cartoon of one of the *Roots* characters tacked to my door, with the words scribbled on it: "Nigger, go home." Some students also anonymously circulated a cassette tape about the black students that we got hold of. On the tape, a voice says in exaggerated southern cadence, "We're going cigar fishing today. No we're not, we're going 'nigar' fishing. What's the bait? Hominy grits!" On another occasion, a white student expressed the wish to place a bottle of sickle-cell anemia in the school's quadrangle to "kill off all the undesirables." So it was very tough for me. I got lost, did some crazy stuff—like helping to devise a system to dial out of the dorm on a phone without a face, allowing me and some friends to call our girlfriends and run up huge bills, which I had to get a second job to pay for while their parents ponied up—didn't do well in school, got expelled, and went back to Detroit a failure after being a golden boy. That was tough to handle. Then I finished night school, which I don't think they have any more, and got my diploma from Northwestern High School.

Almost immediately after I graduated, I met a woman, got her pregnant, married her, and then divorced her. It was a very trying period in my life. I was eighteen years old, she was twenty-six. She eventually had to give up her job as a waitress when she started to show—she had one of those jobs where the waitresses wore hot pants and tiny tops—and I was eventually fired from a job at Chrysler that my wife's uncle helped me to secure (an unjust firing, I might add, as I'll never forget my boss's words, "it had to be somebody's ass, and I'd rather it be yours than mine"). We were forced to live on welfare, since I lost my job a little more than a month before my son was to be born. We got food stamps and government medical assistance to pay the costs of delivering our baby. My wife was enrolled in WIC, or Women, Infants, and Children, and I stood many a day in those long lines and collected packets of powdered milk and artificial eggs—just as I did at the welfare office, where the civil servants were often rude and loud, making the experience that much more degrading.

Why did you marry her, Michael?

I married her because she was pregnant. I suppose those southern values were in effect—my parents were from Alabama and Georgia—and I was, after all, a church boy who believed that if you got a woman pregnant, you should marry her. I didn't want my son to be born out of wedlock. Of course, that was a narrow, naive view, but I suppose I had to learn the hard way. But I really did love Terrie, the woman I got pregnant. I just discovered too late that she didn't love me. She told me two months into our marriage that she didn't love me and should have never married me. I was devastated. By that time, however, she was well into her pregnancy. So we made as good a go of it as possible for young people who were poor, stressed, often unemployed, on welfare, and unequally yoked in affection. We had our son, a wonderful, beautiful boy who is now nineteen years old. I spent quite a bit of time attending to him. I did much of the night duty. I loved my son and wanted to bond with him.

That's a startling contrast to many black fathers today.

I don't know. I think many more black men than are given credit want to love and nurture their children. It is true that I lived in a moral universe with an ethical framework that dictated that one should acknowledge one's responsibility, and in my case, the obligation to marry in the belief that marriage itself would protect and preserve the family. At this time in my life, I think such a belief can be downright wrong. Still, I suppose there's something to be said for wanting to assume responsibility for what one does. But that couldn't prevent our almost inevitable breakup, so after working in a factory, hustling, cutting grass, shoveling snow and painting houses, working as an emergency substitute janitor for the public school system, working as a maintenance man in a suburban hotel, doing construction jobs, getting laid off, getting fired, going on welfare, and seeing my marriage dissolve, I decided right before my twenty-first birthday that I'd had enough, and I wanted to go to college. I had in my late teens felt a call to ministry, and that call, in tandem with my desire to better provide for my son's future, sent me to school. Plus, my desire to fulfill my early promise, which had been greatly tarnished by the events of my life after being kicked out of Cranbrook, goaded me to take my destiny into my own hands.

To many onlookers, I suppose I looked like a loser, a typical, pathological, self-defeating young black male. That may help explain why I empathize with such youth in the hip-hop generation; I was one of those brothers that many social scientists and cultural critics easily dismiss and effortlessly, perhaps literally, write off. In any regard, there were two people in my church who had gone to Knoxville College, a historically black college in Knoxville, Tennessee. I called the college and asked the dean if they had space for a young black man from Detroit. When he replied in the affirmative, the next day I "grabbed me an arm full of Greyhound," as Sam Cooke once sang, and took the fifteen-hour bus trip from Detroit to Knoxville. I went to college there and initially worked in a factory, then pastored three different churches as I completed my undergraduate studies at Carson-Newman, a small, white southern Baptist school. I transferred from Knoxville College because I wanted to study philosophy, and they didn't offer but a few courses in the subject. Carson-Newman was a true baptism in Southern Baptist theology and worldviews, many of which were problematic and sometimes racist, even as members of the academic community encouraged students to nurture their spiritual faculties. But my time in east Tennessee was crucial to my intellectual development, and taught me to navigate some perilous racial and cultural waters.

During the time frame you became a Baptist minister, it seems like there again you were operating on a number of levels. You were obviously fascinated by theology and philosophy, but I detect something else stirred you to commit yourself to that course of study.

No question. I was influenced to enter the ministry by having a pastor who was broadly learned and extremely erudite, who reflected critically on social and spiritual issues and who had read widely and deeply in philosophy and theology. Later on, as a burgeoning scholar, I was also influenced by scholars such as religious historian James Melvin Washington, a renowned bibliophile whom I met in the early '80s in Knoxville, and the great Cornel West, Washington's colleague at New York's Union Theological Seminary, whom I met in early 1984 at Kalamazoo College in Michigan, during a lecture series West was giving at the college. I had driven there from Tennessee, when I was an undergraduate student at Carson-Newman, a junior I believe, and he was a professor of philosophy of religion on his way to teach at Yale Divinity School. Within African American religious studies and theology, I was also influenced by the work and example of scholars like James Cone, Charles Long, J. Deotis Roberts, William R. Jones, Cecil Cone, Jacqueline Grant, and Riggins Earl. These are figures whose commitment to black theology and, to a lesser degree, to black philosophy, had whetted my appetite to study philosophy and religion.

At Carson-Newman, I experienced a growing desire to wed the life of the mind to the life of the heart. As an undergraduate, I was getting quite an introduction to the ministry in pastoring three different churches, and addressing the issues of life and death: I was preaching to my congregation, counseling them, and marrying and burying them. It was exciting, and at times quite stressful, but I increasingly sought a stronger academic vocabulary to express my intellectual goals and interests. Hence my sharpened focus on philosophy, social theory, literary criticism, and what would later be termed critical race theory. But I have never been one to think that religion dulled one's cutting edge or critical capacities. Of course, if one is honest, there are some tremendous difficulties in maintaining one's commitment to a religious tradition that says, "We know by faith and not by sight," while maintaining habits of critical inquiry that rest on relentless interrogation of the warrants, grounds, bases, and assertions of truth put forth in all sorts of intellectual communities, including religious ones. So there are tensions and, in fact, these multiple tensions define my intellectual projects and existential identities: tensions between sacred and secular, tensions between the intellectual and the religious, tensions between radical politics and mainstream institutions, tensions between preaching and teaching, and so on. But I think they are useful, edifying tensions, tensions that help reshape my ongoing evolution as a thinker, writer, teacher, preacher, and activist.

In many ways, I see myself as a rhetorical acrobat, navigating through varied communities of intellectual interest and pivoting around multiple centers of linguistic engagement, since all of these commitments have their own languages, rhetorics, and vocabularies. I view myself as a work in progress, an improvised expression of identity that is constantly evolving through stages and vistas of self-understanding. Such language owes several debts and has many sources, including my religious tradition's plea to, as the James Cleveland song goes, "Please be patient with me, God is not through with me yet"; my musical roots in jazz, and now in hip-hop, where relentless improvisation and restless experimentation are artistic hallmarks; and postmodern philosophical ruminations on the fluidity of identity. Plus, openness to new experience is critical, but you can't be so open that you lose sight of the crucial references, the haunting paths, the transforming traces, and the grounding marks of your identity. But one has got to constantly evolve and regenerate, stretching the boundaries of identity in a way that permits you to integrate new strains, new molds, new themes, and new ideas into the evolving self-awareness that occupies your heart and mind.

When did you know, finally recognize that your star was rising? When did all this start to take shape for you, Michael?

Good question. Throughout my college years, I struggled financially. Early on, I had to live in my car for almost a month because I didn't have a place to live. My pastor would dig into his pocket to help me out. My father was able to give me a used station wagon after my raggedy old car died, but he had no money to give me. For the most part, I paid for my own education. I borrowed money and had loans that I only recently paid back because I was deep in debt as a result of supporting myself through college. I had to make it on my own, which wasn't new since 1'd basically been living away from my parents' home after starting boarding school at sixteen. I knew I'd come a long way when I got to Knoxville and, after working in a factory, I was able to get some acclaim for my preaching and began to pastor. But in my third church, I was booted out for attempting to ordain three women as deacons in the male supremacist black Baptist church, so I went back to school. I had, ironically enough, been kicked out of Carson-Newman because I refused to attend chapel, a mandatory assignment every Tuesday morning. I was protesting the dearth of black scholars and preachers who were invited to campus, especially after it was explained to me by an administrator that, based on the small number of blacks, one speaker a year was all we could expect.

But after my church let me go—and isn't this more than a little ironic, since it was named Thankful Baptist Church?—with a month's severance pay, and with nowhere to land to support my family, since I had remarried and got temporary custody of my son, I headed back to Carson-Newman in 1983 to finish my studies. I received no scholarship money from the school, despite maintaining a straight-A average in philosophy, so I borrowed more money and graduated *magna cum laude,* and as outstanding graduate in philosophy, in 1985. I applied and got into Vanderbilt University's Ph.D. department of philosophy, and into Brown and Princeton's departments of religion. I was interested in Vanderbilt because of Robert Williams, a respected philosopher of black experience, and because I wanted to study with Alisdair MacIntyre, a renowned philosopher whose book *After Virtue* had recently made a huge splash in moral philosophy. I remember meeting with him on my visit to Vanderbilt, and I remember him asking me why anyone who had gotten into Princeton wanted to come to Vanderbilt to study. I told him I was wrestling with whether to become a philosopher with an interest in religion, or a scholar of religion who took philosophy seriously. His eyes lit up, and he uttered, "That's precisely the question you must answer."

I decided on the latter course, and after visiting Brown and Princeton, I chose to attend Princeton. But there was a snag: Carson-Newman refused to release my final transcript to Princeton because I owed them money, a little more than $7,000, a sum that I knew wouldn't exist if they had given me the scholarship help I thought I deserved. I was quite nervous until a dean at Princeton's graduate school told me that I could come to Princeton without my final grades, since they had already accepted me on my documented performance. It was the closing of a widely gyrating circle of promise that had begun in the ghetto of Detroit where my teachers, my pastor, and some of my peers had foreseen, and in many cases, through their contributions, had assured my success. I realized at Princeton, as great a school as it is, that my being there was nothing less than what I should be doing in living out the early promise that they—my teachers, pastor, and peers—detected in me.

As a second-year graduate student at Princeton in 1987, I began to write professionally, if by that it is meant that one is compensated for one's work. I wrote for religious journals of opinion, for newspapers, for scholarly journals, and for mass-market magazines, much of this before completing my master's degree in 1991 and my Ph.D. in 1993. In fact, I wrote the lead review essay in the *New York Times Book Review,* which ran longer than five thousand words, when they had such a feature in the book review back in 1992. I had begun to write book reviews for the *New York Times* in 1990, along with reviews for the *Chicago Tribune* book review. I wrote the "Black America" column for the left-wing *Z Magazine* in the late '80s and early '90s, which I inherited from Cornel West, and during this time, I also wrote op-eds for the *Nation* and later for the *New York Times, Washington Post, Chicago Tribune, Los Angeles Times,* and other papers. I also wrote essays and chapters for several books. So I guess I took off pretty quickly after hitting graduate school, which, while not unique, I suppose was nonetheless rare enough. Interestingly enough, I ended up writing my first book, *Reflecting Black,* before I wrote my Ph.D. thesis. That fact encouraged me to complete my degree before my book was published in 1993. In fact, I received my Ph.D. from Princeton in June 1993, and my book was printed in late May 1993, and published later in June. I just made it!

But weren't there some highly unusual circumstances surrounding your dissertation, particularly the fashion in which you completed it? Rumor has it that your legend still lives at Princeton because of how you finished.

Well, I don't know if "legend" is quite the word; "infamy" may be more like it. The usual process of completing one's dissertation is the submission to one's doctoral committee of a prospectus, a document that details and outlines one's proposed thesis, which can run up to twenty, thirty, or sometimes forty pages. After one is subject to a long, maybe three-hour, oral examination by one's committee members, other professors, and one's peers, one is asked to step out of the room while the committee votes to accept or reject one's prospectus. If it is accepted, often with recommendations for changes, you are then permitted to go about the business of working on the dissertation, which might take anywhere from two to ten years to complete. You then submit the thesis to your committee (which responds with challenges and changes that are integrated into your work), sit for a final oral examination, and, hopefully, your dissertation is approved.

My committee included Cornel West, whose name I had submitted to a search committee to direct the Afro-American Studies program at Princeton before I left to run an antipoverty project and teach at Hartford Seminary in 1988; Jeffrey Stout, a well-respected religious ethicist, and the teacher with whom I spent the most time in the rigors of writing and rewriting papers, taking courses, and critically reading challenging books; and Albert Raboteau, the well-regarded religious historian and author of the classic work *Slave Religion*. Well, I submitted my prospectus in April 1993, and after a three-hour public oral examination, consisting of close questioning by my committee members and a few others in attendance, I was asked to leave the room. Upon being invited back in and taking my seat at the head of the examining table, I was informed that I had passed and that my prospectus had been approved.

Needless to say, I was quite happy, but for more than the usual reasons of having one's intellectual work approved by one's teachers. I had an even bigger investment than usual because of a big risk I had taken. As my teachers, and the others in attendance, verbally congratulated me from where they sat, I reached under the table and pulled out my completed dissertation, handed copies to my committee members, and said, "Here it is." It is true that that was an electrifying moment. There was a collective gasp that was articulated, an "ah" that reverberated through the room, with some of the folk, including members of my committee, clearly stunned. I realized that it was a big risk to do what I had done. After all, they could have rejected my prospectus or asked for huge changes that would have necessitated significant revision of my work. Fortunately, it was approved, and after I submitted my thesis, I responded to the criticisms, integrated them into the final version of my dissertation, sat for my final oral examination, and was awarded my doctoral degree. And it is true that after my prospectus performance, some of my colleagues cornered me and said, "Day-am," in the black vernacular, "that was unbelievable." And when I came back to defend my dissertation in my final oral examination, some of my peers said that I had become a legend in the department. I'm just glad that things turned out the way they did.

But your legend doesn't stop there. You also had a meteoric rise in academe for one so young. Didn't you get your Ph.D. in 1993, and in the very next year, you received tenure at Brown, also an Ivy League university, and became a full professor at the University of North Carolina? That's almost

unheard of in conservative academic circles, where promotion through the ranks often takes years and years.

Yes, that's true. I had been pretty much teaching full time since 1989, when I left Hartford Seminary to become an instructor of ethics, philosophy, and cultural criticism at Chicago Theological Seminary. I taught at CTS for three years, two as an instructor, and when I completed my master's degree in 1991, I got promoted to an assistant professor. I left CTS in 1992 to become an assistant professor of American civilization and Afro-American studies at Brown. In 1993, as you know, I received my Ph.D. from Princeton, and my first book, *Reflecting Black,* was published and received favorable critical attention from both the academy and the broader public, and I was offered several teaching positions, including offers from Northwestern and Chapel Hill. Because of those offers, Brown sped up my tenure decision by about six years, since one normally receives tenure in one's seventh year.

I was extremely gratified to be awarded tenure at Brown and, as it turns out, at Chapel Hill. (Northwestern offered me tenure too, but the president intervened and told me I could come to the university and essentially "try out" for two years; and if after that time I fulfilled my promise, then I would be awarded tenure. He based his decision, he said, on the fact that he had never known a scholar to be awarded tenure less than a year after he completed his Ph.D., with one exception—a scholar who would go on to win a Nobel Prize in economics. I shot back that, first, no one knew at the time the scholar was awarded tenure that he would receive the Nobel Prize, so the decision to grant him tenure was, by those terms at least, a risk, and second, since the president couldn't be sure that I wouldn't achieve equal prominence in my field, it made no sense to deny me tenure either. Needless to say, I rejected Northwestern's offer.) Chapel Hill made the extraordinary step of offering me tenure and a full professorship, in light of the fact that I had completed my next book, which would be published shortly, a study of Malcolm X.

Wait. If it normally takes seven years to get tenure in the first place, it must take at least another seven years, if not longer, to become a full professor, right?

Well, it certainly can. After seven years, a scholar who successfully obtains tenure is usually made an associate professor. When you write the next book or two, depending on where you teach, you can be granted full professorship. And that may take seven to ten years, or in some cases not quite as long, and in other cases, significantly longer. So yes, it's safe to say that I was fortunate enough to do in a year what can in other circumstances take as long as seventeen to more than twenty years to achieve. In a way, I have been driven by the sense that I have to make up for lost tune, which, ironically enough, has put me ahead of the pace of some of my peers. Plus, I felt a sense of responsibility to my peers from my old neighborhood who will never be able to achieve at the levels I have enjoyed, not because they aren't talented, but because they lack opportunity. Or, on my block, most of them are either in prison or dead. I felt blessed by God, and I didn't want to blow it. Plus, a lot of the early writing and speaking I did—which, as it turns out, helped me to climb the academic ladder rapidly—was not only driven by a sense of vocation, but was done as well in the desperate attempt to raise funds for my brother Everett's defense against the charge, and later the conviction, of second-degree murder. Almost the month after I landed in Chicago to teach at CTS, Everett was accused of murdering a young black man in Detroit. I believe he is innocent, and I have expended quite a few resources in trying to prove his innocence, and to free him from prison. He's been there now for eight years. That has given me great incentive to work as hard as I can, and of course, I'm sure there's a good bit of survivor guilt involved as well.

Have you ever talked with John Edgar Wideman? He crossed my mind; as you know, he's had a similar circumstance with his brother.

We've talked, but not about our brothers. Yes, he too has had to deal with that strange and haunting reality that often morphs into a tragic trope of black existence: one brother a prisoner, the other a professor. One of you free to move, the other one caged like an animal. The effect of that thought on one's psyche is like an enormous downward gravitational pull. But I'm grateful to God for the ability to be able to do what I do, because I know it's a tremendous gift and pleasure and leisure to be able to write and think. And I work hard, traveling around the country giving lectures, speeches, and sermons, writing books, articles, and essays, just trying, as the hip-hoppers say, "to represent." So I spend long hours at what I do, but I'm not complaining. I'm a well-paid, highly visible black public intellectual who is grateful for what God has done for him and who wants to pass it on to somebody else. I don't want to keep it for myself. I want to make sure that other people get a chance to express their talents and their visions. I have no desire to be the H.N.I.C., or the "Head Nigger In Charge."

Do you get a sense of that . . . when you are in your flow . . . do you know the impact you're having on a room?

That's a good question. Let's not have any false modesty: I'm a public speaker and I've been trained from a very young age in the art of verbal articulation. I've been seasoned to engage at the highest level of oral expression. So, I'm experienced enough to know when I'm hitting my target and when I'm missing it. There are times when I can feel the electricity of getting things right, because I've known when I failed [laughs]. I know what that feels like. And even when other people think I've done well, I often feel a great need for improvement. There have been very few times when I feel like I absolutely nailed it. There are some moments when I know I'm "representin'" because I know I'm a vehicle. I'm a vessel. My religion teaches me that the gift is not in the vehicle, but in the giver of the gift. I honestly hope to be an instrument of the Lord. I hope that I'm an instrument of God. And I hope, therefore, that I work hard to stimulate the gift God gave me. I'm constantly striving to get better, to get clearer, sharper, and more eloquent. I think one of the ways that occurs is through testing ourselves in situations where people are unpersuaded by our beliefs and we have to make a case for them with as much passion and precision as possible. Crossing swords rhetorically is a great joy to me, and often a great learning experience.

At the same time, I'm attempting to excel at the height of my profession and at the top of my game, like Michael Jordan. I have no bones about that. I want to represent on that level where people go, "DAMN, did you hear what that brother said?" 'Cause I want young people to say it ain't just got to be about sport, it doesn't just have to be about some athletic achievement—as great as that may be—or about Oprah or Bill Cosby, as great and ingenious as they are at what they do. I want young people to say the same thing about intellectual engagement. I want them to have a desire to deploy a variety of jargons, grammars, rhetorics, languages, and vocabularies to articulate views in defense of African American or marginalized identities, as I attempt to do. I want young people to say, as the folk in the '60s and '70s used to say, "Got to be mo' careful," in admiration of such linguistic and intellectual skill. Not for show, but for war, against ignorance, misery, and oppression. I want young folk to say, "I wish I could do that, I wish I could be like Mike!" I have no qualms in hoping for that, because I want to seduce young people unto excellence, since they've often been sabotaged by mediocrity. I have no reservations in seeking to inspire young people to do what I do, only better. So I constantly strive to deepen my vision, broaden my intellectual reach, and expand my repertoire of verbal skills. And at times, you feel the pleasures of the palpable responses you evoke in those who hear or read you.

On the other hand, you're always surprised by people who claim you have influenced them, because you can never accurately or adequately measure such a thing. We are prevented by circumstance and environment and context from knowing the true nature of our own influence, which is why we should really remain structurally humble. Not falsely modest, but structurally humble. For me that means if I am wielding influence, it is because I have tried to be faithful to the gifts God has given to me. Structural humility means that as a matter of principle, we remain cognizant of the need to check our arrogance and bridle our vanity. This recognition must be the very foundation, the very structure, of our public activity, to keep us from taking credit for what only God can give. To be sure, we never know the full extent of our influence, which is why we should also attempt to be vigilant in exercising our gifts. As the rapper Guru says, we never know when someone is watching or listening. I've had people around the country, folk who read my books, articles, and essays, or hear my sermons, lectures, or commentary on radio or television, tell me that something I've said or done has changed their lives. That's a huge responsibility, and we've got to accept it as part of our duties as public intellectuals. And such responsibility doesn't stop at our national borders. I just got a letter from Japan, and some intellectuals want me to come there because they think I'm doing important cultural criticism. And I've just fielded an invitation from London to speak on religion, and from Italy to speak on politics, and from Cuba to talk about African American culture and politics.

In light of all of this, structural humility is surely in order. The best we can do is to represent the truth as honestly and clearly as we understand it, with all the skills at our disposal. Of course, nothing I'm saying means we can't feel good about our achievements, or about the influence we might wield. From my perspective, if we truly believe that our vocations are manifestations of ultimate purpose, we'll want to do our level best to stay at the top of our games as an acknowledgment of the gifts God has given us.

One last thing that ties in is how you'll be able to do that. I can see very clearly your intellectual path. But how are you going to be able to keep your hand on the pulse of the street, because by necessity . . . it doesn't have anything to do with your commitment . . . but, like you said, Japan, Italy, universities, busy . . . How do you maintain that connection? I know that's vital to you.

It is vital. That's one reason I still spend so much of my time on Sunday mornings preaching, and going into communities as a public intellectual and political activist.

You ever just go walk through the neighborhoods?

Lord yes. When I go to neighborhoods all over this country, I'm trying to find the barbecue shack. I'm trying to find where the Negroes hang out. I hang with the bloods. I want the local color, the local flavor, what Geertz calls local knowledge, because black folks are so diverse and profoundly complex, even if we have similarities that bind us together. Black folks fascinate me. I want to continue to learn about us: the different vernaculars we have in different regions; the different ideological and political subcultures we generate; the varied contexts that shape our cultural identities; the varied sexualities we express, especially beneath the radar of racial correctness or mainstream propriety; and the inflections of the black diaspora in our food, fashion, and faith. So, I'm constantly trying to learn more wherever I go. Of course, one of the critiques of intellectuals I often hear is that we're out of touch with "the folk." Well, when I preach, I'm reaching "the folk." Those critics who say that intellectuals per se—not particular intellectuals, mind you, but intellectuals as a category—are out of touch, have often stereotyped "the folk." Further, they feel free to speak for, and identify with, "the folk," and they feel free to attack intellectuals in the name of "the folk." But I've often discovered that "the folk"—these very souls whom critics seek to protect through claims of our irrelevance—are hungry for intellectual engagement.

In the meantime, "the folk" are out-reading, out-thinking, and out-intellectualizing the very people who quite defensively and condescendingly argue in their name that they won't get what we're doing, won't understand what we're up to, or will be automatically suspicious of our aspirations. Now don't get me wrong; there is more than enough warrant for the skepticism, perhaps even the cynicism, which some folk harbor toward intellectuals who've earned the titles Irrelevant, Pedantic, Didactic, or Condescending. On the other hand, when intellectuals prove that they're serious about helping people think deeply and clearly about the problems they confront, their advice, insight, and analysis is more than welcomed by "the folk." I think we have to stop essentializing the folk, as if it's some mythic community. Well, I'm the folk. They're the folk. So my preservation of connection is through the immediate context of preaching, teaching, and activist politics, as well as hanging out in the 'hood and going to the barber shop and the barbecue joint and hanging with "the niggas." And not for ethnographic titillation or anthropological voyeurism, but as a legitimate participant in vibrant black folk culture, the kind from which I sprang and in which I feel most comfortable.

I can't tell you how many black folk I've met who've said, "Brother, we read your book, keep on writing," or, "We saw you on TV, keep on speaking." And these are ordinary, average people, the so-called folk from whom ostensible grassroots gatekeepers attempt to divide us, almost by ontological fiat, as if we're a different species of people. These black folk say to me, "Man, you're speaking to white folk, you're speaking to black folk, you're keeping it real on a level we often don't see." That makes me feel good, when black folk say I'm speaking brilliantly, insightfully, intelligently. But that doesn't mean I can't disagree with what the majority of black folk think, that I'm somehow locked into a rigid perspective because I am committed to their amelioration. I love black folk, which is why I ain't afraid of them. I'm not afraid to disagree with mass black opinion, to call into question beliefs, habits, dispositions, traditions, and practices that I think need to be criticized. I seek to speak truth to power in love, as the Bible suggests. I seek to address the high and low, those on the inside and those locked out. That's my obligation and lifelong objective.

Interview by Lana Williams
Durham, North Carolina, 1997

Two

LETTER TO MY BROTHER, EVERETT, IN PRISON

Soon after I arrived in Chicago in 1989 to teach ethics, philosophy, and cultural criticism at the Chicago Theological Seminary, I learned that my younger brother Everett was arrested and charged with murder. Of course, such a revelation deeply wounded my family. But we rallied to Everett's defense as we concluded, after intense investigation, that he was innocent. As the only college-educated son among five brothers at the time— though still four years from my Ph.D.—it fell to me to generate money to aid in Everett's expensive criminal defense. The process of securing legal counsel, as well as keeping up the family's morale, was genuinely harrowing. In order to raise funds, I took to lecturing, preaching, and writing for a variety of scholarly and popular venues. These efforts lead in large part to the material collected for my first book in 1993, Reflecting Black. *During my brother's trial—he was eventually convicted of second-degree murder and sentenced to twenty-five years to life in prison—the family dog in Detroit was killed and the family house was shot at, presumably in retaliation for my brother's alleged crime. This prompted my mother to leave her job and house and live with me in Chicago for nearly two years before returning home. Everett has now been in prison for fifteen years. He has converted to the Moorish Temple Muslim faith, changing his name to Everett Dyson-Bey. I visit him regularly and continue to work for his release. This open letter to him, though painful to write, was both emotionally cathartic and morally clarifying, helping me to sort through critical domestic and social issues in both our lives.*

Dear Everett:

How are you? I suppose since we've talked almost nonstop on the telephone over the last five years, I haven't written too often. Perhaps that's because with writing you have to confront yourself, stare down truths you would rather avoid altogether. When you're freestyling in conversation, you can acrobatically dance around all those issues that demand deep reflection. After five years, I guess it's time I got down to that kind of, well, hard work, at least emotionally and spiritually.

I've been thinking about you a lot because I've been talking about black men quite a bit—in my books, in various lectures I give around the country, in sermons I preach, even on *Oprah!* Or is it the other way around, that I've been talking about black men because I've been thinking about you and your hellish confinement behind bars? I don't need to tell you—but maybe I'll repeat it to re-mind myself—of the miserable plight of black men in America.

I am not suggesting that black women have it any better. They are not living in the lap of luxury while their fathers, husbands, brothers, boyfriends, uncles, grandfathers, nephews, and sons perish. Black women have it equally bad, and in some cases, even worse than black males. That's one of the reasons I hesitate to refer to black males as an "endangered species," as if black women are out of the woods of racial and gender agony and into the clearing, free to create and explore their complex identities. I don't believe that for a moment.

I just think black women have learned, more successfully than black men, to absorb the pain of their predicament and to keep stepping. They've learned to take the kind of mess that black men won't take, or feel they can't take, perhaps never will take, and to turn it into something useful, something productive, some-thing toughly beautiful after all. It must be socialization—it certainly isn't genetics or gender, at least in biological terms. I think brothers need to think about this more, to learn from black women about their politics of survival.

I can already hear some wag or politician using my words to justify their attacks on black men, contending that our plight is our own fault. Or to criticize us for not being as strong as black women. But we both know that to compare the circum-stances of black men with black women, particularly those who are working class and poor, is to compare our seats on a sinking ship. True, some of us are closer to the hub, temporarily protected from the fierce winds of social ruin. And some of us are directly exposed to the vicious waves of economic misery. But in the final analysis, we're all going down together.

Still, it's undeniable that black men as a whole are in deplorable shape. The most tragic symbol of that condition, I suppose, is the black prisoner. There are so many brothers locked away in the "stone hotel," literally hundreds of thou-sands of them, that it makes me sick to think of the talent they possess going to waste. I constantly get letters from such men, and their intelligence and determi-nation is remarkable, even heartening.

I realize that millions of Americans harbor an often unjustifiable fear toward prisoners whom they believe to be, to a man, unrepentant, hardened criminals. They certainly exist. But every prisoner is not a criminal, just as every criminal is not in prison. That's not to say that I don't believe that men in prison who have committed violent crimes can't turn around. I believe they can see the harm of their past deeds and embrace a better life, through religious conversion, through redemptive social intervention, or by the sheer will to live right.

The passion to protect ourselves from criminals, and the social policies which that passion gives rise to, often obscure a crucial point: thousands of black men are wrongfully imprisoned. Too many black men are jailed for no other reason than that they fit the profile of a thug, a vision developed in fear and paranoia. Or sometimes, black men get caught in the wrong place at the wrong time. Worse yet, some males are literally arrested at a stage of development where, if they had more time, more resources, more critical sympathy, they could learn to resist the temptations that beckon them to a life of self-destruction. Crime is only the most conspicuous sign of their surrender.

I guess some, or all, of this happened to you. I still remember the phone call that came to me announcing that you had been arrested for murder. The disbelief settled on me heavily. The thought that you might have shot another man to death emotionally choked me. I instantly knew what E. B. White meant when he said that the death of his pig caused him to cry internally. The tears didn't flow down his cheeks. Instead, he cried "deep hemorrhagic tears." So did I.

Even so, a cold instinct to suspend my disbelief arose, an instinct I could hardly suppress. I was willing, had to be willing, to entertain the possibility that the news was true. Otherwise I couldn't offer you the kind of support you needed. After all, if you really had killed someone, I didn't want to rush in to express sorrow at your being wrongly accused of a crime you didn't commit. Such a gesture would not only be morally noxious; it would desecrate the memory of the man who had lost his life.

If I wasn't able to face the reality that you might be a murderer, then I would have to surrender important Christian beliefs I preach and try to practice. I believe that all human beings are capable of good and evil. And regarding the latter, wishing it wasn't the case won't make it so. Too often we deny that our loved ones have the capacity or even inclination for wrongdoing, blinding us to the harm they may inflict on themselves and others.

I eventually became convinced that you were innocent. Not simply because you told me so. As one lawyer succinctly summarized it: "To hear prisoners tell it, there are no are guilty prisoners." After discerning the controlled anger in your voice (an anger that often haunts the wrongly accused) and after learning that the police had discovered no weapon, motive, or even circumstantial evidence, I believed you were telling me the truth. Plus, you had been candid with me about your past wrongdoing. And in the wake of your confessions of guilt, you repeatedly bore the sting of my heated reproach. For these reasons, I believed you were not guilty.

I realized then, as I do now, that these are a brother's reasons. They are the fruit of an intimacy to which the public has no access and in which they place little trust. Many of the reasons that led me to proclaim your innocence are not reasons that convince judges or juries. Still, I felt the bare, brutal facts of the case worked in your favor. A young black man with whom you were formerly acquainted was tied up in a chair on the second floor of a sparsely furnished house. He had tape tightly wrapped around his eyes. He was beaten on the head. He was shot twice in the chest at extremely close range, producing "contact wounds."

After breaking free of his constraints, he stumbled down the flight of stairs inside the house where he was shot. Once he made it down the stairs outside the house, he collapsed on the front lawn of the house next door. As he gasped for breath while bleeding profusely, he was asked, first by neighbors, then by relatives who had arrived on the scene, and later by a policeman, "Who did this to you?" Something sounding close enough to your name was uttered. The badly wounded man was pronounced dead a short time later after being rushed to an area hospital.

In the absence of any evidence of your participation, except the dying man's words, I thought you'd be set free. After all, he could be mistaken. Given the tragic conditions in which he lay dying, he might not have had full control of his faculties. Was his perception affected by his gunshots? Was his mind confused because of the large amounts of blood he had lost? Unfortunately, there was no way to be certain that he was right. There was no way to ask him if he was sure that you were one of the culprits (he said "they" a couple of times) who had so barbarically assaulted him. But without his ability to answer such questions, I believed there was no way you would be imprisoned. Surely, I thought, it took more than this to convict you, or anyone, of murder.

I was wrong. The murdered man's words, technically termed a "dying declaration," were admitted into court testimony and proved, at least for the jury, to be evidence enough. I was stunned. In retrospect, I shouldn't have been. Detroiters were fed up with crime, including the ones who peopled the black jury that convicted you. How many times had this apparent scenario been repeated for them: black men killing other black men, then seeking pardon from blacks sitting on a jury in a mostly black city?

When it came time to sentence you, the judge allowed me to say a few words. I felt more than a little awkward. Although I didn't believe you were guilty, I knew that if I said so the judge would ignore my presentation. In his mind, the jury had settled the issue of your culpability. I didn't know how much I should refer to your past, or to the social forces that shape human action. I figured that the last thing I needed to do was sound like a hot-shot intellectual trying to enlighten the masses.

I knew in my heart that I shouldn't avoid mentioning those beliefs I held to be true, for instance, that economic misery can lead to criminal activity. At the same time, I didn't want to be mistaken for defending the belief that social structures alone determine human behavior. I also wanted to avoid inflicting any more pain on the murdered man's family, most of whom believed that you were guilty as sin. And I didn't want to be condescending. I didn't want to sound like the brother who was righteous, who had made it good, making excuses for the brother who had gone completely wrong. I wanted to speak from the heart, so I didn't use a prepared text. I wonder if you remember what I said?

Your Honor, I'm a minister of the gospel and I'm also a scholar, and a teacher at a theological seminary. I, of course, want to express first of all my deep sympathy to the family of the man who died. They have endured enormous hurt and pain over this past year. I want to say to you in my brief remarks that I am deeply aware, in an ironic sense, of why we're here. Sentencing is a very difficult decision. I have been deeply committed over the years to justice in American culture and also to examining the workings of the legal system.

On the other hand, I also understand the societal forces such as poverty and joblessness and structural unemployment and limited social options and opportunities for legitimate employment—that many people of our culture, particularly black men, face. It is also ironic that I'm here because I write in my professional life about . . . social forces which often leave young black men feeling they have no other options but to engage in . . . criminal activity in order to sustain their lives. Unfortunately many make that choice.

I grew up in the urban poverty of Detroit, as did the other members of my family. Therefore I understand not only from a scholarly viewpoint, but from a personal viewpoint, limited life options and the kind of hopelessness and social despair they can breed in a person.

I come here this morning pleading and praying for leniency in my brother's case. As his lawyer has already stated, the mystery that surrounds the events of that day continues to prevail. In any regard, I can attest to my brother's character, that he is not a hardened criminal. He has made unwise choices about the activity of his life in the past. He has made choices which have encouraged him to engage in a lifestyle that I'm sure at this point he is not proud of. At the same time I think this penalty far exceeds any crime that he has been involved in.

Above all, my brother is, I think, ripe for a productive future in our society. Although he has indeed made a noticeable change in jail, a prolonged stay in prison, I feel, will not greatly contribute to any sense of rehabilitation that the Court might think prison offers.

Unfortunately the prisons of our land often reproduce the pathology that they seek to eliminate. Because of his own poor beginnings in our city, the death of our father at a crucial time in his life, and because he's been subjected to the forces I've already referred to, my brother has made poor choices. But he's also shown a remarkable strength of faith and renewed spiritual insight. He's shown a remarkable sense of concern . . . about all the people involved in this case and not just himself . . . . In conclusion, Your Honor, I would plead and pray that . . . your deepest discretion and most conscientious leniency prevail in your sentencing of my brother this morning.

I have rarely been more depressed, or more convinced that my words meant absolutely nothing, than when the judge's words, all-powerful words, revealed your future. Life. In prison. An oxymoron if I've ever heard one.

You have managed to squeeze an ounce of invention, or should I say, self-reinvention, from the pound of cure that prison is said to represent. When I first learned of your new identity, Everett Dyson-Bey, I was neither dismayed nor surprised. Frankly, my position is simple: do whatever is necessary to maintain your safety and sanity in prison without bringing undue harm to another person. You're a strong, muscular fellow, and I didn't think you'd have much trouble staying safe. I took your change of religions—from the Christianity you inherited as a child to the Moorish Temple Muslim belief of your new adulthood—to be an encouraging, even creative defense of your sanity.

I am disappointed, though, by the response of the black church to your predicament. I suppose since I've been to see you countless times over the last five years, it could be claimed that those visits count for my church's mission to those locked away. But we both know that's bogus. That line of reasoning insults the integrity and slights the example of so many who've followed Jesus in "visit[ing] those who are in prison." You haven't been visited a single time in prison by anyone visiting as a Christian minister, or as a concerned church member. Thank God our pastor visited you in jail before you went to prison. But the church is larger than him. I spoke several times to the minister in charge of prison visitation about going to see you. My requests were futile.

I don't know why so many black Christians avoid the prisons. Of course, I realize that hundreds of black churches have prison ministries that make a real difference in inmates' lives. But the average pew sitting member, or for that matter, the regular church minister, rarely gets into the thick of prison life in the same way, say, as members and ministers of the Nation of Islam. Or the Moorish Temple. Perhaps it has something to do with how black Muslims with smaller numbers than black churches must proselytize when and where they can. Since many of their members have served time, they may be more willing to reach back to help those left behind. Then, too, the application to prisoners' lives of the stringent ethical code taught in black Muslim settings often brings welcome relief to the moral chaos into which so many inmates have descended.

Another reason for their success may be that black Muslims take seriously their theological commitments to racial uplift and reconstruction, especially among the poor and imprisoned who are most in need of that message. Perhaps it's a simple class issue. The more legitimacy some black Christian denominations gain, the higher class status they acquire, the less they appear inclined to take care of "the least of these." In the end, I'm glad you've discovered in the Moorish Temple what you couldn't find—or perhaps what couldn't be found in you—through Christian belief.

Many people think the sort of religious change you have experienced is a "foxhole" conversion, a transformation brought on by desperate circumstances that will be rejected as soon as you're set free. That may be the case. If it is true, you certainly won't be the first person it has happened to. But hold on to the hope your religion supplies as long as you can. There will be other desperate situations after you leave prison. Besides, so-called normal religious people experience a series of crises and conversions over the years in settling down to a deeper faith. Even those folk who don't walk through its doors every time church opens often have meaningful conversations with God.

I think our father was one of those people. He was a complex man who worked extraordinarily hard and who believed deeply in God. But he wasn't very religious, at least not in any traditional way. When people discover I'm a Baptist preacher, they often ask if preachers run in my family, if my father was a preacher. I laugh inwardly, sometimes out loud, thinking of what an odd image that is, Daddy as a preacher. It's not that he cussed like a sailor. I know too many preachers who do that as well. And it's not because he had a short fuse. So do most prophets, biblical and current ones too. I guess it's their righteous rage at evil, their ill-tempered tirades translated as holy damnation. But the line between their baptized fussiness and plain old invective is sometimes quite thin.

I think what causes my bemused response is Daddy's genuine humility. Most preachers I know aren't that humble. I don't think that's all bad. Many can't afford to be. The tribulations of their office are enough to shatter a fragile ego. But the annoying hubris found in so many ministers was completely absent in Daddy. Yet this humble man also displayed ferocious anger which frightened me. True, it didn't last long when it surfaced. But its concentrated expression had devastating consequences. And often—I think too often—it had its most harmful effects on his children's behinds, not to mention on their minds.

To be honest, I don't completely understand why Daddy so readily turned to the strap to discipline us. Perhaps he was treated the same way when he was a child. Maybe the humiliations he suffered didn't have any other outlet. I remember once when he and I were working for "Sam's Drugs" as janitors. I was in my middle teens, which meant Daddy was in his late '50s. A light fixture had been broken in the ceiling of the drugstore. In order to reach it, Daddy climbed a step ladder that I was holding as Ben, the Jewish owner, looked on. When Daddy misstepped and slipped down a couple of rungs on the ladder, Ben became angry.

"Oh, Everett," he indignantly declaimed. "You're just like a little boy. Can't you do anything right?"

Daddy didn't say a word. I was so mad at Ben, and humiliated for Daddy at the same time. I remember thinking of how strong Daddy was, how physically domineering he could be. Yet none of that mattered as Ben reduced his humanity, and as I interpreted it then, attacked Daddy's manhood as well. If I felt that as a teen, what did Daddy feel? Where did he put that anger? Is that at least part of the reason he let his rage loose on us?

As you know, the debate about corporal punishment is raging in our nation. There used to be a belief that there was a racial divide on these matters, at least when we were growing up. Black folk in favor, white folk opposed. Even though I don't think it's that simple (where one lives, either in the city or the suburbs, and one's class identification, are important too). I don't deny that racial differences exist.

Recently, though, I think the gulf between black and white views on child rearing has probably narrowed. A new generation of black parents has questioned and often rejected the wisdom of whipping ass. To be sure, you still hear black folk saying, "The problem with white folk is that they let their kids get away with murder, let them talk and act any way they want to without keeping them in check." You also hear black parents and the experts they listen to arguing that corporal punishment encourages aggressive behavior, stymies the development of moral reasoning, hinders self-esteem, and even causes children to be depressed. No such theories prevailed in our household.

I must admit, I tend toward the newfangled school of thought, even though I haven't always put it into practice now that it's my turn to parent. In fact, during your nephew Michael's childhood and early adolescence, I didn't know anything about "time out." As a teen father, I had barely survived the pain of my own rearing and the violence I'd encountered. I knew what I saw, repeated what was done to me. And I regret it.

One of the most painful moments I experienced involving punishment occurred when I was a teacher and assistant director of a poverty project at Hartford Seminary. Brenda (then my wife), my son Mike, and I were in our car as I drove to work to pick up some papers one evening. Down the street from the seminary, Mike had behaved so badly in the car that I pulled over to the side of the road to discipline him—three licks on his hands. In my view, it was a very light and well-deserved spanking. After administering this punishment, I drove the single block to the seminary.

Before I could park my car in front of the seminary two white policemen drove up in a squad car. They got out of the car and one of the policemen approached my door, instructing me to get out of the car. His partner walked up to Brenda's side of our car.

"Can I ask you why you're stopping me, officer?" I asked politely and professionally. I'd learned to do this, as most black men in America have learned, to keep the blue wrath from falling on my head.

"Just get out of the car," he insisted.

As I got out of my car, I informed the policeman that I worked at Hartford Seminary.

"I'm a professor here," I said, pointing to the seminary behind me.

"Sure," the policeman shot back. "And I'm John Wayne."

The policeman instructed me to place my hands against the car and to lean forward. I knew the drill. I'd done it too many times before. I could hear the other policeman asking Brenda if everything was all right, if my son was harmed. Mike was in the back seat crying, afraid of what the police were going to do to me.

"I'm fine, I'm fine," Mike cried. "Why are you doing this to my Dad?"

From the pieces of conversation I heard between the second cop and Brenda, I gathered that someone—a well-meaning white person no doubt—had spotted me spanking Mike and reported me as a child abuser.

Just as Brenda told the cop how ridiculous that was, two more police cars rolled up with four more white men. "Damn," I thought, "if I had been mugged, I bet I couldn't get a cop to respond within half an hour. And now, within five minutes of spanking my son, I've got six policemen breathing down my neck."

As the other cops surrounded our car, the policeman hovering over me refused to explain why he stopped me. He forcefully patted me down as we both listened to Brenda and Mike explain that nothing was wrong, that Mike was fine.

"You sure everything's all right?" the cop talking to Brenda asked once again for degrading emphasis. She angrily replied in the affirmative.

Finally my knight in shining armor spoke to me.

"We got a complaint that someone was hurting a child," he said.

"I can assure you that I love my son, and that I wasn't hurting him," I responded in a controlled tone.

"I spanked my child now so that he wouldn't one day end up being arrested by you."

"We have to check on these things," the second cop offered. "Just don't be doing nothing wrong."

He shoved me against the car to make his point. With that, the six cops got back into their cars, without apology, and drove off.

I don't have to tell you that the situation was utterly humiliating. I resented how I'd been treated. I felt the cops had deliberately intimidated me. They embarrassed me in front of my family under the guise of protecting them. I think their behavior is fairly typical of how many white men with authority treat black men. They are unable to be humane in the exercise of power. They run roughshod over black men in the name of serving a higher good, such as protecting black women and children from our aggression. The irony of course is that white men ignore how their violence against black men has already hurt millions of black families, including black women and children. In fact, the effect of much of white male hostility is not to help black women and children but to harm black males. Fortunately for me, Brenda and Mike understood that truth. Neither of them trusted the cops' motives for a moment.

Still, the incident forced me to imagine the impact my punishments had on Mike. I thought about how he might interpret the discipline I gave him. I wondered how spankings made him feel, despite the reassurances of love I prefaced to any punishments I gave him. The irony, too, is that I was reading social and cultural theorists who were writing about discipline and punishment. While I found many of them extremely enlightening about big social forces and how they molded people's habits of life at home and in the world, I sometimes wondered if they had any children. I continued to talk to Mike about these matters, apologizing to him about my past disciplinary practices, promising him, and mostly living up to it, that I would look for alternatives to physical punishment.

Of course Daddy lived in a world where such considerations were impossible. If you don't control your kids, they'll control you. That's the logic that informed his decisions. If you don't beat their asses, they'll beat yours one day. I guess depending on where you stand on such issues, the rash of recent slayings of parents by their children either proves or undermines such a theory. In any case, I eventually grew to hate Daddy for the violence of his punishments. I can still hear him saying "get me that 'hind pepper,'" referring to the quarter-inch-thick, twelve-inch-long piece of leather he used to whip us. Occasionally, he'd plant his size twelve foot right up my posterior.

I know, of course, that no one on our block would have called that child abuse. And neither did I. Given the black cultural logic of the time during which he was reared, and during which he and Mama reared us, Daddy was simply attempting to keep his brood in line. (What we must not forget is that during an earlier time in our nation, black folk beat their children at home so they wouldn't give white men lip in public. If a black child wasn't strictly disciplined, he might say or do something that might cause him untold danger away from the protection of parents. Even though that logic may be long exhausted, some habits die hard.)

My resentment of his whippings got so bad that he once told Mama that he thought I hated him because he wasn't my biological father. When Mama told me that, I was crushed.

For despite his discipline, I knew he loved me as if I was his very own, like I was your full blood brother. For that reason, I have never made the distinction between any of us five boys who came up together. In my mind, not only did we have the same mother, but we shared the same father. He was as much father as most of my friends had, and often, much, much more. Since he adopted me when I was two, he is the only father I have ever known. He was Daddy to me, just like he was to you.

No, I was very specific about my beef with him. It wasn't blood, it was those beatings. The same ones he gave to you, Anthony, Gregory, and Brian. And probably to John Everett, Etta James, Robert, and Annie Ruth, our late brothers and sisters from Daddy's previous marriages.

My conflict with Daddy came to a head when I was sixteen, the same age Mike is now. He had ordered me to do something, what I can't remember. I do remember feeling the familiar threat of physical punishment behind his words if I didn't immediately obey. I had had enough. We were at the house, upstairs on the second floor. He barked his orders, but I wasn't moving fast enough.

"Move, goddammit, when I speak to you," he bellowed.

The resentment weighed me down, and slowed my legs. I knew instantly that we were heading for a showdown. Daddy jumped up from the bed in his room and moved toward me. Even that gesture failed to speed my pace. This wasn't worker slowdown, a domestic uprising against an unjust guardian. This was sheer frustration, anger, and weariness.

"Move, I said," Daddy repeated. I didn't.

Then he grabbed me by the arm and pushed me against the wall. Something in me exploded. Or did it snap? Either metaphor, or perhaps both of them, captured my state of mind, my state of soul.

"Fuck it, man," I heaved. "You just gonna have to kill me, 'cause I refuse to be scared any more."

I guess he took me seriously. He literally lifted me off the ground with his left arm, his massive chocolate hand sunk deep into my yellow neck as he pinned me against a hallway wall. They didn't call him "Muscles" for nothing. I thought for sure that he might really kill me. I didn't care anymore. I was tired of running. Mama saved me.

"Everett," she hollered. It was all she said. But it was enough to bring Daddy to his senses, to make him drop me to the ground before he completely choked me. Never mind my gasping. I felt free, delivered of some awful demon of fear that no longer had power over me. It was my emancipation proclamation and declaration of independence all rolled into one moment. It was a milestone in my relationship to Daddy.

For the next seven years, his last on earth, Daddy and I got along much better. After I got Terrie pregnant at eighteen and married her, and after Mike was born, Daddy and I grew much closer. In fact, he'd often cook for me and Terrie because we were so poor at times that we didn't eat every day. In fact, at times, we didn't eat for two or three days in a row. But then we'd go by the house, and Daddy would always give us a good meal. I even sent Daddy a Father's Day card in 1981 when I was in Knoxville attending college. I told him how much I loved him, and how much I appreciated the fact that we had overcome our differences now that I was a man with major responsibilities. A few weeks later, he was dead from a heart attack at sixty-six. So young when you really think about it.

But I must confess, even now as a thirty-five-year-old man I have dreams of Daddy doing violent deeds to me, whipping me in vicious ways. The lingering effects of the whippings Daddy administered are illustrated in a story I heard about a boy and his father, who sought to rid his son of his habit of lying. The boy's father hammered nails into a piece of wood for each lie his son told. Finally, when the board was nearly full, the boy pledged to stop lying. And his father promised to pull a nail out each time his son told the truth. When the board was completely empty, the boy began to cry.

"What's wrong, son?" the boy's father asked. "You should be happy. You've stopped lying, and the nails are all gone."

"Yes," the boy replied. "The nails are gone, but the holes are still there."

Well, the holes are still there for me as well. My psyche bears the marks of spiritual and psychological violence. But I am not bitter toward Daddy. I honestly believe he was a good man trying to do his best in a world that was often difficult for him. The older I get, the more clearly I understand the forces he faced.

I guess I'm sharing all of this with you now because we never enjoyed this kind of intimacy before your imprisonment. A shame, but it's true. And even though we grew up in a household where we knew we were loved, we rarely, if ever, heard the words, "I love you." Daddy taught us to be macho men, strong enough to take care of ourselves on the mean streets of Detroit. And though Mama protested, thinking Daddy was trying to make us too rough at times, I'm sure we both appreciate many of his efforts to prepare us for an often cold-hearted, violent world.

I yearned for a home where we could be both strong and vulnerable, tough but loving. Daddy's reading of the world led him to believe it was either one or the other. He chose to teach us how to survive in a city that was known then, in the seventies, as the "Murder Capital of the World." And because I loved books, and not the cars that you and Daddy and Brian loved to work on, he sometimes thought I was "too soft." Daddy was really proud of me later when I excelled at school. He wanted me to be better than he was.

I remember once when I was about eight years old, I was mimicking his pronunciation of the number 4. He pronounced it "foe." I followed suit. But he stopped me.

"Don't you go to school, boy?" he asked.

"Yes," I replied.

"Don't you know how to say that right?"

"Yes."

"Then do that from now on. Okay?"

I've never forgotten that exchange. He didn't have a great education, but he sure wanted me to be learned. Indeed, he wanted the best for all his boys. I imagine if he was alive he'd be heartbroken that you're in prison. Daddy was the complete opposite of so much of what prison stands for. He rose every day before dawn, even after he retired from the factory, and worked until evening, cutting grass, laying sod, painting, or working as a maintenance man. I learned my work ethic from him. I can still hear him saying, "Boy, if you gonna do a job, do it right or don't do it at all." I've repeated that to Mike at least a million times. And of course, his other famous saying was "If you start a job, finish it." That is, other than his maxim: "Laziness will kill yo' ass."

And even when he worked those thirty-three years at Kelsey-Hayes Wheel-brake, and Drum Factory, he often put in sixty or seventy hours. I swear I once saw a stub where he had worked nearly eighty hours, pulling a double shift for an entire week. It was Daddy's example that led me to work two full-time jobs after Terrie got pregnant with Mike. (He warned me then, "The more money you make, the more you spend." He was right, of course.) I'd go to a maintenance job from 1:00 A.M. to 7:30 the next morning, and then work a menial "construction job" (a misnomer, to be sure) from 7:30 to 4:30 in the evening. And I still had to get food stamps while Terrie was enrolled in WIC (Women, Infants, and Children). That stuff saved our lives.

I'm glad that you and I have learned to talk. To communicate. To express our love for one another. It hasn't been easy seeing you cooped up like an animal when I visit you. But the one good thing to come out of all of this is that at least we're getting to know each other better. That's why I feel good about telling the world about you.

Even as I talk about you on television and radio, though, I always try to impress on the audiences and interviewers in the short time I have that ours is no "one son makes good and the other makes bad: what a tragedy" scenario. I'm not trying to pimp your pain or commercialize your misery to make a name for myself. That's because, I believe in my heart, and hope you do too, that it could just as easily be me in your cell. I don't want people using our story as a justification for rewarding black men like me who are able to do well while punishing brothers like you who've fallen on harder times.

No matter how much education I've got, this Ph.D. is no guarantee that I won't be treated cruelly and unjustly, that I won't be seen as a threat because I refuse to point the finger at "dem ghetto niggers" (a statement made by black and white alike) who aren't like me. I'm not trying to erase class differences, to pretend there's no difference in a black man with a Ph.D. and a black man who's a prisoner. I'm simply saying I can't be seduced into believing that because I've got this degree I'm better.

How could I be? I was one of "dem ghetto niggers" myself. Even now I think of myself as a ghetto boy, though I don't live there anymore, and I refuse to romanticize its role in its inhabitants' lives. Not even survivor's guilt can make me that blind. But being from the ghetto certainly leaves its marks on one's identity. Don't get me wrong. I'm all for serious, redemptive criticism of black life at every level, including the inner city. There's a difference between criticism that really helps and castigation that only hurts.

I should close this letter for now. I fear I've touched on many sensitive spots, and you may sharply disagree with some of the things I've written. But that's all right. The important thing is that as black men, as black brothers, we learn to embrace each other despite the differences that divide us. I hope you write me back. I'd really like to know what you think about what I've said. In the meantime, stay strong, and stay determined to renew your spirit and mind at the altar of devotion to God and our people. In the final analysis, it's the only thing that can save us all.

Peace and Love,
Mike

Three

THIS I BELIEVE

This speech was written for an oratorical contest sponsored by the Detroit Optimist Club when I was an eleven-year-old student at Webber Junior High School. I delivered the oration as a twelve-year-old neophyte who saw his award-winning speech published later that year in a Detroit educational magazine. I was also featured in the local newspaper. I can still recall the photo of me gesturing underneath the Detroit News *headlines: "12 Year Old Boy's Plea Against Racism Wins Award." I suppose my fight for social justice and racial equality began quite early. The speech recalls the influence of Martin Luther King's dream for racial harmony. It bears as well the imprint of the social unrest and urban rebellion that seized the nation in the late '60s and early '70s. Given that I spend more than 150 days annually delivering lectures, sermons, addresses, and speeches across the nation, it is ironic to note that my vocation as a public speaker began in trepidation. On Webber Junior High School's loudspeaker, the announcement went forth about an "oratorical contest." After school, I made my way to English teacher Mr. Otis Burdette's room as directed to discover what oratorical meant. When I was told that it had to do with public speaking, I immediately demurred, but Mr. Burdette convinced me to give it a try. I went on to win several contests over the next two years. Last year, I reconnected with Mr. Burdette after not seeing him for nearly thirty years. He told me then what he didn't have the heart to say to me as a twelve-year-old boy: that I had not won a regional oratorical contest because of racist judges. Thus, there was a strange, even poetic, symmetry between my speech, my life, and my subsequent vocation combating injustice as an intellectual insurgent and rhetorical guerrilla.*

NOT OFTEN IS THE SUBJECT OF **BROTHERHOOD** brought up. War, crime, and other various things are often talked about, but not brotherhood. I believe that one day we won't have discrimination or anything relating to it in the world. There shall be, someday, a faith in all people that will make them see, if they have faith in their country and its peace, that they are taking a step toward having a better world.

Our leaders of yesteryear, and our leaders of today all have tried to make a profitable world for us. If we want peace and justice for ourselves, we must also sacrifice to become profitable.

We must look ahead, never back. When I say this I mean we shouldn't think of the time when a man was beaten, or had to go to jail because of the color of his skin. Instead, we should look for a brighter future.

Our motive shall be to seek the day when all men, disregarding the color of their skins, shall be able to stand up and say that they have overcome the act of devaluating other people and that they can live together in continuing harmony, a harmony that will accomplish what leaders before us have tried.

All people, at times, have dreams about how they can improve our world, but some of us can't quite express ourselves because we are young and don't know how to bring these dreams out. If this is your problem, you should get your ideas across to someone who will act upon them, in a way that will make them sensible and conspicuous.

We should construct an enduring faith within ourselves, a faith that can withstand the problems caused by man, a faith that can someday help man solve the problems he has committed, and that faith should be entrenched in understanding!

We can't judge a person because of the way he looks or because he handles situations differently than us. I believe you should judge a person on what he attempts to do, rather than on how he accomplishes it. I believe that he is putting effort into what he is trying to accomplish. Leaders from many nations would agree that it's not how you do it, but what you try to do. That's what counts.

The late Rev. Dr. Martin Luther King, Jr., provided many benefits for people, but the night before he was assassinated he asked, when someone delivers the eulogy at his funeral, not to mention the many awards he won, but to mention that he had tried to clothe, feed, and get equal rights for all people. Sometimes when someone does something little, he looks for a lot of praise, but this brilliant man only wanted people to remember him in a way knowing that he helped humanity. This sets an example for all people. Dr. King struggled for what he thought was right.

If we have dreams that will benefit our world, we must bring them out, or get them across to someone, because if you think they're worth hearing, they must be heard!

All people, young and old, can at least be listened to, to see if they have anything of meaning that will make our world a better place to live. An old saying composed by Benjamin Franklin, "A penny earned is a penny saved," relates to this, because "A dream gained is a dream made into reality."

I believe that true leadership in bringing people together in a way that is understandable and acceptable to them is the first step in having people respecting and sharing their thoughts and beliefs with humanity. When people have reached the time in their lives when they can accept others as they are, then we might have a world fulfilled with tranquillity! This will be the day when all men will be able to transform their oasis of belief into a quality of success.

PART TWO

THEORIES OF RACE

Racism remains the central problem in our culture; its brutal persistence brings out the ugliest features of the national character. I have spent quite a bit of time reading, writing, and thinking about race, and no small effort opposing racism's malevolent expression. We must clearly grasp the difference between race—the culturally determined base of identity upon which social benefit and stigma rests—and racism—the sordid expression of prejudice and hatred against a racial group with the sanction of law and social custom. Otherwise, we won't make much headway in understanding why it is sometimes helpful to take race into account, even as we continue to fight against white supremacy, one of the most destructive forms of racism in history.

Four

THE LIBERAL THEORY OF RACE

*In 1985, Edmund Perry, a Harlem youth who graduated with honors from Phillips
Exeter Academy, won a full scholarship to attend Stanford University. Ten days later, he
was killed on New York's Upper West Side by a white undercover detective, Lee Van
Houten. The plainclothes policeman claimed that Perry and his brother, Jonah, then a
nineteen-year-old engineering student at Cornell, had viciously beaten him during a robbery
attempt. The story caused an immediate uproar. It also provoked a great deal of hand-
wringing about the difficulties of urban youth straddling two cultures—one black and poor,
the other rich and white. In fact, it is the Edmund Perry story that inspired Michael
Jackson's long-form video "Bad." Robert Sam Anson, a noted journalist, penned a book on
Perry that also addressed the racial and personal factors that may have driven him to self-
destructive behavior. I knew one of Perry's former teachers, the respected religious historian
David Daniels, who is interviewed in Anson's book. Daniels was uncomfortable with the
limiting racial lens through which Anson viewed the case. I wrote this review of Anson's
book to explore the intricacies and contradictions of the Perry case. I sought to engage the
liberal racial paradigm that may have ultimately prevented Anson from successfully
explaining a youth like Perry and the cultural and racial predicaments he confronted.*

THE ABYSMAL STATE OF RACE RELATIONS in American culture is a continuing
source of bewilderment and frustration. The reappearance of overt racist activity,
especially on college and secondary school campuses, forces us to reevaluate our
understanding of race as we approach the last decade of the twentieth century. In
particular, the liberal theory of race, which has dominated the American understanding of race relations, has exhibited a crisis of explanation, manifested in its exponents' inability to elucidate persistent forms of Afro-American oppression.

Robert Anson's book *Best Intentions: The Education and Killing of Edmund Perry* (New
York: Random House, 1988), which recently appeared in paperback, reflects the
crisis in liberal race theory. Anson's perspective is rooted in a theory of race that
prevents him from understanding the complex ways in which racism continues to
exert profound influence over the lives of millions of black people. In particular, his
explanation of the social and personal forces that besieged Edmund Perry's life,
and caused his death, is severely limited by Anson's approach. By examining issues
raised in Anson's treatment of Perry's life and death, I want to comment upon the

limits of the liberal theory of race and show how Anson's use of it distorts crucial issues that need to be addressed.

In 1981, Edmund Perry, a black teenager "of exceptional promise," left Harlem for Exeter, New Hampshire, in order to attend one of the nation's most prestigious prep schools. On June 2, 1985, he graduated from Phillips Exeter Academy with honors, having been awarded a full scholarship to Stanford University. Ten days later, a short distance from Harlem on New York City's Upper West Side, Perry was killed by Lee Van Houten, a young white plainclothes police officer. Van Houten reported that Perry and an accomplice had beaten him viciously during a robbery attempt on the night of June 12.

Van Houten stated that after yelling that he was a police officer, he managed, with blurred vision and failing consciousness, to pull his gun from its ankle holster and fire three shots. One attacker, who held him from behind, fled; Perry, who assaulted him frontally, lay on his back on the sidewalk, stilled by a wound to his stomach. At 12:55 A.M., after being taken to nearby St. Luke's Hospital, Edmund Perry was pronounced dead. (Perry's brother Jonah, then a nineteen-year-old engineering student at Cornell University, was said to have been the accomplice that night. Jonah Perry was later formally charged and cleared by a grand jury.)

Robert Anson is a freelance magazine writer and author. At the time of Perry's killing his son was also a student at Exeter and, in fact, had sat behind Perry every day during school assembly. This connection accounts, in part, for Anson's interest in the Perry story, even after widespread public shock over the shooting subsided. An even more powerful motivation, however, was the apparent contradiction Edmund Perry represented. On the one hand, Perry had "all the things anyone was supposed to need to climb out of poverty and make it in America." On the other hand, if Perry had actually died trying to mug Van Houten, then something had gone "dreadfully haywire," despite the "best intentions" of Harlem and Exeter. Anson's book is his search for an understanding of Perry's life, education, and killing, and thereby of racism in U.S. society.

Anson begins by looking for a conclusive account of what happened on the night of June 12. His investigation is fatally compromised by the fact that Lee Van Houten was the only eyewitness to the event. What Anson does is piece together circumstantial evidence that he believes supports Van Houten's story. (The official police inquiry ruled the killing of Edmund Perry "justifiable homicide" and within departmental guidelines.)

Several factors—Perry's personal reputation, the number of shootings of black men by New York City police, and especially the lack of concrete proof against Edmund and Jonah Perry and Van Houten's inability to identify Jonah as one of the two assailants—lead me to conclude we will never be certain about the events of June 12. We should, however, still look seriously at other issues Anson raises (and doesn't raise) in his search for an explanation of Perry's life: the position of racial minorities in predominantly white institutions, the consequences of juggling two cultures, the ongoing racism of American culture, and the inability of most existing race theory to illuminate racism's malignant persistence.

Since Anson's investigation leads him to rule out foul play or police attempts at cover-up, he follows the lead of one of the principal police investigators—a garrulous detective who tells him the streets had eaten Perry alive. Thus, Anson goes to Harlem.

Through a set of interviews that are the greatest strength of the book, Anson tries to piece together a picture of Edmund Perry's life and the environment that produced and shaped him. We hear the proud voices of women who had driven dope dealers from the streets by their sheer physical presence; the admiring voices of friends who were inspired by Perry's discipline and dedication to his ambitious goals; the knowing voices of former co-survivors of the vicious circle of drugs, poverty, and violence, one of whom contended that "Edmund died a natural death up here"; the perceptive voice of a pastor who appreciated Perry's religious values and his ability to maneuver between two cultures; the empathetic voices of other blacks who had struggled with the difficulty and guilt of their departure from desolate and beleaguered circumstances; and the pained voices of former teachers and mentors who identified and nurtured Perry's powerful intelligence and talent.

Above all, we hear the strikingly ambitious and sacrificial voice of Perry's mother. Veronica Perry emerges as a powerful woman who fought tooth and nail the despair and cynicism that too often conform Harlem life to its ugly mold— a woman who sent both her sons to prestigious prep schools, successfully ran for the school board, and worked ceaselessly to raise the quality of life in her neighborhood.

The picture of Edmund Perry that formed was one of an extremely bright, hard worker who possessed a mature vision of life's purpose and an infectious compassion for his people—a vision nurtured by strong religious beliefs. But Anson, sensing a canonizing impulse at work in the stories of friends, teachers, and mentors, searches for a fuller picture. He wants Edmund Perry, warts and all, and so he begins interviewing classmates, teachers, and administrators at Exeter.

Many at Exeter spoke of Perry's intelligence, his eagerness to perform well, his quick wit, his enormous love for his mother, his pride in (and rivalry with) his brother, Jonah. Exeter's chaplain said Perry was guarded, rarely revealing much about himself. Some black classmates, especially women, thought that initially Perry could be "pushy" or "cocky," something they attributed to his neighborhood roots. Some white classmates were disturbed by what they perceived to be an extraordinary "racial sensitivity." David Daniels, then one of only three blacks on the faculty and the adult closest to Perry at Exeter, conceded that point: Perry "was sensitive about race, probably more so than the other black students. I never saw any racial hostility though. Instead, there was frustration, exasperation."

Anson also reports on the year Perry spent in Barcelona, as well as his troubled final year at Exeter. Perry told many people he experienced no racism in Spain, but Anson contends this was deliberate misrepresentation of the facts. He observes that in this case, as in others, "it was becoming apparent that Eddie had a propensity for telling different stories to different people."

During his final year at Exeter, Perry's work fell off, and he became increasingly hostile. Anson details Perry's participation in a club that demanded a sexual initiation, and discusses his (and others') low-level drug dealing. Perry also delivered a "tough and angry" speech to a schoolwide assembly on Martin Luther King's birthday. The speech, written immediately after King's assassination by a former black Exeter student, used Black Power rhetoric to make a bristling declaration of black independence.

Overall, the picture of Perry that emerged from Exeter was one of a deeply troubled young man whose racial identity caused him and, by extension, those around him a great deal of pain. Now Anson is sure: "Edmund Perry had indeed been killed while trying to assault an officer of the law. Why he had done so was less apparent to me."

Unfortunately, the assumptions that Anson brings to his search for an adequate explanation of Perry's death guarantee that he will not find one. The backdrop for most of his reflections on Perry is a scissors-and-paste version of the liberal theory of race—a theory that even in its more sophisticated manifestations has never come to terms with the reality of structural racism.

The liberal understanding of race in the United States is modeled on the white European immigrant experience.[1] In making this experience paradigmatic, liberal theorists have lumped race together with other variables—religion, language, and nationality, for example—and taken them all to constitute a larger ethnic identity that is more crucial than race in explaining the condition of black people. The focus on ethnicity means that liberal theories of race are primarily concerned either with ethnic assimilation or with the maintenance of ethnic identity through cultural pluralism.

Thus lawyer Madison Grant advanced his Anglo-conformity theory of ethnicity in the 1920s, contending that there must be total assimilation and conformity to Anglo-American life in order for white Americans to retain their racial purity. Historian Frederick J. Turner and Jewish immigrant Israel Zangwill composed the melting-pot theory, which asserted that America is best seen as a pot in which all ethnic groups are melting and merging together. Horace Kallen proposed the notion of cultural pluralism, saying that each culture maintains its own character while coexisting with other groups. And Moynihan and Glazer promoted the emerging culture theory, maintaining that cultures interact and the resultant combination produces a political and cultural *tertium quid,* the phenomenon of the hyphenated American (e.g., African-American).

The liberal theory of race has informed the party practices, jurisprudential reasoning, and legislative agendas of its most ardent and aggressive political proponents, the liberal Democrats. Liberal race theory experienced a fragile inception in FDR's New Deal, a tentative strengthening under Truman's Fair Deal, and a substantial solidification in Kennedy's and Johnson's Great Society due to the civil rights movement. In sociopolitical dress, liberal race theory has argued for a greater black share in jobs, for integration of housing and education, and for desegregation of interstate transportation as strategies to assure black inclusion and assimilation in the larger circle of American privilege.

The problem with the theory is that it encounters an insurmountable obstacle: the irreducible reality of race. Because it conceives of race as merely a part of one's broader ethnic identity, liberal race theory is unable to make sense of the particular forms of oppression generated primarily by racial identity. Much of the time, it cannot explain why blacks have failed to "assimilate" because it has not acknowledged the unique structural character of racism or historical content of racial oppression—slavery, Jim Crow laws, structural unemployment, gentrification of black living space, deeply ingrained institutional racism. At this point, however, instead of revising their fundamental assumptions, liberal race theorists tend to explain blacks' failure to "assimilate" successfully by looking almost exclusively at problems *within* black culture and by treating these problems as givens.

More specifically, liberal theory opts for an explanation of the debilitating effects of racism that reduces them to their psychological effects on the black personality. It does not weave its psychological analysis into a dynamic understanding of the persistent social, historical, and political aspects of racism. While it is undeniable that racism's effect on the black psyche is deleterious, to perceive that as racism's *primary* damage obscures the persistent structural factors that enforce and reinforce perceptions of personal inferiority, rage, and hostility. That kind of reductionism hinders our understanding of personal identity as a construct of several different elements—social, psychological, political, and historical—and makes it likely that we will mislocate the causes of black failure to "assimilate."

This psychological reductionism is nowhere more apparent than in the second half of *Best Intentions*. As Anson interviews Perry's classmates, teachers, and administrators, he draws a psychological portrait of Perry as an angry, hostile, and belligerent person. True, but Anson never really tells us why. He does not connect his psychological portrait to any social structural analysis—either of Exeter or of Harlem as Perry experienced them. When we do get hints of an explanation of Perry's actions—from either his white classmates or Anson—they are usually by way of further appeals to psychological factors. His classmates say Ed had a chip on his shoulder because of race, indeed that he was a racist himself. Anson wonders whether the stories of white racism that Veronica Perry told Ed "shaped" him, because he was "impressionable," possibly causing him to attempt to mug a New York police officer.

To his credit, Anson considers the possibility that Ed's psychic turmoil was occasioned by the clash of cultures between Harlem and Exeter. But aside from a brief review of common understandings of race relations, liberal social policy, and Harlem history of the last few decades, he doesn't even begin to cover the moral, political, socioeconomic, and historical ground that psychology shares in a plausible explanation of Perry's life and behavior. The condition of the black underclass, the way in which gentrification of black living space continues to shrink black life options, an understanding of the psychic, spiritual, and physical attack on black men—all these factors would help chart a comprehensive approach to Perry's life and death.

Such an approach would avoid merely personalistic explanations that totally blame Perry. It would also avoid merely structural explanations that totally absolve Perry of any responsibility for the choices he made. In short, it would provide the richest detail possible about the circumstances of Perry's life so that he is rendered as a human being faced with difficult choices, choices that must be made within a complicated configuration of personal and structural constraints. Anson simply has not done this.

Instead, he gets mired in a great myth of liberal theory—the myth of meritocracy—and fails to comprehend how a person of Perry's talent could have failed. The dominant belief that legitimates the central place of achievement in U.S. culture and explains the distribution of goods and privileges is that all things being relatively equal, one gets what one merits, based upon intelligence, industry, and a host of other American character traits. The single most important social issue that has focused the problems and contradictions of the meritocratic approach is affirmative action.

Throughout *Best Intentions* Anson employs Perry as an example of the "legitimate" complaints white Exeter students had against blacks for receiving "preferential treatment." He says that Perry's race helped him gain admission to Stanford and Yale. Furthermore, Anson reports, several Exeter faculty members admitted this point, referring to the experience of the white valedictorian in Perry's senior year "who possessed an academic and extracurricular record far more distinguished than Eddie's," and who applied to Stanford, "but was not admitted." This example is intriguing because throughout the book Anson reports that Perry was, by most accounts, an extremely intelligent, articulate youngster "sought after by name" by places like Princeton and Yale. But its importance lies elsewhere. It reflects the confusion of effect with cause that underlies Anson's view of Perry. Anson seems to forget that affirmative action was instituted to redress inequality of opportunity; whites who inherit the privileges of economic resources, old boy networks, and the like are not making it on "merit" alone.

The kind of assumptions that inform Anson's thinking are precisely what exacerbated Perry's situation as a black student at a predominantly white institution. On the one hand, many "liberals" want to address past wrongs by admitting qualified minority students to elite educational institutions. On the other hand, these same students are then blamed for extending and perpetuating inequality by being the recipients of "preferential treatment." Unfortunately the terrain on which this battle is fought is the lives of minority students. How can Anson grasp Perry when he, too, is a victim of the same limited understanding?

Anson might have overcome the limits of his approach if he had made a more sustained attempt to acquaint himself with Afro-American culture. But as is clear in several places in *Best Intentions*, he just doesn't understand the general concerns or basic themes of Afro-American life.

Anson asks whether the stories Veronica Perry told her son, stories about the evils of white racism and the need not to "judge all whites harshly," had made Perry "racially proud" or "angry enough, possibly, to have vented that rage on a seemingly innocuous white boy on a darkened city street." What Anson apparently doesn't understand is that in telling her son these stories Veronica Perry was performing the tragically necessary task most black parents face: telling her child about the viciousness of racism while ratifying her Christian belief that hate is not the proper response for victimized blacks. Thus, she was preparing Edmund Perry to negotiate the difficult process of identifying and acknowledging racism while channeling the resulting, and justifiable, anger into creative and redemptive strategies for coping.

Anson remarks that Perry told different stories to different people, pointing to the obvious fact that he was "pretending" in order to augment his image as a ghetto street tough. But there is more. As is obvious throughout the book, Perry more easily (although sometimes only after extensive scrutiny) formed close associations with other blacks and especially sympathetic whites, able to tell and share one story with them and another with the rest of Exeter. Perry most likely learned, as do most black people, that he could not afford to bare his soul often— either because truth telling could not be borne by particular moods of the white conscience or because it could not be tolerated by many aspects of the white worldview. For example, when told by a teacher that he needed counseling, Perry said there wasn't anyone on campus he could talk to, that the only people he could talk to were black, and that "anytime he tried to open up to whites and be honest, he always wound up hurting someone's feelings." Or again: a white student who shared many classes with Perry told him that "people are just people," and that "some people are white and some people are black, and if you are going to get bummed out about it, it's pretty dumb."

Thus, in order to avoid a discourse of perpetual blame (whose payoff is usually only increased frustration) and the pain of having to explain oneself, to argue for the logic or legitimacy of one's being, Perry adopted a familiar coping strategy: he knew when, and when not, to open and reveal himself. While, as a maturing youth, Perry undoubtedly "pretended" and lied, it is important not to confuse this with strategies adopted to deal with an environment that is hostile and insensitive to one's identity. Ironically, Anson's psychological perspective does not comprehend this crucial point.

More poignantly, throughout the book Anson quotes and refers to Veronica Perry's strong religious beliefs, which Anson thinks are "extremely intense." He sees Veronica Perry's swing from profound belief in the wisdom of God in taking her son to a bitter denouncement of the police system that killed him as a possible indication of her emotional instability. (She had had a nervous breakdown.) In fact, her "mood swing" may be understood as ad hoc theodicy, an attempt to come to grips theologically as best she could with the evil that killed her child. It is an attempt to vindicate—through faith—belief in a good and loving God who may appear absent or silent in the face of human suffering, without at the same time excusing the human beings who inflict that suffering. It is a theme that runs through the Afro-American Christian engagement with the world, and it is a central problem in Christian theology.

Finally, a most telling moment comes when, in speaking of what led to Perry's death, Anson concludes, "The only villain I found was something amorphous, not a person or thing, just a difference called race." He then checks his conclusion with "the only black friend I really had." It happens that Anson's phantom friend also knew Edmund Perry. The disturbing aspect of this is that Anson checks the viability of his interpretive vision against the understanding, insight, and knowledge of one black man, who, Anson says, offered to "guide me as my reporting went along, not by providing specific leads, but by confirming whether or not what I came up with was correct." We are thus left with the definite impression that Anson does not know very much about the *diversity* of Afro-American thought and culture. In what constitutes an irony of liberalism, he depends upon his only black friend, thereby tokenizing that thought and culture and segregating himself from a powerful tradition that might have deepened his reflections on Perry's life and death.

The upshot of Anson's approach is that even though he unearths the conflicts and consequences of being socially and culturally amphibious, of negotiating the psychological demands of two different worlds, his findings just pass him by. He cannot fashion an understanding of Edmund Perry's life and death. All we hear is the restatement of a "difference called race" without any attempt to explain what difference that difference makes.

Two other approaches to race might have helped Anson understand what made Edmund Perry's life hell. The first is the racial formation theory advanced by Michael Omi and Howard Winant in their book *Racial Formation in the United States.* In going beyond liberal race theory, Omi and Winant want to avoid the economic determinist and class reductionist elements in most progressive and leftist race theory, and conceive race as an irreducible category, like gender and class, for social theorizing about oppression. Racial formation theory, then, seeks to capture the process by which racial categories are formed, transformed, destroyed, and reformed. Furthermore, it treats race as a central axis of social relations that resists being subsumed under a larger category like ethnicity. It takes seriously the psychological, social, political, cultural, and historical as crucial explanatory strands in a full-blown theory of race.

The second theory is Cornel West's analysis of race, first articulated in *Prophesy Deliverance!* and now developed in an essay in his new book, *Prophetic Fragments.*[2] West, like Winant and Omi, seeks to avoid reductionist accounts of racism. West's theory permits him to trace the emergence and development (or genealogy) of the idea of white racism and supremacy in modern Western discourse. Such an approach promotes the unearthing of the material, economic, political, cultural, psychological, sexual, and spiritual forces that express and respond to the social practices of racism within the cultural traditions of Western civilization. West's theory has three stages: (1) a radical historical investigation of the emergence, development, and persistence of white supremacy; (2) an analysis of the mechanisms that develop and maintain the logic of white supremacy in the everyday lives of people of color; and (3) an examination of how class exploitation, state repression, and bureaucratic domination operate in the lives of people of color. Both theories, then, offer an analysis of racism that takes seriously the psychological, social, political, cultural, and historical as crucial explanatory strands. They therefore offer a much more comprehensive picture, in alliance with the broader and deeper perspective of Afro-American culture, of the complex, stubborn reality Edmund Perry faced.

In a revealing passage early in the book, Anson tells of the time Martin Luther King came to Chicago to march for open housing. It was the summer of 1966, and Anson, fresh out of Notre Dame, was a correspondent for *Time*. He marched with King and was present when King was hit on the head with a rock. He was one of the people who "pulled him up and shielded him." The supreme irony may be that twenty years later, while intending to shield King's legacy, Anson has left it more vulnerable and exposed.

Five

WHEN YOU'RE A CREDIT TO YOUR RACE, THE BILL WILL COME DUE: O.J. SIMPSON AND OUR TRIAL BY FIRE

The cultural critic Mark Anthony Neal has written that I "became one of the brightest lights among black public intellectuals in the aftermath of the O.J. Simpson trial, providing commentary during the trial (and immediately after the jury decision) for NPR and appearing as the 'color commentator' on BET, when Ed Gordon sat down with Simpson after his acquittal." My participation that night on BET was surely memorable—it was Simpson's first interview after vacating his famous Los Angeles jail cell. Still, it wasn't as memorable as the call Simpson placed to me on the evening of the fifth anniversary of the Nicole Simpson/Ron Goldman murders. I had appeared earlier that day on NBC's Today Show, along with television host Geraldo Rivera and critic Neal Gabler. "Should I call you Reverend, Professor, or Doctor Dyson?" the famous voice politely quizzed me before launching into an animated forty-five-minute discussion of his innocence, the evidence in his criminal trial, the bias of Marcia Clark, the false accusation that most of his friends were white, and the unheralded work he did on behalf of the black community—especially his participation in a golf tournament sponsored by The Links, an elite black women's service organization. That conversation with Simpson remains one of the most surreal moments I've experienced in all my years of punditry. This chapter from Race Rules *is my attempt to come to grips with one of the most inglorious racial spectacles the nation has endured in the past fifty years.*

Now it says here, "And every white man shall be allowed to pet himself a Negro. Yea, he shall take a black man unto himself to pet and to cherish, and this same Negro shall be perfect in his sight. . . ." The appointee has his reasons, personal or political. He can always point to the beneficiary and say, "Look, Negroes, you have been taken care of. Didn't I give a member of your group a big job?"

—ZORA NEALE HURSTON
"THE 'PET' NEGRO SYSTEM," 1943

THE STUDIO CRACKLED WITH EXCITEMENT. Although I had appeared on Black Entertainment Television (BET) a few times before, this night was special. In fact, it was extraordinary. Former BET anchor Ed Gordon, my Detroit homeboy, had snagged the first televised interview with O.J. Simpson since his acquittal for the murder of his ex-wife, Nicole, and her companion, Ron Goldman. BET asked me to give "color commentary" before and after Simpson's appearance. A large irony, indeed. I'd written about Simpson in my previous book, and I'd discussed his trial on other national television shows. But there was poetic justice in me talking about Simpson's trials and tribulations, and those of black America, on the only television station that caters to black folk.

I must confess that I was an O.J. addict. I watched the trial every day for hours at a time. I was completely mesmerized. I knew it was a vulgar display of American excess. I knew it was the revelation of the gaudiness behind the lifestyles of the rich and famous. (Of course, I took delight in seeing so many rich folk exposed for the shallow people many of us hoped they'd be.) I knew it was the theater of the absurd meets the Twilight Zone. I knew as well that the trial was a painful choreography of black grief—that of O.J. and of every black person who identified with him—before an international audience. I knew it was totally artificial, a sordid drama full of kitsch that fiendishly aspired to the status of morality play. I knew it was the story of a black man who had made good but who had forgotten what made it possible, which made it bad. I knew it was all that and much, much more. And I couldn't stop watching.

Even as questions about O.J.'s guilt or innocence fade from daily debate, we continue to grapple with the wounds the trial exposed, with the trial's revelations of the pernicious rules of race in America, '90s style. That night, as I viewed Simpson on the big screen in BET's green room, I was struck again by how flawless his face is, how smooth his skin is. But I was taken as well by the jagged horrors his eyes never gaze on—how many white folk now hate his name, how they wish he would disappear. And some wish him dead. And how black folk look at him with a mix of pity and disdain. Like the member of the family you have to recognize but hate to, because the recognition embarrasses him as well. I was struck by the size of the denials by which Simpson lives, as if he must now draw energy from the resentment that he can't afford to acknowledge, though its sheer vehemence defines and confirms his every step. Seeing Simpson so resiliently spiteful that night—not in any way bitter against whites, just against the idea that they might not love him—made it painful for me to have to say anything after he spoke. It was the final step in my loss of a hero who had once thrilled me, as he, in Ralph Ellison's words, "slice[d] through an opposing line with a dancer's slithering grace." A part of me was now gone. It was sad, and sadly disorienting.

Something of the same disorientation gripped America when Simpson was set free. When the not-guilty verdicts in the O.J. Simpson double-murder case were handed down, the compass of race went haywire. The Simpson case has made many Americans doubt if we can all get along. The case has rudely reminded us of a gigantic and numbing racial divide. It reminds us, too, that boasting about racial progress often hides racial pain. The response to the verdicts knocked down the floodgates that hold back the waters of racial hostility The Simpson case also taught us a tough lesson: the more settled race relations seem to be, the more likely they are raging beneath the surface.

Americans have become addicted to the Simpson case for more than its grotesque exaggeration of our secret racial fears. From its very beginning the case was overloaded with huge social meanings we claim not to be able to understand under normal circumstances. We have become dependent on the Simpson case to represent complicated truths that we think can only be illustrated by catastrophe. That dependence shows contempt for ordinary signs of ruin. It ignores the experience of common people, especially blacks, whose silent suffering is the most powerful evidence of decay. What their experience shows us is this: a two-tiered universe of perception rotates around an axis defined by race. While good fortune lights one side, despair darkens the other. It is rarely sunny at the same time in white and black America. In a nutshell, that's what the Simpson case reminds us of.

That O.J. Simpson is at the heart of the most ugly racial spectacle to hit America in decades is a symptom of just how crazy things are. For a quarter century, Simpson symbolized the icon-next-door. His athletic genius was revered by many blacks. His athletic skill and "colorless" image were attractive to millions of whites.

Simpson's sleek form and catlike grace as a running back brought glamour to a brutal sport. Simpson beautifully combined judgment and intuition. His sixth sense for where his pursuers were likely to pounce on him allowed him to chisel arteries of escape around heaving bodies.

As with many famous athletes, Simpson's athletic exploits gave him influence beyond the boundaries of his sport. This is hardly natural. After all, why should athletes receive tons of money and notoriety beyond the recognition and compensation they earn in sports? The absurdity of this is masked by the fact that we take for granted that such things should occur. That's not to say sports don't teach us valuable lessons about life. Sports are often a powerful training ground for moral excellence. Take the case of Willis Reed, the injured center for the 1969–1970 New York Knicks who was not expected to play in the seventh and deciding game for the NBA championship. When Reed emerged from the locker room, limping but determined to compete, several virtues were literally embodied: sacrifice of self for the sake of the larger good; the courage to "play through pain"; and the sort of moral leadership that rallies one's teammates and lifts their level of expectation and achievement. These virtues transcend sport. They inspire ordinary people to overcome obstacles in achieving their goals.

There's another way, one wholly beyond his choosing, that the rare athlete has managed to rise beyond the limits of his sport. Some figures have served as heroic symbols of national identity. Others have heroically represented achievement against the artificial restrictions imposed on a group of people. In those cases, a restriction was also placed on competition as an ideal of democratic participation.

Joe DiMaggio, of course, fit the first bill. His fifty-six-game hitting streak in base-ball thrilled America in 1941, a colossal feat of endurance to which the nation would turn its attention time and again as our preeminence as a world power began to fade after World War II. Jackie Robinson fit the second meaning of hero-ism. As major league baseball's first black player, Robinson performed gallantly in the face of bitter opposition. His gifted play paved the way for blacks in his sport and beyond the bounds of baseball.

Joe Louis managed the difficult art of fulfilling both sorts of heroism. He ex-isted in a racial era just as complex—if more violent—as the one Robinson faced. As was true of DiMaggio's Italian world, Louis's black community celebrated its ethnic roots while affirming its American identity. Louis captured the genius of American citizenship and the protest of blacks against their exclusion from full cit-izenship in a single gesture: the punch that sunk German boxer Max Schmeling at the height of Nazism. That punch transformed Louis into an American hero. It also revealed the hidden meaning of Louis's heroic art: beating white men in the ring was a substitute argument for social equality. Louis's prizefighting was an elo-quent plea to play the game of American citizenship by one set of rules.

Simpson never aspired to that sort of heroism. In part, that's because the times didn't demand it. Near the start of Simpson's pro career in the late '60s, the tension between the older civil rights establishment and the newer black power movement produced a more acerbic model of black heroism. Instead of integration, many blacks preferred separating from white society to build black institutions. Black antiheroism gave an angry face to the resentment that festered in pockets of black life. To be an American and a Negro—later still, a black man—were not considered flip sides of the same coin. They were different cur-rency altogether.

Judging from Simpson's behavior during the height of his career, he had no in-terest in claiming whatever remained of Louis's heroic inheritance. Neither was Simpson attracted to the sort of antiheroism championed by his contemporary, Muhammad Ali. Ali's self-promoting verse and brilliant boxing proved to be spar-ring matches for his real battle: the defiance of white authority because of his re-ligious beliefs. And Simpson certainly wasn't drawn to the plainspoken demeanor of fellow athlete-turned-actor Jim Brown. Brown's militant, studly image had Crazy Negro written all over it. It was the opposite of everything Simpson seemed to stand for. That is, until he was charged with brutally slashing his ex-wife and her companion.

Simpson's appeal beyond sports rested on two related but distinct factors: com-merce and the conscious crafting of a whitened image. Simpson came at the be-ginning of an era when athletes began to make enormous sums of money inside sports. (To be sure, Simpson's highest salary was pittance compared to what even mediocre sports figures now make.) He also helped pioneer the entrepreneurial athlete. Simpson hawked everything from tennis shoes to soft drinks. He turned charisma into cash on television. Now that Michael Jordan has eclipsed everyone who came before him, it's easy to forget that Simpson's Hertz commercials used to be the star that athletes aimed for in marketing their fame.

The wide adulation heaped on Simpson beyond his gridiron glory also owed much to his absent, indeed *anti*-racial politics. Simpson soothed white anxieties about the racial turmoil caused by black radicalism. Simpson's Teflon racelessness assured white citizens and corporations that no negative, that is, exclusively black, racial inference would stick to his image. That is Jordan's charm as well. He is a latter-day Simpson of sorts. His universal appeal derives from a similar avoidance of the entanglements of race. As the old black saying goes, it's alright to *look* black, just don't act your color. As Simpson's case suggests, the Faustian bargain of trading color for commercial success may prove devastating in the long run.

Simpson's silence about race didn't necessarily have to be a bad thing. After all, given the history of their relative powerlessness, blacks have a heroic tradition of fighting in ways that cloak their rebellion. They adapt their speech and activity to the language and styles of the dominant society. Silence in the presence of whites was often a crucial weapon in the war to survive. If it looked like blacks were happy to be oppressed, all the better. Such appearances greased the track of covert action on which black freedom rolled. For instance, slaves sang spirituals both to entertain their masters and to send each other coded messages about plans of escape.

Still, Simpson's privileged perch in white America led many blacks to hope that he might cautiously speak about the troubles of ordinary blacks. It soon became clear, however, that Simpson was having none of that. What many blacks wanted from Simpson was no different from what was expected of other blacks. Simpson was not expected to be a politician. At least not in any way that departed from the political behavior required of all blacks in O.J.'s youth, who had to carry themselves with an acute awareness of their surroundings. To do less meant early death. Or, more crushing, it meant a slow, painful surrender of life in gasps of frustrated energy because you just didn't understand the rules of survival in a white world.

It's easy to understand how O.J. and other blacks wanted to escape the demands of being representatives of The Race, its shining symbols. Standing in for the group was a burden. It was also risky. You could never be sure that your efforts were taken seriously. In fact, a law of inversion seemed to apply. For most blacks, only the negative acts seemed to count. Even the positive became a negative good: it only counted as a credit against black liability, against all the Wrong things black folk inevitably did. The good you did simply meant that you, and, by extension, all blacks, didn't mess up this time. When the good was allowed to count, it only underscored one's uniqueness, that one was not like other black folk. For many whites, excellence made blacks exceptions to, not examples of, their race. Ironically, to be thought of as an exception to the race still denied a pure consideration of individual merit. As long as race colored the yardstick, a real measurement of individual achievement was impossible. It is a bitter paradox that the evaluation of individual achievement that blacks yearned for was subordinated to a consideration of any achievement's impact on, and relation to, the race. Blacks were routinely denied the recognition of individual talent that is supposed to define the American creed. This history is barely mentioned now that blacks are made by many whites to look as if they duck individual assessment while embracing group privilege.

The problem of representing The Race is compounded by whites who protest its injustice to famous blacks. "Why should they be made to represent the race?" well-meaning whites ask, as if anonymous blacks had more choice in the matter than their well-known peers. (Besides, such protest releases these whites from the awful burden of confronting racism in their own world. If the representative of The Race is relieved of duty, everybody can party. It also obscures how the need for racial representation was created by white racism to begin with.) The assumption is that fame makes the burden of representation heavier for some blacks. In many ways, that's true. There's more territory to cover. And there are certainly more folk to deal with in countering or confirming destructive views of black life. On the other hand, visible blacks have routes of escape that ordinary blacks will never know. The well-known black can bask in fortunes of fate most blacks will never be tempted by. They can make lots of money, join elite social clubs, live in exclusive neighborhoods, send their kids to tony schools, enjoy the lifestyles of the rich and famous. Famous blacks can cash in on their complaints about having to represent all blacks. They can enjoy the fruits of a situation created by their being black in the first place.

Simpson took the path of least resistance for those looking to dodge the burden of being black: ignoring race. Although ignoring race is often mistaken for self-hatred, they are not the same. Those who confuse them commit what philosophers call a "category mistake." In such cases, shades of meaning slip off the edges of sloppy distinctions. Those who ignore race, and those who hate themselves because they can't, do share self-defeating habits: both deny the differences race makes and the lingering effects of racism. But not all blacks who have these habits hate themselves or consciously set out to ignore race. Some blacks are simply nonconformists who seek to defy the bitter boundaries of race, both within and beyond black life.

Simpson has confessed (not exactly, I'm afraid, what millions of Americans were hoping for) that it wasn't until he got hate mail in jail that he admitted racism hadn't gone away. Simpson concedes that he simply ignored or denied racism for most of his adult life. Simpson's denial, combined with his raceless image, entitled him to a derisive honor: White Man's Negro. Simpson earned his crown by avoiding and forgetting about race. He kept it by lusting after white acceptance at any cost. On the face of it—at least the side of his face he showed on the BET interview—that lust continues to shape his sense of reality. On the BET interview, Simpson said most whites don't believe he's guilty. That suggests more than Simpson's delusional state of mind. It shows how his perception of events squares with the logic of denial that made him useful to the white world. It is a vicious twist of fate for Simpson. The same technique of survival that brought him praise from whites in the past—as he was lauded, no doubt, for bravely resisting the demagogic demand to represent The Race—now causes those same whites to view him as pathological. No wonder O.J. is confused.

Simpson has now been forced to claim his race by default. It is an act that undoubtedly fills him—at least it would the old Simpson—with great regret. And not a little disdain. The blackness Simpson embraced during the trial was foreign to him. Its unfamiliar feel made him clutch it with great desperation. That blackness was molded for Simpson by Johnnie Cochran, who proved to be a shrewd conjurer of a "one size fits all" blackness. After all, it might complicate matters to acknowledge the conflicting varieties of black identity. In Cochran's conjuring, the complexity of race was skillfully shifted to a more narrow, but, on the surface at least, universal meaning of blackness-as-oppression. When applied to Simpson, such a meaning was laughable. It fit him even worse than the gloves prosecutor Christopher Darden tried to make Simpson force over his arthritic joints. But because blackness-as-oppression is often true for most blacks, Simpson benefited from its link to his case.

Darden, on the other hand, was unfairly stigmatized by Cochran's conjuring of blackness during the trial. Darden was viewed by many blacks as a traitor because he dared to call narrow blackness a phony idea in full view of white America. Darden failed because he didn't have Cochran's oratorical or lawyerly skills. (But Darden also had the thankless task of prosecuting a beloved, fallen American hero who was, at the same time, seeking to make a comeback to his black roots. Black folk are too often suckers for this sort of figure. Although blacks resent racial infidelity, we are often open to reconciliation. Even if the forgiven black continues to abuse the privilege of return, as Simpson has done. It's painfully clear that black folk are his fallback, not his first choice.) Darden also goofed when he argued that black jurors would be outdone if they had to hear the dreaded "N" word, particularly if it leapt from the past of star prosecution witness, police detective Mark Fuhrman. Black folk endure that epithet and much worse every day.

Darden's naïveté and strategic mistakes made it easy to believe that he had little understanding of the harsh realities black folk routinely face. Ironically, Darden desperately tried to point out that it was Simpson who had avoided the hardship most blacks confront. In the symbolic war of blackness being waged between Darden and Cochran, Darden tried to make Simpson appear unworthy of the knee-jerk black loyalty he enjoyed but from which Darden had been excluded. But that point was skillfully shredded in rhetorical and legal crossfire with Cochran, both in the courtroom and in the court of public opinion.

Simpson *has* largely sidestepped the indignities imposed on ordinary blacks. His fame and fortune certainly helped. Equally important, Simpson has made a career out of making white folk feel safe. He has been an emissary of blackness-as-blandness. With O.J. present, there was no threat of black rage careening out of control. He made no unreasonable demands—or any reasonable ones for that matter—for change of any sort. He blessed the civility and rightness of the status quo. Indeed, O.J. got a big bonus by comparing favorably not only to black "hotheads," but to figures like Hank Aaron, the baseball legend whose mellow thunder led him to speak gently but insistently about racism in sports. Once Simpson put away his youthful law breaking in San Francisco's Potrero Hill projects, he adopted a winning formula: he would play by the rules within the limits of the Given. The Given amounts to whites being on top. To win, you must act and talk white. In many interviews, Simpson has literally said so.

The extraordinary white hostility aimed at Simpson after the verdicts can largely be explained by the equally extraordinary investment O.J. made in the white world. He was a Good Negro who played by the rules. Many whites returned the favor. They invested in Simpson as a surrogate white. That investment explains their sense of betrayal by O.J. once he was charged, then cleared, of murder. According to the rules of surrogate whiteness, Simpson should have confessed his guilt and taken his punishment like a (white) man. Of course, by breaking the rules of surrogate whiteness, Simpson actually followed the rules of the Given: Those on top—wealthy whites—are not accountable to the system of justice in the same way as those on the bottom. The rules—of justice, fairness, equality—work fine for privileged whites as long as they are applied to a world of experience whites are familiar with. Beyond that territory, their sense of how and when the rules should apply is severely limited. That's the supreme paradox of white power Simpson learned up close.

It's not that white people are inherently more unfair or unjust than others. It's just that the rules are often applied in an arbitrary fashion to those outside the realm of their understanding and sympathy. That's why the barbarity of police brutality against blacks didn't faze many whites until the Rodney King beating and the riots that followed his molesters' acquittal. (Even now many whites still don't get it, as the response to the April 1996 beatings of illegal Mexican immigrants by deputies from the Riverside County Sheriff's office in South El Monte, California, proves.) Once O.J. lost his standing as a surrogate white, once he reverted back to a barbaric blackness, all bets were off. All rules were broken. Simpson began to see, perhaps for the first time, that he was worse than "just another nigger." He was a spurned black member of the white elite, an honorary white who had fallen from grace.

Simpson's celebrity, honorary whiteness, and wealth made him largely immune to the treatment shown the run-of-the-mill black male suspect. He was partly exempted by analogy: just the notion that a person *like* Simpson could murder his wife was hard for many of us to believe. The glow of false familiarity that fit his affable screen image helped too. (If one doubts the transfer between screen roles and real life, ask soap stars, who are constantly taken for their television characters, sometimes with disastrous results.) For a long stretch, Simpson made nice on television, both as a sports commentator and in typecast roles in a string of forgettable films that occasionally surface on late-night rotation. Simpson had only recently managed to find a role whose career benefit exceeded his paycheck: the hilariously unlucky Lt. Nordberg in the three *Naked Gun* films highlighted Simpson's comedic talent.

The sum of Simpson's celebrated parts—plus an unnameably perverse addiction to vicarious disintegration—moved his mostly white fans to cheer "the Juice" as he and pal A.C. Cowlings halfheartedly fled the law up I-5 and, later, the I-405 freeway in Cowlings's infamous white Bronco. (Always wanting to be like Simpson but never quite measuring up, Cowlings, this one time, ended up in the driver's seat.) Here privilege intervened. Any other black fugitive would most likely have been shot or otherwise stomped before he could call his mother, or swing by home to get a swig of orange juice. (At the time of Simpson's ungetaway cruise, L.A.'s freeways had been the setting of the blockbuster adventure flick *Speed.* The similarities are eerie: a chase with an uncertain conclusion; a spectacle involving revenge, murder, and obsession; and the freeway itself as a metaphor for both the resolution and realization of urban trauma.)

If Simpson's celebrity kept him from trauma, it attracted others to his trial to compete for public attention. Understanding that there's only so much understanding to go around—witness the spread of "compassion fatigue" and the backlash against "PC"—abused women, blacks, feminists, and others lobbied for the trial to be viewed through the lens of their suffering. While their pain was legitimate, their perspectives were often depressingly narrow. The scamper for the spotlight ruined some. Plain old greed and self-aggrandizement spoiled others.

Still, the Simpson trial and its aftermath reveal how nefarious social forces intersect and collide, how the suffering these forces breed cuts across every imaginable line of social identity, and how the suffering of some groups outweighs the suffering of others. Domestic violence made a cameo appearance at the trial's center stage. It quickly became a bit player in the judicial drama that followed. It was shattered and swept away by a hurricane of legal strategies and tactical maneuvers. It was clear that the bodies of battered women simply don't count where they should matter most—in the public imagination, and in private spaces where women live, work, play, and, too often, where they die.

True enough, the exposure of his ugly treatment of Nicole rightly shamed Simpson. The halo Simpson wore blinded the public to the darker corners of his character. The trial deglamorized Simpson's gentle, happy-go-lucky public demeanor. At the same time, a more telling symptom of our national hypocrisy emerged. The attack on Simpson as a batterer often degenerated into scapegoating. Such a practice eases consciences. It does little, however, to erase harmful attitudes and behaviors. By demonizing Simpson, many felt they were proving the moral enlightenment of a culture that refuses to tolerate such behavior. Such self-congratulation is groundless. The demonization of Simpson amounted to little more than moral posturing. We permit, sometimes condone, the abuse and killing of women every day. We need look no further than countless courtrooms and morgues for proof. Scapegoating allows us to avoid changing the beliefs and behavior that give domestic violence secret vitality.

If we were to really change our cultural habits, calling Simpson's behavior barbaric would ring true. It would be the extension of, not the exception to, our everyday practice. In our present climate, labeling Simpson's behavior barbaric revives, however remotely, ugly stereotypes of black men as beasts. The less sophisticated version of that stereotype has long been demolished. It is reborn, however, in images of young black males as social pariahs and older black males as rootless, ruthless ne'er-do-wells. Plus, the labeling invokes the ancient taboo against interracial love, whispering to all potential Nicoles: "See, that's what happens when you mess around with a black man."

Let's face it. Beating women is a manly sport in America. It is not a widely reviled practice, at least not before the Simpson trial. (It is helpful to remind ourselves that for years many white stars in every major American sport have beat their wives, too. But without a history of stereotypes to support white male beastliness, the wife-beating issue failed to catch on among the cause célèbre set.) Simpson's treatment of Nicole—manhandling, stalking, surveilling, beating, and tyrannizing her—was vicious. It was the extreme but logical outgrowth of deeply entrenched beliefs about the worth of women's bodies in our culture. Sadly, such beliefs persist in the face of feminist activism.

Part of our problem is that we think we can have it both ways. We think we can detest feminists while lauding the "good" women, those who wouldn't call themselves feminists to save their lives. And often don't. But most men are ignorant of flesh and blood feminism and the lives of the women who fill its ranks. Feminism is what women do when they realize they must struggle to protect the rights and privileges most men take for granted.

Still, Gloria Steinem's appearance on the *Charlie Rose* show immediately after the verdicts—where she recounted taking solace in an apology offered to her, and, presumably, all whites, by an elderly black man who assured her that "not all of us feel this way"—was disappointing. It showed a lack of appreciation for the trial's complexity from a feminist who has heroically struggled for human rights. Steinem's lapse was topped, however, by the pit bull meanness of NOW's Los Angeles head, Tammy Bruce. She was later removed from office because of her relentlessly racist attacks on Simpson.

Steinem's and Bruce's behavior underlines why it is difficult for even battered black women to imagine themselves as feminists. They played the dangerous game of ranking suffering without regard to context. They made their pain, and the greater pain of abused women, the almost exclusive focus of their fiery outrage. Domestic abuse is a legitimate and largely neglected plague. But what Steinem and Bruce overlooked was how race gives white women's pain, and the bodies on which that pain is inflicted, more visibility than the suffering bodies of black women. There are thousands of black women who have gone to their graves at the hands of hateful men. Some of their deaths were more heinous than

Nicole's. (True, they didn't have the dubious advantage of having a famous man charged with their murder.) But these women remain invisible. Even to folk like Steinem and Bruce, who are bravely committed to keeping the memory of abused women alive.

No doubt some of this resentment of unspoken white privilege–of ranking black bodies lower on the totem pole of distress–slid onto the tongues of black women who claimed the Simpson case was not about domestic violence. Technically, that's true. But neither was it, technically, about race. The important ways this case was about race are the same ways it was about domestic violence. And about the benefits and liabilities of class, wealth, fame, and gender. The disavowal of domestic abuse as an issue in the Simpson case by black women reinforces the tragic refusal of many blacks to face the crushing convergence of issues that shape black life. Their disavowal was not simply a way these women remained loyal to the script they've been handed–race first, race finally, race foremost. It was a telling example of how that script writes out their lives as well, often in their own handwriting. The dispute between Clarence Thomas and Anita Hill showcased the futility of thinking about our problems in strictly racial terms.

There is damning evidence too, that Nicole contributed to the brutality that broke her. And in all likelihood, killed her. I'm not arguing that Nicole should have simply left, got out at the first whiff of trouble. The destructive dance of complicity and shame, of cooperation and resistance, of instigation and retaliation, is too complex to blame victims for the brutal behavior of their abusers. And the psychology of identifying with one's abuser is too well established to mock the difficulty of leaving. But Nicole was also obsessed with O.J. Her huge appetites for cash, cocaine, and convenience tied her to a destructive lifestyle that rivaled her relationship to Simpson.

Equally tragic, Nicole's suffering was partially aided by her family's silence and inaction. Time and again Simpson hurled Nicole's body across the room. He crashed her face with his fists, leaving telltale signs almost as large as his anger. Her family surely knew or suspected that there was big trouble between Nicole and O.J. The Browns' not knowing is just as plausible as Simpson not having murdered Ron and Nicole. After Nicole's death, her sister, Denise, insisted that Nicole wasn't a battered woman. That's an excusable lie if we admit that silence, secrecy, and shame choke domestic abuse victims and their families.

Nicole's martyrdom can certainly aid other victims of domestic abuse. Her martyrdom might also help restore her family to wholeness. The Browns' helplessness and willed ignorance about Nicole's abuse–their neglect of her living body, bought in part by O.J.'s generous patronage–helped to make her a symbol of domestic violence. Her bloodied body obviously gave the Browns the energy they needed to speak up, to act. Martyrdom lifts a person's life beyond her body. Her suffering supports those who draw strength from her life's purpose–even if that purpose is only fully realized after death. The Browns must now join with others who identify, beyond blood ties or biology, with the fight against domestic violence to which Nicole's life and martyred body have become connected. Without the Browns' acknowledgment of complicity in Nicole's suffering, her martyred body becomes an empty tablet on which her family's guilt is written.

As serious as the Browns' failure was, Simpson's was by far the greater sin. His beating of Nicole marked a vile sexual obsession. Simpson apparently believed he owned Nicole. She was a trophy. She was a commodity O.J. bought with his considerable earnings. Such logic might suggest that Nicole was interchangeable with most of the other women to whom Simpson was attracted. Like her, they had blonde hair and big breasts.

But sexual obsession is not offset by potential—by what one might have or get in the future to replace what one lost or can't have. This makes it difficult to defend Simpson by saying that he didn't have to kill Nicole because he could have had any woman he wanted. Sexual obsession can never be satisfied. The obsessor fixes on the object of desire as a way of realizing his own desire. Hence, sexual obsession is a disguised form of narcissism. It ultimately refers back to itself. Such self-reference contains the seed of the obsessor's dissatisfaction. By projecting his desire onto an erotic interest, the obsessor surrenders the means of achieving fulfillment to a force outside himself. Hence, the obsessor employs various forms of control, including seduction and violence, to bring the erotic interest in line with his wishes.

The obsessor ultimately requires the collapse of the erotic interest into himself. This feat is rarely possible, and certainly not desirable, at least not from the erotic interest's point of view. It means that the erotic interest will have to surrender her self and identity completely to the obsessor. In the obsessor's eye, to be rejected by the erotic interest is to be rejected by himself. This is a narcissist's nightmare. Such rejection is perceived as a form of self-mutilation. Or, more painfully, it is a form of self-denial. Nicole's final rejection of the sickness of her own, and O.J.'s, obsession a month before she died was the doorway to her freedom and her martyrdom. If the same act of independence led to her liberty and her death, it suggests something of the lethal obsession that millions of women live with and die from.

A similarly lethal obsession—compounded by an even more sinister and convoluted history—shapes the course of race in this country. The responses to the verdicts were misrepresented in the media as an avalanche of emotion determined exclusively by color. Such simple scribing must never be trusted. Nevertheless, the responses showed just how sick and separate race makes us. O.J.—the figure, the trial, the spectacle, the aftermath—was a racequake. It crumbled racial platitudes. It revealed the fault lines of bias, bigotry, and blindness that trace beneath our social existence. The trial has at least forced us to talk about race. Even if we speak defensively and with giant chips on our shoulders. Race remains our nation's malevolent obsession. Race is the source of our harmony or disfavor with one another. Black and white responses to O.J. prove how different historical experiences determine what we see and color what we believe about race.

For instance, even as many blacks defended O.J., they knew he had never been one of black America's favorite sons. He didn't remember his roots when his fame and fortune carried him long beyond their influence. (Or, as a black woman wrote to me, "O.J. didn't know he had roots until they started digging.") On the surface, the black defense of Simpson can be positively interpreted. It can be viewed as the refusal of blacks to play the race authenticity game, which, in this instance, amounts to the belief that only "real" blacks deserve support when racial difficulties arise. But black responses to O.J. can also be read less charitably. They can be seen as the automatic embrace of a fallen figure simply because he is black. If you buy this line of reasoning, Simpson has a double advantage. He is eligible for insurance against the liability of racism, and he is fully covered for all claims made against him by whites, including a charge of murder. But all of these readings are too narrow. Black responses to Simpson must be viewed in light of the role race and racism have played in our nation's history. Race has been the most cruelly dominant force in the lives of black Americans. Racism exists in its own poisoned and protected world of misinformation and ignorance. Its fires of destruction are stoked by stereotype and crude mythology.

That history may help explain black support for figures like O.J. and Clarence Thomas, who have denied the lingering impact of race. Many black folk know that, in the long run, such figures remain trapped by race. Still, it is unprincipled for blacks like Thomas and Simpson to appeal to race in their defense when they opposed such appeals by other blacks in trouble. Many blacks support such figures because they think they discern, even in their exploitative behavior, a desperation, a possible seed of recognition, a begrudging concession even, that race does make a difference.

The ugly irony is that such figures get into a position to do even more harm to blacks because of the black help they receive. (Look at Thomas's judicial opinions against affirmative action and historically black colleges and universities.) For many whites, the example of race exploiters symbolizes how black Americans use race in bad faith. The problem is many whites see this only when their interests are being undermined. Simpson's offense—allowing race to be used on his behalf— is as obvious to many whites as Thomas's injury to blacks is obscured. By contrast, Thomas looks just fine to many whites. His beliefs and judicial opinions protect conservative white interests. But Thomas's cry of "high-tech lynching" when he was seeking confirmation to the Supreme Court choked off critical discussion of his desperate dishonesty. Thomas's comment was a callous, calculated attempt to win Senate votes and public sympathy by using race in a fashion he had claimed was unjust. Thomas's dishonest behavior—gaining privilege because of his blackness only to unfairly deny the same privilege to other blacks highlights the absurdity of race for black Americans.

A small sense of the absurdity of race came crashing down on many whites when the not-guilty verdicts were delivered. A surreal world prevailed. Clocks melted. Time bent. Cows flew over the moon. The chronology of race was forever split: Before Simpson and After Simpson. October 3, 1995, became a marker of tragedy. For many whites, it is a day that will live in the same sort of infamy that Roosevelt predicted for the day Pearl Harbor was bombed. It is hard to adequately describe the bewilderment many blacks felt at white rage over the verdicts. As difficult, perhaps, as it is for whites to understand how so many blacks could be deliriously gleeful at Simpson's acquittal. For perhaps the first time, the wide gulf between legality and morality became real to many whites. At least real in a way that most blacks could see whites cared about. That gulf is one blacks have bitterly protested for years, with only moderate support from most whites. The day of the verdicts, many white people were forced to think of themselves as a group—one denied special privilege rather than guaranteed it—for the first time. As a group, these whites tasted the dread, common to blacks, that follows the absolute rejection of the faith one has placed in a judicial ruling's power to bring justice. The fact that the decision officially took four hours only heaped insult on the injured souls of white folk.

In reality, however, that decision was much longer in the making. *That jury decision was set in motion the first time an American citizen, acting on behalf of the state and supported by public sentiment, made a legal judgment about a human being where an interpretation of the facts was colored by a consideration of race.* The O.J. verdicts are an outgrowth of the system started in that moment. They are, too, a painful exposure of, and a stinging rebuke to, the unjust operation of the judicial system for blacks throughout the history of our nation.

One might conclude from what I've just said that I believe the jury's decision was a rightful thumb in the justice system's eye. That it was sweet black revenge for white wrongdoing. I don't. Nor do I believe that that's the best way to read the jury's verdict. The confusion surrounding the verdicts, indeed the entire trial, reflects the confusion about the meanings of race in our culture. As far as I can see, race is being used in at least three different ways to explain the trial, especially the meaning of the verdicts. But since we haven't taken the time to figure them out, we end up collapsing them into one another in ways that are confusing and harmful. That confusion exaggerates the differences between blacks and whites. It also masks differences within black and white communities, especially where class privilege and gender are concerned.

The three uses of race I have in mind are race as *context*, race as *subtext*, and race as *pretext*. Race as context helps us to understand the *facts* of race and racism in our society. Race as a subtext helps us to understand the *forms* of race and racism in our culture. And race as a pretext helps us to understand the *function* of race and racism in America. Of course, these categories are not absolute. They are impure and flexible. They often bleed into one another. But if we're aware such distinctions exist, we have a better chance of reducing the anxiety around a highly charged subject. I'm using these categories as a tool to analyze race and as a way to describe how race and racism have affected American life. I'll briefly explore these uses of race before explaining how they might help us sort through the racial mess that the verdicts revealed.

Race as context shows how arguments have been used to clarify the role race and racism have played in our nation's history. To view race as a context leads to *racial clarification*. With racial clarification, we get down, as nearly as we can, to the facts of race. When did the idea of race emerge? Why did America choose to make distinctions among people based on race? What happened during slavery? What was Reconstruction really about? What were Abraham Lincoln's motives in freeing the slaves? How did the civil rights movement get started? What was the role of black women in the black freedom struggle of the '60s? How was black sexuality viewed during the early part of this century? How many black men were lynched before 1950? When did affirmative action start? And so on. By having these facts in hand, we're more likely to weave them into an accurate account of how race has shaped our culture. Such an account helps us tell the complex, compelling story of how race influenced ideas like democracy, justice, freedom, individuality, and equality. It also helps us to understand how racism began and spread. The most valuable use of racial clarification may be the vibrant historical framework it gives our discussions about race. It is stunning how much ignorance about what really happened in our racial past poisons present debates about race. Of course, we don't benefit from a Joe Friday "just the facts, ma'am" perspective of the past. There will be disputes about the facts and what they mean. But we certainly need to work as hard as possible to figure out what happened as we interpret the history of race.

Race as subtext highlights how arguments have been used to mystify, or deliberately obscure, the role of race and racism in our culture. To view race as a subtext aids our understanding of racial mystification. With this view of race, we can describe the different forms that racism takes, the disguises it wears, the tricky, subtle shapes it assumes. Race and racism are not static forces. They mutate, grow, transform, and are redefined in complex ways. Understanding *racial mystification* helps us grasp the hidden premises, buried perceptions, and cloaked meanings of race as they show up throughout our culture. (I realize that race and racism are not living organisms. But they have, besides an impersonal, institutional form, a quality of fretful aliveness, an active agency, that I seek to capture.)

For instance, terms like "enlightened" and "subtle" racism have been used to describe one transformation of racism: the shift from overt racism to covert forms that thrive on codes, signals, and symbols. And racial mystification was certainly at play when Charles Stuart in Boston and Susan Smith in South Carolina deflected attention from murders they had committed—Stuart of his wife, Smith of her two sons—by claiming a black man was at fault. What made their stories believable was not the fact, but the perception, of black crime. Statistically speaking, blacks overwhelmingly murder blacks, just as whites overwhelmingly murder whites. Since black males have become racially coded symbols for pathological, criminal behavior, the Stuart and Smith stories found millions of white believers. Such beliefs about black males are subtle updates of an ancient belief about black men as beasts and sexual predators. Race understood as a subtext allows us to get a handle on the changing forms of racist belief and behavior in our culture.

Finally, race as pretext shows how arguments have been used to justify racial beliefs and to defend racial interests. If the context of race is tied to history and the subtext to culture, then the pretext of race is linked, broadly speaking, to science. Race viewed as a pretext increases our understanding of *racial justification*. The stress in racial justification is on how race functions to give legitimacy to racial ideas. The proponents of racial justification drape their arguments about race in the finest garbs of science: objectivity and neutrality. After all, they are dealing in the realm of the empirical, those things that can be proved true or false by experiment and observation. Their work is often developed in the name of the sciences, natural or social. In some cases, racial justification simply seeks to supply a reasoned argument for racial preconceptions. Such arguments form a pretext to justify deeply rooted racial passions, and often give a scientific glow to racist beliefs.

For instance, Charles Murray and Richard Herrnstein's *The Bell Curve* claimed to be a work of science, a work of cool, dispassionate reason. Murray and Herrnstein simply translated racist beliefs into empirical arguments about the limits of black intelligence. Their book has been widely debunked as pseudoscience. But the enormous interest that greeted it suggests the intellectual appeal of the claims they make. The case of black psychiatrist Frances Cress-Welsing is instructive as well. In her book, *The Isis Papers*, she argues for the Cress Theory of color–confrontation and racism. She links the development of white supremacist ideology to white fear of genetic annihilation. It is a biologically based argument, linked to the superiority of black skin because of its ability to produce melanin, to explain the rise of white supremacy. Cress-Welsing's theory is certainly an example of contorted reasoning used to justify racial beliefs. Viewing race as a pretext helps us to identify scientific, empirical work that attempts to justify racist beliefs.

These three uses of race and racism might help us figure out key elements of the trial. Take the bitter dispute over the "mountain of evidence." For most whites and some blacks, there was more than enough evidence to convict Simpson. Simpson had brutally battered Nicole. The blood of the victims was in his Bronco. Simpson's blood was at the crime scene. A bloody glove was found at the crime scene, its match on Simpson's estate. And above all, there were highly sophisticated DNA tests that seemed to prove Simpson's guilt beyond a reasonable doubt. But for most blacks and some whites, there was substantial doubt about the validity of the evidence, for several reasons. The reckless manner in which the evidence was collected and tested. Defense experts who testified that the evidence was questionable, inconclusive, or plain contrary to the prosecution's interpretation. And above all, the star prosecution witness, police detective Mark Fuhrman, a major collector of evidence against Simpson, who turned out to be a bigot of the worst sort.

Most whites and blacks conceded that Fuhrman's bigotry was awful. Both whites and blacks admitted that the police work was sloppy. But for most whites and a few blacks, these factors didn't matter enough to keep them from believing in Simpson's guilt. Most blacks and some whites believed that Fuhrman's mean-spirited bragging about harming, possibly killing, blacks in the past—plus the fact that he collected crucial evidence—was reason enough to doubt Simpson's guilt.

What are we to make of how black folk viewed the evidence?

Right away, race as pretext, or racial justification, makes it clear that evidence never speaks for itself. Evidence never exists in a vacuum. It is used for particular purposes.

In the Simpson case, as in any case where race is a source of contention, how we see evidence is shaped by ideological and racial interests. Evidence must be viewed through a lens of interpretation. Such a lens is surely colored by the history of race. Race as context, or racial clarification, helps us understand the facts of race that might influence how blacks view the evidence in the Simpson case in sharply different fashion from whites. There are many. The unjust treatment thousands of blacks have received at the hands of the justice system. The manufacturing of evidence against black defendants in the past. Judicial indifference to compelling evidence of a black defendant's innocence. The unequal application of punishment to black and white defendants convicted of the same crime. And repeated instances of police brutality in black communities.

Of course, the Rodney King case had already made Los Angeles blacks, indeed blacks throughout the nation, skeptical about the uses of evidence in the judicial system. Particularly when black bodies were at stake. There was, as far as most black folk were concerned, indisputable proof—if not quite the mountain of evidence amassed in the Simpson case—that police brutality was the plague they claimed it to be. After all, nobody saw Simpson murder two people. But the world saw King getting his skull smashed over and over and over again. Millions of black folk, along with the outrage they felt at the King beating, breathed a sigh of relief. Finally, here was the case that would ring the death knell for police brutality and bring the curtain down on the terror that millions of blacks feel when they're stopped by a white cop. But it was not to be. With a barrage of shrewd legal arguments, lawyers for the cops accused of King's beating made the white jury disbelieve what they saw with their own eyes. Neither could millions of blacks believe what they saw. At the trial where King's molesters were acquitted, the roar of evidence barely whimpered. Objectivity was crushed. Reason was sullied. Racial justification abounded.

To be sure, Los Angeles didn't catch fire because of a highfalutin debate about race as a pretext for the brutal treatment of blacks. It didn't erupt over intellectual disputes about the twisted uses of reason, objectivity, and evidence in the justification of racial violence. Yet these factors surely played their part in the L.A. riots of 1992. The seams of black civility finally burst because black folk concluded that even when they played by the rules, they could expect nothing in return—when the evidence was clear as day, it could be explained away. Of course, race as pretext and subtext converge at King's body. King was termed "bearlike," "hulklike," and "like a wounded animal" by his molesters. In view of King's assault, these terms revealed a racially mystified description that appealed to old be-

liefs, as I've argued above, about black males as animals. And of course, by portraying him in such racially mystified terms, the cops were able to justify their vicious treatment of King: treatment befitting a beast.

This history must be kept at the forefront of any discussion of how black folk—
including the jurors—viewed the evidence against Simpson. Black response to the
evidence in the Simpson case might be viewed as an example of reasonable black
suspicion of the uses—really misuses—of the Enlightenment and its towering offspring: objectivity and reason. Both have been used to justify black suffering and
death around the globe. Both, or at least twisted versions of the two, have led rational white folk to treat rational black folk in irrational, inhumane ways, or to
overlook evidence of such behavior in their fellow whites. Plus, many blacks are
suspicious of medical technology. Think of the infamous Tuskegee Study begun
in 1932, when three hundred black men were used as guinea pigs to test the long-
term effects of untreated syphilis. Of course, there's no direct link between such
cases and the Simpson case. But such cases leave millions of blacks suspicious of
the uses of sophisticated scientific technology. Especially when it is employed to
prove black inferiority or to experiment with blacks as animals. A potent mix
of reasonable suspicion, conspiracy theories, and paranoia thrives in pockets of
black America. In the light of real abuse and suspected offenses, it is not difficult
to understand how highly educated blacks could believe, for instance, that AIDS
was invented to destroy black folk. Or that evidence cooked up by sophisticated
science could be manufactured, distorted, or tainted to nab an innocent black
man. As remote as it might seem to whites, that possibility loomed large in the
Simpson case for millions of blacks. There are a thousand Mark Fuhrmans in
black history. Race as context makes that fact crystal clear.

The three uses of race I've sketched might also clear up confusion about the so-
called race card. The "race card" invariably referred to Johnnie Cochran's introduction of race as a factor in Simpson's trial. It referred especially to the defense's
intended blasting of Mark Fuhrman, and to Cochran's statements outside the
court about the pervasive nature of race in our nation. But we should make distinctions. First, the charge that Cochran played the race card is a charge of racial
justification. That is, it is a charge that he used race as a pretext to argue Simpson's
lack of guilt because of Fuhrman's racist behavior. That charge against Cochran is
a separate issue from the validity of his point about the pervasiveness of race,
which is a question of the context of race—of whether the facts, or at least an interpretation of the facts, warrant Cochran's assertion about how pervasive race is.

During the trial, and in commentary since the trial ended, the two meanings
have been blurred. Cochran's point about racial pervasiveness was taken as a justification for his use of race in Simpson's defense. In fact, I think it was an attempt
at racial clarification, an attempt to clarify the huge impact of race in our culture.
By discussing the pervasiveness of race, Cochran sought to do a difficult thing: to
talk about white racism and the privileges and penalties it bestows. It is certainly
possible to disagree with Cochran's use, or interpretation, of the facts. One can

argue that Cochran used legitimate facts in a distorted way. But one cannot ignore the truth of his statements about the prevalence of race in our culture. By keeping the two meanings of race separate, we won't automatically confuse speaking about the facts of race or racism with an attempt to justify unprincipled arguments or exploitative behavior.

For many whites, racial clarification and racial justification are the same. This is especially true when talking about race goes against white beliefs about the disappearance or absence of racism. The question, of course, is whether race made a difference in Simpson's case. For Cochran and millions of blacks, the reasonable answer was yes. The reasonableness of that answer is partially determined by an undeniable fact: the bad treatment of blacks by the police. Mark Fuhrman's bigoted behavior only reinforced the belief among millions of blacks that he might have framed O.J.

If we look closely, it will become clear that the race card (racial justification) was played in the Simpson trial from the beginning. The question of which jurors to select was racially motivated. Both the defense and the prosecution took race into account. The decision to bring Christopher Darden onto the prosecution team was driven by race. The prosecution's decision to stick with Fuhrman, even when it was apparent that he was a racist, carried racial overtones. The race card had been drawn and dealt long before Cochran even came on the scene. It should be evident that the "race card" metaphor is a limited way to understand how race operates. As an instance of racial justification, the race card metaphor leaves aside the context and the subtext of race. The race card metaphor fails to account for the complexity of race. It fails to show how racism poisons civic life and denies the worth of human beings because of their color. Race is not a card. It is a condition. It is a set of beliefs and behaviors shaped by culture, rooted in history, and fueled by passions that transcend reason.

Understanding the complexity of race can throw light on the actions of the black jurors in the Simpson case. The jurors' verdicts were widely viewed as a failure to transcend race. They were also viewed, in the words of a '70s James Brown hit, as the "big payback" to whites for all the wrong they've done. Furthermore, the jurors were accused of failing to critically weigh the evidence in the case. Racial clarification helps to identify a historical paradox of race for blacks relating to claims of this sort: when dealing with their peers, blacks are seen as fair—that is, neutral, just, and transcending race—only when they oppose perceived black interests. For many whites, the black jurors could only transcend race, and satisfy the demands of justice and good citizenship, by finding Simpson guilty of murder. Because the jury found Simpson not guilty, many whites believed their decision was an instance of racial justification, that the verdicts were a biased judgment, a pretext for racial solidarity.

But blacks routinely convict black defendants. (I should know. I saw my brother sentenced to life in prison by an all black jury.) Neither are whites viewed as unfair when they fail to send a white defendant to jail. Whites are not viewed in such cases as expressing white solidarity. Unless, of course, the defendant is accused of a crime against a black person. Even then, whites defend their decisions as just. They often claim their decisions are made without regard to color. Whites are rarely asked to consider the role race plays in the decisions they make. This is especially the case when their decisions involve unconscious expressions of group loyalty.

Racial mystification may help to explain veiled, and not-so-veiled, references to the black jurors' intelligence. The subtext of criticisms aimed at the black jurors was drenched in race: they were uneducated, hence, intellectually inferior. It's interesting to note how dismissed white juror Francine Florio-Bunten's story casts light on racial mystification in the trial. Florio-Bunten claims she would have voted to convict Simpson. She has been celebrated, in coded terms, as a white heroine who would have saved the day by representing the "truth"—that is, "white" interests. Florio-Bunten was lauded for being the only juror who knew what "DNA" stood for at the beginning of the trial. (The subtext is that the black jurors, by contrast, were dumb.) Florio-Bunten also claims that she had decided Simpson's guilt long before the trial had ended. Yet, unlike the black jurors, who were viciously attacked for arriving at a hasty decision (after four hours of deliberation), Florio-Bunten has been exempt from harsh criticism. Florio-Bunten is even more ingratiating to whites when she claims that no amount of deliberation by her cohorts would have swayed her opinion. (Subtext: she would have resisted "black interests" and stood firm for "white interests.") The stigma black jurors wear—dumb, race loyalists, un-American—is the stigma attached to many blacks who risk white rage by reaching decisions that upset white interests and beliefs.

In the final analysis, what race as context, race as subtext, and race as pretext cannot help us gain is certainty about the motives that lurk in the hearts of human beings. We don't know what intentions or motivations people have apart from the behavior we can observe. (That is the frustration for blacks confronting subtle forms of racism that are not manifest in overt action.) Despite every effort to explain the jury's actions, it may be that race, of whatever sort, was the motivation for their decision in the Simpson trial. No amount of knowledge or insight can protect against that possibility. Black folk already know this because they have been on the losing end of that proposition too many times before. As this case proves, it's a bitter lesson few whites are familiar with. It may be that the jurors' decision confirmed the worst fears of whites and blacks: Despite what many whites think about blacks—that they are morally inferior—or what many blacks think about themselves—that they are morally superior to whites—blacks and whites may be very much the same.

Oddly enough, that might be a basis for moving beyond the prism of race. Not by denying race, but by taking it into account. That is the lesson we learn from clarifying our understanding of race. Those whites who claim it is unfair, even absurd, for blacks to enjoy racial preferences deny that whites have always enjoyed such preferences on a much larger scale. Now that many whites seek to use the absurdity of racial preferences as a justification for axing programs like affirmative action, they fail to make use of history. True enough, they highlight the absurdity of the idea of race. But they remove it from a context—racial clarification—that explains its historical function—to justify white privilege. The bitter history of black struggle, the facts, are what make the idea that race is absurd valid and compelling. To take that idea out of context and to turn it against blacks without regard for history is crass and dishonest.

Then too blacks must be honest about the manner in which we have been vulnerable to race exploiters who deny the importance of race. If racial justice is our dominant concern, then the cases of prisoners Geronimo Pratt and Mumia Abu-Jamal should have goaded us to action long before the superrich Simpson captured our attention. And our large disinterest in the trials of rappers Snoop Doggy Dogg, Tupac Shakur, and Dr. Dre reveals a huge class and generational bias in black America. In fact, millions of blacks believed the hostile portrayals of these young blacks in the media. (I'm not suggesting that each didn't deserve criticism for his actions. I'm simply referring to hostile black reaction to the category of "young, black male" or "rapper.") Millions of blacks believed in these rappers' probable guilt simply because they were rappers. Millions of blacks didn't rally around these rappers, who probably had more cash than Simpson. Many blacks wrote them off. Why? They weren't the right kind of blacks. They weren't "our" kind of role models. Yet such figures, given the wide public hostility aimed at them, are more likely to be targets of white fear and police misconduct than a rich, well-loved black sports icon like O.J. Class divisions in black life are huge and growing.

In the end, we can only have racial progress if we take the lessons of this case seriously. Despite the undeniable advances we have made, despite the enormous strides taken, we remain a deeply divided society. (Although this case framed our racial problems in black and white, we must certainly realize that there are all sorts of racial and ethnic tensions brewing that involve Asian, Native American, and Latino communities.) We cannot wish our differences away. We must work to increase our understanding of the contexts, pretexts, and subtexts of race. Then we must do something concrete about racial suffering and racial injustice. We have the negative examples of O.J. Simpson and Mark Fuhrman, the two men at the center of this trial, to spur us on past their, and our, tragic limitations and failures. Simpson, in particular, is a man without a country. The white folk who once adored him, and whose acceptance Simpson still seeks, now despise him. The blacks Simpson has never shown much interest in, and who have welcomed him, do not inspire his allegiance.

In perhaps one of the most tragic ironies this case has served up, a black man who lived his life avoiding black culture was ultimately set free because of a white bigot who hated blacks and worked at the core of urban black life. The cruel symmetry of their fates at the hands of a black culture that each, in his own way, found troubling is nearly biblical. If we are not careful, their fates will be the nation's as well.

PART THREE

AFFIRMATIVE ACTION

There is little doubt that affirmative action is a controversial public policy that has been bitterly debated in the nation's long and chaotic battle for racial justice. I think it is best to tell the truth about affirmative action: that it is not a cure-all for our racial miasma; that it is not fair for whites who have enjoyed centuries of unchallenged social advantage to carp about the relatively small benefits distributed to minorities; and that too often the discussion of racial justice is yanked out of a truthful political context and smothered by amnesia. If we ever ginned up the courage to speak honestly about race, we might also open up unexpected avenues of racial healing.

Six

DEBATING AFFIRMATIVE ACTION

A headline in the University of Pennsylvania's student newspaper, the Daily
Pennsylvanian, *barely captured the tenor of the debate between me and University of
Michigan professor Carl Cohen when it declared: "Taping of 'Justice Talking' Turns
Heated." The debate, moderated by Margot Adler, took place at Penn's Wistar Institute,
and was edited for broadcast on NPR's* Justice Talking. *Although the finished version
screened some of our most acrimonious exchanges, a vibrant measure of our fundamental
disagreement survives on the pages of our transcribed and edited debate. Cohen, a
Michigan philosophy professor, helped instigate the anti–affirmative action movement at
the university that led to two lawsuits targeting the institution's undergraduate and law
school admissions policies, both of which were heard before the Supreme Court in 2003.
I received quite a bit of correspondence after this debate aired shortly before the cases
were argued before the Supreme Court on April 1, and again after the Court's decision
in June. Besides a widely viewed debate on C-SPAN between me and black
conservative activist Ward Connerly, this encounter with Cohen provides my most
extensive response to the issues surrounding this critical racial policy.*

Moderator: From the Annenberg Public Policy Center at the University of
Pennsylvania, I'm Margot Adler. Welcome to *Justice Talking.* Do we still
need affirmative action? The United States Supreme Court will rule this
term on whether the University of Michigan can consider race when
evaluating applicants to its undergraduate and law schools. Like many
prestigious colleges and universities, Michigan takes the position that diversity itself has an important educational value, and that the school
must maintain its academic freedom to create a student body with the
widest range of people, ideas, and experiences. U of M gives African
American applicants additional points just for being black, and whites
who didn't get in have sued, claiming reverse discrimination . . . Affirmative action—will it prevent the resegregation of our country's institutions of higher learning? Is diversity a value so important in the twenty-
first century that colleges may discriminate against whites?

    I'm joined by Carl Cohen, who has taught philosophy at the Univer-
sity of Michigan since 1955. Professor Cohen's request for these policies

under the Freedom of Information Act is credited with sparking the movement to end race-based admissions at the university. He is the author of a book called *Naked Racial Preference*. Michael Eric Dyson is also with us. He's the Avalon Foundation Professor in the Humanities at the University of Pennsylvania. Known as a hip-hop intellectual, Professor Dyson is also a Baptist minister and the author of *Race Rules: Navigating the Color Line*. We're thrilled to have both of you here on *Justice Talking*.

Moderator: So Carl, how do the University of Michigan's affirmative action policies work? And how does race figure into the equation?

Cohen: Race figures into the equation heavily, both on the undergraduate level and in the law school. There are two different systems, and that's why there are two different cases. In the undergraduate case, additional points are actually given on a scale, which one hundred points eventually assures admission. Twenty points are given for color of skin. I find that, of course, deeply wrong. In the law school, a point system is not used, but a critical mass of minority students is sought.

Moderator: Michael, President Bush criticized this policy as a quota system. Is it? Is it discrimination?

Dyson: Absolutely not. Twenty points granted, as Professor Cohen has indicated, is part of a number of points granted for a number of categories and considerations other than color, or even academic achievement. So that if we give twenty points for race, we give points for legacy; we give points for being an athlete; we give points for being from a diverse part of the country. So race is *a* consideration, *a* factor, not the exclusive factor, and certainly not the dominant factor.

Cohen: Of course it's not the exclusive factor. No one thinks that. But it is wrong to consider race, morally wrong and legally wrong, to give preference in our country on the basis of skin color or national origin.

Dyson: I agree, and Carl, as a white man, you would understand that more than anyone else in this room, because racial preferences have been predicated upon pigment. We live in, as some scholars call it, a pigmentocracy [where] the distribution of goods, like employment and education, [is] based upon white skin privilege. So I certainly agree [we've got to attack] racial preferences. However, speaking to affirmative action, that's different than racial preference.

Cohen: Oh no, we're talking about racial preference. That's the issue before the courts right now.

Dyson: Let me finish my point. Affirmative action is about conceding the fact that the historical practices of white supremacy have excluded people, *unfairly*, based upon race, and we cannot now pretend that race shouldn't be a consideration in trying to redistribute those goods.

Moderator: Carl, U.S. Supreme Court Justice Powell, in the majority opinion in the *Bakke* case, wrote that "achieving diversity on campus is an

important and legitimate part of the university's educational mission."
Was he wrong?

Cohen: I think diversity is a very genuine value, and I think the university
is right to seek diversity of all kinds, not just racial and ethnic diversity,
but intellectual diversity. I think that's a genuine merit. But I don't think
that it justifies discriminating by race.

Moderator: Michael, isn't there something a little elitist and even patronizing in the university's argument? They seem to be implying that the
presence of minorities enhances the educational experience offered to the
white majority, and that blacks will get a better education in the presence
of whites. You're an African-American professor on a majority *white* campus. What do you think?

Dyson: Well, I think that in the abstract these arguments may appear to be
patronizing, condescending, and altogether typical of the liberal attempt
to engineer social diversity. But in the concrete context in which we find
ourselves, given the diminution of any intense interest in racial justice for
many students of color on predominantly white campuses, I think it's a
salient point that needs to be reinforced. And diversity in this case,
racially speaking, is a compelling interest, because A, it allows majority
students to interact with, yes, minority students; B, it does allow minority students to engage with those students with whom they will be working in the future; but [C], and most important, it provides an intellectual
context to demystify some of these prejudices and biases that feed racial
injustice. So I think that there are a variety of ways in which diversity is
a compelling interest, both to the college and the university, and to the
society at large.

Cohen: You don't want to suppose that absent these preferential programs
there would be no minorities on campus? There are a very substantial
number of very able minority students and faculty members who would
be, and who are, on our campus, quite without preference. What's at
issue is the increment in the degree of diversity which is provided, by a
degree of deliberate racial preference. And that increment, it is supposed,
is sufficient to justify deliberate discrimination by race.

Dyson: No, I'm not suggesting that absent these so-called, what you termed
preferences, what I call racial modifications, black students will not
thrive. What it suggests is that there are other considerations than intelligence and test scores that play into the acceptance or rejection of students of color. For instance, a recent study just showed that the *name* of
an African-American person is sufficient grounds for excluding them
from even being brought in to *compete* for the job. So don't tell me, Professor Cohen, you've been living in a cocoon, somehow, in the United
States of Amnesia, where you have rejected the legitimacy of the fact that
racial preferences have historically accorded white men, first of all, and

white people secondly, extraordinary access to the goods and resources that are available.

Cohen: With respect, I am not being ahistorical. I am keenly aware of the long history of racial discrimination in our country, and I think we cannot approach this question without attending to it. I share with you, Professor Dyson, a concern for the way in which race, as you put it in your book, has poisoned the atmosphere in our country in many respects. But the way to bring that to an end is not to take another dose of the same medicine.

Moderator: Let me butt in here a second. Carl, you've been at the University of Michigan for nearly fifty years. Over the five decades that you've been teaching, hasn't the growing presence of African-American students in your courses made a qualitative difference to the kinds of discussions your students had in class?

Cohen: I don't know that one could say a very substantial difference. There's been a growing number of minority students over the years. That's a good thing. There was a growing number of minority students in the '60s before preferential programs began. One of my colleagues at the University of Michigan Law School, Terrance Sandalow, remarked after many years of teaching at the law school, that he never found that any one of his minority students contributed in the discussion an idea or a point of view that wasn't contributed by others.

Dyson: If you've been, for instance, subject to police brutality, and you're discussing police brutality in your classroom, it makes a heck of a difference if you're a white man who has had the ability to teach at the University of Michigan for 50 years without the compunction of the law, as opposed to a person of color who has been subject to police brutality, like myself, where the marks are borne in the body. That makes a *heck* of a difference epistemologically, as well as existentially.

Cohen: We are not going to be without that representation when preference is done away with. It's not as though we were choosing between the presence of minorities and the absence of minorities. We're choosing between the presence of minorities in a substantial degree, and the presence of minorities in a somewhat greater degree. And that increment is the only thing that can justify this system. Now I want to say, the way to transcend our tradition, our unhappy tradition, of racial prejudice and discrimination, is to cease to do it, to resolve never again to use race and national origin as the criterion for judgment. That is what I think it is time for us to resolve.

Dyson: I would agree with [the latter part of your statement], except to say *racism* is a key distinction. Not race.

Moderator: Carl, some studies show that *without* affirmative action, enrollment of African-Americans at highly selective schools like the U of M, would drop from 9 percent to 2 percent. The state of Michigan is 14 percent black, has three of the ten most segregated cities in the country. Are you saying that the university would be a better place with only a token presence of black students?

Cohen: I don't believe that the result of the elimination of preference would yield a token presence of minority students. The numbers will drop because they have been artificially inflated. I think they will drop, but there will be a substantial number of minority students, as there *were* a substantial number of minority students before the introduction of preference. But I do think the university will be a better place when the hostilities and the tensions that are created by preference are no longer there, and when all the minority students who are on campus are recognized as being there on their own merits. I think we do the minorities a great service when we eliminate preference in their behalf.

Dyson: Well, let me respond to that by saying, first of all, thank you so much for your concern about the psychological state of African-American students who, in the embrace of so-called racial preferences, are thought to be somehow inferior. Surely Professor Cohen, as a teacher of philosophy, is aware of the long legacy of the disbelief in the essential humanity and intelligence of black people—long before affirmative action, I might remind you. So when I went to Carson-Newman College, a historically Southern Baptist school, [a] white school, I got a Ph.D. fellowship to go to Princeton University. I made straight A's in philosophy, [and] graduated at the top of my class in philosophy. A white man—whose son was graduating with me—at an awards banquet came up to me and said, "Son, you know, you're not just going to Princeton because you're black." Now he excluded all of the evidence and the data that suggested that my superior academic standing was the basis, was indeed the engine that drove my acceptance into Princeton. I'm suggesting to you that if we ever stoop to perceptions of minority students as the basis from which to include or exclude them, we will reproduce the very pathology you're seeking to avoid. I think that affirmative action has been a credible tool and a critical tool to implement real diversity, and therefore real racial justice.

Moderator: Carl, Derek Bok, the former president of Harvard, wrote that "no applicant has a right to a certain college. Instead the school has an obligation to choose students carefully so as to advance the purposes it seeks to serve." Aren't the white students suing the University of Michigan, essentially asserting a right to go there?

Cohen: Most certainly not. These students—I happen to know them—are not claiming that they have a right to enter the University of Michigan. What they're claiming very clearly is they have a right to have their credentials viewed in a race-neutral system. They have a right not to have the color of their skin counted against them.

Moderator: Let's bring our audience now into the debate.

Question: My question is for Professor Cohen. If you believe that race should be eliminated as a specific preference in college admissions, do you *also* believe that race affected factors like legacy students, or geography even, should also be somehow altered to reflect the race-neutral idea that you seem to be advocating? Is that something that you would also support?

Cohen: I would support the elimination of these other preferences. But you really have to see that they are quite a different kettle of fish from race, because race has a role–the Constitution speaks to race in a way it doesn't speak to legacies, it doesn't speak to athletics or to playing music. But I happen to believe, in fact, that the legacy is a bad sort of preference, and I think we probably ought to eliminate it. But it's not something which is constitutionally required.

Question: In view of the fact that I feel as though we are still suffering the consequences of the African Holocaust, which was called slavery, which lasted for over 300 and some odd years, how is it that you could have affirmative action for such a short period of time and feel as though it has solved everything? And quite often there are situations where there is not a painless solution, where some people might be inconvenienced. But when you look at the greater majority of the people that were inconvenienced strictly on race, how is it all of a sudden race should not matter?

Moderator: Carl, I think that's for you.

Cohen: No one will deny that there has been a long history of racial oppression in our country. The issue before the Supreme Court is the use of race preferences for admission in universities. And even the University of Michigan does not argue that those preferences can compensate for the long history of oppression. The only issue before the Court is whether the diversity of the class can justify special preference by race.

Dyson: If you look at the rhetorical legerdemain deployed by Professor Cohen–who continues to talk about racial preferences, *not* in regard to white supremacy, or racial preferences to white men–what's interesting [is that] he avoids your question by engaging in what they call in philosophy a logical fallacy. He refuses to acknowledge the legitimacy of your claim by suggesting that what's before the Court is only a narrow consideration. That he's absolutely right about. But what's interesting is that in the broader picture of justice in America, of course . . . the legitimacy of talking about the African Holocaust, or the incredible discrimination that was suffered by African-American people, is already ruled out. I too will focus my comments upon diversity, which for me, is a compelling interest. But let it be noted that the broader picture cannot be talked about, simply because those who dominate the conversation are the very people who have historically been responsible for putting us in the position we are in, in the first place.

Question: Given that one of the goals of affirmative action is supposedly to bring disadvantaged students access to higher education, I wonder if you both could comment on the argument that the policies wrongly focus on race when they should actually be focusing on class, for example.

Dyson: What's amazing to me is that many Americans who have been self-confessed conservatives, even, become Marxist when it comes to race. All of a sudden the incredible outpouring for poor white people—I've never seen it [before]. The incredible upsurge of, "Oh, we're concerned about the poor." [Yet we] devastate them every day; refuse to reinforce their communities with economic policies that can uplift them. But when it comes to race, all of a sudden there's a historic legacy of pitting poor whites, and working-class whites, against poor blacks and working-class blacks. It's not either/or, it's both/and.

Cohen: Whether we should give preference on the basis of socioeconomic disadvantage as the question asked, is an important question. Certainly there is no constitutional objection in doing so. There is a constitutional objection to giving preference on the basis of race.

Moderator: Carl, let me ask you this: Even if this is not the question of the past, and the question of, let's say, slavery, cannot be an argument before the Supreme Court, on some level, isn't that still the point? Blacks and whites don't yet have a level playing field. Affirmative action in higher education might not be the first or best place to close the gap. But isn't it in some way the last chance for justice?

Cohen: In the first place, those who get advantage from preference in admission to universities are not those who have been damaged by the tradition of history. The advantage goes to the wrong people. And those who have been damaged never get to apply to the law school at the University of Michigan, so that the instruments do not address the issue of injury in the first place. And the second reason is that these programs are instituted by universities, and universities are not competent, they have not the authority, to decide who has been hurt, and who shall be remedied. I mean, Justice Powell in the *Bakke* decision made it clear that you can only award compensation after a court or a legislature has made a finding that there has been a constitutional injury, and universities are not in a position to do that. The University of Michigan understands all of this very well, and therefore does not make the compensatory argument at all.

Moderator: Let me ask Michael a question also. If diversity is critical to a college education, how much diversity is optimal? When you say diverse, don't you really just mean black? For example, why shouldn't a Vietnamese-American applicant be given the same number of points as an African-American or Latino?

Dyson: Well, first of all, I believe in a diversity of diversities. I believe in a cosmopolitan view of complex integration. But secondly, all diversities are not equal. Vietnamese people, who have certainly been subject to historical forces of oppression, have not in this country been slaves, seen as three-fifths human, [and] used as chattel to reproduce the mechanisms of capitalism, and furthermore, to underwrite the very leisure to engage in white supremacist thinking that slavery provided.

Question: When I think of getting rid of affirmative action, it's not that colleges shouldn't be able to decide who they want and who they don't want. If the college wants more black people, then they accept more black people. They already do that. They shouldn't get an automatic point that makes it a rule that the college has to follow. It's not up to the college anymore.

Dyson: Sure. When we talk about points, you say automatic. It's not automatic. This is something that has been historically fought over for a long time. The University of Michigan case has used a system of granting points along a continuum, and that's the point I'm trying to reinforce here, that race is but one consideration. If I saw white Americans who were equally outraged at the fact that we have a president who himself has been the recipient of legacy, geographical distribution—with patent mediocrity, and yet is the president of the United States—if we had the ability to acknowledge that . . . and go equally as aggressively after that unfair distribution of a social good like an education and an admission slot, I would say I would be much more willing to listen to the argument [against considering race]. Unfortunately, for many of our white brothers and sisters, they are not equally aggressive in pursuing litigation against those who have been treated to unfair advantages that only reproduce their already unfair advantage.

Moderator: Carl, Michael, what do you think about economic figures [cited by Ted Cross of the *Journal of Blacks in Higher Education,* who argues that for the last forty years, the median income of black families has been 60 percent of whites, but that when blacks hold a college diploma, their income is 90 percent of whites, so that college is the engine of racial equality in the country]? How would you comment, Carl, on what Ted said?

Cohen: We have a fundamental social and economic problem, of course. And we're going to change that only when we transform the education of minorities in the public schools. We're not going to change that by putting a thumb on the scale, as you put it, in admission to a University of Michigan or similar universities. That's just a Band-Aid which is not going to do any real good at all. And, in fact, is going to create hostility and division within the universities, and more tension for the minorities than would otherwise be the case.

Moderator: Michael.

Dyson: Well, I think what those statistics reveal—and they have been derived from Oliver and Shapiro's study of the difference between black wealth and white wealth—reinforces the perception that affirmative action is part of a larger piece of the pie here. When black students get an education, they're still making only 90 percent of what whites are making. What that statistic didn't tell you is that sometimes college-educated black people still make less than what white people who have only gone to high school and graduated make. So what it suggests to me, however, is that equaling the playing field by a compelling interest in diversity is not only good for diversity as an inherent educational good; it's also good for redressing the historic legacy of inequality in the society at large. And if we can get two birds with one stone like that, what an amazing thing to do.

Question: During slavery, a system of classification was begun that established that one drop of black blood rendered one black, and so I want to sort of explore the ambiguity of the racial categories that affirmative action sort of enforces. And I was wondering how black or Latino one must be to garner the benefits of affirmative action.

Cohen: It is in fact a dreadful consequence of systems of preference by race that the public institution is placed under the burden of deciding who *is* a member of the minority being preferred. And indeed, *what* minorities ought to be preferred, and whether they are to be preferred in equal degree. How much to each? And how many drops of blood make one a member of this or that race? That is the ugly and disgusting quality of divisions by race that has permeated our society lo these many generations, and that is what we must transcend. No longer attending to whether your grandfather or your great-grandfather, or your great-great grandfather was black or Hispanic or whatever, or Hispanic from Spain, or Hispanic from Argentina, or Hispanic from Mexico. It's crazy to draw distinctions of that sort in a country of this sort and allow them to weigh in admission to universities.

Question: Paul Dickler. I teach at University of Pennsylvania and Nashaminy High School. Professor Cohen, you seem to be opposing the Michigan plan because you see it as a quota plan. You have indicated before that you do approve of some affirmative action plans. I'd like our two speakers to give an example of an affirmative action plan that they both agree with, whether it's the state of Texas plan or some other.

Cohen: Well, that's easy. There are many affirmative action plans that I have supported from the outset. Affirmative action is concrete steps taken to eliminate discrimination. When President Johnson and his executive order insisted upon affirmative action for federal contracts, he insisted that the contractors say that they will not discriminate by race, to eliminate residual discrimination. So, for example, [the nation was encouraged to begin] eliminating examinations which are inappropriately biased. Or eliminating old boy networks, which inappropriately keep people out, or engaging in all sorts of activities, which under the table discriminate by race. Such elimination is affirmative action, honorable and right. What affirmative action is not, is deliberately using race. Affirmative action was originally intended to eliminate the vestigial uses of race, the remnants of race, and that honorable spirit I supported from the outset.

Dyson: Martin Luther King Jr. said, if the nation has done something special *against* the Negro for 200 some odd years, the nation must now do something special *for* the Negro. And I think . . . affirmative action . . . was to address both the vestigial remnants of racial oppression, but also to address concrete examples of *present* forms of racial discrimination, to prevent them from poisoning the pool of resources from which minorities could draw now in order to represent more equality in the country.

Moderator: What do you both think about programs like in Texas and Florida that essentially take a percentage of the top students in high schools, and therefore try to get a balance that way?

Dyson: Well, I think that on the face of them, *prima facia* evidence suggests that that's an interesting [approach]. It may be a *supplement* to affirmative action programs, but not a *substitute* for [them]. There's a kind of re-segregation afoot in this country, and I think what we're not addressing here is that the re-segregation of black and brown students in poor schools that don't have equal resources only reproduces the very thing he's worried about—that is, students who are not competent or capable of competing or performing in our broader educational system. So I agree with him in this sense, that we must not simply start at the higher educational level, we must begin at K–12 to fix the system. But, again, it's a both/and, not an either/or.

Moderator: Carl do you believe . . .

Cohen: Do I get a chance to respond to that? Good.

Moderator: I just wanted to know whether you think those systems are fair.

Cohen: The problem with these Texas-like plans, these 10 percent plans, is first of all, that they are based on segregated high school systems. They only work because the schools are segregated. And if we succeed in eliminating the segregation of the schools, these programs won't accomplish what they were intended to. Moreover, they only work if you have a state system. But the worst thing about these percentage plans is that they are fundamentally ways of trying to do what you may not lawfully do. And if these plans have been devised to achieve a certain amount of deliberate racial preference without calling it that, then they are indeed constitutionally weak, and I think probably will fall.

Question: Getting back to the question of admissions, Professor Cohen, I'm curious, you say that you think that acceptance to a university is not a right. But at the same time you advocate a system that depends on a definition of merit, which reinforces white privilege, and at the same time disallows minority students from presenting themselves and their experi-

ences in an honest and respectful manner. I'm curious how you
of reconcile that.

Cohen: With respect sir, I don't support a system of merit that specially benefits white students. I support an admission system which is race neutral.
You want to consider leadership. You want to consider character. You
want to consider attainment. You want to consider socioeconomic disadvantage. Maybe all of those things admissions officers may appropriately
weigh if they think it applies for their institution. What they may *not*
under our Constitution, and under our civil rights laws, and under the
principles of morality themselves—what they may not weigh is the color
of people's skin.

Question: I'm an Asian-American person who went to a small private liberal
arts college. I have a couple of comments to make, one to Professor
Dyson: Your comment in regards to gauging how . . . the various minorities have been persecuted by the white man, I don't think is relevant
in this conversation.

Dyson: Well, let me just say very quickly, I did not say that the "white man"
had held anybody down. That's an old boogie man deployed by black
nationalists from the '60s. I'm much more sophisticated about the detec-
tion of . . .

Question: You made a comment about the Vietnamese-Americans not having been persecuted enough to warrant twenty points.

Dyson: No. I said as the basis of slavery and the reproduction of American
society and privilege. I'm saying Vietnamese people weren't here shuck-
ing corn and digging and planting . . .

Question: They were violated and raped in their own land.

Dyson: No doubt about that. And I'm saying affirmative action should be
going on in their own land. What I'm suggesting here in America is that
we deal with the people who have been historically . . .

Question: You just lost me. You lost everything. You lost me.

Dyson: God bless you, and I'm saying to you . . .

Question: I'm disappointed in you.

Dyson: I'm very disappointed that you're disappointed in me. But what I'm
suggesting to you . . .

Question: You're not. You don't care about me. All you care about is you
and the black population, and that's fine, because that's what you're arguing for. But I'm here to represent Asian-Americans.

Dyson: Very good, and I want you to represent Asian-Americans in their diversity. And there's a diversity of viewpoints among Vietnamese people,
and Asian people. When we talk about Asians, we are talking about an
enormously broad swath of people. What I'm suggesting to you is that
I'm not insensitive to Asian-American or Asian claims about restitutional
justice . . .

Question: But you made that comment.

Dyson: Let me finish. I made a comment that said Asian people were not here in America as slaves. Professor Cohen continues to refer to the Constitution, and the basis of race as a consideration of distribution of goods.

Question: Okay . . .

Dyson: Let me finish . . . I said specifically Vietnamese people were not here as slaves in this country. I'm not denying the historic legacy of oppression.

Question: They don't deserve twenty points?

Dyson: I didn't say that Asians didn't deserve twenty points. In fact, the quota system has been used against Asians in California to keep Asian students out of the university system because white people could not compete against Asian students. And therefore it would have been disproportionate representation. I ain't the one ranting against Asians; that is not me. I'm suggesting to you that you're conflating issues of personal bias and perception of oppression—which I agree with . . .

Question: Personal bias?

Dyson: The perception of personal bias.

Question: Wow.

Cohen: Is it my turn, Professor Dyson?

Moderator: Okay.

Dyson: When you can jump in it will be your turn.

Moderator: Carl.

Cohen: My turn?

Moderator: Yes.

Cohen: The argument we just heard between our black speaker and our Asian member of the audience . . .

Dyson: Our black speaker? Our *black* speaker? Are you a Jewish speaker? What are you?

Cohen: Yes, that's right. You're the one who is calling attention to that. You are the one who said I'm a black man. Now let me finish.

Dyson: I said black man, not black speaker.

Cohen: The argument we have just heard is an example of the kinds of quarreling over racial lines to which preference leads. Because it is inevitable, once preference is given to one race or to one cultural group or to another, [the other will say]: "Well what about us? How much are we getting? You didn't get your share." It's just that kind of spoils system that we ought to eliminate by seeking to pay attention to those lines.

Question: Professor Cohen, if you had two absolutely equally qualified applicants, one white, one black, would you flip a coin to determine who gets in, or would you be willing to go with the black person?

Cohen: I don't know how I would respond in that situation. But I have served on admissions committees, sir, both for the undergraduate college at the University of Michigan, and for the medical school, and I've never seen a case in which we had two absolutely equal candidates. When we got into difficulties about who should be admitted to medical school, we sat there and we talked about these different candidates, and we looked at their credentials, and we finally decided, largely by consensus that it ought to be X rather than Y. And I don't think there is ever a case in which two people are absolutely equal.

Moderator: Michael and Carl, brief response to [director of polling for ABC News] Gary Langer's poll [which found that Americans support or oppose affirmative action, depending on how they are asked: two-thirds of Americans oppose preferential programs, whereas more than two-thirds of Americans supported programs of assistance for minorities, with blacks expressing considerably greater support for such programs than whites]. Carl.

Cohen: I think it's perfectly clear that most people do not want to give preference by race or color, and I think that will come to an end. The Court won't have it, and the people won't have it. Whenever it's been put to a public vote, the people don't want it and they won't have it. In this country race and national origin and color are not appropriate grounds for preference.

Dyson: It's no surprise to me that many white Americans, when told it's a preference versus assistance, are against it when it's preference, and for it when it's an assistance, because of the altruism of the human spirit in America. And I think that it's no surprise that African-Americans and all others are much more supportive of these policies than others, because after all, they have borne the brunt of discrimination upon which rests the necessity for affirmative action.

Moderator: Michael, if universities did more to reach out, to recruit and retain black students without race-based preferences in admissions, and *not* just athletes, would you be willing to let go of affirmative action?

Dyson: No, because I don't think it addresses the fundamental issue here. . . . A special outreach program is itself predicated upon at least racial sensitivity, or racial consciousness. After all, we have to remember, it's not just test scores, it's not just grade point average–there are other intangible considerations that go into the makeup of a student body, and that determine whether or not we accept or reject a student. Ten thousand white people can apply for 1,000 slots at Harvard. . . . And if they're all smart, with relatively equal grade point averages, you have to recognize that there will be other kinds of considerations [determining their admission]–legacy, athletics, whether they come from North Dakota, because we only have one student from there, and we've got ten from Iowa. All kinds of considerations play into the distribution of that good, and I think we have to be honest about that.

Cohen: There is a difference between race and those other considerations.

Dyson: Absolutely, because race has been the very tool to keep people out more than those others.

Cohen: There's a constitutional difference.

Dyson: The constitutional difference . . .

Cohen: There is a legal difference.

Dyson: The legal and constitutional difference is predicated upon the history of slavery, *Carl.*

Question: I wanted to speak directly to the legal question that's before the Court: Does diversity increase how we learn in our culture? And I think Professor Cohen, you said specifically that our society is segregated. Our society has a history of racism that you will not deny. How is that going to be fixed? It has to be fixed by the legislature, by public policy. If people do not integrate, if they do not speak, if white students have never met a student of color who has been discriminated against, how will we fix those problems?

Cohen: But the problem is that you seem to suppose that without preference there would be simply no opportunity for whites and blacks and other minorities to mingle. That's simply not the case. It's almost to the contrary because the presence of these preferential programs, I have to tell you in honesty often creates a certain amount of tension and hostility between the groups on campus and tends to divide and isolate them. Now I've been at the University of Michigan for a long time, and I will tell you that race relations at the University of Michigan are not all that good today. They were much better before preferential programs became paramount. And the reason for that is that people in different racial groups tend now less to trust one another than once they did. And do not credit one another as once they did. So it's not the case that these programs are really helpful in advancing the objective that you and I would share.

Dyson: Let me tell you this: [It is good] when we have classes, as the class I teach here at the University of Pennsylvania, where we have Latino, Native American, Asian, African-American, and a whole host of other "others" congregating together, to hash out problems of difference . . . of talking about the vicious varieties of identity politics and those edifying ones. When we talk about issues of class and culture in society, this is one of the last few places where such conversation can be had without the vicious consequences of racial animus that goes on. The race conversation on the streets of Brooklyn or anyplace in New York, is about a young black man reaching for his wallet, and four white policemen shooting at him forty times, hitting him nineteen. That's the race conversation in the larger society. The race conversation at a university is rather much more interesting, insightful, enlightened, heated to be sure, but we also know that this is one of the places where we can forge the sort of national solidarity that we claim we want in the aftermath of 9/11.

Cohen: We can do it better without preference. We can do all of that much better without preference.

Dyson: White preference does need to go, I agree absolutely. [Laughter]

Question: Tukufu Zuberi, University of Pennsylvania. I teach here. I'm a professor here. It seems to me that Professor Cohen does admit that, for example, his own position in life has been heavily influenced by the affirmative action which has been attributed to white men, especially when he was going to school. His whiteness was a factor that actually aided him in getting into school. Yet, now he ends with a point of saying, "Let's not consider race"–understanding that the legacy of using race has contributed to the differences in race that we see today. So if both speakers could speak to the role of history and the continued practice, both in their lives and in the society's life, of racism?

Cohen: Yes. The history of race in our country is painful and terribly important in understanding what is going on. As constitutional scholars have remarked again and again, the great lessons of our history, the great lessons of the Supreme Court decisions in this matter, has been again and again that using race as a dividing line has been the source of misery and anger and hostility. And the great steps that have been taken in our country, in the adoption of the Fourteenth Amendment, in the adoption of the Civil Rights Act of '64, and in the *Brown* case, was the elimination of the race line. What I am urging is that at the universities also, we eliminate the line that divides by race, and all history teaches us that eliminating that race will improve our society, and using that racial categorization will injure us and set back the cause of racial relations.

Dyson: The substance of race in terms of its history would suggest [by analogy] that if we've denied tall people access to a certain kind of good, and all of a sudden we say we're going to be equal, short and tall people can come into consideration, and yet we've produced privileges, [for example] where buildings are made for one [height category] of people, not the other–you're going to have to adjust the size of your building to accommodate the people who now can get in! [Laughter] And I'm saying that American society has to accommodate the ways in which race has played a significantly detrimental factor in the distribution of a good like education. And I'm glad that Professor Cohen is willing to admit that racial preferences should go, because again, as a white man, he has historically been able to take advantage of the preferences afforded to white men in this society. The reality is that those racial preferences about which Professor Cohen has spoken have continued to accumulate around white men in predictable fashion. We live in the United States of Amnesia. The theme song is provided by Barbra Streisand: "What's too painful to remember/ we simply choose to forget." [Laughter] And we have to overcome that.

Cohen: We *do* need to eliminate preference for whites as well as for blacks. And since you make reference to me personally, Professor Dyson, I rise to a point of personal privilege. I served for many years as chairman of the American Civil Liberties Union in Washtenaw County in Michigan, and then chairman of the Michigan ACLU, and then as a member of the National Board of the American Civil Liberties Union. And I have struggled all my life to eliminate preferences for whites. I have struggled against preferences for whites, because I have believed all my life that preference on the basis of skin color was wrong, whether it was whites or blacks or greens or blues. And the way to begin the transcending process is to stop doing it now.

Dyson: [Professor Cohen's statement evokes the memory of Dr. King's argument with white liberalism.] What I'm suggesting to you is that Martin Luther King Jr. said one of his great problems was the way in which white liberals failed to understand the incredibly difficult process by which racism operates in American society. It's not just the formal ways in which racial restrictions operate; it's the informal collection of beliefs and sentiments and passions that continue to inform the citizenry, and that continue to pollute the population, vis-à-vis race. And I think that's the thing we haven't dealt with here.

Question: Dr. Cohen, authors who are admittedly historians, and not philosophers, have said that every day is affirmative action for white men. And when you look at the preferential treatments that are accepted in this country—farm subsidies, legacies, old boy networks, and taxpayer benefits for homeowners—these benefits disproportionately benefit white people. So how can you take race out of the equation?

Cohen: I think your question is fair, and I want to address it frankly. Ours is a country which is beset by racism, still. It really is. And the unfairness of racism in our country is very painful to one who reflects upon it, and one who tries, as I have tried, to combat it. But most respectfully I urge you to see you do not overcome that, or transcend it, by finding new ways to give preferences to other groups. You and I want the same thing. We want to eliminate preferences for groups by virtue of their skin color or their group. The way to do that is to cease to use categories of that kind.

Moderator: It's time for us to give our debaters a chance to share a final remark. First, Michael Eric Dyson.

Dyson: There's a compelling interest of the nation to continue to invest in programs that recognize racial diversity as a common good, a common good that is apparent, a common good that is worthy of support, and a common good that will reinforce the best virtues of American democracy. We live in a nation where the distribution of social goods like employment and education continues to be driven by racial preferences for white majorities, who often unconsciously, and without awareness, benefit from those advantages. So I suggest that the compelling interests of the state, and especially of the higher educational institutions that we populate, and that we support, is that we will be able to engage in reasoned and reasonable dialogue about difference; come to an appreciation for the radical ethnic, racial, moral, civil, gendered, sexual orientation differences that constitute our nation at its best; and then appreciate the beauty and harmony that may result from that diversity. But without taking race into consideration, I'm afraid, given the history of this country, that that will not be achieved in our institutions of higher education.

Moderator: And now a word from Carl Cohen.

Cohen: The central issue before the Supreme Court of the United States in the Michigan admissions cases now on their desks is discrimination by race. Discrimination by race, by skin color, and by national origin is wrong. It's a violation of the equal protection of the laws guaranteed by the Constitution of the United States. And race preference is also a plain violation of the Civil Rights Act of 1964, which unambiguously forbids racial discrimination by institutions receiving federal financial assistance. But above all, race preference is morally wrong–always was morally wrong. And good motives do not make it right. We Americans, I think, reject now, and will reject forever more, every form, *every* form of discrimination by race. And the Michigan admissions cases, *Gratz* and *Grutter*, give our Supreme Court the opportunity to say this now crisply and forcefully. And I think they will.

Moderator: University of Michigan Professor Carl Cohen and University of Pennsylvania Professor Michael Eric Dyson. Thank you both and thanks to our audience here at the Wistar Institute. . . . And before we say goodbye, I'd like to leave you with this closing thought from President Theodore Roosevelt: "Our aim is to recognize what Lincoln pointed out: The fact that there are some respects in which men are obviously not equal, but also insist that there should be an equality of self-respect and of mutual respect, an equality of rights before the law, and at least an approximate equality in the conditions under which each man obtains the chance to show the stuff that is in him when compared to his fellows." I'm Margot Adler, thanks for listening to *Justice Talking.*

Seven

A REPRIEVE FOR AFFIRMATIVE ACTION

On April 1, 2003, I traveled to Washington, D.C., to join thousands of other activists surrounding the Supreme Court to voice our support for affirmative action as the nine justices inside heard oral arguments on the two University of Michigan cases that severely questioned the policy's legal standing. Along with figures like Reverend Al Sharpton, Martin Luther King III, and Reverend Jesse Jackson, I spoke that day about the poisonous legacy of white supremacy and the multiracial quest for racial justice, a fight whose timing was even more poignant since it took place in the centennial year of the publication of W.E.B. Du Bois's magisterial book, The Souls of Black Folk *(1903). The Michigan cases were the fiercest challenge to affirmative action in a generation, dating back to 1978's* Bakke *case, when the Supreme Court held by a narrow margin that race could play a factor in choosing a diverse student body. Once again in 2003, the Supreme Court, by a 5–4 margin, contended that race could be one of many factors in the admissions process to select a diverse student body. The policy is barely safe for the moment. However, the intense opposition to affirmative action suggests that its advocates must double their efforts to educate the public about the value of educational diversity and enlarge the fight for racial justice, points I make in this essay from the* Philadelphia Inquirer.

WELL, THE SUPREME COURT GOT IT HALF RIGHT. It voted 5–4 to uphold the use of race in University of Michigan law school admissions, but rejected by a 6–3 margin the particular plan that Michigan was using to achieve diversity in its undergraduate admissions. But in this political climate of racial amnesia compounded by hostility to progressive and enlightened views of race, the Court's split decision in the University of Michigan cases may be a greater victory than appears with the law school, and not as great a defeat as it seems at the undergraduate level.

The Court was right to uphold Michigan's law school admissions process that seeks to enroll qualified minority students in the belief that diversity is a compelling *educational* interest. Diversity is an educationally compelling interest because it helps to destroy racial stereotypes; it erodes the ignorance upon which bias rests; it facilitates positive interracial experiences that establish lifelong patterns of such interaction; and it enriches classroom discussion and learning.

As history has amply proved, without strategic pressure and clearly expressed goals, there is little incentive for even educational institutions to act in their best long-term interests when it comes to race. And since diversity is a critical means to maintain educational health, the interests of minority students dovetail nicely with the interests of higher education to create viable and visionary learning environments.

If this is the case, race-conscious remedies are an indispensable means to achieve such diversity. The advocates of the race-conscious remedy known as affirmative action—including the leaders of the University of Michigan—contend that considerable leeway in the use of race is necessary to implement the goals of racial justice. Hence, educational institutions must be free to employ a creative mix of programs and policies that bring them—and our society—closer to racial parity.

The opponents of affirmative action contend that such programs and policies are unjust. This conclusion results from a faulty premise: that the enemy of racial justice is racial consciousness, and not the wretched uses of race in the past—and sometimes, in the present. For affirmative action's opponents, any sign of racial consciousness is wrong, even the awareness that our racial history is fatally flawed and stands in need of remedying through racially conscious methods.

Further, the opponents of affirmative action believe that all forms of racial consciousness are created equal, confusing democratic principle with constitutional practice. They assert that the race-conscious remedies of affirmative action grow from the same tree as lynching and Jim Crow law and housing segregation. Surely we possess sufficient ethical insight to carefully distinguish between racial injustice aimed at preventing minority progress and the conscientious efforts of good citizens to combat the legacy of bigotry in our educational and social institutions. Those who contend that there is no difference between the Ku Klux Klan and the NAACP because they both evoke black identity in their respective attempts to shape social policy and affect political change, are dead wrong. Fortunately, if by a slim margin, the Supreme Court rejected such arguments in siding with Michigan's law school that it is a legitimate and laudable goal to assemble "a class that is both exceptionally academically qualified and broadly diverse."

In the undergraduate case, Michigan has sustained a blow, but it is far from a fatal one. The Supreme Court ruled that awarding minority students points in the admissions process undercuts the Court's precedent in the *Bakke* case of using race in a flexible and fair fashion, and not, in the words of Justice Sandra Day O'Connor—the swing vote in the law school case and the author of its majority opinion—in a way that is "nonindividualized [and] mechanical."

But two things are overlooked by the Court. First, a fixed number of points were also given to applicants for other factors, including geography, athletics, and alumni connections. The Michigan undergraduate affirmative action admissions program only used race as *one* of several considerations. They also took into account—as do most other colleges and universities—grade point averages, standardized test scores, personal essays, musical talent, and teacher recommendations. Moreover, despite the evaluation of these criteria, the admissions process is far from objective. A given admissions officer may place varying emphasis on one ingredient over the others. Also, each candidate for admission will be subject to a given admissions officer's subjective evaluation of the student file. While wildly aberrant admissions decisions rooted in obviously unfair criteria are easily spotted, it is more likely that subtle gradations of judgment come into play. But it is precisely those gradations that often determine the success or failure of potential candidates for admission to colleges and universities.

Second, it is highly ironic that the Court should restrict Michigan's use of points for minority status on the basis that such minorities—including blacks, Latinos, and Native Americans—are not viewed as individuals. We must not forget that the very basis of racial injustice is to stigmatize minority individuals in an unjust fashion by treating all of them, regardless of merit, talent, or achievement, in the same, unfair manner. It is both logically and morally confused to deny the legitimacy of recognizing the group status imposed on minority groups through racial prejudice, group bias, and social stigma. The only way in the present to counteract such prejudice, bias, and stigma is to take group identity and interests into account as we seek remedies for racial injustice's virulent persistence. We must not fall prey to the notion that all forms of racial consciousness are identical.

Moreover, racial injustice is not simply a relic, but a living, breathing animal. One of the greatest hindrances to the realization of true equality for racial minorities is the dangerously persistent belief that unjust racial practices—and the equally noxious ideas and perceptions that feed them—have been completely eradicated. Nothing could be further from the truth. As Justice Ruth Ginsburg eloquently reminds us in her dissenting opinion: "We are not far distant from an overtly discriminatory past, and the effects of centuries of law-sanctioned inequality remain painfully evident in our communities and schools." But this ruling is no reason for advocates of affirmative action to lose heart. It is true that Michigan's method was rejected, but its mission remains constitutionally in place: to achieve a racially diverse student population.

While the victory in the Michigan case should further embolden affirmative action's advocates to stand tall, its slim margin should goad us to work hard to provide constitutional guarantee to its existence, and to deepen the public's awareness of the extremely useful benefits that racial diversity entails.

PART FOUR

MULTICULTURALISM

In the October 2001 issue of the Village Literary Supplement, I argued that the most vexing moment in the literary landscape over the last twenty years was, "hands down, the publication of Allan Bloom's The Closing of the American Mind. It made snobbishness fashionable, bigotry acceptable, and intellectual imperialism a thing to be imitated in a slew of trailing tomes." Bloom's book was indeed the rallying cry to war against a host of "enemies" of Western culture: blacks, lovers of rock & roll, leftists, feminists, and basically whoever else didn't uncritically co-sign the superiority of dead white men. Although it is true that even worthy causes sometimes flail in the crosswinds of cultural fads, our culture is helped by robust multiculturalists who pursue their aims without apology—in part, because the love of dead white men is not foreign to those who want to open the canon beyond their books. It has never been a question for multiculturalists of whether one should love Whitman or Wright, but rather, how the resistance to widening our view of greatness and nobility in the culture tells on our flawed and biased literary custodians.

Eight

LEONARD JEFFRIES AND THE
STRUGGLE FOR THE BLACK MIND

At the height of the culture wars in the early 1990s, Leonard Jeffries was a lightning rod for controversy because of a widely cited speech he gave claiming that Jews and Italians had worked collaboratively to undermine the black image in Hollywood. He also argued that Jews had financed the slave trade. Predictably, Jeffries became anathema to the conservative junta in higher education even as he was embraced by certain groups of black students and activists. In this chapter, I evaluate Jeffries's challenge to Eurocentric biases in public and higher education. I also critique a claim advanced by Jeffries and other scholars that skin pigment melanin plays a crucial role in shaping racial behavior among blacks and whites. This chapter, which first appeared in the now defunct and sorely missed Emerge *magazine, earned me the 1992 award for magazine writing from the National Association of Black Journalists.*

THE WHIRLWIND OF CONTROVERSY THAT surrounds the figure of Dr. Leonard Jeffries obscures the complex problems that must figure in an understanding of the nerve he has struck deep in the decadent cavity of race in America. The outspoken chairman of the black studies department of the City College of New York is the lightning rod for a gaggle of issues that embody a contemporary cultural crisis: theories of biological or environmental determinism, the rise of Afrocentric education, and claims about the African origin of civilization.

A speech Jeffries made in July 1991, in which he said Jews and Italians had collaborated in Hollywood to denigrate blacks and that Jews had financed the slave trade, drew outrage from many whites who felt that such alleged bigotry and anti-Semitism warranted disciplinary action from the college. On October 28, 1991, the trustees effectively put Jeffries on probation as department head, although his employment was protected by his tenured status. However, further allegations that Jeffries had also threatened the life of a Harvard student journalist during an interview put Jeffries in danger of being dismissed for "conduct unbecoming a member of the staff." City College had announced that it would investigate the allegations, which Jeffries called "scurrilous" and part of "a media lynching."

Jeffries continues to be a popular figure among black students on campus and certain activists in the community. What seems to draw their interest are his alleged

statements about the role of the skin pigment melanin in shaping culture and behavior and his provocative use of the metaphor of sun people (who are warm, cooperative, and community-minded) versus ice people (who are cold, territorial, and
aggressive). Few realize that the popular contemporary source of the sun people/ice
people typology is a 1978 book, *The Iceman Inheritance: Prehistoric Sources of Western
Man's Racism, Sexism, and Aggression*, by white Canadian author Michael Bradley.[1]

The melanin theory, however, has its genesis in a broad body of literature published mostly by independent or black presses and in highly technical studies in
scientific and medical journals. Black authors like psychiatrist Richard King, in his
book titled *African Origin of Biological Psychiatry*,[2] Carol Barnes in his privately published monograph *Melanin*, and lecturers such as Baltimore psychiatrist Patricia
Newton have stimulated interest in the role of melanin in biological, mental, and
racial development. Newton and King have also been a motivating behind-the-
scenes force in organizing a series of "Melanin Conferences," held annually since
1987 in San Francisco, New York, Washington, D.C., Dallas, and Los Angeles.
Each conference has drawn more than five hundred participants—laypeople and
community activists joining with scholars.

But the most prominent figure to introduce a consideration of the possible behavioral and cultural consequences of melanin to broad public discussion has been
black psychiatrist Frances Cress-Welsing. Cress-Welsing first articulated in 1970 the
Cress Theory of color confrontation and racism (white racism), which links the development of white supremacist ideology to white fear of genetic annihilation. Her
theory maintains that "whiteness is indeed a genetic inadequacy or a relative genetic deficiency state, based upon the genetic inability to produce the skin pigments
of melanin (which is responsible for all skin color). The vast majority of the
world's people are not so afflicted, which suggests that color is normal for human
beings and color absence is abnormal. . . . Color always 'annihilates' (phenotypi-
cally and genetically speaking) the non-color, white."[3] Cress-Welsing further states
that because of their "color inferiority," whites respond with a psychological
vengeance toward people of color, developing "an uncontrollable sense of hostility
and aggression," an attitude that has "continued to manifest itself throughout the
history of mass confrontations between whites and people of color."[4]

Ironically, Cress-Welsing now says she believes that the recent preoccupation
with her melanin theory is a diversion from the more immediate problem facing
people of color: white supremacy. "I put the discussion of melanin on the board
in order to [describe how pigmentation] was a factor in what white supremacy
behavior was all about," she says. "If I had my way, there wouldn't be all the discussion about melanin. I would say discuss white supremacy. White supremacy
has guided the discussion to multiculturalism, diversity, to anything [but white
supremacy]."[5]

Indeed, white supremacy is a theme that Cress-Welsing single-mindedly pursues in her book *The Isis Papers: The Keys to the Colors*, a text that has sold nearly
40,000 copies, principally through black-owned retail outlets. But despite her cur-

rently stated interest in refocusing her message on white supremacy, she continues to develop her melanin theory, for example, by expounding on the neuro-
chemical basis of soul and evil. Moreover, since her theory links white injustice
with the inability of whites to produce melanin, her focus on white racism leads
ineluctably to a concern with melanin.

Jeffries, too, has been attempting to distance himself from possible racist implications of the melanin theory. When he appeared on *Donahue* last fall, his first
time on a national TV show, he said, "We do not have a theory of melanin that
says black people are superior. It's a joke. But it's been run and run and run into
the ground." Jeffries contends that melanin is subsidiary to "the larger awakening
of African peoples in terms of their real history," because there is "an African primacy to human experience."

But he just as often stressed the need for comprehending the crucial function of
melanin in cultural and biological evolution. Jeffries noted that *Civilization or Barbarism: An Authentic Anthropology*, the landmark book by the late Senegalese scholar
Cheikh Anta Diop, characterizes melanin as "the phenomenon which helps us establish that there's only one human race, and that human race is African. Melanin
is that phenomenon that comes about as a result of the sun factor."

Jeffries says Diop links the development of melanin to a more involved theory
about the origins of human civilization in Africa's Nile River valley, where important distinctions in the qualities of persons and cultures would have been developed—hence his use of the reductionist sun people/ice people dichotomy to explain perceived differences in persons from the northern and southern cradles.
"The value system of the northern cradle [ice people] . . . that rough survival
value system, produces a premium on male physical strength and has produced
this warrior value system," Jeffries opined, "whereas [in] the value system of the
south [sun people] where you can look at the spiritual relationship within the
human and the cosmic family . . . you see the male and female principle in harmony and balance, you see nature in harmony and balance, you see the relationship of the sky and the moon and the sun to human development." This amounts
to biological, ecological, and racial determinism, and can hardly be substantiated.

Although Jeffries views himself as an Afrocentrist, Molefi Kete Asante, chairman of Temple University's Department of African American Studies and often
described as the "father of the theoretical and philosophical movement of Afrocentricity" (he is the author of *Afrocentricity*, published by Africa World Press), contends that Afrocentricity itself "is not a theory of biological determinism [but] essentially the idea that African people must be seen as subjects of history and of
human experience, rather than objects." Asante finds the melanin theory "intriguing" but disavows it as an Afrocentric theory.

Rigid categories based on essential, unvarying characteristics melt in the face of
actual experience and human history. "Blacks are just as intellectual [as whites],
and whites in some situations are just as feeling [as blacks]," says Cornell University professor Martin Bernal, author of *Black Athena: The Afroasiatic Roots of Classical*

Civilization.[6] "My study of human societies and the way in which whites and blacks behave in their societies makes me believe that you can explain these things more satisfactorily in terms of society and social relations than you can in terms of physiology."

Bernal, a white Briton whose recent scholarship explores the Egyptian roots of Greek civilization, admits a personal affinity for Egypt in part because "here is an African culture [that is] analytical and intellectual. You can have African societies of both types, just as you can have European societies of both types." Bernal says his study of Egypt and Greece has taught him that both were such a "mixed culture."

Egypt was one of the great civilizations of the ancient world, but so were China, Mesopotamia in the Middle East, and other cultures in Central America. So in attempting to overcome the bruising absence of constructive discourse about Africa, Jeffries and his cohorts have distorted the variety and legitimacy of other ancient civilizations through the lens of a compensatory racial and cultural hierarchy that assigns Africa artificial and romantic superiority.

Indeed, it was Jeffries's courageous attempt to reverse the harmful effects of Eurocentrism through educational reform in the New York State school system that first brought him to national attention. Jeffries served as a consultant to the first of two task forces charged by the New York State Commission on Education with correcting deficiencies in the curriculum in regard to people of color. Not surprisingly, Jeffries and many of the task force members concluded that the experiences, histories, and contributions of nonwhite people were gravely underrepresented in New York's educational curriculum. Brutal internecine battles developed, especially between Jeffries and his ideological opponents, historian Arthur Schlesinger, Jr., and educator Diane Ravitch, but many of Jeffries's ideas were adopted in the committee's final report, "A Curriculum of Inclusion."

Schlesinger issued his dissenting opinions in *The Disuniting of America: Reflections on a Multicultural Society.*[7] In it he invoked the timeworn metaphor of national unity forged as ethnic groups melted into the American character, in contrast to what he saw as the vicious ethnic tribalism evinced by people of Jeffries's ilk. Apparently for Schlesinger, anyone who appeals to racial or ethnic identity as the basis of making radical social, political, or moral claims is what may be termed an ethnosaur, a recalcitrant ethnic loyalist who has not acknowledged the legitimacy of a superior and more sweeping national identity. Schlesinger contends that many Afrocentrists "not only divert attention from the real needs but exacerbate the problems."

The call by Schlesinger and others for more "objective" historical scholarship fails to address the persistent historical patterns of racist exclusion of minority perspectives that are manifest in varying degrees from the elementary school to university education. "[Schlesinger] probably really believes that he and his contemporaries have been writing objective history," says Bernal. "He seems to me remarkably lacking in self-consciousness and awareness and still sees white middle-aged men as the only people capable of rendering acceptable historical judgments."

In this context, Afrocentric attempts to articulate credible intellectual conceptions of the nature and shape of black racial experiences and to express profound disenchantment with the silence of majoritarian histories on the suffering and achievements of minority peoples are praiseworthy indeed. But while Jeffries's diatribes against Eurocentrism are sometimes accurate, his embrace of various ideas in support of his version of Afrocentrism seems plain wrongheaded. Jeffries is promoting a rigid and romantic notion of racial identity.

Ironically, Jeffries is arguing for the same sort of unanimity of vision and experience that racism has artificially imposed upon African-American life. Perhaps he would do well to heed the words of fellow Afrocentrist Asante that "the virtue of Afrocentrism is pluralism without hierarchy." Asante emphasizes that "Afrocentricity is not about valorizing your position and degrading other people. Whites must not be seen as above anyone; but by the same token they've got to be seen alongside everyone."

Moreover, Jeffries's romanticization of Egyptian culture as the seat of human civilization incorrectly views history through the idyllic lens of uncritical racial pride and narrow nationalist goals. Such simplistic distortions overlook the conflicts and corruption spawned by Egyptian civilization and repeat the fantastic egocentrism and therapeutic fables of Eurocentric history at its worst. "Eurocentric history as taught in schools and universities has had a very large ego-boosting, if not therapeutic, purpose for whites," acknowledges Bernal. "It's in a way normal for the idea that blacks should have some confidence building in their pedagogy." But he cautions against an uncritical celebration of racial and cultural roots. "I think there should be research history as well, and that will sometimes reveal facts that you don't like."

As mature African-American scholars, teachers, students, and citizens, we must embrace the rich and varied racial past that has contributed to our making. We must also acknowledge the profound degree to which we have alternately enjoyed and endured a terrible but sometimes fruitful symbiosis with European American culture how we have helped shape many of its cultural gifts to the world, even against its will; and how those expressions emerged in the crucible and turmoil of our uniquely African American experience.

Nine

SHAKESPEARE AND SMOKEY ROBINSON:
REVISITING THE CULTURE WARS

This is one of my favorite essays. I first delivered it as a keynote address at a symposium on language and identity held at the Mark Twain House in 1994, featuring Frank Rich, Christopher Hitchens, Jeff Greenfield, and Gloria Naylor. In this essay (an excerpted version appeared on the back page of the New York Times Book Review*) I embrace the vital intellectual and cultural traditions of African American and European American life. At the same time, I nod to the vibrant popular cultures from which I learned a great deal while appreciating the classics of literary culture. I see no essential contradiction in embracing the poetry of Hughes and Tennyson, the novels of Morrison and Hemingway, the essays of Baldwin and Ozick, the drama of Wilson and O'Neill, the criticism of Gates and Gass—or, for that matter, the insights of the Harvard Classics or hip-hop culture. They all help deepen one's awareness of what it means to be human and intellectually engaged with the questions of truth, beauty, goodness, evil, suffering, life, and death.*

I CAN HARDLY THINK OF A SUBJECT MORE strained by confusion and bitterness than the relation of race to identity. Our anguish about this matter is at least three centuries older than the current turmoil stamped in the culture wars. American views on race and identity have wearily tracked our Faustian bargain with slavery, an accommodation of moral principle to material gain that has colored national history ever since.

The paradox of our situation is that Americans are continually fatigued and consumed by race. We sense, indeed fear, that its unavoidable presence is the truest key to our national identity. Yet we are as easily prone to deny that race has any but the most trivial affect on human affairs, and that it has little to do with personal achievement or failure. Therefore, the people whose lives have been shaped by the malicious meanings of race—to be sure, there are ennobling ones as well—must now endure the irony of its alleged disappearance in silence.

If they speak of the continued effect of racial bigotry, for instance, they are accused of exploiting unfairly their status as victims. If they talk of the injury inflicted by coded speech that avows neutrality even as it reinforces bias, they are called supporters of political correctness. If they appeal to black, or Latino, or Native American heritage as a source of security in the face of hostility or neglect, they are said to practice the distorting politics of identity. And if they argue that Emerson be joined by, say Baldwin, in getting a fix on the pedigree of American literary invention—if they insist that the canon jams, occasionally backfires when stuffed with powerful material poorly placed—they are maligned for trading in a dangerous multicultural currency.

All of this makes clear that language is crucial to understanding, perhaps solving, though at other times even intensifying, the quandaries of identity that vex most blacks. Speaking and writing are not merely the record of our quest to conquer illiteracy or ignorance (they are not the same thing). Neither are they only meant to hedge against the probability of being forgotten in the future by marking our stay with eloquent parts of speech that add up to immortality. Language simply, supremely, reminds us that we exist at all.

Whether this is positive or negative, an uplifting or degrading experience, depends largely on how language—plus the politics it reflects and the power it extends—is used on our behalf or set against us. This is especially true for blacks. Early in American life the furious entanglements of ideology and commerce caused disputes about black folk to follow a viciously circular logic; slaves deprived of the mechanics of literacy for fear of their use in seeking liberation were judged inhuman and unintelligent because they could neither read nor write. Even those blacks who managed to show rhetorical or literary mastery were viewed as exceptional or hopelessly mediocre. However unfair, language became the most important battlefield upon which black identity was fought. This is no less true today.

The most important concerns of black life are intertwined in the politics of language—from the canon to gangsta rap, from the debate about welfare reform to the fracas about family values, from the roots of urban violence to the place of black religion. In my view, a happy though unintended effect of the culture wars is that they force Americans to see that from the beginning our language has been indebted to political transaction.

It is not just now that ideological intimidation has allegedly ruined the prospect of objective judgment, or that its advocates have crashed the party and lowered the American standard of artistic achievement. Our literary traditions and rhetorical cultures eloquently testify to the influence of class upon taste, and reveal how power shapes the reception of art.

Black culture lives and dies by language. It thrives or slumps as its varied visions, and the means elected to pursue them, are carefully illumined or deliberately distorted. The threats, of course, are not entirely from the outside. The burden of complexity that rests at the heart of cultures across the black diaspora is often avoided in narrow visions of racial identity within black life. Its earnest proponents evoke the same old vocabulary of authenticity and cry of purity in their defense. But such moves echo as a hollow chant when voiced in league with the resounding complexity of identities expressed in the literature and music, the preaching and art of black culture.

Likewise, prolonged concentration on a fictitious, romantic black cultural purity obscures the virtues of complex black identity. An edifying impurity infuses black experiments with self-understanding and fires the urge to embrace and discard selves shaped in the liberty of radical improvisation. Fiction and jazz, for instance, urge us to savor the outer limits of our imagination as the sacred space of cultural identity. When advocates of particular versions of Afrocentrism and black nationalism claim a common uniqueness for black life, they deny the repertoire of difference that characterizes African cultures.

Such conflicts teach us to spell black culture and language in the plural, signifying the diversity that continually expands the circumference of black identities. If this is true for black culture, it is even more the case with American culture. The two are intimately joined, forged into a sometimes reluctant symbiosis that mocks the rigid lines of language and identity that set them apart. American culture is inconceivable without African-American life.

Can we imagine the high art of fusing religious rhetoric with secular complaint without Martin Luther King Jr. and Malcolm X? Their craft lifted freedom and democracy from their internment in ink and unleashed them as vital motives to social action. Can we think of contemporary American fiction, and its fiercely wrought negotiations with the cataclysmic forces of modernity, without the magisterial art of Morrison, Naylor, Wideman, and Walker?

Can we imagine the will to spontaneity, and what anthropologist Melville Herskovits termed the "deification of Accidence," that threads through American music without the artistry of Armstrong, Coltrane, and Ellington? And can we think intelligently about the American essay, that venerable form of address that splits the difference between opinion and art with felicitous abandon, without the elegiac anger of Baldwin and the knowing sophistication of Ellison?

These few examples point up the resolute dismissiveness that mark knee-jerk responses to multiculturalism at its best. Opponents to the opening of the American mind would have us believe that multiculturalism is the graffiti of inferior black art scrawled against the pure white walls of the American canon. This claim reveals how black cultural purists have nothing on the defenders of an equally mythic American literary tradition.

Among other influences, the American voice carries a British accent, even as it rallies to sublime expression the coarser popular elements of the times it both inhabits and transcends. It must be remembered that *Moby-Dick*, claimed by critics to be a work of Shakespearean magnitude by a writer of Shakespearean talent, gained such stature because Melville hitched the bard's cosmic grandeur to the motifs and genres of mid-nineteenth-century popular literature. Imagine Hemingway doing a number on Jacqueline Susann, or Doctorow remaking Sidney Sheldon. The hybrid textures of the American grain are the most powerful argument for relinquishing beliefs in American orthodoxies and for celebrating the edifying impurity behind democratic experiments with culture and identity.

In this strict sense, multiculturalism doesn't argue for a future state of affairs to come into being. It simply seeks to bring to light the unacknowledged history of the trading back and forth along racial, and by extension, gender, class, and sexual lines. Multiculturalism is a request by minorities for this nation to come out of the closet, to own up to its rich and creolized practice in every corner of American life. In such an environment, it makes sense to ask, as Shelly Fisher Fishkin's poignant book about Twain's character does, *"Was Huck Black?"*

In a broader sense, though, multiculturalism cannot proceed painlessly. It must topple conventions precisely because they are erected on myths that exclude traditions and distort histories. The struggle over language and identity—over which work is legitimate and which is not, and over who gets to decide—is unmistakably a struggle of power. Plus, all the naysaying and hem-hawing that goes on around debates about multiculturalism neglect the manner in which African-American artists have often investigated both sides of the hyphen.

Ellison owed the habit of a critical style of reading, and the title of his first book of essays, to T. S. Eliot. Baldwin's essays draw equally from the gospel sensibilities and moral trajectory of the black sermon and the elegant expression of the King James Bible. And so on.

The fear of radical anti-multiculturalists that a democratized canon will trash Western tradition is mostly unfounded. At their best, multiculturalists expose the shifting contours of literary taste and the changing ways in which literacy is judged. (For instance, Homer could neither read nor write, but he is hardly frowned upon in our culture.) Multiculturalists also embrace the superior achievements of talented, towering figures. Such an operation bears little resemblance to hyperventilated protests that an ethic of racial compensation guides the selection of worthy work, and that its bad consequences will, in the words of Harold Bloom, "ruin the canon." I think of my own early education as an illustration of the possibility of black and white books together shaping a course of wide learning.

In the fifth grade I experienced a profound introduction to the life and literature of black people. Mrs. James was my teacher, a full-cheeked, honey brown skinned woman whose commitment to her students was remarkable. Mrs. James's sole mission was to bathe her students in the vast ocean of black intellectual and cultural life. She taught us to drink in the poetry of Paul Laurence Dunbar and Langston Hughes. In fact, I won my first contest of any sort when I received a prized blue ribbon for reciting Dunbar's "Little Brown Baby." I still get pleasure from reading Dunbar's vernacular vision:

> *Little brown baby wif spa'klin' eyes,*
> *Who's pappy's darlin' an' who's pappy's chile?*
> *Who is it all de day nevah once tires*
> *Fu' to be cross, er once loses dat smile?*
> *Whad did you get dem teef? My, you's a scamp!*
> *Whah did dat dimple come f'om in yo' chin?*
> *Pappy do' know you- I b'lieves you's a tramp;*
> *Mammy, dis hyeah's some ol' straggler got in!*

Mrs. James also taught us to read Margaret Walker Alexander. I can still remember the thrill of listening to a chorus of fifth-grade black girls reciting, first in turn and then in unison, the verses to Alexander's "For My People."

> For the cramped bewildered years we went to school to learn to know the reasons why and the answers to and the people who and the places where and the days when, in memory of the bitter hours when we discovered we were black and poor and small and different and nobody cared and nobody wondered and nobody understood.

The girls' rhetorical staccatos and crescendos, their clear articulation and emotional expressiveness, were taught and encouraged by Mrs. James.

Mrs. James also opened to us the lore and legend of the black West long before it became stylish to do so. We read about the exploits of black cowboys like Deadwood Dick and Bill Pickett. We studied about great inventors like Jan Matzeliger, Garrett Morgan, and Granville T. Woods. The artists and inventors we learned about became for us more than mere names, more than dusty figures entombed in historical memory. Mrs. James helped bring the people we studied off the page and into our lives. She instructed us to paint their pictures, and to try our own hands at writing poetry and sharpening our own rhetorical skills. Mrs. James instilled in her students a pride of heritage and history that remains with me to this day.

Before it became popular, Mrs. James accented the multicultural nature of American culture by emphasizing the contributions of black folk who loved excellence and who passionately and intelligently celebrated the genius of black culture. She told us of the debates between W.E.B. Du Bois and Booker T. Washington, and made us understand the crucial differences in their philosophical approaches to educating black people. There was never a hint that we could skate through school without studying hard. There was never a suggestion that the artistic and intellectual work we investigated was not open to criticism and interpretation. There was never even a whisper that the work we were doing was second-rate. There was no talk of easing standards or lowering our sights.

On the contrary, Mrs. James taught us that to really be black we would have to uphold the empowering intellectual and artistic traditions that we were being taught to understand and explore. Mrs. James was extraordinarily demanding, and insisted that our oral and written work aspire to a consistently high level of expression. And neither did she reproduce some of the old class biases that shaped black curricula around "high culture." She taught us the importance of Roland Hayes and Bessie Smith. She taught us to appreciate Marian Anderson and Mahalia Jackson. She encouraged us to revel in Paul Robeson and Louis Armstrong.

This last element of Mrs. James's pedagogy was particularly important since so many of her students lived in Detroit's inner city. She provided us a means of appreciating the popular culture that shaped our lives, as well as extending the quest for literacy by more traditional means. Thus, we never viewed The Temptations or Smokey Robinson as the raw antithesis to cultured life. We were taught to believe that the same musical genius that animated Scott Joplin lighted as well on Stevie Wonder. We saw no essential division between "I Know Why the Caged Bird Sings" and "I Can't Get Next to You." Thus the postmodern came crashing in on me before I gained sight of it in Derrida and Foucault.

But Mrs. James's approach to teaching her students about black folk did not go over well with many of her black colleagues. Still bound to a radically traditionalist conception of elementary school curricula, many of Mrs. James's colleagues blasted her for wasting our time in learning ideas we could never apply, in grasping realities that would never give us skills to get good jobs. (This was still the late 1960s, and the full impact of the civil rights revolution had not yet trickled down to the classrooms, nor the psyches, of many black teachers.) But Mrs. James's outstanding example of intellectual industry and imagination has shaped my approach to education to this day.

Another event in my adolescence also shaped my quest for knowledge. I can vividly remember receiving a gift of *The Harvard Classics* by a generous neighbor, Mrs. Bennett, when I was in my early teens. Her husband, a staunch Republican (a fact which, despite my own politics, cautions against my wholesale reproach of the right), had recently died, and while first inclined to donate his collection to a local library, Mrs. Bennett gave them instead to a poor black boy who couldn't otherwise afford to own them. I was certainly the only boy on my block, and undoubtedly in my entire ghetto neighborhood, who simultaneously devoured Motown's music and Dana's *Two Years Before the Mast*.

I can barely describe my joy in owning Charles Eliot's monumental assembly of the "world's great literature" as I waded, and often, drowned, in the knowledge it offered. I memorized Tennyson's immortal closing lines from "Ulysses:"

> *Tho' much is taken, much abides; and tho'*
> *We are not now that strength which in old days*
> *Moved earth and heave, that which we are, we are;*
> *One equal temper of heroic hearts,*
> *Made weak by time and fate, but strong in will*
> *To strive, to seek, to find, and not to yield.*

I cherished as well the sad beauty of Thomas Gray's poem "Elegy (Written in a Country Churchyard)," reading into one of its stanzas the expression of unrealized promise for black children in my native Detroit:

> *Full many a gem of purest ray serene*
> *The dark unfathom'd caves of ocean bear;*
> *Full many a flower is born to blush unseen,*
> *And waste its sweetness on the desert air.*

I pored over Benjamin Franklin's *Autobiography* and exulted in Marcus Aurelius; I drank in Milton's prose and followed Bunyan's *Pilgrim's Progress*. I read John Stuart Mill's political philosophy and read enthusiastically Carlyle's essays (in part, I confess, because his quote, "No lie can live forever" had become branded on my brain from repeated listening to Martin Luther King Jr.'s recorded speeches). I read Lincoln, Hobbes, and Plutarch; the metaphysical poets; and Elizabethan drama. (This last indulgence led a reviewer of my first book to chide me for resorting to Victorian phrases—which in his view was patently inauthentic—to describe a painful incident of racism in my life; I was tempted to write him and explain the origin of my faulty adaptation, but, alas, I concluded that "that way lies tears.")

The Harvard Classics whetted my appetite for more learning, and I was delighted to discover that it opened an exciting world to me, a world beyond the buzz of bullets and the whiplash of urban violence. One day, however, that learning led me right to the den of danger. Inspired by reading the English translation of Sartre's autobiography *Les mots (The Words)*, I rushed to the corner store to buy a cigar, thinking that its exotic odor would provide a whiff of the Parisian cafe life where the aging master had hammered out his existential creed on the Left Bank.

My fourteen-year-old mind was reeling with anticipation as I approached the counter to confidently ask for a stogie. Just then, I felt a jolt in my back; it was the barrel of a sawed-off shotgun, and its owner ordered me and the other customers to find the floor as he and his partners robbed the store. Luckily, we survived the six guns brandished that day to take our money. Long before Marx and Gramsci would remind me, I understood that consciousness is shaped by the material realm, that learning takes place in a world of trouble.

I was later thrilled to know that the new pastor of my church, Frederick Sampson, a Shakespearean figure if there ever was one, shared my love of learning. An erudite man trained to speak the King's English to the Queen's taste, he would, at a moment's notice, embellish his sermons and conversation with long stretches of Shakespeare or Wordsworth. Even at funerals, as he led the procession out of the church, he would recite Longfellow;

> *Life is real! Life is earnest!*
> *And the grave is not its goal;*
> *Dust thou art, to dust returnest,*
> *Was not spoken of the soul . . .*
> *Let us, then, be up and doing,*
> *With a heart for any fate;*
> *Still achieving, still pursuing*
> *Learn to labor and to wait.*

But like Mrs. James, Dr. Sampson read widely in black letters. Time and again, his eloquent pulpit art indexed the joys and frustrations of black and religious identity. He ranged between unlikely sources to make his points. He called on

Bertrand Russell ("the center of me is a wild curious pain . . . [the search for God] is like passionate love for a ghost") and W.E.B. Du Bois:

> It is a peculiar sensation, this double-consciousness, this sense of always look-ing at one's self through the eyes of others, of measuring one's soul by the tape of a world that looks on in amused contempt and pity. One ever feels his twoness—an American, a Negro; two souls, two thoughts, two unreconciled striv-ings; two warring ideals in one dark body, whose dogged strength alone keeps it from being torn asunder.

Mrs. James, Dr. Sampson, and my early habits of reading are to me models of how the American canon can be made broad and deep enough to accommodate the complex meanings of American identity. To embrace Shakespeare, we need not malign Du Bois. To explore black identity, we need not forsake the learning of the majority culture. And even if Dostoyevsky never appears among the pyg-mies, great culture may nonetheless be produced in unexpected spots.

The difficulties of gaining clarity about cultural and racial identity are only in-creased with the introduction of theory into the mix, a move bitterly debated among black intellectuals. The application of theory to black culture has pro-voked resistance from the right and left alike, mimicking patterns of response to theory in larger literate culture. Now what is meant by theory is literary theory, not a theory of progressive politics, say, or a theory of quantum mechanics, though both have come under attack for sharply different reasons.

The notion of theory itself, however, is not suspect. How could it be? Even its opponents have theories about the problems with theory. Some Marxists and feminists have theories about why deconstructionists need to be more realistically grounded in the world and politically engaged. Defenders of the Great Books have ideas about why theorists romp in pedantry and obfuscation, their jargon a sign of poor writing, or worse yet, muddled thinking. African-Americanists have theories of why black intellectuals should spurn European theories and stick to more traditional ways of criticizing books and culture. In their opposition to the-ory, at least, usual opponents find full agreement. With some adjustments, I think theory may help to explain black culture. We must have at least two skills to make it a go.

The first skill is *translation*. What's said meaningfully in one place must often be restated to make sense in another setting. Among initiates, subtleties of theory will be transparent, while those outside the theoretical loop will inevitably miss out. But if theory is to serve or undermine traditions of interpreting books and culture, the moral of the story (even if the point is that there isn't one) must at crucial points become clear. Admittedly, that is sometimes communicated by writ-ers whose politics of expression lash out at simple, given meaning. In order to be successful, though, such an act should not be hindered by sloppy execution. As with all writing, there are good and bad ways to do theory.

The second skill is *baptism*. I know the phrase evokes volatile responses because of its religious association, but then I've got a theory or two about that. For Lyotard, Derrida, and Foucault to be useful to me, they can't be dragged whole-hog into black intellectual debates without getting dipped in the waters of African-American culture. Strategies of play, notions of "difference," and ideas about the relation of knowledge to power can illumine aspects of black culture when applied judiciously.

But theory must be reborn in the particular cultural forms that shape its use; it must reflect the cultural figures fixed in its gaze. Jazz and science fiction, hip-hop culture and collagist painting, and broad intellectual imagination—embodied in folk like Betty Carter and Octavia Butler, Snoop Doggy Dogg and Romare Bearden, C. L. R. James and Zora Neale Hurston—all have something to gain from, and to give to, theory. Bertrand Russell believed that the goal of education is to help us resist the seductions of eloquence. At its best—in translation and baptized—theory can do just that.

The controversies surrounding hip-hop bring us full circle in grappling with how race, language, and identity are joined, and how their contradictory meanings sometimes collide. Because of its extraordinary visibility, indeed, vilification in the larger society—and because of the strong veto it has aroused in many black quarters as well—rap perfectly symbolizes the failure of neat, pure analysis to illumine the complex workings of black culture. The debates about hip-hop culture strike the deepest nerves in black culture—how we name ourselves; how the white world views us; how we shape images and identities that are tied to commerce and exploitation; how black culture preserves itself while continually evolving; and finally, and perhaps, most important, how survival is linked to the way words are used for and against us. Like the black culture that produces it, rap is both a new thing, and the same ol' same ol'. That is the crux of black culture's gift and burden.

As debates about the canon continue, and as currents of suspicion about the wisdom of multiculturalism endlessly swirl, the example of black culture's constant evolution and relentless self-re-creation is heartening. At its best, African American culture provides an empowering model of education that combines the impetus to broad learning and experimentation with new forms of cultural expression. The ongoing controversies generated by identity politics, hip-hop culture, and racial politics, and the insurgence of a host of other minority voices, insures that African-American intellectual and cultural life remains an important resource in addressing not only marginal traditions, but in reconceiving and expanding the very framework of American literature and democracy.

PART FIVE

WHITENESS STUDIES

Over the last decade, the recognition that white folk make up a racial group, much like black and red and brown folk, has spurred some powerful, progressive scholarship. Writers on whiteness have examined the very notion of what makes someone white, as well as how that identity is used to justify an alarming variety of destructive practices. Some of the best insight has come from folk who have been the victims of whiteness as it has metastasized across the globe. I hope that as the scholarship on whiteness grows, it will provide even greater inspiration to the nation to turn away from the road of white supremacy and to follow the path of racial justice.

Ten

THE LABOR OF WHITENESS, THE WHITENESS
OF LABOR, AND THE PERILS OF WHITEWISHING

*On October 3–4, 1996, at Columbia University, a historic gathering of labor activists
and academics convened under the theme, The Fight for America's Future: A Teach-in
with the Labor Movement. The two-day meeting included labor leaders like AFL-CIO
president John Sweeney, philosopher Richard Rorty, and feminist Betty Friedan. I was
privileged to speak on a panel entitled The Wages of Race: Unions and Racial Justice,
moderated by University of Pennsylvania historian Thomas Sugrue and featuring legal
theorist Derrick Bell, labor historian and whiteness studies pioneer David Roediger, and
activist Mae Ngai of the Asian Pacific American Labor Alliance of the AFL-CIO. The
teach-in also highlighted thinkers with profound disagreements. For instance, there was
also a panel on Culture, Identity, and Class Politics that featured, along with UNITE'S
Jo-Ann Mort, a vigorous exchange between NYU professors Robin D.G. Kelley, a
prominent historian, and Todd Gitlin, a noted cultural critic. My paper actually addresses
a critical issue taken up by Kelley and Gitlin: the function of identity politics in the labor
movement, and in progressive circles more broadly. Too many critiques of identity politics
take minority communities to task for undermining a fictional national and ideological
unity while reinforcing the invisibility of white identities, thus exempting them from close
scrutiny. This chapter, which appeared in* Audacious Democracy, *a collection of
presentations from the teach-in, briefly provides a historical framework to the debate over
identity politics in the labor community.*

BITTER CONFLICTS OVER THE POLITICS OF IDENTITY are at the heart of
contemporary debates about the labor movement, the political left, and the American academy. Such debates are often burdened by a truncated historical perspective that overlooks crucial features of the story of how identity politics, and the alleged special interests upon which such politics is said to rest, have come to
dominate our intellectual and cultural landscape. This essay, then, has a modest
ambition: to provide a small corrective to such stories by emphasizing how whiteness—which has reflexively, if unconsciously, been defined in universal terms—is
composed of particular identities. These particular white identities have, until recently, been spared the sort of aggressive criticism that minority identities routinely
receive. I will also argue that some critics of identity politics ignore these facts, and

this ignorance smoothes the path for false accusations against blacks, women, and other minorities as the source of strife and disunity in the labor movement. Finally, I will suggest that, based on the uses of whiteness in the labor movement, the politics of identity was a problem long before the fuller participation of blacks and other minorities. Indeed, identity politics is most vicious when it is invisible, when it is simply part of the given, when it is what we take for granted.

One of the unforeseen, and certainly unintended, consequences of recent discussions of race is that we have come to question the identities, ideologies, and institutional expressions of whiteness.[1] For most of our national history, the term race has meant black. The collapse of the meanings of blackness into the term race has led to a myriad of intellectual blind spots, not only in the narrow conceptualization of black identity, but in the severe lack of attention paid to how whiteness serves as a source of racial identity. The result of this is a cruel irony: whiteness, the most dominant and visible of American racial identities, has been rendered intellectually invisible, an ideological black hole that negates its self-identification as one among many other racial identities. In the absence of viewing themselves as having a race, many whites latched onto citizenship as a vital means of self-definition. Whites were individuals and Americans; blacks, Latinos, Native Americans, and other minorities were collectively defined as members of racial and ethnic subgroups. Whiteness had a doubly negative effect: it denied its racial roots while denying racial minorities their American identities.

Prior to conceiving of whiteness as a social construct—as a historically mediated cultural value that challenges the biological basis of white identity—most blacks and whites viewed whiteness as a relatively fixed identity. For blacks, the meaning of whiteness was singularly oppressive. The varied expressions of whiteness were viewed as the elaboration of a single plot: to contain, control, and, at times, to destroy black identity. For whites, their racial identities were never as concretely evoked or sharply defined as when the meanings of blackness spilled beyond their assigned limitations to challenge white authority. In part, whiteness was called into existence by blackness; a particular variety of whiteness was marshaled as a defensive strategy against black transgression of sanctified racial borders. At the least, whiteness was tied to blackness, its hegemonic meanings symbolically linked to a culture it sought to dominate. As a result, blackness helped expose the dominant meanings of whiteness and helped reveal the meaning of whiteness as domination.

To be sure, whiteness as domination had many faces, though the body of belief they fronted shared profound similarities. White supremacist ideology united poor whites in the hoods of the Ku Klux Klan and sophisticated scholars in robes in the halls of academe. Still, if domination was the hub of the meaning of whiteness, there were many spokes radiating from its center. First, there was *whiteness as the positive universal versus blackness as the negative particular*. On this view, the invisibility of whiteness preserved both its epistemic and ethical value as the embodiment of norms against which blackness was measured. White styles of speech, behavior, belief, and the like were defined as universal standards of human achievement; their origins in particular ethnic communities were successfully masked. Through this meaning of whiteness, whites were able to criticize blacks for their failure to be human, not explicitly for their failure to be white, although in principle the two were indistinguishable.

Then there was *whiteness as ethnic cohesion and instrument of nation making.* This meaning of whiteness consolidated the fragmented cultures of white European ethnics and gave social utility to the ethnic solidarity that the myth of whiteness provided. The genius of unarticulated, invisible whiteness is that it was able to impose its particularist perspective as normative. Thus, the resistance of blacks, Latinos, and Native Americans to absorption into the white mainstream was viewed by whites as viciously nationalistic, while white racial nationalism managed to remain virtuously opaque.

Next, there was *whiteness as proxy for an absent blackness it helped to limit and distort.* The accent in this mode of whiteness is on its power to represent the ideals, interests, and especially the images of a blackness it has frozen through stereotype, hearsay, and conspiracy. In important ways, this use of whiteness parallels Renato Rosaldo's description of imperialist nostalgia, where a colonial power destroys a culture, only to lament its demise with colonialism's victims.[2] In the present case, whiteness claims the authority to represent what it has ruined. The exemplars of this function of whiteness voice, instead of nostalgia, a presumptive right to speak for a minority it has silenced. Thus, there is a coercive representation by whiteness of the blackness it has contained. Needless to say, coercive representation often presents images that are feeble, distorted, or the idealizations of domesticated, colonized views of black life.

Finally, there was *whiteness as the false victim of black power.* This mode of whiteness is the ultimate strategy of preserving power by protesting its usurpation by the real victim. The process was driven as much by the psychic need of whites for unifying inclusion as it was by a need to find a force to combat the exaggerated threat of black power. Thus, whites were able to make themselves appear less powerful than they were by overstating the threat posed by blacks. D. W. Griffith's film *Birth of a Nation* exaggerated black male threats to white womanhood to justify the lynching of black men and to increase membership in white hate groups like the White Knights of Columbus. And in our own day, widely voiced complaints by "angry white males" about unfair minority access to social goods like education and employment often misrepresent the actual degree of minority success in these areas.

These strategies of dominant whiteness, as well as the orthodox views of race on which they are premised, held sway until the recent rise of constructivist views of race. One fallout from such constructivist views—challenging the racial stereotyping of minorities by dominant communities, as well as criticizing the romantic representations of minorities within their own communities—has been the wide denunciation of identity politics. It is not, I believe, coincidental that identity politics, and its alleged ideological cousins, political correctness and multiculturalism, has come under attack precisely at the moment that racial, sexual, and gender minorities have gained more prominence in our culture.

Although I favor forceful criticism of vicious varieties of identity politics–the sort where one's particular social identity is made a fetish, where one's group identification becomes an emblem of fascist insularity–the rush to indiscriminately renounce group solidarity without fully investigating the historical contexts, ideological justifications, and intellectual reasons for identity politics is irresponsible and destructive. If the labor movement, the left, the academy, and communities of color are to enjoy a renewed alliance, such investigations are crucial.

Still, taking history into account is no guarantee that the outcome will be just, or that it will profit the sort of balanced perspective for which I have called. Many critics have launched sharp attacks on identity politics as, among other things, the source of sin and suffering within the academy, the left, and the labor movement.[3] Many critics argue that the left–including civil rights groups, feminists, gays and lesbians, and elements of the labor movement–has, through its self-destructive identity politics, undermined the possibility of progressive consensus and community. The Hobbesian war of all against all–pitting minority groups against the majority, blacks against whites, gays against straights, and the handicapped against the able-bodied–results in each group talking (or, more likely, hollering) past the other, leading to a destructive politics of purity. Many critics suggest that the energy squandered on identity politics is nothing less than an American tragedy, because it negates a history of left universalism even as it supports a bitter battle over select identities. On this view, the larger tragedy is that the right, long identified with privileged interests, increases its appeal by claiming to defend the common good.

Like these critics, I am certainly worried about the plague of the politics of identity when it is unleashed without concern for the common good.[4] I, too, lament the petty infighting and shameless competition for victim status among various groups. Still, such analyses inadequately explain how we got into the mess of identity politics to begin with. Such critics of identity politics fail to grapple with the historic meanings and functions of whiteness, especially the harsh stigma that whiteness brings to those identities and social ideals which fall outside its realm. Moreover, they do not account for the narrow definition of universality and commonality on which such a project of left solidarity often hinges. To paraphrase Alasdair MacIntyre, "Whose universality and which commonality?"

But if such critics' efforts at explicating our national malaise fall short, Michael Tomasky's similar story falls far shorter.[5] In trying to figure out where the left has gone wrong, Tomasky is even more unrelenting in assailing the lefts "identity politics, and how those [intellectual] underpinnings fit and don't fit the notions about a civil society that most Americans can support." According to Tomasky, "the left has completely lost touch with the regular needs of regular Americans." He contends that the left "is best described as tribal, and we're engaged in what essentially has been reduced to a battle of interest-group tribalism." Further, Tomasky claims that "solidarity based on race or ethnicity or any other such category always produces war, factionalism, fundamentalism." He concludes that "particularist, interest-group politics—politics where we don't show potential allies how they benefit from being on our side—is a sure loser." Tomasky warns that "will never do the left any good, for example, to remonstrate against angry white men." Tomasky says that this "is not to say angry white men don't exist. But what's the use in carrying on about them?"

Tomasky is certainly right to criticize the left for its failure to show possible fellow travelers how they might be helped by tossing in with our project. And he's within reason to decry the destructive tribalism of the left. But he fails to comprehend that creating a civil society that has the support of most Americans cannot be the goal of any plausible left in America. The role of a marginalized but morally energized American left is to occupy an ethical register that counters injustice, especially when such injustice passes for common sense. The welfare debate is only the most recent example of how the left should gird its loins to defend those who are unjustly stigmatized against the advocates of universal values and common sense. But nowhere is Tomasky's fatal lack of balanced historical judgment seen more clearly than in his dismissal of the political and social effect of "angry white men." Tomasky fails to understand that such anger often grows from the historical amnesia encouraged by the ideology of white supremacy and by the politics of neoliberal race avoidance as well.

Tomasky, and other critics of his ilk, are, to varying degrees, victims of what I term *whitewishing*. In my theory, whitewishing is the interpretation of social history through an explanatory framework in which truth functions as an ideological projection of whiteness in the form of a universal identity. Whitewishing draws equally from Freud and Feuerbach: it is the fulfillment of a fantasy of whiteness as neutral and objective, the projection of a faith in whiteness as its own warrant against the error of anti-universalism because it denies its own particularity. Whitewishing is bathed, paradoxically enough, in a nostalgia for the future: too sophisticated simply to lament a past now gone (and in some ways that never was), it chides the present from an eschatological whiteness, the safest vantage point from which to preserve and promote its own "identityless" identity.

Tomasky's and other critics' whitewishing permits them to play down and, at times, erase three crucial facts when it comes to the labor movement. First, identity politics has always been at the heart of the labor movement, both to deny black workers, for instance, their rightful place in unions and as wage earners in the workplace, and to consolidate the class, racial, and gender interests of working elites against the masses of workers. The identity politics now allegedly ripping apart the labor movement—as well as Balkanizing the academy and the left in general—is a response to a predecessor politics of identity that was played out without being identified as such because of its power to rebuff challenges brought by racial, ethnic, and gender minorities. Even white proletarians enjoyed their secondhand brands of universalism. This shows how the move to decry "special interests"—that is, blacks, Latinos, Asian Americans—within the labor movement denies a fundamental fact: all interests are special if they're yours.

Second, as the work of David Roediger has shown,[6] race and class were integrally related in shaping the (white) working class in America. The class interests of white workers were based on their developing a sense of whiteness to help alleviate their inferior social status: they derived benefits from not being black. This simple fact is a reminder that, from the very beginning in the labor movement and in working-class organizations, race played a significant role in determining the distribution of social and economic goods. Such a fact flies in the face of arguments that the labor movement must reclaim its identity by retreating from identity politics to focus once again on class.

Finally, many debates about labor and identity politics are ahistorical in another way: they presume a functional equivalency between the experiences of all workers who are presently making claims about the weight certain features of identity should carry in a consideration of getting work, keeping work, and job advancement. The real history of racial and gender discrimination in the labor movement, and in the job sector, means that the affirmative action claims of blacks, Latinos, Asian Americans, Native Americans, and women are not special-interest pleadings, but a recognition of their just due in arenas that were segregated by race and gender. To think and behave as if these differences are equal to the forms of disadvantage that white workers face is to engage in another form of whitewishing.

The only way beyond vicious identity politics is to go through it. As with race, we can get beyond the nefarious meanings of racism only by taking race into account. We cannot pretend in the labor movement that significant barriers have not been erected to prevent coalition and cooperation between minorities and the mainstream. Many of those barriers remain. Only when we engage in honest conversation, accompanied by constructive changes in our social practices, will we be able to forge connections between labor, the left, the academy, and communities of color that have the ability to empower and transform each partner in the struggle.

Eleven

GIVING WHITENESS A BLACK EYE

This interview, conducted by gifted DePaul University educational scholar Ronald E. Chennault when he was a graduate student at Penn State, is my most in-depth exploration of white identities, institutions, and ideologies. It situates the rise of whiteness studies in America while exploring the philosophical and theoretical underpinnings of white racial practices. The white scholars and activists associated with whiteness studies—especially David Roediger, Mab Segrest, Theodore Allen, and Peggy McIntosh—are among the most courageous American intellectuals who seek to challenge the unquestioned superiority that an investment in whiteness breeds. While I may have disagreements with some whiteness studies thinkers at points, they are minor, strategic differences. Whiteness studies present a unique opportunity for our nation to rethink the meanings of whiteness, and to resist easy reliance on the destructive implications of whiteness.

Let me start by just talking a little bit about what other authors have done. Generally, they have tried to describe what they understand whiteness to be or what the content of whiteness is, identified some of the forms that whiteness takes in the multiple locations in which it manifests itself, and attempted either to redefine what whiteness should be or to spell out ways to combat the oppressiveness that is a part of whiteness, thus trying to rescue the productive content of whiteness. Based on that synopsis of the work of the others, why don't we start, if it's okay with you, with what you perceive whiteness to be or what you understand whiteness to mean.

I think when we talk about whiteness in the context of race in America, we have to talk about whiteness as *identity*, whiteness as *ideology*, and whiteness as *institution*. These three elements are complex and impure; they bleed into one another. Still, as categories of analysis they can help us get a handle on the intensely variegated manifestations of whiteness.

In speaking of whiteness as identity, I am referring to the self-understanding, social practices, and group beliefs that articulate whiteness in relationship to American race, especially in this case, to blackness. I think whiteness bears a particularly symbiotic relationship to redness and blackness; in one sense, whiteness is called into existence as a response to the presence of redness and blackness. Only when red and black bodies—from colonial conquest and slavery on to the present—have existed on American terrain has whiteness been constituted as an idea and an identity-based reality. White people's sense of themselves as being white is contingent on a negation of a corollary redness and blackness, and, for my present purposes, the assertion of that blackness as the basis of a competing racial identity.

White people who understand themselves through narratives of race often do so in response to the presence of African "others" on American terrain. As a result, I think that white identities have been developed unconsciously and hence, for the most part, invisibly, within the structures of domination in American society. For the most part, whiteness has been an invisible identity within American society, anal only recently—with the deconstruction and demythologization of race in attacks on biologistic conceptions of racial identity—has whiteness been constituted as a trisected terrain of contestation: over ethnicity, over ethnocentrism, and over the way groups manufacture and reproduce racial identity through individual self-understanding. I think whiteness in that sense has only recently been called into existence as a result of questions about the social construction of race, the social reconstruction of biology, and, in general, how we have come to talk about race in more complex terms.

When I talk about whiteness as ideology, I'm referring to the systematic reproduction of conceptions of whiteness as domination. Whiteness as domination has been the most powerful, sustaining myth of American culture since its inception. In other words, the ideological contamination of American democracy by structures of white domination is indivisible from the invention of America. Another way of saying this is that the invention of America and the invention of whiteness are ideologically intertwined because the construction of narratives of domination are indissolubly linked to the expansion of the colonial empire: America as the new colony. America found its roots in response to an *intraracial* struggle with Europe over the power of representation (i.e., how citizens should be granted official voice and vote in the polls) and the representation of power (i.e., how cultural institutions like churches and schools should no longer be exclusively regulated by the state). The United States was brought into existence as a result of an intraethnic war between white, Anglo-Saxon Protestants and American colonists who rejected their political deference to Europe and defended their burgeoning sense of nationhood and personal identity.

In that sense, there is a fissure in whiteness that is not articulated as such because it happens within the borders of ethnic similarity. This civil war of white ethnicity generated the fissuring of the state at the behest of procreative energies of emancipation. But that emancipation, at least in terms of its leaders' self-understanding, was not ethnically or racially constituted; it was viewed as the ineluctable conclusion to a fatal disagreement over issues of primary political importance, like freedom, justice, and equality.

At the same time, ironically enough, the expansion of American culture, especially the American state, was fostered primarily through the labor of black slaves and, to a lesser degree, the exploitation of white indentured servants and the oppression of white females. From the very beginning of our nation's existence, the discursive defense and political logic of American democracy has spawned white dominance as the foundational myth of American society—a myth whose ideological strength was made all the more powerful because it was rendered invisible. After all, its defenders didn't have to be conscious of how white dominance and later white supremacy shaped their worldviews, since there was little to challenge their beliefs. Their ideas defined the intellectual and cultural status quo. In that sense, the white race—its cultural habits, political practices, religious beliefs, and intellectual affinities—was socially constructed as the foundation of American democracy.

In terms of the genealogy of American nationality, whiteness and democracy were coextensive because they were mutually reinforcing ideologies that undergirded the state. When we look at the Constitution and the Declaration of Independence, the implicit meanings of white domination were encoded in state discourse. State discourse was articulated in the intellectual architecture of the Constitution and the Declaration of Independence; it was also written into the laws of the land that eroded the social stability of African-American people, first as slaves and then as subjugated victims of the state through debt peonage, sharecropping, Jim Crow law, the assault on the welfare state, and so on.

Also written into the laws of the land was the explicit articulation of black racial inferiority and the implicit assumption of white racial superiority. These two poles were reproduced ideologically to justify white supremacy; the mutually reinforcing structures of state-sponsored racial domination and the ideological expression of white racial superiority solidified the power of white people, white perspectives, and white practices. As a result, whiteness in its various expressions was made to appear normative and natural, while other racial identities and ideologies were viewed as deviant and unnatural.

The final component of my triad is the institutional expression of whiteness. The institutions I have in mind—from the home to the school, from the government to the church—compose the intellectual and ideological tablet on which has been inscribed the meanings of American destiny. Let's focus on one example of how whiteness has been institutionally expressed: the church. First, "manifest destiny" found an institutional articulation in the church, even though our country's founders ingeniously disestablished state-sponsored religion and thereby encouraged radical heterogeneity within American religion. While ostensibly free from state rule, religious communities were not impervious to secular beliefs; the theological discourse of many faiths actively enunciated the ideology of white domination.

Not only did manifest destiny bleed through the theological articulations of the churches, but the belief in blackness as an innately inferior identity galvanized the missionary activities of most religious communities as they sought to contain and redeem the black slave's transgressive body; many believed blacks didn't have a soul. With the overlay of theological verity added to embellish the ideology of

white supremacy, black identity became the ontological template for the reproduction of discourses of racial primitivism and savagery. The black body became
a contested landscape on which the torturous intersections of theology and ideology were traced: it was at once the salvific focus of the white missionizing project
and the foremost example of what unchecked transgression could lead to.

These elements of whiteness—identity, ideology, and institution—are articulated
and reinforced over space and time. They substantiate the argument that whites
don't understand themselves in abstraction from the cultural institutions and the
critical mythologies that accrete around whiteness. What we've witnessed over the
last decade is a crisis in the myth of whiteness; that is, it has been exposed as a visible and specific identity, not something that is invisible and universal. Whiteness
has been "outed," and as a consequence of its outing, it has to contend with its own
genealogy as one race among other races. We are now seeing a proliferation of
ideas, articles, books, plays, and conferences that question the meanings and significations of whiteness. As part of that process, we've got to understand what whiteness has meant and specify what it can or should mean in the coming century.

**Given this "outing" of whiteness, would it be your opinion that the concept
of whiteness will continue to be studied, that it won't be just a fleeting academic interest?**

That's right. I think we can rest assured that the extraordinary interest in whiteness
won't taper off too much. First, there are masses of whites who are absorbed by the
subject, a sure index of its staying power. There are also a great number of African
Americans, Native Americans, Latinos, and Asians—as well as other subaltern, aboriginal, and colonized peoples—who are deeply invested in reversing the terror of
ethnography: of being the disciplined subject of an often intellectually poisonous
white anthropological scrutiny. Many minorities yearn to return the favor of interrogation, if you will, though not in nearly as punishing a manner as they've received. Many members of these groups simply seek to unveil the myths of universality and invisibility that have formed the ideological strata of white supremacy.

They also seek to reveal a fundamental strategy of white supremacy: forging
belief in the omnipotence of whiteness. This belief maintains that whiteness se-
cretes a racial epistemology whose function is akin to omnipotent narration in fiction: it unifies the sprawling plot of white civilization; it articulates the hidden
logic of mysterious white behavior; it codifies the linguistic currency through
which the *dramatis personae* of white cultures detail their intellectual idiosyncrasies
and emotional yearnings; and it projects an edifying white racial denouement to
the apocalyptic conflict between whiteness and nonwhiteness. One consequence
of an investment in the omnipotence of whiteness, and in the unitary racial sentiment that it enforces, is that many minorities have been ontologically estranged
from what might be termed the *Dasein* of American race—the racial order of being
that defines national and, more fundamentally, human identity.

The great irony of American race—within the discursive frame of whiteness as an invisible entity—is that the condition for racial survival is racial concealment, a state of affairs that produces a surreal racelessness that stigmatizes all nonwhite identities. Thus racial and ethnic minorities face a triple challenge: they must overcome the history and ongoing forces of oppression; they must eradicate the demonization of racial identity-qua-identity that whiteness generates; and they must help excavate the historical and ideological character of whiteness in the sedimenting fields of cultural and social practice.

Another reason I think that the examination of whiteness will not diminish quickly is the sheer variety of white identities, behaviors, texts, and practices that the current phase of whiteness studies has uncovered. Such variety gives the lie to whiteness as a singular and fixed phenomenon. Whiteness must be viewed as destabilized loci of contested meanings that depend on different articulatory possibilities to establish their identities and functions. Whiteness is now up for grabs; it is being deeply retheorized and profoundly rearticulated. Whiteness is no longer simply good or bad: either formulation is a *reductio ad absurdum* that underwrites a rigid, essentialist view of race.

Contemporary studies of whiteness explore the complex character of white racial identity and practice. Such studies examine whiteness in multifarious modes: as domination *and* cooperation, as stability *and* instability, as hegemony *and* subordination, and as appropriation *and* co-optation. By no means am I suggesting that a narrow ideological binarism lies at the heart of whiteness; I simply mean to accent the interactive, intersectional, and *multilectical* features of whiteness with other racial and ethnic identities as they are elaborated in intellectual inquiry. Even if such studies are viewed as faddish, we must remember that many substantive intellectual engagements began as trends.

One of the advantages of the *subject(ed)s* of whiteness now *objecting* it (constituting it as a legitimate object of discursive interrogation and thereby objecting to the power of whiteness to iterate domination by remaining amorphous and invisible) is that we demystify the mechanisms by which whiteness has reproduced its foundational myths. We also get a better sense of how whiteness has helped construct blackness, and how whiteness has helped to construct Latino/a, Native American, and Asian identities as well.

We must recognize that current studies of whiteness—especially the groundbreaking writings of white scholars such as David Roediger, Theodore Allen, Noel Ignatiev, and others—are building on the often unacknowledged tradition of black critical reflection on the ways and means of whiteness. To be sure, whiteness studies in its present modes—in terms of the scopes of interrogation, disciplinary methodologies, paradigms of knowledge, theoretical tools of analysis, historical conjunctions, and material supports that make this an ideal intellectual climate for scrutinizing white identities—unquestionably marks a significant scholarly, perhaps even disciplinary, departure in cultural studies of race and ethnicity. But such studies would be impossible, or at least highly unlikely, without the pioneering work of figures like W.E.B. Du Bois, Langston Hughes, Zora Neale Hurston, Fannie Lou Hamer, and on and on.

To be fair, a number of the "new abolitionist" writers have scrupulously acknowledged their debt to this hidden black intellectual tradition. For instance, David Roediger acknowledges that Du Bois was the first to write, in his magisterial tome *Black Reconstruction*, about the "psychic wages of whiteness," arguing that even poor workers derived a psychological benefit from their whiteness. Current whiteness studies will only be strengthened as they refer to those texts and figures in black life, and in other minority communities, which have aided in the demythologization of a homogeneous, uniform whiteness.

I think that the study of whiteness will be around for some time because it can give us crucial historical insight into current cultural debates. For example, contentious discussions about the labor movement and its relationship to identity politics would be greatly benefited from a vigorous examination of the role white racial identity played in the formation of the American working class. Despite their economic disadvantage, poor white workers appealed to the surplus value that their whiteness allowed them to accumulate in the political economy of race. Many poor workers invested their surplus valued whiteness into a fund of psychic protection against the perverse, impure meanings of blackness. They drew from their value-added whiteness to not only boost their self-esteem but to assert their relative racial superiority by means of what may be termed a *negative inculpability*: poor whites derived pleasure and some cultural benefit by *not being the nigger*.

Their negative inculpability prevented poor whites from being viewed as the ultimate cause of harm to white civilization—despite the social problems to which their poverty and class oppression gave rise. Their negative inculpability redeemed poor whites, at least partially, by granting them powers to deflect their degraded status through a *comparative racial taxonomy*: poor whites could articulate the reasons for their superiority by naming all the ways they remained white despite their economic hardship. Negative inculpability and comparative racial taxonomy were racial strategies by which poor whites appropriated the dominant meanings of whiteness, and the ideology of white domination, while obscuring the intellectual and material roots of their own suffering. Of course, in objective, empirically verifiable ways, poor whites had much more in common with poor blacks: degraded social status, depressed wages, and stigmatization through social narratives of "the deserving poor" that blamed the poor for their plight. Such studies are of utmost importance in explicating the complex intersections of race, gender, and class in the labor movement, as well as in contemporary cultural politics.

In order to solidify the intellectual foundation of whiteness studies, we should distinguish among at least three economies within whiteness: an *economy of invention*, an *economy of representation*, and an *economy of articulation*. Economies of invention explore how and when the multiple meanings of whiteness are fashioned. Economies of invention permit us to excavate, for instance, the construction of Irish as a white ethnicity, as Noel Ignatiev has done; the making of the white working class, as David Roediger has done; and the invention of the white race, about which Theodore Allen has written. Economies of invention address the foundational myths of white ethnicity as they are articulated through metaphysical claims of white superiority. Economies of invention help us narrate the means by which culture has colluded with ideology to reproduce whiteness. They help us understand how cultural privilege is assigned to an accidental racial feature like whiteness, and how such privilege gives credence to philosophical arguments about the inherent goodness and supremacy of white identity.

Economies of invention encourage critics to stress how the project of whiteness was constructed on a labor base of exploited indigenous Americans and enslaved blacks. The irony is that enslaved blacks supplied material support and social leisure to white elites as they constructed mythologies of black racial inferiority. Economies of invention also accent a factor I discussed earlier: the symbiotic relationship between white and black identities, practices, and cultures in the construction of the material and cultural means to express whiteness.

In this matter, Orlando Patterson's important book *Freedom* is crucial in pinpointing the intellectual function of an economy of invention in interrogating the historically and socially constituted meanings of whiteness. Patterson argues that Western conceptions of freedom—as well as the epistemic crucible of Western culture and identity—are contingent on, indeed articulated against, the backdrop of slavery. In other words, there's no such thing as Western freedom without a corresponding articulation of slave identities; there's no ideal of freedom within American culture in particular, and Western cultures in general, without the presence of the corollary slave subject that was being constructed and contained within the narrative of freedom to begin with. Economies of invention help us comprehend the extraordinarily intricate construction of white identities in the interstices of hybrid cultural contacts.

Economies of representation examine how whiteness has been manifest, how it has been symbolized, how it has been made visible. Economies of representation highlight how whiteness has been embodied in films, visual art, and branches of culture where public myths of white beauty and intelligence have gained representative authority to rearticulate the superiority and especially the desirability of whiteness. Economies of representation pay attention to the erotic visibility of white identities and images—how whiteness has been fetishized as the ideal expression of human identity.

Economies of representation also underscore the cultural deference paid to white identities, images, styles, and behaviors even as they cast light on the scorn heaped on nonwhite identities in a key strategy of defensive whiteness: demonizing the racialized other as a means of sanctifying the white self; devaluing nonwhite racial identities through stereotypical representations as a means of idealizing white identities; and bestializing the expression of eroticism in nonwhite cultures while eroticizing racial others for white pleasure and consumption.

Finally, economies of articulation name the specific sites of intellectual justification for white superiority and supremacy. From selected writings of Thomas

Jefferson, David Hume, Immanuel Kant, Abraham Lincoln, and Woodrow Wilson to the writings of Dinesh D'souza (a white superiorist in brown skin), Charles Murray, Arthur Jensen, William Shockley, and Richard Herrnstein, beliefs in the pathologies and corruptions of black culture, and by extension in the inherent rightness of whiteness, have deluged our intellectual landscape.

Economies of articulation specify how, from the Enlightenment to *The Bell Curve*, ideas of black inferiority have been expressed with vicious consistency. Indeed, *The Bell Curve* argues black intellectual inferiority through a tangle of pseudo-scientifically manipulated data, leading to what Raymond Franklin has termed "statistical myopia." Economies of articulation isolate the philosophical architecture and rhetorical scaffolding that joins white superiorist and supremacist thinking to social and cultural practices. Economies of articulation show how myths of value neutrality, ideals of Archimedean-like objectivity, conceptions of theory-free social science, notions of bias-free scholarship, and beliefs in heroically blind moral explanations are deployed to defend (and to coerce others outside of its ideological trajectory to defer to) white civilization. These three economies help us determine, define, and demystify the meanings of whiteness and make sure that the study of white identities, images, and ideologies rests on a critical intellectual foundation.

What about whiteness being discussed outside the confines of academia, or what about the influence of these scholarly discussions on others not in the academy? How can that happen or how is that happening?

I think it certainly is happening. One flagrant example is in the cultural discourse about "white male anger," which, according to its apologists, is the legitimate bitterness of white men who have been unfairly denied employment because of affirmative action. Debates about white male anger take place in employment arenas, especially fire and police stations, where white men, we are told, have had enough. White male anger has focused on black bodies as its *objet de terror*, its target of rage. In the minds of such men (and their wives and daughters), blacks occupy wrongful places of privilege in the job sector because of their color. Black progress symbolized in affirmative action policies constitutes reverse racism for many whites. This is an extremely volatile occasion outside of the academy where the meanings of whiteness are being fiercely debated.

There were also discussions—sometimes explicit, more often veiled and coded—about whiteness in the recent ordeal of the bombing of the Murrah federal building in Oklahoma City, and in its aftermath, the trial of Timothy McVeigh. McVeigh became a flashpoint in the resurfacing of a virulent, violent whiteness that had to be contained for at least three reasons. First, the racial violence that McVeigh symbolized transgressed its historic ethnic limits by, in significant measure, being directed toward other whites. Second, by intentionally targeting the American government, McVeigh's white racial violence shattered an implicit social contract where the nation absorbed (i.e., excused, overlooked, downplayed, underestimated, etc.) extralegal racial violence more readily if it was aimed at black or other minority bodies. This was an ideological relic from earlier generations when extralegal white racial violence actually served the interests of the state, or at least multitudes of its officials, by discouraging black insurrection, protest, or rebellion against the legal strictures of white supremacy. Finally, McVeigh's violence had to be contained, even eradicated, because his poor white rebellion against state authority threatened to symbolically contaminate "purer," more elite expressions of white ethnicity.

One really gets a sense, from many of the white cultural discussions of McVeigh, of the ethnic betrayal many whites feel in the Oklahoma City bombing. Judging by what I've read, McVeigh viewed himself as part of a tiny outpost of pure patriotic rebels whose patriotism was expressed in the logic of radical *antipatriotism*: one must blow up the state as it is to get to the state as it should be. I think that McVeigh believed he was reviving a heroic vision of whiteness that he thought was being suppressed within the institutional matrices of American democracy and "legitimate" government. Apparently in McVeigh's thinking, the only legitimate government was to be found in the guerrilla gangsterism of his supremacist, antistatist comrades. They are the real Americans, not the namby-pamby politicians and state officials who cater to racial minorities, who endanger the freedom of religious minorities like the followers of the late cult leader David Koresh.

What's fascinating about McVeigh is that his actions articulate in the extreme the logic of repressive, hegemonic whiteness that hibernates within the structures of legitimate government: vicious attacks on welfare and its recipients; brutal attacks on black progress and its advocates; heartless attacks on the crime-ridden black ghetto; and exploitative attacks on the alleged pathologies of black culture. All of these claims and more have been launched by governmental officials. The cumulative effect of such attacks is the implementation of policies that punish the black poor and stigmatize the black middle class as well as the legitimation of crude cultural biases toward black citizens.

Figures like Timothy McVeigh become hugely discomfiting manifestations of the hidden animus toward blackness and civility that such discourses of attack encourage. McVeigh is the rabid reification of the not too abstract narratives of hatred that flood segments of white talk radio. Bob Grant, Rush Limbaugh, and many other lesser lights discover a living embodiment of their vitriolic, vituperative verbiage in McVeigh. McVeigh is the monster created by the Frankensteins of white hatred. And there's a great deal of shame in him because he's out of control and destroying his creators. In this regard, it's crucial to remember a salient fact: Frankenstein is not the name of the monster but the name of the monster's creator. The real terror, then, is the mechanisms of reproduction that sustain and rearticulate ideologies of white supremacy, and that sanction the violent attack on black and other minority identities.

Finally, debates on whiteness beyond the academy occur in the construction of cultural conversations about "poor white trash." Interestingly enough, Bill

Clinton figures as a key subject and subtext of such conversations. For many, Clinton is our nation's *First Bubba*, our country's *Trailer Trash Executive*, our nation's *Poor White President*. It tells on our bigoted cultural beliefs and social prejudices that Clinton—a Georgetown University alumnus, a Rhodes Scholar, an Oxford University and Yale University Law School graduate, and a president of the United States—could be construed in many quarters as a poor white trash, "cracker" citizen. The study of whiteness prods us to examine the means by which a highly intelligent man and gifted politician is transmuted into "Bubba" for the purposes of intraethnic demonization.

Clinton, or at least his legal representatives, relied on the same prejudice that befell the president in their legal battles over sexual harassment with a very different victim in the poor white trash wars: Paula Jones. The intriguing subtext in Clinton's fight against Jones's suit was not simply about the hierarchy of gender, where a male's prerogative in defining a sexual relationship is under attack through the discourse of sexual harassment. An even more powerful subtext is that Jones was a "po'white trash'ho." By being so designated, Jones's claim to sexual ownership of her body was much less prized in the popular mind-set than Clinton's ownership of his sexual self. As a result, Jones's believability was unfairly compromised by her degraded social and gender status. Beyond considerations of her relationship to political forces that oppose Clinton, Jones's status reinforced the perception that gender and class cause one to be assigned a lower niche on the totem pole of poor white identity. And there are many, many more places where whiteness is being discussed far beyond the boundaries of the academy in ways that scholarly studies of whiteness are barely beginning to catch up to.

What do you think about President Clinton's addresses on this issue of race? Did they serve in your mind as useful or productive means of expanding the public discourse on whiteness and race?

I think it's important that the president of the United States help set the tone for how discourse about race will proceed. If we have any chance of rescuing the productive means by which race is articulated, we certainly have to have the "First Pedagogue" in place. And Clinton in that sense became a figure of estimable symbolic and even moral worth in setting a healthy tone for the debate about race. The means that he ingeniously seized on (which has been discussed in not altogether dissimilar ways in philosophical circles by Michael Oakeshott, Richard Rorty, and others) is that of conversation. The will to converse about race is motivated by an overriding concern: How can we adjudicate competing claims about race without tearing the essential fabric of American democracy that is embodied in the slogan, *E Pluribus Unum*, "Out of many, one"? If we're already fractured at the level of identity, and this fractured identity is reproduced through mythologies of racial superiority and inferiority (or through narratives of whites being victimized by blacks in identity politics, affirmative action, multiculturalism, or political correctness), how can we justly resolve disputes about relative victimization within the larger framework of American democracy? It's a very messy business, and one that certainly calls for the president to become a leader in these matters. But his shouldn't be the only or even the dominant voice. Still, Clinton created space for the conversation to take place.

It was important that Clinton open up the space of conversation about race; talking is infinitely better than shooting or stabbing or killing one another. It's better than black men killing each other in the streets of Detroit or Chicago. It's better than black people being beaten and killed by white policemen in New York or Los Angeles. It's better than Latinas being victimized by the ideology and institutional expressions of anti-immigrant sentiment. Conversation certainly is superior to destroying one another and our nation.

Still, we mustn't be naive. One of the supreme difficulties of discussing race in America is our belief in the possibility of morally equivalent views being reasonably articulated and justly examined. The implicit assumption of Clinton's ideology of race conversation is debates among equals, or at least among people who have been equally victimized in American culture. But this is a torturous belief that obscures history and memory. We've got to unclog the arteries of collective American political memory.

In regard to race, we are living in the United States of Amnesia. We've got to revoke our citizenship in what Joseph Lowery terms "the 51st state, the state of denial." That's an extraordinarily disconcerting process, partly because what is demanded is the rejection of a key premise of liberal racial discourse: whites, blacks, and others share a common moral conception of racial justice, an ideal that regulates social practice and promotes the resolution of racial disputes. The politics and history of race have not supported this belief. To shift metaphors, what we've got to do is graft the skin of racial memory to the body of American democracy. That demands skillful rhetorical surgery and the operation of an intellectual commitment to truth over habit. In the conversation of race, we really must be willing to discover new ideas and explore ancient emotions. We can't simply shout our prejudices louder than someone else's defense of their bigotry.

If we're going to have real progress in thinking and talking about race, we must not reduce racial issues to black and white. Race in American culture is so much more profound and complex than black and white, even though we know that conflict has been a major artery through which has flowed the poisonous blood of white supremacy and black subordination. There are other arteries of race and ethnicity that trace through the body politic. The tricky part is acknowledging the significant Latino, Asian, and Native American battles with whiteness that have taken place in our nation while admitting that the major race war has involved blacks and whites.

The political centrality and historical legitimacy of dealing with the mutual and dominant relations of whiteness to blackness in the development of what Michael Omi and Howard Winant call "racial formation" is simply undeniable. But such a view must be balanced by paying attention to other racial and ethnic conflicts, as well as the intraracial, interethnic differences that reconstitute racial and ethnic identity and practice. It's extremely important to get such a complex, heated, and potentially useful dialogue started.

A nagging question, however, remains: Who gets a chance to come to the race table to converse? Will poor people's voices be heard? What about young people's voices? In the conversation on race, there is the danger that we merely reproduce a liberal ideology of racial containment and mute the radical elements of race that might really transform our conversation and practice. Such a prospect appears inevitable if we refuse to shatter our ideological and intellectual grids in order to hear the other. What we don't need is the crass and deceitful politics of toleration that masks the sources of real power that conceals the roots of real inequality, that ignores the voices of the most hurt, and that is indifferent to the faces of the most fractured. What we need is *real* conversation, the sort where hidden ambitions are brought to light, where masked motives are clarified to the point of social discomfort.

Such an aim of honest, hard conversation is what the so-called opponents of political correctness should have in mind when they launch their sometimes pedantic, always pejorative broadsides against the assertion of racial, ethnic, gender, class, and sexual difference. Instead, their ostensible desire to push beyond received racial truths ends up being an operation of rhetorical sleight of hand: they end up reasserting in new terms much older, biased beliefs. That's why I'm so skeptical about many of the critics of so-called political correctness—they simply dress up bigotry in socially acceptable form by calling it "anti-PC," when indeed it's the same old political correctness: the poppycock of socially sanctioned racial disgust.

What we have to do, then, is to aim at a raucous debate where the impoliteness of certain people must be permitted because their pain is deep and unheeded. We must surely shatter the rituals of correctness and civility in order to hear from those whose voices have been shut out, where the ability to even articulate pain and rage has been delegitimized through social stigma. That's the only way we have a chance of striking a just racial contract with our citizens. Taking all of what I've discussed into consideration, I think the conversation on race is a step in the right direction.

That gets us away from what Toni Morrison refers to as the "graceful" liberal practice—in the past, at least—of talking about people as if they were raceless, which we at one time thought was the best way. But what you're suggesting is that that doesn't work.

That's right, such a move simply doesn't work. As Du Bois said, there's no way to deal with race without going through race; there's no way of overcoming race without taking race into account. What we've had in our nation for too long is a willed ignorance about race; on one reading, it's a perverse application of philosopher John Rawls's notion of the "original position" in the social contract where we are placed behind a veil of ignorance in order to execute justice in the social realm. When we've misapplied this model to race, it has been quite disastrous. It's failed primarily because we can't justly assume a statutory ignorance about race and because the means to apply racial justice fall disproportionately into the hands of those against whom claims of injustice have been convincingly levied.

Further, the assumption of racelessness fails to account for the contents and identities of race that have always played a role in fashioning American views of justice. This is why I think identity politics must be given a historicist, materialist, and genealogical reading. Identity politics has been going on from the get-go in American culture, indeed, in cultures the world over. Aristotle and Plato and their followers were ensconced in identity politics; Descartes and Kant and their followers merely negotiating identity politics; Foucault and Derrida and their followers are embroiled in identity politics; and Julia Kristeva and Luce Irigaray and their followers are unquestionably involved in identity politics, though they, as I suspect the others I've named, would vehemently deny it.

That's because many of them are or were transfixed by the dream of transcendental truth, Enlightenment rationality, deconstructive practice, or semiotic analysis that, for the most part, severs questions of identity from questions of racial politics. What we must come to see is that even when we deal with intellectual or theoretical issues, they refer to—although by no means are they reduced to or equated with—considerations of identity, even if such considerations are not explicitly articulated. The disingenuous character of too many debates about identity in America is that they deny this process.

After generating a genealogy of identity—which places our own accounts of universalism versus difference into historical context and acknowledges that identity politics occur in a variety of intellectual and social settings—we can press forward to an adequate and fair criticism of identity politics. As things stand, too many critics wrongly argue that we must move beyond narrow frameworks of identity to get to this universal identity. I have in mind the most recent writings of Todd Gitlin and Michael Tomasky. I share some of Gitlin's and Tomasky's concerns about the cultural dead ends of vicious identity politics that enshrine tribal preferences over the common good. But right away I disagree with them about what constitutes tribal preferences, how they can be justly eradicated, and what constitutes successful expressions of universal identities in the social and cultural realm.

In regard to whiteness, Gitlin and Tomasky fail to acknowledge that the particular identities of white people were rendered universal by a cultural and political process that punished blacks and other minorities for seeking to come into their own: their own identities, their own cultural repertoires, their own linguistic and rhetorical facilities, their own styles of survival, and so on. Until we are able to concede this point, we won't get far in this debate about identity, about racelessness, and about the proper role that race should play, both in the American public sphere and in private institutions.

Do you see any contradiction between Clinton's inviting everyone to the table to talk about race and yet not listening to all those voices in making policy—welfare reform, for instance—and excluding the very voices that we need to be hearing from?

There's no question that there's a deep contradiction in Clinton's methodology. Further, there's no question that in the past Clinton has not been above race baiting through very subtle semantic distortions and ideological gyrations. This surfaced in Clinton's first run for the presidency, when his crass opportunism got the best of him as he attacked Sister Souljah for her violent racism without providing a thicker account of the conditions that shaped her comments, something Clinton was clearly capable of effectively pulling off. It surfaced when Clinton, during his first campaign, sent coded signals to alleviate white fears by suggesting that he and Gore would focus their policies on rescuing suburbia and middle America. It surfaced as well when Clinton failed to justly read the complex writings of his close friend, Lani Guinier, thereby encouraging her unjust demonization as a "quota queen." It surfaced with Clinton's support for a heinous crime bill that, like the welfare reform he supported, targeted black men and women with vicious specificity. And on and on.

More important, Clinton failed to understand that if we as a nation are to have a successful conversation about race, it must be seconded at the level of public policy and political implementation. The conversation about race must perform a crucial educational function as well. I think that too often Clinton caved in to the American tendency to demonize what Malcolm X termed the "victims of democracy." Clinton heartily advocated a neoliberal rearticulation of the ideology of racial tolerance that has largely served to hurt the black and Latino poor. One of the great problems with neoliberal race theory is that it writes the check of its loyalty to the black and Latino poor against the funds of conservative rhetoric and social policy. Bill Clinton certainly has a troubled history when it comes to race, a matter about which we must be forthright.

Clinton symbolizes, ironically enough, many white Americans who are well intentioned about race but constantly make faux pas in their quest to do the right thing. Of course, in Clinton's case, his mistakes have cost millions of blacks, Latinas, Native Americans, and other minorities dearly. Clinton's political position, his peripatetic bully pulpit, has given him the authority to amplify his intentions as well as the contradictions of his racial beliefs. But he is as representative of the misguided rhetoric of neoliberal race thinking as we're likely to get. The mixed blessing of such representation is that we get a clear glimpse of just how difficult it will be for the average white American to adequately confront the history and continued function of white supremacy, especially as it is manifested in neoliberal intolerance of radical black insurgence against racism. The bitter irony is that in Clinton black folk are being hurt by friendly fire. The bitter reality is that we have no choice but to find ways to work with him, as limiting as that may be, in the hope of reconstructing racial destiny in American culture.

In addition to what you've already mentioned, how do you in specific ways talk about whiteness, such as in your writing, your public lectures, and your classroom?

As I've lectured across the country, I've witnessed the resistance by many whites to identify and name whiteness in its supremacist ideological mode. Many whites believe that white supremacy is old news, which it is, but they fail to see how it's also today's news. Many believe that pointing to it is divisive and adds to the racial and cultural Balkanization that we're told we're living through. It's extremely difficult to break the hold such a perception has on many whites. So, one of the strategies I try to adopt—in lectures, sermons, speeches, op-eds, articles, book reviews, and books—is the imaginative redescription of white supremacy in its cultural and ideological manifestations.

I also think it's important to emphasize the heterogeneity of whiteness, to stress how the meanings of whiteness are not exhausted by discussions of domination or supremacy. One of the good results of constructivist views of race—and in American culture, "race" has usually signified "black"—is that whiteness is increasingly viewed as a source and site of racial identities and practices. As much as I admire and appreciate the important work of David Roediger, Noel Ignatiev, Mab Segrest, and other new abolitionist thinkers, I think we have to proceed cautiously with the project of reconstituting white identities through their abolition. We have to pose a multipronged question: Do we want to abolish whiteness, or do we want to destroy the negative meanings associated with white identities? I think the latter is what we should aim for.

Of course, Roediger, Ignatiev, Segrest, Allen, and other new abolitionist writers would concede that the whiteness they have in mind to abolish is precisely the socially constructed, culturally sanctioned, ideologically legitimated value of white supremacy that has been a scourge to our nation. In that sense, perhaps they'd agree that we don't want to destroy white identity—because then we'd have to destroy those meanings of whiteness that have been mobilized to resist supremacist thought, or, for that matter, to abolish whiteness. Rather, we want to abolish the lethal manifestations of white identity. The salient issue is whether we can completely and exclusively identify whiteness with destruction, negativity, and corruption. In any case, I applaud their desire to reject white skin privilege and to historicize social and racial identities.

Moreover, Roediger, Allen, Ignatiev, and the new abolitionists have got an extremely useful point: whiteness has been manifest in our nation in hegemonic, destructive, and at times evil ways. Although many whites are loath to admit it, whiteness in its supremacist mode, which has been its dominant mode, has polluted our moral ecology through slavery, colonialism, imperialism, and genocide. Still, I'm uncomfortable with the notion of destroying white folks and cultures, which, by the way, isn't what Ignatiev and the folks around the journal *Race Traitor* have argued. I do think we have a moral obligation to destroy white supremacy. We must speak and think about the rearticulation, reconstitution, and recasting of whiteness to expand, enhance, and embrace its more redemptive, productive features.

This is why cultural studies and theoretical interrogations of whiteness are crucial. Besides the work of the new abolitionists—including Roediger, Allen, Ignatiev, Segrest, John Garvey, Alexander Saxton, and many others—we should remember the important work of W.E.B. Du Bois, C.L.R. James, Thomas Kochman, Eric Foner, Lerone Bennett Jr., bell hooks, Toni Morrison, George Lipsitz, Marilyn Frye, Vron Ware, Ruth Frankenberg, Adrienne Rich, and Peggy McIntosh. And much of the recent work on whiteness is indispensable in coming to terms with its complex cultural manifestations: the brilliant books of Henry Giroux and Tukufu Zuberi, and the important work of Fred Pfeil, Linda Powell, Becky Thompson, Michelle Fine, John Dovidio, Lois Weis, John Hartigan Jr., Robin D.G. Kelly, Annalee Newitz, Ron Sakolsky, James Koehnline, Jesse Daniels, Melvin L. Oliver, Thomas M. Shapiro, Eric Lott, Michael Rogin, Upski Wimsatt, Barbara Ching, Mike Hill, Paul Kivel, Patricia Hill Collins, Sean Wilentz, Jennifer Hochschild, Nancy Hartsook, Michele Wallace, Jose Saldivar, Matt Wray, Laura Kipnis, and on and on.

We should also scrutinize, for instance, white studies of the underclass, which address, reflect, or extend the pathologization of the black poor. Many also reveal how white critics make use of blackness—which is an intellectual strategy worthy of examination—and how they construct the ghetto and articulate black identity and moral norms against a rhetorical backdrop of implicit whiteness.

Or think of a brilliant text like Ann Douglas's *Terrible Honesty: Mongrel Manhattan in the 1920s*. Douglas shows in her book how black and white figures were working, playing, loving, and thinking together, how they were engaging across the white-black divide in ways that have been relatively hidden. Douglas's book is crucial to excavating a cultural tradition of interaction, exchange, appropriation, and influence between various forms of whiteness and blackness. Such works help us accent the stratified and complex character of whiteness while paying attention to the history of how whiteness became a socially useful, racially valued, and culturally hybrid identity.

I'm glad you brought that up because I did want to talk about rescuing that productive content because that's an important dimension, so that we get away from some of the accusations of talking about whiteness in terms of an essentialized notion, or of oversimplifying what whiteness is, or of only allying it with domination.

That's right. The importance of the studies of whiteness I've discussed above is that they uncover—indeed, recover—the contradictory, contested meanings of whiteness from hidden histories of racial practice. If we don't speak about the productive, transgressive, subversive, edifying meanings of whiteness, we're being intellectually dishonest. If we don't narrate those stories, we're doing a great disservice to the moral trajectory that our work of historical reclamation often follows. One of the most powerful ways of challenging and ultimately destroying the ideology of white supremacy, the myth of white superiority, and the narrative of white domination is to unearth sites of resistive memory, history, and practice. One way to rescue the productive meanings of whiteness is to accent transgressive whiteness: how whites cooperated with racial "others" in the unmasking of white skin privilege, the subversion of forms of white power, and the destabilization of forces of white oppression.

I think that people tend to essentialize white identities because whiteness has been a consistently malevolent force in a great number of cultures over a long period of time. It is also true that white allies to racial emancipation have often sacrificed blood and body in expressing a redemptive disloyalty to oppressive meanings of whiteness. Hopefully, in a future that still appears too far away, white disloyalty to unjust privilege and power will fuse with the liberation struggles of oppressed people around the globe as we create a world where we can lay down the burden of race.

I want to return to something you mentioned earlier: that is, some other ways of discussing intragroup differences within whiteness, other than focusing on ethnic variation, like, "I'm Irish and you're Italian," but focusing on gender difference and class difference.

One of the benefits of, for instance, ethnographies of white cultures, practices, and identities is that we begin to get a fuller picture of differentiated whiteness. The fissuring and fracturing of whiteness, especially along axes of class and gender, gives us greater insight into how white cultures have adapted, survived, and struggled in conditions where their dominance was modified or muted.

It's also important to explore histories of white difference to highlight how whiteness has not been made by whites alone. Part of what it means to be white in America is to be black. To paraphrase Ralph Ellison: "I don't want to know how 'white' black folk are, I want to know how 'black' white folk are." If we completely, indiscriminately destroy whiteness, we're also destroying what blacks and other racial minorities contributed—sometimes covertly, sometimes symbiotically, often in hybrid interactions, and occasionally in extravagant fashion—to white behaviors, identities, styles, and intellectual traditions. One of the great paradoxes of race is that whiteness is not exclusively owned or produced by whites. White is also black. As we discover how black whiteness is, we discover how interesting and intricate whiteness is. We discover how whites and blacks have cooperated in very shrewd ways to produce alternative structures, rituals, and cultures to dominant whiteness.

Interrogating whiteness in the manner I've just outlined opens discursive space for a post-appropriationist paradigm of cultural and racial exchange. Such a paradigm accents the unbalanced power relations, racial inequality, and economic injustice that often mediates, say, black-white artistic exchanges, where black ideas, products, styles, and practices are stolen, borrowed, or appropriated without attribution or reward. But it also accents the revisioning of whiteness through the prism of black cultural practices, especially as white subjectivities are reconceived and recast in the hues of transgressive blackness.

That's why it's important to explore racialized *communitas* and *habitas* where whites live and commune—to understand the productive meanings of whiteness through the reproduction and rearticulation of the productive meanings of blackness. In this connection, it makes sense to examine the phenomenon of the substitute nigger or the "wigger"—the white nigger, whites who have been viewed, or view themselves, as black. What uses have they made of blackness? How has blackness allowed them to alter dominant modes of whiteness? How have their knowledges and cultural practices pitted ontological contents of racial identity against strictly biological or phenotypical ones? All of these lines of inquiry are opened up by fracturing and fissuring, by differentiating, whiteness.

In what ways has whiteness in the American context spread its tentacles globally or had some effect at the international level, in productive or in oppressive ways?

Let me answer your question in two ways. First, I'll briefly address how the oppressive meanings of whiteness in the American context have global implications. Then I will address black skepticism about the uses of even productive whiteness to unmask and unmake itself.

There's no question that one of the most powerful claims—though it is often dressed in racially essentialist terms—that certain postcolonialist, black separatists make is that whiteness has screwed things up the world over. It's relatively easy to supply historical verification for such a claim; after all, the oppressive meanings of whiteness have destroyed minority hearth and home, and kith and kin, around the globe. Wherever it has taken root, oppressive, colonizing, imperialistic whiteness has subjugated or tyrannized native peoples, indigenous populations, and aboriginal tribes. Along these lines, American visions of white supremacy have exported well, inspiring, for instance, South African apartheid and modern varieties of European neocolonialism.

The problem with certain criticisms of oppressive whiteness is that they are grounded in discourses of biological determinism and genetic inheritance, turning out to be *The Bell Curve* in reverse: whites are genetically incapable of humane behavior and sane social interaction. Other varieties of racial geneticism and biological determinism—such as that found in Frances Cress-Welsing's *The Isis Papers*, a perennial best-seller in black communities—maintain that white supremacy grows from whites' fear of genetic annihilation because they lack melanin, while blacks, who possess it in abundance, are guaranteed survival. In such versions of reductive pseudo-science, white supremacy is genetically encoded and biologically reproduced. In light of such theories, it's understandable that antiracist critics of new abolitionism shudder when they hear of the need to abolish the white race, even if it is conceded that it's a social construction the abolitionists aim to destroy.

One of the most ingenious, deceitful strategies deployed by white supremacists is to insulate themselves from knowledge of white supremacy's evil, of its thoroughgoing funkiness. In this mode, a crucial function of whiteness is to blind itself to its worst tendencies, its most lethal consequences. And one of the ways that dominant whiteness does this is by adopting a facade of ignorance, innocence, or naïveté in the face of claims of its destructiveness. Whether such a facade covers the deep knowledge its advocates possess of white supremacy's ill effects is, and is not, relevant to how racial or ethnic minorities interact with whites in general. On one reading, such knowledge is irrelevant because even if the intent to harm does not exist, the malevolent consequences of white supremacy are just as real.

On the other hand, such knowledge is relevant when racial or ethnic minorities seek to forge coalitions with whites who reject the perspectives, practices, and privileges of white supremacy. How can blacks or Latinas be sure that such a rejection is abiding? The immediate response, of course, is that one must judge white allies, as one judges all people, by their actions. But this is precisely where matters get tricky: it is sometimes the actions of even the most devoted white allies that surprise, stun, shock, hurt, and disappoint blacks, Latinos, or Asians. The claim to ignorance, innocence, or naïveté by white allies in the face of offensive action is the cause of no small degree of discomfort in the relations between whites and racial minorities.

What is even more uncomfortable is when white allies make a merit badge of their resistance to what is increasingly thought of as the hypersensitivity of racial minorities. As a result, alleged white allies of blacks—for instance Bill Clinton—parade their racial accomplishments as a gateway to legitimacy in black communities and as a passport to do harm. The new white abolitionists and other progressive white allies are the first to decry this variety of neoliberal racial manipulation. A more difficult suspicion to overcome in many black communities is the historic pressure of whiteness to make virtues of its vices—and vice versa—even as it creates discursive space to deconstruct and demythologize its own socially constructed meanings.

That may explain why some blacks are skeptical of even progressive versions of white studies: it may be a sophisticated narcissism at work, another white hoax to displace studies of, but especially by, The Others at the height of their popularity and power with an encroaching obsession with the meanings, identities, practices, anxieties, and subjectivities—and hence the agendas, priorities, and preferences—of The Whites. On such a view, whiteness once again becomes supreme by trumpeting its need for demystification, dismantling, or abolition. Thus the cultural capital of otherness is bleached; to thoroughly mix metaphors, the gaze of race is returned to sender.

We've got to keep such skepticism in mind as we attempt to unmake and remake whiteness. As we scan the globe where whiteness has left its mark, the most remarkable fact is not the willingness of whites to become disloyal to their white-ness, but the courageous rebellion of native, colonized, or enslaved folk who fought and, as best they could, remade the meanings of the whiteness they inher-ited or confronted. Their stories are worthy of serious study.

Related to that, let's talk about in particular a place you just came from—Cuba—and how you see that disguising of the "funkiness" of whiteness func-tioning in U.S. relations with Cuba and the role that whiteness might play in our relationship with that country.

I'll answer that in a couple of ways. First, the political measures that America has employed against Cuba are simply obscene. It is indefensible for America to treat a neighboring nation of beautiful people ninety miles away with such contempt while it grants China most favored nation status. Our relations with Cuba are hostile for one overriding reason: America has been unable to kill Castro. Like that little Energizer bunny, he just keeps on going. Our foreign policy with the Soviet Union is far better, a fact that is more than a little ironic. We have thawed the thick ice that once froze Soviet-U.S. relations, and in our post–Cold War generosity, we've embraced the big bear we used to fear and hate, but we still can't embrace her cubs in Cuba.

The Helms-Burton Act extends unjust American policies to their logical, impe-rialist conclusion. The embargo we have against Cuba not only punishes that na-tion but punishes other nations that might cooperate with Cuba. Our bullying has cost the people of Cuba dearly: extreme poverty, severely curtailed luxuries, evap-oration of resources, shrinking of capital, and the deprivation of essential goods and services. In the guise of ostensibly just foreign policy, our relation with Cuba, especially as driven by Helms, is white supremacy in its reckless, destructive mode. America is not killing Castro; he's living well. We're hurting decent, beautiful everyday folk who love their country and are proudly trying to extend the most democratic features of the Revolution: universal literacy, political representation of the poor, and government rooted in historical memory and national pride.

Finally, I think what's interesting is that most Cubans have a very different un-derstanding of race than we have in the United States. Many white Cubans, and black ones as well, denied that they had a race problem. To our American eyes and ears, to mix metaphors, that was a hard claim to swallow. The Cubans had undeniably worked to remove vestiges of discrimination from their official quar-ters; still, many of the members of our delegation of black Americans understood that the rhetorical and representational battles that bewitch racial equity were still being fought. It is equally undeniable that white and black Cubans have been able to forge a Cuban national identity that overcomes in important ways the schisms of ethnic tribalism.

Even if it is not what we black Americans, imbued with the rhetoric of our own racial difficulties, think is altogether just, black and white Cubans at least have the real possibility of negotiating a livable racial situation. It may be what Ernest Becker termed a "vital lie": a necessary deception that preserves the social fabric and keeps at bay the forces that destroy identity and community. The embargo has led to what the Cubans term a "special period," the time of austerity that has thrown their culture into sustained crisis. In such a period, it is perfectly reasonable that Cubans understand race in the fashion they do to preserve the very survival of their nation. In many ways, they've done a much better job with race than we have under conditions of relative material prosperity.

Any closing comments on the past, present, or future of the study of whiteness?

I have just one observation. As we look to the next century of whiteness studies, the field will mature and reconstruct its genealogy by pointing b(l)ack—to those great figures from W.E.B. Du Bois to Zora Neale Hurston, from Langston Hughes to Ralph Ellison, and from Nella Larsen to James Baldwin. Such a genealogy for white studies brings to mind something Fannie Lou Hamer said. She argued that the mistake white folk made with black folk is that they put us behind them, not in front of them. Had they placed us in front of them, they could have observed and contained us.

Instead, white folk placed us behind them in what they deemed an inferior position. As a result, we were able to learn white folk—their beliefs, sentiments, contradictions, cultures, styles, behaviors, virtues, and vices. Black survival depended on black folk knowing the ways and souls of white folk. It's only fitting now that we turn to African American, Latino, Asian, and Native American scholars, workers, intellectuals, artists, and everyday folk to understand whiteness.

Interview by Ronald E. Chennault
New York, New York, 1998

PART SIX

GENDER VIEWS

In the same way that many whites have no idea that their whiteness gives them a racial identity, many men don't realize they have a gender. I have spent a great deal of my writing life exploring masculinity and its edifying and harmful meanings. I have also probed the simple yet remarkably unassimilated view that our culture holds ancient beliefs about how men should enjoy privileges and powers that women should not. On that foundation rests all sorts of vicious behaviors that have garnered the support of social convention and legal precedent. Moreover, a great deal of controversy has surrounded interracial relations, especially between black men and white women, whose erotic liasions have spawned hostile debate on all sides. It is vital to the nation's moral health to unravel patriarchy's seductive webs while weaving an understanding of the intricate interactions of men and women.

Twelve

THE PLIGHT OF BLACK MEN

This was the first article I wrote for a regular "Black America" column (that I inherited from Cornel West) for the left-wing Z Magazine, beginning in February 1989. I was still a graduate student at Princeton, although I was also serving as assistant director of Hartford Seminary's Action Plan on Poverty, working with local congregations to shepherd resources to combat the enormous poverty in Hartford, Connecticut. In this chapter, I chart the sufferings and struggles of black men while refusing to elevate their heartaches above those of black women. Throughout my writing career, I have written a great deal about the triumphs and tragedies, and the joys and sorrows, of black males: athletes and hustlers, preachers and professors, leaders and prisoners, wise men and foolish boys. I have striven to write about masculinity in a way that reaffirms the humanity of black men while challenging our patriarchal pitfalls and self-destructive behavior. This chapter embodies that aim.

ON A RECENT TRIP TO KNOXVILLE, I VISITED Harold's barbershop, where I had my hair cut during college, and after whenever I had the chance. I had developed a friendship with Ike, a local barber who took great pride in this work. I popped my head inside the front door, and after exchanging friendly greetings with Harold, the owner, and noticing Ike missing, I inquired about his return. It had been nearly two years since Ike had cut my hair, and I was hoping to receive the careful expertise that comes from familiarity and repetition.

"Man, I'm sorry to tell you, but Ike got killed almost two years ago," Harold informed me. "He and his brother, who was drunk, got into a fight, and he stabbed Ike to death."

I was shocked, depressed, and grieved, these emotions competing in rapid-fire fashion for the meager psychic resources I was able to muster. In a daze of retreat from the fierce onslaught of unavoidable absurdity, I half-consciously slumped into Harold's chair, seeking solace through his story of Ike's untimely and brutal leave-taking. Feeling my pain, Harold filled in the details of Ike's last hours, realizing that for me Ike's death had happened only yesterday. Harold proceeded to cut my hair with a methodical precision that was itself a temporary and all-too-thin refuge from the chaos of arbitrary death, a protest against the nonlinear progression of miseries that claim the lives of too many black men. After he finished, I thanked Harold, both of us recognizing that we would not soon forget Ike's life, or his terrible death.

This drama of tragic demise, compressed agony, nearly impotent commiseration, and social absurdity is repeated countless times, too many times, in American culture for black men. Ike's death forced to the surface a painful awareness that provides the chilling sound track to most black men's lives: it is still hazardous to be a human being of African descent in America.

Not surprisingly, much of the ideological legitimation for the contemporary misery of African-Americans in general, and black men in particular, derives from the historical legacy of slavery, which continues to assert its brutal presence in the untold suffering of millions of everyday black folk. For instance, the pernicious commodification of the black body during slavery was underwritten by the desire of white slave owners to completely master black life. The desire for mastery also fueled the severe regulation of black sexual activity, furthering the telos of southern agrarian capital by reducing black men to studs and black women to machines of production. Black men and women became sexual and economic property. Because of the arrangement of social relations, slavery was also the breeding ground for much of the mythos of black male sexuality that survives to this day: that black men are imagined as peripatetic phalluses with unrequited desire for their denied object—white women.

Also crucial during slavery was the legitimation of violence toward blacks, especially black men. Rebellion in any form was severely punished, and the social construction of black male image and identity took place under the disciplining eye of white male dominance. Thus healthy black self-regard and self-confidence were outlawed as punitive consequences were attached to their assertion in black life. Although alternate forms of resistance were generated, particularly those rooted in religious praxis, problems of self-hatred and self-abnegation persisted. The success of the American political, economic, and social infrastructure was predicated in large part upon a squelching of black life by white modes of cultural domination. The psychic, political, economic, and social costs of slavery, then, continue to be paid, but mostly by the descendants of the oppressed. The way in which young black men continue to pay is particularly unsettling.

Black men are presently caught in a web of social relations, economic conditions, and political predicaments that portray their future in rather bleak terms.[1] For instance, the structural unemployment of black men has reached virtually epidemic proportions, with black youth unemployment double that of white youth. Almost half of young black men have had no work experience at all. Given the permanent shift in the U.S. economy from manufacturing and industrial jobs to high-tech and service employment and the flight of these jobs from the cities to the suburbs, the prospects for eroding the stubborn unemployment of black men appear slim.[2]

The educational front is not much better. Young black males are dropping out of school at alarming rates, due to a combination of severe economic difficulties, disciplinary entanglements, and academic frustrations. Thus the low level of educational achievement by young black men exacerbates their already precarious employment situation. Needless to say, the pool of high school graduates eligible for college has severely shrunk, and even those who go on to college have disproportionate rates of attrition.

Suicide, too, is on the rise, ranking as the third leading cause of death among young black men. Since 1960, the number of black men who have died from suicide has tripled. The homicide rate of black men is atrocious. For black male teenagers and young adults, homicide ranks as the leading cause of death. In 1987, more young black men were killed within the United States in a single year than had been killed abroad in the entire nine years of the Vietnam War. A young black man has a one in twenty-one lifetime chance of being killed, most likely at the hands of another black man, belying the self-destructive character of black homicide.

Even with all this, a contemporary focus on the predicament of black males is rendered problematical and ironic for two reasons. First, what may be termed the "Calvin Klein" character of debate about social problems—which amounts to a "designer" social consciousness—makes it very difficult for the concerns of black men to be taken seriously. Social concern, like other commodities, is subject to cycles of production, distribution, and consumption. With the dwindling of crucial governmental resources to address a range of social problems, social concern is increasingly relegated to the domain of private philanthropic and nonprofit organizations. Furthermore, the selection of which problems merit scarce resources is determined, in part, by such philanthropic organizations which highlight special issues, secure the services of prominent spokespersons, procure capital for research, and distribute the benefits of their information.

Unfortunately, Americans have rarely been able to sustain debate about pressing social problems over long periods of time. Even less have we been able to conceive underlying structural features that bind complex social issues together. Such conceptualization of the intricate interrelationship of social problems would facilitate the development of broadly formed coalitions that address a range of social concern. As things stand, problems like poverty, racism, and sexism go in and out of style. Black men, with the exception of star athletes and famous entertainers, are out of style.

Second, the irony of the black male predicament is that it has reached its nadir precisely at the point when much deserved attention has been devoted to the achievements of black women like Alice Walker, Toni Morrison, and Terry McMillan.

The identification and development of the womanist tradition in African-American culture has permitted the articulation of powerful visions of black female identity and liberation. Michele Wallace, bell hooks, Alice Walker, Audre Lorde, and Toni Morrison have written in empowering ways about the disenabling forms of racism and patriarchy that persist in white and black communities. They have expressed the rich resources for identity that come from maintaining allegiances to multiple kinship groups defined by race, gender, and sexual orientation, while also addressing the challenges that arise in such membership.

Thus discussions about black men should not take place in an ahistorical vacuum, but should be informed by sensitivity to the plight of black women. To isolate and examine the pernicious problems of young black men does not privilege their perspectives or predicament. Rather, it is to acknowledge the decisively deleterious consequences of racism and classism that plague black folk, particularly young black males.

The aim of my analysis is to present enabling forms of consciousness that may contribute to the reconstitution of the social, economic, and political relations that continually consign the lives of black men to psychic malaise, social destruction, and physical death. It does not encourage or dismiss the sexism of black men, nor does it condone the patriarchal behavior that sometimes manifests itself in minority communities in the form of misdirected machismo. Above all, African-Americans must avoid a potentially hazardous situation that plays musical chairs with scarce resources allocated to black folk and threatens to inadvertently exacerbate already deteriorated relations between black men and women. The crisis of black inner-city communities is so intense that it demands our collective resources to stem the tide of violence and catastrophe that has besieged them.

I grew up as a young black male in Detroit in the 1960s and 1970s. I witnessed firsthand the social horror that is entrenched in inner-city communities, the social havoc wreaked from economic hardship. In my youth, Detroit had been tagged the "murder capital of the world," and many of those murders were of black men, many times by other black men. Night after night, the news media in Detroit painted the ugly picture of a homicide-ridden city caught in the desperate clutches of death, depression, and decay. I remember having recurring nightmares of naked violence, in which Hitchcockian vertigo emerged in Daliesque perspective to produce gun-wielding perpetrators of doom seeking to do me in.

And apart from those disturbing dreams, I was exercised by the small vignettes of abortive violence that shattered my circle of friends and acquaintances. My next-door neighbor, a young black man, was stabbed in the jugular vein by an acquaintance and bled to death in the midst of a card game. (Of course, one of the ugly statistics involving black-on-black crime is that many black men are killed by those whom they know.) Another acquaintance murdered a businessman in a robbery; another executed several people in a gangland-style murder.

At fourteen, I was at our corner store at the sales counter, when suddenly a jolt in the back revealed a young black man wielding a sawed-off, double-barreled shotgun, requesting, along with armed accomplices stationed throughout the store, that we hit the floor. We were being robbed. At the age of eighteen I was stopped one Saturday night at 10:30 by a young black man who ominously materialized out of nowhere, much like the .357 Magnum revolver that he revealed to me in a robbery attempt. Terror engulfed my entire being in the fear of imminent death. In desperation I hurled a protest against the asphyxiating economic hardships that had apparently reduced him to desperation, too, and appealed to the conscience I hoped was buried beneath the necessity that drove him to rob me. I proclaimed, "Man, you don't look like the type of brother that would be doin' something like this."

"I wouldn't be doin' this, man," he shot back, "but I got a wife and three kids, and we ain't got nothin' to eat. And besides, last week somebody did the same thing to me that I'm doin' to you." After convincing him that I really only had one dollar and thirty-five cents, the young man permitted me to leave with my life intact.

The terrain for these and so many other encounters that have shaped the lives of black males was the ghetto. Much social research and criticism has been generated in regard to the worse-off inhabitants of the inner city, the so-called underclass. From the progressive perspective of William Julius Wilson to the archconservative musings of Charles Murray, those who dwell in ghettos, or enclaves of civic, psychic, and social terror, have been the object of recrudescent interest within hallowed academic circles and governmental policy rooms.[3] In most cases they have not fared well and have borne the brunt of multifarious "blame the victim" social logics and policies.

One of the more devastating developments in inner-city communities is the presence of drugs and the criminal activity associated with their production, marketing, and consumption. Through the escalation of the use of the rocklike form of cocaine known as "crack" and intensified related gang activity, young black men are involved in a vicious subculture of crime. This subculture is sustained by two potent attractions: the personal acceptance and affirmation gangs offer and the possibility of enormous economic reward.

U.S. gang life had its genesis in the Northeast of the 1840s, particularly in the depressed neighborhoods of Boston and New York, where young Irishmen developed gangs to sustain social solidarity and to forge a collective identity based on common ethnic roots.[4] Since then, youth of every ethnic and racial origin have formed gangs for similar reasons, and at times have even functioned to protect their own ethnic or racial group from attack by harmful outsiders. Overall, a persistent reason for joining gangs is the sense of absolute belonging and unsurpassed social love that results from gang membership. Especially for young black men whose life is at a low premium in America, gangs have fulfilled a primal need to possess a sense of social cohesion through group identity. Particularly when traditional avenues for the realization of personal growth, esteem, and self-worth, usually gained through employment and career opportunities, have been closed, young black men find gangs a powerful alternative.

Gangs also offer immediate material gratification through a powerful and lucrative underground economy. This underground economy is supported by exchanging drugs and services for money, or by barter. The lifestyle developed and made possible by the sale of crack presents often irresistible economic alternatives to young black men frustrated by their own unemployment. The death that can result from involvement in such drug- and gang-related activity is ineffective in prohibiting young black men from participating.

To understand the attraction such activity holds for black men, one must re-member the desperate economic conditions of urban black life. The problems of poverty and joblessness have loomed large for African-American men, particu-larly in the Rust Belt, including New York, Chicago, Philadelphia, Detroit, Cleve-land, Indianapolis, and Baltimore. From the 1950s to the 1980s, there was severe decline in manufacturing and in retail and wholesale trade, attended by escalating unemployment and a decrease in labor force participation by black males, partic-ularly during the 1970s.

During this three-decade decline of employment, however, there was not an ex-pansion of social services or significant increase in entry-level service jobs. As William Julius Wilson rightly argues, the urban ghettos then became more socially isolated than at any other time. Also, with the mass exodus of black working and middle-class families from the ghetto, the inner city's severe unemployment and job-lessness became even more magnified. With black track from the inner city mim-icking earlier patterns of white flight, severe class changes have negatively affected black ghettos. Such class changes have depleted communities of service establish-ments, local businesses, and stores that could remain profitable enough to provide full-time employment so that persons could support families, or even to offer youths part-time employment in order to develop crucial habits of responsibility and work. Furthermore, ghetto residents are removed from job networks that operate in more affluent neighborhoods. Thus, they are deprived of the informal contact with em-ployers that results in finding decent jobs. All of these factors create a medium for the development of criminal behavior by black men in order to survive, ranging from fencing stolen goods to petty thievery to drug dealing. For many black fami-lies, the illegal activity of young black men provides their only income.

Predictably, then, it is in these Rust Belt cities, and other large urban and met-ropolitan areas, where drug and gang activity has escalated in the past decade. De-troit, Philadelphia, and New York have had significant gang and drug activity, but Chicago and Los Angeles have dominated of late. Especially in regard to gang-related criminal activity such as homicides, Chicago and L.A. form a terrible one-two punch. Chicago had forty-seven gang-related deaths in 1987, seventy-five in 1986, and sixty in 1988. L.A.'s toll stands at four hundred for 1988.

Of course, L.A.'s gang scene has generated mythic interpretation in the Dennis Hopper film *Colors*. In the past decade, gang membership in L.A. has risen from 15,000 to almost 60,000 (with some city officials claiming as much as 80,000), as gang warfare claims one life per day. The ethnic composition of the groups in-clude Mexicans, Armenians, Samoans, and Fijians. But gang life is dominated by South Central L.A. black gangs, populated by young black men willing to give their lives in fearless fidelity to their group's survival. The two largest aggregates of gangs, composed of several hundred microgangs, are the Bloods and the Crips, distinguished by the colors of their shoelaces, T-shirts, and bandannas.

The black gangs have become particularly dangerous because of their associa-tion with crack. The gangs control more than 150 crack houses in L.A., each of which does over $5,000 of business per day, garnering over half a billion dollars per year. Crack houses, which transform powdered cocaine into crystalline rock form in order to be smoked, offer powerful material rewards to gang members. Even young teens can earn almost $1,000 a week, often outdistancing what their parents, if they work at all, can earn in two months.

So far, most analyses of drug gangs and the black youth who comprise their membership have repeated old saws about the pathology of black culture and weak family structure, without accounting for the pressing economic realities and the need for acceptance that help explain such activity. As long as the poverty of young black men is ignored, the disproportionate number of black unemployed males is overlooked, and the structural features of racism and classism are avoided, there is room for the proliferation of social explanations that blame the victim. Such social explanations reinforce the misguided efforts of public officials to stem the tide of illegal behavior by state repression aimed at young blacks, such as the sweeps of L.A. neighborhoods resulting in mass arrests of more than four thousand black men, more than at any time since the Watts rebellion of 1965.

Helpful remedies must promote the restoration of job training (such as Neighborhood Youth Corps [NYC] and the Comprehensive Employment and Training Act [CETA]); the development of policies that support the family, such as child care and education programs; a full employment policy; and dropout prevention in public schools. These are only the first steps toward the deeper structural transformation necessary to improve the plight of African-American men, but they would be vast improvements over present efforts.

Not to be forgotten, either, are forms of cultural resistance that are developed and sustained within black life and are alternatives to the crack gangs. An example that springs immediately to mind is rap music. Rap music provides space for cultural resistance to the criminal-ridden ethos that pervades segments of many underclass communities. Rap was initially a form of musical play that directed the creative urges of its producers into placing often humorous lyrics over the music of well-known black hits.

As it evolved, however, rap became a more critical and conscientious forum for visiting social criticism upon various forms of social injustice, especially racial and class oppression. For instance, Grandmaster Flash and the Furious Five pioneered the social awakening of rap with two rap records, "The Message" and "New York, New York." These rap records combined poignant descriptions of social misery and trenchant criticism of social problems as they remarked upon the condition of black urban America. They compared the postmodern city of crime, deception, political corruption, economic hardship, and cultural malaise to a "jungle." These young savants portrayed a chilling vision of life that placed them beyond the parameters of traditional African-American cultural resources of support: religious faith, communal strength, and familial roots. Thus, they were creating their own aesthetic of survival, generated from the raw material of their immediate reality, the black ghetto. This began the vocation of the rap artist, in part, as urban griot dispensing social and cultural critique.

Although rap music has been saddled with a reputation for creating violent outbursts by young blacks, especially at rap concerts, most of rap's participants have repeatedly spurned violence and all forms of criminal behavior as useless alternatives for black youth. Indeed rap has provided an alternative to patterns of identity formation provided by gang activity and has created musical vehicles for personal and cultural agency. A strong sense of self-confidence permeates the entire rap genre, providing healthy outlets for young blacks to assert, boast, and luxuriate in a rich self-conception based on the achievement that their talents afford them. For those reasons alone, it deserves support. Even more, rap music, although its increasing expansion means being influenced by the music industry's corporate tastes and decisions, presents an economic alternative to the underground economy of crack gangs and the illegal activity associated with them.

However, part of the enormous difficulty in discouraging illegal activity among young black men has to do, ironically, with their often correct perception of the racism and classism still rampant in employment and educational opportunities open to upwardly mobile blacks. The subtle but lethal limits continually imposed upon young black professionals, for instance, as a result of the persistence of racist ideologies operating in multifarious institutional patterns and personal configurations, send powerful signals to young black occupants of the underclass that education and skill do not ward off racist, classist forms of oppression.

This point was reiterated to me upon my son's recent visit with me at Princeton near Christmas. Excited about the prospect of spending time together catching up on new movies, playing video games, reading, and the like, we dropped by my bank to get a cash advance on my MasterCard. I presented my card to the young service representative, expecting no trouble since I had just paid my bill a couple of weeks before. When he returned, he informed me that not only could I not get any money, but that he would have to keep my card. When I asked for an explanation, all he could say was that he was following the instructions of my card's bank, since my MasterCard was issued by a different bank.

After we went back and forth a few times about the matter, I asked to see the manager. "He'll just tell you the same thing that I've been telling you," he insisted. But my persistent demand prevailed, as he huffed away to the manager's office, resentfully carrying my request to his boss. My son, sitting next to me the whole time, asked what the problem was, and I told him that there must be a mistake, and that it would all be cleared up shortly. He gave me that confident look that says, "My dad can handle it." After waiting for about seven or eight minutes, I caught the manager's figure peripherally, and just as I turned, I saw him heading with the representative to an empty desk, opening the drawer and pulling out a pair of scissors. I could feel the blood begin to boil in my veins as I beseeched the manager, "Sir, if you're about to do what I fear you will, can we please talk first?" Of course, my request was to no avail, as he sliced my card in two before what had now become a considerable crowd. I immediately jumped up and followed him into his office, my son trailing close behind, crying now, tearfully pumping me with "Daddy, what's going on?"

I rushed into the manager's office and asked for the privacy of a closed door, to which he responded, "Don't let him close the door," as he beckoned three other employees into his office. I angrily grabbed the remnants of my card from his hands and proceeded to tell him that I was a reputable member of the community and a good customer of the bank and that if I had been wearing a three-piece suit (instead of the black running suit I was garbed in) and if I had been a white male (and not a black man) I would have been at least accorded the respect of a conversation, prior to a private negotiation of an embarrassing situation, which furthermore was the apparent result of a mistake on the bank's part.

His face flustered, the manager then prominently positioned his index finger beneath his desk drawer, and pushed a button, while declaring, "I'm calling the police on you." My anger now piqued, I was tempted to vent my rage on his defiant countenance, arrested only by the vision terrible that flashed before my eyes as a chilling premonition of destruction: I would assault the manager's neck; his coworkers would join the fracas, as my son stood by horrified by his helplessness to aid me; the police would come, and abuse me even further, possibly harming my son in the process. I retreated under the power of this proleptic vision, grabbing my son's hand as I marched out of the bank. Just as we walked through the doors, the policemen were pulling up.

Although after extensive protests, phone calls, and the like, I eventually received an apology from the bank's board and a MasterCard from their branch, this incident seared an indelible impression onto my mind, reminding me that regardless of how much education, moral authority, or personal integrity a black man possesses, he is still a "nigger," still powerless in many ways to affect his destiny.

The tragedy in all of this, of course, is that even when articulate, intelligent black men manage to rise above the temptations and traps of "the ghetto," they are often subject to continuing forms of social fear, sexual jealousy, and obnoxious racism. More pointedly, in the 1960s, during a crucial stage in the development of black pride and self-esteem, highly educated, deeply conscientious black men were gunned down in cold blood. This phenomenon finds paradigmatic expression in the deaths of Medgar Evers, Malcolm X, and Martin Luther King, Jr. These events of public death are structured deep in the psyches of surviving black men, and the ways in which these horrible spectacles of racial catastrophe represent and implicitly sanction lesser forms of social evil against black men remains hurtful to black America.

I will never forget the effect of King's death on me as a nine-year-old boy in Detroit. For weeks I could not be alone at night before an open door or window without fearing that someone would kill me, too. I thought that if they killed this man who taught justice, peace, forgiveness, and love, then they would kill all black men. For me, Martin's death meant that no black man in America was safe, that no black man could afford the gift of vision, that no black man could possess an intelligent fire that would sear the fierce edges of ignorance and wither to ashes the propositions of hate without being extinguished. Ultimately Martin's death meant that all black men, in some way, are perennially exposed to the threat of annihilation.

As we move toward the last decade of this century, the shadow of Du Bois's prophetic declaration that the twentieth century's problem would be the color line continues to extend itself in foreboding manner. The plight of black men, indeed, is a microcosmic reflection of the problems that are at the throat of all black people, an idiomatic expression of hurt drawn from the larger discourse of racial pain. Unless, however, there is vast reconstitution of our social, economic, and political policies and practices, most of which target black men with vicious specificity, Du Bois's words will serve as the frontispiece to the racial agony of the twenty-first century as well.

Thirteen

ANOTHER SATURDAY NIGHT, OR HAVE ALL THE BROTHERS GONE TO WHITE WOMEN?

This is one of the most controversial pieces I have written. The title joins Sam Cooke's lament of "Another Saturday night / and I ain't got nobody"—the plea of many talented and beautiful black women—with a query many of them raise to me in seeking an explanation for the disinterest of many eligible black men: "Have all the brothers gone to white women?" In this chapter, from my book Why I Love Black Women, *I explore the reasons given for why black women are alone—reasons of their own making and those having to do with societal forces. I conclude that black women are often unfairly stigmatized as overbearing and "too choosy." Moreover, despite claims that their often superior education makes it difficult for black men to get along with them, black women often date and marry men with far less training. The most controversial aspect of this chapter is the contention that some black men, due to the racist cues they inherit from mainstream society, spurn their own and turn to white women as the ideal representatives of womanhood. I also argue that, in terms of socioeconomic status, many black men marry "down" when they marry white women. When I appeared on the ABC television talk show* The View, *most of the hosts charged that I was a racist for making this empirically grounded claim. They interpreted "marry down" to mean that I believed black men who married white women chose racially inferior women. Despite my vigorous attempts at clarification, the hosts—with the exception of guest host Kathie Lee Gifford—maintained their views. My only consolation is that I was able to publicly praise host Star Jones, about whom I had written in the book. Another host, Joy Behar, called me the "Barry White" of black romantic literature because of my appreciation for Star's beauty. In light of the great singer's death last year, it was the highest compliment I received that day.*

"LOOK AT ME," THE SISTER BLURTED IN EXASPERATION. "It's Saturday night, and I can't buy a date."

I was at a black-tie event for Chicago's 100 Black Men, an organization devoted to improving the lot of young black males. The event drew many of Chicago's black elite, including prominent clergy, physicians, entrepreneurs, and politicians. After the ceremonies were over, my frustrated female had spotted me across the cavernous room in the Hyatt Hotel. She was a tall, statuesque woman, voluptuous in the way that sends black men hankering after something to hold on to because they've been waylaid by breathtaking beauty. Her skin was brown and smooth—all sweet chocolate dipped into sensuous ebony hues—and her sparkling eyes set like flaming candles above her arching cheekbones. Her hair was a stylish black splash, with her limbs elegantly gesturing and her hands delicately pointing as her painted, manicured nails punctuated her message.

As we talked for half an hour, it was clear that she was not only drop-dead gorgeous, but also bright as all outdoors, down-to-earth but schooled, witty and urbane but a true homegirl, used to the corporate game she played as an executive but wearing her status loosely. Highly intelligent, educated, perceptive, in love with her people, down for the cause, a lover of black men—and she was alone, by herself, without a date in sight on a Saturday evening that brimmed with romantic promise.

"What am I supposed to do?" she asked me. "I'm not trying to get married tomorrow—I'm not pressuring black men that way. I just want somebody to spend some time with, someone with whom I can have a good discussion and a good meal, and somebody I can laugh with. I just want a date, for God's sake, not a husband!"

She had nothing against husbands, should a relationship develop in that direction. My lovely interlocutor simply sought to underscore her lack of desperation, a desperation that she had to defend herself against because of the frequent complaint by black men that they feel the noose of matrimony tightening around their necks on the second date. Besides, an equally stunning Afro-Cuban executive who was barely five feet accompanied her. She was highly articulate and scrumptiously attractive. Her very pretty, cocoa-brown face was lit by a radiant smile. And her petite but exquisitely crafted figure pressed warmly against the soft fabric of her evening gown as her charismatic glow haloed her curly, flowing locks.

"I'm extremely fortunate," my magnetic Afro-Cuban conversationalist enthused. "I found a wonderful man who recognized my worth. It's extremely important to be with someone who appreciates and respects you, someone who's comfortable with himself, and who'll therefore be comfortable with you, a man who's not threatened by a strong black woman." As if by cue, he approached, and true to his wife's word, he was a splendid symbol of black masculinity: tall, dark, and handsome, and like his wife, Ivy League trained, and from my hometown, to boot.

"Sister, I just don't understand it," I confessed. "'Cause you finer than the print at the bottom of a contract whipped up at midnight by a shady lawyer. You should have brothers beating down your door—or at least standing in line to take a number so they can catch five minutes of your time. I don't know what I can do in your case, but I've got to think about this problem because if I've heard it once, I've heard it thousands of times from incredible black women who simply want a little love." It was true. I had traveled across much of the nation for the past decade, and beautiful, bright black women from every walk of life repeated her story with frightening regularity.

I was frustrated by my failure to adequately explain the painful mystery of why perfectly wonderful black women are often by themselves. Perhaps they are punished for their success, reviled for their strength and independence, feared for their security, hated for their heart, loathed for their determination to survive, and yet still loyal to black men. I didn't have to romanticize black women to appreciate them. After all, I had married three black women with wildly differing results. But I knew the tough situation they confronted was not mostly of their own making, despite what social theorists or barbershop pundits concluded.

The statistics seem to reinforce the gloomy outlook for black women. In essence, black women are less likely than other women to marry in the first place, more likely to divorce, and less likely to remarry. Only 50 percent of black women are expected to be married by the age of twenty-eight, compared to 80 percent of white women. Black women are less likely to remarry after a divorce than white women. Only 32 percent of black women remarry within five years of divorce, while 54 percent of white women and 44 percent of Latina women get married again. As if to underscore how tight and complicated relationships are for black folk, even when marriages are broken, they don't necessarily lead to divorce. Many sisters experience a marital breakup without having their relationships legally terminated. Just 67 percent of black women who were separated from their husbands were divorced three years later. Although this statistic might be interpreted as 33 percent of black women try to work out their relationships during separation, it is just as likely that the high percentage of sisters who don't terminate their relationships suggests an inclination—perhaps the desperation—to hold on as long as possible.

When the Centers for Disease Control issued a report in 2002 highlighting some of these numbers, a journalist friend—I'll call her Dorothy—shared with me her e-mail exchange with a black male colleague—let's call him Henry—who had some interesting things to say about why black men over thirty-five find it tough to be in relationships with black women. Henry said that his college-educated, high-professional male friends in their late thirties and early forties are quite comfortable being single and feel no compulsion to marry. Henry and his friends are wary of women over thirty-five who've never been married. They figure that any reasonably attractive woman who is bright and not angry at men is likely to have lived with someone or been married by thirty-five, even if the relationship failed and she's in circulation again. When Henry's women friends describe their negative behavior and attitudes toward men, he lets them know, when pressed, that "no man is going to stick around for that."

Henry wrote that while we hear a great deal about men being the cause of women's failure to find a mate, there is little discussion of how women are responsible for their fates. Henry tried to avoid discussions with his never-married, over-thirty-five female friends because the truth is painful, and only when they are pushed will they admit they have issues that keep them single. Moreover, Henry believed that "too many women view themselves as perpetual victims; the stories they tell about their previous relationships usually involve them as the victims of male treachery and the narrative doesn't allow any possibility that maybe they had some personal qualities that would make a man not want to be in a long-term relationship with them." Besides the decreased prospect of fertility for women over thirty-five, Henry said that many women are overweight, and that trying to force black men to find plus-size women attractive "is like trying to convince a guy who is indifferent to spectator sports that a baseball strike matters."

In one of her responses, Dorothy, who is forty-something and married for the second time, told Henry that she could sympathize with many of his observations, though she was mystified by the double standard. "Perfectly acceptable-looking sisters sit at home on Saturday nights because they don't look like Vanessa Williams (either of them!), Ananda Lewis, or Halle Berry—yet these same men who are insisting that they have to have fit and trim women have pot bellies, raggedy nails, and shoes that are run down at the heels. Maybe they think their Jaguars make up for it? Maybe they figure the numbers are so in their favor they don't have to, in Archie Bunker's words, "run to catch the bus." It's at the stop, doors open, motor running, waiting for them to hop aboard.'" Dorothy reminded Henry of the quote from journalist George Curry, who once told her "any brother could get over in D.C. long's he can read, write and don't have no running sores." Dorothy confessed that were she single, she'd have to throw in the towel. "All I know is I'd be home by myself with a book before I'd allow myself to wait on some of these brothers to lower their impossibly high standards and ask me out!"

There are many social scientists, armchair analysts, ghetto critics—and some black women themselves—who believe that it is black women who set impossibly high standards for potential partners. To be sure, there are many other reasons besides high standards that keep black women from marrying, including their educational achievements and socioeconomic standing, both of which are higher on average than black men's; the substantial mortality gap between men and women; the disproportionate incarceration of black men; the poor labor force participation of black men; black men's lower occupational status; the dramatically decreasing rate of black men seeking higher education; and the increasing rate of interracial marriage among black men.

The incarceration of black men is a huge problem, especially when it is a zero-sum game between brothers in prison or in school. In what seems an eon ago in hip-hop years, rapper turned actor/director Ice Cube proved hip-hop's prescience when he asked the question, "Why more niggas in the pen than in college?" It's taken more than a decade for social science to match the science Cube dropped when he was a bad-boy rebel, long before he became a mainstream media darling in comedies like *Friday* and *Barbershop*.

According to the Justice Policy Institute (JPI) report "Cellblocks or Classrooms? The Funding of Higher Education and Corrections and Its Impact on African American Men," hip-hop has been on the money. And cash is precisely what is at stake in the booming prison industry that lusts to house more blacks in local penitentiaries. The more black bodies are tossed in jail, the more cells are built, and the more money is made, especially in the rural white communities where many prisons thrive. In 1995 alone, 150 new prisons were constructed and filled, while 171 more were expanded.

But money is also at stake when it comes to making a crucial choice: to support blacks in the state university or the state penitentiary. As the report makes clear, we have chosen the latter. During the 1980s and 1990s, state spending for corrections grew at six times the rate of state spending on higher education. By the end of last century, there were nearly a third more black men in prison and jail than in colleges and universities. That means that the number of black men in jail or prison has increased fivefold in the last twenty years. In 1980, at the dawn of the prison construction boom, black men were three times more likely to be enrolled in college than incarcerated.

In 2000, there were 791,600 black men in jail or prison, while only 603,032 were enrolled in colleges or universities. In 1980, there were 143,000 black men in jail or prison and 463,700 matriculating in higher educational institutions. In effect, the cell block or classroom choice boils down to a policy that, whether intended or not, is genocidal. We would permit no other population of American citizens to be locked away with such callous disregard for the educational opportunity that might help stem the tide of incarceration.

It is hardly a coincidence that, as blacks have become cogs in the machinery of the prison economy, their chances of being college educated have been drastically reduced. The engine of the prison-industrial complex is fueled by the containment of black upward mobility and the disenfranchisement of black citizenry. In many states, felons are ineligible to vote once they leave prison. First we deny these men a solid education, and then we deprive them of the right to help reshape the policies that have harmed them.

One of the tragedies of this state of affairs is that it undercuts the advances of black males in higher education over the last two decades. Between 1980 and 2000, three times as many black men were sent to prison as were enrolled in college or the university. In 2000, at least thirteen states had more black men in prison than in college, and from 1980 until 2000, thirty-eight states, along with the federal system, increased the prison population more than they swelled the ranks of higher education. If the planners of state budgets continue this destructive trend, they will compensate for a loss of revenue by cutting spending on education and social services, two critical means by which blacks escape poverty and the prison trap. If black men are in prison and not in college, they have two strikes against them in their bid to become viable partners to black women. Black male imprisonment has a double-whammy effect on black women finding mates among their male peers: it separates black men from society, and it severely erodes their prospects for higher education.

Even with these facts supporting the diminished choices faced by women, there is still the perception that they are just too picky. *Ebony* magazine has through the years addressed the issue, in articles such as "How Black Women Can Deal with the Black Male Shortage," "Black Women/Black Men: Has Something Gone Wrong Between Them?" and "Do Black Women Set Their Standards for Marriage Too High?" The black male shortage article, from the May 1986 issue, cited Census Bureau statistics that there were at the time 6.4 million more females than males in the United States, and that there were 1.4 million more black females than black males.

According to the article, Dr. Ann Ashmore Poussaint and other experts suggested that black women stop blaming black men and society for their dilemma. The experts argued that women should take a closer look at themselves, their attitude about men, and their approach to finding a mate. "There are many single women who complain about loneliness, but when they do meet interesting men, they project a negative attitude or seem to always get into debates over feminist issues. Others aren't shy about flaunting their professional and financial successes, giving men the impression that they either don't need or have time for a meaningful relationship."

These sentiments appear to be informed by the reluctance to embrace feminist principles as a viable alternative for black women, or by a presumption that female success is the catalyst for the downfall of black men. But Poussaint also argued that too many black women eliminated suitors for superficial reasons, including profession, skin color, height, weight, income, education, family background, and social graces or contacts. She said that if a woman felt she was lowering her standards by dating or marrying a particular kind of man, she should reconsider her priorities. Poussaint and others were not suggesting that black women lower their standards, the article said, but that they should broaden their outlooks, including, some experts said, dating men outside their culture, although other experts strongly opposed interracial relationships.

In the higher standards article, printed in January 1981, *Ebony* explored the black male complaint that black women are more interested in what black men do than who they are. It also grapples with the black male perception that black women are more concerned with professional stature, high income, college degrees, and good looks. They tested this perception—which was really a hypothesis about black female behavior put forth by black men—by engaging twenty-five young women at Spelman College in a group discussion. To the question, "Is a man's status really important to a Black woman thinking about marriage?" *Ebony* reports there "was a resounding 'Yes' from the group."

Some of the students claimed that they were attending college to better themselves, and thus, they seek mates who match their efforts and achievement. The gap between a black male bus driver and a black female attorney would be hard to surmount. Since the vast majority of black men in 1981 held blue-collar jobs—a statistic that remains unchanged to this day—and because black women's route to professional achievement was not as difficult as that of black men, the magazine contended, the tensions between the genders would only increase. Many of the young Spelman women recognized that they might have difficulty in finding mates with comparable achievements, and hence believed they could afford to wait. The article explores the class rift between high-achieving, highly motivated black females, and black males hampered by persistent racism and differing socialization.

If the issue of black women having higher standards for relationships was a concern twenty years ago, it is even more prevalent now. According to some research, black women have been less willing than white women to marry men with lower status and undesirable traits—those who are younger, previously married, less educated, or unattractive. In short, black women prefer attractive men who are near their age and who have a stable career. For those black women who have never been married, they prefer mates with no previous wives or children. The younger the black woman, the greater her expectation that her man meet the criteria she deemed important. Further, black women who have higher status are more invested in building careers and less urgent about finding a mate. The economic independence of high-achieving black women, and the deteriorating economic conditions of black males, severely depletes the pool of potentially marriageable black men.

In our nation, people tend to marry folk who have similar educational backgrounds. That poses a huge problem for black men and women, since the ratio of highly educated black men to women has been said to be as small as sixty men available for every one hundred women. There are nearly 400,000 more black women than men enrolled in higher education. Black women are now earning more than 63 percent of all college degrees awarded to blacks. There are nearly 4 million black married couples in the United States, and among them, just under 10 percent have marriages where both spouses have a college degree. Slightly more than 1 percent of them are marriages where both spouses had graduate degrees.

Moreover, black women with higher levels of education are disproportionately affected by the shortage of black men with similar levels of education. In the 1930s, only 11 percent of black women were expected not to marry; today, less than 40 percent of black women are expected to marry. One might conclude in analyzing these statistics that there is no shortage of black men for black women to marry, but that black women choose to remain single rather than marry partners who do not meet their expectations. Further, educated professional black women seek to marry only those men they find acceptable by high standards; thus, lack of motivation, not availability, is the critical issue.

But that would be extremely shortsighted. While it is true that such numbers might translate to black women being "picky," the reality is that black women seek to meet and marry those men with whom they have the greatest degree of compatibility. Black male resentment of black female achievement, especially among black men who have not enjoyed the opportunity to succeed, may translate to unwarranted hostility toward black women. Many brothers feel that black women are the pawns of a white establishment that seeks to hold them down. As a result, black female movement through educational and professional ranks is to some black men a symptom of black women's complicity with a racist system. Rather than offer an astute analysis of our condition—that in a patriarchal culture, black men do represent a specific threat to white male power that black women don't, and hence, in some instances, white men prefer the presence of black women in professional settings—black men often confuse the consequences of racism with a desire of black females to undercut them.

Further, for a black man to reach beneath his class station to embrace a black woman reinforces the status quo: as breadwinner, he can provide for his family, and thus remain "head of the house." For a black woman to behave similarly up- sets the status quo: if she makes more money and is better educated than her partner, the resentment of her man can become burdensome, sometimes abusive. I know a lot of brothers who felt they could take a woman making more money than them, but once the reality of her higher status set in, it usually took on so- cial meanings beyond a paycheck. Issues of control inevitably arose, and the question of who was in charge followed in its wake. Since black men struggle with a society that sets up expectations for appropriate masculine behavior—take care of one's family, be gainfully employed, be a financial success—and then un- dermines their attainment, black women are often the psychological scapegoat of our anger. The rise in black male domestic violence is poignant testimony to such tensions in the black home.

It would be hard to blame black women for wanting to be "equally yoked," but that does not mean there aren't sisters who are dismissive of black men outside of their income or educational bracket. In my early twenties, a young lady I had grown quite fond of and with whom I had become intimate, bluntly told me, "I'm attracted to you physically, and I think you're very smart, but you're a minister, and you won't make a lot of money. I need a man who will be financially well-off, so I don't think we can have a relationship."

I was stunned and hurt, and from that day forward, robbed of any illusions about how poorly some sisters can behave. Still, the grim reality is that black men often despise women's success as the unfailing predictor of domestic trouble. I will never forget a black man who told me that his wife's education had hurt their re- lationship because she no longer understood her place. "She became a 'phenom- enal woman,'" he declared with bitter irony, citing in his resentful put-down the fa- mous Maya Angelou poem of the same name. I have heard similar comments repeated by brothers time and time again.

Despite all of this, many college-educated black women marry black men with significantly lower levels of education. In marriages where black women have a col- lege degree, only 45.9 percent of their husbands also have a college degree. More than one-quarter of black women who have a college degree are married to men who have never gone to college. And 4 percent of black women with a college de- gree are married to black men who didn't graduate from high school. By compar- ison, nearly 70 percent of white women with a college degree married men who also had a college degree, and only 12 percent of white women with a college degree married men who never went to college. While black women may prefer mates who are educationally compatible, they have often chosen mates whose lower achievement makes their marriages vulnerable to divorce and spousal abuse.

Other black men complain bitterly that many black women prefer the hardcore, thugged-out brother, the bad boy, the player. A brilliant young Vanderbilt University professor of mathematics, whom this thinking victimized, wrote an essay about his experience for *Essence* magazine. Jonathan Farley is a tall, slim, attractive brown-skinned young man, a summa cum laude graduate of Harvard who took a doctorate in mathematics from Oxford University and is an outspoken advocate for the Black Panthers. In his essay, he recalls a painful episode: a young lady with whom he fell in love only wanted to be his friend. But the worst of it is that she took him to dinner to heal his wounds by telling him why he struck out. "She outlined the difference between men like me and the men Black women preferred, between mere African Americans and 'niggaz': African-Americans are safe, respectable, upwardly mobile and professional Black men. Niggaz are strong, streetwise, hard Black men."

Jonathan pointed out that his erstwhile love had a question posed to her by a friend: if she was walking down a dark street at night, who would she want by her side, an African-American or a nigga? She told Jonathan that black women sought a strong protector. Jonathan writes that he "tried to explain that physical strength had ceased to be a survival trait back in the Stone Age." Further, he warned her that women who prefer niggaz to African-Americans were making a costly mistake since African-Americans, by virtue of their "higher social and economic status"—and wasn't this what black women wanted?—could better protect them and give them the security they desired. Since many young black women grow up without fathers in the home, even college-educated black women often settled for dropouts and drug dealers.

Because of his experience, Jonathan found himself "resisting my own impulses to open a door, start a conversation or even say hello to many young black women I meet, for fear of appearing too gentlemanly and hence unworthy of their attention." Jonathan argued that even black men who were "raised in the suburbs don the attire and attitude of street thugs so that they, too, will be chosen." He concluded his essay by admonishing sisters to "leave the players in the playground. . . . Knights in shining armor don't have to have gold teeth."

Many black women have admitted that this is far too frequent a flaw among their sisters. Many sisters claim to have outgrown such an inclination, chalking it up to their youth and their failure to know what kind of man would really be a good partner. Once they mature, many black women are attracted to brothers whose stability and substance are prized above the flashy danger of destructive black men.

If some black men chafe under the restrictive mythology of the ghetto tough, many more black women are passed over for an equally nefarious reason. Recently, when I lectured at a northeastern college, a young lady approached me after my lecture. As we chatted about a number of issues, we began to discuss the dating situation at her college for black women. That's when she dropped the bombshell on me.

"Professor Dyson, my boyfriend broke up with me earlier this year," the attractive chocolate sister told me.

"Why'd he do that?" I asked her, noticing that her heart was heavy, her eyes tearing up as she spoke.

"He said I was too dark," she said lowly.

"That can't be right," I protested on her behalf. "Did he actually tell you that?"

"Right to my face," she replied, as if still in shock.

Although many black men are rarely that blunt, their actions speak just as harshly. The preference for light-skinned women finds painful precedent in black culture. It dates back to slavery when the lightest blacks—whose skin color was often the result of rape by white slave masters—were favored over their darker kin because they were closer in color and appearance to dominant society. Unfortunately, despite the challenge to the mythology of inherently superior white standards of beauty, there persists in black life the belief that light is preferable to dark. Music videos have historically presented light-skinned black women as the most desirable women. Even as browner women have more recently won space in the culture of representation within our race—a few of them, like Carla Campbell, Angela Basset, and Valerie Morris appear in videos, film, and on television news, respectively—there is an undeniable subordination of darker-skinned black women to lighter sisters in everyday life.

A bright, beautiful, and brown friend of mine—I'll call her Renee—recently told me that she dated for a year a famous football star, a very dark brother, who told her that he almost didn't ask her out because she was so dark. One of his gridiron colleagues, an equally chocolate brother, said within her earshot that Renee was not the kind of girl he usually dated since his other women had been much fairer. Renee also reported to me that an all-star NBA player told her that in order to fit in, he had to have the same car, same house, and same-looking woman as most of the other basketball players—meaning women who are very light-skinned or of mixed heritage, since these women are "hot" now.

Renee shared with me a painful e-mail missive from an intern who worked in her office that testifies to the persistence of virulent beliefs about skin color in black America. The young lady said that she and her friends felt that "as normal/average looking young black women, we are no longer desirable." She has "many friends who are dark-skinned and have natural hair who complain that they can never get attention from black men." She also commented on what she and her friends have termed "hybrid chicks," girls who are showcased and admired in music videos because they "are exotic looking, either half black and Asian or half Hispanic."

What is remarkable is that such self-defeating prejudice persists despite the growing prominence in some circles of beautiful dark-skinned black women.

There is Ingrid Saunders Jones, the enormously gifted corporate executive who, from her perch as a senior vice president of Coca-Cola and head of its foundation, has funneled tens of millions of dollars into black America in aid of charitable, civic, and cultural causes. Ingrid is a glamorous woman with flawless, honey-dipped ebony skin; healthy, sculpted eyebrows; soulful and sexy eyes; cascading, jet-black hair that is often pulled back into a ponytail; a blinding smile; perfectly lined lips; and a '50s-style sensuality. There is Vanessa Bell Calloway, the intelligent and strikingly beautiful actress and co-host of the BET talk show *Oh Drama*. Vanessa is a shapely, buff sister with a dewy, espresso-brown complexion; clear, bright eyes; perfect white teeth; and a glittering sexuality—and a laugh as strong as her personality. There is Darlene Clark Hine, a brilliant Northwestern University historian—and former president of the Organization of American Historians—who has written several path-breaking books on black women's life and history. Darlene is a deep, rich maple-colored beauty with entrancing features: big, expressive eyes; succulent cheeks; sexy, full lips; and milk-smooth skin, framed by a flow of layered, shining, silky, silvery hair. And among the younger generation, there is Aunjanue Ellis, a superbly talented actress with Ivy League credentials—she attended Brown University—and graduate training at New York University. Aunjanue is a smoky, sultry chocolate stunner whose megawatt smile, thick black tresses, chiseled cheeks, sweetly burnished flesh, alluring eyebrows, riveting dark eyes, luscious and life-affirming lips, svelte and taut physique, and comely legs make the gorgeous thespian a vision of soulful sensuality.

The continued preference for lighter sisters among blacks bears witness to psychic wounds that are not completely healed. The poisonous self-hatred that pours freely in the rejection of dark blackness is painful evidence of our unresolved racial anxieties about our true beauty and self-worth. Dark black women have often been cast aside and looked down upon because they embody the most visible connection to a fertile African heritage whose value remains suspect in our culture and nation.

As long as black men continue to spurn the root of our reality—summed up, perhaps, in the saying, "the darker the berry, the sweeter the juice"—the longer we will be separated from the source of our survival. While we are wise not to envision our blackness in literal terms—it is not simply about skin, but about sensibility, aesthetics, culture, style, and the like—it would be foolish to deny that the debasing of blackness is often about the debasing of blacks in our skin, through our skin, because of our skin. While race is more cosmic than epidermis and flesh—encompassing politics, social structure, class, and region—our place in the world, and our reward and punishment too, are profoundly shaped by color.

As big a barrier to the flow of love between black men and women as the issues I've discussed are, perhaps none is more controversial, or as hurtful, as the rejection many black women experience when black men date and marry white women. As I lecture and preach across the country, black women of every station corner me, or ask me before an auditorium of hundreds, sometimes thousands, a version of the question: "Why do so many brothers despise us and chase white women?"

Of course, I am always reluctant to speak for all black men, especially when it comes to something as personal and subjective—though obviously not without serious social overtones—as who one likes or loves. And many of my heroes—Quincy Jones and Sidney Poitier among them—married white women at a time when doing so bravely challenged the nation's apartheid. In the '60s and '70s, interracial marriage, whether intended or not, represented a rejection of white supremacist values and indicated that love was a matter between individuals, not races. Few could miss the heroic gesture of loving across racial lines. Those who did often risked their reputations and social status while enduring cultural stigma. In short, it was apparent that interracial romance was unavoidably interpreted in political terms.

But if we are honest, interracial love has rarely, if ever, been simply about love. It has always borne political implications. From the very beginning of the black presence on American soil, stereotypes have distorted relations between the races, including those involving sex. Black males were brought to this nation in chains to be studs. Their virility was placed in the service of slavery. Black females were raped at will; their wombs became the largely unprotected domain of white male desire. Their sexuality was harnessed to perpetuate slavery through procreation. Later, of course, many more stereotypes of black men and women flourished, from the docile Uncle Tom, the fiery "field nigger," the compliant "house nigger," and the uppity buck, to the nurturing Mammy, the sarcastic sapphire, the promiscuous Jezebel, and now, in our day, the sex-crazed Lothario, the unrepentant rapist, the welfare queen, and the hoochie mama.

These stereotypes revolve largely around sex—how black people have it, under what conditions, for what reasons, how frequently, and if it can be read as a symptom of their debased nature and perverted character. Hence, these stereotypes often expressed the stunted social perceptions of black identity put forth by a white culture that refused to own up to its heavy hand in their creation.

Moreover, white society was ambivalent about black sexual identity—they wanted their blacks highly sexed to support slavery and white male pleasure. Otherwise, they wanted blacks to be constrained, even sexless if possible. Black men were feared and envied for their mythically large sexual organs. White male sexual desire was linked to strengthening patriarchal culture. As a result, white men sought to exploit black female eroticism, and to minimize sexual competition by outlawing black male sexual interactions with white women. The rise of lynching and castration are tied to the white male attempt to control the exaggerated threat of black male sexual desire. Long after the demise of such vicious social acts, the strong taboo on interracial sex prevails.

While black men were being constructed as studs, and black women as inherently lascivious—basically it was guilt by association, since black women must be hyper-sexed to be able to satisfy the sexual desire of their men—white women were being projected as paragons of sexual virtue and placed on pedestals of purity. White female sexual desire, as much as possible, was segregated from public view. It was exclusively directed toward the bedroom of their white husbands, whose carousing outside the home—whether in the slave quarter or the whorehouse—was for the most part exempt from ethical scrutiny. There was minimal sexual contact between black men and white women during slavery. However, during Reconstruction there was a noticeable increase in these relations, although interracial marriages remained rare.

Antimiscegenation laws prohibiting interracial marriage between whites and people of color existed in forty states until 1967, when the U.S. Supreme Court struck down these laws as unconstitutional in the landmark—and aptly named—*Loving v. Virginia*. Moreover, after emancipation, vicious sexual stereotypes served in part as a smoke screen to divert attention from how white men sought to prevent black men from enjoying the privileges of economic stability, middle-class status, and the freedom to raise their families. Still, the white woman defined the norm of beauty for the culture. She remained the prized erotic possession to be fought over by black and white men. Black women were largely excluded from this economy of desire, except in the crudest fashion.

This history must be kept in mind as we ponder the sexual fault lines in black America, and the tensions between black men and women around the perception that black men are aggressively marrying white women. Interracial marriage among black men and white women has risen dramatically in the last few years. Nearly 8 percent of all black men between the ages of twenty-five and thirty-four who were married in 1990 married nonblack women, compared to just 4 percent for white men in the same age cohort who married outside their race. Region, occupation, and education play a huge role in determining the interracial marriages of black men. In the Pacific Northwest, 32 percent of black men marry white women; in California, it's 20 percent; in the Rocky Mountain states, it's 30 percent; and in the New England states, 19 percent of black men marry white women. Military service hikes the numbers for black men marrying women outside their race, as 14 percent of black males in the military are married to nonblacks.

By contrast, only 7 percent of black men who didn't serve in the military married nonblacks. More than 10 percent of black men who complete college marry outside of their race, compared to only 6 percent for black men who didn't complete high school. And for black men who have attended graduate school, the number jumps to 13 percent who marry nonblack women. In fact, black men with graduate school experience are 30 percent more likely to marry outside their race than even black men with a college degree. Overall, more than 200,000 black men are married outside their race, mostly to white women.

On the surface, despite the soaring rates of intermarriage for black men, that number might not seem particularly disturbing, but from the perspective of educated black women, it represents a significant draining of the pool of available black men from which to choose a potential mate. As more black men go to prison, die early from crime or from AIDS, are severely unemployed or underemployed, or choose an alternative sexual lifestyle, the numbers of compatible black men begin to significantly diminish for educated black women. And given the hostility that black men without higher education often harbor toward educated black women, the numbers of black men available for black women dwindle even more.

Young black women face a crisis in available black men unlike that faced by their grandmothers, who found marriageable black men in relatively plentiful numbers. The GI Bill altered the educational and employment landscape for black men of the post–World War II generation. Black men who had been closed out of white-collar and professional jobs found new opportunities beyond the school teaching to which they had been formerly relegated. While black women, especially in the South, held many of the teaching jobs, blue-collar jobs were at the time a far better source of income, including waiting on tables in five-star restaurants and hotels, jobs that many college-educated black males took, along with serving as Pullman porters.

In the South's segregated black schools, black men held most of the principals' jobs. For those black men who didn't go to college, especially since it was tough in the rigidly segregated job market for black men to reap benefit from higher education, they went to work immediately after high school in the jobs that college-educated men coveted as well. Under Jim Crow, the educated and uneducated alike met and mixed, and black women enjoyed a much larger pool of available and socially attractive black men from which to choose a mate.

Today, not only are the economic opportunities severely shrunk for black men who don't obtain higher education, but the overwhelming majority of black students who attend college—80 percent of them—are matriculating in predominantly white schools. In contrast to black students of earlier generations who attended historically black colleges and universities, black students now have far greater access to white culture, tastes, opportunities, values, and goals. And they mix with white peers far more frequently than black students at black colleges and those black youth who end their education at high school.

The situation I have just outlined has in its own right negatively affected the prospects of black women finding a mate. But when one takes into consideration the persistence of the belief that white women are the ideal embodiment of beauty in our culture, and the prize that *all* men seek, the situation for black women is even more dismal. They not only fight against trends in the economy, employment, and education, but they fight a far more elusive opponent: the mythological eroticization of a standard of beauty that by definition excludes them from competition. Furthermore, black women are subject to stereotypes among black men about their being "difficult," "demanding," "bossy," "full of attitude," "aggressive," and the like, ruling them out of play as possible mates, often by the relatively small pool of highly educated, or highly achieving, black men.

Thus, when black women express anger at being abandoned by black men in favor of white women, they are neither being irrational, unfair, nor unduly hostile.

Rather, they are taking stock of an abominable cultural condition over which they have little control. When highly educated or visible black men consistently make choices of partners or mates outside of the race, it appears to be far more than coincidence or the capricious stirrings of affection. In fact, it hardly seems to be arbitrary at all. Rather, there seems to be an undeniable wall of separation between desirable black men and the educated and beautiful black women they are turning away from in droves. White women are often unconsciously elevated as the erotic payoff—the sexual reward—for those black men who seek elevated status in our society, or alternatively, who want to cement their position as outstanding men.

Hence, the spurning of black women cannot be considered an exclusively personal or private choice of black men in an erotic and emotional vacuum. In light of the factors that drive this trend, it must be seen as part of a deeply rooted, if often unconscious, process of pursuing the emblem of beauty and status from which black men have been historically barred. I am not suggesting that all black men who pursue or marry white women are the victims of an unconscious adoration of white standards of beauty. But it is difficult to ignore the compelling evidence that it is often more than happenstance or coincidence that drives interracial relations between black men and white women.

Of course, it is hardly a one-way street. Many white women find black men desirable too, obviously for purely personal reasons—as is the case many times with the black male attraction to white women—but also for more complex social reasons as well. A black female student at George Washington University, where I had gone to lecture, explained to me her theory about why many black men and white women are magnetized to each other.

"See, Professor Dyson, I think it has to do with the ideals both black men and white women represent," the beautiful brown-skinned woman said to me in a circle of black female students. "White women are allegedly the ideal expression of beauty: blonde hair, blue eyes, keen nose, thin lips, big breasts, and flat behind. And black men are the ideal expression of the ultimate physique: muscular, dark and handsome, sexually aggressive, and of course, having a large sexual organ. So naturally, when they get together, it's pretty explosive. It's the meeting of two ideals." That certainly was part of the answer, although neither the student nor I would reduce the complexity of erotic and interpersonal attraction to sheer physical chemistry. It also has to do with the way that chemistry is determined by deeply held social beliefs about features that we are told are attractive and those we are told we should avoid or that we can live without. Too often, those beliefs are shaped by racial considerations, driven by troublesome and often unexamined assumptions about white and black women that pass for common sense, but which, upon reflection, turn out to be little more than projections, stereotypes, or scapegoating.

For some black men, having a white woman or wife amounts to enjoying a level of liberation from erotic or social restrictions that is downright intoxicating. For some, it involves the complicated choreography of racial revenge, as they seek—as I once heard it explained of a black nationalist who justified his relationships with white women—"to punish their fathers." For others, having a white wife or woman is a way into the club of white patriarchy, as if to say, "I've got what it takes to snag one of your women, now let me have some of your power."

Of course, such a move might backfire, only increasing the likelihood of white male resentment, perhaps retaliation. But sometimes, in the strange machinations of the patriarchal imagination, the pursuit and capture of the white ideal of beauty signifies to white men a level of erotic and social competence that augurs well for transracial alliance in the business world. A black woman wrote to me about how her "sons' biological father (nothing more) married a woman who was thirty years older than him, just so he could move up in the ranks of his job and have a 'trophy white wife.' Then he proceeded to have children with other women while he stayed married to his security blanket." Of course, one might argue that this is merely the sour grapes of a woman who lost her man to a white woman. Still, her belief that some black men prize white women as stepping-stones is not far-fetched. Some social scientists have pointed out that members of a stigmatized social group, or those bereft of prestige, often trade characteristics when choosing a mate. That might mean that black men have a better chance of winning the affections of a white woman if they offer, for instance, higher socioeconomic status in return. In fact, white women marry up more often when they marry a black man than when they marry a white man. A black man has higher socioeconomic status to offer in exchange for the elevated esteem he might achieve, in his own eyes, or in the eyes of those he seeks to please, by marrying a white woman. Interestingly, black men marry down more often when marrying a white woman than when marrying a black woman.

This research may support the perception of many black women that many white women seek only those black men who are well educated, or whose high visibility and social status are compensation for the status conferred by white womanhood. Professional athletes and entertainers, among others, are noteworthy for a high, or at least visible, degree of interracial partnering and marriage. Many black women resent the fact that they are precluded access to such men because they do not offer the status of white skin, blue eyes, or blonde hair. Nor do they simply cater to the unreasonable demands of the black male star or prominent figure, as some black women contend is true of many of their white female counterparts.

There is, too, a great deal of hypocrisy involved in the spurning of black women by well-known black men. For instance, some black men claim that their preference for white women—besides the fact that they are, according to these men, devoid of the bitterness, harshness, and drama of black women—has to do with the relative ease with which they yield to the sexual desires of black men. The irony, of course, is that if black women give in easily, they are marked as "ho's," and if they refuse black men's sexual advances, they are often seen as "bitches." By contrast, many white women are rewarded for the same behavior with permanent partnership or marriage. Further, many of the white women who aggressively pursue high-profile black men are viewed as appropriately assertive, endearing, and supportive. On the other hand, black women who are equally aggressive are viewed as "gold diggers" and materialistic hoochies.

Perhaps one of the greatest furors among black women in recent memory was sparked when an outraged white woman—she signed her missive "Disgusted White Girl"—who was engaged to a black man penned a letter to Jamie Brown, editor of the popular gossip magazine *Sister 2 Sister*. Disgusted wrote to Jamie to "challenge some of your Black male readers," saying she was engaged to a good-looking, educated, and loving black male, and that she didn't understand "a lot of the Black females' attitudes about our relationship." Disgusted wrote that her man "wanted me because the pickings amongst Black women were slim to none. As he said, they were either too fat, too loud, too mean, too argumentative, too needy, too materialistic, and carrying too much excess baggage." Disgusted said that before she was engaged, she was "constantly approached by Black men, willing to wine and dine me and give me the world. If Black women are so up in arms about us being with their men, why don't they look at themselves and make some changes."

Disgusted said that she was tired of the dirty looks and snide remarks she got, that she "would like to hear from some Black men about why we are so appealing and coveted by them. Bryant Gumbel just left his wife of 26 years for one! Charles Barkley, Scottie Pippen, the model Tyson Beckford, Montel Williams, Quincy Jones, James Earl Jones, Harry Belafonte, Sidney Poitier, Kofi Annan, Cuba Gooding Jr., Don Cornelius, Berry Gordy, Billy Blanks, Larry Fishburne, Wesley Snipes . . . I could go and on." Disgusted admonished black women not "to be mad with us white women because so many of your men want us. Get your acts together and learn from us and we may lead you to treat your men better."

Then she challenged black men and appealed to an unstated compact that has been seemingly forged by many black men and white women, when she confidently wrote, "If I'm wrong, Black men, let me know." This hurtful diatribe exposed the racial logic and, unwittingly, the unconscious white female privilege that work against black women, and to white women's advantage. By arrogantly lecturing black women about their shortcomings, Disgusted failed to account for the elevated status she enjoyed—and the exaggerated value she had conferred on her—because of her white skin and the social and historical meanings of white female identity.

But it isn't just the famous or visible black man who is the object of white female desire. In 1995, seven black female students at Brown University started in their dormitory a "Wall of Shame," which listed the names of the black males who were dating white women, when they became angry that many of the black males on campus favored white women while spurning their affections. It would be easy to make these and other black women look frustrated, irrational, jealous, foolish, or plain loony when they point to the pathological behavior of their black men avoiding or stigmatizing them. And yet, the trends suggest that increasingly, black males in college are doing just that.

As a result, perhaps, college-educated black women are increasingly turning to white men and others outside the race in seeking companionship. Black women are often more constrained in the choice of partners or mates by a profound sense of racial loyalty. Between 1960 and 1980, the number of black women married to white men was relatively static, inching from 26,000 to 27,000. By 2000, it had grown to 80,000, and the number is bound to increase with the crisis of available black men only getting worse for the foreseeable future. To be sure, there is the possibility of the romanticized white male suitor—the one capable of providing life's best, unlike the bulk of struggling black men, or the white man who fits the bill of what is sexy and romantic in ways that black men are rarely permitted—playing an equally problematic role in the black female imagination as the idealized white woman plays for black men. And as with many black men, simple attraction to the opposite race might be in effect. For the most part, black women are perceived as coupling with white men out of necessity more than preference.

A recent spate of articles, in *Essence* and *Ebony* magazines, and in newspapers like the *Atlanta Journal-Constitution*, has commented on the phenomenon. The *Journal-Constitution* article, entitled "Could Mr. Right Be White?" raised the ire of journalist Nathan McCall. The article quotes twenty-nine-year-old Melanie Robinson, a black woman who has dated three white men, as saying that black men take black women for granted since the numbers favor men, and that white men are "more romantic and willing to go on dates like walking in the park or visiting a museum." Robinson also wishes that black men would do more than offer to take her for a drink or go to "Red Lobster for all-you-can-eat crab legs on Monday."

In a letter to the newspaper, McCall wrote that he found the article "appallingly racist and typically shallow." McCall argued that it's "one thing to say that some black women date white men because there is a shortage of available black men," but quite another to "suggest that the very group that created and perpetuated that shortage—white men—are also the most sensitive and romantic people on God's great earth." He suggested that it would have been as easy to find women to "testify that white men are insecure, and that given a dating choice between an all-you-can-eat crab legs special and an evening at the museum, white men will opt for Red Lobster every time." McCall concluded that he was thankful for shows like *Jerry Springer* and *Ricky Lake*, because, as "insane as their programs are, at least they demonstrate that human frailties are as much a reality for whites as for anyone else."

Perhaps the most recent controversy involving a white man enjoying the pleasures of black female companionship erupted around the film *Monster's Ball*, starring Halle Berry as a waitress who becomes involved with a racist sheriff—played by Billy Bob Thornton—who executes her convict husband on death row before falling in love with her. The film includes an extended and explicit sex scene where Thornton's character makes love from behind to Berry's waitress. Many blacks were torn when Berry won the Oscar for her powerful portrayal: they were rooting for her to be acknowledged for her superior skill, but reluctant to praise a part that even indirectly suggested that her character's sexual liaison was a reward for hating black people and executing her husband, played by Sean "P. Diddy" Combs.

A few weeks after the Oscars, actress Angela Bassett—whom Berry had graciously mentioned by name in her acceptance speech as one of "the women that stand beside me"—criticized the role Berry played even as she was careful to praise Berry for her performance. Bassett said, "I wasn't going to be a prostitute on film," and that "I couldn't do that because it's such a stereotype about black women and sexuality," concluding that "Meryl Streep won Oscars without all that." Bassett said that she loved Berry's performance, and that she didn't begrudge Berry her success, but that it "wasn't the role for me." Bassett said that she wanted an Oscar, but "for something I can sleep with at night." The issue of stereotypes is extremely important, especially for black women in a powerful medium like film involved sexually with white men. But so is the freedom to choose roles that stretch the boundaries of sexual propriety and challenge the limitations imposed on black female sexuality.

In her acceptance speech, Berry challenged the stereotypes of how a black woman who has been honored by the powers-that-be should behave. Instead of being safe, Berry was bravely political. She gave the millions who watched around the globe not only a sorely needed history lesson, but also a lesson in courageous identification with the masses. Berry tearfully declared that her award was for "every nameless, faceless woman of color" who now had a chance since "this door has been opened." Berry's remarkable courage and candor are depressingly rare among famed blacks with a lot on the line: money, prestige, reputation, and work. Many covet the limelight's payoffs, but cower in light of its demands.

Even fewer speak up about the experiences their ordinary brothers and sisters endure—and if they are honest, that they themselves too often confront—on a daily basis. To be sure, there is an unspoken tariff on black honesty among the privileged: if they dare cut against the grain, they may be curtailed or cut off from reward. Or they may endure stigma. What Berry did was brave and generous: on the night she was being singled out for greatness, she cast her lot with anonymous women of color who hungered for her spot, and who might be denied for no other reason than that they were yellow, brown, red, or black. Her achievement, she insisted, was now their hope. Her performance that night was a stereotype buster.

No matter how you cut it, sex between the races is a complicated affair. Many black men honestly love white women, and many black women honestly love white men. But the history of traumatic interaction between the races shapes the patterns of love and sex across racial lines. As a social taboo that has been shattered, interracial sex is a healthy and edifying occurrence. As the symptom of the attempt to escape or avoid intimate contact with the women who have loved and nurtured our race, it can be a sign of utter self-hatred, and hatred of our group's

most powerful and loyal members. One of the most vicious legacies of white supremacy is the belief that our women are not beautiful, desirable, intelligent, and
worthy of our love.

The factors that rob black men and women of more love between us—imprisonment, early death, educational disparities, and self-destructive habits such as
snobbishness, skin-color bias, the preference for "bad boys," and worship of white
standards of beauty—can be combated through conscientious response to our
plight. There are millions of black women from every walk of life who simply
want, like every other group of women alive, to be wanted and loved by the men
who issued from their mothers' wombs. To dishonor that wish is the seed of our
destruction.

Fourteen

IN O.J.'S SHADOW:
KOBE BRYANT'S PREDICAMENT

On July 6, the Eagle County Sheriff's Office in Colorado made an announcement that shook the world: twenty-four-year-old basketball superstar Kobe Bryant had been arrested on suspicion of felony sexual assault and false imprisonment of a nineteen-year-old college student at an elite Edwards, Colorado, spa where she worked, and where Bryant had been staying in preparation for knee surgery. Bryant wasn't formally charged until July 18, but by then the media circus and rumor mill had already spun wildly out of control. Later that day Bryant appeared highly emotional at a news conference in Los Angeles, with his wife Vanessa by his side, proclaiming his innocence of the charges while admitting he had had an adulterous—and, according to him, consensual—liaison with his accuser. And although major news outlets generally observe a policy of not revealing an (alleged) rape victim's identity, her name and picture—as well as those of a falsely identified woman—had by then been plastered all over cyberspace. Bryant's accuser, an attractive, white, blonde former cheerleader, was employed as a concierge at the Cordillera Lodge & Spa, which was where the fateful encounter took place, on June 30, just before midnight.

It appears unavoidable that Bryant's case would be compared to the Simpson criminal case, despite spectacular differences: Bryant's is not a murder case; Simpson intimately knew one of the two victims in his alleged crime, whereas Bryant met his accuser that night; and Bryant is not a former star, but a widely celebrated athlete not yet at the height of his projected place as one of basketball's best players of all time. Still, the elements of race and gender suggest striking parallels: a handsome black athlete pitted in court against a white woman, and polls that suggest a strong racial divide in the public's belief in Bryant's guilt or innocence. Whatever the outcome, the case will have permanently altered the lives of Bryant and his accuser and has already provided a glimpse into persistent stereotypes of white female identity and black sexuality, and the continuing difficulty of interracial relationships. This brief essay from my column in Savoy *magazine is my take on these issues.*

IF KOBE BRYANT'S ATTORNEYS HAVE THEIR WAY, it will be several months, perhaps even a year, before the NBA superstar goes to court to defend himself against sexual assault charges. But within the court of black public opinion, there has already been a long and brooding deliberation, and a fair amount of dramatic signifying based on the fact that Bryant's accuser is a nineteen-year-old white woman. "That's what happens when you mess with a white girl," goes the quiet chorus. It's a harsh sentiment, but one buttressed by an even harsher history of sexual mistrust, suspicion, and fear between the races. Even without an assault charge, the sex between white women and black men has often been volatile. Sometimes it's been downright fatal. If we're to understand Kobe's case, we've got to know that history, since it may determine his fate in the national imagination, and most important, in a Colorado courtroom.

Interracial sex is haunted by entrenched beliefs about how black and white folk should live and treat one another. Until a few decades ago, we lived in stifling segregation that was supported by custom and law. Whites convinced themselves and many others that they were superior in every way. We were led to believe that the only way blacks could be saved was to accept white culture and to adopt their view of the world. But once we were baptized in the rivers of white life, sometimes to be drowned, at other times to be washed of our blackness, we saw the ironies that pollute the mainstream.

No irony was clearer than how white women were at once celebrated and dismissed. White women have long been seen as pure and chaste. During slavery and beyond, white wives were for the most part spared the duty of recreational sex; that was the job of the whore or the slave. Instead, they were saved for what can only be thought of as Darwinian sex: if not the origin, then at least the perpetuation of the species was at stake. White women were in truth "respected" into sexual confinement and robbed of erotic freedom. For white men, pleasure and social privilege came wrapped in one neat package: if they ran the world, they could enjoy it as they liked. For white women, these realms were strictly separated, and besides, they had less of both.

That was even truer for slaves. Black women were victims of the erotic whims of white men who bedded them as they pleased. Black men, too, were sexually vulnerable. White culture harnessed the black penis to fertilize black wombs and to fortify white rule. But if black women were a thrill—typecast as the erotic equals of their insatiable men—black men were a threat. Black men's legendary prowess made white men jealous and even erotically competitive. White men feared the free black phallus, and spread that fear to their wives and daughters. The idea of the potent black male was so scary that it drove D.W. Griffith in 1915 to unleash *Birth of a Nation,* a film that throbbed with conspiracy in warning that the social contract would unravel if black men were permitted to satisfy their lust for white women. It made little difference that such paranoia was fueled more by stereotype than by science. The point was to protect white women, control black men, and exploit black women.

The history of sexual relations between black men and white women is part romance novel, part Greek tragedy, and part horror story. In slavery, interracial sex was plainly forbidden, even though such unions probably took place far more than ol' Massa knew. Even in emancipation, the erotic ties between black men and white women were forged in secrecy. The assault on interracial sex in the name of white supremacy made such discretion necessary. Black men could be lynched for just looking at a white woman, or, equally as savage, they could, like Emmett Till, be beaten and tossed into a river and left for dead. White women sometimes cried rape to escape the stigma or alienation that dogged those who slept with black men. And even when black men and white women were brave enough to defy social convention and expose their love to ridicule, they still faced ugly comments, hateful stares and certain ostracism in the mainstream. Politics and history are never far away in the interracial bed.

It is these politics and history that flare up in our consideration of Kobe's case. On the face of it, the charge of sexual assault against Bryant is a bitter legal dispute between two young adults. And yet, right away, there are complicating factors. Bryant is a married man whereas his accuser is single. Bryant is a wealthy athlete whose skill and charisma have made him hugely popular around the globe. Although his gender and celebrity may tip the case in Bryant's favor, race is a perennial wild card. Bryant is a big black man; his accuser, by all accounts, is a much smaller white blonde. The idea of a black man in a tryst with a white woman still spooks bigots who oppose interracial sex. And there may be hidden resentments and subtle resistance even among those who don't view themselves as prejudiced. This may be as true for those blacks tired of our men tripping up with, and on, white women, as it is for whites with little experience of blacks, much like those in the Colorado town with a miniscule black population where Kobe may have sealed his fate.

It might turn out that Kobe's wealth and fame are trumped by his accuser's race and gender. That comforts those who think that Bryant's status dupes people into believing he couldn't assault anyone. To others, it's proof that the word of an anonymous white woman is enough to bring a brother down, even a brother of Kobe's standing, which, in their view, would be tragic, as his flawless record, and more important, the law, says he deserves the benefit of the doubt. Of course, this is assuming that there is no clear evidence of Bryant's or his accuser's guilt forthcoming at trial. If no damning proof is presented, it's her word against his. In such a case, race shapes our views of what looks like reasonable doubt or even the evidence of wrongdoing.

Bryant finds himself in the deadly shadow of a racial catastrophe that was burned into the nation's collective psyche: the O.J. Simpson case. The disappointments and frustrations of that twisted drama have set the stage for Bryant's prosecution in the court of public opinion, and most likely in the legal arena as well. Black and white reactions to the Simpson case made it seem as if each group lived in bitterly opposed worlds of racial perception. Early polls in the Bryant case mirror this trend: blacks are much more likely than whites to think that the charge against Bryant is false. And although 40 percent of whites are "very" or "somewhat" sympathetic to Bryant, nearly two-thirds of blacks feel that way. One can hardly be blamed for spotting in some whites' insistence on Bryant's guilt a hunger for revenge of the Simpson verdict.

When the mainstream embraced Bryant, it did so because of his athletic genius, his good looks, his magnetic smile, his clean image, his easy rapport with the public—and, as with Simpson, because of the widely shared belief that he has transcended race, or more to the point, that he has escaped the stigma of blackness. (Let's not forget that Bryant has been hailed for being the Anti-Iverson, peeling away the thug image glued to the Philadelphia 76ers corn-rowed, tattooed, and hip-hop loving superstar. In addition, Bryant is considered a "Renaissance man" because he is fluent in Italian, even as the more impressive multilingual talent of athletes like Hakeem Olajuwon and Dikembe Mutombo is discounted because their roots, and the source of their mastery, are African). Like Michael Jordan before him, and Simpson before them both, Bryant made millions by making it safe for whites to consume blackness.

It remains to be seen whether Bryant will fall from grace as wildly and sharply as Simpson did after his acquittal on murder charges. But the two are joined in grisly solidarity because a white woman screams from the heart of their crises. An alleged crime against a white woman also led them both to embrace blackness in a manner they either never knew or had long forgotten. One of the first things Simpson did after he found his freedom was to descend on a Los Angeles soul food eatery.

Because his tribulation has just begun, Bryant is not yet desperate to deepen his ties to loyal blacks. But he is already "blacker" than he was before tragedy struck, in part because his problems reveal racial cleavage in public opinion, and because, to many, he has proved to be no better than the athletes to whom he was once favorably compared—and indeed, he might now be seen as much worse. Perhaps most striking, Bryant has publicly identified with the greatest symbol of black struggle. At an awards show where he was named favorite male athlete of American teens, Bryant paraphrased Martin Luther King, Jr., while alluding to his troubles: "An injustice anywhere is an injustice everywhere." It is too soon to tell whether, in the spirit of the song that carried the civil rights movement, Bryant can overcome.

PART SEVEN

AFRO-BAPTIST
RADICALISM AND RHETORIC

A number of groups have compared their social activism to the valiant example of the black church to bolster the moral stature of their struggles, from those who protest legal abortion to conservatives who oppose affirmative action. Much of this comparison has been wretchedly ill-informed, driven more by political expediency than a genuine embrace of the spirit of resistance to injustice that, at its best, characterizes the black church. From before the nation's founding until the present day, religious rhetoric has been heard in sacred and secular circles as leaders expressed the moral and political dimensions of black religious belief. Among the greatest voices for social change have been black Christian Baptists, most notably Martin Luther King, Jr., who have articulated to the nation the stirring themes of Afro-Baptist radicalism. Both the rhetoric, and the radical social thought, of black Baptists is worthy of greater study.

Fifteen

"GOD ALMIGHTY HAS SPOKEN FROM WASHINGTON, D.C.": AMERICAN SOCIETY AND CHRISTIAN FAITH

A version of this chapter was first presented at a conference entitled the First Amendment and Religion, held in 1991 at the DePaul University Law School, in response to a paper by the formidable theological ethicist Stanley Hauerwas. Hauerwas, named in 2001 by Time *magazine as "America's best theologian," was also praised by the magazine as "contemporary theology's foremost intellectual provocateur." Hauerwas is a brilliant thinker whose mind ranges across an impressively wide range of subjects from medical ethics to gossip, in supporting his insistence that the gospel prophetically preach to liberal society rather than tailor its demands to the political order. In the present chapter, I argue that the black religious tradition offers a powerful example of the redemptive relationship between religious belief and social transformation. Although, as this chapter makes clear, Hauerwas and I have some serious differences of belief about religion and the public square, I consider him one of the bravest voices in Christendom, and one of the greatest theological minds of the last half of the twentieth century.*

As usual Stanley Hauerwas (this time with Michael Baxter) has, in "The Kingship of Christ: Why Freedom of 'Belief' Is Not Enough," given us a great deal to think about in wrestling with the persistent problems growing out of the church–state debate. Arguing that there are irresolvable tensions between American society and Christian faith, the authors deliver a tough rebuke to those theologians who "posit some kind of harmony between the two by means of a so-called church–state theory."[1] The authors further maintain that most Christian theologians conspire to "privatize and subordinate Christianity," especially when they assume that "Christianity consists of a set of beliefs (mere belief) that can be abstracted from practices and actions (conduct)."[2] The danger, as the authors see it, is that Christian belief gets removed from its legitimate social context in the church and becomes conceived as a matter of individual freedom. The remedy that Hauerwas and Baxter propose is for Christians to reclaim their ecclesiastical and social identity as "the people who acknowledge the Kingship of Christ."[3]

One need not accept (and indeed I don't) the authors' arguments about the value and function of church–state debates in discussions of religious freedom to affirm that the Kingship of Christ is crucial for the health of Christian churches. Still, I remain deeply suspicious of their claims about the social form that best serves and expresses Christian belief. Their arguments about the church's role in society suffer from the same flight from social embodiment that they claim characterizes their opponents in the church–state debate. And the intellectual road Hauerwas and Baxter travel inductively from their conclusion of Christ's Kingship—leading through arguments about freedom and political practice, the insuperable conflicts introduced by church–state debates, and the relation of civil religion to authentic Christian belief—is marked by signs of confusing detours and confounding dilemmas.

In my response to Hauerwas and Baxter's position, I will show how their narrow focus on secondary, less helpful issues in the history of church–state debates obscures more compelling and primary points of concern that have a better chance of illumining these debates. Then I will show how Hauerwas and Baxter's views of religious indifferentism rest on faulty analogies between free speech and freedom of religion, reveal an inadequate theory of politics, and are plagued by insurmountable dilemmas. In the end, their worries about indifferentism pale in comparison to the specter of irrelevance posed by Hauerwas and Baxter's beliefs to the lives of everyday Christians perplexed by the right relation between religion and politics.

Finally, I will argue that their understanding of the Christian tradition implies a homogeneous idea of faith that excludes from consideration other relevant examples of the relation between church and society that might challenge or support their views. Among other helpful models, the example of the prophetic black church presents a vital vision of the relationship between faith and politics that preserves Christian identity while expanding the possibilities of democracy, an unjustifiable task for Christians from Hauerwas's point of view, but a central claim of black prophetic Christianity.[4]

Hauerwas and Baxter's misgivings about the First Amendment in their present essay derive partially from a narrow interpretation of church–state relations by columnist George Will.[5] As Hauerwas and Baxter explain, for Will the "heart of the constitutional understanding of 'religion,'" is the "distinction between 'conduct' and 'mere belief.'"[6] According to the authors, Will elaborates this distinction by saying that the Founding Fathers sought to avoid the religious controversies that plagued Europe by establishing in religion's stead the commercial republic of capitalism. Influenced by John Locke, who maintained that the truth of religion cannot be established by reason, Thomas Jefferson shaped the American doctrine of the free exercise of religions, which made religions private and subordinate to the political order. As long as religion is mere belief and private, the logic goes, it is free and unrestricted. But when it becomes a matter of conduct or behavior, religion is subject to the rule of law. For Will, this represents the Founders' genius; for Hauerwas and Baxter, it is sheer anathema, an intolerable rub.

But Will has a severely limited and self-serving view of the First Amendment. Even if we acknowledge the distinctions many Founders made between belief and behavior, we are not automatically bound to Will's interpretation of their views. Indeed Hauerwas and Baxter's worries are legitimate only if Will's argument about the Founders' beliefs turns out to be the crucial distinction in the constitutional view of religion. But the most important distinction is not between conduct and mere belief, but between freedom of conscience and the coercion to believe. This distinction is made clear when we carefully consider in historical context the easily misinterpreted terms of James Madison and Thomas Jefferson, the prime architects of the constitutional concept of freedom of religion.

James Madison, who contributed key phrases to the important Virginia Declaration of Rights, an exemplary document defending freedom of religion, proposed the language of the First Amendment that was eventually revised and enacted by the First Congress.[7] In proposing the First Amendment, Madison was as greatly influenced by the suffering of religious dissenters at the hands of the Church of England as by enlightenment ideals of reason's superiority and the doctrine of natural rights.[8] These ideals led Madison to declare that religion "can be directed only by reason and conviction."[9] And the brutal battles fought over religious freedom led him to conclude that "all men are equally entitled to the free exercise of religion according to the dictates of conscience."[10]

Such religious battles also convinced Madison that religious belief must not be established or imposed by the state. This was especially true for a revealed religion like Christianity, whose claims to the exclusive possession of truth also opened the possibility of religiously justified claims to political power.[11] To circumvent this possibility in the embryonic nation, Christianity had to be shorn of its potential political authority, a strategy achieved by challenging Christianity's biblical authority and asserting its status as a reason-governed discourse, a transformation that profoundly shaped Madison's views of religion, and Jefferson's as well.[12]

Indeed, Jefferson, in the strong embrace of Lockean liberalism, natural rights philosophy, and enlightenment rationality, also rejected Christianity's status as revelation.[13] With Madison and other similarly enlightened men, Jefferson declared religion to be a matter of opinion.[14] This view led him to proclaim that, should the neighbors of Americans say that there are twenty gods, or no God, such a statement would neither "break their legs or pick their pockets," precisely because it is not backed by the force of law.[15] For Jefferson and the Founders, such an opinion is distinguished from officially established and recognized beliefs. Since the government is derived from the natural rights of human beings and not divine revelation, such opinions would neither mandate punishment nor require exceptional protection for their utterance. To act otherwise, as if the religious opinion that there was no God or that there were twenty gods could cause injury to be inflicted upon its bearer, is to acknowledge that such an utterance fractured a legally sanctioned belief about God. But this would be contrary to the constitutional view of religion.

And more important for the fledgling nation, Christianity was no longer to be protected from challenge or dissent under cover of legal sanction. Thus, the interests of nonbelievers, unorthodox believers, and dissenting Christians converged around the disestablishment of religion and the establishment of religious freedom. In view of this history, the central distinction in the constitutional view of religion is indeed between freedom of conscience and the coercion to believe. Hauerwas and Baxter's acceptance of Will's distinction between mere belief and conduct as the primary constitutional religious issue causes them to overlook the bitter cultural and interpretive wars fought over the freedom of religion by citizens oppressed by the intolerant behavior of the established church. By viewing the issue of the freedom of religion in relation to the historical events I have just sketched, Hauerwas and Baxter might be led to accentuate the struggles of oppressed Christians and other citizens against the power of the church when it is officially entrenched by law in a classic Constantinian contract with the state.[16] Ironically, the Constantinian compromise of the church is a favorite theme of Hauerwas's ethical reflections, and invites vigorous exposition in the present context.[17] But Hauerwas and Baxter's pursuit of a less important constitutional distinction has diverted their attention from a suitable occasion to press one of Hauerwas's more powerful charges.

Even a cursory reading of the events precipitating the development of the First Amendment suggests that it was a brilliantly preemptive and bloodless resolution of religious conflict. By disestablishing religion and establishing religious freedom, the Founders translated an a priori denial of privilege to any one religion in particular as the principle for extending privilege to them all. The crucial distinction in the constitutional view of religion is the one between enforced religious views and the freedom to practice the religion of one's choice or community. Viewing the freedom of religion debate in this manner allows us to understand what really was at stake for citizens who endured hardship because of their opposition to the politically protected claims of official and legal Christianity.

But Hauerwas and Baxter's silence on this aspect of the church–state debate is rooted perhaps in a presumption of the homogeneity of the Christian experience, a point I will take up in greater detail later. For now, it is enough to say that the freedom of religion debate pointed to the vibrant religious diversity, especially within Christianity itself, that was mocked by the rigid constraints and narrow practices of the Church of England and by established religion in the colonies. Established religion defined the church in the singular, but the existence of New Light Presbyterians, Strict Congregationalists, Separate Baptists, and even Methodists demanded that it be reconceived in the plural.[18]

Conflicts created by the quest for the tolerance of religious pluralism is an inescapably key theme that must be addressed in any credible account of the events surrounding and leading to the First Amendment. Their avoidance is certain to lead to truncated and self-serving versions of events that shaped, in principle, the democratic destiny of our nation. Indeed, the religious question played a crucial role "in the beginning of free government. No question was then more important, none played so prominent a role in the thought of the pertinent theorists—Hobbes, Locke, Spinoza, Bayle, and, to a lesser but still significant extent, even Montesquieu—and even if it could be said that they solved it, or answered it, in principle, it was left to the American Founders to be the first to solve it, or to try to solve it, in practice.[19]

Of course, as Hauerwas and Baxter's discussion of *Employment Division, Dept. of Human Resources of the State of Oregon v. Smith and Black* proves, freedom of religion has met limitations in the form of state proscription of religious beliefs that intersect the nebulous area between important aspects of law and faith. We have also seen the opposite effect in the case of the Jonestown mass suicides, where the failure of state intervention in the name of freedom of religion perhaps inadvertently aided the economic and religious exploitation and deaths of over nine hundred persons.[20] But uses of freedom of religion have largely safeguarded the religious liberties of faith communities to pursue the practice of their beliefs in a society where religious prejudice, bigotry, and intolerance were not given legal underpinning.

The glaring exception, of course, is chattel slaves, who were for most of their enslavement legally barred from free worship without white supervision. But even black Christians came to cherish the First Amendment because it protected their hard-won freedom to worship without governance, while also giving legal expression to their concern that other groups not suffer similar penalties of social and religious intolerance. The formulation of the First Amendment by the Founders presented a tenable solution to the religious suffering created by the legalization of Christianity. It may be cogently argued that with the First Amendment, a large and vital Christian purpose was served, that the ideals of Christian love and tolerance were ironically promoted through the government's refusal to cede Christianity official status. By keeping believers from maiming one another over religious dispute, the government instituted in law what Christian belief aimed for in principle but failed to practice. It would not be the last time the government intervened in the face of the failure of Christians to act on their beliefs, a topic about which I shall have more to say later.

Overall the First Amendment has been very good for Christianity. It forced Christian churches to appeal to potential adherents on the basis of persuasive preaching, sound theology, superior ways of life, and sacrificial action.[21] Once they were cut from the strings of official obligation, independent Christian churches were free to prophetically address the state and to criticize practices that were offensive to moral principles to which churches strongly adhered. The benefits of the separation of church and state are nicely summarized by John Bennett, who says that it fulfills the "need of religious institutions to be free from control by the state," that it satisfies the "need to protect citizens from interference with their religious liberty" by either state power or religious groups, and that it "is favorable to the health and vitality of churches."[22]

The alarm set off in Hauerwas and Baxter by Will's insistence that the free exercise of religion rests on religion's privatization and subordination is largely unnecessary. Perhaps we can reach a clearer understanding if we examine the two terms of Will's contention separately. To proclaim that religion will not carry the weight of law by being disestablished is not the same as saying religion will be made private.[23] It is very important not to collapse the two as Will has done, a move Hauerwas and Baxter fail to challenge. Indeed, many of the Founders promoted the advantage of the public expression of religion even as they asserted the necessity for religion's disestablishment.

Because the Founders were not orthodox Christians, the views they held about the role of religion in the republic had more to do with its preservative function in national life and its support of political institutions than its strictly redemptive role as envisioned by partisan believers.[24] Benjamin Franklin, for instance, saw the virtue of what he called "public religion," the forerunner of what we know today as civil religion.[25] Martin Marty says that by public religion Franklin "meant not the end of sects but of sectarianism, not the end of their freedoms but the increase of their duty to produce a common morality. Wherever he saw churches agreeing, he encouraged their support of the commonweal, and he opposed their spats over their peculiarities. His faith . . . was in . . . the need to do good."[26] Franklin's views resonated with other Founders, who sought to fashion a public polity based on the premise that a common moral community underlay the republic. As Marty says: "Fortunately for later America, the Founding Fathers, following the example of Franklin, put their public religion to good use. While church leaders usually forayed only briefly into the public arena and then scurried back to mind their own shops, men of the Enlightenment worked to form a social fabric that assured freedom to the several churches, yet stressed common concerns of society."[27]

George Washington, too, subscribed to a belief in the public utility of religion, asserting the link between religion and public morality as the foundation of national flourishing. In his farewell address, Washington stated:

> Of all the dispositions and habits which lead to political prosperity, religion and morality are indispensable supports. In vain would that man claim the tribute of patriotism who should labor to subvert these great pillars of human happiness, these firmest props of the duties of men and citizens. The mere politician, equally with the pious man, ought to respect and to cherish them. . . . Whatever may be conceded to the influence of refined education on minds of peculiar structure, reason and experience both forbid us to expect that national morality can prevail in exclusion of religious principle.[28]

And even Thomas Jefferson, despite his unorthodox Christian beliefs and his individualization of religious faith, demonstrated appreciation for religion's public function in the republic, especially since the proliferation of religious bodies would serve as a built-in check and balance to American religious life. According to Jefferson, the function of "several sects perform the office of a Censor morum over each other."[29] He also valued religion for lending moral support to political liberty when he queried, "And can the liberties of a nation be thought secure when we have removed their only firm basis, a conviction in the minds of the people that these liberties are the gift of God?"[30]

Of course, it is exactly the public expression of religion along these lines that disturbs Hauerwas and Baxter, who hold that national or civil religion is "counterfeit" Christianity uprooted from an account of the good. Even if one maintains this view, however, it doesn't negate the fact that there is nothing in the First Amendment that prohibits the public expression of religion, including Christianity, in the republic. Thus, as Hauerwas and Baxter present his case, Charles Taylor's arguments about religion and political life are on target: there was neither intent nor need in the separation of church and state to exclude God or religion from the republic.

Similarly, the subordination of religion to the political order is not as bad as Hauerwas and Baxter deem it to be, because it doesn't mean what they fear it to imply. I have already hinted at my response earlier by suggesting that one virtue of the separation of church and state is Christianity's enhanced potential to address the state on politically independent terms. But Will's claim is also legitimate, that religion was to be made subordinate to the political order. The tension that arises from these apparently contradictory claims can be relieved by examining the two ways in which we can read religious subordination: either functionally or morally.

First, since American society was deliberately constructed upon secular principles to avoid the fatal conflicts occasioned by established religion in the England of the Founders' recent memory, the subordination of religion to the state went hand in hand with the creation of the nation and the establishment of the freedom of religion. Saying that religion is subordinate to the political order is the positive statement of its more generally repeated negative formulation: that religion will not be established, or politically justified, in American society. What is meant is that religion will not function officially to adjudicate national disputes, will not occupy legal status to enforce civil codes, and will not be the means by which social goods are distributed. These functions are left to the political realm. Hence, in a legal sense, religion is functionally subordinate to politics.

On the other hand, if by subordinate it is meant that religion will surrender its independence to the political order to merely justify, or even sanctify, its practices; that religion will abdicate its role as critic of governmental and state practices; that religion will no longer provide moral visions and ethical principles by which advocates of justice may call society to judgment, then religion is without question morally insubordinate to and politically independent of the political realm. Its functional subordination by no means entails its moral subordination.

The difference is that functional subordination is the very premise by which American religions can claim their freedom to express faith and exercise their belief, especially in the social and public sphere. But moral insubordination is the way religions preserve their integrity and viability and perform their real worth to the republic by calling it to judgment in relation to their specific moral visions.

Moreover, as I will more fully argue later, if the moral visions of religion are to have public persuasion, they must be cast in terms that transcend narrow or sectarian religious language and concern, demonstrating their relevance by their prophetic judgment of, or application to, the nation in compelling public terms.[31]

Given these distinctions, Hauerwas and Baxter's worries that religion becomes private and subordinate to the state in the First Amendment are dissolved when we bring more precision to our understanding of the terms of religion's relation to the state. If Hauerwas and Baxter's real concern is to resist the privatization and moral subordination of Christianity, their fight is not with constitutional views of religion, but with forms of Christian experience and belief that claim that the church's most perfect social expression is limited to ecclesial expressions, as Hauerwas and Baxter proclaim.

Ironically, then, it is Hauerwas and Baxter who turn out to be the real opponents of the full social embodiment of Christianity. By refusing to acknowledge the legitimate expression of Christian faith outside the perimeters of the church, Hauerwas and Baxter contribute to a fatal narrowing of religious belief, a position that has led to Hauerwas being characterized (fairly I think) as a sectarian.[32] Their sectarian belief conflicts with Hauerwas and Baxter's intent to resist the privatization, and indirectly, the subordination of Christianity.

Their views also lead them to deemphasize the crucial features of the church–state debate that have the best chance to illumine the historical conflicts over religious tolerance, plurality, difference, and diversity, issues that also clearly affect our contemporary religious and cultural scene. More important, their position also reduces the potential impact of the gospel on the lives of Christians struggling to understand the proper role of faith in contemporary political debates.

Hauerwas and Baxter's deficiencies are further magnified in the way they make analogies between freedom of speech and freedom of religion in pressing their case. Drawing on an essay by Stanley Fish, the authors claim that just as freedom of speech has paved the way for "indifferentism" in speech, so freedom of religion has led to "religious indifferentism." According to Hauerwas and Baxter, Fish claims that speech has become a matter of indifference because it has been severed from an account of the good that assigns value to "free speech," which in reality has built-in limits against those expressions its exponents deem harmful to its flourishing.

In this view, freedom of speech is really an illusion. Furthermore, all the distinctions that Will made about religion find analogous expression in "a private sphere not only of speech and ideas, but also of 'mere speech' and 'mere ideas,' of speech and ideas understood apart from any substantive account of the good which they serve."[33] The same holds for religion. As Hauerwas and Baxter say, "Inherent in Christian convictions is a substantive account of the good," an account that is in tension with "all so-called 'political' accounts of the good."[34] Moreover, when political accounts of the good underwrite a vision of God and Christianity that are rooted in civil religion, there is conflict with genuine Christianity. Hauerwas and Baxter state that when Christianity gets separated from its embodied social form,

Christian belief becomes "asocial" and degenerates into mere belief, while a "counterfeit" religion, a religion of the nation, rises to take Christianity's place.

On the face of it—judging from the passages they cite—Hauerwas and Baxter's use of Fish's work appears consonant with their project, an act of untroubled appropriation. But closer reading of Fish's essay suggests that there are irresolvable tensions between his views and Hauerwas and Baxter's, tensions that have to do primarily with theological presumptions in Fish's work that are diametrically opposed to Hauerwas and Baxter's beliefs. Such tensions place Hauerwas and Baxter in a confounding dilemma. As a result, for Hauerwas and Baxter to successfully adopt Fish's arguments, they will either have to substantially alter their positions or give up their present beliefs about the appropriate social expression of Christian faith.

The tensions between Fish's analysis and Hauerwas and Baxter's use of it are glimpsed in Fish's discussion of the possible objections to his view of free speech as articulated by its defenders. What the defenders of free speech could say, Fish hypothesizes, is that he has not appropriately anticipated future revisions to his specific account of the good for which speech stands, thus prematurely closing possible valid interpretations to future generations: "My mistake, it could be said, is to equate the something in whose service speech is with some locally espoused value (e.g., the end of racism, the empowerment of disadvantaged minorities), whereas in fact we should think of that something as a now inchoate shape . . . we cannot now know . . . and therefore we must not prematurely fix it in ways that will bind successive generations to error."[35] But Fish demurs from this position on the First Amendment, saying that it "continues in a secular form the Puritan celebration of millenarian hopes, but it imposes a requirement so severe that one would expect more justification than is usually provided."[36] Fish continues: "The requirement is that we endure whatever pain racist and hate speech inflicts for the sake of a future whose emergence we can only take on faith. In a specifically religious vision like Milton's, this makes perfect sense (it is indeed the whole of Christianity), but in the context of a politics that puts its trust in the world and not in the Holy Spirit, it raises more questions than it answers."[37]

For Fish, this alternative to his view makes "perfect sense" only if it is rooted in a Christian interpretation of events that he implies does not prevail in our culture, or at least not in the political realms where decisions about the First Amendment are debated and resolved. Such a Christian interpretation of events, which would counsel enduring the present penalties imposed by free speech, could only be supported by belief in a future guaranteed by religious faith. Moreover, such a Christian perspective is only coherent within a political framework that puts its trust in the Holy Spirit. Thus, the key features of this opposing view to Fish's position are dependent upon the premises of a religious worldview to make its claims cogent.

Also, such a religious perspective would influence the political expression of the alternative to Fish's position, and could therefore in no way be identical to his views of free speech or, by extension, free religion. As Fish has already indicated, one such crucial difference between his position and its alternative might be that free speech in the abstract must be protected, even though it means the present and concrete suffering by blacks and minorities, because of a future disclosure of truth that in retrospect will alter how we perceive present suffering. The good to be revealed in the future guaranteed by faith, we can infer, will compensate for, or at least justify, the present suffering.

The point is that Fish's view is predicated upon an explicitly secular view that would seem to severely contradict Hauerwas and Baxter's views. The sorts of evidence that count in the realm of faith will not do for the secular realm—the requirement, as Fish says, is too severe. The opposite is also true, that the sorts of evidence sufficient in the secular realm will not wash in the realm of faith. The severe requirement that Fish cannot imagine bearing derives from its linkage to a Christian worldview where evidence is supplied by faith and trust in the Holy Spirit. This latter alternative—which Fish says requires that we acknowledge "the (often grievous) consequences, but that we . . . suffer them in the name of something that cannot be named"—is the second of two unacceptable alternatives (and the one not mentioned by Hauerwas and Baxter) to his position. The first is the alternative Hauerwas and Baxter do mention, the position that makes speech inconsequential and a matter of indifference.

This second alternative to Fish's position seems ideally suited for Hauerwas and Baxter, and given their religious outlook—which emphasizes the social expression of Christianity in the church and opposition to secular liberal society as the "politics that know not God"[38]—the one that they would logically adopt. The only problem is that by adopting such a view Hauerwas and Baxter immediately face a dilemma. In accepting the religious basis of society signified by trust in the Holy Spirit and the Kingship of Christ, they are identified with a position that Fish claims is opposed to the sort of secular logic that clinches the case that he makes for speech inconsequentialism and that Hauerwas and Baxter by analogy extend to religious indifferentism. On the other hand, if Hauerwas and Baxter reject the secular logic of Fish's position, they have destroyed the basis of their argument for the indifferentism of freedom of religion and would have to forfeit their claim that it has corrupted the church–state debate, because it is rooted in the sort of reasoning they find offensive to Christian belief. Either way, Hauerwas and Baxter are caught in a damning dilemma.

There is yet another point of tension between Hauerwas and Baxter and Fish. Fish contends that both alternatives to his views—speech as inconsequential, and present suffering for the sake of a nameless something—are unpersuasive. But he admits that "many in the society seemed to have bought them."[39] Why? Because such persons avoid facing

what they take to be the alternative. That alternative is politics, the realization (at which I have already hinted) that decisions about what is and is not protected in the realms of expression will rest not on principle or firm doctrine but on the ability of persons and groups to so operate (some would say manipulate) the political process that the speech they support is labeled "protected" while the speech inimical to their interests is declared to be fair game.[40]

To those who respond that politics would render the First Amendment a "dead letter," or that it deprives us of norms in determining "when and what speech to protect," or that it effaces the distinction between speech and action, Fish argues for the primacy of politics.[41] Fish responds that

> the First Amendment has always been a dead letter if one understood its "liveness" to depend on the identification and protection of a realm of "mere" expression or discussion distinct from the real of regulatable conduct; that the distinction between speech and action has always been effaced in principle, although in practice it can take whatever form the prevailing political conditions mandate; that we have never had any normative guidance for marking off protected and unprotected speech; rather, that the guidance we have had has been fashioned (and refashioned) in the very political struggles over which it then (for a time) presides.[42]

In sum, for Fish the "name of the game has always been politics, even when (indeed, especially when) it is played by stigmatizing politics as the area to be avoided."[43]

As if Hauerwas and Baxter's arguments were not already on the ropes because of their earlier dilemma, this last argument of Fish's deals a fatal blow to their aspirations to make Christianity social but not political, especially because so much of their argument hinges on the effective correlation between Fish's views on free speech and the conclusions Hauerwas and Baxter draw from them about the perils of free religion. Fish explicitly endorses politics as the means by which claims of free speech are made intelligible and cogent, precisely because politics has been the implicit basis of understanding and applying the amendment from the very beginning. The same, presumably, should hold for the application of politics to free religion claims. But Hauerwas and Baxter are unwilling to cede the primacy of politics in making the claims of Christianity cogent or in adjudicating religious conflict, which is the obvious application of Fish's position to their own. Again, they are faced with a dilemma: if they give up politics, they give up the punch line to Fish's arguments, severely compromising the force of his contentions and, by extension, their arguments. But if they adopt politics, they abort their arguments about the primacy of a confessional God and ecclesial religion to politics. Either way, a principle they cherish is surrendered.

In some places in their essay, it appears that Hauerwas and Baxter will stick with Fish all the way through. They say that with "the indifferentism which inevitably ensues when speech is considered apart from the Good, 'freedom of speech' enjoys a protection in the United States according to arbitrary patterns of political influence and power as much as according to any consistent application of constitutional principles."[44] It seems as though they are on the verge of acknowledging that value-laden, good-dependent notions of free speech, and by analogy free religion, need to be negotiated by politics, which in this case amounts to the struggle to assign value to goods defined in the abstract.

But Hauerwas and Baxter dismiss such hopes by saying that only "within the ecclesial context, that is, only within a context in which the social landscape is imbued with the presence of Christ, can Christianity emerge as an alternative both to liberal freedom and civic freedom, and more generally, to the political project we call the United States of America."[45] For Hauerwas and Baxter, the task is to "provide an alternative vision to the political vision of America, one that is shaped by the acknowledgment that true political authority is to be found not in any republican virtues, new or ancient, nor in any set of governmental procedures, but in Jesus Christ who is our true King."[46] So much for politics!

By refusing to enter the fray, to give political justification and arguments for their beliefs about the Christian good, Hauerwas and Baxter not only repudiate their connection with the sort of social activity that Fish describes as necessary for those who refute nebulous concepts of the freedom of speech, but they also risk a more serious setback with disturbing consequences for the Christian Church: they fail to offer to everyday Christians stuck in the gritty interstices of politics adequate resources and substantive recommendations for moving beyond paralysis, confusion, or wrong practice. Just when Christians caught in the punishing political dilemmas of contemporary society need a note of reveille, retreat is sounded. Thus, the most harmful effect of Hauerwas and Baxter's views of free speech and free religion may not be the indifferentism they worry over, but the sheer irrelevance of their views to the church to which they are committed.

This irrelevance is pegged on the peculiar social but apolitical vision Hauerwas and Baxter have of Christian faith. By failing to take politics seriously, they can do little more than lament, for instance, the loss of rights by Smith and Black in the Supreme Court case they cite. At best, they can make intellectual moves to reject the distinctions that have made religion a matter of indifference. Because they refuse to engage a public beyond the church, Hauerwas and Baxter have little chance to affect the manner in which discussion is formed around these issues in the public sphere. More poignantly, Hauerwas and Baxter's modus operandi cannot affect future legal and political decisions that similarly impact other citizens' lives and their freedom of religious beliefs.

Hauerwas and Baxter's problems are also rooted in yet a third dimension of their discussion of religious indifferentism that they themselves seem not to take seriously: a substantive account of the good that is the background to their notion of Christian faith. Not only should speech have an account of the good, as Hauerwas and Baxter contend, but by extension of their analogy between free speech and free religion, so should Christian faith. The point here is not to highlight an account of the good to which Christian faith can be said to generally refer—Christian love, peace, or justice, for instance—but to elaborate the specific cultural contexts and social visions that have decisively shaped and made possible specific faith communities. I suspect this is not high on Hauerwas and Baxter's agenda because their procedures and assumptions imply a homogeneity about the Christian faith that masks the social roots and cultural contexts of the ecclesial embodiment of religious belief.

Hauerwas and Baxter's approach mutes the radical diversity and complex pluralism within the Christian faith, a situation that long ago made it untenable in certain sociological and theological senses to speak primarily of The Church.[47] Because of their procedures, Hauerwas and Baxter have failed to take into consideration, or even argue against, an expression of Christian faith that has creatively confronted many of the problems discussed by the authors: the black church.[48] By turning now to this example, I intend to illumine the relation between religion and politics in one of the most helpful but neglected models available.

Black Christian churches have had quite a different approach to the First Amendment than the position argued by Hauerwas or Baxter, largely because of the prominence of legal issues in determining the status, fate, and humanity of African-Americans for much of our history. And with the central importance of religion to African-American culture, the strong and vital connections between civil and religious concerns has been well established. Not only has religion helped sustain black survival in times of racial and national crisis, but it has furnished principles and persons to justify black claims to equal humanity and social justice in government, church, and school.[49]

Although it is by now common to cite the black Christian experience in debates about the relationship between religion and politics, the black church is rarely viewed as a genuine source of information about these matters in ways that count. As Cornel West has stated:

> Ironically, the black church experience is often invoked as an example of the religion/politics fusion, but rarely as a source to listen to or learn from. Instead, it is simply viewed as an instance that confirms the particular claims put forward by the respective sides. The black experience may no longer be invisible, but it remains unheard—not allowed to speak for itself, to be taken seriously as having something valuable to say.[50]

The black church view of the relationship between religion and politics has roots in the denominational affiliations that shaped it, the ongoing experiences of oppression in national life that black religion ceaselessly addresses, and broad experiments in American civil religion.

Black Christians are overwhelmingly Baptist and Methodist, a legacy that extends back to slave culture.[51] Because it was illegal to baptize and preach to slaves during much of slavery, the process of exposing slaves to Christianity was gradual.

As slaves were eventually incorporated into Christianity on limited terms in the mid-1700s, they were deeply affected by Methodists and especially by Separate Baptists. The Separate Baptists were viewed with suspicion by both the established church and society at large during their initial stages of growth in the early 1700s.[52] Deeply disinherited, poor, without formal training, and broadly suspicious of external authority, the Separate Baptists naturally appealed to slaves who were even more ostracized from American culture than the Baptists because of their legal status as personal property.

But as they grew, Separate Baptists continued to exhibit two traits that marked their early years: their opposition to slavery and their enthusiastic leadership of the fight against established religion.[53] Thus, at the base of the denomination to which slaves were overwhelmingly drawn, and in which they eventually established independent churches in the mid-1800s, was an emphasis on the strong relation between political and civil issues and personal and communal religious belief. The arguments that radical religious dissenters made for freedom from slavery and freedom of religion prefigured the legal and social arguments advanced by black intellectuals, organizers, and leaders in the fight against institutional racism in two important ways.[54]

First, the religious dissenters' arguments expressed religious themes of social justice linked to belief in God. The arguments of Isaac Backus and John Allen against slavery and religious intolerance pictured these injustices as offenses not only to civil society, but to authentic Christian belief.[55] Second, although their arguments were unquestionably motivated by religious concern, dissenters cast their arguments in the language of civic piety and civil responsibility in making moral claims on the state to act justly. These two narrative strategies were adopted and ingeniously expanded by black Christians, especially the prophetic wing of the black church. This vital branch of black Christianity has relentlessly explained and justified the moral and religious claims of black Christian belief in the language of civic piety, whose vocabulary includes legal redress, moral suasion, civil rights, and political proclamation.

This last point reveals as well African-Americans' participation in and expansion of traditions of American civil religion. Although for Hauerwas and Baxter it is "counterfeit" religion, a progressive, largely liberal version of civil religion is critically celebrated within African-American prophetic Christianity.[56] As Charles Long says, "The distinction between civil religion and church religion is not one that looms large for us."[57] He continues:

> In the first place, it is the overwhelming reality of the white presence in any of its various forms that becomes the crucial issue. Whether this presence was legitimated by power executed illegally, or whether in institution or custom, its reality, as far as blacks were concerned through most of their history, carried the force of legal sanction enforced by power. The black response to this cultural reality is part of the civil rights struggles in the history of American blacks.[58]

Long further argues that it is not incidental that black churches have been the locus of civil rights struggle because it "represented the black confrontation with an American myth that dehumanized the black person's being."[59] Furthermore, the "location of this struggle in the church enabled the civil rights movement to take on the resources of black cultural life," such as organization, music, artistic expression, and proficiency in collecting limited economic resources.[60]

In appropriating and improvising upon a vocabulary of civic piety, black Christians have appealed to the sacred symbols of national life and its democratic principles, which find literate expression in the Constitution and the Declaration of Independence. Perhaps the most famous example of this long-standing black church tradition is symbolized in the brilliant career of Martin Luther King Jr. Like his Separate Baptist predecessors and his Black Baptist ancestors, King employed the language of civic piety (particularly civil rights) in articulating at once the goals of African-American religion and a version of liberal democracy.[61] Although he remained rooted in his religious base, King transcended the narrow focus of sectarian and myopic religious concerns to embrace a universal moral perspective in addressing, first, the specific suffering of black Americans and, eventually, the economic exploitation and racial oppression of other "minorities."

But King's genius lay in his ability to show how increased democracy for African-Americans served the common good by making democracy hew closer to its ideals than its performance in the distant and recent past suggested. King spoke a language of civic piety (especially civil rights) that resonated with crucial aspects of American moral self-understanding, particularly since such self-understanding was closely linked to ideals of justice, freedom, and equality. King and his colleagues creatively reinterpreted documents of ultimate importance in national life—particularly the Declaration of Independence and the Constitution—in extending the goods at which they aimed (including democracy, justice, and equality) to blacks and others excluded from their original intent.[62]

Shaped profoundly by the black Christian Church and rooted in black theological perspectives on love, justice, equality, and freedom articulated in the rich history of black resistance to racism, King and his cohorts forged empowering connections between their religious beliefs and the social, civic, and legal goals to which they believed their faith committed them. Indeed, they translated their religious efforts into the language with the best chance to express their goals in the national arena. For the black church, justice is what love sounds like when it speaks in public, civic piety is love's public language, equality its tone of voice, and freedom its constant pitch. For Hauerwas and Baxter, such translation may prove problematic, but for black Christians it has meant survival.

Such acts of translation also rest on the black Christian belief that the entire world belongs to God, that religious truth is not bound to the sanctuary, and that God often employs apparently disinterested or even hostile persons, forces, and institutions to achieve the divine prerogative. This truth can be partially glimpsed in the popularity of the scripture "You meant evil against me; but God meant it for good."[63] This often quoted passage forms one of the most visible hermeneutic strategies employed in the black church, one that reflects a strong doctrine of providence and a serviceable theodicy geared toward black survival and a momentous confrontation with suffering and evil.

For prophetic black Christians, not only is speaking the language of civil society not taboo, but the messages of God are likewise not limited to homiletical proclamation, theological discourse, or other ecclesial expressions of God talk. Since the world belongs to God, and the powers that exist, even if evil intentioned, may have good consequences in the eyes of faith, God can use whatever forum necessary to deliver divine gift or judgment. This whole theological approach is implicit in the statement by a jubilant black person who, upon hearing of the 1956 Supreme Court decision declaring segregated transportation in Montgomery, Alabama, unconstitutional, exclaimed, "God Almighty has spoken from Washington, D.C."[64] For black Christians, God is the original and ultimate polyglot. The language of civic piety (especially civil rights) serves God's purposes, as does the language of theological study and religious devotion. Thus, the civil rights movement helped foster a progressive understanding of the relation between religion and politics that rested on precedents of such interaction in American civil religion.

I have given this severely abbreviated genealogy and justification of the positive relation of religion to politics in African-American Christianity to suggest the rich resources it contains for critical thinking about the relation between church and society. The progressive and prophetic black church, as I have sketched it here, rejects the premises of Hauerwas and Baxter's arguments about the relation of faith and politics. Faith has a large part to play in the public arena, but only if it will redescribe its goals in languages that are publicly effective, accompanied by the politics with the best chance to make those goals concrete and relevant. Black Christianity avoids attempts to impose Christianity on the world, a strategy as old as religious establishment and as new as national attempts to manipulate God for political favor.[65] Rather, it retains the strengths and insights of religious belief while making arguments for the common good and public interest that are subject to criticism and open to revision because they are neither final nor infallible.

Its history prevents black Christianity from endorsing Hauerwas and Baxter's pessimistic views about the ability of Christian faith to mix with politics without losing its soul, without surrendering its capacity to criticize liberal democracy. Hauerwas and Baxter are right to remind us that Christian faith is in perennial tension with all political accounts of the good. Indeed, the history of African-American prophetic Christianity is the story of the relentless criticism of failed American social practices, the constant drawing attention to conflicts between political ideals and realities, and the ageless renewal of a commitment to broaden the bounds of liberty so that democracy is both noun and adjective, both achievement and process. But some political accounts of the good are better than others, and only those Christian communities willing to risk the erosion and expansion of certain aspects of their Christian identity in secular affairs have the opportunity to affect the public interest for the better.

This, of course, is why Hauerwas and Baxter's views of the various problems associated with the freedom of religion are viewed suspiciously by the prophetic black Christian Church. By avoiding the nasty and brutal sphere of politics, Hauerwas and Baxter cannot adequately account for the black struggle and suffering endured to receive the freedoms the First Amendment guarantees. Black Christians have always understood that the batteries are not included, that American ideals, principles, and promises are never given, but must be secured through political struggle in the public realm. With Fish, they recognize that the "game has always been politics."[66] Hauerwas and Baxter's account not only masks the social and political roots of their own faith, but it effectively discounts the experience of black Christians who provide precisely the sort of example of the relation between church and politics that might have a chance of bringing greater clarity to this complex debate.

Finally, black prophetic Christians are wary of theological discussions that reduce the social embodiment of Christianity to the church and that portray the state as the enemy of Christian freedom. If theological justifications of slavery had not done so before, white Christian opposition to the civil rights movement chastened black Christian expectation of white Christians' moral and religious support of the goal of African-American liberation.[67] While arguing that the role of the church was to attend to the spiritual aspects of life in the church while avoiding the acrimonious and schismatic business of politics at all costs, many white Christian churches ironically furnished ideological and theological support to the forces that impeded the progress of the civil rights movement.[68]

The greater and more tragic irony, however, is that often white Christians actively opposed black progress by participating in White Citizens' Councils, the Ku Klux Klan, or other hate groups that harassed and even murdered black Christians. Even if they didn't actively participate in such heinous crimes, many white Christians "retreated into the womb of an ahistorical piety."[69] By adopting positions similar to those that Hauerwas and Baxter suggest, these white Christians were rendered impotent to affect the lives of their black Christian colleagues because their theological stance was deeply apolitical and hence unable to make claims on the public good in ways that were immediately helpful to black Christians.

Moreover, it was not the white church-qua-church that called for the end of such barbaric and evil practices or that actively intervened to prevent the murder and maiming of black life. It was the sustained social and political struggle of a tiny band of black prophetic Christians and their allies who, by sacrificial action, civil disobedience, and appeals to the American conscience by means of the language of civic piety, forced the *state* to intervene through legal and political measures. As in the religious situation of colonial America during Revolutionary times, the state intervened to prevent one group of Christians from killing others.

Once again, civil protest and political power had put into law what Christian belief had professed but failed to practice. And black Christians interpreted such intervention as an extension of the providence of God over even secular political structures, as black Christians heard God Almighty speaking from Washington, D.C. This does not mean that the state is uncritically praised as the unwavering instrument of divine deliverance. It is, however, one of the legitimate means available to black Christians seeking to secure and protect their freedom, so long denied by law and Christian practice.

The poverty of Hauerwas and Baxter's vision of the social embodiment of Christianity becomes even more evident when they return to one of the bleakest epochs in modern Catholic Christendom, the papacy of Pope Pius XI, to draw examples of Christ's Kingship. Pope Pius XI, according to Hauerwas and Baxter, "boldly and bluntly asserts the importance of publicly recognizing and celebrating the Kingship of Christ in reconstituting the entire social order."[70] The whole point behind the feast celebrating Christ's Kingship was to emphasize that "the common good is to be defined by Christ."[71] Furthermore, Hauerwas and Baxter claim that, in opposition to Will's celebration of the secularism that led to the subordination of religion to politics, "Pope Pius XI sees such a subordination as the undoing of any true politics."[72] Finally, Pope Pius XI, according to Hauerwas and Baxter, "resists the temptation to conceive of politics in anything less than soteriological terms."[73]

But Pope Pius XI is precisely the sort of figure who is an example of Hauerwas and Baxter's worst fears: he promoted the moral subordination of Christianity to the political order. By signing a concordat with Mussolini in 1929, Pope Pius XI made Mussolini's regime the first government in modern Catholic history to receive official recognition by the Vatican, thus supplying theological justification to the dictator's murderous Fascist maneuvers.[74] Pius XI "deliberately sabotaged democracy, the strongest opponent of Communism, for the politically and morally ruinous experiment of Fascism."[75] Pius XI was also a particularly cruel foe of religious tolerance and diversity.

Pius XI facilitated the "marriage of convenience" between Catholicism and Fascism that helped to destroy the Popolari (the Christian Democratic party), the People's party, which was the second legitimate party in parliament and the only real alternative to the Fascists.[76] More viciously, he requested the resignation of priest Don Sturzo as general secretary of the Popolari, banishing him from Rome at the height of the Popolari's fight against Mussolini. After his departure, the Fascists moved to expand their efforts to "wipe out the 'white' trade-unions, co-operatives, and youth organizations."[77] Pius XI also used his proximity to Mussolini to repress the freedom of religious minorities, urging Mussolini to restrict Protestant missions in Italy and to outlaw Freemasons. Pius XI was also pleased when Mussolini prevented the building of a Muslim mosque in Rome and when the dictator persecuted Waldensians, Pentecostalists, the Salvation Army, and eventually Jews.[78] After the Concordat of 1929, Mussolini exempted priests from taxation and employed public funds to prevent the financial collapse of Catholic banks.[79]

Most appallingly, the official pact between Mussolini and Pius XI led to the Vatican's declaration that the dictator was a man "sent by providence."[80] Pius XI compromised the politically independent, socially prophetic, and morally insubordinate voice of the church by officially colluding with Mussolini's Fascist Party to stamp out democracy, restrict the religious freedom of other denominations and religions, and betray some of the church's own priests and members in an effort to placate Mussolini. As Denis Mack Smith says, Mussolini claimed that "the Church, as a result of their treaty, was no longer free but subordinate to the State."[81] During Mussolini's dictatorship, and because of Pope Pius XI's fatal compromise, this was tragically true.

The concordat with Mussolini is the infamous political legacy of Pius XI's reign. He is hardly the figure to whom we should turn in thinking about Christ's Kingship. Even Hauerwas and Baxter's statements about Pius XI's insistence on the link between soteriology and politics seems more appropriately elaborated, and less severely compromised, by contemporary exponents of that belief, especially liberation theologians.[82] And although most liberation theologians are completely committed to the radical transformation of society in light of Christ's Kingship–and are equipped with penetrating social analysis, progressive political activity, and broad historical investigation–few are willing to exclusively identify the Kingdom of Christ with the kingdom of this world. Pius XI failed to remember Hauerwas and Baxter's lesson: that Christianity is in extreme tension with all accounts of the political good.

Given Hauerwas's belief in the unity of the virtues, the choice of Pius XI–a pope who was antidemocratic, unfaithful in fateful ways to the church and its Lord, and intolerant of religious and political freedom–as the best exponent of the Kingship of Christ is not only unfortunate; it is no less than tragic.[83] But then, given the dilemmas I have shown Hauerwas and Baxter to be trapped by, and their refusal to engage the nitty-gritty world of real politics, their misled–and misleading–choice is sadly predictable.

Hauerwas and Baxter have largely missed the major areas of concern in the struggles to relate church and state, and religion and politics, because they have not viewed these matters from the perspective of those who suffered for the freedom to worship and practice their beliefs. The political struggle to implement democratic ideals in our society is the real story behind the First Amendment. It is about much more than the wall that separates church and state. If the truth be told, however, the real wall of separation most grievous to American Christianity and the Church of Christ is not between church and state; it remains the wall between black and white. About that, Hauerwas and Baxter have nothing to say.

Sixteen

GARDNER TAYLOR: THE POET
LAUREATE OF THE AMERICAN PULPIT

One of my most enjoyable moments as a writer came when I interviewed the Rev. Dr. Gardner Taylor for this profile, published first in the Christian Century, *which I serve as a contributing editor. Taylor is one of the nation's foremost preachers and certainly one of the twentieth century's homiletical giants. He preached in sanctuaries around the world and served as the president of the Progressive National Baptist Convention. And for more than forty years, Taylor was pastor of the Concord Baptist Church of Christ in Brooklyn, making it one of the legendary pulpits in American Christendom. Besides being a master wordsmith, Taylor is a man of great humility. He is also a sly wit and a sage bristling with insight and wisdom. In order to fully appreciate his many gifts, one has to hear Taylor, like all great orators, in person, or at the very least, on audio recording. I encourage readers to purchase the multivolume* The Words of Gardner Taylor, *edited by Edward L. Taylor, which features Taylor's written words accompanied by compact discs of his sermons and lectures (Judson Press).*

"GARDNER TAYLOR IS THE GREATEST PREACHER living, dead, or unborn," Wyatt Tee Walker proclaimed as he introduced Taylor in the fall of 1993 at a service marking Walker's twenty-fifth anniversary as pastor of Harlem's Canaan Baptist Church. (Walker gained fame while serving as one of Martin Luther King's trusted lieutenants.) Among black Baptists, the pastoral anniversary forms a distinct genre of religious appreciation. It is an often lavishly orchestrated event joining praise and pocketbook in feting a congregation's spiritual head.

But on the crisp October morning of his celebration, Walker shared the spotlight with the man *Time* magazine in 1980 dubbed "the Dean of the Nation's black preachers," a phrase that then New York Mayor David Dinkins would later repeat in his remarks at the service. After acknowledging Taylor's role as an adviser ("he used to tell me, 'Dave, you've got to bite bullets and butter biscuits'"), Dinkins declared Taylor's preaching could be described in "only two ways: good and better."

These free-flowing compliments might appear to be the natural excesses of a feel-good service where the spirit is high and such praise, no matter how heartfelt, is by design the order of the day. But they mirror the sentiments of many more—black and white, religious and secular, preaching authorities and laypeople—who have been entranced, even transformed, by Taylor's legendary oratorical gifts.

Taylor, however, is more modest about his protean pulpit work. When I mentioned *Time*'s declaration, he deflected the tribute with characteristic humor. "You know what they say a Dean is, at least of eastern schools?" he asks, playing me with the instincts and timing of a seasoned comic. "Somebody too smart to be president, but not smart enough to teach." He smiled, shrugged his shoulders in self-deprecation, and deadpanned, "So much for being Dean."

His humor and refreshing lack of hubris, combined with a preaching genius of extraordinary duration, have won the energetic seventy-seven-year-old Taylor a legion of admirers during his half century of ministry. Most of his career has been spent as pastor of Brooklyn's 14,000-member Concord Baptist Church of Christ. He made that pulpit perhaps the most prestigious in black Christendom before retiring in 1990 after forty-two years of service. The imposing, block-long gray brick church is a massive monument to black Christianity's continuing vitality in the midst of the well-documented decline of mainline religion. Under Taylor's leadership, Concord built a home for the aged, organized a fully accredited grade school (headed for over thirty years by Taylor's late wife, Laura), and developed the Christ Fund, a million dollar endowment for investing in the Brooklyn community.

For Taylor, his success is an example of how God works in human life. "It is as if God said 'I'm going to take this unlikely person from the Deep South and I'm going to open opportunities for him to show [the world] what I can do,'" he says.

Taylor was born poor in Baton Rouge, Louisiana, in 1918, the only son of the Rev. Washington and Selina Taylor. "My father was a huge, tall, ebony man who had no trace of anything but Africa in him," Taylor says. "And he was extraordinarily arrogant about it." By contrast, his mother "looked white." After her husband's death, Selina Taylor attended "normal school" to become a teacher, later earning a degree from Southern University through extension courses. In one of his four books of sermons, Taylor writes that despite his parents' lack of formal education, they "had a natural feel for the essential music of the English language wedded to an intimate and emotional affection for the great transactions of the Scriptures." The same is true of their son.

Although his father died before Taylor was thirteen, his father's influence, more than that of any other preacher's—especially his eloquent declamation and his wide range of reference—marks his son's preaching style. "Dad didn't finish high school, but he read voraciously. Sixty years ago, he spoke about Darwin's survival of the fittest and the battle of Thermopylae."

"Wash" Taylor enjoyed a wide reputation among Louisiana blacks for his brilliant preaching. Carl Stewart, Gardner Taylor's lifelong friend and a former basketball coach at Southern University, has for several years hosted a Baton Rouge radio show devoted exclusively to broadcasting the younger Taylor's sermons. Stewart illustrates Wash Taylor's preaching appeal by telling the story of a discussion between two Louisianans about an upcoming funeral. "'Hey, are you going to the funeral today?' one person asked. And his friend said, 'Who's dead?' And the other fella retorted, 'It really doesn't matter. Wash Taylor is preaching.'"

Despite his father's influence, Taylor attended Louisiana's Leland College in hopes of becoming a lawyer. "Clarence Darrow fascinated me," Taylor says in explaining his career choice. And because an aunt who helped raise him held the ministry in contempt, Taylor confesses that his view of religion wasn't exalted. "I didn't have the healthiest attitude about black preachers," Taylor says. "I thought preaching was a foolish way for people of normal intelligence to waste their lives."

But Taylor's plans changed dramatically when he survived a deadly automobile accident in which two white men died. Taylor experienced his "call" in that event, discerning God's claim on his life. "I thought that God must have wanted me to be his lawyer." Instead of enrolling at the University of Michigan law school where he had been admitted, Taylor ventured north to the now defunct Oberlin School of Theology. At Oberlin he read avidly, following writers ranging from Heywood Broun to Walter Lippmann. Their "literary styles affected me," he says. He also served as pastor of a church in nearby Elyria, Ohio, and after graduation, he pastored one in Baton Rouge, before being summoned at the tender age of thirty to Brooklyn's Concord Baptist Church, then with a membership of more than 5,000.

In New York Taylor joined an elite fellowship of ministers. "I don't think ever in the history of these two millennia have so many pulpit geniuses come together in one setting as I found in New York in the early '50s. . . . My God, it was unbelievable," he says. Taylor's multiracial aggregate included such preaching luminaries as Adam Clayton Powell Jr., George Buttrick, Paul Scherer, Robert McCracken, Sandy Ray, and Fulton J. Sheen. Taylor has fond memories and wonderful stories about them all.

"Adam . . . with his angry oratory . . . was withering, blazing," he says of Powell, the controversial and colorful former pastor of Abyssinian Baptist Church and a longtime congressman. "He was a bon vivant. Adam had hair he could throw over his brow." Powell's nonkinky, straight mane, along with his pale color, led to his being called "light, bright and almost white." "While we [black people] talk about the exaltation of our features, there was still [in the admiration of Powell's features] a lot left in us that adored white society," Taylor says.

"Buttrick [possessed] the poetry of the English Romantic poets. He was Wordsworth in the pulpit. He had a probing mind and relentless logic, and a gift for aphorism. For example, he said that the past ought to be a milestone, not a millstone." Paul Scherer, a former professor of homiletics at Union Theological Seminary, had a thespian bent. "Scherer was grand in manner. He had a great voice and a magnificent head of hair. As Jim Fry, a former student of his used to say, 'When Scherer said good morning, it was an occasion.'"

When Scherer was invited to deliver the prestigious Lyman Beecher Lectures at Yale University, "He said to a former classmate who was then a faculty member at Yale, 'You know, it's a great honor for them to have me here. I can't tell you how honored I feel. But why did they wait so long?'" Taylor relates, laughing at the story. Taylor delivered the 100th installment of the Beecher Lectures, which were published in 1977 as *How Shall They Preach*.

Taylor's unique blend of gifts may place him at the forefront of even this great cadre of preachers. His mastery of the technical aspects of preaching is remarkable. He brilliantly uses metaphor and has an uncanny sense of rhythmic timing put to dramatic but not crassly theatrical effect. He condenses profound biblical truths into elegantly memorable phrases. He makes keen use of parallels to layer and reinforce the purpose of his sermons. His stunning control of narrative flow seamlessly weaves his sermons together. His adroit mix and shift of cadences reflects the various dimensions of religious emotion. He superbly uses stories to illustrate profound intellectual truths and subtle repetition to unify sermons. And his control of his resonant voice allows him to pliantly whisper or prophetically thunder the truths of the gospel. What was once alleged of southern Baptist Preacher Carlyle Marney may be equally said of Taylor: he has a voice like God's—only deeper.

Taylor's commanding physical presence, hinged on a solid 6'1" frame, suggests the regal bearing of pulpit royalty. His broad face reveals seasoned character. His wide set eyes are alive to the world around him. Taylor's forehead is an artistic work of chiseled complexity. Furrows furiously cross-hatch his bronze brow, extending to the receded areas of his exposed, upper cranium where a shock of grey hair fastidiously obeys its combed direction. Taylor's massive hands are like finely etched soft leather. They function as dual promontories that stab the air in the broad sweep of pulpit gesture or clasp each other in the steadied self-containment of quiet reflection.

Taylor's snappy sartorial habits, though, hint more at Wall Street executive than Baptist preacher. For a class on homiletics that he occasionally teaches at Princeton Theological Seminary, Taylor wore a dark-blue, double-breasted wool suit with a windowpane design, a burgundy-striped shirt, and a paisley tie. And at Wyatt Walker's pastoral anniversary, he wore a charcoal-gray pin-striped suit, with a white shirt and burgundy tie.

But it is not his sharp dressing which draws most attention to Taylor. The preacher's magnetism lies in his intimate and unequalled command of the language and literature of the English-speaking pulpit.

James Earl Massey, himself a noted preacher, professor of homiletics, and dean of Anderson School of Theology in Indiana, ranks Taylor "as one of the top five unique pulpit geniuses of any generation in American life." Massey contends that the gifts such figures as Harry Emerson Fosdick, Phillips Brooks, and Henry Ward Beecher brought to the American pulpit scene, "Taylor has brought in one person." Taylor possesses Beecher's "prolix ability to spin words," Brooks's "earnestness of style and breadth of learning," and Fosdick's "ability to appeal to the masses and yet maintain a dignity in doing so."

Preaching authority Henry H. Mitchell, author of the widely cited *Black Preaching*, points to Taylor's familiarity with the preaching tradition as a key to his appeal. "He's not only master of black preaching as such. He knows all the great white preachers and quotes them [as well]."

Carolyn Knight, a professor of preaching at Union Theological Seminary and highly regarded pastor of a New York church, recalls a conversation she had with Taylor that displayed his endless pursuit of preaching excellence. "He told me last year—and he advised me to do it—that in preparation for his Beecher Lectures, he went down into the stacks of Union's library and read every set of published Beecher lectures."

Taylor's reputation as the "poet laureate of American Protestantism" is a considerable achievement. Throughout its history, black preaching has been widely viewed as a form of public address brimming with passion but lacking intellectual substance. Like black religion in general, black preaching is often seen as the cathartic expression of pent-up emotion, a verbal outpouring that supposedly compensates for low self-esteem or oppressed racial status. Not only are such stereotypes developed in ignorance of the variety of black preaching styles, but they don't take into account the black churches that boast a long history of educated clergy.

James Weldon Johnson's classic poem *God's Trombones* provides a literary glimpse of the art and imagination of the black folk preacher. C. L. Franklin's recorded sermons, spread out over sixty albums for Chess Records, brought the vigor and ecstasy of the black chanted sermon—dubbed in black church circles as "the whoop"—to the American public. By and large, however, Americans have remained insulated from the greatest rhetorical artists of the black pulpit.

Of course, broad segments of American society have sampled the richness of black preaching through the brilliant political oratory of Martin Luther King Jr. and Jesse Jackson. Both King's and Jackson's styles of public speech—their impassioned phrasing, intellectual acuity, and imaginative metaphors—reflect their roots in the black church. And their involvement in civil rights and politics extends the venerable tradition of black preachers serving as social critics and activists.

But their oratory—like that of preacher-politicians from Adam Clayton Powell to William Gray—has been shaped by the peculiar demands of public life and informed by a mission to translate the aspirations of black Americans to the larger secular society. The aims of their public speech have led them to emphasize certain elements of the black preaching and church tradition such as social justice, the institutional nature of sin, and the redistribution of wealth, while leaving aside such others as the cultivation of the spiritual life, the nurturing of church growth, and the development of pastoral theology. Such varying emphases are usually framed as the differences between "prophetic" and "priestly" religion. If the former has been most visible to American society in the guise of church-based civil rights activists, the latter has been closer to the heart of the religious experience of most black Christians.

Though Taylor has combined both approaches—he was active in the civil rights movement in New York, and was a close friend and preaching idol of Martin Luther King, Jr.—he realizes that his life work has ruled out the kind of visibility that comes from high-profile activism. "I recognized early that the [kind of] work I do is not attention grabbing. . . . When I came along . . . college presidents were the lords of black America. Later, it became civil rights [leaders]. Still later, it became [holders of] political office."

Taylor humorously admits that with every attempt he made to "do something else [other than pastor], I got trapped. . . . They put the whole board of education off when I was a member," he says. "Governor Rockefeller wiped it out."

As James Massey maintains, "Taylor has stuck with the church. He has been busy handling the themes of the gospel, busy heralding what it was that Jesus came to do. He's been busy honoring the name of his Lord, shaping a community around that name and seeking to effect society in ways that are consonant with the gospel purpose. This is not newsworthy, like leading a sit-in."

Don Matthews of Washington's First Baptist Church, the church of fellow Baptists Bill Clinton and Al Gore, agrees. "We're in a time when the pulpit and the church in general are not particularly admired by anybody else that isn't in it. The only place it is perceived as powerful is in the political world. . . . But the people who have the spiritual word to speak aren't paid much attention by the *New York Times* or the *Washington Post*."

William Augustus Jones, noted pastor of Brooklyn's Bethany Baptist Church, contends that Christians are "resident aliens" who have a radically different perspective on the world than secular citizens. "For a preacher to be regarded as popular means that his faithfulness to the word is not what it ought to be."

Ironically, Taylor's most bitter disappointments and defeats have come within the church world to which he has been single-mindedly devoted. Over dinner at Greenwich Village's popular Spanish restaurant El Charro's, Taylor, joined by his wife Laura—a shock of healthy black hair loosely pinned atop her hauntingly beautiful ebony face of high cheek bones and deep-set eyes—recalls the 1952 fire that destroyed Concord Church.

"It was devastating. And were it not for this lady I don't know what I would have done," Taylor confesses. "She fooled me, innocently. The architect sat in our home, and . . . I asked him how much it was going to cost [to rebuild the church]. He said it would cost a million dollars. My heart went straight down. Black people in Bedford-Stuyvesant in 1952 couldn't raise a million dollars. But Laura said, 'Don't pay any attention to him. It won't cost a dime over $750,000.'" Taylor says that he was so anxious to believe her that for a year and a half he "traveled on that delusion." He laughs heartily as he reports that it cost nearly $2 million. In his view, his wife's figure turned out to be a "merciful deception."

Though naysayers said that Concord would never rebuild, the congregation not only erected an edifice on the very grounds of the fire but also added a gymnasium, an educational building, and a full space underneath the sanctuary, doubling the church's seating capacity.

Less satisfying was the outcome of the bitter 1960 confrontation between Taylor and J. H. Jackson, then president of the National Baptist Convention, USA,

Inc., the nation's third largest Protestant denomination and the group to which most black Baptists belong. Jackson's conservative social and political views put him at odds with Martin Luther King Jr. and those ministers sympathetic to the cause of civil rights. Because of their disagreements about civil rights, and the issue of incumbency (Jackson had been president of the convention since 1953 and in the process broke convention limits on presidential tenure), Taylor agreed to run for the convention presidency at its annual meeting in Kansas in 1960.

A bitter fracas ensued. Hundreds of supporters of each candidate physically struggled and fought, leading to the accidental death of a loyal Jackson supporter and certain defeat for Taylor's team. The next year Taylor joined with King and other ministers who seceded from the convention to form the Progressive National Baptist Convention, Inc., which currently has a membership of more than 2 million people.

More than 30 years after this painful period, Taylor harbors no animosity toward Jackson, who died in 1991 at eighty-four. "Jackson had an ingenious and peculiar appeal to black people, as Reagan had to white people: J. H. Jackson could weep with the idea . . . that he was being put upon by powerful people . . . who were attacking [him], and he was weak. He had a gift for that."

Taylor even manages to find humor in illustrating this dimension of Jackson's appeal, which turned on his great gift of storytelling. H. H. Humes, a childhood friend of Jackson's, recalls hearing Jackson preach about the hardships that afflicted his parents in attempting to send Jackson to college. "When it looked like he couldn't go back to college, his mother said, 'The boy must go.' And the father said, 'We don't have anything but a mule.' But she said, 'The boy must go to college.' And the father said, 'We won't have any way to get the crop.' But the mother said, 'The boy must go to college,' and they finally sold the mule. Humes was weeping as he came out of the church. And someone said to him, 'Well you grew up with him. What did they do for a crop [since] they sold the mule? [Taylor's voice affects a weepy tone] 'Oh,' Humes said, 'Jack's people never did own a mule, but I just can't stand to hear him tell that story.'" Taylor breaks into laughter, trailing it with "Lord, have mer . . . " The last syllable of his plea is erased by more laughter.

Taylor's enormous gift of humor, his ability to acknowledge the humanity of his opponents, gives him the grace to accept and overcome his own failings. When I asked him about the thorny problem confronting the black church in its treatment of women in the ministry, Taylor confessed that he had to grow into his enlightened position.

"As with the white male, an exclusive preserve [of black male power is] under threat of invasion . . . I had to have a conversion myself. I knew theoretically this was wrong, but prejudice is not a rational thing."

Taylor's conversion occurred in the late '60s at Colgate Rochester Divinity School, where he was teaching a class on preaching. There Taylor encountered white female students whose fresh viewpoints helped change his views on women in the ministry. "As they presented the gospel, I saw a new angle of vision ... I had an interesting, and to me a humorous, thing happen. The young women of Colgate came to me and said, 'You know, you're just like all these other people here. You use all this sexist language.' Well, I was really stung. Who am I, having suffered from being excluded so long, to [exclude others]? And so I worked on it."

Taylor reports that after he delivered the Luccock Lectures at Yale Divinity School, a female faculty member thanked him for his inclusive language. Feeling good about the acknowledgment, he went back to Colgate to report this fresh triumph to his female students. "I saw some of the young women in the hall, and I told them what had happened. And I said, 'You know, I want to thank you girls ... ' 'Oh,' they said, 'you don't say girls. Say women,' 'Well,' I said. 'It takes a little learning.'"

Since that time, Taylor has developed an acute analysis of gender relations, particularly in black culture. "I was greatly troubled by the Anita Hill–Clarence Thomas situation, and more troubled than almost anything by the attitude of [many] black women. I reached the conclusion that black women have been so put upon that they have developed a kind of psychological scar tissue, so that they've learned to take in stride things that ought to outrage them. And that distresses me. I am tired of the way black men misuse black women, and the way black women apologize for and accept what black men do."

It is above all Taylor's unsurpassed ability to preach to preachers—his keen sense of the preaching mission and its encumbrances and opportunities, its joyous peaks and its seemingly bottomless sorrows—that make him a popular presence among seminarians and seasoned preachers alike. In his homiletics class at Princeton, Taylor ranges through the history of the English pulpit with formidable ease, sharing stories of history's great divines. He whips out tattered pieces of newspaper, whose margins are covered with notes drawn from a massive and virtually infallible memory bank of preaching lore and legend.

On one of the days I attend his class, Taylor produces a snatch of paper ripped from the previous Sunday's *New York Times Book Review,* which he reads religiously, along with the *New Republic* ("I despise almost every word in it, but it gives me good targets to shoot at"), the *New York Review of Books,* and the daily *New York Times* and *Newsday.* Taylor reads a review describing the ingredients of a great novel—from its descriptive power to its presentation of a wide view of humanity without losing its link to individual characters. He reminds them that great preaching contains the same elements.

His desire to help other preachers has endeared Taylor to audiences across the nation. It has made his sermons to ministers legendary. Black preachers, especially, collect sermons with the zeal of avid fans of baseball cards. At conventions of black denominations, the tapes of famous ministers sell briskly. These tapes are especially circulated and reproduced among younger preachers, serving as models of preaching excellence and training in the high art of sacred speech. Some even preach the sermons to their own congregations, trying out fresh ideas and new words they have gleaned from master storytellers. Frederick Sampson's "Dwelling on the Outskirts of Devastation," Jeremiah Wright's "Prophets or Puppets," Charles Adams's "Sermons in Flesh," William Jones's "The Low Way Up," and Caesar Clark's "Elijah Is Us," have all acquired canonical status in a genre of religious address that treats the plight of the preacher. Several of Taylor's own sermons, including "Seeing Our Hurts with God's Eyes," and "A Wide Vision Through a Narrow Window," neither of which appear in his books of published sermons, are classics of the genre. They amply illustrate the astonishing range of his pulpit gifts.

In "A Wide Vision Through a Narrow Window," Taylor, speaking on a text from Job, details for his audience of preachers at Bishop College's L. K. Williams Institute in 1980, the price of authentic preaching. In an arresting metaphor he reminds us that for eighteen chapters Job's friends had turned against him, "driving cold steel into his already bleeding spirit." The nineteenth chapter—the chapter containing Taylor's text—is Job's "reply to their gloomy countenances, and their long, bitter indictment of his calamity, as they sit around the pallet of his misery."

Taylor employs and repeats the sermon's theme to sharpen his portrayal of Job's predicament, a condition where "the window has narrowed out of which he looks upon the landscape of life. Once there had been the homes of children, and fruitful fields, and lowing cattle and bleating sheep. But now, the window has narrowed." As if being forsaken by earthly friends were not enough, Job faces, as do all ministers, the prospect of feeling forsaken by God. Speaking through the voice of Job, Taylor says that "it seems that God has overthrown me. Now here is where the window does narrow to a slit. If God be for us, then what difference does it make, who is against us? . . . But, my father, if G-a-w-w-d be against us, what else is there left? I don't know why, in the solemn appointments of God, that there are times when it does indeed seem as if we've got not a friend in earth—or in heaven!" Taylor thunders. And then he emphatically completes the sentence, with a staccato verbal surge, "left!"

Taylor eloquently rephrases the theme of his sermon in question form. "And my brother preachers, you say that you want great power to move among men's heartstrings?" Taylor incants in almost mournful tones. "You cannot have that, without great sorrow. G-a-w-w-d can fill only the places that have been emptied of the joys of this life." He then challenges them with examples drawn from the lives of other suffering servants. "Dale of Carr's Lane in Birmingham [England] had particularly toward the end a terribly lonely existence. Charles Spurgeon in the Metropolitan Tabernacle [London] had rheumatism and gout that made life unbearable for him. Frederick W. Robertson of Brighton [England] was so sensitive that the least thing shattered him like the piercing of an eye. George Truett, who charmed the American South in the first four decades of this century lived in the after-memory of a hunting accident in which a friend was killed by his own gun."

Taylor restates his theme later in the sermon. He then implores his congregation of preachers to look beyond the peripheral signs of preaching greatness to the real source of pastoral insight—the common bond with one's hearers provided by suffering. "Now you may tickle people's fancies, but you will never preach to their hearts, until at some place, some solemn appointment has fallen upon your own life, and you have wept bitter tears, and gone to your own Gethsemane and climbed your own Calvary. That's where power is!"

Taylor rhythmically measures his speech, repeating the forces that cannot by themselves make for great preaching. He builds up tension for the ultimate release in the announcement of what constitutes the power of proclamation. "It is not in the tone of the voice. It is not in the eloquence of the preacher. It is not in the gracefulness of his gestures. It is not in the magnificence of his congregation. It is in a heart broken, and put together, by the eternal God!"

Taylor wrestles with some of the inevitable sadness that life brings—for instance, the suffering that comes with aging. "I have reached a very unflattering and unenviable time. I have more money than I have time. And that's not good. It was much better the other way. But then I'll take it—what can I do?"

As we discussed his fifty-two years of marriage to Laura, he said, "I sometimes see her lying in repose now, and [he pauses], a great sadness comes over me because I know one of us must leave the other. I don't know which I fear the most. [He pauses again]. But, what can we do?"

Tragically Laura was struck and killed by a New York sanitation truck in February 1995. Despite this great loss, one suspects that Taylor will do what he has always done, whether life favored him or assaulted him. He will, as long as he is able, preach the Word of God. That has been his peculiar gift and burden, his bread and butter for more than fifty years. And out of his own suffering, he has shaped a ministry that has spoken to the hearts of men and women throughout the world. And because of his peculiar gift for making mortals see the light of God, no matter how dimmed by human frailty and failure, who can doubt that it will continue to shine on him in the hour of his greatest need.

Seventeen

"SOMEWHERE I READ OF THE FREEDOM OF SPEECH": CONSTRUCTING A UNIQUE VOICE

There is little doubt that the most controversial book I've written is I May Not Get There with You: The True Martin Luther King Jr. *Many black readers were outraged that I spoke openly about Dr. King's shortcomings in the book, especially allegations that he was a plagiarist and an adulterer. Ironically, many of my critics never read the book. Only when I appeared in the media and explained my love and admiration for King did the attacks subside. I argued that we must confront King's failures honestly since they are part of the historical record, but that his flaws cannot diminish his legendary status. I was also keen on being frank about King's failures so that the younger generation might believe that they didn't have to be perfect to be useful. In fact, the failure to address King's all-too-human behavior only strengthens the hand of his enemies, since they will be free to distort King's memory with their own jaundiced and bigoted views of his life. Better to tell the truth and still claim King's greatness, than pretend that King wasn't a human being who had shortcomings like the rest of us. This chapter addresses the rich oral traditions from which King drew in developing his style of speaking, while confronting King's plagiarism in academic circles. I make a distinction between King's oral borrowing—part of a well-established tradition of verbal sharing that, while not exclusive to black culture, does have unique resonance—and his literary lapses on the page. I also attempt to explain the psychological elements that may have driven his actions, while offering an account of the racial pressures that may help explain his behavior. Perhaps the greatest vindication of my efforts was supplied by Andrew Young, who told me that my book was honest and necessary, and that I had gotten King and his courageous cohort right. Coming from one of King's most trusted lieutenants, Young's words have been a blessed source of peace.*

AT A RECENT CONFERENCE ON BLACK MALES, I shared keynote responsibilities with two other speakers. One of them was a forty–something civil rights leader and Baptist preacher. It was February, known in my circles as "National Rent-a-Negro Month"[1] in homage to the flurry of Black History Month activities that colleges and corporations cram into those twenty-eight days (as if no other time was appropriate to recognize black achievement). I hustled into the conference late, arriving just in time to hear the closing comments of the civil rights leader, who by now was "putting on the rousements"—firing the crowd up with his astute analysis of the crises confronting black men. He was sailing fast now, punctuating his speech with powerful phrases he knew would elicit the audience's approval, an old trick that we Baptist preachers use to send our congregations out to do the Lord's work.

Just as the speaker reached the climax of his oration, I was whisked to the back entry of the stage to await my turn to speak, since all three keynoters were presenting in rapid succession. As I watched my colleague finish, I got an even better sense of the glorious rapport he had established with his audience, a sublime connection that gives both parties a rush that few other events can match. As he offered his husky-voiced parting thoughts, the crowd leaped to its feet, and so did I, gleefully grabbing him as he came off stage in a brotherly bear hug, wrapping him in the audience's affection as their unofficial emissary.

"Hey, Doc, how ya doin?" my colleague brightly greeted me.

"Man, you tore it up," I enthused. "I got a hard act to follow, boy."

"Aw, man," he graciously responded, "you know you gonna turn it out."

"I don't know, brother," I shot back. "You look like you killed every*thang* in there. And what ain't dead, you done put in intensive care."

We both cracked up, bathing each other in the occasionally obnoxious mutual admiration to which Baptist preachers are eagerly given. As I was being introduced, my colleague offered his regrets about having to leave for another engagement. I readily understood, since I would have to leave right after my speech for the next town in my Black History Month tour.

As the crowd warmly greeted me, I let on that my colleague was difficult to follow but that I'd try to do my best (a Baptist preacher way of begging for sympathy and winning the crowd). My grasp at pity seemed to be working, as the crowd urged me on with "amens" and "go 'heads." I slid easily enough into my speech, but at a crucial period—or, more exactly, at a crucial three-minute passage that I had used in many of my speeches over the past year—I felt the enthusiasm of the audience flag. Usually my passage drew uproarious guffaws and penetrating "humhs," but now I was greeted with sprinkled laughter and moderate "huhs," the kind that feel more obligatory than genuine. I pressed on, not giving it much thought, chalking the lukewarm response up to my poor delivery or to having misjudged my audience. But the rest of my speech went well. I too got a standing ovation and was grateful for the audience's loving endorsement. But after my speech, I wondered again why my passage hadn't gone over as hugely as it usually did. Not until later did I discover what had gone wrong.

Three weeks after my keynote speech, I had a speaking engagement in a nearby town. The woman who picked me up from the airport for the hour-long drive to the university remarked that she had attended the conference on black males and had enjoyed all of our speeches.

"I know you must have wondered why, when you got to a certain point in your speech, people didn't respond as enthusiastically as you perhaps thought they would," my host offered, impressing me with her savvy while piquing my interest.

"Yeah, I did wonder what had happened," I confessed.

"Well, the speaker before you had gone through the same routine in his speech," she revealed. "And since the audience had just heard it, their response was certainly muted."

"O-h-h-h-h," I said. "Now I get it."

Although I was friendly with the civil rights leader, I took it as a matter of pride to point out to my host that *he* had ripped *me* off, and not vice versa. As soon as my host's comments hit my ears, I recalled that the civil rights leader's wife had heard me preach a few months before at a black Baptist church, and since her husband couldn't attend, she promised that she would give him a tape of my sermon. I had used my dramatic passage in that sermon, and of course, he had obviously listened to the tape and lifted my passage for his speeches. In spite of my brief fit of ego, I couldn't stay sore at my colleague. After all, Baptist preachers are always ripping each other off and using the stories, illustrations, phrases, verbal tics, mannerisms—and in some cases, whole sermons—we glean from other preachers. That's how we learn to preach; by preaching like somebody else until we learn how to preach like ourselves, when our own voice emerges from the colloquy of voices we convene in our homiletical imagination. And in the end, the only justification for such edifying thievery among preachers is that the Word is being preached and the ultimate Author of what we say is being glorified.

In fact, the line I had used about the civil rights leader having "killed every*thang* in there" was torn straight from the transcript[2] of a thousand other conversations between black Baptist preachers congratulating one another for their rhetorical might. Then, too, I knew the humorous three-step rhetorical rule of citation by which many black Baptist preachers operate. The first time they repeat something they hear, they say, "like Martin Luther King said . . ." The second time they repeat it, they say, "like somebody said . . ." The third time they repeat it, they say, "like I always say . . ." None of this means that there aren't rules of fair play—that one shouldn't work exceedingly hard in preaching with a Bible in one hand, the newspaper in the other (an idea ripped off from theologian Karl Barth),[3] that one shouldn't hunt for inspiration in all sorts of unusual places, and that one shouldn't feed one's flock with the fruits of rigorous intellectual and spiritual engagement. At their best, the practices of black Baptist preachers[4] remind us that knowledge is indeed communal, that rhetoric is shaped in the interplay of a rich variety of language users, and that what is old becomes new again by being recast in forceful and imaginative ways.

All of this is crucial if we are to make sense of the recent revelation that Martin Luther King, Jr., borrowed other people's words in his published and preached sermons.[5] Of course, nothing I have said can account for the even more disturbing charge that King was a plagiarist in his academic work. It is now clear that he plagiarized huge chunks of his dissertation and graduate school papers and that he carelessly cited sources in his seminary and undergraduate papers. This news is especially jarring to those who view King as an American original, a figure whose social vision came wrapped in brilliant metaphors and memorable phrases. The notion that a figure who commanded the English language with such authority was in truth a borrower of other people's words is too hard for King's admirers to swallow. For many Americans, King's example is law, his words scripture. In fact, King's memory has become a racial Esperanto. His life has been made into a moral language that allows whites to translate their hopes and fears about black life into meanings that black folk intuitively understand. Much of King's power hinged on his use of language, indeed, his use *as* language. His moral authority was largely rooted in his unique ability to express eloquently the claims of black freedom.

In that light, understanding what King did with language—that is, getting at his complex rhetorical habits and the presuppositions he brought to his spoken and written work—will give us a better sense of how to judge his achievements and failures. By explaining how King absorbed and recycled rhetorical sources and how he creatively fused a variety of voices in finding his own voice, one may be charged with excusing his verbal theft by "converting King's blemish into a grand achievement."[6] Worse yet, one may be charged with appealing to some mythic racial practice to justify his borrowing, but certainly not borrowed, genius. But that is to confuse explanation with justification. Such a conclusion clings desperately to the naive belief that we must ignore context and circumstance in making moral judgments.

King's borrowing, and at times, outright theft, of others' words must be viewed in two arenas: his sermons in the pulpit and in print, and his scholarly writing in the academy before that. The most sophisticated arguments to date about King's use of language in the pulpit and in print have been made by scholars Keith D. Miller and Richard Lischer. Miller, in his insightful *Voice of Deliverance*, persuasively argues that King heavily borrowed from white liberal preachers in his published sermons to further the cause of civil rights.[7] He ingeniously seized on the ethical and political dimensions of white liberal sermons—including their emphasis on the Christian social gospel, their antimilitarism, their critiques of capitalism and communism, and even their inchoate antiracism—to cast his own arguments for black emancipation in terms that white liberal listeners would find irresistible.[8] By fusing his voice with white liberal voices, King practiced, in Miller's term, the black oral art of "voice-merging," an ancient practice in black religious circles.[9] Miller argues that in such circles, speech is seen not as private but as communal property. In black oral culture black folk learn to refine rhetoric and shape identity by joining their voices to the voices of their ancestors and their contemporary inspirations. Thus, King didn't view such an art as verbal theft but as a time-honored, community-blessed tradition with deep roots in black culture.

Richard Lischer agrees in substance with this aspect of Miller's argument. His brilliantly argued *The Preacher King* explores the rich rhetorical resources that King inherited as a prince of the black church.[10] While Miller analyzes King's written sermons and speeches, Lischer pays close attention to King's spoken word, poring over the unedited audiotapes and transcripts of King's sermons and speeches.

Lischer argues that King's real voice was edited out of his published sermons[11] as he and his publisher sought to appeal to as wide an audience as possible. Where Miller finds virtue in such a strategy, Lischer smells trouble. Not only is King's spoken voice missing—a voice full of cultural allusion, racial wisdom, and black rhythms that were muted under the dogma of pen and page—but his theological and ideological evolution—a full-blown radicalism that was especially apparent in his highly personal, magnificently improvised, and deeply colloquial black sermonizing—is completely whitewashed. Lischer disagrees with the notion that "in his plagiarism King was simply adhering to the standards of African-American . . . preaching."[12] He claims that it "is one thing to assert" that language is a shared commodity in black culture,[13] which he concedes, but "it is quite another to translate that generalization into a rationale for academic falsification." Finally, Lischer thinks that Miller overstates the extent to which King borrowed.[14] After all, he argues, white liberal ministers borrowed freely from each other (Miller also makes this point).

Despite their disagreements, Miller and Lischer offer persuasive arguments about how King used his intellectual and rhetorical gifts to bring about social change. Both authors help us understand exactly how King went about the formidable task of drawing on black cultural and religious traditions while shaping a message of liberation that could sway the conscience of white America. By digging deep into the history of black oral traditions, they help us understand a much celebrated but little understood practice: black preaching. Their brilliant explorations of the mechanics, methods, and modes of black sacred rhetoric help us see that black preachers often give their listeners reason to hope and fuel to survive by spinning words into the Word. Black preachers coin phrases, stack sentences, accumulate wise sayings, and borrow speech to convince black folk, as the gospel song says, to "run on to see what the end is gonna be." King had a genius for knowing what intellectual and spiritual resources to bring together, and to know when such a fusion would make the most sense and the greatest impact on his hearers.

As Miller and Lischer make clear, King's borrowing had a noble purpose. For Miller, it was nothing less than the reflection back to liberal white America of the ideals it cherished in comforting and familiar language.[15] For Lischer, King's borrowing helped to subvert the status quo as King's speech progressively filled with rage in denouncing racial optimism.[16] Miller is right to emphasize King's brilliant reworking of white liberal religious themes and to suggest that King's success, at least the success of his early years, was surely linked to the perception by liberal whites that he and, by extension, most other blacks, was very much like them. King possessed the unique ability to convince liberal whites, through phrases and sermon plots they were familiar with, that black freedom was a legitimate goal because it was linked to social ideals they embraced each Sunday morning. By embracing liberal orthodoxy through the rhetoric of its main exponents, King was able to send the message that he and the blacks he represented were committed to the same goal of social reform as white Protestants. Miller also convincingly argues

that through the rhetoric at hand, King constructed a public persona–a social self–
that expressed blackness in a fashion that appealed to the white mainstream.[17]

Lischer complains that Miller's notion of self-making makes King appear du-
plicitous.[18] But Miller discerns in King's public persona the tough but inevitable
choice that all minorities in a dominant culture face: how to put one's best face
forward. Given that King was concerned or, early on, even obsessed with what
would work in white America, he was perhaps compelled to mold a public persona that pleased liberal whites while reinforcing black self-respect, a virtually
impossible task. But Lischer usefully reminds us that King faced Du Bois's
famed dilemma of twoness–to be "an American, a Negro."[19] Even in this light,
mask wearing or self-making need not be read as mere duplicity. Instead, it may
be viewed as a renewal of the ancient black effort to survive through creating
durable, flexible personalities. Making selves and wearing masks is not merely a
defensive device to deter white intrusion. It is also the positive means by which
blacks shape their worlds and make their identities. Lischer is right to argue that
Miller's reading skews King's later, more radical preaching by not attending to
the sermons and speeches that rarely made it to print. And he renders invaluable
service by excavating a neglected version of King's public persona that remains
buried beneath the rubble of feel-good rhetoric that distorts his memory. Like
Miller, Lischer shows us how King used rhetorical formulas to argue for racial
justice, but with a different bent. He explores how King ingeniously employed
the rhythms, cadences, and colloquialisms of the black vernacular to inspire his
black audiences to disobey unjust laws. Thus, King made speech a handmaiden
of social revolution.

Both authors' arguments illumine King's borrowing habits by placing his
speech making and sermon giving in broad cultural and racial context. Black
preachers–for that matter, all preachers–liberally borrow themes, ideas, phrases,
and approaches from one another, although most would not pass off in print a
sermon heavily borrowed from another preacher as their own. But many of the
same preachers would not hesitate to preach a heavily borrowed sermon in their
pulpits. Many critics are skeptical about the claim that speech is so freely shared
in black communities, and even more skeptical of the notion that cribbing others'
work is such a common practice.[20] But in an oral culture where, as Miller argues,
authority is prized above originality, the crucial issue is not saying something new
by saying something first, but in embracing the paradoxical practice of developing
one's voice by trying on someone else's voice, and thus learning by comparison
to identify one's own gift. If imitation and emulation are the first fruits of such an
oral culture, its mature benefits include the projection of a unique style–a new
style–that borrows from cultural precedents but finds its own place within their
amplifications.

King spoke much the way a jazz musician plays, improvising from minimally or
maximally sketched chords or fingering changes that derive from hours of practice
and performance. The same song is never the same song, and for King, the same

speech was certainly never the same speech. He constantly added and subtracted, attaching a phrase here and paring a paragraph there to suit the situation. He could bend ideas and slide memorized passages through his trumpet of a voice with remarkable sensitivity to his audience's makeup. King endlessly reworked themes, reshaped stories, and repackaged ideas to uplift his audience or drive them even further into a state of being–whether it was compassion or anger, rage or reconciliation–to reach for justice and liberation. King had a batch of rhetorical ballads, long, blue, slow-building meditations on the state of race, and an arsenal of simmering mid-tempo reflections on the high cost of failing to fix what fundamentally ails us–violence, hatred, and narrow worship of tribe and custom. King knew how to play as part of a rhetorical ensemble that reached back in time to include Lincoln and Jefferson and stretched across waters to embrace Gandhi and Du Bois in Ghana.[21] But he played piercing solos as well, imaginatively riffing off themes eloquently voiced by black preachers Prathia Hall and Archibald Carey.[22] In the end, King brilliantly managed a repertoire of rhetorical resources that permitted him to play an unforgettable, haunting melody of radical social change.

Even if one holds that King's creative uses of borrowed words amounted to verbal theft (a view I heartily reject), one might still conclude that, in King's case, there was a moral utility to an immoral act. A greater good was served by King's having used the words of others than might otherwise have been accomplished had he not done so. This utilitarian calculus takes into account Miller's insistence that King was weighed down[23] with so much to do that it would have been impossible for him to achieve the worthy goal of racial revolution without appealing to such resources. And even if one concludes that King's unattributed use of sentences and paragraphs from others' sermons in his printed sermons was plagiarism (a view I do hold), one can still acknowledge the pressures under which King performed–not simply pressures of time and commitment, but the pressure to resist white supremacy in a manner that maintained black dignity while appealing to white conscience. As if that were not formidable enough, King also had to balance the militant demand for social change early on while making certain that the manner in which black folk demanded their due would not lead to mass black destruction. Given such pressures and in the light of King's moral aims, it is certainly not unforgivable to produce a book of sermons, *Strength to Love*, that includes unacknowledged sources.[24] In fact, there is some poetic justice in King's use of orthodox liberal ideas to undermine orthodox racial beliefs and even more justice in his having breathed new life into these words while expanding their moral application, fulfilling them in ways their owners might never have conceived but to which they would certainly have no objections. As Lischer argues, *Strength to Love* was published to consolidate King's white liberal audience, a goal he certainly achieved.[25] But as Lischer also notes, unedited audiotapes of King's sermons and speeches[26] are not only more representative of King's rhetorical output, but are a more reliable index of his sophisticated oral practices. In the main, King was more Miles Davis than Milli Vanilli.[27]

King's academic work is another matter altogether. From the scant evidence that exists, even in his undergraduate days at Morehouse College, King was sloppy in formally citing the sources of ideas he propounded in his papers.[28] King began college at age fifteen, swept in on an early admissions policy for bright students to compensate for the drain of black men during World War II. King graduated from college at nineteen, the same age at which he preached his trial sermon.[29] The sermon that King would preach that night became one of his favorite homilies and was greatly dependent on a sermon by a well-known white minister. King sailed into seminary with supreme confidence, the son of a solidly middle-class minister whose future promise had begun to blossom as he embraced graduate school at an age when most male students were gearing up for girls and guzzling beer. King's work at Crozer Theological Seminary in Chester, Pennsylvania, was often distinguished enough to earn him high marks from his professors (except, ironically enough, in a couple of public speaking courses)[30] and the confidence of fellow students, who voted him class president. But King's formal citation habits continued to be sloppy.[31] In most cases, his errors might have easily been corrected had he taken more time to place quotation marks around material amply cited in his notes and had he refined his skills of paraphrasing others' work. King's work at Crozer, especially his use of books and articles from which he drew many of his ideas, proves that he used these sources to bolster his burgeoning theological beliefs about God, human nature, evil, and sin.

The same holds true for his work at Boston University, where King matriculated after graduating from Crozer. Initially enrolled in the philosophy department to work with renowned philosophical theologian Edgar Brightman, King transferred to the school of theology when Brightman died. There King worked under the tutelage of L. Harold DeWolf and, to a lesser degree, S. Paul Schilling, both of whom were influenced by Brightman's conception of personalism, which holds that God is a living being with the characteristics of human personality. King put his own stamp on personalist theology[32] even as he wrestled with other great theological and philosophical figures, some of whom he first read in seminary—Kant, Hegel, Marx, Nietzsche, Barth, Niebuhr, Tillich, and Wieman. Throughout his Boston University career, it is now evident that King plagiarized large portions of his course papers and his dissertation, "A Comparison of the Conceptions of God in the Thinking of Paul Tillich and Henry Nelson Wieman," completed in 1955.[33] King plagiarized the two principal subjects of his dissertation, but the bulk of his theft concentrated on large portions of Jack Boozer's dissertation, "The Place of Reason in Paul Tillich's Conception of God," written just three years before King's thesis and supervised by L. Harold DeWolf, King's major adviser.[34] Interestingly, King used plagiarized thoughts to reinforce his theological convictions. He stole words for at least three reasons: first, to explore the character of a God who was personal and loving, and not simply, as Tillich argued, the "ground of being"; second, to investigate the complex nature of human identity and sinfulness, as King struggled between neo-orthodox theology, with its emphasis on original sin, and liberal religious views, which hold that myths and symbols dot the biblical landscape; and, finally, to probe the origin and persistence of evil—was it allowed by God, who in yielding to human will, decided to limit herself, or was God not really all-powerful?[35] As historian Eugene Genovese notes, King's plagiarism contained a "curious feature"[36] since it was not characterized by "laziness and indifference" but showed that King "constantly wrestled with difficult subject matter." And most of his teachers agreed with his seminary professor's assessment that King possessed "exceptional intellectual ability."[37] Moreover, there is no evidence that King cheated on his examinations, which he constantly passed with high marks. Then why did he plagiarize?

No one knows, although many scholars and critics across the ideological spectrum have ventured reasons. Theodore Pappas's edited volume, *Martin Luther King Plagiarism Story*, is a relentless assault on King's reputation, a bitterly moralizing anthology that assays to unveil King's moral deficits through his stolen words.[38] Instead, Pappas's tome, with the exception of contributions by Genovese, Gary Wills, and Jacob Neusner, is a throb of journalistic overkill with little relief or balance. Its ominous blue tones seek to warn us that King's sordid act of intellectual treachery reveals his inherently flawed character—information intended, no doubt, to flatten King's naive boosters. Pappas's attack reveals just how persistent are the pockets of intellectualized attacks on Martin Luther King's reputation in our nation, although he does document the reluctance of media and academic critics to publicize King's plagiarism. King's first scholarly biographer, David Levering Lewis, was "appalled" at the news of his virgin subject's literary misdealings, decrying King's "repeated act of self-betrayal and subversion of the rules of scholarship," which, in the light of Lewis's estimate of King's ability, was wholly unnecessary.[39] Lewis detects in King's psychic makeup the "angst of strivers in the melting pot," whether they came by immigration or slavery.[40] He plausibly posits that an "alert striver" like King might have sensed a racial double standard in his professors' treatment of him, and thus, "finding himself highly rewarded rather than penalized"[41] for his apparent mistakes, "he may well have decide[d] to repay their condescension or contempt in like coin." That may be true, although it may not help us understand why King cheated in the first place. Then, too, such a reading depends on denying that King's scholarly habits were influenced by the verbal promiscuity of black culture, an argument Lewis finds "wholly incredulous."[42] Another exhaustive King biographer, David Garrow, is more willing than Lewis to concede the relevance of black cultural factors in understanding King's practices, at least on the sermonic front. Garrow holds that the discovery of King's plagiarism will not only "alter our understanding of the young Martin Luther King,"[43] but that the consequences of such a finding will "complement and further strengthen two interpretive themes" that have found support among civil rights scholars. The first is that King "was far more deeply and extensively shaped"[44] by the black church tradition that nurtured him than by the thinkers and teachers he engaged in graduate school. And second, "the black freedom movement was in no way the simple product of individual leaders and national organizations."[45] Like King scholars James Cone, Lewis Baldwin, and Taylor Branch, Garrow underscores the powerful influence of the black church on King's theological framework and his habit of verbal borrowing.[46] Although none of these scholars is an apologist for King's scholarly plagiarism, they bring a vital balance to criticism that fails to acknowledge the cultural and racial forces that shaped King's rhetorical choices.

Still, it is one thing to argue that King's habits of verbal borrowing drew from cultural practices (which I think is true) and another to argue that King simply carried these habits into the academic arena. Such an argument dishonors King's sophistication and shrewdness and ignores the intellectual gifts and scholarly talents that got King admitted to graduate school in the first place. But even those who argue that King's academic habit of taking others' words without attribution was pure and simple plagiarism (which I believe it was) have unconvincing arguments about what drove him to do it. The suggestion that King's teachers gave him a break because he was black—that they engaged in "reverse racism" or, even worse, as Lewis and Genovese argue, that his professors engaged in racial paternalism—seems implausible.[47] After all, Boston University produced, during or immediately after King's tenure, distinguished scholars like Major Jones, Samuel Proctor, Evans Crawford, Cornish Rogers, and C. Eric Lincoln.[48] That does not rule out the possibility that King's case was an exception, but for that logic to work, King would had to have been a marginal student whose limited skills prevented his success. There is too much evidence that King mastered the mechanics of academic survival and was bright, diligent, and highly disciplined. David Garrow's surmise that King was in his Boston years "first and foremost a young dandy whose efforts to play the role of a worldly, sophisticated young philosopher were in good part a way of coping with an intellectual setting that was radically different from his own heritage and in which he might well have felt an outsider,"[49] may go further in capturing King's conflicting emotions about graduate school and his doubts about whether he belonged. The most highly gifted black student[50] could harbor insecurities about his talents in a white world that insisted on his inferiority, even in a relatively benign environment like Boston University, which had a reputation for nurturing bright black students. Garrow suggests that the King of Boston University may have been "a rather immature and insecure man,"[51] who did not fully become "himself" until he left graduate school, a reasonable speculation not only in the light of King's subsequent career but in the light of how most of us who have trod a similar path have developed. (Did anyone really expect Michael Jordan to become the greatest basketball player ever after viewing him in college, where he never averaged twenty points a game?) We often forget that King was only twenty-six when he became what Hegel termed a world-historical figure.[52] Boston University certainly was a proving ground for him, a place where he fought personal and institutional demons and succumbed to the temptation to represent others' work as his own. I think there are at least two complex and interrelated reasons behind King's scholarly plagiarism.

First, part of the explanation may reside in what Cornish Rogers, a contemporary of King at Boston University, says was King's primary goal: to become a first-rate preacher and pastor of a distinguished black southern church. Rogers says that "King told me the main reason he was getting a doctorate was so he could get that church—Dexter Avenue, which wanted a minister with a doctorate."[53] Rogers says that despite the fact that King's application for Boston University indicated his desire to become a scholar of theology, it was not surprising that King "changed his perspective as he got older and sensed where his real heart and best gifts lay."[54] This confirms Miller's and Lischer's arguments that King was first and foremost a preacher of extraordinary skill and resources, and by comparison, at best a competent theologian. Rogers also argues that theological education was "alien in the sense that it really did not provide [King] with the tools for ministry in the black community,"[55] even though King would use "some of the titillating ideas that he got in his studies if he thought they would preach well." For King, as for many "evangelical divines," preaching was the supreme skill one must possess and develop to render the greatest service as a Christian minister. Among black preachers, there is the often repeated mantra dressed up as a question: "But can he tell the story?" referring to homiletical skills honed in the black pulpit. And, as Lischer argued about King, every item of experience is made grist for the preacher's mill, as preachers often remark about a compelling story or idea "that will preach."

Undoubtedly, there is a profound conflict in such circles about formal theological education. Although it is viewed as necessary to critical thinking about religious matters, theological education is often viewed as a hindrance to the true worship of God, since liberal scholarship in particular challenges evangelical faith. This skepticism often translates into a paralyzing anti-intellectualism, a phenomenon not unknown in black and white preaching circles. But even as such preachers despise the process of theological education—both its demanding intellectual regimen and its relentless criticism of received theological views—they cherish its value to their upward mobility and hunger after its symbolic rewards. This is why, perhaps, there are so many self-anointed, self-appointed, self-administered "doctors" in the Christian ministry, including the black pulpit (especially, perhaps, the black pulpit). The doctor deficiency among black clergy—the result of racist strictures against formal and higher education for most of our history—has led to its diseased exaggeration in such quarters. King certainly got major cachet from his degree.[56] How many times would black folk derive pride from announcing that their leader was "*Doctor* Martin Luther King Jr.," almost as if his title were part of his given name? And liberal white folk were pleased with themselves in pronouncing a title that King had collected from one of their schools. Calling him "*Doctor* King" was a way for them to participate vicariously in his achievement while perhaps unconsciously lauding themselves for having had the good sense to recognize his gifts. The anti-intellectualism of the clergy, the alienation of a white academic setting, the appeal of becoming a "doctor," the desire to serve the black church, and a change in vocational aspiration in midstream might certainly have ganged up on a young black scholar who sought to relieve the intense pressure of being simultaneously vain, gifted, ambitious, and insecure. Neither can we gainsay King's pride in being able to pull it all off—not simply the deception that the work he stole was his, which wasn't difficult (after all, as his dissertation's second reader, S. Paul Schilling commented, there were other student-scholars whose plagiarism was far worse than King's)[57]—but the more difficult task of managing the competing demands of two worlds that, in the words of Bernice Johnson Reagon, King sought to "straddle."[58] In this sense, King's plagiarism, though still tragic, was among the least of his worries. That is a profound commentary on the racist world King sought to penetrate, the conflicted black world from which he emerged, and the uncertain world into which he would be thrust as an educated agent of social change. Not to get the degree would be a greater failure than cheating to get it. The fault lies not simply with King, although he bears a lion's share of the blame, but with a world that demanded that he and others perform under such conditions. The wonder is not that King cheated under these conditions, but that C. Eric Lincoln, Samuel Proctor, Evans Crawford, Cornish Rogers, Major Jones, and thousands of other blacks, did not.

Second, King's plagiarism may have had to do with his aversion, one shared by many black students of his generation, to write a dissertation on race.[59] Of course, that aversion is not the driving force in King's cheating but its symptom. The racial climate that made race a scholarly taboo and encouraged the embrace of already validated European subject matter might have been the predicate for his plagiarism. The aversion to write about race was not accidental, but reflected the dilemma that all black students faced: if they wrote about race, they risked being pigeonholed or stereotyped; if they avoided it, they risked failing to develop critical resources to combat arguments about black inferiority. Even today, such a stigma persists, particularly in the light of the bitter culture wars still being fought. For instance, Eugene Genovese, in an otherwise tough and eminently fair review of King's work, let slip that "King passed over the chance to take courses on social Christianity, Gandhi, race relations, and other trendy subjects, preferring courses on Plato, Hegel, formal logic, and modern philosophy."[60] If such courses were deemed trendy then, it is no wonder that rigorously exploring the ideas that pushed or prevented racial justice would be strongly discouraged in white academic settings. At Boston University, the stigma of "race scholar" was one that few students appeared willing to risk. As James Cone notes, King did "not even mention racism in most of his graduate papers that dealt with justice, love, sin, and evil."[61] Cone also argues that in "six years at Crozer and Boston, King never identified racism as a theological or philosophical problem or mentioned whether he recognized it in the student body and faculty."[62]

Such issues were broached in the Dialectical Society, an organization of black graduate students founded by King and Cornish Rogers to offer their peers an intellectual forum to debate ideas relevant to black communities.[63] The need for such a group underscores the schizophrenia that many black scholars faced, and often still do, in seeking to address the painful circumstances of black life while satisfying the demands of a white academy. Cone's conclusion that King, like most other integrationists of his time, "appeared to be glad merely to have the opportunity to prove that Negroes could make it in the white man's world,"[64] is borne out by Rogers's observation that "the only reason many students stuck around (and did everything that was required of them) was to get the degree which in the black community makes you equal to the man, to white folks, if you've got your degree from a white institution, the same degree that whites get."[65] In such an environment, King concluded that he would never set the world on fire with his scholarly gifts. And as he perhaps battled his own self-doubt in confronting the rigorous demands of scholarly work—work he couldn't do as well as the work his genius had suited him for in the pulpit and the public stage, work of which he was not yet fully aware or capable—it is likely that cheating became a way to save face back home, satisfy "the man" at school, and sail off into the sunset of pastoral duties with no one having been the wiser about his grave sin. After all, as David Levering Lewis points out, no one, not even King himself, knew then that he would become *Martin Luther King Jr.*[66] Neither did King or, for that matter, his admirers and detractors, realize that his failures, like his successes, would gain such wide attention.

Recent scholarship in the psychology of race may provide a small glimpse onto King's tortured psychic landscape. This is by no means an attempt to excuse King's misdeed. Neither is it an attempt to suggest that most of those blacks victimized by the problem I will discuss would ever resort to stealing others' words as their own. Still, I think it opens a window onto King's mental processes that might help us understand a bit better why he cheated. Studies by Stanford University psychologist Claude Steele and his colleagues suggest the existence of a problem that King most likely engaged.[67] Steele and his colleagues have attempted to answer a difficult question: Why do able black college students fail to perform as well as their white colleagues? Throughout the 1990s, Steele says, "the national college-dropout rate for African-Americans has been 20 to 25 percent higher than that for whites. Among those who finish college, the grade-point average of black students is two thirds of a grade below that of whites."[68] Steele says that "the under-performance of black undergraduates is an unsettling problem" that may "alter or hamper career development, especially among blacks not attending the most selective schools."[69]

Steele says the answers have resulted in an often "uncomfortably finger pointing . . . debate. Does the problem stem from something about black students themselves, such as poor motivation, a distracting peer culture, lack of family values, or—the unsettling suggestion of the *The Bell Curve*—genes?"[70] Steele adds to that list a host of other factors relating to the "conditions of blacks' lives: social economic deprivation, a society that views blacks through the lens of diminishing stereotypes and low expectation, too much coddling, or too much neglect?"

What stumped researchers even more is that middle-class black students, who have had the social and economic resources to lift them above the social plight of their poorer peers, underperform as do disadvantaged blacks, garnering lower standardized-test scores, lower college grades, and lower graduation rates than their white peers. What forces could possibly account for such underperformance, even among middle-class black students? At the risk of oversimplifying and reducing Steele's argument, it all boils down to what he and his colleagues termed "stereotype threat": the "threat of being viewed through the lens of negative stereotype, or the fear of doing something that would inadvertently confirm that stereotype."[71]

Steele develops his theory to apply to differential performance among black undergraduate students and their white peers. I apply it to King's own possible mind-set and suggest that he cheated in part to escape or relieve "stereotype threat"—the enormous pressure of feeling under relentless white scrutiny and living with the fear of confirming stereotypes of black identity. In a telling passage, nineteen-year-old graduate student King (at an age when most young men are college sophomores) is described as being

> terribly tense, unable to escape the fact that he was a Negro in a mostly white world. He was painfully aware of how whites stereotyped the Negro as lazy and messy, always laughing, always loud and late. He hated that image and tried desperately to avoid it. "If I were a minute late to class," he said, "I was almost morbidly conscious of it and sure that everyone noticed it. Rather than be thought of as always laughing, I'm afraid I was grimly serious for a time. I had a tendency to overdress, to keep my room spotless, my shoes perfectly shined and my clothes immaculately pressed."[72]

King was certainly not alone as a black student who confronted an egregiously unfair academic situation. Neither can we be sure that he wasn't simply the sort of person who would have cheated no matter his race or age. But since we only know him as we did—a black man confronting his self-doubt in a majority white culture—we can only reasonably speculate with the facts at hand. From King's own description of the psychic and emotional torture he confronted, I think it is reasonable to suggest that a possible reason for his cheating had to do with the attempt to please the white professors who judged him and to measure up to the standards of the white society in which he competed academically. I am not suggesting that most black students respond similarly; they obviously do not. I am, however, arguing that it is plausible that King responded to stereotype threat, perhaps even "stereotype fatigue," and surrendered the fight on the academic end to preserve his mental health on the emotional end. The fight was just that costly that plagiarizing course papers and a dissertation—as awful and lethal a flaw as it is—was deemed less harmful than facing the consequences of failing to meet the challenges of the white world.

King's plagiarism at school is perhaps a sad symptom of his response to the racial times in which he matured. His plagiarism is made even sadder by the realization that King's heroic efforts as a civil rights leader relieved for others some of the pressures that he faced as a graduate student, pressures that no one should have to face but that thousands of blacks have managed with amazing grace. It is not unbelievable that such figures were gifted, but that they could perform under the punishing conditions of rigid racial apartheid. Their success deflects attention from the horror of the conditions they learned to master. It is bitterly ironic that of all people, Martin Luther King, Jr., should be found out as a plagiarist since his huge rhetorical gifts helped to create a world of opportunity for millions. But then his genius for mastering the white world through mastering its languages, and for portraying so compellingly the pained psychic boundaries of black life, may derive from the tortured memory of his sore temptation on an isolated battlefield of conscience where he wrestled with, and failed, himself. As a *New York Times* editorial eloquently reminded our nation, King may have plagiarized words, but he could never plagiarize the courage he displayed on countless occasions:

> But however just it may be to denounce his scholarship,[73] that should not be confused with his leadership. Whether or not, as a student, he wrote what he wrote, Dr. King did what he did. . . . Some say he solicited the assistance of others . . . but even if so, that's no more to be faulted than John Kennedy turning to Theodore Sorensen, or George Bush to Peggy Noonan. . . . What the world honors when it honors Dr. King is his tenacity on behalf of racial justice—tenacity equally against gradualism and against violence. He and many with him pushed Americans down the long road to racial justice. That achievement glows unchallenged through the present shadow. Martin Luther King's courage was not copied; and there was no plagiarism in his power.

PART EIGHT

RELIGION AND SEXUALITY

The sexuality of black peoples has been a source of mythology, stereotype, fear, and fascination since our arrival in "the New World." Black folk have waged fierce campaigns against the exploitation of our sexual identities even as we have sought to enjoy, with varying degrees of success, erotic liberty. Although black religions have been instrumental in fostering social and spiritual freedom, they have been less adept in encouraging black folk to break the shackles of repression and the sexual conformity imposed on us by a white supremacist society. And when it comes to alternative lifestyles and sexual practices, stalwarts of black religion have been just as homophobic in their outlook as the members of dominant, heterosexist culture. Black folk whose heterosexuality has been demonized should be the last folk on earth to dump stigma on our gay, lesbian, bisexual, and transgender brothers and sisters. The challenge to black believers is to embrace a just vision of black sexuality that emphasizes a love and acceptance of all human beings, whatever their sexual orientation.

Eighteen

WHEN YOU DIVIDE BODY AND SOUL, PROBLEMS MULTIPLY: THE BLACK CHURCH AND SEXUALITY

Some black preachers were angry with me for writing this essay and "telling tales out of school." It only helped a little that I was honest about my own shortcomings as well. But the black church must engage black sexuality on every front: the sometimes hypocritical assaults by the white mainstream that have over the years caused us to deny our sexual beauty; the sometimes repressive sexual practices of black religious communities that deny the sacredness of sexual identity; and the homophobia that feeds the AIDS pandemic, which has torn through black communities with destructive fury. In this chapter, I combat the legacy of white supremacy that brings shame to black embodiment, even as I exhort the black church to develop a theology of eroticism that freely embraces our God-given sexual gifts. Otherwise, the church will be mired in sanctimonious pronouncements that offer little help to struggling believers, and our children will be further alienated from an institution that, were it honest and courageous, might literally save their lives.

He healed my body, and told me to run on.

—GOSPEL SONG
"CAN'T NOBODY DO ME LIKE JESUS"

Love . . . gives you a good feeling. Something like sanctified.

—MARVIN GAYE
"LET'S GET IT ON," 1973

Sexual healing is good for me.

—MARVIN GAYE
"SEXUAL HEALING," 1982

THE VISITING PREACHER, A BRAWNY BROWN MAN with smooth skin and teeth made of pearl, was coming to the close of his sermon, a ritual moment of climax in the black church. It is the inevitable point to which the entire service builds. Its existence is the only justification for the less dramatic rites of community—greeting visitors, collecting tithes, praying for the sick, reading scripture, and atoning for sins. These rites are a hallway to the sanctuary of zeal and vision formed by the black sermon. The furious splendor of the preacher's rhythmic, almost sung, speech drove the congregation to near madness. His relentless rhetoric stood them on their feet. Their bodies lurched in holy oblivion to space or time. Their hands waved as they shrieked their assent to the gospel lesson he passionately proclaimed. His cadence quickened. Each word swiftly piled on top of the next. The preacher's sweet moan sought to bring to earth the heavenly light of which his words, even at their most brilliant, were but a dim reflection.

"We've got to keep o-o-o-o-on keepin' on," he tunefully admonished. The preceding wisdom of his oration on Christian sexuality, arguing the link between passion and morality, turned this cliché into a sermonic clincher.

"We can't give up," he continued. "Because we've got God, oh yes, we've got Go-o-o-o-d, um-humh, on our side."

"Yes," members of the congregation shouted. The call and response between the pulpit and the pew escalated as each spurred the other on in ever enlarging rounds of emotion.

"We've got a friend who will never forsake us."

"Yes sir, Reverend."

"We've got a God who can make a way outta no way."

"Yes we do."

"He's a heart fixer, and a mind regulator."

"Oh, yes He is."

"I'm here tonight to tell you whatever moral crisis you're facin', God can fix it for you."

"Thank you, Jesus."

"If you're facin' trouble on the job, God can make your boss act better."

"Tell the truth, Reverend."

"If your kids won't act right, God can turn them around."

"Hallelujah!"

"If you're fornicating, and I know some of y'all been fornicatin', God can turn lust to love and give you a healthier relationship with Him."

"Hold your hope! Hold your hope!"

"If you're committin' adultery, and I know some of y'all are doing that, too, God can stop your rovin' eyes and keep you from messin' up. Won't He do it, church?"

"Yes! Yes He will!"

"If your marriage is fallin' apart, and there's no joy—I said there's no jo-oy-oy-oy at your address, God can do for you what He did for David. David asked God:

'Restore unto me the joy of Thy salvation.' I'm a witness tonight, children. God can do that, church. God can restore your joy. Won't He do it, children?!"

"Yes He will! Thank you, Jesus! Thank you, Jesus!"

"I'm closin' now, but before I go, I just stopped by to let you know that you can't find salvation in things. You can't find salvation in clothes. You can't find salvation in your car. You can't find salvation in your wife or husband. And you certainly can't find salvation in sex. Did y'all hear me? You can't find salvation in sex. You can't find it in sleepin' around, tryin' to fill the empty places of your life with pleasure and loose livin'."

"Thank you, Jesus!"

"You can only find salvation in our Lord and Savior, Jesus Christ! Do y'all hear me? Jesus, that's who you need! Jesus, that's who can save you. Jesus, the author and finisher of our faith. Jesus! Jesus! Jesus!"

"Thank ya! Oh, hallelujah!"

The congregation erupted in waves of shouting and hand clapping as the minister withdrew from the microphone and dramatically spun to his seat. He was thoroughly spent from a forty-five-minute exercise in edification and enlightenment. As soon as he was done, his fellow ministers on the dais, including me, descended on the preacher's chair to thank him for his thoughtful, thrilling message. Sex, after all, is a difficult subject to treat in the black church, or, for that matter, in any church. This is indeed ironic. After all, the Christian faith is grounded in the Incarnation, the belief that God took on flesh to redeem human beings. That belief is constantly trumped by Christianity's quarrels with the body. Its needs. Its desires. Its sheer materiality. But especially its sexual identity.

I got a glimpse that night, or, I should say, a reminder, of how deeply ambivalent Christians are about sex. I learned, too, how dishonest we're sometimes made by the unresolved disputes between our bodies and our beliefs.

After the service was over, after the worshipers had time to greet and thank the preacher, we ministers, five in all, retired to the pastor's study.

"Doc, you blessed me tonight," beamed the pastor, a middle-aged preacher of no mean talent himself. (Among black ministers and their circle of intimates, "Doc" or "Doctor" is an affectionate term given to preachers. It began, perhaps, as a way of upgrading the minister to the level of respect his gifts deserved, especially at a time when black ministers were prevented from completing their formal education.)

"Thank you, man," the preacher gently replied with a kind of "aw shucks" smile.

"Yeah, Doctor, you were awful, just terrible, boy," a second minister enthused, heaping on the guest the sort of congratulation black preachers often give to one another.

"Revrun, it was judgment in here tonight," another minister chimed in with yet another line of black preacherly praise. "You killed everythang in here. And if it wasn't dead, you put it in intensive care." At that, we all laughed heartily and agreed that the preacher had hit his mark.

As a young minister in my early twenties, I was just glad to be in their number, bonding with ministerial mentors, men standing on the front line of spiritual warfare, or, as the black church memorably refers to it, "standing in the gap": carrying and crying the judgment of the Almighty, opening opportunity for salvation, proclaiming the soul's rescue and the requirements of redemption, and edifying believers with the inscrutable, wholly uncompromising, tell-it-like-it-is, to-be-preached-in-season-and-out-of-season gospel of the living God. I was simply enjoying this magical moment of fraternal friendliness. And it was just that. No women were there. No one thought it odd that they weren't. We never remarked once on their absence, and, indeed, we counted on their absence to say things, manly things, that we couldn't, didn't dare say, in mixed company. Still, I wasn't prepared for what followed.

"Revrun, I need to ask you something," the visiting preacher begged the pastor. His eyebrows were raised, a knowing look was on his face, and his voice affected, if not quite a mock seriousness, then a naughty whisper that clued us that his curiosity was more carnal than cerebral.

"Who is that woman with those big breasts who was sitting on the third aisle to my left?" he eagerly inquired. "Damn, she kept shouting and jiggling so much I almost lost my concentration."

"She is a fine woman, now," the pastor let on.

"Well, Doc, do you think you could fix me up with her?" the visiting preacher asked with shameless lust.

"I'll see what I can do, Revrun," the pastor promised.

The married preacher's naked desire shocked me. To my surprise, it also made me secretly envious. The fact that he could seek an affair less than an hour after he had thundered against it offended my naive, literal sense of the Christian faith. I thought immediately of how angry I'd been in the past when I heard preachers justify their moral failings, especially their sexual faults. Such ministers chided their followers with a bit of theological doggerel dressed up as a maxim: "God can hit a straight lick with a crooked stick."

But in ways I didn't yet completely understand, I envied the preacher's sense of sexual confidence. He was able to zoom in on his desire and, to borrow a favorite neo-Pentecostal catchphrase, "to name it and claim it." The preacher—and he was surely aware of it, since he didn't let principle stand in the way of his pleasure—had apparently made his peace, however temporary, with the war between Christian ideals and delights of the flesh. I hadn't.

Still, I'm glad I didn't mount a high horse that night to trample the preacher. I've developed enough failures in the sometimes bloody management of erotic desire. So have many other black Christians. Especially those seeking, like most people of faith, to close the gap between what they believe and how they behave. That night, I was nearly tortured by questions I couldn't answer. Was the preacher's theology off? Did he have a flawed understanding of how a Christian should view the body and its sexual urges? Was his extreme sexual libertarianism just plain out of order? Was he simply a hypocrite? Or was he acting out, however crudely, a confused sense of black Christian sexuality that is, by turns, repressed and excessive? Or all of the above?

The answers to these questions are not as simple as we might believe, despite the rigid certainty of self-anointed arbiters of Christian Truth. And neither are the answers relevant simply for cases, like the one I've described, where everyone can agree that something was wrong. It's much more difficult to figure out how we can have a healthy sense of black Christian sexual identity in a world where being black has been a sin, where black sexuality has been viewed as a pathology, and where the inability to own—and to own up to—our black bodies has led us to devalue our own flesh. We must recover the erotic uses of our bodies from the distortions of white racism and the traps of black exploitation. We must liberate ourselves to embrace the Christian bliss of our black bodies.

At the beginning of the African presence in the New World, black bodies were viewed in largely clinical and capitalist terms. The value of black slave bodies was determined by their use in furthering the reach of Western colonial rule; expanding the market economies of European and American societies; institutionalizing leisure for white cultural elites; deepening the roots of democracy for white property-owning gentry; and providing labor for the material culture that dominates the American landscape. Interestingly, when Christianity poked its nose in, chattel slavery, already a vile and dehumanizing affair, got even uglier.

Christianity insisted there was a need to save the savages from their own cultural deficits. White Christians sought to rescue slaves from perdition by making sure what little soul they had was made suitable for the Kingdom of God. Christianity gave theological legitimacy, and racial justification, to widely held beliefs about black inferiority. It also sanctified the brutal methods deemed necessary to tame the beastly urges of black Africans. White society exploited black labor. White Christianity made it appear that God was behind the whole scheme. Some argued that God used slavery as a tool to bring backward Africans to America. They believed God used white slavers to save black souls by subjugating their bodies. Christian theology shook hands with slavery and sailed off into the sunset of white supremacy.

A key to keeping blacks under white control was the psychological poison pumped into the intellectual diets of slaves. Whites viewed black bodies as ugly, disgusting, and bestial, and blacks were made aware of this. Black bodies were spoken of in the same breath as, say, horses and cows. As if being viewed as an animal wasn't bad enough, blacks were also considered property. Because of Western beliefs about the connection between moral and aesthetic beauty, the belief in the ugliness of black bodies carried over to attitudes about black souls.

Black sexuality sat at the heart of such judgments. If black bodies were demeaned, black sexuality was demonized. Unless, of course, it was linked to breeding black babies for slavery, or, in the case of black women, satisfying the lust of white men. Thus, a central paradox of black sexuality began. Even as whites detested black bodies for their raw animalism, they projected onto those same black bodies their repressed sexual yearnings. Black bodies provided recreational and therapeutic relief for whites. Although that paradox has certainly lessened, it has not entirely disappeared.

For the most part, black sexuality was cloaked in white fantasy and fear. Black women were thought to be hot and ready to be bothered. Black men were believed to have big sexual desires and even bigger organs to realize their lust. White men became obsessed with containing the sexual threat posed by black men. The competition for white women was mostly mythical. It was largely the projection of white men's guilt for raping black women. Even after slavery, white men beat, burned, hung, and often castrated black men in response to the perceived threat black men represented. White men also repressed white female sexuality by elevating a chaste white womanhood above the lustful reach of black men. Well before gangsta rap, the crotch was the crux of black masculine sexual controversy.

During slavery and after emancipation, blacks both resisted and drank in sick white beliefs about black sexuality. Some blacks sought to fulfill the myth of unquenchable black lust. The logic isn't hard to figure out: if white folk think I'm a sexual outlaw, some blacks perhaps thought, I'll prove it. Other blacks behaved in exactly the opposite fashion. They rigidly disciplined their sexual urges to erase stereotypes of excessive black sexuality. During slavery, many black women resisted sexual domination through abortion, abstinence, and infanticide. They interrupted white pleasure and profit one body at a time.

The rise of the black church, first as an invisible institution and then as the visible womb of black culture, provided a means of both absorbing and rejecting the sexual values of white society. Black religion freed the black body from its imprisonment in crude, racist stereotypes. The black church combated as best it could the self-hatred and the hatred of other blacks that white supremacy encouraged with evil efficiency. It fought racist oppression by becoming the headquarters of militant social and political action in black communities. The black church produced leaders who spoke with eloquence and prophetic vigor about the persistence of white racism. It was the educational center of black communities, supporting colleges that trained blacks who became shock troops in the battle for racial equality. Black churches unleashed the repressed forces of cultural creativity and religious passion. The church also redirected black sexual energies into the sheer passion and emotional explosiveness of its worship services.

I'm certainly not saying, as do those who argue that black religion compensates for racial oppression—we can't beat up the white man so we cut up in church—that the displacement of black sexual energy by itself shaped black worship. I'm simply suggesting that the textures, styles, and themes of black worship owe a debt to a complicated sexual history. In sharp contrast to the heat of most black worship experiences, there emerged almost immediately in black churches a conservative theology of sexuality. In part, this theology reflected the traditional teachings of white Christianity. Out of moral necessity, however, black Christians exaggerated white Christianity's version of "PC"–Puritan Correctness. Later, many black Christians adopted white Christianity's Victorian repression to rebut the myth of black sexuality being out of control.

The contemporary black church still reflects the roots of its unique history. It continues to spawn social action, though not on the same fronts as it once did. The increased secularization of black communities, and the rise of political leadership outside of the black church, has blunted the focus of the church's prophetic ministry. Some things, however, have changed very little. There remains deeply entrenched in black churches a profoundly conservative theology of sexuality. Like all religious institutions where doctrine is questioned, rejected, perhaps even perverted by members, the black church faces a tense theological situation. Unlike, say, the Catholic or Episcopal Church where an elaborate and more unyielding hierarchy prevails, historically black churches have a real opportunity to bring lasting change more quickly to their religious bodies. Such change is sorely needed in black communities and churches where issues of sexuality have nearly exploded.

Of course, there are problems that are easily identified but are difficult to solve. Earlier and earlier, black boys and girls are becoming sexually active. Teen pregnancy continues to escalate. Besides these problems, there are all sorts of sexual challenges that black Christians face. The sexual exploitation of black female members by male clergy. The guilt and shame that result from unresolved conflicts about the virtues of black sexuality. The continued rule of black churches by a mainly male leadership. The role of eroticism in a healthy black Christian sexuality. The revulsion to and exploitation of homosexuals. The rise of AIDS in black communities. The sexual and physical abuse of black women and children by black male church members. The resistance to myths of super black sexuality. And the split between mind and body that leads to confusion about a black Christian theology of Incarnation. What should be done?

For starters, the black church should build on a celebration of the body in black culture and worship. Ours, quite simply, is a body-centered culture. Sharp criticism by black intellectuals, including me, of essentialism–the idea that there is such a thing as black culture's essence, and that we get at it by viewing blacks as a monolith, ignoring differences made by region, sexuality, gender, class, and the like–has made many critics reluctant to highlight persistent features of black life. But in many African and black American communities, colorful, creative uses of the body prevail. (Unfortunately, as we have learned with resurgent slavery and genital mutilation of females in Africa, destructive and oppressive uses of the body mark our cultures as well.) Many black folk use vibrant, sometimes flamboyant, styles and colors to adorn their bodies. Johnnie Cochran's purple suit and Dennis Rodman's weirdly exotic hairstyles and body tattoos reveal a flare for outrageous, experimental fashion. Plus, the styling of black bodies for creative expression–Michael Jordan's gravity-rattling acrobatics, singer Anita Baker's endearing tics, Denzel

Washington's smoothly sensuous gait, and Janet Jackson's brilliant integration of street and jazz dance—underscores the improvisational uses of black bodies.

The black church, too, is full of beautiful, boisterous, burdened, and brilliant black bodies in various stages of praising, signifying, testifying, shouting, prancing, screaming, musing, praying, meditating, singing, whooping, hollering, prophesying, preaching, dancing, witnessing, crying, faking, marching, forgiving, damning, exorcising, lying, confessing, surrendering, and overcoming. There is a relentless procession, circulation, and movement of black bodies in the black church: the choir gliding in and grooving to the rhythmic sweep of a grinding gospel number; members marching aisle by aisle to plop a portion of their earnings in the collection plate; women sashaying to the podium to deliver the announcements; kids huddling around the teacher for the children's morning message; the faithful standing at service's start to tell how good the Lord's been to them this week; the convicted leaping to their feet to punctuate a preacher's point in spiritual relief or guilt; the deliberate saunter to the altar of the "whosoever wills" to pray for the sick and bereaved, and for themselves; the white-haired, worldly wise deacon bowing down at his seat to thank God that he was spared from death, that "the walls of my room were not the walls of my grave," his bed "sheet was not my winding sheet," and his bed was not "my cooling board"; the church mother shaking with controlled chaos as the Holy Ghost rips straight through her vocal cords down to her abdomen; the soloist's hands gesturing grandly as she bends each note into a rung on Jacob's ladder to carry the congregation "higher and higher"; the ushers' martial precision as they gracefully guide guests to a spot where they might get a glimpse of glory; the choir director calling for pianissimo with a guileless "shhhh" with one hand as the other directs the appointed soprano to bathe the congregation in her honey-sweet "ha-lay-loo-yuh"; and the preacher, the magnificent center of rhetorical and ritualistic gravity, fighting off disinterest with a "you don't hear me," begging for verbal response by looking to the ceiling and drolly declaring "amen lights," twisting his body to reach for "higher ground," stomping the floor, pounding the pulpit, thumping the Bible, spinning around, jumping pews, walking benches, climbing ladders—yes literally—opening doors, closing windows, discarding robes, throwing bulletins, hoisting chairs, moaning, groaning, sweating, humming, chiding, pricking, and edifying, all to better "tell the story of Jesus and his love." In the black church, it's all about the body: the saved and sanctified body, the fruitful and faithful body, working and waiting for the Lord.

The body, too, is at the center of what Christian theologians have long termed the "scandal of particularity": the very idea that an unlimited, transcendent God would become a human being, time-bound and headed for death, was just too hard for nonbelievers to swallow. That scandal has special relevance for black Christians, who draw courage from a God who would dare sneak into human history as a lowly, suffering servant. From the plantation to the postindustrial city, suffering blacks have readily identified with a God who, they believe, first identified with them.

The black church has helped blacks find a way to overcome pain, to live through it, to get around it, and, finally, to prosper in spite of it. Black religion has often encouraged black folk to triumph over tragedy by believing that undeserved suffering could be turned to good use. That idea sparked the public ministry of Martin Luther King Jr., a towering son of the black church. The radical identification with Jesus' life and death, which happened, after all, in his body, has permitted black Christians to endure the absurd violence done to their bodies. Through church sacraments, black Christians nurtured and relieved their bodies' suffering memories. On every first Sunday of the month, or whenever they celebrated the Lord's Supper, black Christians broke bread and drank wine, knowing that Jesus' crucified body was their crucified body, and that Jesus' resurrected body could be theirs as well. Every time the words of Holy Communion were repeated, "this do in remembrance of me," black Christians remembered those lost warriors who once fought mightily against oppression but who now slept with the ancestors.

Above all, the Incarnation revealed to black folk a God who, when it came to battling impossible odds, had been there and done that. Because black Christians inevitably had to pass through the "valley of the shadow of death," they could take solace from a God who had faced a host of ills they faced. Divine abandonment. Cruel cursing. Ethnic bigotry. Religious marginalization. Unjust punishment. Spiteful epithets. And most important, vicious death. Just knowing that God had walked this same earth, eaten this same food, tasted this same disappointment, experienced this same rejection, fought this same self-doubt, endured this same betrayal, felt this same isolation, encountered this same opposition, and overcome this same pain often made the difference between black folk living and dying.

It is indeed ironic that, with so much staked on the body, many black Christians continue to punish themselves with the sort of extreme self-denial that has little to do with healthy sexuality. To a large extent, the black church has aimed to rid the black body of lascivious desires and to purge its erotic imagination with "clean" thoughts. All the while, the black worship experience formed the erotic body of black religious belief, with all the rites of religious arousal that accompany sexual union.

Indeed, the story of the visiting minister that begins this chapter portrays the erotic intensity of the black worship experience: the electric call and response between minister and congregation; the fervent temper of the preacher's words of wisdom and warning; the extraordinary effort by the minister to seduce the audience onto God's side through verbal solicitation; and the orgasmic eruption of the congregation at the end of the sermon. It requires no large sophistication to tell that something like sexual stimulation was going on.

Perhaps that's because there is a profound kinship between spirituality and sexuality. Great mystics figured that out a long time ago. More recently, so have black singers Marvin Gaye, the artist formerly known as Prince, and R. Kelly. Black Christians are reluctant to admit the connection because we continue to live in Cartesian captivity: the mind-body split thought up by philosopher Descartes flourishes in black theologies of sexuality. Except it is translated as the split between body and soul. Black Christians have taken sexual refuge in the sort of rigid segregation they sought to escape in the social realm—the body and soul in worship are kept one place, the body and soul in heat are kept somewhere else. That's ironic because, as critic Michael Ventura has argued, black culture, especially black music, has healed, indeed transcended, the split between mind and body inherited from Descartes and certain forms of Christian theology. Segments of secular black culture have explored the intimate bond of sexuality and spirituality. The black church has given a great deal to black culture, including the style and passion of much of black pop music. It is time the church accepted a gift in return: the union of body and soul.

The sensuality of our bodies must be embraced in worship. That sensuality should be viewed as a metaphor for the passion of our sexual relations as well. And vice versa. The link between sexuality and spirituality was hinted at when the Bible talked of the church as Christ's bride, and alternately, as the body of Christ. Because Christian belief is rooted in the Incarnation, Anglican theologian William Temple held that Christianity is literally the most material of all religions. The sheer materiality of our faith is not simply a protection against those versions of Christianity that get high on the soul's salvation and forget about the body's need to eat. It is also a rebuke to those who believe that God is opposed to our sexual pleasure. To twist literary critic Roland Barthes, we should celebrate the pleasure of the text, especially when the text is, literally, our bodies.

Simply put, the black church needs a theology of eroticism. Admittedly, that is a hard sell in an Age of Epidemic, where panic and paranoia, more than liberty and celebration, set our sexual moods. Of course, black sexuality has always thrived or suffered under a permanent sign of suspicion or revulsion. Still, that's no reason to be cavalier about sex when its enjoyment can kill us. A theology of eroticism certainly promotes safe sex. Our definition of safety, however, must include protection against the harmful sexual and psychic viruses that drain the life from our desire. Further, a theology of eroticism looks beyond the merely physical to embrace abstinence as a powerful expression of sexuality.

In the main, a theology of eroticism must be developed to free black Christian sexuality from guilty repression or gutless promiscuity. Sermon after sermon counsels black Christians to abstain from loose behavior. To sleep only with our mates. To save sex for permanent love. And to defer sexual gratification until we are married. In black churches, as with most religious institutions, hardly anyone waits for marriage to have sex. People sleep with their neighbor's spouse. Casual sex is more than casually pursued. And because the needs of their bodies make them liars with bad consciences, some drown their demons in a sea of serial monogamies. Little of this is highly pleasurable, but it's pleasurable enough to make us unhappy. Ugh!

What's even more intriguing is that the sermons pretty much stay the same. Black Christians pretty much tell their children and each other that that's how things ought to be. And consistency is seen as a substitute for tradition. But it certainly isn't. Vital, living traditions leave space for people to change bad habits because they have a better understanding of what the tradition should mean. As one wise churchman put it: *tradition* is the living faith of dead people, while the *traditional* is the dead faith of living people. Too often, the latter has ruled black churches. While we may share our forebears' faith, we can certainly leave aspects of their theologies behind.

A theology of eroticism is rooted in simple honesty about black sexuality. While we tell our kids not to have sex, more and more of them do. They are making babies, having babies, and dying from AIDS. The black church should lay off the hard line on teen sexuality. Sure, it must preach abstinence first. It should also preach and teach safe sex, combining condoms and common sense. It should tell kids from ages twelve through seventeen that when it's all said and done, human sexuality is still an enlarging mystery, a metaphor of how life seeks more of itself to sustain itself, of how life, as black theologian Howard Thurman remarked, is itself alive. (Of course, we adults could use a reminder of this as well.) Our sexuality is one way life reminds itself of that lesson. In the hands of groping teens, sex is often little more than bewilderment multiplied by immaturity, despite growing, groaning body parts that seem fit for the job. In an era when music videos, television commercials, daytime soaps, and nighttime cable movies exploit our kids' urges, it's no wonder that they, and indeed, all of us, have sex on the brain. If only we could use *that* organ more in our erotic escapades.

The bottom line, however, is that traditional black church methods of curbing teen sex aren't working. We must make a choice. Either we counsel our kids about how to have sex as safely as they can, or we prepare to bury them before their lives begin. The cruelty of contemporary sex is that the consequences of our kids' mistakes, the same mistakes we made, are often swift and permanent. Most black preachers and parents who tell kids they shouldn't have sex had sex as teens. If not, most of them surely tasted carnal pleasure before they were married. The guilt or embarrassment stirred by their hidden hypocrisy often makes them harsh and unyielding in their views on teen sexuality. The black church's theology of eroticism should place a premium on healthy, mature relations where lust is not mistaken for affection. It must make allowances for our children, however, to learn the difference, and to safely experiment with their bodies in pursuit of genuine erotic health. The black church should pass out condoms on its offering plates. At the least, it should make them available in restrooms or in the offices of clergypersons or other counselors. The days of let's-pretend-the-problems-will-go-away, never-fully-here-anyway, are now most certainly gone.

We must find remedies, too, for angst-ridden black preachers. Many of them stir anxiety in their congregations because of their own conflicted theology of sexuality. The visiting minister I spoke of earlier was bewitched by the erotic double bind that traps some ministers. He preached a theology of sexuality that satisfied the demands of black church tradition. But he was also moved by erotic desires that are rarely openly discussed in black churches, or in the seminaries that prepare men and women to pastor. The sexual exploitation of black women by black preachers, and the seduction of preachers by female members, rests on just this sort of confusion. (Of course, it also rests on a gender hierarchy in black churches where women do much of the labor but are largely prevented from the highest leadership role: the pastorate. The ecclesiastical apartheid of the black church, which is more than 70 percent female, continues to reinforce the sexual inequality of black women.) In many cases, both parties are caught in the thralls of unfocused erotic desire. Such desire doesn't receive reasonable, helpful attention. It is either moralized against or it lands on the wagging tongues of church gossips.

As a very young pastor—I was all of twenty-three years old—I sometimes participated in the sort of sex play that mocks healthy erotic desire. Once, after assuming the pastorate of a small church in the South, I received a call from a desperate female parishioner.

"Reverend Dyson, I need to see you right away," the soft, teary voice on my phone insisted. "It's an emergency. I can't discuss it on the telephone."

It was seven o'clock at night. Since I lived nearly a hundred miles from the city where my church was located, it would take me at least an hour and a half to reach her home.

"All right, Ms. Bright (not her real name)," I replied. "I'll be there as soon as I can."

I told my fiancée Brenda, with whom I was living, that a member needed me to come immediately. I tore up the highway in a frantic race to Ms. Bright's home. I was a young, relatively inexperienced pastor, new on the job, and eager to please. When I arrived at Ms. Bright's home, her parents greeted me at the door. Judging by the surprised look on their faces, her parents had no idea of their daughter's distress, or her urgent request to see me. When she appeared a few minutes later, I didn't let on that I'd just zoomed to their house to help relieve their daughter of whatever problem she had. To them, I guess it looked like I had come courting on the sly. After all, neither of us were married, and Ms. Bright was only a few years older than me. Although I was in a committed relationship with Brenda, my members didn't know that we were, as the '70s R&B hit goes, "living together in sin." (Already living in the Bible Belt, perhaps on its buckle, I was caught in the cross fire between sex and soul almost before my career as a pastor began.)

Ms. Bright suggested that we go upstairs to her room to talk. We excused ourselves from pleasant chitchat with her amiable parents. We soon found ourselves alone in her stylish, sweetly scented bedroom. I felt awkward. I'd never spent time alone with her before outside of the few occasions we spoke in church. Besides, I didn't know what signal my presence in her boudoir might send. But I soon found out what was weighing on her heart and mind.

"Reverend Dyson, I think I'm in love with you," she blurted out.

I was genuinely startled. I had never been a Don Juan. And despite the crude stereotypes of ministers as lotharios out to bed every woman within speaking distance, I certainly hadn't been promiscuous. I could count the number of girlfriends I'd had on one hand. And I'd never been led to think of myself as irresistibly handsome. I wasn't a guy, like many I'd known, for whom women seemed to pant and pine. I was just Mike Dyson, the poor kid from Detroit who worked hard, studied long, and mostly lived out his sexual fantasies with a few beautiful women.

"Well, Ms. Bright, I, um, I, well, I'm very flattered," I barely managed. By now my yellow face was flushed and my eyes were boring holes in the floor. "I don't know what to say."

Then it hit me. My pastor, Frederick Sampson, knowing that the advice would one day come in handy, had given me a stern warning.

"Never let a woman down harshly, Mike," Dr. Sampson said. "Always be gentle and considerate." Eureka! Here was my out.

"You know, Ms. Bright, what you've said makes me feel good," I uttered with more conviction. "I'm truly honored that a woman like you would even be interested in me. But you know I'm in love with Brenda."

I saw the disappointment in her eyes. Quickly extending Sampson's rule, I was determined not to make Ms. Bright feel foolish.

"But if I was available, you're the kind of woman I would definitely like to be with."

And I wasn't just blowing smoke, as they say. Ms. Bright was a very intelligent, inquisitive woman, as our few conversations revealed. She was also a beautiful woman; a tall five feet ten inches, she dwarfed my five-foot-nine-inch frame. She had flawless chocolate skin, an incandescent smile, a sensuous voice, and a voluptuous figure.

"Really?" she replied.

In retrospect, I guess that gave her an opening. And despite denying it then, I probably wanted her to find it. Although each of us had been sitting on chairs in her room, Ms. Bright stood up and, well, descended on me. Standing directly above me, she confessed that she'd spent a great deal of time daydreaming about me.

"I just can't get you off my mind," she said. "I really think I'm in love with you, Reverend Dyson. I don't know what I'm going to do."

As the words rolled off her tongue, which I began to notice more and more, she began to run her fingers through my hair. I was embarrassed, ashamed, almost mortified, and extremely turned on.

"Well, I don't know either, Ms. Bright," I muttered. "I guess, well, I don't know, I guess we'll just have to . . . "

Before I could finish, she was kissing me. Before long, we were kissing each other. Our tongues dueled with more energy than we'd been able to devote to resolving her problem. Except now, it was our problem. I wasn't in love with her, but my lust was certainly piqued. Talk about not letting a woman down roughly; I certainly wasn't flunking that test. But I felt bad for cheating on Brenda. I yanked myself free from Ms. Bright's luscious lip lock and came up for air, reaching as well for a little perspective.

"Look, Ms. Bright, I didn't mean for this to happen," I said through my heavy breathing. "After all, I'm your pastor, and I should be counseling you, not trying to get down with you."

She simply smiled. Then, before I could protest, she was out of her blouse. Next her bra fell to the floor! The queenly, regal pose she struck, part Pam Grier and part British royalty, made me feel like a lowly subject. And gawking at the sheer magnificence of her breasts, I was glad to be in her majesty's service. We groped each other like high school teens stranded in a hormonal storm. After nearly a half hour of this pantomimed intimacy, guilt suddenly overtook me. Better yet, the thought of having sex with her parents able to hear the bed creak and groan quenched my erotic fire. I recovered what little pastoral authority I had left—I think it was mixed up with my jacket and tie on the floor—and insisted that we quit. So we fixed up our clothes. Ms. Bright retouched her makeup, and without saying much—what could we say?—we went back downstairs to make small talk with her parents. After fifteen minutes or so, I bid them farewell and drove home far more slowly than I'd driven to my appointment. I was more disappointed at myself than angry at Ms. Bright. Despite what she said—and even she probably didn't really believe it—I didn't think Ms. Bright was in love with me. She simply had a crush, though, admittedly, it was a big one. Plus, she had a healthy dose of sexual desire, a subject we should have been able to talk about, not only in her house but in our church. We should have been able to refer to sex education classes, sermon series, Sunday school discussions, Sunday night forums, and a host of other ways that erotic desire might be addressed in the black church. Some churches are doing this, but they are far, far too few in number.

I was flattered that Ms. Bright wanted me. At the same time, I was ashamed that I'd given in to wanting her. I'd come to pray. I'd ended up the prey—the willing prey, as it turned out. Maybe Ms. Bright had seen the desire in my eyes, which failed to be disguised as pastoral concern. Maybe she was simply the first to act on what she knew we both wanted. Maybe she was just more honest.

On my way home, I couldn't help thinking of the visiting preacher. I got a lot more humble. Still, I kept thinking about my erotic encounter with Ms. Bright. Despite trying to feel bad about it, I found myself getting aroused all over again. I hadn't yet figured out that it's all right to enjoy erotic desire—to own up to the fact that you can be horny and holy—as long as you don't live at the mercy of your hormones. But if we can't talk about sex at home, and we can't talk about it at church, black Christians end up lying to ourselves and to the people to whom we're sexually attracted. And too often, we end up being much more destructive because of our erotic dishonesty.

Because so many black Christians have taken up the task of being sexual saviors—of crucifying the myths of black hypersexuality and sexual deviance—we abhor out-of-bounds sexuality. This social conservatism expresses itself as a need to be morally upright. Beyond reproach. (Unsurprisingly, gangsta rappers are high on the list of sinners. If its detractors actually ever listened to more than snippets of gangsta rap lyrics, they'd probably have a lot more grist for their critical mills.) Oh, if it was only that simple. If the black church—for God's sake, if any religious institution—was erotically honest, it would admit that the same sexual desire that courses through rappers' veins courses through the veins of its members. If many of the black ministers who wail against the sexual improprieties of hip-hop culture would be erotically honest, they'd admit that the same lust they nail rappers for breaks out in their own ranks. And there aren't too many sermons pointing that out.

The standard religious response has been: "Of course we have the same desires, but we fight them and put them in proper perspective." That's partly true. The desire is certainly fought. Why, you can see the strain of erotic repression on unmade-up faces, in long dresses that hide flesh, and in the desexualized carriage of bodies (notice the burden is largely on the women) in the most theologically rigid of orthodox black churches. But that's just the point: mere repression is not the proper perspective. We've got to find a mean between sexual annihilation and erotic excess. Otherwise, the erotic practices of church members will continue to be stuck in silence and confusion.

Neither are there many sermons that assail ministers for exploiting women. To be sure, there are women who think they were put on earth to please the pastor. For them, embracing his flesh is like embracing a little bit of heaven. Pastors should study their books on transference and help spread light on this fallacy. Of course, there are just as many women who simply get in heat over a man who can talk, especially if they've dealt with men for whom saying hello in the morning is an effort. So let's not romanticize the put-upon, helpless female who's charmed by the wiles of the slick, Elmer Gantry–like, minister-as-omnicompetent-stud-and-stand-in-for-God.

Too often, though, there are women who come to the minister seeking a helping hand who get two instead. Plus some lips, legs, arms—well, you get the picture. The black church is simply running over with brilliant, beautiful black women of every age, hue, and station. Pecan publicists. Ebony lawyers. Caramel doctors. Mocha engineers. Beige clerks. Bronze businesswomen. Brown housewives. Redbone realtors. Yellow laborers. Coffee teachers. Blueblack administrators. Copper maids. Ivory tellers. Chocolate judges. Tan students. Often these women are sexually pursued by the church's spiritual head, so to speak.

This fact makes it especially hard to endure the chiding of black preachers, veiled in prophetic language, launched at the sexual outlaws of black pop culture. In reality, the great Martin Luther King Jr. is the patron saint of the sexual unconscious of many black ministers, but for all the wrong reasons. For most of the time he lived in the glare of international fame, King, as is well known, carried on affairs with many women. He wasn't proud of it. He confessed his guilt. He said he'd try to do better. But he just couldn't give it up. Plus, he was away from home for 28 days of most months. Lest too many critics aiming to bring King down a notch or two for his moral failings get any ideas, bear in mind that he spent that kind of time away from his wife and children, under enormous stress and at great peril to his life, leading the war against racial inequality.

Many black ministers have absorbed King's erotic habits, and those of many white and black ministers before and after him. But they have matched neither his sacrifice nor his achievements. Not that such factors excuse King's behavior. But they do help us understand the social pressures that shaped King's erotic choices. One must remember, too, the ecology of erotic expression for civil rights workers. The wife of a famous civil rights leader once told me civil rights workers often went to towns where their presence reviled whites and upset many complacent blacks. She said it was natural that they sexually fed off of each other within their tight circles of sympathy and like-minded perspective. That squares as well with King's comment that a lot of his philandering was a release from the extraordinary pressures he faced. That's probably a large part of the story, though it can't be the complete story. King's behavior apparently predates his fame. His philandering was a complex matter.

In some senses, King's erotic indiscretions were the expression of a Casanova complex, pure and simple. That complex is especially present in famous men whose success is a gateway to erotic escapades. Indeed, their fame itself is eroticized. Their success is both the capital and the commodity of sex. It procures sexual intimacy and is the gift procured by (female) sexual surrender. Then, too, for black men there is a tug-of-war occurring on the psychosexual battlefield. Black men occupy a symbolic status as studs. That stereotype is one of the few that black men refuse to resist. They embrace it almost in defiance of its obvious falseness, as an inside joke. (How many times did King tell white audiences that blacks wanted to be their brothers, not their brothers-in-law, even as white women flaunted themselves before him? King was even set to marry a white woman when he was in seminary, but she was sent away, and King was warned by a mentor that he would never be able to be a black leader with a white wife.)

There is also a specific psychology of the ministerial Casanova. He believes he merits sexual pleasure because of his sacrificial leadership of the church community. Ironically, he sees the erotic realm as an arena of fulfillment because it is forbidden, a forbiddance that he makes a living preaching to others. (Yes, the cliché is certainly true that "That which is denied becomes popular.") But erotic forbiddance is a trap. The very energy exerted against erotic adventure becomes a measure for ministerial integrity. It becomes the very force the minister must resist if he is to be erotically honest. Erotic desire both induces guilt in the minister and is his reward for preaching passionately about the need for the denial of erotic exploitation! Self-delusion and self-centeredness mingle in this arena of sexual desire.

All of this sets up an erotic gamesmanship between minister and the potential—often willing—object of his erotic desire. One of the rules of the game is, "Let's see if I can get him to fall, to act against what he proclaims as truth." This is more than simply a case of Jezebel out to seduce the minister. It is a case of erotic desire being expressed in a way that reflects the unequal relation between male leaders and female followers.

Many ministers who travel on the revival circuit—delivering sermons and giving a lift to the sagging spirits of churches across the nation—too often settle into comfortable habits of sexual exploitation. Their regimen of erotic enjoyment gets locked in early in their careers. They travel to churches, preach the gospel, meet a woman or women, have sex, return home, go back the next year and do the same. Even ministers who stay in place can roam their congregations, or the congregations of their peers, in search of erotic adventure. What it comes down to is that the Martin Luther King Jrs., and the Snoop Doggy Doggs of black culture all want the same thing. The Snoops are up front about it. Most of us in the black church aren't.

The same erotic dishonesty applies to another sexual identity: homosexuality. The notorious homophobia of the black church just doesn't square with the numerous same-sex unions taking place, from the pulpit to the pew. One of the most painful scenarios of black church life is repeated Sunday after Sunday with little notice or collective outrage. A black minister will preach a sermon railing against sexual ills, especially homosexuality. At the close of the sermon, a soloist, who everybody knows is gay, will rise to perform a moving number, as the preacher extends an invitation to visitors to join the church. The soloist is, in effect, being asked to sing, and to sign, his theological death sentence. His presence at the end of such a sermon symbolizes a silent endorsement of the preacher's message. Ironically, the presence of his gay Christian body at the highest moment of worship also negates the preacher's attempt to censure his presence, to erase his body, to deny his legitimacy as a child of God. Too often, the homosexual dimension of eroticism remains cloaked in taboo or blanketed in theological attack. As a result, the black church, an institution that has been at the heart of black emancipation, refuses to unlock the oppressive closet for gays and lesbians.

One of the most vicious effects of the closet is that some of the loudest protesters against gays and lesbians in the black church are secretly homosexual. In fact, many, many preachers who rail against homosexuality are themselves gay. Much like the anti-Semitic Jew, the homophobic gay or lesbian Christian secures his or her legitimacy in the church by denouncing the group of which he or she is a member, in this case an almost universally despised sexual identity. On the surface, such an act of self-hatred is easy. But it comes at a high cost. Homophobic rituals of self-hatred alienate the gay or lesbian believer from his or her body in an ugly version of erotic Cartesianism: splitting the religious mind from the homosexual body as a condition of Christian identity. This erotic Cartesianism is encouraged when Christians mindlessly repeat about gays and lesbians, "we love the sinner but we hate the sin." A rough translation is "we love you but we hate what you do." Well, that mantra worked with racists: we could despise what racist whites did while refusing to despise white folk themselves, or whiteness per se. (Of course, there were many blacks who blurred that distinction and hated white folk as well as they pleased.) But with gay and lesbian identity, to hate what they do is to hate who they are. Gays and lesbians are how they have sex. (I'm certainly not reducing gay or lesbian identity to sexual acts. I'm simply suggesting that the sign of homosexual difference, and hence the basis of their social identification, is tied to the role of the sex act in their lives.)

The black church must develop a theology of homoeroticism, a theology of queerness. (Well, if we want to be absolutely campy, we might term it a theology for *Afriqueermericans*.) After all, if any group understands what it means to be thought of as queer, as strange, as unnatural, as evil, it's black folk. A theology of queerness uses the raw material of black social alienation to build bridges between gay and lesbian and straight black church members. The deeply entrenched cultural and theological bias against gays and lesbians contradicts the love ethic at the heart of black Christianity. Virulent homophobia mars the ministry of the black church by forcing some of our leading lights into secret and often self-destructive sexual habits. James Cleveland, considered the greatest gospel artist of the contemporary black church, died several years ago, it is rumored, from AIDS. Aside from embarrassed whispers and unseemly gossip, the black church still hasn't openly talked about it. Perhaps if gay and lesbian black church members could come out of their closets, they could leave behind as well the destructive erotic habits that threaten their lives.

The black church should affirm the legitimacy of homoerotic desire by sanctioning healthy unions between consenting gay and lesbian adults. After all, promiscuity, not preference, eats away at the fabric of our erotic integrity. Are gays and lesbians who remain faithful to their partners committing a greater sin than married heterosexuals who commit adultery? The ridiculousness of such a proposition calls for a radical rethinking of our black Christian theology of sexuality.

Central to the doctrine of Incarnation in the black church is the belief that God identified with the most despised members of our society by becoming the most despised member of our society. Sunday after Sunday, black ministers invite us to imagine God as, say, a hobo, or a homeless person. Well, imagine God as gay. Imagine God as lesbian. Is the gay or lesbian body of God to be rejected? Better still, isn't God's love capable of redeeming a gay or lesbian person? The traditional black theological answer has been yes, if that person is willing to "give up" his or her sin—in this case, being gay or lesbian—and turn to God. But a more faithful interpretation of a black theology of love and liberation asserts that God takes on the very identity that is despised or scorned—being black, say, or being poor, or being a woman—to prove its worthiness as a vehicle for redemption. We don't have to stop being black to be saved. We don't have to stop being women to be saved. We don't have to stop being poor to be saved. And we don't have to stop being gay or lesbian to be saved. Black Christians, who have been despised and oppressed for much of our existence, should be wary of extending that oppression to our lesbian sisters and gay brothers.

The black church continues to occupy the center of black culture. Although most black folk have never officially joined its ranks, the influence of the black church spreads far beyond its numbers. The black church raised up priests to administer healing to wounded spirits in slavery. It produced prophets to declare the judgment of God against racial injustice. The black church has been at the forefront of every major social, political, and moral movement in black culture. It remains our most precious institution. It has the opportunity to lead again, by focusing the black erotic body in its loving, liberating lens. A daughter of the black community, Jocelyn Elders, attempted to bring the sharp insight and collective wisdom of our tradition to a nation unwilling to ponder its self-destructive sexual habits. Let's hope that her advice won't be lost on those closer to home. Like Marvin Gaye, black churches and communities need sexual healing. If we get healed, we might just be able to help spread that health beyond our borders.

Nineteen

HOMOTEXTUALITIES: THE BIBLE, SEXUAL ETHICS, AND THE THEOLOGY OF HOMOEROTICISM

The issue of homosexuality has reaped a whirlwind of controversy and acrimonious debate in most Christian communities. I believe that one of the explanations for black homophobia is the realization that if heterosexuality—the supposed "normal" sexuality— has been demonized in the West for centuries, then surely black homosexuality will only up the ante of black oppression. Thus, ironically enough, blacks identify with mainstream sexual values—the very mainstream that has censored and castigated black heterosexuality—when they practice homophobia. I am not arguing that homophobia has no homegrown black varieties; I am simply suggesting that such homophobia allows blacks to forge solidarity with a culture that has excluded them. Thus one form of bigotry is traded for another. In this interview, conducted by the very sharp cultural critic and gay activist Kheven LaGrone, I argue that lesbians, bisexuals, gays, trans- gender, and all other-sexed people have a right to the "tree of life," and that they can find theological and biblical support for their religious and sexual existence. Although I have written elsewhere about gay, lesbian, bisexual, transgender, and other-sexuality, I have never been as extensive, analytical, wide-ranging, or as daring in discussing the subject as I am in this interview, a tribute to the provocative questions posed to me by LaGrone.

Please elaborate on your theology of homoeroticism.

What I mean by theology of homoeroticism is a theology that is grounded in the biblical admonition to acknowledge sexuality as a crucial function of human iden- tity, and as a symbol of the interpenetration of the divine and the human, signi- fying a fusion of planes. Since we are grounding our sexual ethics in a theology that speaks poignantly to human experience, it is natural to turn to the Bible to justify, legitimate, or sanction our beliefs. I believe that there is theological and biblical space for the articulation of a homoerotic instinct, homosocial ideas, and a homosexual identity. People who happen to be same-sex identified can certainly find support within our churches.

Furthermore, I sought, in my notion of a theology of homoeroticism, to underscore an implicitly homoerotic moment within the ecclesiastical order of black Christendom. Think, for instance, of men claiming to love Jesus standing on their feet in fully enthralled ecstasy, emoting about their connection to a God who became flesh and dwelled among us, as a man. For men to publicly proclaim their intense, unsurpassed love for a God who became a man leaves the door open for homoerotic identification and communion within the liturgy of the black ecclesial universe. In short, the black church provides space for men and women to love their own gender in erotic ways with biblical and theological sanction. My conception of the theology of homoeroticism is an attempt to develop a theologically sound and biblically justified relationship of love that is the underlying ethic within any sensual order, regardless of one's orientation, whether it is bisexual, transsexual, transgendered, gay, lesbian, or heterosexual. The prevailing ethic in any sexuality ought to always highlight the precise function of love in the adjudication of competing erotic claims. Whenever there is a contest between destructive incarnations of lust and righteous expressions of erotic communion, love promotes the latter. That doesn't mean that lust or fantasy cannot embody an ethically justifiable sexual urge. But it does mean that we have to pay attention to how a relationship of justice is exercised within the context of a sexual ethic. Sexual relations are related to the theological and moral ideals to which we subscribe.

When I think about homosexuality or any sexual identity, the prevailing idea is not simply satisfaction of the erotic drive and the sexual urge, but the manner in which the human being is recognized as the center of one's sexual ethic. Corporeal identity, theologically speaking, should exist in relationship to the divine order that prescribes human activity. A homoerotic theology is an acknowledgment that there are legitimate means to express same-sexuality, and the fantasies and erotic desires that grow from it. It also holds that there's a way of theologically asserting love as the predicate of such unions, since love ought to be the central principle of any sexual orientation. The question should be, regardless of orientation: How does this relationship enable the flourishing of an ethic of self-concern and other-regard? If that basic test is met within a sexual ethic, then the content of one's sexual identity should not be dictated by traditional theological proscriptions of homoerotic union. Even in the black church we can affirm the sexual legitimacy of brothers and sisters who do not meet the heterosexual norm, and still support them as fellow members of a religious community.

A theology of homoeroticism points to the effort to embody the full expression of God's sexual gifts to us, and to find legitimate theological support for the articulation of a broad erotic order within the context of our religious beliefs. If we can't do it there then we can't do it anywhere. Sex and salvation should be seen as neither mutually exclusive nor identical. However, they are often mutually reinforcing, since sexual union within a religious ethic is often a symbol of God's care and love for the other. Erotic unions at their best engender the salvific function of intimate contact between God and believer, a relationship often pictured as one between a lover and his beloved. In that light, a believer's sexual identity should be fully supported within an ecclesial context that embraces the erotic as a symbol of divine presence and affirmation.

A theology of homoeroticism combats recalcitrant prejudice against alternative sexualities—prejudices, by the way, that parallel bigotry against the black body in Western thought and culture. That makes it even more painful to observe the failure of the black church to embrace the full range of sexual identities that have been mobilized and manifested within our communities. In so doing, we have mimicked the sexual bigotry that has bedeviled us. I suppose such behavior is to be expected, since we have failed to be just and fair with gender relations in the black church. If the gendered character of heterosexual ethics has presented a profound challenge to the black church, God knows that homosexuality and homoeroticism present a formidable challenge. That's even the case for theologies of liberation that have been promulgated and, in limited form, adapted in the black church.

Of course, we can account for such resistance to a liberating sexual ethic by tracing it to the schism between body and soul that many black believers adapted in the face of feeling that they had to defend themselves against a charge of sexual profligacy, perversion, and impurity. Thus the black church bought into the division of the body and soul that the white church foisted on us to justify its psychic, moral, and material investments in chattel slavery and racial hegemony. The white church justified its assault on black humanity and its evil experiment in slavery by saying, "at least we're taking care of their souls," a goal they sought to achieve by containing and controlling the black body. In the minds of white Christians, the black body was a savage body. In a white Christian prism, the ethical end, the moral telos, of slavery was the social, psychic, and theological subordination of the African savage to European Christianity. This ideological matrix provided the crass ethical utilitarianism for European-American Christianity's justification of slavocracy: "As long as we're addressing their soul's salvation, we can do what we will to their bodies." But this theological schizophrenia that rested on the artificial division of body and soul was more Greek than Hebraic, since the latter insists on the essential unity of corporeal and spiritual identity. Such theological schizophrenia introduced into our culture some vicious beliefs that have negatively impacted our racial self-perceptions, not only as subjects of our own sexuality but also as objects of the criminalization of our sexuality by white culture. The black church hasn't done a good job of resisting the worst elements of theological schizophrenia, leading us to suppress alternative, unconventional, and transgressive sexualities in the black church and beyond.

So that almost leads directly to my next question: Do you think that black homosexuals can use the Bible for sexual healing? If yes, how, and what kind of healing?

Black homosexuals can definitely use the Bible for sexual healing. They can do so because the biblical texts are a reflection of historical struggles with enlightened revelation. God has placed on the hearts and minds of human beings beliefs about how we should live our lives, even though such beliefs are fallible since they are mediated by the human voice and cognition. The Scriptures reflect the attempt of human beings to wrestle with divine revelation within the context of our particular histories, given cultures and local traditions. In interpreting biblical texts, we must always pay attention to what biblical scholars call the *Sitz im Leben*—the historical context within which scriptural revelations emerged.

Consequently, we must always be on the lookout for the political hermeneutic of a biblical text. What I mean by political hermeneutic is that the horizon of interpretation is always shaded by the social order in which readers and hearers discover themselves. We must remember that the Bible was compiled over the course of a few centuries. That means that there are an incredibly diverse array of identities, intentions, ethical limits, and political philosophies articulated within the discursive and theological perimeters that shape the interpretation of the Bible and God's revelation. Even though some of us think of the Bible as the inspired word of God—the transcendental truth of eternity mediated through written revelation—we must not forget the critical role of the amanuensis. Whether it was Matthew, Mark, Luke, or John, or the scribes of the Pentateuch, or one of the ostensible authors in the JEDP documentary hypothesis, the truth is, they were secretaries—or as Mary J. Blige might say, and I'll pronounce this phonetically, seck-uh-taries! And secretaries can get stuff wrong, sometimes by mistake! They can leave the i's undotted, the t's uncrossed, or they may occasionally impose on a document their own beliefs or shades of their own meaning.

Remember that Paul says at one point in the Scriptures—and I'm paraphrasing—"Now this is what God says, and this is what I'm telling you." So he at least tried to gesture toward a hermeneutical ethic that acknowledged the implicit human character that shapes the record of God's inspiration. He at least tried to distinguish between human interpolations and divine revelation—a notion that is fraught with peril, to be sure, since providence and revelation are concepts often manipulated by religious elites or those with claims to esoteric knowledge. Moreover, Paul metaphorically suggested the human limitations of comprehending divine revelation and the fallibility of interpreting God's word when he declared, "We have this treasure in earthen vessels."

I note all of this as a backdrop to saying, yes, as with any of us, I think gay, lesbian, transgendered, transsexual, bisexual, and all other-sexed black Christians can certainly turn to the Bible for sexual healing. After all, this is the great book of love that points to the appropriate ethical etiquette for our sexual behavior. As such, it points back to God. The mores, folkways, and moral traditions that shape us inevitably impinge on our consciousness and color our understanding of what we should do and how we should behave. Conscience is the product of a historical encounter with ethical ideals. One's conscience is always shaped by the culture in which one is reared. Therefore our beliefs about the Bible, about ethical behavior, about good and bad, and about how we should adhere to certain principles are unavoidably shaped by the political and social and moral contexts we inherit and create. Depending on how it has been deployed and interpreted, the Bible has been both the Ur-text and Err-text of black ethical existence. It has been the great, grand narrative thread that has been weaved throughout the collective history of African American people and through the individual consciousness of millions of blacks, even if they didn't officially join the church. "The Book" has been the dominant interpretive touchstone for the ethical behavior of African people in America and other parts of the black diaspora.

Black homosexuals can turn to the Bible for sexual healing, just as many of us heterosexuals have, because it tells us that God loves us, that God created us in God's image, and that we should learn to accept ourselves as we are. Of course, I realize that the process of self-acceptance is an index of our evolving spiritual maturity. It takes profound spiritual and moral wisdom to claim with our own lives on full theological display that what God made is good. We can make such a claim despite the critical modifications introduced into Christian thought through Augustinian themes of original sin and the ethical miasma that was its consequence in "the fall." We must accentuate the positive dimensions of human identity and self-conception as the admittedly distorted reflection of the *imago dei*. Still, we can affirm our re-created goodness through discourses of redemption open to *all* human beings. There is no asterisk in the biblical promise of redemption that excludes homosexuals. We have to reclaim the primordial goodness of God that ultimately took human form in Jesus. As they say in Christian circles, God didn't make any junk, and that means that whomever God has made, whether homosexual or heterosexual, is a good person.

I realize there are debates about biological determinism versus social construction in sexuality. I know there's a dispute about whether gay and lesbian sexuality, indeed all sexualities, reflect an inherent predisposition biologically implanted in the human genetic code that regulates sexual orientation, or if sexual identity is the result of human choice. I happen to believe that gays and lesbians can no more get up tomorrow morning and be heterosexual than heterosexuals can get up tomorrow morning and be gay or lesbian. I'm not gainsaying the fluidity of sexual identity, the elasticity of erotic urges, the changeability of passionate proclivities, or the broad continuum of sensual engagements and stimuli. And I'm not suggesting that biological urges are not socially constructed. After all, even homosexuals who grow up in a culture where their identity and self-perception is shaped in the crucible of heterosexism, internalize the belief that it is a sin or an unbearable stigma to be gay or lesbian. Thus they often suppress their sexual desires and erotic urges, whether they are conceived to be "natural" or constructed.

That is why the coming-out process is often especially volatile: it involves the painful irony of self-identification with the very sexual identity that has been culturally demonized. That's why there's so much self-hatred among gays and lesbians. The coming-out process must address the fact that the self has been artificially split off from self-consciousness, at least a self-consciousness that is socially supported. This accounts for why the homosexual ego is coerced into epistemic and ethical isolation, or the proverbial "closet." In the closet, one must subordinate one's "natural sexuality" to society's accepted sexual norms, to its entrenched mores. So the Bible should help Christians liberate the sexual urge from artificially imposed restrictions and repressions. In the case of homosexuals, such restrictions and repressions are fueled by heterosexist values, but these values, I believe, can be critiqued by an appeal to a progressive sexual ethic, an enlightened biblical hermeneutic, and a humane theological tradition. How can black homosexuals use the Bible for sexual healing? They can do as all Christians should do: express their sexuality in the context and pursuit of a right relationship with God, which is the predicate of all sexual ethics.

But critics who seek to proof-text their opposition to homosexuality often neglect to interpret such biblical passages in their larger theological meaning. For instance, the story of Sodom and Gomorrah is more about underscoring the necessity for hospitality to strangers than it is about homosexual perversion. In essence, the larger pericopes in which biblical texts are contained are either neglected, severed from their interpretive frameworks through theological ax grinding, or subject to hermeneutical myopia. Hence the practice of biblical interpretation reinforces the heterosexist culture from which the theological repression of sexual difference has emerged. What's fascinating about black Christian appeals to the Bible to justify suppression of homosexuality is that such appeals are quite similar to those made by whites to justify slavery. Then again, that was already a familiar hermeneutical move in black religious circles, since it had been employed to justify theological strictures against the ecclesial expression of female authority. Those of us promulgating a theology of homoeroticism must engage in hermeneutical warfare and interpretive battle, not only with the text but also with the heterosexist presuppositions that shaped the biblical narratives and their subsequent mainstream interpretation.

Finally, I think that Jesus states the bottom line when he says that all of the law and prophets were contained in his summary of the ethical aim of Christian belief. "Thou shalt love the Lord thy God with all thy heart, and with all thy soul, and with all thy mind. This is the first and great commandment. And the second is like unto it, Thou shalt love thy neighbor as thyself. On these two commandments hang all the law and the prophets."

That means that we must embrace and affirm all brothers and sisters regardless of where we stand on the mysteries of sexual identity. Too often we have focused on a subsidiary accounting of sexual identity and thrust it into primary consideration to determine legitimate standing within the religious community. Being in right relationship with God and our neighbor is the crucial factor in our Christian existence. Once that issue is settled, then sexual orientation becomes subsidiary.

Sacred orientation is more important than sexual orientation. When the Bible is read through that liberating lens and through the prism of self-acceptance in light of God's offer of the gift of love and affirmation, it can be read as a source of sexual healing for homosexuals.

One of the most crucial issues a liberating interpretation of the Bible can address is the culture of dishonesty that smothers alternative sexualities. Gays and lesbians, as well as all other-sexed people, often have had to deny to themselves they were homosexual. They denied their sexuality to others who might have perceived it even before they did, a perception that might have caused them great discomfort. They often have had to stay in an epistemological closet, a theological closet, a sociological closet, and to some degree, even a biological closet, because they didn't want to suffer the consequences of coming out. The culture of deceit imposed on gays and lesbians has to be relieved by the church's open affirmation of their legitimacy, so that they don't have a distorted consciousness and a bruised conscience about their own sexuality. In the final analysis, we are liberated into self acceptance by a loving and forgiving God.

Okay. You are going to change everybody's mind.

We can hope.

Well, I think so. You've already largely answered my next question, but I'm going to ask it in case there is something you want to add. How do we reread the Bible as a guide to promoting complete and healthy homosexual relationships?

As I've stated, in order to skillfully interpret the Bible, we've got to get at the social, political, and ideological history of the time during which its constitutive texts emerged. By so doing, we get a sense of the philosophical reflections on race, gender, culture, class, and of course, sexuality as well, that penetrated the discursive frames and theological views of the Bible. Some of these reflections were egalitarian, but many more were authoritarian. Then, too, we've got to acknowledge that the culture in which we live shapes our self-understanding, as well as our understanding of our relationship to the Bible, and what role it should play in regulating our intellectual and moral lives. Our cultural situations even affect how we think we are capable of transforming our self-understanding through a new interpretation, perhaps even radical reinterpretation, of the Bible in light of the moral aspirations that we learn to claim as legitimate components of our individual and collective identities.

But it's equally important to understand there are multiple textualities within revelation's household. Of course, the Bible is the crucial, significant, and central text that shines on other texts interpreted in its light, and within the circumference of its ethical imagination. But a crucial implication of revelation is the belief in the variegated modalities through which it is articulated, which means that God speaks and is revealed to us in a number of ways. Even though the Bible is the hermeneutical ground of all textualities and modalities of revelation, it is not the exclusive or exhaustive medium of revelation. I think fundamental Christians in particular fail to comprehend this point, or at least they strongly disagree with this theological belief and interpretive principle. As a result, there is often in such circles a species of bibliolatry, or worship of the Bible. In my view, we should only worship the God who inspired the Bible. Bibliolatry is a way to foreclose wrestling with the complex demand of responsible assessment of the contradictory data of human experience in light of religious belief. Bibliolatry resolves all complexity, nuance, ambiguity, and so on.

Other Christians believe that we can't worship the Bible on the premise that God continues to speak. When we close the Bible, we have neither shut God's mouth nor closed God's mind. The radical openness of the mouth and mind of God means there is ongoing revelation in our times. It means that God is still speaking to us. That means that we have scriptural-like, biblical-like revelations that need to be taken seriously. The backdrop of such critical reflection is the understanding that the Bible is, besides a book of faith, also a book of history. It is a text that belongs to time and circumstance. Even though it claims to mediate eternal truth—a claim I take seriously—its medium is birthed in contingency. God's word is true, but the means by which we know it are limited, finite, and fallible. That means we've got to confront the historical conditions of biblical production. We've got to ask the questions: Why were all the books in the Bible written by men? Why was the canon largely shaped by masculinist sensibilities? In many ways, the canon reflects a patriarchal code rearticulated as theological necessity. In truth, historical contingency has been recapitulated as transcendental inevitability. Those of us believers who are skeptical, even suspicious of human claims of divine revelation, also believe that God continues to speak to liberated—and liberating—people.

Therefore, in spite of occasional biblical crankiness about (alternative) sexualities, one can conceive of the biblical worldview as an interpretive canvas on which to sketch a liberating ethical intentionality. We must account for the manner in which writers smuggled their biases into the biblical text, even as the biblical landscape accommodated the social perspectives and cultural norms of societies that shaped its construction. We must also take the risk of reinterpretation and posit the principle of extended canonicity. I think we have to appeal to the extrabiblical textualities—of experience, suffering, and oppression—that shape the lives of believers and affect the modalities and anatomy of revelation. It is extrabiblical revelation because it is not contained in the Bible, but the Bible is contained in the believer's arc of experience. But blacks, women, gays, lesbians, and other minorities have to risk reinterpreting the words of the Bible in light of the Word—to whom the text points and who legitimates the experience of these minorities.

That covers the Bible, but what about the Qu'ran and other sacred Scriptures?

Sure, the same applies to the Qu'ran, the Bhagavad-Gita, the Torah, and other holy texts by which religious believers abide. And what I say is significant for all religious communities, whether they believe God speaks through Moses or Muhammad.

I wrote a story years ago about a black man who was rescued by Jesus, and they made love. So basically, it was very erotic, with brown skin to brown skin. What is your reaction to that type of story?

I think that there's space in our fantasy lives for the fusion of autonomous human eroticisms and divinely ordered sexual identities, especially as we struggle to imagine the dynamic and complex nature of our relationship to God. We have to remember that the intimate relation between believers and God is deeply and profoundly erotic at points, a perception that is reinforced in biblical texts and in theological and religious literature of all sorts throughout the ages. It makes sense that erotic communion is the analogical predicate for the intimate relation between the divine and the human. After all, we start with what we know—intimate human communion—and analogize to what we imagine—God's identity. Since erotic relations that take place in the context of a committed relationship is one of the most profound unions on earth, it is the basis for understanding the intensity of God's presence.

I think that whether it's your story or the story I read once, I think, in the book, *Spirituality for Ministry*, by Urban T. Holmes, more than twenty years ago—where some nuns were either fantasizing about making love to Jesus or dreaming about him in a sexual fashion—the notion of erotic engagements with God appear to be honored by sacred precedent. Communion with God takes multiple forms. I don't think we can, in an a priori fashion, determine any sexual orientation per se as off-limits when it comes to understanding our relationship to God. It's important in this context to view our erotic relations in a metaphoric vein, that is, as attempts to analogize the highest moment of human ecstasy in regard to the ecstatic communion with God. Penetration of the flesh, among other erotic gestures, becomes a vehicle for a realized spiritual communion. I think all forms of edifying, nondestructive erotic play can ultimately become true grist for the mill of our sexual imaginations and express true hunger for God.

Let me ask you this then: I shared this story with a friend of mine, and he was offended. He called it blasphemy and he didn't want to touch the story; he didn't want to finish it. It was almost as if he were being contaminated or getting the evil spirit from the story itself, almost like he was afraid of it. What do you think about that?

Beliefs or fantasies that are radically dissimilar to our normal beliefs, behavior, and identity are certainly dangerous. They're taboo. They are contaminating, but perhaps in a good sense. It conjures for me the title of Mary Douglas's magisterial work, *Purity and Danger*. In some religious communities, the sexual relation is never to be thought of in relationship to God; the purity of God's identity is not to be enmeshed in the passionate, erotic communion. And yet God creates human beings with sexual organs and orientations. I think it is very dangerous and disturbing for many of us to imagine a different sexual order than the one that supports and governs our everyday existence. Plus, let's face it, we often fear what we don't understand. Or as Stevie Wonder phrased it, "when you believe in things that you don't understand, then you suffer"—but he added a key phrase that the dominant society should take to heart: "Superstition ain't the way." We could replace superstition with hate, fear, intolerance, bigotry, and the like. America once feared blacks and oppressed us and, when forced to accept us, discovered either that we weren't so different or that we presented a valuable difference that the nation eventually learned to embrace. The inability to embrace sexual difference says more about a culture or tradition that strangles innovation and creativity in our relationships to one another and to God, than it says about the sinful character of the fantasy or imagination that might offend us. Beliefs and passions that fall outside of the norm often bring terror, perhaps even the terror of self-recognition, which may be the ultimate terror. The possibility that the very thing I despise may represent a suppressed fantasy is all the more cause to outlaw that fantasy.

How important is fantasy to our sexuality?

I think fantasy is extraordinarily important to sexuality. Fantasy draws from the collective or individual expressions of one's historically shaped erotic and sexual desire. Fantasy is the projection of a possible erotic or sexual engagement with another human being or entity that is driven by our socially constructed and biologically driven conception of what is desirable. So fantasy, in one sense, is indivisible from the political and historical contexts in which our identities are shaped. We learn to desire the things we're taught to believe are desirable. Sometimes desire cuts across the grain of the socially sanctioned and "appropriate" fantasy. Certain fantasies are ruled as legitimate and others as illegitimate and, unsurprisingly, the rules follow a broadly patriarchal and heterosexist vein. It's just fine for young men to want to make love to young women at the appropriate age, but it's reprehensible for men and women to gravitate to their own gender, regardless of age. This notion falls into the realm of permissible fantasy. Permissible fantasy is an index of the sexual relations that may not be explicitly or overtly encouraged, but are nonetheless tolerated because they fall within the realm of heterosexual erotic identity. I'm thinking here, for example, of illicit sex between a married man and a woman. Even though there is a taboo to such sex, it causes nothing like the fear or revulsion of homosexual relations. In fact, the notion of a same-sex union is so profoundly offensive that its very existence is thought to be the mark of perversion, while adultery is viewed as a "sin." At that level, homoerotic fantasy cuts across the socially constructed object of desire and becomes a subversive political gesture in a heterosexist universe.

Fantasy nurtures the erotic life and permits the idealization of possibly perfect unions. If fantasies are read as both political projections and individual assertions of unrealized potential, or even remembered achievement, they become more than neo-Freudian expressions of suppressed sexualities. Of course, fantasy is also a crucial philosophical plank in the argument over offensive, transgressive sexual behavior. For instance, in the Catholic Church right now, the scandal over pedophilic priests is linked in the minds of some critics with outlaw sexual fantasies of illicit sex between men and boys. The fact that at least one accused priest was actively involved in NAMBLA, the North American Man/Boy Love Association, only served to cement the belief in the minds of millions that priests were little more than closeted gay pedophiles out to seduce altar boys. The perception among many straight Catholics is that this is a homoerotic fantasy that needs to be restricted, that if the fantasy didn't exist then the sexuality couldn't flourish. And even if the fantasy exists, the behavior should be outlawed.

Sexual fantasies present a template for erotic desire that is reproduced in bodily behavior. The fantasy is literally the prelude to the kiss. If one can control the fantasy life of a human being, then one might control the behavior that issues from the fantasy. Still, one might reasonably question if there is strict causality between fantasy and fulfillment. One is reminded of Jesus' words of warning that to even imagine an act of adultery is to essentially commit it: "But I say unto you, that whosoever looketh on a woman to lust after her hath committed adultery with her already in his heart." Few critics of homosexuality are likely to remonstrate with equal passion against millions who have lusted after a woman in their hearts, and who have, by Jesus' standards, already committed adultery. (One thinks unavoidably here of Jimmy Carter's confession in the pages of *Playboy* that he had lusted in his heart and therefore sinned.) Jesus is aiming here not simply at causality, but at the necessity to discipline one's imagination according to the ethical standards of a monogamous, committed relationship.

Hence, it wasn't the sexual identity that was the cause of sin—after all, it was articulated within the logic of heterosexuality—but a sexual imagination or fantasy that subverted faithful relations. One supposes, therefore, that one's sexual orientation would not necessarily alter the ethical prescriptions that regulate one's fantasies when one is in a committed relationship. One's moral practice seems more important in the fantasy life than one's sexual orientation. But I do think that fantasies play a legitimate, even crucial, function in sexual identity by nurturing a vision of the ideal relations in one's mind that one may not ever live up to. In this positive sense, fantasy is the picture of perfection against which practices are measured. That can be quite punishing because in a heterosexual world, where erotic ideals of perfection crowd the fantasies of many men, the collective imaginary, politically speaking, is often a pornographic one. Most women cannot live up to that ideal and perhaps they shouldn't have to even try to reach that unattainable goal.

(The reason for my qualification here is that I don't want to rule out all acts of pornography as problematic, such as those enjoyed within a healthy erotic relationship among committed adults.)

My comments and observations are equally applicable to gays and lesbians. Ironically enough, in the humdrum, mundane, quotidian relations among homosexuals, gays and lesbians end up depressingly similar in their lives to heterosexuals. The lion's share of that depression is experienced by close-minded heterosexuals who come to realize that in most regards, there's no big difference in gays and lesbians and straight folk in their day-to-day existence. They just happen to have sex differently and may have the same sexual fantasies as heterosexuals, just with different partners. I'm not suggesting that all fantasies are good, healthy, or edifying, but that has nothing to do with sexual orientation. When they occur in a context of erotic and sexual health, as well as ethical strength, fantasies are just fine.

On an individual level, do you think there are such things as illegitimate fantasies?

For anybody, any group, I think that there are obvious limits. If you are a gay or lesbian person and you fantasize about murdering somebody in the process of having sex, I think that's a deeply disturbing, perhaps even potentially destructive fantasy, just as it is for straight folk. So yes, there are always ethical norms and limits generated within the logic of a given sexual ethic. You don't have to step outside of gay or lesbian sexuality to find a restrictive norm that could be imposed as a legitimate one. Within all orientations, sexual liberty should be shaped by moral responsibility. However, I don't think responsibility is determined by an ahistorical and depoliticized appeal to a transcendental norm of respect for the other, although I'm not knocking Kantian ethics, just disagreeing with aspects of its description of how morality works. I think that responsibility is a highly nuanced ethical concept, shaped by an ethic of respect that finds expression in historically specific and culturally conditioned relations to others. It causes one to ask the questions: How can one seek one's best while acting in a way not to harm others? How can the flourishing of one's erotic desire be checked by a sense of community that respects the integrity of the other? For example, rape is wrong, period, and the fantasy of rape that one intends to act on is highly destructive, regardless of one's sexual orientation. So yes, I think that . . .

Let me step in. There are some fantasies that are not acted on. Or let's think about if a fantasy is one that imitates or plays out behavior that some find offensive, say a woman who might have a fantasy about being raped . . .

Oh sure, sure. I thought about that immediately, as soon as I made my comments on rape. When it comes to fantasy, the sky's the limit, and if you tell no one your fantasy, or if you share your fantasy with someone of like mind, or act on it with consenting partners in a noncoercive, nonviolent fashion, it's all good. I certainly think that it's important to acknowledge the irreverence and the transgressive potential of autonomous sexual desire and fantasy within one's own mind. I think that the landscape of the psyche should be scouted for fantasies that allow people to uninhibitedly embrace their healthy erotic identities. I suppose even so-called illicit fantasies of rape, or of being raped, within a nonviolent context of reciprocal affection—or as a solitary fantasy nurtured within one's solipsistic universe of erotic desire—may be fine as long as one doesn't act on that fantasy in a violent fashion. For instance, we've got to allow for the pantomime of rape by couples as an erotic stimulation within the moral boundaries of their relationship. But I'm rather more libertarian about these matters and believe in a kind of autonomous sexuality within the limits of fantasy that allows people to sustain a range of irreverent, transgressive beliefs as long as they don't turn violent.

Years ago I was at a party and I saw a black man walking through the party wearing a leash behind a white man. This was in the Castro, in San Francisco, which at the time was very white supremacist, was very white. And I remember I wrote about it, and it got a lot of reaction. One of the questions that came up was: Does sexual fantasy imitate reality, or does reality imitate fantasy?

It's a dialectical process, isn't it? It's a give-and-take. Can we really divorce Robert Mapplethorp's *Man in a Gray Suit*—is that the name of it?

Polyester suit.

Man in a Polyester Suit, right. I'm mixing up Mapplethorp and Gregory Peck, who starred in the film *Man in the Gray Flannel Suit* [which I'm actually conflating with a film he did a decade earlier, *A Gentleman's Agreement*], which was about another form of bigotry: anti-Semitism. Anyway, as erotically charged as *Man in a Polyester Suit* is, and as full of transgressions against the heterosexual norm as that photo is, can we really divorce Mapplethorp's imagination from the political context of a socially constructed black male sexuality, with the large black organ it features as the site and source of so much fantasy and fear within the white heterosexual world?

I read in Mapplethorp's biography that he had fantasies about the black male animal. So that shaped my view of his photography.

Right, right. Technically, that may be true as a precise term of the mammal—the animal—but we both know that "animal" signifies racial primordialism and a savagery of sorts within the context of an eroticized black masculine subjectivity. But even individual fantasies reflect the political context in which people are shaped and in which they mature. The same is true for homoerotic desire, even as it thrives on articulations of nonnormative desire. So it's dialectical: fantasies shape behaviors and behaviors are shaped by fantasies, though I'd still resist the strict one-to-one correlation between the two, since it fails to account for other causative factors. Fantasies are related to politics, and politics to the articulation of not only the possible—as in politics is the art of the possible—but also to the ideal one holds in one's mind.

When I think of the black man being led around on the leash by the white man, I think of the Hegelian dimension of the master-slave dialectic—or the relationship between the dominant and the dominated—illustrating, in this case, that there's a reciprocity of means that promotes a mutual reinforcement of fantasy and its fulfillment. They feed each other and sustain each other, even if in unequal fashion. On the one hand, the white man has the power because he can pull the black man. On the other hand, if the black man is stronger, he can resist; so there's give-and-take. Even in a relation of inequality, there's tension. That's not only Hegelian, it's downright Foucaultian. Whereas traditional theories of power located authority in conventional spots of domination in a rigid hierarchical schemata, Foucault contended that power breaks out everywhere. Its locus classicus is not simply in an institution or in hegemonic power, but in varied and complex relations and negotiations among and between the powerless as well.

That having been said, there's no question that when white men dominate black men, even within a homoerotic context, that can certainly be the corollary of a white supremacist ethic, or perhaps its direct expression. White supremacist domination, or fantasies of domination, may fuse with homoerotic desires of union with black men. I'm not suggesting that white gays and lesbians cannot be white supremacists, or that they cannot derive benefits, pleasures, and perks from white skin privilege. In fact, their white supremacist fantasies can be projected onto black bodies. For instance, the big black dick can be sought by gay white men who possess vicious, stereotypical views of black sexuality, aping—pun intended, I suppose—the behavior of some white straight communities. The relations of power and domination, although eroticized within a same-sex framework, can nevertheless express a white supremacist fantasy that is prior to the sexual fantasy, or at least coterminous with it. I think this is relatively untheorized in certain white gay and lesbian communities. Still, I must add, without essentializing them, that white gays and lesbians seem more aware in general of the complex racial dynamics of both intimate and social relations than their heterosexual counterparts. That's not a law or rule, just an informal ethnographic observation about how one minority is sometimes sensitive to the plight of another minority—although the exact opposite is also true, since we know that in straight black communities and among gay and lesbian white communities, there's plenty of ignorance and bigotry to go around.

One thing I was thinking about was in terms of the black male's perspective, and his eroticizing of white supremacy . . .

Oh sure. If heterosexual blacks can internalize white supremacist views where we hate our big black lips, our broad noses, or our big behinds—although there ain't that much black self-hatred around that, thank God!—and seek to modify features of our God-given beauty through cosmetic surgery, then certainly gay black men can absorb a white supremacist identity that subordinates black sexuality to dominant white sexualities. There's no homosexual exemption to racial self-hatred. In fact, for the black other-sexed, there's an exacerbating effect of self-hatreds, an exponential increase in multiple self-abnegations: with the black self and the gay self in tandem, there are potentially more selves to despise, resent, even hate. (I'm not playing into the additive theory of multiple minority statuses here, where folk don't integrate their various constituent identities into a "person." I'm simply trying to highlight how, among those prone or vulnerable to self-hatred, there's more to hate of one's self when it integrates a variety of identities and fights a variety of battles.)

Thus there is a reinscription of a pattern first generated within the context of patriarchal heterosexism's sexual fantasies, so that gay white communities rearticulate dominant whiteness. Some gays get off on white supremacist fantasies, which could conceivably fuse with rough-trade homoeroticism that may be a cognate of white supremacist domination of the other. I'm not suggesting that the two are necessarily the same thing, or that they share a reciprocal relationship. I am simply saying that the two can merge. Homosexuality has modalities that extend the white supremacist's desire to subordinate the black sexual identity to himself, and the acceptance of that by black men is no less problematic because it occurs in the context of a homoerotic union. Just because the white fist up your ass gives you pleasure doesn't mean that it's not meant to rip out your guts.

But is the black man's fantasy an illegitimate fantasy?

It's not necessarily illegitimate, it's just troubling. It is legitimately problematic, even self-destructive. One cannot, by entering a homoerotic union, escape the ethics of relationality that should govern any healthy relationship.

Now how about educated, successful black men who have prison fantasies?

Again, I don't think anything is off-limits in terms of the autonomy of desire within the context of fantasy, so I am not interested in restricting such fantasies, even for those who may subordinate themselves to white men because they have internalized a white supremacist worldview. To be sure, I would find such fantasies problematic and self-destructive, even if they are literally instrumental to one's erotic existence. I don't have any desire to impose an ontologically grounded black ethic of propriety on the homosexual mind. Still, if such fantasies ultimately prove to be dehumanizing to gay black men, it diminishes the community; and if it diminishes the community, it impacts all of us in some measure. Self-loathing often has social repercussions.

Yeah, but see, I'm thinking that when these black men have prison fantasies, a lot of times their fantasies remind me of inverted white supremacy, where

they are taking the ideas of black masculinity being animalistic, and so on, and they are eroticizing that.

That's different. It's like the state of nature meets the myth of the black savage as Jean-Jacques Rousseau shakes hands with Carl Van Vechten, the gay white patron of black artists during the Harlem Renaissance. In many ways, Van Vechten was a great guy, and incredibly supportive of black writers like Langston Hughes. But at his worst (and remember, as with most of us, the best and the worst live on the same block, in the same house, and when you get one you get the other), he seemed to go trolling among the Negroes to get in touch with the primitive state of man that was signified in blackness. Indeed, the genealogy of the eroticized primitivism and fetishized animalism of black masculinity stretches back to our first moments on Western soil as slaves in 1619, down to educated gay black men seeking the ideal savage type and the archetypically most unreconstructed black masculinity available—the black prisoner.

What may be erotically attractive to educated gay black men, even in the straight black male prisoner, is the prospect of situational homosexuality, since at any moment in prison, heterosexual agency is redirected into homosexual channels, given the restricted erotic commerce available. By definition, prison sex in male prisons among prisoners is sex between men, excluding the occasional heterosexual alliance in various guises. In prison, the black heterosexual male is often transformed into a vulnerable or victimizing gay man, at least in provisional, situational terms, his body marked by ad hoc homoeroticism. The idealization of the prisoner as the black savage is nothing but the postmodern urban update of the state of nature primitive with a huge sexual organ grinding in the fantasies of an erotically omnivorous culture.

This is a deep conversation. One last topic. I'm thinking about the word "queer." In your essay on the black church and sexuality in *Race Rules*, you mentioned "Afriqueermericans." Queer is a word that is really debated in the black gay and lesbian community. I see queers of color, younger gays and lesbians, and I guess they use that word because it's supposed to be co-opting it, and it's not white, and it's not male. When I was growing up, the term queer was used by white people, and it was used in reference to boys—little boys were "queer." I don't know where I'm going with this . . .

Where you are going with it, at least in my mind, is that the change in the use of queer points to the dynamic character of linguistic transformation, signifying that words change over space and time. Moreover, they mean one thing to one group, something different to another group, much like "nigger" or "bitch." Queer is not as demonizing as nigger, or as bitch for that matter, but it carries an ontological negativity that is mediated through its enthralling witness against the norm. Queer: not normal. The riot against normalcy that queer betokens makes it a highly explosive and useful weapon in the politics of publicity for gay and lesbian causes. I think here the hierarchy of race makes a huge difference even in gay and lesbian communities. Black gays and lesbians, as well as other-sexed people, have been caught in the crosswinds of seeking acceptance in predominantly white gay and lesbian communities that provide erotic and intellectual succor, but which may close them out culturally; or hunting for love in a black culture that provides familiar rituals of home while alienating, stigmatizing, and even demonizing them because of their sexual preferences. They've been caught betwixt and between; it has been especially difficult for minority gays, bisexuals, and lesbians to find an appropriate grammar of erotic identification and communion.

Although "queer" has the resonance of a specific time and cultural identification, it has interpretive flexibility and can be used to signify a transgressive, even playful, resistance to the term's negative connotations. Queer can be a terminological rallying point to galvanize multiple constituencies within gay and lesbian communities. There can be a postmodern sense of *jouissance* as well, as in, "Damned right, I'm queer," or "Damned right, I'm a fag"—the latter expression, perhaps, a more tolerable or racially resonant signifier among a certain generation of blacks. Such terms represent the articulation of ethical agency among gays and lesbians that says, "We refuse to be put off by your negative language; in fact, we are going to rearticulate it positively in our world in our own way." The same was done, of course, by some blacks with the word "nigger," and by some women with the word "bitch." Whether that works or not, I think, is an open question. I think it's more difficult to talk about among gays and lesbians of color because they have dramatically participated in multiple kinship groups in their quest for a home. Only when you find a home can you enjoy the leisure of self-parody or the luxury of grounding a derisive term in the history of your community's response to bigotry. There has not been, by and large, a stabilization of black gay and lesbian communities. Individual examples of success abound, but authentic homosexual community has been much more difficult to attain.

One thing that I think is different between the words "nigger" and "queer" is that, when I hear rappers use the word nigger, I don't think they are really changing its meaning. They are reinforcing and personifying what it means. Years ago, we couldn't point to what a nigger was. If someone called you a "nigger," you said, "Well I'm not a dumb person, I'm not a nigger." Now you have these black men acting ignorant, acting loud, cursing, swearing, and so on, and saying, "By the way, I'm a 'nigger' and I'm black." So they personify what "nigger" is. I think what "queers" are doing—even though I hate the word, it sounds nasty—is that they are at least projecting intelligence and projecting respect.

Right, right, right. That is a very interesting point. You've touched on one of the great contentions in black life, especially with the rise of hip-hop culture. Some critics, however, would disagree with you; they would say that there were dumb, ignorant people to whom we could point all along in black history. They would tell you that there have always been people who could justify the stereotype. But they will also tell you that "nigger" as an epithet never represented the complexity of black identity, and that to isolate a minor personality type—the so-called nigger—within the behavioral norms of blackness to justify the demonization of all black people was patently unjust. As a result, blacks questioned the legitimacy of the claim that the epithet was deployed by whites to define the behavior of people who fell outside the norm of good behavior. That's because every black person in the eyes of most whites was a nigger.

In that light, we might be able to concede the racial daring and subversive attempt among some blacks to appropriate the linguistic negativity of "nigger" and to recirculate, recontextualize, recode, refigure, refashion, and rearticulate the term for their purposes. At least now when it came to that word, the "niggas"—the term as it is baptized in black linguistic subversion—were in control, challenging whites and bourgeois blacks who could never consider using the term in any incarnation. In the eyes of the contemporary "niggas," bourgeois blacks do not exercise the same level of discretion over their rhetorical and linguistic self-representation as do the folk, say, in hip-hop.

So the argument could be made that there is indeed a flip, that the people who were supposed to be dumb are not dumb at all. Instead, they are playing the culture to the hilt. They are reinforcing certain stereotypes while challenging others. They're reaping economic remuneration from trying to parody and stigmatize what "nigger" is or saying, "Yeah, if you call me a nigger, I'm going to live up to that, I'm going to be a larger-than-life nigger, and I'll show you what that might mean." Or they might say, "I dare you to keep calling me 'nigger' in the face of my embracing this term in such a fashion as to not only reinforce the negative behaviors that you think characterize the term, but to deploy it as a rhetorical weapon against the white supremacy that seeks to deny black people the opportunity to choose their own destinies." So I think the use of "nigga" is much more complex than the either/or absolutism that bewitches too many black critics in their discussion of the term.

I understand your point in terms of queer. But your perception that "queers" are engaging in their linguistic subversion in an intelligent way has to do with the fact that gay and lesbian people have not been subject to the same stereotype of being unintelligent that blacks have been saddled with. For centuries now, blackness has signified stupidity and ignorance in the West. But gays and lesbians have not been perceived as intellectually inferior to heterosexuals. In fact, the opposite is true: gays have been tied, at least in the West, to the Greeks, who were viewed as exceedingly intelligent. So what you face as a queer minority is the improbable complexity of black gay identities because you're dealing with both stereotypes collapsing on your head: dumb nigger and smart queer. Although I'm sure an exception is made for black queers, whose race may cancel out their sexual orientation, at least in the intelligence sweepstakes. How much more de-graded and contradictory can one get in one body? So I think that black gays and lesbians would certainly be much more sensitive to the nomenclature of self-disclosure and self-description than even most white gays and lesbians might ever imagine.

One last topic: class issues. By most people's account, we would be considered bourgie. I think, like W.E.B. Du Bois's notion of "the talented tenth," we're leading the masses. Don't you feel that as such we should set an example . . .

Set an example for whom?

In general for the masses of African Americans, since we're going to be lead-ers. Say for instance, earlier you mentioned bourgie blacks, and it was kind of in a derogatory sense. In fact, I think most "bourgie blacks" are doing pos-itive things.

Sure, sure. What I mean by "bourgie"—which is a pejorative term shortened from bourgeois—is not simply middle class. I mean by bourgie the construction of a self-determined persona that is hostile to, and scornful of, ordinary black people. You can be rich and not be bourgie. Class in black America has been less about how much money you make or how many stocks you have than the politics of style. Still, your overall point is well taken. I think that those of us who are privileged—and that includes gays and lesbians who have high levels of education—have an ab-solute obligation to "give back" to the less fortunate. I think we are bound by blood, history, and destiny to our brothers and sisters, especially to those who will never know the privilege or positive visibility that many in the middle class enjoy. And we should cross all lines—sexual, economic, religious, gender, geographical, genera-tional—in speaking for the oppressed. For instance, that's why I think it's incumbent on me as a heterosexual black man to speak against the bigotry and injustice faced by my black brothers and sisters who are gay, lesbian, bisexual, and other-sexed. And it's equally important for educated, upwardly mobile blacks to not forget those who have been entombed in permanent poverty and miseducation.

It is part of the hidden courage of black gays and lesbians that despite the stigma they have endured, they continue to work within the arc of black identity and com-munity in fulfillment of their sense of personal and political destiny. I think that's a beautiful thing. Being "queer" or "gay" is a tremendous struggle, but even before the enemies of black people see a fey snap of the wrist or the "butch" dress of les-bian women, they see black pigment. So pigment may trump sexual orientation in a manner that many black gays and lesbians intuitively understand in their bodies, even though deeply inscribed in their bodies at the same time is the recognition of their unalterable sexual identities that need to be sustained, affirmed, and prized. To the degree that black gays and lesbians struggle with the complex convergence of racial, sexual, gender, and class issues, they already represent courageous role models of negotiating differences in one body at one site. They represent to us what blackness will look like well into the twenty-first century.

What a beautiful ending.

Thanks, brother.

Interview by Kheven LaGrone
Chicago, Illinois, 2002

PART NINE

BIOCRITICISM AND BLACK ICONS

Over the last decade, I have occasionally embraced a genre of writing I term "biocriticism," a critical examination of a figure's career and cultural impact through the prism of biographical details and life episodes. With biocriticism I hope to open an intellectual window onto the cultural and intellectual landscape that shapes a figure's life, using biography as a means to social and cultural criticism. I have used a biocritical approach to probe the lives and times of black icons like black nationalist revolutionary Malcolm X, civil rights leader Martin Luther King, Jr., and hip-hop immortal Tupac Shakur. The virtue of biocriticism is a wide-ranging exploration of the forces and figures that define a particular movement or era through the lens of a single figure, combining the best of biography, cultural analysis, historical examination, and social criticism. I am presently at work on a biocritical analysis of Marvin Gaye, the legendary artist whose work altered the American musical and cultural landscape.

Twenty

X MARKS THE PLOTS: A CRITICAL
READING OF MALCOLM'S READERS

This critical analysis of how Malcolm X has been conceived and interpreted by scholars and writers was initially written for the late Joe Wood's fine 1992 anthology, Malcolm X: In Our Own Image. *I had written several drafts of the essay and had sharpened my arguments, honed my analysis, and deepened my engagement with the vast body of literature on Malcolm that fit under the four categories of interpretation I developed. Wood was quite pleased, but suddenly, at the end of this arduous process, he told me that he wouldn't be using my essay. I was quite disappointed. Wood offered little explanation except to ask if I hadn't been involved in other projects where my work, having been assigned, was not ultimately used. It was only later, a few years before Wood's tragic death in 1999 on a solo hiking expedition in the Longmire area of Mount Rainier—a real loss for black letters—that I discovered that he had been heavily influenced in his decision by a mentor from his Yale days whose essay did appear in Wood's collection—Adolf Reed Jr. Reed's great disdain for me and my work, and that of other black scholars, would be later aired in an infamous* Village Voice *diatribe against black public intellectuals.*

Fortunately, what began badly proved to be a boon. A "popular" version of this chapter, under the mighty advocacy and pen of editor Rosemary Bray, appeared in November 1992, as a 5,000-word lead essay for the New York Times Book Review. *Further, my rejection led me to write my own book on Malcolm, a decision that resulted in two auspicious events: the publication of* Making Malcolm: The Myth and Meaning of Malcolm X, *which was named a Notable Book of 1994 by the* New York Times *and* Philadelphia Inquirer, *and one of the "outstanding black books of the twentieth century" by* Black Issues Book Review. *My partnership with Liz Maguire as my editor and intellectual compatriot, a professional relationship that blossomed into a friendship, has lasted over eight books and four publishing houses! This chapter is the first section of* Making Malcolm, *and is one of the scholarly efforts of which I am most proud.*

I think all of us should be critics of each other. Whenever you can't stand criticism you can never grow. I don't think that it serves any purpose for the leaders of our people to waste their time fighting each other needlessly. I think that we accomplish more when we sit down in private and iron out whatever differences that may exist and try

> and then do something constructive for the benefit of our people. But
> on the other hand, I don't think that we should be above criticism.
> I don't think that anyone should be above criticism–Malcolm X.
>
> –MALCOLM X: THE LAST SPEECHES

THE LIFE AND THOUGHT OF MALCOLM X have traced a curious path to black cultural authority and social acceptance since his assassination in 1965. At the time of his martyrdom–achieved through a murder that rivaled in its fumbling but lethal execution the treacherous twists of a Shakespearean tragedy–Malcolm was experiencing a radical shift in the personal and political understandings that governed his life and thought.[1] Malcolm's death heightened the confusion that had already seized his inner circle because of his last religious conversion. His death also engendered bitter disagreement among fellow travelers about his evolving political direction, conflicts that often traded on polemic, diatribe, and intolerance. Thus Malcolm's legacy was severely fragmented, his contributions shredded in ideological disputes even as ignorance and fear ensured his further denigration as the symbol of black hatred and violence.

Although broader cultural investigation of his importance has sometimes flagged, Malcolm has never disappeared among racial and political subcultures that proclaim his heroic stature because he embodied ideals of black rebellion and revolutionary social action.[2] The contemporary revival of black nationalism, in particular, has focused renewed attention on him. Indeed, he has risen to a black cultural stratosphere that was once exclusively occupied by Martin Luther King Jr. The icons of success that mark Malcolm's ascent–ranging from posters, clothing, speeches, and endless sampling of his voice on rap recordings–attest to his achieving the pinnacle of his popularity more than a quarter century after his death.

Malcolm, however, has received nothing like the intellectual attention devoted to Martin Luther King Jr., at least nothing equal to his cultural significance. Competing waves of uncritical celebration and vicious criticism–which settle easily into myth and caricature–have undermined appreciation of Malcolm's greatest accomplishments. The peculiar needs that idolizing or demonizing Malcolm fulfill mean that intellectuals who study him are faced with the difficult task of describing and explaining a controversial black leader and the forces that produced him.[3] Such critical studies must achieve the "thickest description" possible of Malcolm's career while avoiding explanations that either obscure or reduce the complex nature of his achievements and failures.[4]

Judging by these standards, the literature on Malcolm X has often missed the mark. Even the classic *Autobiography of Malcolm X* reflects both Malcolm's need to shape his personal history for public racial edification while bringing coherence to a radically conflicting set of life experiences and coauthor Alex Haley's political biases and ideological purposes.[5] Much writing about Malcolm has either lost its way in the murky waters of psychology dissolved from history or simply substituted—given racial politics in the United States—defensive praise for critical appraisal. At times, insights on Malcolm have been tarnished by insular ideological arguments that neither illuminate nor surprise. Malcolm X was too formidable a historic figure—the movements he led too variable and contradictory, the passion and intelligence he summoned too extraordinary and disconcerting—to be viewed through a narrow cultural prism.

My intent in this chapter is to provide a critical path through the quagmire of conflicting views of Malcolm X. I have identified at least four Malcolms who emerge in the intellectual investigations of his life and career: Malcolm as hero and saint, Malcolm as public moralist, Malcolm as victim and vehicle of psychohistorical forces, and Malcolm as revolutionary figure judged by his career trajectory from nationalist to alleged socialist. Of course, many treatments of Malcolm's life and thought transgress rigid boundaries of interpretation. The Malcolms I have identified, and especially the categories of interpretation to which they give rise, should be viewed as handles on broader issues of ideological warfare over who Malcolm is, and to whom he rightfully belongs. In short, they help us answer: Whose Malcolm is it?

I am not providing an exhaustive review of the literature, but a critical reading of the dominant tendencies in the writings on Malcolm X.[6] The writings make up an intellectual universe riddled with philosophical blindnesses and ideological constraints, filled with problematic interpretations, and sometimes brimming with brilliant insights. They reveal as much about the possibilities of understanding and explaining the life of a great black man as they do about Malcolm's life and thought.

HERO WORSHIP AND THE CONSTRUCTION OF A BLACK REVOLUTIONARY

In the tense and confused aftermath of Malcolm's death, several groups claiming to be his ideological heirs competed in a warfare of interpretation over Malcolm's torn legacy. The most prominent of these included black nationalist and revolutionary groups such as the Student Nonviolent Coordinating Committee (SNCC, under the leadership of Stokely Carmichael), the Congress of Racial Equality (CORE, under the leadership of James Farmer and especially Floyd McKissick), the Black Panther Party, the Republic of New Africa, and the League of Revolutionary Black Workers.[7] They appealed to his vision and spirit in developing styles of moral criticism and social action aimed at the destruction of white supremacy. These groups also advocated versions of Black Power, racial self-determination, black pride, cultural autonomy, cooperative socialism, and black capitalism.[8]

Malcolm's death also caused often bitter debate between custodians of his legacy and his detractors, either side arguing his genius or evil in a potpourri of journals, books, magazines, and newspapers. For many of Malcolm's keepers, the embrace of his legacy by integrationists or Marxists out to re-create Malcolm in their distorted image was more destructive than his critics characterizing him in exclusively pejorative terms.

For all his nationalist followers, Malcolm is largely viewed as a saintly figure defending the cause of black unity while fighting racist oppression. Admittedly, the development of stories that posit black heroes and saints serves a crucial cultural and political function. Such stories may be used to combat historical amnesia and to challenge the deification of black heroes—especially those deemed capable of betraying the best interests of African-Americans—by forces outside black communities. Furthermore, such stories reveal that the creation of (black) heroes is neither accidental nor value neutral, and often serves political ends that are not defined or controlled by black communities. Even heroes proclaimed worthy of broad black support are often subject to cultural manipulation and distortion.

The most striking example of this involves Martin Luther King, Jr. Like Malcolm X, King was a complex historic figure whose moral vision and social thought evolved over time.[9] When King was alive, his efforts to affect a beloved community of racial equality were widely viewed as a threat to a stable social order. His advocacy of nonviolent civil disobedience was also viewed as a detrimental detour from the proper role that religious leaders should play in public. Of course, the rise of black radicalism during the late 1960s softened King's perception among many whites and blacks. But King's power to excite the social imagination of Americans only increased after his assassination.

The conflicting uses to which King's memory can be put—and the obscene manner in which his radical legacy can be deliberately forgotten—are displayed in aspects of the public commemoration of his birthday. To a significant degree, perceptions of King's public aims have been shaped by the corporate sector and (sometimes hostile) governmental forces. These forces may be glimpsed in Coca-Cola commercials celebrating King's birthday, and in Ronald Reagan's unseemly hints of King's personal and political defects at the signing of legislation to establish King's birthday as a national holiday.

King's legacy is viewed as most useful when promoting an unalloyed optimism about the possibilities of American social transformation, which peaked during his "I Have a Dream" speech. What is not often discussed—and is perhaps deliberately ignored—is how King dramatically revised his views, glimpsed most eloquently in his Vietnam era antiwar rhetoric and in his War on Poverty social activism. Corporation-sponsored commercials that celebrate King's memory—most notably, television spots by McDonald's and Coca-Cola aimed at connecting their products to King's legacy—reveal a truncated understanding of King's meaning and value to American democracy. These and other efforts at public explanation of King's meaning portray his worth as underwriting the interests of the state, which advocates a distorted cultural history of an era actually shaped more by blood and brutality than by distant dreams.

Many events of public commemoration avoid assigning specific responsibility for opposition to King's and the civil rights movement's quest for equality. On such occasions, the uneven path to racial justice is often described in a manner that makes progress appear an inevitable fact of our national life. Little mention is made of the concerted efforts—not only of bigots and white supremacists, but, more important, of government officials and average citizens—to stop racial progress. Such stories deny King's radical challenge to narrow conceptions of American democracy. Although King and other sacrificial civil rights participants are lauded for their possession of the virtue of courage, not enough attention is given to the vicious cultural contexts that called forth such heroic action.

Most insidious of all, consent to these whitewashed stories of King and the 1960s is often secured by the veiled threat that King's memory will be either celebrated in this manner or forgotten altogether. The logic behind such a threat is premised on a belief that blacks should be grateful for the state's allowing King's celebration to occur at all. These realities make the battle over King's memory—waged by communities invested in his radical challenge to American society—a constant obligation. The battle over King's memory also provides an important example to communities interested in preserving and employing Malcolm's memory in contemporary social action. As with King, making Malcolm X a hero reveals the political utility of memory and reflects a deliberate choice made by black communities to identify and honor the principles for which Malcolm lived and died.

For many adherents, Malcolm remained until his death a revolutionary black nationalist whose exclusive interest was to combat white supremacy while fostering black unity. Although near the end of his life Malcolm displayed a broadened humanity and moral awareness—qualities overlooked by his unprincipled critics and often denied by his true believers—his revolutionary cohorts contended that Malcolm's late-life changes were cosmetic and confused, the painful evidence of ideological vertigo brought on by paranoia and exhaustion.

All these interpretations are vividly elaborated in John Henrik Clarke's anthology *Malcolm X: The Man and His Times*.[10] Clarke's book brings together essays, personal reflections, interviews, and organizational statements that provide a basis for understanding and explaining different dimensions of Malcolm's life and career. Although its various voices certainly undermine a single understanding of Malcolm's meaning as a father, leader, friend, and husband (after all, it includes writers as different as Albert Cleage and Gordon Parks), the book's tone suggests an exercise in hero worship and saint making, as cultural interpreters gather and preserve fragments of Malcolm's memory.

Thus even the power of an individual essay to critically engage an aspect of Malcolm's contribution or failure is overcome by the greater urgency of the collective enterprise: to establish Malcolm as a genuine hero of the people, but more than this, a sainted son of revolutionary struggle who was perfectly fit for the leadership task he helped define. But moments of criticism come through. For instance, in the course of a mostly favorable discussion of Malcolm's leadership, Charles Wilson insightfully addresses the structural problems confronting black protest leaders as he probes Malcolm's "failure of leadership style and a failure to evolve a sound organizational base for his activities," concluding that Malcolm was a "victim of his own charisma."[11]

At least two other writers in the collection also attempt to critically explore Malcolm's limitations and the distortions of his legacy by other groups. James Boggs deplores both the racism of white Marxist revolutionaries who cannot see beyond color and the lack of "scientific analysis" displayed by Malcolm's black nationalist heirs whose activity degenerates into Black Power sloganeering. And Wyatt Tee Walker, King's former lieutenant, criticizes Malcolm for "useless illogical and intemperate remarks that helped neither him nor his cause," while emphasizing the importance of Malcolm's pro-black rhetoric and his promulgation of the right to self-defense.[12] At the same time, Walker uselessly repeats old saws about the vices of black matriarchy.

But these flutters of criticism are mostly overridden by the celebrative and romantic impulses that are expressed in several essays. Fortunately, Patricia Robinson's paean to Malcolm X as a revolutionary figure stops short of viewing black male patriarchy as a heroic achievement. Instead, she sees Malcolm as the beginning of a redeemed black masculinity that helps, not oppresses, black children and women. But in essays by W. Keorapetse Kgositsile, Abdelwahab M. Elmessiri, and Albert Cleage, Malcolm's revolutionary black nationalist legacy is almost breathlessly, even reverentially, evoked.

Cleage especially, in his "Myths About Malcolm X," seeks to defend Malcolm's black nationalist reputation from assertions that he was becoming an integrationist, an internationalist, or a Trotskyist Marxist, concluding that "if in Mecca he had decided that blacks and whites can unite, then his life at that moment would have become meaningless in terms of the world struggle of black people."[13] Clarke's book makes sense, especially when viewed against the historical canvas of late '60s racial politics and in light of the specific cultural needs of urban blacks confronting deepening social crisis after Malcolm's death. But its goal of redeeming Malcolm's legacy through laudatory means makes its value more curatorial than critical.

Similarly, Oba T'shaka's *The Political Legacy of Malcolm X* is an interpretation of Malcolm X as a revolutionary black nationalist, and *The End of White World Supremacy: Four Speeches by Malcolm X*, edited by Benjamin Karim, attempts to freeze Malcolm's development in the fateful year before his break with Elijah Muhammad and the Nation of Islam.[14] T'shaka is an often perceptive social critic and political activist who believes that "the scattering of Africans throughout the world gave birth to the idea of Pan-Africanism," and that the "oppression of Blacks in the United States cannot be separated from the oppression of Africans on the African continent and in the world."[15]

Such an international perspective establishes links between blacks throughout the world, forged by revolutionary black nationalist activity expressed in political insurgency, material and resource sharing, and the exchange of ideas. In this context, T'shaka maintains that Malcolm was a revolutionary black nationalist who "identified the world-wide system of white supremacy as the number one enemy of Africans and people of color throughout the world." He argues that Malcolm's internationalist perspective on revolutionary political resistance was specifically linked to African experiments in socialist politics, contending that Malcolm rejected European models of political transformation. Not surprisingly, T'shaka is sour on the notion that after his trip to Mecca, Malcolm accepted and expressed support for black-white unity, and he characterizes beliefs that Malcolm began to advocate a Trotskyite socialism as "farfetched statements."[16]

Although he gives a close reading of Malcolm's ideas, T'shaka's treatment of Malcolm is marred by largely uncritical explorations of Malcolm's rhetoric. He fails to challenge Malcolm's philosophical presuppositions or even critically to juxtapose contradictory elements of Malcolm's rhetoric. In effect, he bestows a canonical cloak on Malcolm's words. Nor does T'shaka give a persuasive explanation of the social forces and political action that shaped Malcolm's thinking in his last years. Understanding these facts might illuminate the motivation behind Malcolm's utopian interpretations of black separatist ideology, which maintained that racial division was based on blacks possessing land either in Africa or in the United States. Although T'shaka, following Malcolm's own schema, draws distinctions between his long-range program (that is, return to Africa, which he claims Malcolm never gave up) and short-term tactics (that is, cultural, psychological, and philosophical migration), he doesn't prove that Malcolm ever resolved the ideological tensions in black nationalism.

Karim's *The End of White World Supremacy* is an attempt to wrench Malcolm's speeches from their political context and place them in a narrative framework that uses Malcolm's own words—even after his break with the Nation of Islam—to justify Elijah Muhammad's religious theodicy. Such a move ignores Malcolm's radically transformed self-understanding and asserts, through his own words, a worldview he eventually rejected. Karim, who as Benjamin Goodman was Malcolm's close associate through his Nation of Islam phase until his death, says in his introduction that Muhammad gave Malcolm "the keys to knowledge and understanding," that this is "one key point in Malcolm's life that is still generally misunderstood, or overlooked," and that these speeches "represent a fair cross section of his teaching during that crucial last year as a leader in the Nation of Islam."[17]

Karim's introduction to the speeches winks away the ideological warfare that helped drive Malcolm from the Nation of Islam, and ignores evidence that Malcolm grew to characterize his years with Muhammad as "the sickness and madness of those days."[18] Here we have Malcolm the master polemicist telling twice-told tales of Mr. Yacub and white devils, a doctrine he had long forsaken. Here, too, is Malcolm the skillful dogmatist deriding Paul Robeson for not knowing his history, when in reality Malcolm grew to admire Robeson and tried to meet him a month before his own death.[19] The political context Karim gives to the speeches attempts to transform interesting and essential historical artifacts from Malcolm's past into a living document of personal faith and belief.

Karim's shortcomings reveal the futility of examining Malcolm's life and thought without regard for sound historical judgment and intellectual honesty.

Serious engagement with Malcolm's life and thought must be critical and balanced. The most useful evaluations of Malcolm X are those anchored in forceful but fair criticism of his career that hold him to the same standards of scholarly examination as we would any figure of importance to (African-) American society. But such judgments must acknowledge the tattered history of vicious, uncomprehending, and disabling cultural criticism aimed at black life, a variety of criticism reflected in many cultural commentaries on Malcolm's life.[20]

The overwhelming weakness of hero worship, often, is the belief that the community of hero worshipers possesses the *definitive* understanding of the subject—in this instance, Malcolm—and that critical dissenters from the received view of Malcolm are traitors to black unity, inauthentic heirs to his political legacy, or misguided interpreters of his ideas.[21] This is even more reason for intellectuals to bring the full weight of their critical powers to bear on Malcolm's life. Otherwise, his real brilliance will be diminished by efforts to canonize his views without first considering them, his ultimate importance as a revolutionary figure sacrificed to celebratory claims about his historic meaning. Toward this end, Malcolm's words best describe the critical approach that should be adopted in examining his life and thought:

> Now many Negroes don't like to be criticized—they don't like for it to be said that we're not ready. They say that that's a stereotype. We have assets—we have liabilities as well as assets. And until our people are able to . . . analyze ourselves and discover our own liabilities as well as our assets, we never will be able to win any struggle that we become involved in. As long as the black community and the leaders of the black community are afraid of criticism and want to classify all criticism, collective criticism, as a stereotype, no one will ever be able to pull our coat. . . . [W]e have to . . . find out where we are lacking, and what we need to replace that which we are lacking, [or] we never will be able to be successful.[22]

THE VOCATION OF A PUBLIC MORALIST

Within African-American life, a strong heritage of black leadership has relentlessly and imaginatively addressed the major obstacles to the achievement of a sacred trinity of social goods for African-Americans: freedom, justice, and equality. Racism has been historically viewed as the most lethal force to deny black Americans their share in the abundant life that these goods make possible. The central role that the church has traditionally played in many black communities means that religion has profoundly shaped the moral vision and social thought of black leaders' responses to racism.[23] Because freedom, justice, and equality have been viewed by black communities as fundamental in the exercise of citizenship rights and the expression of social dignity, a diverse group of black leaders has advocated varied models of racial transformation in public life.

The centrality of Christianity in African-American culture means that the moral character of black public protest against racism has oscillated between reformist and revolutionary models of racial transformation. From Booker T. Washington to Joseph H. Jackson, black Christian reformist approaches to racial transformation have embraced liberal notions of the importance of social stability and the legitimacy of the state. Black Christian reformist leaders have sought to shape religious resistance to oppression, inequality, and injustice around styles of rational dissent that reinforce a stable political order. From Nat Turner to the latter–day Martin Luther King, Jr., black Christian revolutionary approaches to racial transformation have often presumed the fundamental moral and social limitations of the state. Black Christian revolutionary leaders have advocated public protest against racism in a manner that disrupts the forceful alliance of unjust social privilege and political legitimacy that have undermined African-American life.

In practice, black resistance to American racism has fallen somewhere between these two poles. At their best, black leaders have opposed American racism while appealing to religion and politics in prescribing a remedy. Whether influenced by black Christianity, Black Muslim belief, or other varieties of black religious experience, proponents of public morality combined spiritual insight with political resistance in the attempt to achieve social reconstruction. Any effort to understand Malcolm X, and the cultural and religious beliefs he appealed to and argued against in making his specific claims, must take these traditions of prophetic and public morality into consideration.

Of the four books that largely view Malcolm's career through his unrelenting ethical insights and the moral abominations to which his vision forcefully responded, Louis Lomax's *When the Word Is Given: A Report on Elijah Muhammad, Malcolm X, and the Black Muslim World* and James Cone's *Martin and Malcolm and America: A Dream or a Nightmare?* treat the religious roots of Malcolm's moral vision. Peter Goldman's *The Death and Life of Malcolm X* and Lomax's *To Kill a Black Man* expound the social vision and political implications of Malcolm's moral perspective. Moreover, both Lomax's and Cone's books are comparative studies of Malcolm and Martin Luther King, Jr., Malcolm's widely perceived ideological opposite. The pairing of these figures invites inquiry about the legitimacy and usefulness of such comparisons, questions I will take up later.[24]

Lomax's *When the Word Is Given* is a perceptive and informal ethnography of the inner structure of belief of the Nation of Islam, a journalist's attempt to unveil the mysterious concatenation of religious rituals, puritanical behavior, and unorthodox beliefs that have at once intimidated and intrigued outsiders. Although other, more scholarly critics have examined Black Muslim belief, Lomax is a literate amateur whose lucid prose and imaginative reporting evoke the electricity and immediacy of the events he describes.[25]

Lomax is also insightful in his description of the cultural forces that helped bring Black Muslim faith into existence. He artfully probes how the Nation of Islam proved essential during the 1950s and 1960s for many black citizens who were vulnerably perched at the crux of the racial dilemma in the United States, seeking psychic and social refuge from the insanity of the country's fractured urban center. In Lomax's portrait, it is at the juncture between racist attack and cultural defense that Malcolm X's moral vocation emerges: he voices the aspirations of the disenfranchised, the racially displaced, the religiously confused, and the economically devastated black person. As Lomax observes, the "Black Muslims came to power during a moral interregnum"; Malcolm "brings his message of importance and dignity to a class of Negroes who have had little, if any, reason to feel proud of themselves as a race or as individuals."[26]

Despite the virtue of including several of Malcolm's speeches and interviews, which compose the second half of the book (including an interview during Malcolm's suspension from the Nation), the study's popular purposes largely stifle a sharp analysis of Malcolm's moral thought. Lomax provides helpful historical background of the origins and evolution of the Black Muslim worldview, linking useful insights on the emergence of religion in general to Islamic and Christian belief in Africa and in the United States. But his study does not engage the contradictions of belief and ambiguities of emotion that characterized Malcolm's moral life. In fairness to Lomax, this study was not his final word on Malcolm. But his later comparative biography of Malcolm and King is more striking for its compelling personal insight into two tragic, heroic men than for its comprehension of the constellation of cultural factors that shaped their lives.

Cone's *Martin and Malcolm and America*, on the contrary, is useful precisely because it explores the cultural, racial, and religious roots of Malcolm's public moral thought.[27] Cone, the widely acknowledged founder of black theology, has been significantly influenced by both King and Malcolm, and his book is a public acknowledgment of intellectual debt and personal inspiration. In chapters devoted to the impact of Malcolm's northern ghetto origins on his later thought, the content of his social vision, and the nature of his mature reflections on American society and black political activity, Cone discusses Malcolm's understanding of racial oppression, social justice, black unity, self-love, separatism, and self-defense that in the main constituted his vision of black nationalism.[28]

Cone performs a valuable service by shedding light on Malcolm's religious faith and then linking that faith to his social ideals and public moral vision, recognizing that his faith "was marginal not only in America as a whole but in the African-American community itself."[29] Cone covers familiar ground in his exposition of Malcolm's views on white Americans, black Christianity, and the religious and moral virtues of Elijah Muhammad's Black Muslim faith. But he also manages to show how Malcolm's withering criticisms of race anticipated "the rise of black liberation theology in the United States and South Africa and other expressions of liberation theology in the Third World."[30]

The most prominent feature of Cone's book is its comparative framework, paralleling and opposing two seminal influences on late-twentieth-century American culture. It is just this presumption—that Malcolm and Martin represented two contradictory, if not mutually exclusive, ideological options available to blacks in combating the absurdity of white racism—that generates interest in Cone's book, and in Lomax's *To Kill a Black Man*.[31] But is this presumption accurate?

As with all strictly imagined oppositions, an either-or division does not capture what Ralph Ellison termed the "beautiful and confounding complexities of Afro-American culture."[32] Nor does a rigid dualism account for the fashion in which even sharp ideological differences depend on some common intellectual ground to make disagreement plausible. For instance, the acrimonious ideological schism between Booker T. Washington and W.E.B. Du Bois drew energy from a common agreement that something must be done about the black cultural condition, that intellectual investigation must be wed to cultural and political activity in addressing the various problems of black culture, and that varying degrees of white support were crucial to the attainment of concrete freedom for black Americans.[33] Although Washington is characterized as an "accommodationist" and Du Bois as a "Pan-African nationalist," they were complex human beings whose political activity and social thought were more than the sum of their parts.

The comparative analysis of King and Malcolm sheds light on the strengths and weaknesses of the public-moralist approach to Malcolm's life and career. By comparing the two defining figures of twentieth-century black public morality, we are allowed to grasp the experienced, lived-out distinctions between King's and Malcolm's approaches to racial reform and revolution. Because King and Malcolm represent as well major tendencies in historic black ideological warfare against white racism, their lives and thoughts are useful examples of the social strategies, civil rebellion, religious resources, and psychic maneuvers adopted by diverse black movements for liberation within American society.

The challenge to the public-moralist approach is to probe the sorts of tensions between King and Malcolm that remain largely unexplored by other views of either figure. For instance, it is the presence of class differences within black life that bestowed particular meanings on King's and Malcolm's leadership. Such differences shaped the styles each leader adapted in voicing the grievances of his constituency— for King, a guilt-laden, upwardly mobile, and ever-expanding black middle class; for Malcolm, an ever-widening, trouble-prone, and rigidly oppressed black ghetto poor. These differences reflect deep and abiding schisms within African-American life that challenge facile or pedestrian interpretations of black leaders, inviting instead complex theoretical analyses of their public moral language and behavior.

The comparison of King and Malcolm may also, ironically, void the self-critical dimensions of the public-moralist perspective, causing its proponents to leave unaddressed, for instance, the shortcomings of a sexual hierarchy of social criticism in black life. Although Cone is critical of Malcolm's and Martin's failures of sight and sense on gender issues, more is demanded. What we need is an explanation of how intellectuals and leaders within vibrant traditions of black social criticism seem, with notable exception, unwilling or unable to include gender difference as a keyword in their public-moralist vocabulary. A comparative analysis of King and Malcolm may point out how *they* did not take gender difference seriously, but it does not explain how the public-moralist traditions in which they participated either enabled or prevented them from doing so.

By gaining such knowledge, we could determine if their beliefs were representative of their traditions, or if other participants (for example, Douglass and Du Bois, who held more enlightened views on gender) provide alternative perspectives from which to criticize Malcolm and Martin without resorting to the finger-pointing that derives from the clear advantage of historical hindsight.

As Cone makes clear, Malcolm and Martin were complex political actors whose thought derived from venerable traditions of response to American racism, usefully characterized as nationalism and integrationism. But as Cone also points out, the rhetoric of these two traditions has been employed to express complex beliefs, and black leaders and intellectuals have often combined them in their struggles against slavery and other forms of racial oppression.

Lomax, by comparison, more rigidly employs these figures to "examine the issues of 'integration versus separation,' 'violence versus nonviolence,' 'the relevance of the Christian ethic to modern life,' and the question 'can American institutions as now constructed activate the self-corrective power that is the basic prerequisite for racial harmony?'"[34] Lomax is most critical of Malcolm, leading one commentator to suggest that Lomax's assessment of Malcolm betrayed their friendship.[35] Lomax points out the wrongheadedness of Malcolm's advocacy of violence, the contradictions of his ideological absolutism, and the limitations of his imprecisely formulated organizational plans in his last year. His criticisms of King, however, are mostly framed as the miscalculations of strategy and the failure of white people to justify King's belief in them. Lomax's vision of Malcolm loses sight of the formidable forces that were arrayed against him, and the common moral worldviews occupied by King and his white oppressors, which made King's philosophical inclinations seem natural and legitimate, and Malcolm's, by that measure, foreign and unacceptable. One result of Lomax's lack of appreciation for this difference is his failure to explore King's challenge to capitalism, a challenge that distinguished King from Malcolm for most of Malcolm's career.

Another problem is that we fail to gain a more profitable view of Malcolm's real achievements, overlooking the strengths and weaknesses of the moral tradition in which he notably participated. Malcolm was, perhaps, the living indictment of a white American moral worldview. But his career was the first fruit as well of something more radical: an alternative racial cosmos where existing moral principles are viewed as the naked justification of power and thought to be useless in illumining or judging the propositions of an authentically black ethical worldview. Not only did Malcolm call for the rejection of particular incarnations of moral viewpoints that have failed to live up to their own best potential meanings (a strategy King employed to brilliant effect), but, given how American morality is indivisible from the network of intellectual arguments that support and justify it, he argued for the rejection of American public morality itself. Malcolm lived against the fundamental premises of

American public-moralist judgment: that innocence and corruption are on a continuum, that justice and injustice are on a scale, and that proper moral choices reflect right decisions made between good and evil within the given moral outlook.

Malcolm's black Islamic moral criticism posed a significant challenge to its black Christian counterpart, which has enjoyed a central place in African-American culture. Malcolm challenged an assumption held by the most prominent black Christian public moralists: that the social structure of American society should be rearranged, but not reconstructed. Consequently, Malcolm focused a harshly critical light on the very possibility of interracial cooperation, common moral vision, and social coexistence.

A powerful vision of Malcolm as a public moralist can be seen in Goldman's *The Death and Life of Malcolm X*. Goldman captures with eloquence and imagination the Brobdingnagian forces of white racial oppression that made life hell for northern poor blacks, and the Lilliputian psychic resources apparently at their disposal before Malcolm's oversized and defiant rhetoric rallied black rage and anger to their defense. Goldman's Malcolm is one whose "life was itself an accusation—a passage to the ninth circle of that black man's hell and back—and the real meaning of his ministry, in and out of the Nation of Islam, was to deliver that accusation to us." Malcolm was a "witness for the prosecution" of white injustice, a "public moralist." With each aspect of Malcolm's life that he treats—whether his anticipation of Black Power or his capitulation to standards of moral evaluation rooted in the white society he so vigorously despised—Goldman's narrative skillfully defends the central proposition of Malcolm's prophetic public-moralist vocation.[36]

Goldman's book is focused on Malcolm's last years before his break with Muhammad, and tracks Malcolm's transformation after Mecca. Goldman contends that this transformation occurred as process, not revelation, and that it ran over weeks and months of trial and error, discovery, disappointment. Additionally, Goldman sifts through the conflicting evidence of Malcolm's assassination.[37] Goldman maintains that only one of Malcolm's three convicted and imprisoned assassins is justly jailed, and that two other murderers remain free.[38] Goldman says about Malcolm's Organization of Afro-American Unity (OAAU), which he founded in his last year, that its "greatest single asset was its star: its fatal flaw was that it was constructed specifically as a star vehicle for a man who didn't have the time to invest in making it go."[39]

When it was written in 1973, and revised in 1979, Goldman's was the only full-length biography of Malcolm besides Lomax's *To Kill a Black Man*. The virtue of Goldman's book is that it taps into the sense of immediacy that drives Lomax's book, while also featuring independent investigation of Malcolm's life through more than a hundred interviews with Malcolm himself. Goldman's treatment of Malcolm also raises a question that I will more completely address later: Can a white intellectual understand and explain black experience? Goldman's book helps expose the cultural roots and religious expression of Elijah Muhammad's social theodicy, an argument Malcolm took up and defended with exemplary passion and fidelity. He describes Malcolm's public moral mission to proclaim judgment on white America with the same kind of insight and clarity that characterized many of Malcolm's public declarations.

Explaining Malcolm as a public moralist moves admirably beyond heroic reconstruction to critical appreciation. The significance of such an approach is its insistence on viewing Malcolm as a critical figure in the development of black nationalist repudiations of white cultural traditions, economic practices, and religious institutions. And yet, unlike hero worshipers who present treatments of Malcolm's meaning, the authors who examine the moral dimensions of Malcolm's public ministry are unafraid to be critical of his ideological blindnesses, his strategic weakness, his organizational limitations, and his sometimes bristling moral contradictions.

But if they display an avidity, and aptitude, for portraying Malcolm's moral dimensions and the forces that made his vision necessary, Malcolm's public-moralist interpreters have not as convincingly depicted the forces that make public morality possible. The public-moralist approach is almost by definition limited to explaining Malcolm in terms of the broad shifts and realignment of contours created within the logic of American morality itself, rarely asking whether public-moralist proclamation and action are the best means of effecting social revolution. This approach largely ignores the hints of rebellion against capitalist domination contained in Malcolm's later speeches, blurring as well a focus on King's mature beliefs that American society was "sick" and in need of a "reconstruction of the entire society, a revolution of values."[40]

This approach also fails to place Malcolm in the intricate nexus of social and political forces that shaped his career as a religious militant and a revolutionary black nationalist. It does not adequately convey the mammoth scope of economic and cultural forces that converged during the 1940s, 1950s, and 1960s, not only shaping the expression of racial domination, but influencing as well patterns of class antagonism and gender oppression. As Clayborne Carson argues in his splendid introduction to the FBI files on Malcolm X, most writings have failed to "study him within the context of American racial politics during the 1950s and 1960s."[41] According to Carson, the files track Malcolm's growth from the "narrowly religious perspective of the Nation of Islam toward a broader Pan-Africanist worldview," shed light on his religious and political views and the degree to which they "threatened the American state," and "clarif[y] his role in modern African-American politics."[42]

Moreover, the story of Malcolm X and the black revolution he sought to effect is also the story of how such social aspirations were shaped by the advent of nuclear holocaust in the mid-1940s (altering American ideals of social stability and communal life expectation), the repression of dissident speech in the 1950s under the banner of McCarthyism, and the economic boom of the mid-1960s that contrasted starkly to shrinking resources for the black poor. A refined social history not only accents such features, but provides as well a complex portrait of Malcolm's philosophical and political goals, and the myriad factors that drove or denied their achievement.

Malcolm's most radical and original contribution rested in reconceiving the possibility of being a worthful black human being in what he deemed a wicked white world. He saw black racial debasement as the core of an alternative moral sphere that was justified for no other reason than its abuse and attack by white Americans. To understand and explain Malcolm, however, we must wedge beneath the influences that determined his career in learning how his public-moralist vocation was both necessary and possible.

PSYCHOBIOGRAPHY AND THE FORCES OF HISTORY

If the task of biography is to help readers understand human action, the purpose of psychobiography is to probe the relationship between psychic motivation, personal behavior, and social activity in explaining human achievement and failure. The project to connect psychology and biography grows out of a well-established quest to merge various schools of psychological theory with other intellectual disciplines, resulting in ethnopsychiatry, psychohistory, social psychology, and psychoanalytic approaches to philosophy.[43]

Behind the turn toward psychology and social theory by biographers is a desire to take advantage of the insight yielded from attempts to correlate or synthesize the largely incompatible worlds of psychoanalysis and Marxism carved out by Freud and Marx and their unwieldy legion of advocates and interpreters. If one argues, however, as Richard Lichtman does, that "the structure of the two theories makes them ultimate rivals," then, as he concedes, "priorities must be established."[44] In his analysis of the integration of psychoanalysis into Marxist theory, Lichtman argues that "working through the limitations of Freud's view makes its very significant insights available for incorporation into an expanded Marxist theory."[45]

Psychobiographers have acknowledged the intellectual difficulties to which Lichtman points while using Marxist or Freudian theory (and sometimes both) to locate and illumine gnarled areas of human experience. For instance, Erik Erikson's *Gandhi's Truth: On the Origins of Militant Nonviolence*, one of psychobiography's foundational works, weds critical analysis of its subject's cultural and intellectual roots to imaginative reflections on the sources of Gandhi's motivation, sacrifice, and spiritual achievement.[46]

As they bring together social and psychological theory in their research, psychobiographers often rupture the rules that separate academic disciplines. Then again, if the psychobiographer is ruled by rigid presuppositions and is insensitive to the subject of study, nothing can prevent the results from being fatally flat. Two recent psychobiographies of Malcolm X reveal that genre's virtues and vices.

Eugene Victor Wolfenstein's *The Victims of Democracy: Malcolm X and the Black Revolution* is a work of considerable intellectual imagination and rigorous theoretical insight.[47] It takes measure of the energies that created Malcolm and the demons that drove him. Wolfenstein assesses Malcolm's accomplishments through a theoretical lens as noteworthy for its startling clarity about Malcolm the individual as for its wide-angled view of the field of forces with which Malcolm contended during his childhood and mature career.

Wolfenstein uses an elaborate conceptual machinery to examine how racism falsifies "the consciousness of the racially oppressed," and how racially oppressed individuals struggle to "free themselves from both the falsification of their consciousness and the racist domination of their practical activity."[48] For Wolfenstein's purpose, neither a psychoanalytic nor a Marxist theory alone could yield adequate insight because Freudianism "provides no foundation for the analysis of interests, be they individual or collective," and Marxism "provides no foundation for the analysis of desires." Therefore, a "unifying concept of human nature was required."[49]

Wolfenstein's psychobiography is especially helpful because it combines several compelling features: a historical analysis of the black (nationalist) revolutionary struggle, an insightful biographical analysis of Malcolm X's life, and an imaginative social theory that explains how a figure like Malcolm X could emerge from the womb of black struggle against American apartheid. Wolfenstein accounts for how Malcolm's childhood was affected by violent, conflicting domestic forces and describes how black culture's quest for identity at the margins of American society—especially when viewed from the even more marginal perspective of the black poor—shaped Malcolm's adolescence and young adulthood.

Wolfenstein also explores Malcolm's career as a zealous young prophet and public mouthpiece for Elijah Muhammad, revealing the psychic and social needs that Malcolm's commitments served. Wolfenstein's imaginative remapping of Malcolm's intellectual and emotional landscape marks a significant contribution as well to the history of African-American ideas, offering new ways of understanding one of the most complex figures in our nation's history.

Undoubtedly, Wolfenstein's book would have benefited from a discussion of how black religious groups provided social and moral cohesion in northern urban black communities, and from a description of their impact on Earl Little's ministry. Although Wolfenstein perceptively probes the appeal of Marcus Garvey's Universal Negro Improvement Association to blacks—and the social, psychological, and economic ground it partly shared with the Ku Klux Klan and white proletarian workers—his psychoanalytic Marxist interpretation of Earl Little and Malcolm would have been substantially enhanced by an engagement with black Protestant beliefs about the relationship between work, morality, and self-regard.[50]

Wolfenstein is often keenly insightful about black liberation movements and the forces that precipitated their eruption, but his dependence on biological definitions of race weakens his arguments.[51] The value of more complex readings of race is that they not only show how the varied meanings of racism are created in society; but prove as well that the idea of race has a cultural history.[52] More complex theories of race would permit Wolfenstein to illumine the changing intellectual and social terrain of struggle by groups that oppose the vicious meanings attributed to African-American identity by cultural racists.

In the end, Wolfenstein is too dependent on the revelations and reconstructions of self-identity that Malcolm (with Haley's assistance) achieved in his autobiography. In answering his own rhetorical questions about whether Malcolm and Haley represented Malcolm accurately, Wolfenstein says that from a "purely empirical standpoint, I believe the answer to both questions is generally affirmative."[53] The problem, of course, is that Malcolm's recollections are not without distortions. These distortions, when taken together with the book's interpretive framework, not only reveal his attempts to record his life history, but reflect as well his need to control how his life was viewed during the ideological frenzy that marked his last year. By itself, self-description is an unreliable basis for reconstructing the meaning of Malcolm's life and career. Still, Wolfenstein's work is the most sophisticated treatment to date of Malcolm's intellectual and psychological roots.

But Bruce Perry's uneven psychobiographical study, *Malcolm: The Life of a Man Who Changed Black America*, which reaches exhaustively beyond Malcolm's self-representation in his autobiography, possesses little of the psychoanalytic rigor and insight of Wolfenstein's work.[54] Although Perry unearths new information about Malcolm, he does not skillfully clarify the impact that such information should have on our understanding of Malcolm. The volume renders Malcolm smaller than life.

In Perry's estimation, Malcolm's childhood holds the interpretive key to understanding his mature career as a black leader: Malcolm's "war against the white power structure evolved from the same inner needs that had spawned earlier rebellions against his teachers, the law, established religion, and other symbols of authority."[55] Perry's picture of Malcolm's family is one of unremitting violence, criminality, and pathology. The mature Malcolm is equally tragic: a man of looming greatness whose self-destruction "contributed to his premature death."[56] It is precisely here that Perry's psychobiography folds in on itself, its rough edges puncturing the center of its explanatory purpose. It is not that psychobiography cannot remark on the unraveling of domestic relations that weave together important threads of personal identity, threads that are also woven into adolescent and adult behavior. But Perry has a penchant for explaining complex psychic forces—and the social conditions that influence their makeup—in simplistic terms and tabloid-like arguments.

Still, Perry's new information about Malcolm is occasionally revealing, though some of the claims he extracts from this information are more dubious than others. When, for instance, Perry addresses areas of Malcolm's life that can be factually verified, he is on solid ground. By simply checking Malcolm's school records Perry proves that, contrary to his autobiography, Malcolm was not expelled from West Junior High School but actually completed the seventh grade in 1939. And by interviewing several family members, Perry establishes that neither Malcolm's half-sister Ella nor his father Earl were, as Malcolm contended, "jet black," a claim Perry views as Malcolm's way of equating "blackness and the strength his light-skinned mother had lacked."[57] Despite Malcolm X's assertion of close friendships with Lionel Hampton, Sonny Greer, and Cootie Williams during his hustling days, Perry's interviews show that the "closeness Malcolm described was as fictitious as the closeness he said he had shared with the members of his own family."[58]

But when Perry addresses aspects of Malcolm's experience that invite close argument and analytical interpretation, he is on shakier ground. At this juncture, Perry displays an insensitivity to African-American life and an ignorance about black intellectual traditions that weaken his book. For instance, Perry depicts Malcolm's travels to Africa—partially in an attempt to expand his organization's political and financial base, but also to express his increasingly international social vision—as intended solely to fund his fledgling organization. Perry also draws questionable parallels between the cloudy events surrounding a fire at Malcolm's family farm during his early childhood in 1929 (which Perry concludes points to arson by Earl Little) and the fire at Malcolm's New York house after his dispute with Nation of Islam officials over ownership rights.

A major example of the limitation of Perry's psychobiographical approach is his treatment of Malcolm's alleged homosexual activity, both as an experimenting adolescent and as a hustling, income-seeking young adult. Perry's remarks are more striking for the narrow assumptions that underlie his interpretations than for their potential to dismantle the quintessential symbol of African-American manhood. If Malcolm did have homosexual relations, they might serve Perry as a powerful tool of interpretation to expose the tangled cultural roots of black machismo, and to help him explain the cruel varieties of homophobia that afflict black communities. A complex understanding of black sexual politics challenges a psychology of masculinity that views "male" as a homogeneous, natural, and universally understood identity. A complex understanding of masculinity maintains that male identity is also significantly affected by ethnic, racial, economic, and sexual differences.

But Perry's framework of interpretation cannot assimilate the information his research has unearthed. Although the masculinist psychology that chokes much of black leadership culture needs to be forcefully criticized, Perry's observations do not suffice. Because he displays neither sensitivity to nor knowledge about complex black cultural beliefs regarding gender and sexual difference, Perry's portrait of Malcolm's sex life forms a rhetorical low blow, simply reinforcing a line of attack against an already sexually demonized black leadership culture.

The power of psychobiography in discussing black leaders is its potential to shed light on its subjects in a manner that traditional biography fails to achieve. African-American cultural studies, which has traditionally made little use of psychoanalytic theory, has sacrificed the insights such an undertaking might offer while avoiding the pitfalls of psychological explanations of human motivation. After all, psychobiography is also prone to overreach its capacity to explain.

In some ways, the psychobiographer's quest for (in this case) the "real Malcolm" presumes that human experience is objective and that truth is produced by explaining the relation between human action and psychic motivation. Such an approach may seduce psychobiographers into believing that they are gaining access to the static, internal psychic reality of a historical figure. Often such access is wrongly believed to be separate from the methods of investigation psychobiographers employ, and from the aims and presumptions, as well as the biases and intellectual limitations, that influence their work.

Because both Wolfenstein and Perry (like Goldman) are white, their psychobiographies in particular raise suspicion about the ability of white intellectuals to interpret black experience. Although such speculation is rarely systematically examined, it surfaces as both healthy skepticism and debilitating paranoia in the informal debates that abound in a variety of black intellectual circles. Such debates reflect two crucial tensions generated by psychobiographical explanations of black leaders by white authors: that such explanations reflect insensitivity to black culture, and that white proponents of psychobiographical analysis are incompetent to assess black life adequately. Several factors are at the base of such conclusions.

First is the racist history that has affected every tradition of American scholarship and that has obscured, erased, or distorted accounts of the culture and history of African Americans.[59] Given this history (and the strong currents of anti-intellectualism that flood most segments of American culture), suspicion of certain forms of critical intellectual activity survive in many segments of black culture. Also, black intellectuals have experienced enormous difficulty in securing adequate cultural and financial support to develop self-sustaining traditions of scholarly investigation and communities of intellectual inquiry.[60]

For example, from its birth in the womb of political protest during the late 1960s and early 1970s, black studies has been largely stigmatized and usually underfunded. Perhaps the principal reasons for this are the beliefs held by many whites (and some blacks) that, first, black scholars should master nonblack subjects, and second, that black studies is intellectually worthless. Ironically, once the more than 200 black studies programs in American colleges and universities became established, many white academics became convinced that blacks are capable of studying only "black" subjects.

At the same time, black studies experienced a new "invasion" by white intellectuals. This new invasion—mimicking earlier patterns of white scholarship on black life even as most black scholars were prevented from being published—provoked resentment from black scholars."[61] The resentment hinged on the difficulty black scholars experienced in securing appointments in most academic fields beyond black studies. Black scholars were also skeptical of the intellectual assumptions and political agendas of white scholars, especially because there was strong precedence for many white scholars to distort black culture in their work by either exoticizing or demonizing its expression. Black intellectual skeptics opposed to white interpretations of black culture and figures employ a variety of arguments in their defense.

Many black intellectuals contend that black experience is unique and can be understood, described, and explained only by blacks. Unquestionably, African-American history produces cultural and personal experiences that are distinct, even singular. But the *historical* character of such experiences makes them theoretically accessible to any interpreter who has a broad knowledge of African-American intellectual traditions, a balanced and sensible approach to black culture, and the same skills of rational argumentation and scholarly inquiry required in other fields of study.

There is no special status of being that derives from black cultural or historical experience that grants black interpreters an automatically superior understanding of black cultural meanings. This same principle allows black scholars to interpret Shakespeare, study Heisenberg's uncertainty principle, and master Marxist social theory. In sum, black cultural and historical experiences do not produce ideas and practices that are incapable of interpretation when the most critically judicious and culturally sensitive methods of intellectual inquiry are applied.

Many intellectuals also believe that black culture is unified and relatively homogeneous. But this contention is as misleading as the first, especially in light of black culture's wonderful complexity and radical diversity. The complexity and diversity of black culture means that a bewildering variety of opinions, beliefs, ideologies, traditions, and practices coexist, even if in a provisional sort of way. Black conservatives, scuba divers, socialists, and rock musicians come easily to mind. All these tendencies and traditions constitute and help define black culture. Given these realities, it is pointless to dismiss studies of black cultural figures simply because their authors are white. One must judge any work on African-American culture by standards of rigorous critical investigation while attending to both the presuppositions that ground scholarly perspectives and the biases that influence intellectual arguments.

Psychobiographies of Malcolm X's life and career represent an important advance in Malcolm studies. The crucial issue is not color, but consciousness about African-American culture, sensitivity to trends and developments in black society, knowledge of the growing literature about various dimensions of black American life, and a theoretical sophistication that artfully blends a variety of disciplinary approaches in yielding insight about a complex historic figure like Malcolm X. When psychobiography is employed in this manner, it can go a long way toward breaking new ground in understanding and explaining the life of important black figures. When it is incompetently wielded, psychobiographical analysis ends up simply projecting the psychobiographer's intellectual biases and limitations of perspective onto the historical screen of a black figure's career.

VOICES IN THE WILDERNESS:
REVOLUTIONARY SPARKS AND MALCOLM'S LAST YEAR

To comprehend the full sweep of a figure's life and thought, it is necessary to place that figure's career in its cultural and historical context and view the trends and twists of thought that mark significant periods of change and development. Such an approach may be termed a trajectory analysis because it attempts to outline the evolution of belief and thought of historic figures by matching previously held ideas to newer ones, seeking to grasp whatever continuities and departures can be discerned from such an enterprise. Trajectory analysis, then, may be a helpful way of viewing a figure such as Martin Luther King Jr., whose career may be divided into the early optimism of civil rights ideology to the latter-day aggressive nonviolence he advocated on the eve of his assassination. It may also be enlightening when grappling with the serpentine mysteries of Malcolm's final days.

Malcolm's turbulent severance from Elijah Muhammad's psychic and world-making womb initiated yet another stage of his personal and political evolution, marking a conversion experience. On one level, Malcolm freed himself from Elijah's destructive ideological grip, shattering molds of belief and practice that were no longer useful or enabling. On another level, Malcolm's maturation and conversion were the result of his internal ideals of moral expectation, social behavior, and authentic religious belief. His conversion, though suddenly manifest, was most likely a gradual process involving both conscious acts of dissociation from the Nation of Islam and the "subconscious incubation and maturing of motives deposited by the experiences of life."[62]

Many commentators have heavily debated the precise nature of Malcolm's transformation. Indeed, his last fifty weeks on earth form a fertile intellectual field where the seeds of speculation readily blossom into conflicting interpretations of Malcolm's meaning at the end of his life. Lomax says that Malcolm became a "lukewarm integrationist."[63] Goldman suggests that Malcolm was "improvising," that he embraced and discarded ideological options as he went along.[64] Cleage and T'shaka hold that he remained a revolutionary black nationalist. And Cone asserts that Malcolm became an internationalist with a humanist bent.

But the most prominent and vigorous interpreters of the meaning of Malcolm's last year have been a group of intellectuals associated with the Socialist Workers Party, a Trotskyist-Marxist group that took keen interest in Malcolm's post-Mecca social criticism and sponsored some of his last speeches. For the most part, their views have been articulately promoted by George Breitman, author of *The Last Year of Malcolm X: The Evolution of a Revolutionary* and editor of two volumes of Malcolm's speeches, organizational statements, and interviews during his last years: *Malcolm X Speaks: Selected Speeches and Statements* and *By Any Means Necessary: Speeches, Interviews, and a Letter, by Malcolm X.* A third volume of Malcolm's speeches, *Malcolm X: The Last Speeches,* was edited by Bruce Perry, who claimed "ideological difference with the publisher.[65]

Breitman's *The Last Year of Malcolm X* is a passionately argued book that maintains Malcolm's split with Elijah took Malcolm by surprise, making it necessary for him to gain time and experience to reconstruct his ideological beliefs and redefine his organizational orientation. Breitman divides Malcolm's independent phase into two parts: the transition period, lasting the few months between his split in March 1964 and his return from Africa at the end of May 1964; and the final period, lasting from June 1964 until his death in February 1965. Breitman maintains that in the final period, Malcolm "was on the way to a synthesis of black nationalism and socialism that would be fitting for the American scene and acceptable to the masses in the black ghetto."[66]

For Breitman's argument to be persuasive, it had to address Malcolm's continuing association with a black nationalism that effectively excluded white participation, or else show that he had developed a different understanding of black nationalism. Also, he had to prove that Malcolm's anticapitalist statements and remarks about socialism represented a coherent and systematic exposition of his beliefs as a political strategist and social critic. Breitman contends that in the final period, Malcolm made distinctions between separatism (the belief that blacks should be socially, culturally, politically, and economically separate from white society) and nationalism (the belief that blacks should control their own culture).

Malcolm's views of nationalism changed after his encounters with revolutionaries in Africa who were "white," however, and in his "Young Socialist" interview in *By Any Means Necessary*, Malcolm confessed that he "had to do a lot of thinking and reappraising" of his definition of black nationalism.[67] Breitman argues that though he "had virtually stopped calling himself and the OAAU black nationalist," because others persisted in the practice, he accepted "its continued use in discussion and debate."[68] Malcolm said in the same interview, "I haven't been using the expression for several months."[69]

But how can Breitman then argue that Malcolm was attempting a synthesis of black nationalism and socialism if the basis for Malcolm's continued use of the phrase "black nationalism" was apparently more convenience and habit than ideological conviction? What is apparent from my reading of Malcolm's speeches is that his reconsideration of black nationalism occurred amid a radically shifting worldview that was being shaped by events unfolding on the international scene and by his broadened horizon of experience. His social and intellectual contact with activists and intellectuals from several African nations forced him to relinquish the narrow focus of his black nationalist practice and challenged him to consider restructuring his organizational base to reflect his broadened interests.

If, therefore, even Malcolm's conceptions of black nationalist strategy were undergoing profound restructuring, it is possible to say only that his revised black nationalist ideology might have accommodated socialist strategy. It is equally plausible to suggest that his nationalist beliefs might have collapsed altogether under the weight of apparent ideological contradictions introduced by his growing appreciation of class and economic factors in forming the lives of the black masses.[70] For the synthesis of black nationalism and socialism that Breitman asserts Malcolm was forging to have been plausible, several interrelated processes needed to be set in motion.

First, for such a synthesis to have occurred, a clear definition of the potential connection of black nationalism and socialism was needed. The second need was for a discussion of the ideological similarities and differences between the varieties of black nationalism and socialism to be joined. And the third need was for an explicit expression of the political, economic, and social interests that an allied black nationalism and socialism would mutually emphasize and embrace; the exploration of intellectual and political problems both would address; and an identification of the common enemies both would oppose. But given the existential and material matters that claimed his rapidly evaporating energy near the end of his life, Malcolm hardly had the wherewithal to perform such tasks.

Breitman also maintains that Malcolm's final period marked his maturation as "a revolutionary—increasingly anti-capitalist and pro-socialist as well as anti-imperialist," labels that Breitman acknowledges Malcolm himself never adopted.[71] Breitman reads Malcolm's two trips to Africa as a time of expansive political reeducation, when Malcolm gained insight into the progressive possibilities of socialist revolutionary practice. After his return to the United States from his second trip, Malcolm felt, Breitman says, the need to express publicly his "own anti-capitalist and pro-socialist convictions," which had "become quite strong by this time."[72] He cites interviews and speeches Malcolm made during this period to substantiate his claim, including Malcolm's speaking at the Audubon Ballroom on December 20, 1964, of how almost "every one of the countries that has gotten independence has devised some kind of socialist system, and this is no accident."[73]

Such a strategy, one that seeks to predict probable ideological and intellectual outcomes, may shed less light on Malcolm than is initially apparent. Breitman's contention that Malcolm was becoming a socialist; Cleage's that he was confused; T'shaka's that he maintained a vigorous revolutionary black nationalist stance; and Goldman's that he was improvising can all be proclaimed and documented with varying degrees of evidence and credibility.

This is not to suggest that one view is as good as the next or that they are somehow interchangeable, because we are uncertain about Malcolm's final direction. It simply suggests that the nature of Malcolm's thought during his last year was ambiguous and that making definite judgments about his direction is impossible. In this light, trajectories say more about the ideological commitments and intellectual viewpoints of interpreters than the objective evidence evoked to substantiate claims about Malcolm's final views. The truth is that we have only a bare-bones outline of Malcolm's emerging worldview. In "The Harlem 'Hate-Gang' Scare," contained in *Malcolm X Speaks* (and delivered during what Breitman says was Malcolm's final period), Malcolm says that during his travels he

noticed that most of the countries that had recently emerged into independence have turned away from the so-called capitalistic system in the direction of socialism. So out of curiosity, I can't resist the temptation to do a little investigating wherever that particular philosophy happens to be in existence or an attempt is being made to bring it into existence.[74]

But at the end of his speech, in reply to a question about the kind of political and economic system that Malcolm wanted, he said, "I don't know. But I'm flexible. . . . As was stated earlier, all of the countries that are emerging today from under the shackles of colonialism are turning toward socialism."[75]

This tentativeness is characteristic of Malcolm's speeches throughout the three collections that contain fragments of his evolving worldview, especially *Malcolm X Speaks* and *By Any Means Necessary*. Even the speeches delivered during his final period showcase a common feature: Malcolm displays sympathy for and interest in socialist philosophy without committing himself to its practice as a means of achieving liberation for African-Americans.

Malcolm confessed in the "Young Socialist" interview, "I still would be hard pressed to give a specific definition of the overall philosophy which I think is necessary for the liberation of the black people in this country."[76] Of course, as Breitman implies, Malcolm's self-description is not the only basis for drawing conclusions about his philosophy. But even empirical investigation fails to yield conclusive evidence of his social philosophy because it was in such radical transformation and flux.

Malcolm was indeed improvising from the chords of an expanded black nationalist rhetoric and an embryonic socialist criticism of capitalist civilization. Although Breitman has been maligned as a latecomer seeking to foist his ideological beliefs onto Malcolm's last days, there is precedence for Trotskyist attempts to address the problem of racism and black nationalism in the United States.[77] And the venerable black historian C. L. R. James became a Marxist, in part, by reading Trotsky's *History of the Russian Revolution*.[78] Although Malcolm consistently denounced capitalism, he did not live long enough to embrace socialism.

The weakness of such an interpretive trajectory, then, is that it tends to demand a certainty about Malcolm that is clearly unachievable. An ideological trajectory of Malcolm's later moments is forced to bring coherence to fragments of political speech more than systematic social thought, to exaggerate moments of highly suggestive ideological gestures rather than substantive political activity, and to focus on slices of organizational breakthrough instead of the complex integrative activity envisioned for the OAAU. In the end, it is apparent that Malcolm was rapidly revising his worldview as he experienced a personal, religious, and ideological conversion that was still transpiring when he met his brutal death.

But the thrust behind such speculation is often a focus on how Malcolm attempted to shape the cultural forces of his time through the agency of moral rhetoric, social criticism, and prophetic declaration. Just as important, but often neglected in such analyses, is an account of how Malcolm was shaped by his times, of how he was the peculiar and particular creation of black cultural forces and American social practices. Armed with such an understanding, the focus on Malcolm's last year would be shifted away from simply determining what he said and did to determining how we should use his example to respond to our current cultural and national crises.

IN THE PRISON OF PRISMS: THE FUTURE OF MALCOLM'S PAST

The literature on Malcolm X is certain to swell with the renewed cultural interest in his life. And although the particular incarnations of the approaches I have detailed may fade from intellectual view or cultural vogue, the ideological commitments, methodological procedures, historical perspectives, cultural assumptions, religious beliefs, and philosophical presuppositions they employ will most assuredly be expressed in one form or another in future treatments of his life and thought.[79]

The canonization of Malcolm will undoubtedly continue. Romantic and celebratory treatments of his social action and revolutionary rhetoric will issue forth from black intellectuals, activists, and cultural artists. This is especially true in the independent black press, where Malcolm's memory has been heroically kept alive in books, pamphlets, and magazines, even as his presence receded from wide visibility and celebration before his recent revival. The independent black press preserves and circulates cultural beliefs, intellectual arguments, and racial wisdom among black folk away from the omniscient eye and acceptance of mainstream publishing.

Shahrazad Ali's controversial book, *The Blackman's Guide to Understanding the Blackwoman*, for instance, sold hundreds of thousands of copies without receiving much attention from mainstream newspapers, magazines, or journals. The mainstream press often overlooked Malcolm's contributions, but black publications like *The Amsterdam News*, *The Afro-American*, *Bilalian News*, and *Black News* scrupulously recorded his public career. The black independent press, in alliance with various black nationalist groups throughout the country that have maintained Malcolm's heroic stature from the time of his assassination, is a crucial force in Malcolm's ongoing celebration. Such treatments of his legacy will most likely be employed by these groups to actively resist Malcolm's symbolic manipulation by what they understand to be the forces of cultural racism, state domination, commodification, and especially religious brainwashing that Malcolm detested and opposed.

The enormous influence of the culture of hip-hop on black youth, coupled with the resurgence of black cultural nationalism among powerful subcultures within the African-American community, suggests that Malcolm's heroic example will continue to be emulated and proclaimed. The stakes of hero worship are raised when considering the resurgent racism of American society and the increased personal and social desperation among the constituency for whom Malcolm eloquently argued, the black ghetto poor. Heightened racial antipathy in cultural institutions such as universities and businesses, and escalated attacks on black cultural figures, ideas, and movements, precipitate the celebration of figures who embody the strongest gestures of resistance to white racism.

Moreover, the destructive effects of gentrification, economic crisis, and social dislocation; the expansion of corporate privilege; and the development of underground political economies—along with the violence and criminality they breed—means that Malcolm is even more a precious symbol of the self-discipline, self-esteem, and moral leadership necessary to combat the spiritual and economic corruption of poor black communities. With their efforts to situate him among the truly great in African-American history, hero worshipers' discussion of Malcolm will be of important but limited value in critically investigating his revolutionary speech, thought, and action.

Malcolm's weaknesses and strengths must be rigorously examined if we are to have a richly hued picture of one of the most intriguing figures of twentieth-century public life in the United States. Malcolm's past is not yet settled, savaged as it has been in the embrace of unprincipled denigrators while being equally smothered in the well-meaning grip of romantic and uncritical loyalists. He deserves what every towering and seminal figure in history should receive: comprehensive and critical examination of what he said and did so that his life and thought will be useful to future generations of peoples in struggle around the globe.

Twenty-One

MIXED BLESSINGS:
MARTIN LUTHER KING, JR., AND THE
LESSONS OF AN AMBIGUOUS HEROISM

Martin Luther King, Jr., is, perhaps, the greatest influence on my life outside of the mentorship of my beloved pastor, the late, great rhetorical genius, theological giant, and political mystic, the Rev. Dr. Frederick George Sampson II. I was nine years old when King was murdered in Memphis, and though I had never heard of him, his death affected me profoundly. I scrounged around for every personal recollection about him I could find, sent off for recordings of his most famous speeches, and read every article and book about him that the library contained. This chapter from Reflecting Black *is among my first published attempts to wrestle with the intellectual and moral legacy, as well as the clear but complex social heroism, of a man I consider the greatest American in our nation's history.*

THE ESTABLISHMENT OF A NATIONAL HOLIDAY to honor the life and achieve-ments of Martin Luther King, Jr., is a reason for critical celebration. Only the sec-ond American and the first African-American to be feted with this singular honor, the celebration of King's birthday is an occasion of national, religious, and racial significance. It acknowledges that King was the supreme embodiment of American citizenship and political engagement, the highest manifestation of the American re-ligious genius, and the richest expression of the multifaceted character of the black experience in America.

On the other hand, the King birthday celebration also presents the danger of losing the challenging and uncomfortable dimensions of King's thought and life by romanticizing his career. The nature and scope of King's accomplishments, which center in nothing short of a specific revolution in how black people live and are perceived in American culture, inevitably invite historic embellishment and social myth. But neither a puerile romanticization of King as Safe Negro nor a car-icatured mythologization of King as Great American Hero will do. King's life was too complex, his achievements too profound, and his thinking too provocative to warrant such naive responses. We must transcend such unrealistic assessments of King and concentrate on the substantive contributions of his life and thought.

An especially helpful and illuminating way to view King's life and justly assess his accomplishments is through a reflection upon the ethics and politics of hero celebration. This context permits us to examine the beneficial and harmful uses to which the King holiday may be put in creating or preserving images of King that avoid disturbing history or dodge painful truth. This context also provides a healthy framework in addressing recent revelations about King's character, including charges of plagiarism and womanizing. In this chapter, I will examine some characteristics of heroism, exploring the ways it makes sense to call King a hero, treat two central tensions that arise in asserting that King's heroism is ambiguous, and briefly suggest that King's birthday is indeed worth celebrating.

In my brief examination of some characteristics of heroism, I do not intend to provide a theory of heroism or trace its varied genealogy. Rather, I will discuss heroism within the limits of existing understandings of the concept and then seek to apply them to King in analyzing the effects of hero worship on the ideals for which he gave his life.

In his work on George Washington, cultural critic and historian Gary Wills reminds us that hero worship "is a hard assignment for many people today—one they think they cannot fulfill, or should not. Hero worship is elitist. It reduces the science of history to mere biography, if not to anecdote. It suggests that individual talent is a more important force than large economic processes. . . . The attitude of many in our time is captured by Bertolt Brecht's *Galileo,* who says: 'Unhappy the land that needs a hero.'"[1] While Wills's larger point about the suspicion of many Americans toward hero worship may be valid, explaining the diminished field of activity over which heroism is spread, it is equally true that American hero worship is presently focused in two social spheres: competitive sports and the military.

Contemporary forms of American heroism are often displayed within the context of sports competition, where individual or team exploits are lauded for embodying particular virtues, skills, and mastery. For example, basketball heroes are often said to embody the virtues of rigorous habits of practice, expert skills of physical dexterity, and mastery of the overall complexity of their craft necessary to perform excellently and unselfishly in a team sport.

Military heroes, as well, figure prominently in the comparatively constricted sphere of heroism celebrated today. America's recent war in the Gulf shows how eager Americans are for clear embodiments of American values of national patriotism, personal valor, and sacrifice for the common good. That Generals Norman Schwarzkopf and Colin Powell are instant heroes testifies to the peculiar hunger of many Americans for reassurance about the integrity and rightness of this country's values and ways of life.

Perhaps this last point clearly demonstrates a telling feature of heroism: it is intimately related to ideals felt to be worthy of support because they say something important about national self-identity. Part of the difficulty in deciding upon a genuine and truly national hero is connected to the increasing diversity of American culture. Because of the bewildering pluralization of perspectives about what it means to be an American, growing dispute about what goods are worthy of pursuit, strong disagreement about how to measure various forms of moral and social excellence, and the unraveling of a unified concept of the public good, the virtuous as well as the heroic is subject to radical revision and heated debate. Occasionally, however, a person or movement so decisively captures the nation's imagination that a variety of Americans come to believe that their truest selves and deepest beliefs are embodied in the vision and life of that figure or movement. Such was the case for many Americans in relation to Martin Luther King, Jr., and the civil rights movement.

The civil rights movement provided a social context, cultural framework, and racial worldview for blacks and other similarly excluded Americans to argue for inclusion within the larger circle of privilege, rights, and status from which they had been socially and legally barred. Civil rights leaders and activists built upon the symbol systems of black religion, the resonant traditions of radical protest within black culture, and a progressive understanding of liberal democracy in articulating demands for equality, justice, and freedom. Because of this potent mix of elements, the civil rights movement had the advantage of appealing to specific values nourished within a black cultural cosmos, while linking them to the iconic structures, symbolic worldviews, and heroic values that undergirded much of American society. As symbolic representative of the civil rights movement, Martin Luther King, Jr., embodied the virtues of black religious culture and black traditions of protest, as well as the best impulses of Western liberal democracy.

On the other hand, King wove into his rhetorical and strategic tapestry threads of prophetic religious utterance and radical social criticism that sorely tested the limits of liberal tolerance of forces of fundamental social challenge and transformation. The fact that some state and national politicians who represent the forces of stasis and regression that King opposed are now in part responsible for presiding over the public rituals to commemorate his memory only attests to the ambiguous character of the heroism King embodies.

King figures prominently in a distinct line of social prophets whose ideals can sometimes only be truly honored by their remaining, in significant measure, outside of the totemic processes of official acceptance, which cloak their status as prophetic characters whose memory judges American moral practice. The ambiguity that surrounds King's memory is healthy because it creates suggestive tensions within the developing edifice of King worship and draws attention to those troubling aspects of King's thought that have the potential to shatter the rigid constructions of official truth.

In reflecting on the ambiguity of King's heroism, it will be helpful to discuss some characteristics of heroism and explore how King can be usefully understood as an American hero. A heroic figure undeniably possesses the ability to substantially alter and influence the course of events because of her mix of personal traits, skills, talents, and visions. This definition, of course, rests on the distinction that

Sidney Hook made between two types of persons who qualify as potential heroes. After defining the hero in history as "the individual to whom we can justifiably attribute preponderant influence in determining an issue or even whose consequences would have been profoundly different if he had not acted as he did," Hook describes the difference in "eventful" persons and "event-making" persons.[2]

> The *eventful* man in history is any man whose actions influenced subsequent developments along a quite different course than would have been followed if these actions had not been taken. The *event-making* man is an eventful man whose actions are the consequences of outstanding capacities of intelligence, will, and character rather than of accidents of position. This distinction tries to do justice to the general belief that a hero is great not merely in virtue of what he does but in virtue of what he is.[3]

By Hook's measure, King certainly qualifies as a genuine hero, as someone whose combination of talents, intelligence, and vision considerably altered the course of events. This does not mean that King was the only person in the civil rights movement who possessed high degrees of intelligence, discipline, and skill. Numerous participants in the civil rights movement exhibited extraordinary leadership ability and qualities, ranging from the ingenious strategic skills of Bayard Rustin, the penetrating philosophic skills of Bob Moses, the uncanny organizational skills and folk wisdom of Fannie Lou Hamer, and the creative nonviolent theory of James Lawson.[4] While others possessed sharper skills than King in particular areas, King possessed a unique ability to inspire masses and maintain the loyalty of an impressive host of talented men and women. Perhaps this was best expressed by Benjamin Mays when he wrote:

> It may be that only one man in ten million could have led the Montgomery boycott without that city exploding into one of the worst race riots in history. . . . If the Montgomery Improvement Association had chosen a person other than King to communicate the Negroes' grievances to the city fathers, Dr. King might have gone through life as a successful Baptist preacher and no more. His rare ability to lead and inspire the classes as well as the masses, in a crusade for social justice, might never have been called forth.[5]

Furthermore, it may be argued that the force of King's personality, intelligence, and gifts helped create the conditions for social change in regard to race relations. King thus exhibited what Hook meant in a further clarification of the eventful versus the event-making person.

> The event-making man, on the other hand, finds a fork in the historical road, but he also helps, so to speak, to create it. He increases the odds of success for the alternative he chooses by virtue of the extraordinary qualities he brings to

bear to realize it. At the very least, he must . . . display exceptional qualities of leadership. It is the hero as event-making man who leaves the positive imprint of his personality upon history—an imprint that is still observable after he has disappeared from the scene.[6]

As Lerone Bennett observed, King's ability to create the conditions that led to social transformation was clearly demonstrated in Birmingham, Alabama, where it is widely believed that the civil rights movement gained its greatest symbolic victory because of a highly publicized clash with Sheriff Bull Connors's violent tactics to repel the civil rights demonstrators.

> No leader, of course, can create an event the time is not prepared for. But the genius of the great leader lies precisely in his apprehension of what the times require and in carrying through in the teeth of great opposition an act that changes the times. In Birmingham, King approached that kind of greatness, creating the occasion of the "Negro Revolution" by an act almost everyone said was ill-timed and ill-chosen. Birmingham . . . was cbosen, not stumbled upon. It was created by a man who knew exactly what he wanted and how much he would probably have to pay to get it.[7]

King was certainly a figure who often precipitated change through conscious, decisive action.

The hero, particularly the one who advances an agenda of trenchant social criticism and sweeping ethical reform, also possesses the ability to create a situation in which it is untenable to remain unchanged or unchallenged by the hero's vision of how things should be. The hero, in short compass, forces us to make moral choices. As James Hanigan says:

> One thing that makes the hero's course a precarious one is that the very nature of the hero's role in history requires the more ordinary among us to make choices. It is not simply a matter for us of liking or disliking, of admiring or ignoring the hero. Rather, we are forced to choose for or against the hero, for or against the vision, or dream, or message, or course of action the hero proposes to us. One hallmark of the hero's authenticity as a hero is precisely that he or she forces us to choose; we cannot remain indifferent to this presence among us, even if we would. For not to be with the hero is automatically to be against him or her.[8]

This aspect of heroism was quite evident in King's life. He constantly envisioned America as a work in progress, a nation constructed by the redemptive or destructive choices it would make about its moral and social future. In this regard, King was quintessentially American, placing the notion of experiment and pragmatic moral revisionism at the heart of his creed of American social life.

The primary impact of King's life and career may consist in the clarity he brought to the choices that Americans must make in "living out" the principal ideals of the American creed, particularly as embodied in the Constitution and the Declaration of Independence. King's genius and heroic stature derived from his adroit skill at pointing out the disintegration of the American Dream and dramatically portraying the distance between American ideals of justice and equality and its contradictory antidemocratic practices. But it was his willingness to die for American ideals that made King so dangerous, because he forced America to examine itself with the instruments of equality, justice, and social morality America claimed as its own. Because of this quality in King's leadership, we may concede that "the possibility for heroism in our time will be tempered by the ideals we propose to ourselves—a thing proved in the heroic age of civil rights, when Dr. King and many others suffered and died for the concept of equality we profess but have not lived up to."[9]

Moreover, King's martyrdom also linked him to other American heroic figures, like Abraham Lincoln and John and Robert Kennedy, whose deaths made them the subjects of national memory through eulogies and memorials, and gained them even greater status as the vehicles of American moral and social redemption. As Conrad Cherry perceptively notes in writing about Robert Kennedy's funeral, and by extension other funerals of national significance:

> In this funeral Americans joined in a sacred ceremony, the scope of which crossed denominational religious boundaries. Many citizens had participated in another such ceremony only a few weeks earlier at the funeral for Dr. Martin Luther King Jr., and in still another only a few short years earlier at the funeral for President John F. Kennedy. American history is, in fact, replete with leaders who have been canonized in the national consciousness as exemplars of American ideals and as particular bearers of Americans' destiny under God. When those leaders have met their deaths they have become, in the national memory as well as in the ceremonies and speeches that surround their deaths, martyrs for the American cause, even in some cases redeemers.[10]

Equally important, heroism often enables ordinary people to make a critical difference in their social and personal existence by linking their lives to larger social goals and movements that embody the virtues to which they aspire. The ideals of equality, justice, and freedom had for so long been uttered in public discourse and written in the creeds of American society and had in varying degrees been realized for particular segments of American culture. But freedom, equality, and justice often remained unrealized for many others, and King both envisioned how these ideals could be enfleshed and boldly envisioned how enormous obstacles to their realization could be overcome. In this scenario, the individual hero functions as an enabler for a group of people to rise above their limiting circumstances and participate in a drama of redemption, reconstruction, or transformation in which their roles, however small, are perceived as necessary and vital. Thus I will speak of this further when I discuss King's means of nonviolent transformation.

But the hero also looks to the group for insight and inspiration. Indeed, the group often serves a heroic function itself, engaging in what Max Weber called social heroism:

> Max Weber claimed that the Reformation and the attendant rise of capitalism were the last examples of middle class heroism. He is not alluding by this to the highly individualized gallantry of a John Wayne. Heroism for Weber is a social act. It occurs when a group of people no longer simply stand up for the system, but stand out against it. They critique the present and act to reclaim control over the future. The bourgeoisie of the Reformation era changed the circumstances of their existence and freed themselves from the dominance of aristocratic, social, political, and economic structures.[11]

In this scenario, the hero often functions to recall great past deeds as the basis for present and future action by masses of people. King understood this, and acted on it.

But the prospect of King's heroism becomes more problematic as we reflect on why he is presently being officially canonized, while near the end of his life he was roundly dismissed as a hopeless romantic and an irrelevant idealist. What was the real nature of King's achievements? In this section, I want to explore the nature of King's genius, and then proceed to address two tensions that further reinforce the ambiguity of King's heroism. Although King possessed many gifts, I think his genius lay in his moral vision and the choice of nonviolent means in attempting to achieve equality and real democracy for black Americans.

The idea that Martin Luther King was a man of moral vision raises questions about the nature of moral arguments, the particular content of moral statements, and the proper adjudication of competing moral claims. In our day, simply put, morality has fallen on hard times. This difficulty, though, does not absolve us of the responsibility to engage our every energy and resource in clarifying what we mean by morality and advancing a moral vision. King was willing, and able, to perform such a task. In fact, the historical conditions under which he and his comrades labored elicited from King and the civil rights movement a moral vision to guide and regulate its tasks and purposes.

Although King's moral vision may be variously conceived, I think, for my present purposes, it may be helpfully viewed in the following two ways. First, King's moral vision was not the work of one man; it expressed the hopes and aspirations of a long tradition of confrontation with and critical reflection upon the existential and social circumstances of black people in America. King did not invent or discover, but rather inherited, the imperative to rectify the evils of racism and impoverishment embedded in the legal, social, political, economic, and religious structures of American society.

King was the son, grandson, and great-grandson of Baptist preachers, so the very texture of his life from birth was religious and spiritual. He was reared under the powerful preaching of his father, the Rev. Martin Luther King Sr., pastor of the Ebenezer Baptist Church of Atlanta, Georgia. Martin Luther King, Jr., attended Morehouse College and came under the influence of, among others, the late Dr. Benjamin Elijah Mays, president of Morehouse, and Dr. George Kelsey, who is now professor emeritus at Drew University. These men, both scholar-preachers, provided for King the paradigm of ministry as an intellectually respectable, socially engaged, and emotionally satisfying vocation. At nineteen Martin was ordained to the ministry and became associate pastor of Ebenezer, and later its co-pastor, after serving six years as the pastor of Dexter Avenue Baptist Church in Montgomery, Alabama.

Given this background, King was firmly rooted in the institution that lies at the heart of Afro-American life, the black church. Throughout their history religion has been and remains the central ordering influence upon the vast majority of Americans of African descent. Albert Raboteau, in his groundbreaking work on the religion of Afro-American slaves, titled *Slave Religion*, writes,

> Black religious institutions have been the foundation of Afro-American culture. An agency of social control, a source of economic cooperation, an arena for political activity, a sponsor of education, and a refuge in a hostile white world, the black church has been historically the social center of Afro-American life.[12]

From its inception the black church identified racism (whether embedded in vicious slavery or embodied in white Christianity's segregationist ethos) as a heinous sin, and resolved to make its extirpation a primary goal of the black church's existence. The black church's message that all people are children of God and that everyone deserves to be treated with decency and respect found ample application in King's moral vision. The notion in the black church that God sides with the oppressed, as God sided with Israel against Egyptian bondage, inspired King's actions and was a central part of his moral vision, as reflected in his belief that Afro-Americans had "cosmic companionship" in the struggle for liberation.

The Afro-American religious notion of loving and praying for one's enemies, despite their decadence, hate, or brutality, had a strong affinity with the Gandhian philosophy of nonviolence as a teaching technique and lifestyle that King ardently preached and assiduously practiced. The black church understanding that all people, regardless of social standing, educational attainment, political sophistication, or cultural refinement, are equal heirs to God's promises found expression in King's concept of the beloved community where black and white, rich and poor, and powerful and powerless would be united in peace and harmony.

In these and many more significant ways King was organically linked to the living tradition of Afro-American religion. One aspect of King's genius was his ability to project this profoundly Afro-American religious sensibility into the American sociopolitical ethos and employ it as a base from which to argue for and, to a degree, effect social, political, and economic transformation.

This ability reflects the second characteristic of King's moral vision: it countered the narrow exclusivism of a vulgar patriotism and put forward a creative reinterpretation of America's central political concepts and documents. King's moral hermeneutic understood these concepts generally in relation to American moral improvement and specifically in relation to Afro-American freedom and liberation. In short, King appealed to the very documents that are central to American civil life—the Constitution, the Declaration of Independence—and pointed out their basis for a moral understanding and interpretation of concepts like equality, justice, and freedom. Furthermore, he employed these documents as a yardstick to judge the actual attainment by American society of the goals, norms, and ideals they articulated.

Not only does King's moral vision have a religious moment, but it extends itself into the national and civic realm, constituting its political moment. King's moral vision was predicated upon, in part, what he understood to be the best in American religious, civil, legal, social, and political history. He deemed his moral vision to be commensurate with American historic and national goals set forth in the Constitution and the Declaration of Independence, which help regulate American ideas about issues like freedom, justice, and equality.

In fact, in his famous "I Have a Dream" speech, King clearly stated that his dream was "deeply rooted in the American dream."[13] When King confronted the massive and abusive legal, social, and political structures that thwarted the materialization of Afro-American freedom, justice, and equality in any concrete sense, he appealed to these documents in calling for the realization of the norms and ideals they espoused. King said in Washington, "I have a dream that one day this nation will rise up and live out the true meaning of its creed, 'We hold these truths to be self-evident that all men are created equal.'"[14]

King believed, despite the fact that black people were slaves when this creed was written, that any fair-minded interpreter would be bound to enlarge its vision of liberty and equality to include all people. The principles articulated in the Constitution and the Declaration of Independence struck an authentic chord of truth for King that could not be nullified even by the shortsightedness of their original authors in regard to people of color. These documents provided a substantial foundation for American society to accord all people the status of persons with rights. King stated: "When the architects of our Republic wrote the magnificent words of the Constitution and the Declaration of Independence, they were signing a promissory note to which every American was to fall heir. This note was the promise that all men, yes black men as well as white men, would be guaranteed the unalienable rights of life, liberty and the pursuit of happiness."[15]

King refused to permit the interpretation of democracy, liberty, justice, and freedom to be monopolized by those who would truncate and distort the understanding of American history and ideals. King refused to allow either the overt barbarity of bigoted segregationists like the Ku Klux Klan and the White Citizens' Council or the covert but no less pernicious racism of prejudiced politicians to define democracy. On the rhetorical battleground of American public ideology, King wrested from them the prerogative of describing and defining what is authentically American, and in the process transformed the terms of American political and civil discourse. Martin Luther King's moral vision, then, which was rooted in Afro-American religion and which advanced a creative American moral hermeneutic, was a powerful and often persuasive means for structuring a protest movement to secure basic rights for black Americans.

Another way of accounting for King's heroic character and genius is his insistence on militant nonviolence as the means of obtaining freedom, justice, and equality for black people. King's advocacy of militant nonviolence was important for two interrelated reasons. First, it appealed to the African-American religious heritage of black culture, while linking that heritage to other powerful models of resistance and social transformation. Second, it presumed the heroic character of everyday black folk to resist evil and located transformative agency within their grasp.

King's advocacy of nonviolence was deeply anchored in an African-American religious ethic of love that promoted the fundamental dignity of all creatures because of their relationship to a loving, all-powerful God. As I have already indicated, norms and values developed in the black church influenced King's theological ideals, but they also shaped his strategies of social reform and his beliefs about human potential for progress and change. What is crucial for the African-American religious ethic of love in relation to nonviolent means to attain social, economic, and political freedom is that in King's worldview, nonviolence was a *way of life* and not simply a strategy of social transformation.

This distinction is key to understanding how King maintained a consistent moral stance toward various forms of violence, including war and domestic policies that reinforced poverty and classism. King saw nonviolent resistance to oppressive social structures, policies, and persons as a means of acquiring basic necessities such as food, clothing, and shelter, as well as being the only viable and ethically legitimate way to obtain freedom, justice, and equality. Although the destruction of racism was a major goal of African-American nonviolent resistance, it was only one goal of the nonviolent lifestyle. As King matured politically, he began to expand his field of moral vision to include classism, poverty, and militarism as legitimate objects of social protest. He believed that conceiving of nonviolence as both a lifestyle and a means of resisting a variety of social and moral problems was consonant with the affirmation of life, liberty, and equality in the black religious experience.

But King's advocacy of nonviolence was also the result of disciplined study of its applications in a variety of national, social, and moral contexts. He examined the principled resistance to taxpaying advocated by Henry David Thoreau, as well as his seminal essay on civil disobedience. It is widely known that King also diligently studied the principles, methods, and lifestyle of Mohandas Gandhi, whose "experiments with truth" had a powerful impact on King's thinking.

Gandhi's leadership of millions of Indians to resist the systemic social oppression of British colonialism inspired King to adapt Gandhi's methods of nonviolent resistance to American society.

Second, King's advocacy of nonviolence presumed the heroic character of everyday black people. Although this presumption contained romantic notions of black self-identity, it also located forms of transformative agency within the grasp of often powerless ordinary black folk. It is important to remember that at the beginning of the civil rights movement the lot of everyday black people remained even more circumscribed by the forces of segregation, race hatred, and class inequality from which the black middle class had only occasionally, and precariously, escaped. The civil rights movement provided an enormous boost to the self-identity of black people who had long believed that they were relatively powerless to change their condition.

However, Cornel West points out that King's presumption that black people could wield nonviolence as a means to social liberation contained a romantic notion of superiority over other racial groups, particularly white Americans. West also contends that King's doctrine of nonviolence

> tends to assume tacitly that Afro-Americans have acquired, as a result of their historical experience, a peculiar capacity to love their enemies, to endure patiently suffering, pain, and hardship and thereby "teach the white man how to love" or "cure the white man of his sickness." King seemed to believe that Afro-Americans possess a unique proclivity for nonviolence, more so than do other racial groups, that they have a certain bent toward humility, meekness, and forbearance, hence are quite naturally disposed toward nonviolent action. In King's broad overview, God is utilizing Afro-Americans—this community of caritas (other-directed love)—to bring about "the blessed community." . . . The self-image fostered . . . is defensive in character and romantic in content.[16]

While I think West's assessment is just, there is another dimension to King's assumption that must not be overlooked: his belief in the moral heroism of black people also assumed that the power to affect their destiny and to exercise transformative moral agency was achievable by ordinary black folk. Like that of Marcus Garvey before him and Malcolm X during his own day, the genius of King resided in the ability to appeal to his followers' heroic potentials by placing strict demands on their shoulders, challenging them to live up to a standard of moral excellence that neither they nor their opponents realized they possessed. King believed that black people could muster the resources they already had at their disposal, such as moral authority and a limited but significant economic base, to foster legitimate claims to social goods like education, housing, and enfranchisement.

Moreover, the standards of moral excellence that King expected through disciplined participation in nonviolent demonstrations, which included rites of self-examination and purification, were of inestimable worth not only in fighting for denied social privileges and rights, but in the healthy enlargement of crucial narratives of racial self-esteem. King understood the virtues of "everyday forms of resistance," and appealed to the "weapons of the weak" in opposing unjust social forces.[27]

While the above discussion specifies how it makes sense to call King a hero, now I want to explore two tensions that flow from the assertion of King's ambiguous heroism, which may be summed up in the following way: while King's contributions were heroic and significant, many African-Americans, particularly the working poor and the underclass, still suffer in important ways; and while King deserves great honor and praise of a particular sort, he is indebted to traditions of African-American religious protest, social criticism, and progressive democracy.

It must be conceded that despite the significant basic changes that King helped bring about, the present status of poor black Americans in particular presents little cause for celebration. Their situation does not mean that King's achievements were not substantial. Rather it reflects the deep structures of persistent racism and classism that have not yet yielded to sustained levels of protest and resistance.

In order to judge King's career, we must imagine what American society would be for blacks without his historic achievements. Without basic rights to vote, desegregated public transportation and accommodations, equal housing legislation, and the like, American society would more radically reflect what Gunnar Myrdal termed the "American Dilemma." King and other participants in the civil rights movement wrought heroic change, but that change was a partial movement toward real liberation.

If it was once believed that King's vision was only a beginning, a mere foot in the door of civil rights, political empowerment, and economic equality, the tragic reality now is that the door has been shut fast in the face of many Afro-Americans. This is displayed particularly in two areas: the persistence of racism and the disintegration of postindustrial urban life.

It is fair to say that a climate of hostility has been generated toward those who assert that this country has not achieved the ideals of freedom, justice, and equality in any significant structural manner, as envisioned by the mature Martin Luther King Jr. The early Martin Luther King was preoccupied with securing inclusion in American society as it is, without questioning the means by which wealth is distributed; without probing the mechanisms that determine privilege, prestige, and status; and without challenging the growing classism that shattered the notion of a monolithic black community.

The mature Martin Luther King Jr., however, understood that economic injustice was just as great an impediment to black liberation as racial injustice. As I will show later, King's mature career was spent in attempting to draw out the implications of a coalition politics that transcended race to speak of economic injustice and class oppression. His Poor People's March was the first real attempt to enact a coalition politics that bound together the interests of various marginalized groups, including Latinos, poor blacks and whites, and peace activists.

Part of King's great frustration resulted from the fact that racism was much more complex and multifaceted than he realized at the beginning of his career, and he sought to educate himself and his colleagues about the structural, socially embedded nature of institutional racism and the structural nature of class oppression. This accounts in part for how we can claim that King's contributions were heroic while acknowledging that they were neither perfect nor permanent. Some of the gains King helped secure were structurally permanent, such as legally desegregated public housing and transportation. Other gains must be continually ratified by law, such as the civil rights bill, which must be renegotiated through legislation. Moreover, the logic of racial progress is subject to perennial reexamination and justification.

The project to make King a particular sort of hero has often presented a picture of completion and satisfaction with regard to the structural obstacles to African-American racial progress. However, a suggestive and subversive side of King's heroism views him as an iconic figure who inspires continued battle to implement the goals and dreams for which he gave his life. It is consistent to suggest that although the general perception of blacks has changed, the actual legal barriers to social mobility have been removed, and particular categories of blacks have made substantial gains economically, King's life equally symbolizes the continued battle for the truly disadvantaged, the ghetto poor. It is heroic in a distinctly Kingian sense to resist official efforts at King canonization that both whitewash actual racial history and deny the work that remains, and to support the belief that much more progress must be made before real liberation can be achieved.

To suggest this, however, is to counter the self-image of the reigning political view of things that is the framework of contemporary conservative and liberal American sociopolitical ideology. Conservative political thought as construed here maintains that the struggle for black self-determination is largely over and that sufficient energy has been devoted to the eradication of racism in American life. Liberal political thought, even when it acknowledges the continuing expression of certain forms of racial and economic inequality, rarely effectively examines the reasons for their malignant persistence.

The predominant political ideology shrinks space for radical dissent and marginalizes, absorbs, or excludes voices asserting that the American condition is in terrible disarray. In short, the ideological horizon and sociopolitical landscape have been dominated by conservative and liberal visions that constitute political realism, effectively preventing radical alternatives to their often mundane and pedestrian achievements.

Conservative ideology and politics have the effect of both offering limited and narrowly conceived options to Afro-American suffering and ensuring the continued hegemony of white, upper-middle-class politics. Liberal alternatives, while certainly an improvement, are nevertheless plagued by an inability to move beyond a provincial vision of what economic and political measures are necessary to better Afro-American life. Liberalism attends to symptoms rather than to root causes.

The tragic reality of the Afro-American condition is that, while in many respects blacks are certainly better off, in other respects many blacks continue to suffer. For instance, the disintegration of the moral, economic, and civic fabric of poor black communities is stunning and entails lethal social consequences. The arising of a subculture of crime, which thrives on the political economy of crack, is threatening to destroy the inner city. Also the gentrification of black urban living space means that inner-city residents are being squeezed out of marginal neighborhoods by an escalating tax rate that forces the working poor into even poorer neighborhoods.

Poverty, for example, affects black people in an especially pernicious manner. Since the 1970s, there has been an enormous increase in poverty in America. In 1970, 14.9 percent of all children were poor. Today the figure is almost 21 percent. For minorities, it is even worse. Two out of every five Hispanic children are poor, and almost one out of every two black children is poor. For black children under six, the poverty rate is a record high 51.1 percent. There is a continually widening gap between the wealthy and the poor in America, and this year it is the highest ever since the Census Bureau began collecting statistics in 1947. Last year, two-fifths of the population received 67 percent of all national income, the highest ever recorded. The poorest two-fifths, on the other hand, received only 15.7 percent of all income, the lowest ever recorded. Even worse, one-third of all black America remains below the poverty line.[18]

Another factor that has contributed to the current condition of black America for the better part of the eighties is the legacy of the Reagan era. The Reagan administration symbolized, and ominously expressed, a new breed of racism, generating policies pervaded by subtle forms of discrimination and prejudice that have had a devastating impact on black America. The Reagan administration's laissez-faire attitude toward the enforcement of laws and governmental policies that protect minorities and its outright attack on the hard-won rights of America's poor and dispossessed helped set the tone for an almost unmitigated viciousness toward these groups.[19] The Reagan years have fueled a subversive shift in the modus operandi of American racism. Often no longer able to openly express racial hatred through barbaric deeds, racists have found subtle and insidious forms of expression.

This racism not only is evident in upper-middle-class America, with its staunchly conservative values and sensibilities that problematize Afro-American progress, and in the white working and underclass, with its tightly turfed communities that cling to racial and ethnic identification as a means of exclusion and survival (e.g., Howard Beach and Bensonhurst);[20] but it also has, in a cruelly ironic twist, engendered a new reactionary group of black neoconservative political and intellectual figures. This group rejects civil rights as a means to black progress and naively contends that such measures as affirmative action cripple rather than aid black freedom by creating negative stereotypes about inferior black performance in education and employment. All of this suggests the deep dimensions of our current crisis.

The second tension in regard to King's heroism rests on the fact that, although his achievements merit praise and honor, those accomplishments are related to a larger tradition of African-American protest, as well as traditions of liberal democracy. For instance, the King Holiday reminds us that by celebrating King's life, and career in particular, America celebrates the profound accomplishments of black America in general. This recognition offers to American intellectual life the vital resources of a living Afro-American intellectual tradition that can continue to inform, challenge, and even transform American discourse about race, class, justice, freedom, and equality. More specifically, since, as I have stated above, King's life was developed and shaped in the ethos of a black church worldview and since the locus classicus of his moral vision was the Afro-American religious experience, our attention is redirected back to that experience as a crucial resource for the maintenance and extension of King's moral vision, in alliance with other progressive sociopolitical, historical, and economic thought.

Indeed, the notion that King himself was the producer, not the product, and the cause, not the effect, of Afro-American liberation potentials that had been long latent, and at times vitally visible, in the fabric of our national experience is entirely alien to King's thought. Although he believed historical forces, under the direction of a demanding but loving providence, had arranged his ascension to a leadership position, he always believed that he articulated what many black people thought, knew, and held to be true. King obviously understood that he was the voice for a protest movement that had been growing for a long while and that had finally gathered the strength to resist the cumulative evils visited upon black people by the apartheid-like conditions in the American South. In fact, in speaking about the experience that initially catapulted him into international fame, King wrote:

> When I went to Montgomery, Alabama, as a pastor in 1954, I had not the slightest idea that I would later become involved in a crisis in which nonviolent resistance would be applicable. After I had lived in the community about a year, the bus boycott began. The Negro people of Montgomery, exhausted by the humiliating experiences that they had constantly faced on the buses, expressed in a massive act of noncooperation their determination to be free. They came to see that it was ultimately more honorable to walk the streets in dignity than ride the buses in humiliation. At the beginning of the protest the people called on me to serve as their spokesman.[21]

The recognition that King was part of a larger tradition disallows America to escape its obligation to those King represented by relegating his thought to the fixed and static past. Instead, it forces America to critically engage and constantly examine the dynamic contemporary expressions of the thought and practices emerging from the tradition that birthed and buttressed King.

Furthermore, the need for a reinvigorated moral vision can only be immediately strengthened by portraying the explicit relationship among King, the civil rights movement, and the most recent and powerful popular expression of the Afro-American intellectual and religious tradition: the Jackson campaigns for president. No honest and complete assessment of the movements and forces made possible by King's and his comrades' achievements can be performed without mention of the Jackson candidacy. The Jackson campaigns, which have already in a fundamental way transformed the shape and contours of modern American politics, were made possible by a host of historical ingredients, not the least of which was the tradition of sociopolitical insurgency stimulated by the Afro-American religious tradition and the civil rights movement.

The Jackson campaigns in part enact a profound transformation in the ideas we inherit from the mature Martin Luther King. They underscore the need for a transition from an initial emphasis on civil rights to an appreciation of issues of class and economic inequality.[22] Thus the relationship between King and Jackson, as participants in the same tradition and in active pursuit of the goals of economic empowerment, racial harmony, and universal justice, regulated by a vision developed in an Afro-American religious perspective, must not be lost as we celebrate King's birthday.

Indeed, as we celebrate his birthday we must exercise extreme caution in retrieving images of King, especially those that avoid the painful truth of recent revelations about King's character. The latter includes charges that King plagiarized portions of his dissertation, that he was a womanizer, and that he possibly physically abused a woman the night before his death. In the face of these revelations, how can we proceed celebrating King's life?

First, it is important to remember that the celebration of King's achievements is not predicated upon a notion of human perfection. Before these revelations, it was well known that King was a great but flawed human being. He admitted on several occasions his own guilt over sexual indiscretions and pledged to remedy his infidelity with all the strength to resist temptation that lay in him. King's obvious recognition of his finitude and limitation serve as a worthy model of emulation for us as we seek to celebrate his moral legacy of protest for civil and social rights. But his legacy of self-examination, admission of fault, and the attempt to concretely rectify the wrong, even if it is not always successfully done, is a model we can usefully incorporate as responsible and mature moral agents.

Second, the charges of King's alleged plagiarism are disturbing and inexcusable. To use someone else's written work without proper recitation is a form of verbal thievery. This painful truth, however, forces us to raise even more questions about why it occurred. Since we cannot question King, we can only surmise, infer, and speculate. King's dissertation was completed while he was pastoring his first church in Montgomery and during the beginning of the Montgomery bus boycott. Undoubtedly, the pressures of the burgeoning movement tempted King to plagiarize Jack Boozer's dissertation in order to complete his own doctoral studies.

Moreover, although many black scholars had passed through Boston University's doctoral program in religion, one peculiar and tragic legacy of racism involved the pernicious self-doubts that could have plagued any developing black scholar. Qualities of self-worth, competence, talent, and skill are not developed in a vacuum, but are in part socially constructed and reproduced. In the mid-fifties it is certainly conceivable that a young talented black doctoral student who was uncertain of his real worth, despite the encouragement of professors and colleagues, and who was faced with an unpredictable and unfolding social crisis, could be tempted to rely on work that had already been accepted and viewed as competent.

The best approach to these charges, as well as charges about King's possible physical abuse, can be made by developing a healthy and realistic framework of assessment of King's life and career that will remain consistent even in the event of other revelations about his person and character. The power of King's achievements, the real force of his genius, consisted in his passion for justice to be done for the most lowly and oppressed inhabitants of American society. His moral authority as a spokesperson for truth, equality, and the embodiment of a particular slant on the American Dream cannot be compromised by revelations about his personal and student life.

What these revelations do achieve, however, is a sad reminder of the forces of wrong and dishonor by which we are all subject to be tempted and corrupted. King serves as a reminder that no figure establishes an Archimedean point of moral perfection from which to argue for social change, that all argument for transformation is immanent criticism rooted in the faults and limitations of being human, but those limitations do not ultimately destroy the truth for which limited and faulty humans stand. Although the vehicle for that truth is tarnished, enough of the truth's power and persuasion can emerge to convince others of its necessity and worth. We must view King in such a realistic fashion. These revelations show that King was an enormously complex human being, confirming what we know of him as we study his ideological evolutions and his political maturation.

As has been much remarked on, toward the end of his life King began to discern inadequacies in his former analyses of racial antipathy, social injustice, and economic inequality. He discovered that these problems were much more deeply rooted and structurally expressed than he had initially surmised.

As a result he focused his considerable critical skills on the larger national and international economic, political, and social contexts of Afro-Americans', and other oppressed people's, plight. King began to speak about the redistribution of resources, guaranteed incomes for the poor, and forming a multiracial coalition of the unemployed and the poor. This signified his changing perspective. In an article written just before his assassination and published after it, King wrote:

> We call our demonstration a campaign for jobs and income because we feel that the economic question is the most crucial that black people, and poor people generally, are confronting . . . . We need an economic bill of rights. This would guarantee a job to all people who want to work and are able to work. It would also guarantee an income for all who are not able to work . . . . I hope that

a specific number of jobs is set forth, that a program will emerge to abolish unemployment, and that there will be another program to supplement the income of those whose earnings are below the poverty level.[23]

King had already begun to speak out against the war in Vietnam, decrying the lamentable manner in which resources for the poor were being pilfered by an ever increasing war chest. He was criticized within the civil rights movement for squandering its social influence and political capital with the Johnson administration. He was attacked outside the movement for delving, even "meddling," into larger domestic and foreign affairs that were not the legitimate concern of a civil rights leader.

King's moral vision, however, could not abide the spurious schizophrenia that compartmentalized moral concern into distinct and separable spheres. Morality was of a piece to King, and his moral vision was integrated and unified. The whole of life fell under its searching purview and rigorous scrutiny. King's later efforts to unite poor blacks, whites, and other minorities, as well as labor and other progressive concerns, marked him as a highly dangerous man who was greatly feared in many governmental, political, and social quarters.

These facts must be recalled as we engage in the rituals of remembrance and rites of recovery of the meaning of King's moral vision. We must refuse those who would commodify King's career into acceptable packages of comfortable, and not dangerous, memory, to be consumed by the American public in the name of a mythologization project intent on subverting King's radical and disturbing memory. In short, we must engage in hermeneutical combat and interpretive warfare over the future of King's memory, making certain that the custodians of the King canon include and remember his provocative words and oppositional ideas, as well as his comforting thoughts and hopeful beliefs. Martin Luther King, Jr., was a man who possessed a profound moral vision that was rooted in the Afro-American religious experience and that advanced a creative American moral hermeneutic. Remembering his life and thought challenges us to examine the present condition of American moral life and discover it wanting in regard to its treatment of those King represented: the black, the poor, and the oppressed.

Construed in the above manner, King's birthday serves as an outpost in progressive terrain, creating space in which to collect the energies of protest and struggle as they are related to the visionary revival and recovery of the moral tradition within which King lived and labored. King Day can facilitate a broadly conceived coalition of the oppressed and suffering who have a desperate interest in recovering the symbol and substance of King's moral vision.

Celebrating Martin Luther King's birthday as an official holiday promises a poignant and profound change in the rhythm of public rituals commemorating events of ultimate national and historical significance. King Day structures in the recurring cycle of American holidays a period of time that concentrates attention upon the meaning of King's life and thought. It also extends beyond King, transcending his personal and individual meaning, and celebrates the ingenuity of black survival in an American political, social, and cultural ethos often inimical to Afro-American existence.

King Day also points us back to that Afro-American religious tradition that produced King and that continues to thrive in the midst of American religious, social, and political life. It also provides a means of reconstituting King's moral vision by challenging us each year to more closely approximate in our national and individual life and thought the goals and purposes for which he gave his life. In this sense, the name Martin Luther King, Jr., no longer merely represents the time and place of his life and body on earth, but symbolizes the hope of oppressed people everywhere that the dignity and worth of human life will be universally respected and uplifted.

Twenty-Two

"GIVE ME A PAPER AND PEN":
TUPAC'S PLACE IN HIP-HOP

*The death of Tupac Shakur also hit me hard. I had been a fan of his political thug
gnosticism, even as I had been critical of his occasionally harsh treatment of women in his
songs and his will to self-destruction. I found his brutal honesty refreshing, and his
intellectual engagement with the most pressing social issues of the day through his lyrics a
cause for wonder and broad celebration. After all, Tupac was a high school dropout. But
he read widely and voraciously, and his work stands head and shoulders above that of
most of his peers. I was attracted to Tupac because he is the perfect embodiment of his
generation's virtues—the desire to tell the truth, the love for poor blacks, the quest for
authenticity—and its peculiar troubles, including a romance with social carnage, the
worship of tribal social deities in mystified geographies of "East Coast" and "West
Coast," and the bloody investment in a painfully narrow view of blackness. Above all,
Tupac is at once what we hope for and pray against in every black man. In this chapter,
I evaluate how Tupac became the most influential rapper of our time. He was an artist
consumed with telling his story, and by extension, the story of millions of black youth,
with as much fire and force as he could summon from the short twenty-five years that
were his. Considering that he has released and sold more albums dead than alive, his
genius will not soon be extinguished in the cultural landscape.*

WHEN I VISITED WITH EASTSIDAZ RAPPER Big Tray Dee, he surprised me
with his frank discussion of his fallen colleague's art. "I'm real critical and skeptical about lyrics or what people say and how they put it from an artistic standpoint," Dee says. "It would be maybe like thirty percent of Tupac's songs that I
wouldn't really feel all the time. I would be like, 'That's all right.'" Dee speaks of
Tupac's method of creation, highlighting in the process what made him such a big
force in hip-hop. "But [his songs] wound up in my head because they would grow
on me, and I would see where he was coming from. I had to get that feeling or be
in that mood to really relate to what he was saying at that particular time, on that
particular song. He showed me how he created music through his heart and
through his spirit, showing me that you have to have a certain vibe and continuity. You are not going to appeal to everybody."

Dee's comments underscore a crucial paradox: Tupac's art as a hip-hop emcee was an acquired taste among the genre's cognoscente, even as the masses embraced him through huge record sales and he gained international notoriety as a symbol of rap's fortunes and follies. Tupac was not hip-hop's most gifted emcee by any of the criteria that define the form's artistic apotheosis. He did not, for instance, possess the effortless rhythmic patterns of Snoop Dogg, the formidable timing and breath control of the incomparable KRS ONE, the poetic intensity of Rakim, the deft political rage of Chuck D, the forceful enunciation of M. C. Lyte, or the novelistic descriptions and sly cadences of Notorious B.I.G.–the "mathematician of flow," according to hip-hop luminary Mos Def. Still, Tupac may be the most influential and compelling rapper of them all. It is not that Tupac lacked supreme talent in writing lyrics, composing dramatic stories, and manipulating his voice to haunting effect. But he was more than the sum of his artistic parts. A considerable measure of Tupac's cultural heft was certainly extramusical, especially his well-publicized clashes with the law and his shamanistic thespian efforts. Above all, Tupac was a transcendent force of creative fury who relentlessly articulated a generation's defining moods–its confusion and pain, its nobility and courage, its loves and hates, its hopelessness and self-destruction. He was the zeitgeist in sagging jeans.

"I wasn't a big Pac fan when he was out," Mos Def lets on. "But I'll tell you why people loved him: because you *knew* him." Tupac was easy to know because he was the ghetto's everyman, embodying in his art the horrors and pleasures that came to millions of others who were in many ways just like him–except they lacked his protean genius and a microphone to amplify tragedy and triumph. Despite being pegged a "gangsta rapper," Tupac ranged freely over the lyrical landscape of hip-hop, pursuing themes that bled through a number of rap's subgenres, among them conscious rap, political hip-hop, party music, hedonism rap, thug rap, and ghettocentric rap. Tupac was equally adept at several modes of address within hip-hop, from the dis rap ("Hit 'Em Up") to the hip-hop eulogy ("Life Goes On"), from the maternal missive ("Dear Mama") to the pastoral letter ("Keep Ya Head Up"). There is something fiercely eloquent and haunting about Tupac's accomplished baritone: Its regal, distinct register vibrated directly to the heart and gave him an intimacy and immediacy of communication that are virtually unrivaled in hip-hop. If one were confined to a desert island with the choice of taking only one artist to capture rap's range of expression, Tupac could hardly be surpassed. Tupac's genius can be understood only by tracing the contours of contemporary rap and placing him within its rapidly expanding boundaries.

Hip-hop culture has come a long way since its fledgling start in the late 1970s. Early hip-hoppers were largely anonymous and could barely afford the sound systems on which the genre is built. By contrast, contemporary artists reap lucrative contracts, designer clothing lines, glossy magazine spreads, fashionable awards, global recognition, and often the resentment of their hip-hop elders. If there is a dominant perception about today's rap superstars among hip-hop's purists, it is that they have squandered the franchise by being obsessed with shaking derrieres, platinum jewelry, fine alcohol, premium weed, pimp culture, gangster rituals, and thug life. Although hip-hop has succeeded far beyond the Bronx of its birth, it has, in the minds of some of its most ardent guardians, lost its soul. To paraphrase an ingenious storyteller whose haunting tales elevated and examined the poor—Charles Dickens—these are for hip-hop the best of times and the worst of times. In his embattled soul, Tupac embodied both.[1]

Contemporary rap is filled with stirring reminders of why the marriage of the spoken word to music has revolutionized black culture. Figures like Lauryn Hill, Common, Mos Def, Talib Kweli, and Bahamadia generate black noise to spur the eruption of social conscience. Gifted wordsmiths like Jay-Z, Nas, DMX, and the assorted rappers of the Wu-Tang Clan use their pavement poetry to probe urban existence in gripping detail. But there is still strong criticism of rap's musical vampirism and its dulling repetitiousness. Those who claim the mastery of instruments through the production of original music is the only mark of genuine artistry offer the first criticism. Such purists ignore the severely depleted funding of arts in public schools since the late 1970s, a fateful development that kept many inner-city students from learning to play musical instruments. The critics also overlook the virtuosity implied in the technical manipulation of existing sounds to create new music. Although hip-hop was vulnerable to the claim that it lacked original music at its birth, Tupac was fortunate to have producers who gave melody to his rage. The sounds that bathed his beautiful baritone were often striking. "I loved the kind of tracks that were put together for him to rap over," says contemporary jazz musician George Duke. "They had a lot of the old-school vibe in there. I thought what he did was interesting in terms of the chords. It just felt like something I could play over." Moreover, the fact that so many rappers repeat tired formulas that have been successful for other artists cannot possibly distinguish rap from, say, contemporary rhythm and blues or rock music. And neither can the gutless, uninspiring imitation on which too many raps thrive be said to be unique to hip-hop. After all, contemporary American classical music and smooth jazz—a misnomer worth fighting over, according to jazz purists—do the same.

To be sure, there are more serious criticisms of hip-hop. It is easy to understand the elements of rap that provoke consternation: its violence, its sexual saturation, its recycling of vicious stereotypes, its color-coded preference for light or nonblack women, its failure to engage politics, its selling out to corporate capitalism, and its downright ugly hatred of women. Tupac has come to symbolize the blights on hip-hop's troubled soul. His self-destructive behavior and premature death inspired a great deal of hand-wringing over hip-hop's influence on black youth. Unfortunately, many critics divide the wheat from the chaff in hip-hop by separating rap into its positive and negative expressions. That distinction often ignores the complexity of hip-hop culture and downplays rap's artistic motivations. Instead, rap is read flatly, transmuted into a sociological phenomenon of limited cultural value. Rap is viewed as a barometer of what ails black youth. It is apparent that a great deal of bitterness and anger clutter the disputes between rap's advocates and its critics. It is equally obvious that black youth are under attack from many quarters of our culture. In hip-hop, as with most youth music, that is nothing new. "All art created by young people is despised by adults," says Toni Morrison. "Whether it's Mozart or Louis Armstrong, if it's young, it always has to fight . . . . And what shakes out of that, of course, becomes the best." From its origins, rap music was dismissed or denigrated, even by blacks. The point here is not to berate blacks for missing the boat on what has turned out to be one of the most popular, creative, and commercially viable art forms in many decades. I am simply suggesting that there was a love–hate relation between many black folk and hip-hop culture long before Tupac and long before rap's controversial headlines, its tragic deaths, and its worldwide influence.

Early seeds of suspicion have often bloomed into outright rejection of hip-hop as a vital source of art and imagination for black youth. That is why black wags of every stripe have stepped up to denounce the music as misguided, poisonous, and inauthentic, since music that gyrates into the spotlight has little truck with the revolutionary thrust of, say, Gil Scott-Heron or the Last Poets. In other words, hip-hop is not really black music. On such a view, hip-hop is but the seductive corporate packaging of the vicious stereotypes black folk have tried to defeat since our ancestors were uprooted and brought to America in chains. Except now, critics of hip-hop claim, the chains that bind us are more mental and psychological than physical. And the great-great-great-grandchildren of slaves who fought to be free and who hoped that their seed would escape rather than embrace enslavement create the images that destroy our standing in society. "Thanks to music videos, the image people all over the world now have of African Americans is of violence-prone misogynists, preoccupied with promiscuous sex and conspicuous consumption," says writer Khephra Burns. "Despite years of striving to distance ourselves from the negative ways in which white folk once portrayed us, we have come at last to the point of portraying ourselves to the world in this way." Stanley Crouch sees an even more sinister effect of the relentlessly negative and stereotypical portrayal of blacks. "You can talk to people who have traveled around the world, and they'll tell you the contempt that has developed for black people over the last twenty years is mightily imposing," he says. "You and I might have a completely different experience, but if we were in our early twenties, that's another vibration. People would say, 'Uh-oh, here they come,' and people would be suspicious and cross the street. That's going on all over the world."

Burns and Crouch make powerful arguments about the lethal consequences of flooding the airwaves and video screen with self-defeating visions of black life.

There is little doubt that the effect is exactly as they describe it, with the caveat, however, that the global portrayal of black life surely cannot rest on the images or words of barely postadolescent entertainers. This is not to deny that a single video by a rap artist can more successfully shred international boundaries than a hundred books by righteous authors. Neither is it to deny the huge responsibility such artists bear in confirming or combating hateful and ignorant beliefs about black folk that circulate around the globe. But that is just it: These beliefs are part of the ancient legacies of colonialism, racism, and regionalism, legacies that persist despite the efforts of intellectuals, artists, and leaders to destroy them. Is it fair to expect DMX to achieve what W E.B. Du Bois could not, or for Tupac to succeed where Archbishop Tutu failed? The complex relationship between art and social responsibility is evident, but we must be careful not to place unrealistic, or even unjust, demands on the backs of artists. Their extraordinary influence cannot be denied, but the very argument that is often used against them—that they are not politicians, leaders, or policymakers, just entertainers who string together lines of poetic meter—is often conveniently forgotten when it might work to hip-hoppers' advantage.

This recognition does not discount the troubling manifestations of youth culture that merit consideration. One such instance is Tupac's vigorous embrace of "thug life." In the interview taped in 1995 when he was in prison, Tupac explained that "it's not an image; it's just a way of life; it's a mentality." He claims that thug life is "a stage that we all go through. It's just like that for white kids and rich kids. They get to go to the military academy or ROTC, or they take all the risk, energy, and put it into the armed forces. And for a young black male, Puerto Rican, or Hispanic person, you've got to put this in the streets; that's where our energies go." Speaking of his thug life mentality, Tupac says, "The way I was living and my mentality was a part of my progression to be a man." In outtakes from an interview he did with Snoop Dogg for MTV, Tupac clarifies what he means by "thug life." "It's not thugging like I'm robbing people, 'cause that's not what I'm doing," Tupac said. "I mean like I'm not scared to say how I feel. Part of being [a thug] is to stand up for your responsibilities and say this is what I do even though I know people are going to hate me and say, 'It's so politically un-correct,' and 'How could you make black people look like that? Do you know how buffoonish you all look with money and girls and all of that?' That's what I want to do. I want to be real with myself." Tupac's thug life mentor, West Coast rapper Big Syke, eloquently and simply defined for me "thug" and "outlaw," another word Tupac embraced and transformed. "I call thugs the nobodies," Syke says, "because we really don't have nobody to help us but us. And then outlaw is being black and minority. Period."

In a conversation with cultural critic Vijay Prashad, I learned a great deal more about the complex roots of thug. "It's very clear that the word 'thuggee' is a north Indian word," Prashad tells me. "Probably from Murati, from western India, but it's not clear." A British man by the name of General Sleeman made it his mission to eradicate thugs in India. During the early years of the British Empire, there was an increase in the trade of bullion, and brigands roamed the countryside robbing merchants and stealing revenue transactions. Sleeman claimed these thugs were the disciples of the goddess Kali. The thugs used to attach themselves to merchant caravans, claiming to have some talent, like cooking or preparing drinks. They would often drug the merchants and then strangle them with a handkerchief called a *rumal*, leaving a mark on the necks of the victims. Prashad conjectures that there are three possible ways the word entered the United States. "The easiest way is that Sleeman's work was well-known in the U.S.," Prashad says. Sleeman authored a popular nonfiction account of India. But this was mainly to the white mainstream. Prashad thinks the word may have reached black audiences through excerpts in the *Colored American* and other newspapers that were tied in some way to the black church, as the black religious press was deeply interested in India. The third way is through the Caribbean, since there was a large transit of people from eastern India coming into the Caribbean after the 1840s. Given the strong link between black and eastern Indian religions—between Rastafarianism and Shavism, the worship of Shaiva—there were also cultural exchanges, with "thug" passing into the Caribbean lexicon.[2]

In light of the heavy Caribbean influence on the development of rap—its founding light, D. J. Kool Herc, emigrated from the Caribbean to the Bronx, where he transplanted West Indian outdoors parties to the backyards of his American neighborhood—the word "thug" has a specific resonance in black popular culture. "It sounds perfect, in musical terms," Prashad says. "It is better than gangster, which puts you too much in the lineage of the Mafia. This is an alternative kind of thug; it's 'our' kind of thug. It's a unique word; it is known and not known at the same time. It has a flavor to it." When I tell Prashad that Tupac had actually made an acronym of "thug life" ("the hate you gave little infants fucks everyone"), he is in full agreement with the rapper's forcefully subjective interpretation. "It is beautiful, because the word, even though it is an indigenous word to these fellows who were out there to begin with, means the 'hate you gave.' After all, it's the currency transactions that begin because of the empire's influence that will bring the brigands. There is truth there." Prashad ends our conversation by telling me of his experience with some African-Caribbean and African-American youth. They were sitting on his porch when one of them said, "I'm thugged out." It caught Prashad's attention. "I remember having a chat with them, saying, 'Do you know this word? It's familiar to me.'" The youth were making fun of Prashad's eastern Indian accent, and as a result Prashad and the students began "playing around with words and language." Prashad gave them a brief history of the word they were using, the word that bound at least three cultures together. "They found it fascinating, the story I told them, and we had this interchange, and I said, 'We are inside each other.'"[3]

Toni Morrison, too, has "respect for the genre, because of what it does with language." Morrison is not oblivious to the "bad influence" of "people who are driving [rap] to make it sensational," but she understands the crucial role to youth of an art form that transmits important information. "It is a conversation among and between black youth from one part of the country to another: 'What is it like in Detroit, as opposed to L.A., as opposed to New York?'" Morrison's view of hip-hop is admirably international, giving her an appreciation of the genre's inspiring, and subversive, global reach. "Just seeing what happened to it in Europe is astonishing," Morrison told me. "When I was in Frankfurt—the center of rap music in Germany—I got some unbelievable rap discs from a Turkish girl who was singing in German." Morrison argues that what unifies hip-hop throughout the world is its emergence from "the 'others' within the empire"—for instance, the Turks in Germany and the Algerians and North Africans in France—who ring profound changes in the nation's discourse. "First of all, they're changing the language, although nobody admits it," she says. "But that's where the energy comes from . . . . It is the necessity for young people to talk to one another in language that is not the fake language of the press. That sort of conversation curtails thought altogether. So it is a dialogue." But Morrison does not neglect the essential *musical* element that frames the use of language. "The fact that it also is the music you can't sit down to—you really do *get up*—is what has made it so fetching." Morrison is, of course, completely aware of the controversial subject matters broached in hip-hop. "It is always up for grabs about sexuality and violence," she says. Morrison argues that the establishment accepts such discourse only when "it's separate, like when Shakespeare does it, or Chaucer, or Boccaccio—those are the most outrageously provocative stories and language in the *Decameron*. They say they want safe language, but that's just the way the establishment is: It [rap discourse] wouldn't be outlawed or policed unless it had that quality." As a parting thought, Morrison raises an intriguing question—humorously, to be sure, as she chuckles all the way through it, but, as is evident, it seizes me by the pen. "Are there any other groups of gangsters or robbers or whatever you want to call them who made music? The whole notion of making an art form while you're doing it is . . ." Before she can finish, we're both cracking up at her brilliant thought, her deliriously righteous question, which she caps with a nod to the genius of the folk. "I mean only black people could figure that out. I don't know how far you can go with that! There are sagas about medieval thugs and Robin Hood, but [it's fascinating] to actually invent your own art form while you're in the life, so to speak."[4]

Tupac, Syke, Prashad, and Morrison bring to light the complex fashion—one full of signification and play—in which the thug, the outlaw, the pimp, and the like are evoked in hip-hop. It is true that Tupac tried to make the world believe he really was who he announced on his albums. But at some levels—it is important to stress *some* levels—even that was an act, in the best sense of that word, an ingenious artistic strategy to create a persona. Persona making, after all, is the province of art—and of politics, preaching, and every realm where performance is crucial to self-definition and the transmission of ideas. Too often, however, we deny the artistic milieu in which rappers operate and descend instead into a thudding literalism. The historian Robin Kelley makes this point when discussing Miles Davis and the necessity of a more complex vision of art and persona, even those involving controversial figures like the pimp. "Why is it that we still love Miles despite the fact that he's such an evil figure?" Kelley asks. "It's because the stuff that's so romantic, and evil, can be reconciled in the pimp. And so my thing is, turn the mirror around and look at yourself when you look at the music. And it's deeply romantic, because that's what the pimps are, the great ones." Kelley is not offering an apology for pimping. Instead, he is suggesting that cultural creations have multiple meanings, none of which can be exhausted or suspended by appeals to the responsible behavior of the artist. (Indeed, many of art's meanings exist beyond the intent or desire of its creators.) "I guess I'm tired of this question of what's redeeming or problematic," Kelley says. "We don't have to go to hip-hop to find it. We can actually invent something." Kelley contends that an artistic representation "does both of those things simultaneously" and that a more important question is "Why are we still drawn to it?" As Kelley says, "moralizing [and] saying there's nothing redemptive about this, so therefore we should just critique it, doesn't really tell us anything about how people are thinking."[5]

Taking the time to learn what our youth are thinking and why they create the art they do demands a capacity for deferred justification that most adults lack. They seek to ensure the legitimacy of their moral critique by rendering quick and easy judgments about the art form. Many critics of hip-hop do not have the ethical patience to empathize with the formidable array of choices, conflicts, and dilemmas that many poor black youth confront. Tupac is deeply attractive to millions of young people because he articulates the contradictory poses of maturing black identity with galvanizing exuberance and savage honesty. "Most of my music [tells the truth]," Tupac says in the interview he did in prison. "I'm just trying to speak about things that affect me and about things that affect our community. . . . Sometimes I'm the watcher, and sometimes I'm the participant, and sometimes it's just allegories or fables that have an underlying theme." Tupac's allegories and fables largely estranged his elders, underscoring how the generation gap has grown more menacing.

By almost any measure, the gaps between older and younger blacks are flagrant, even frightening. To be sure, there have always been skirmishes between the generations. Many older blacks have often found the dress, language, and hair of younger blacks offensive. In turn, many younger blacks have often soured on the conservative values and accommodating styles of social existence favored by a majority of their elders. These tiffs have certainly not disappeared.

Indeed, every era seems obligated to draw from local circumstance and color in painting a fresh picture of generational malaise. Where the Afro hairstyle raised dander in the '70s, the '90s outbreak of hair twists and braids provoked dread in corporate and conservative colored circles alike. And as if the boom in '70s clothing had not already offended by dredging up bell-bottom pants and platform shoes, the baggy fashions sported by youth—oversized shirts, unlaced shoes, beltless pants sagging to the upper gluteus for maximum exposure—have riled their seniors, especially since such styles are purportedly inspired by prison gear. Although the specific circumstances of black life in the new millennium—unprecedented growth of the black middle class, devastating expansion of the ghetto poor, restructuring of industries that employ large numbers of blacks, sustained drug and criminal activity, capital flight, increased technologization of the workforce—shape our understanding of these conflicts, they appear, in one form or another, in each generation.[6]

What *is* new and particularly troublesome is the sheer hostility that bruises relations between older and younger blacks. For perhaps the first time in our history, blacks over thirty have fear and disdain for black youth. Such a perception turns graver when we consider that *half* of black America, some 17 million citizens, is below the age of thirty. That means, too, that half of black America has come to maturity in an age of bewildering black "posts": post–civil rights, postmodern, postindustrial, and post–baby boom. A great deal of the age chasm in black communities can be explained by the chaos that blacks over forty confronted in seeking racial equity, personal status, and social justice. Blacks who cut their teeth on the sinewy fibers of violent racial oppression have little tolerance for cries of injustice from quarters of relative privilege: young black urban professionals who can't hail a cab or coddled college students who seethe at the racist slights encountered on elite campuses. Neither do older blacks, whether strong integrationists or radical nationalists, cotton easily to "the devil made me do it" theory of criminal behavior and social disintegration that plagues many black communities. The purpose of the civil rights and black liberation movements, after all, was to foster healthy black communities unfettered by white supremacy. Such struggles were not meant to justify thugs who hurt other blacks. Neither did those struggles intend to ignore the moral deficiency of persons who use racism to deflect attention from their own failings.[7]

For many blacks over the age of forty, Tupac represents the repudiation of ancient black values of hope and positive uplift that tied together black folk across geography and generation. His studied hopelessness—and he affirmed his depressive status by repeatedly declaring "I'm hopeless"—and his downward-looking social glance only aggravated the generational warfare that looms large in black America. As "a brother from another generation, I can't help but hear Tupac, if not totally objectively, at least from a broader perspective—the bird's-eye view of the forest as opposed to being in the trees, so to speak," says Khephra Burns.

"And what I hear generally are words that rip through our communities, our families, and our lives like automatic weapon fire." Burns says that Tupac is full of "discord, death, and revenge." Bishop T D. Jakes sees Tupac as an emblem of fin de siècle black social disintegration, a state of affairs markedly different from what previous generations bequeathed to their offspring. Jakes says that the twentieth century "ended with the sound of gunshots reverberating in the streets of the American black culture." Speaking of Tupac, Jakes laments how the "hearse wheels rolled away the remains of a young man who our children watched, admired, and perhaps emulated to some degree." Jakes argues that the "gunshots should have been a wake-up call to us that somehow our cultural pace and our agenda was now being set by young men whose rhythm is at best unsteady." Jakes contrasts such a scenario with an earlier epoch of black achievement and struggle. He says that our present predicament is "a far cry from the previous decades, when the role models that we were awed by were world shakers like Martin Luther King, Rosa Parks, Medgar Evers, and many others": Unfortunately, these "giants of black faith have in their latter years been replaced by young men whose talent has lifted them to a height whereby they gained the ear of America prematurely, having more talent than statement."

Although youth music has always outraged parents who refused to listen—because it was morally offensive or sexually suggestive, from jazz to rock—the depressing note of hatred and fear of black youth that is being sounded has dire consequences. Sadly, it suggests there is agreement between the regressive forces that target black folk in general—conservative critics who decry our moral laxity, our sexual looseness, our racial obsessions—and black folk who think that hip-hop channels our pathologies into broad daylight. Many older blacks fail to see that the same folk who thought it was just fine to keep black life segregated and economically inferior are now leading the charge to incarcerate their children. And often, with a black authority figure standing literally or symbolically in tow, they point to hip-hop's excesses to justify their actions. Tupac was an irresistible example of how self-destructive and utterly irredeemable our youth had become. Too often the explanations we seek for the disturbing behavior of youth like Tupac are insufficiently sophisticated. As proof we bog down in the understandable but lamentable question: Has hip-hop caused or reflected the violence we should detest?

Even that question buys into the either-or worldview that undermines a sane response to our predicament. Of course hip-hop has become intoxicated with danger, as Tupac's life and career amply testify. Its violent metaphors, profane lyrics, and real-life embodiment of thug fantasies are at some levels chilling. It does no good to reprimand black youth for their addiction to violence. Our nation suffers the addiction in spades, as even a cursory read of pop culture suggests. But it is not just pop culture that is implicated. American society was built on violence, from the wholesale destruction of Native American culture to the enslavement of Africans. "It's violence in America," Tupac says in his interview from prison. "What did the USA just do, flying to Bosnia? We ain't got no business over there." Comparing America's actions to the destructive effects of gang violence, Tupac argued, "America is the biggest gang in the world. Look at how they didn't agree with Cuba, so . . . [they] cut them off." That is surely no justification for hip-hop's artistic elevation of gang-banging or murder, as glimpsed in Tupac's lyrics. "As a rapper, Tupac represented many of the most despicable elements of America's youth on account of the Afro-American extension of what I call anarchic individuality," Stanley Crouch says, "which is: me first." For Crouch, Tupac's anarchic individualism showed most destructively in the glamorization of the gangster in lyrics promoting murder and mayhem, thereby lowering the threshold of resistance for impressionable youth. "You can't pile all of this on Tupac," Crouch says. "But I'm saying that his life and his death and his behavior and the behavior of the people in his circle represent something deeply disturbing."

Crouch's argument underscores the urgent need to address not only rhetorical but literal violence, the causes of which cannot be exclusively or primarily located within hip-hop culture. Although Crouch is tough on Tupac, he avoids blaming him directly for the scourge of violence in the culture or even in black communities. "None of this is to say that there shouldn't be some voicing of the terrible ways in which certain people in this society have to live due to poverty," Crouch says. "That's not something that's supposed to be ignored. That's absolutely irresponsible." Blaming black youth for social violence reeks of the worst kind of scapegoating. Since hip-hop culture is barely a generation old, and black violence is much older, the charge that hip-hop jump-started violence lacks merit. But even if hip-hop didn't invent violence, it can be held accountable for promoting violence. Indulging violence as a reaction to more lethal but less visible forms of violence (for instance, racism and economic inequality) is not excusable, but it is surely a reason to tackle the issues to which black youth are responding.

Neither should we overlook the double standard that prevails in addressing societal violence or its pop culture parallel. It is by now a cliche to state that Bruce Willis, Arnold Schwarzenegger, Tom Cruise, and a host of other big white stars don't come in for nearly the rhetorical drubbing that hip-hop stars regularly endure. "Like with Quentin Tarrantino, when he puts out his pictures, they're all gangster pictures and they're all good and they're all critically acclaimed . . . and they're very creative," Tupac said in the outtakes from his 1996 MTV interview. "But when we do that same thing without the visuals, all wax, just as compelling . . . we get treated like the bad messengers and he gets treated like King Solomon." Tupac also spoke of the video he was directing for the rap song he did with Snoop Dogg, "2 of America's Most Wanted." Tupac said the video's concept drew from the criticism he and Snoop received for portraying gangsters and dirtying the airwaves with their gangsta rap. "We wanted to put the mirror up to show you where we got these gangster ideas," Tupac said. "So we took all these scenes out of classic movies with gangsters in them . . . not gangsters named Doo Dirty and Snoop and Tupac . . . but gangsters named Lucky Luciano and Don Corleone and John Caddy, Al Capone and Smitty."

The ready response, of course, is that these white stars don't seek to imitate the roles they play in real life. "James Cagney, Edward G. Robinson, Clint Eastwood, John Wayne, Sylvester Stallone, Arnold Schwarzenegger, Bruce Willis, not one of them has ever had one bullet fly at them in public," Crouch says. When I bring up *The Sopranos,* the hugely successful and much beloved cable television series, Crouch pounces immediately. "Tony Soprano remains a monster from the first episode to last night's episode," he says. "See, the brilliance of it is he shows you, yes, this man is a human being, but he's a sociopath. He's a predator. He's sadistic. He's a murderer. [Series creator] David Chase doesn't duck any of that, and he doesn't make it seem to you that you're supposed to like it. It's just you see the complexity of what's going on." Crouch contends that Tony Soprano, the lead character in the series, is full of angst about the life he leads. "He still has all of this guilt, because what he's doing is fundamentally fucked up. But none of that justifies what he does." Crouch presses me. "I mean, you're an expert on this material. There's nobody in rap that I'm aware of in which real questions are asked by the rappers themselves about what the hell they're doing."

Taken in his full lyrical sweep, I maintain that Tupac is such a figure. One of the reasons he stands out in rap is precisely because he offered such a powerful, complex, panoramic view of the young black experience. "If you were going on the path of a social activist, there is something for you in his lyrics," says Everett Dyson-Bey, a Moorish Temple minister and prisoner. "If you were on the path of a straight thug, there is something there for you, too. So to bridge that gap from one end to the next, to run that polarity, from the positive to the negative, spoke to so many people of so many different backgrounds." But Tupac constantly questioned his direction by filling his lyrics with characters who were both the victims and perpetrators of crime, characters who were thugs begging God for guidance through the minefields of self-destruction, characters leaving the ghetto while others stayed, characters who asked why they suffered even as they imposed suffering. In that haze of morbid contradictions, Tupac shone the light of his dark, brooding, pensive spirit, refusing to close his eyes to the misery he saw, risking everything to bear witness to the pain he pondered and perpetuated. In a word, *The Sopranos* offers, in Ernest Becker's term, an "anthropodicy," where we hold each other accountable for the suffering and evil imposed, whereas Tupac wrestles with a theodicy, the effort to square belief in God with the evil that prevails, which is at root an attempt to explain the suffering of those he loved.

Crouch may be right about the motley fellowship of gangster actors who never saw a gun aimed at them off-camera, but it is likely that just as great a percentage of white actors and singers get into trouble with the law as do black rap artists. The list includes Robert Downey Jr., James Caan, George Michael, Hugh Grant, and Axl Rose, among countless others. And in case Tupac and Biggie seem totally anomalous, one must remember James Dean, Sal Mineo, Kurt Cobain, and Bob Kane. And earlier black stars that are now revered had their troubles, including Little Willie John, Frankie Lymon, and Sam Cooke. In their personal foibles and destructive habits, Flavor Flav, Old Dirty Bastard, Bobby Brown, and their cohort have got nothing on legends Marvin Gaye, Wilson Pickett, or for that matter James Brown. None of this explains away the undeniable sadness of the violent captivity of segments of hip-hop culture. It simply gives a broader context to our concerns and cautions against seeing hip-hoppers as uniquely plagued. It is true that the violence that increasingly gets spoken about in hip-hop is self-inflicted and racially perpetuated. Then, too, the violence is so cartoonish and caricatured that fewer and fewer vulnerable minds take it seriously, at least not literally. The biggest knock on hard-core hip-hop may be its tired, cliché-ridden exploration of a subject that demands subtlety, artistic courage, and the wisdom to refrain from using a sledgehammer where a scalpel will do. But the big picture must not be neglected: The real-world violence too many hip-hoppers and black youth confront is so much more troubling than the violence they romanticize, even eroticize, on records and screen.[8]

Needless to say, the rhetorical violence that is directed at black women is altogether troubling. To be sure, there is a great deal of parody, signifying, and raucous humor that fills a lot of hip-hop's more vulgar lyrical traditions. Those who believe that hip-hop invented these practices have only to listen to blues music from the early twentieth century. Old-school blues bawdiness was every bit as vulgar and sexually explicit as what disturbs contemporary defenders of black morality. Many critics now claim that black youth have lost their way by forsaking earlier visions of ethical caution and racial care. But a review of the concerns of black leaders in the early 1900s confirms that many of them thought their youth were just as morally wayward as the youth of our day. And many of those leaders indicted popular culture for its vicious effects on black youth. The remarkably humbling point to remember is that those youth who were seen as heading to hell in a hand basket became the grandparents and great-grandparents whose behavior is held up as the example we should aim for.

Still, the crude misogyny and sexism that are rampant in hip-hop are deeply disturbing. The sheer repetition of "bitch" as the proper name of females is not only distressing but destructive. It sends the message to young girls and women that their price of admission to hip-hop culture is the acceptance of self-denigration. Unlike the use of the word "nigga" in hip-hop, "bitch" fails to come across as resistant. An argument can be made that the circulation of variants of "nigger" serves to deprive the term of its negative meanings. "You my nigga" becomes a way of bonding around a term that was historically used by whites to degrade blacks. Thus, it deprives racist whites of the prerogative of naming blacks in harmful ways, since blacks have adapted it to their culture in playful or at least signifying fashion. Of course many black folk disagree and insist that the word can in no sense be redeemed. But the logic of those who contend that the word has use is clear, if unacceptable. The use of "bitch," by contrast, is less compelling. The majority of those using it are the men who continue to dominate hip-hop culture. Thus, its negative meanings are largely held in place. Even when males intend "bitch" to be positive, such as Notorious B.I.G.'s "Me and My Bitch," the term is still loaded with hurtful connotations. It is not clear that women in hip-hop who use the term have sought to use it in ways that question male power or perspectives on women. Their use of bitch usually does little more than second the female bashing of their male counterparts.

Likewise, the sexual saturation of hip-hop reflects the sexual obsessions that haunt the culture. It seems that nearly every rap video has a stock character: a woman bouncing her bosom, gyrating her gluteus, or otherwise occupied in fulfilling the sexual fantasies of millions of adolescents and adults. Such a specter surely degrades women by reducing them to their lowest erotic denominator. It also suggests to young women that the only viable assets they can exercise are their behinds and not their brains. Hence, Lil' Kim and Foxy Brown spin lustful, lascivious tales that rival their male counterparts in raunchy abandon. Place that in the company of hustling, drug-selling, death-dealing, sex-crazed lotharios who increasingly dominate the imagination of hip-hop and, well, the picture is rather grim. For many critics, it simply repackages the stereotypes that black folk have spent centuries resisting: the whorish black woman, the studly black man. The cruel caveat, however, is that now these stereotypes are brashly amplified in the mouths of history-starved misfits whose political illiteracy masquerades as defiant art. Of course there is some truth to this rather harsh, dismissive, and unjust diatribe. Too many black youth have no idea where black folk have been and only dimly know what we've had to do to get where we are. But it isn't primarily their fault. We have reneged on our responsibility as black adults to keep the culture vital by making it relevant to contemporary struggles. That means translating the terms of past struggle into present action. Instead, older blacks often nostalgically rehash romantic memories of the past, failing to acknowledge just how remarkably similar our failures and prospects for triumph are to those of the hip-hop generation.

That shouldn't stop us from admitting that we are much more attracted to the basest, simplest elements of our artistic makeup than to its brightest, most demanding features. This is true for the culture as a whole. That is why *Mission Impossible* outpaces *Boys Don't Cry* and why Britney Spears outsells Bonnie Raitt. The fact that Common, Mos Def, Talib Kweli, Bahamadia, Black Eyed Peas, Jurassic

Five, and the Roots don't chart as highly as Jay-Z, Juvenile, Master P, or the lat-est posthumous effort by Tupac is certainly a problem. But is it hip-hop's problem or ours? Another way of putting the question is to ask whether that trend doesn't reflect a general resistance to art that is explicitly political, sharply critical of the status quo even inside black life, and self-reflective in a way that only mature art will risk. There is no denying that the ethical aspirations of Mos Def, for instance, directly counter the corporate capitalism that commits bigger budgets to market and distribute the latest butt-shaking record. Or another tired, trite, and uninter-esting "bling-bling" (the sight produced by light reflecting off diamond-laced or platinum jewelry) video lauding the virtues of material or commercial culture. In that sense, there is a real war going on in hip-hop. On the one side are purists who stake the future of the form on lyrical skill, narrative complexity, clever rhymes, and fresh beats. On the other side are advocates of commercialized hip-hop, marked by the mass production of records that sell because they are crassly ac-cessible. They neither challenge their audience nor move them to reflect on social, racial, or cultural ills. But the issue has never been as simple as politics versus art or positive versus negative.

Mos Def, praised as one of the leaders of "conscious rap," refuses to think in such narrow terms. "They've got their little categories, like 'conscious' and 'gangsta,'" says Mos Def. "It used to be a thing where hip-hop was all together. Fresh Prince [Will Smith's old moniker] would be on tour with N.W.A. [Nig-gas With Attitude, featuring Dr. Dre and Ice Cube]. It wasn't like, 'You have got to like me in order for me to like you.' That's just some more white folks trying to think that all niggas are alike, and now it's expanded. It used to be one type of nigga; now it's two. There is so much more dimension to who we are. A monolith is a monolith, even if there's two monoliths to choose from." Mos Def sees the danger, however, in having only one dimension of the black experience get airplay, which in present terms is usually of the bling-bling or thug variety. "I ain't mad at Snoop. I'm not mad at Master P; I ain't mad at the Hot Boyz. I'm mad when that's all you see. I would be mad if I looked up and all I saw on TV was me or Common or the Roots, because I know that ain't the whole deal. The real joy is when you can kick it with everyone. That's what hip-hop is all about."

Another rapper lauded for his rhetorical brilliance and revolutionary passion, Common, similarly sees the virtue of the range in hip-hop. "I can't put a line be-tween us," Common says about the difference between him and hardcore rap. "Because we are speaking our experiences and we are speaking our voice in hip-hop. Tupac was talking about smoking weed, guns, and so on, and we can't ig-nore that. I talk about other subjects [than hard-core rappers], but [conscious rap-pers] still have flaws, and we are not afraid to show those flaws." Mos Def is careful to avoid accepting the praise—and the typecasting—of corporate interests that deny the complexity of black identity and culture. "They keep trying to slip the 'conscious rapper' thing on me," he says. "I come from Roosevelt Projects, man. The ghetto. I drank the same sugar water, ate hard candy. And they try to get me because I'm supposed to be more articulate, I'm supposed to be not like the other Negroes, to get me to say something against my brothers. I'm not going out like that, man." In light of his thug persona, it may be hard to consider Tupac a "brilliant poet as great as any medieval writer," as he is regarded by Arvand Elihu, a talented young graduate student who taught a course on the felled rapper at the University of California–Berkeley.

There is another dimension to the debate as well: Some of the best-intentioned hip-hop, politically speaking, is simply boring or lyrically void of imagination or inspiration. Or it is just musically dead, a real drawback to what folk in the midst of heated argument often forget is first and foremost a musical form. And some of the most apolitical rap is lyrically clever and musically compelling. (Why should it be any different in hip-hop than it is in, for instance, R&B, where Luther Vandross's ethereal love notes rise higher than a musical complaint about racism, though few folk assail that branch of black music for its bourgeois sensibilities that are decidedly apolitical, noninterventionist, and downright misleading in its portrayal of romantic love?) It may well be that we should expand our understanding of what politics is, since hip-hop as an art form has been embroiled in the politics of culture and the culture of politics since its beginnings. In light of Senate hearings about rap's violent effects, it has little choice but to be political, even when its politics have to do with its right to exist at all.

The debate about hip-hop's complexity as well as Tupac's role in rap underscores the need for genre justice. We ought to recognize that there are all sorts of rap music, that not all of rap can do what some of it can do, and that the best rap is the rap that sticks to what it does best. The power of Tupac's raps is that they encompass a variety of hip-hop genres. One of the liabilities of blanketing rap in general terms is that we fail to recognize its diversity. That means that we also fail to see how many of the debates we try to force on hip-hop culture from outside are occurring with regularity on the inside. Take, for instance, the bravado and posturing that clutter hip-hop and the profanity that is often mistaken for authenticity, for keeping it real. Lauryn Hill, as a member of the Fugees, offered a biting commentary in as brilliant and pithy a fashion as might be imagined when she rhymed: "And even after all my logic and my theory / I add a 'muthafucka' so you ignorant niggers hear me." There are many moods and styles in hip-hop. There is griot rap, including figures like Common, Mos Def, Talib Kweli, Bahamadia, and the Roots. There is radical rap, characterized by the Coup and most recently by Dead Prez. There is materialistic/hedonistic rap, presented by Juvenile, Cash Money Millionaires, and a hundred offshoots. There is ghettocentric hip-hop, including figures as diverse as Jay-Z and the Wu-Tang Clan. There is gangsta rap, including Snoop Dogg and Dr. Dre. There is pop rap, symbolized most powerfully by Will Smith. There is Bohemian hard core, as glimpsed in Outkast and Goodie Mobb. And of course some of these figures and groups bleed into several genres. And many of these genres can be divided not only by theme and style but also by region. So the Dirty South of Atlanta's Outkast and Master P of New Orleans can be contrasted to the West Coast rap of South Central's Ice Cube or Compton's DJ Quick or the Upsouth rhymes of Nelly of St. Louis.

Our expectations of hip-hop's genres should be rooted in an appreciation of their intents. We should not expect pop rap to give us a peek into the inner workings of capitalism or white supremacy. Will Smith will never be Dead Prez. At the same time, Will Smith can beautifully celebrate fatherhood and welcome us to Miami (and to the dance floor) with his delightful pop confections. And that doesn't mean that we cannot be rocked by Dead Prez's brilliant critiques of racial amnesia and cultural genocide in black American life. It's not either-or. And we must not be afraid to enjoy the many intriguing transgressions of Lil' Kim and Foxy Brown, even as we lament their lyrical existence almost exclusively in sexualized zones. Not only are there many genres of hip-hop, but one artist can give us many different looks, feels, sensibilities, styles, and themes. Tupac could both "get around" by sexually exploiting his star status (a fact that hardly makes him unique) and admonish poor young women to "keep ya head up." The edifying and terrifying in this singular artist lived on the same block.

Like Tupac, perhaps its most embattled icon, hip-hop culture lives in conflict and thrives on contradiction. It is both a highly commercialized, corporate-sponsored venture as well as an indigenous art form that reflects (on) the brutal realities of black youth existence. That white corporate types have gotten into the mix doesn't negate the ghetto sensibilities and themes that drive—and sometimes drag down—hip-hop. As Toni Morrison says, "The fact that rap is so attractive to white kids in the suburbs is the risk that all discourses that black people invent have." Hip-hop is a barometer of black youth taste, style, and desires—as they are created and disseminated in local communities and by force of corporate distribution. It is also a sure test of our ability to embrace the best of our youth while engaging in critical conversations about their future. Given its universal popularity and its troubling effects, hip-hop is a vital cultural language that we had all better learn. To ignore its genius, to romanticize its deficits, or to bash it with undiscerning generalities is to risk the opportunity to engage our children about perhaps the most important cultural force in their lives.

Tupac may be the most influential rapper to have lived. His voice rings through our cultural landscape and hovers over our spirits with formidable intensity. Nearly five years after his death, his posthumously released double compact disc, *Until the End of Time*, dwarfed its nearest competition and sold over 400,000 copies in its first week of circulation. It may be that Tupac's bold voice is more necessary now than when he lived. He embraced the history of rap and operated within its limits while always pushing against them, reshaping rap's conventions while blurring the lines between his art and life. His stunning baritone was filled with surprising passion and urgency. He narrated his life as a road map to suffering, wrenching a brutal victory from the ghetto he so loved, and the fame and fortune that both blessed and cursed him. As the supreme symbol of his generation, he embodied its reckless, audacious liberties and its ominous hopelessness. Above all, he was as truthful as we can expect any human being to be about his evolving identity and his expanding artistic vision. "My music is spiritual, if you listen to it," Tupac said in his prison interview. "It's all about emotion; it's all about life. Not to dis anybody, but where other rappers might paint a perfect picture of themselves, I would tell my innermost, darkest secrets. I reveal myself in every one of my records. From 'Dear Mama' to 'Shed So Many Tears,' I tell my own, personal problems, and people can relate to what I believe."

PART TEN

CINEMA NOIR

In the mid-eighties, a new era in black cinema dawned. Director, actor, and writer Spike Lee led the way with his provocative, brilliant, and idiosyncratic films, including the highly charged racial drama, Do The Right Thing, *and his masterpiece, the bio-picture,* Malcolm X. *Not far behind Lee were Reginald and Warrington Hudlin with their fresh, hip urban musical,* House Party; *John Singleton, with his poignant and moving coming-of-age film,* Boyz N The Hood; *Mario Van Peebles and his riveting drug drama,* New Jack City; *and Ernest Dickerson's powerful urban morality tale,* Juice. *These figures were joined by Euzhan Palcy, Julie Dash, Matty Rich, Leslie Harris, and other black directors eager to explore the complex dimensions of black life that have been historically neglected on film. Twenty years later, a new stable of supremely gifted directors, including Kasi Lemmons* (Eve's Bayou), *Carl Franklin* (Devil in a Blue Dress), *Millicent Shelton* (Ride), *Gina Prince-Bythewood* (Love & Basketball), *F. Gary Gray* (Set It Off), *Theodore Witcher* (Love Jones), *Malcolm Lee* (Best Man), *Rick Famuyiwa* (Brown Sugar), *and Antoine Fuqua* (Training Day) *have expanded the cinematic canvass on which black life is drawn.*

Twenty-Three

SPIKE LEE'S NEONATIONALIST VISION

When I went to see Spike Lee's brilliantly disturbing film Do the Right Thing *in New York, the tension in the theater was palpable. After all, warnings had gone out that the film might provoke racial melees because of its volatile topic and approach. Of course, nothing of the sort happened. However, the June 1989 film proved to be a powerful conversation piece in the culture, especially in light of racial tragedies connected to white ethnic New York neighborhoods in the recent past (the infamous Howard Beach incident, where twenty-three-year-old Michael Griffith was chased to his death by white teens pursuing him with baseball bats and tree limbs) and in the near future (the murder of sixteen-year-old Yusuf Hawkins in August 1989 in Bensonhurst, shot twice in the chest by a white youth who was part of a mob assembled to seek revenge for a neighborhood girl's interracial dating). This review of Lee's film, originally published in* Tikkun *magazine, charts his attempt to meld two competing ambitions: to narrate the complex humanity of black folk and to specify the political implications of his neonationalist perspective. Although I emphasized Lee's tremendous strengths while pointing to the film's flaws, in retrospect, I think* Do the Right Thing, *and Lee, deserve even more praise than I gave them fifteen years ago. I think it is perhaps his second greatest movie—the greatest is the monumental* Malcolm X, *which is still in my mind underrated—and a signal accomplishment in American film. As critic Roger Ebert wrote at the time,* Do the Right Thing *"comes closer to reflecting the current state of race relations in America than any other movie of our time." It is a tribute to Lee's huge gifts and aesthetic courage that the film remains a provocative portrait of its times. It is also a warning against the racial amnesia that clouds our national racial memory and threatens true racial harmony and equality.*

IN 1986, A DISTINCT PHASE IN CONTEMPORARY African-American cinema commenced. Spike Lee wrote, produced, directed, and acted in *She's Gotta Have It,* an independently made sex comedy that cost $175,000 but grossed over $6 million after distribution by Island Pictures. Since then Lee, and an expanding cadre of black filmmakers, including Robert Townsend, Keenan Ivory Wayans, and Euzhan Palcy, have written and directed a number of films that explore various themes in black life. Lee in particular creates films that are part of a revival of black nationalism (neonationalism), a movement that included provocative expressions in the cultural sphere (elements of rap music, the wearing of African medallions), interesting interventions in the intellectual sphere (articulation of Afrocentric perspectives in academic disciplines), and controversial developments in the social sphere (symbolized by Louis Farrakhan's Nation of Islam ideology, which enjoys narrow but significant popularity among blacks). Lee, foremost among his black director peers, is concerned with depicting the sociopolitical implications of his Afrocentric film aesthetic and neonationalist worldview.

But he is also determined to display the humanity of his characters, and he insists upon exploring the unacknowledged diversity and the jarring and underappreciated contradictions of black life. Lee, however, is confronted with a conflict: how to present the humanity of black folk without lapsing into an ontology of race that structures simplistic categories of being for black people and black culture that are the worst remnants of old-style black nationalism. Such constructions of black character and culture fail to express the complex diversity of black humanity.

On the one hand, because Lee is apparently committed to a static conception of racial identity, his characters appear as products of an archetypal mold that predetermines their responses to a range of sociohistorical situations. These characters are highly symbolic and widely representative, reflecting Lee's determination to repel the folkloric symbols of racism through racial countersymbol. On the other hand, Lee must revise his understanding of racial identity in order to present the humanity of black characters successfully. He must permit his characters to possess irony, self-reflection, and variability, qualities that, when absent—no matter the high aims that underlie archetypal representation—necessarily circumscribe agency and flatten humanity. It is in the electric intersection of these two competing and at times contradictory claims, of black cultural neonationalism and black humanism, that Lee's art takes place.

In *Do the Right Thing,* Lee's black neonationalism leaps off the screen through brilliant cinematography and riveting messages. As most Americans know, *Do the Right Thing is* about contemporary racism. The film's action is concentrated in a single block of Brooklyn's "Bedstuy" neighborhood on a scorching summer day. The heat, both natural and social, is a central metaphor for the film's theme of tense race relations. The pivotal place of social exchange in this compact, ethnically diverse, and highly self-contained community is Sal's Famous Pizzeria, the single vestige of white-owned business in Bedstuy. Sal (Danny Aiello) owns and operates the restaurant along with his two sons, Pino (John Turturro) and Vito (Richard Edwon), proud Italians who make the daily commute from the suburb of Bensonhurst. Lee plays Mookie, the hardworking but responsibility-shirking delivery man for Sal's and the primary link between the community and the pizzeria. Mookie seems able to maneuver easily between two worlds—until late in the film, when the community erupts in a riot at Sal's, prompted by an egregious instance of police brutality.

In choosing to explore the racial tension between Italian-Americans and African-Americans, Lee makes explicit reference to Howard Beach, employing it as an ideologically charged conceptual foil for his drama about American racism.

Lee makes allusions to the Howard Beach incident throughout the movie: Sal brandishes a baseball bat in conflicts with various black patrons; the crowd chants "Coward Beach" at the riot. Lee wants his movie to provoke discussion about racism in the midst of a racially repressive era, when all such discourse is either banished to academia (although not much discussion goes on there, either) or considered completed in the distant past. Lee rejects the premises of this Reagan-era illogic and goes straight to the heart of the mechanism that disseminates and reinforces racial repression: the image, the symbol, the representation. *Do the Right Thing* contains symbols of racism and resistance to racism, representations of black life, and images of black nationalist sensibilities and thought.

Lee creates symbols that reveal the remorseless persistence of racism in quotidian quantity, exposing the psychopathology of everyday racism as it accumulates in small doses, over the course of days not unlike the one we witness in *Do the Right Thing*. Lee shows us the little bruises, the minor frustrations, and the minute but myriad racial fractures that mount without healing. There is the riff of the prickly relations between the black residents and the Koreans who own the neighborhood market. There is the challenge of Radio Raheem (Bill Nunn), a menacing bundle of brawn who wields his boom box as a weapon to usurp communal aural space as he practices his politics of cultural terrorism. But the central symbol of racial conflict is the ongoing tiff between Buggin' Out and Sal over the latter's refusal to place photos of black people on Sal's Wall of Fame, reserved for the likes of DiMaggio, Stallone, and Sinatra. Sal and Buggin' Out's battle over the photographs, over the issue of *representing* black people, makes explicit the terms of the film's representational warfare.

Lee's decision to provoke discussion about racism is heroic. He exposes a crucial American failure of nerve, a stunning loss of conscience about race. But beyond this accomplishment, how much light does he shed by raising the question of racism in the manner that he does? Lee's perspective portrays a view of race and racism that, while it manages to avoid a facile Manichaeanism, nevertheless slides dangerously close to a vision of "us" and "them," in which race is seen solely through the lens of biological determinism.

The problem with such biological determinism is that it construes racial identity as a unidimensional, monocausal reality that can be reduced to physically inheritable characteristics. Racial identity is an ever-evolving, continually transforming process that is never fully or finally exhausted by genetics and physiology. It is constantly structured and restructured, perennially created and re-created, in a web of social practices, economic conditions, gendered relations, material realities, and historical situations that are themselves shaped and reshaped. As the feminist critique of Freud asserts, anatomy is not destiny; likewise, biology is not identity.

Black cultural neonationalism obscures the role of elements such as gender, class, and geography in the construction of racial identity, and by so doing limits its resources for combating racial oppression. Consider the film's end, in which

Lee juxtaposes quotes from Martin Luther King, Jr., and Malcolm X that posit the harm versus the help of violence in aid of black liberation. Lee has not stumbled serendipitously toward an interpretive framework that summarizes the two options open to black folk in fighting racism: Lee's neonationalist perspective has regulated his presentation of the problem of racism in the movie all along.

Furthermore, Lee's neonationalism determines which quotes he uses. As Lee knows, it can be argued that, before their deaths, King and X were converging in their understanding of race and racism. Both of them were developing understandings of racial identity and racism that were much more complex, open-ended, ecumenical, and international than the views they had previously held. King was changing because of his more radical comprehension of the relationship between race and class, and thus began to promote a more aggressive version of nonviolent resistance. X was changing, too, because of his visit to Mecca and his expanding conception of the possibilities of interracial solidarity. Each man also borrowed elements of analysis from the other, appropriating those lessons in ways that had the potential to chart a much different path for resistance to oppression in the '70s and on. By using these quotes from King and X, free of context, Lee gives an anachronistic and historical reading of the two figures. Presenting these quotes as a basis of present options may provide some conceptual and emotive resources for debate, but does little to enlighten. Lee freezes the meanings of these two men, instead of utilizing their mature thought as a basis for *reconceiving* the problem of racism to address *our* particular set of historical circumstances.

Lee's neonationalist leanings also affect his characters, who become mere archetypes. Buggin' Out (Giancarlo Esposito) is the local radical, a caricature of deep commitment, who is more rabblerouser than thoughtful insurgent. Smiley (Roger Gueneveur Smith) is the stuttering conscience, first seen in front of the Yes Jesus Can Baptist Church. He hawks photographs of the famous meeting between King and X to reluctant passersby. Ossie Davis plays Da Mayor, the neighborhood drunk, who represents older black men who were scathed by economic desperation and personal failure, and whose modus vivendi is shaped by the bottle. Ruby Dee (Davis's real-life wife) is Mother Sister, a lonely black woman who represents the neighborhood's omniscient eye. She is a possible victim of desertion by a man like Da Mayor, or a woman who was determined and independent before her time (or perhaps both). Joie Lee, Spike's real-life sister, plays Mookie's sister Jade, and represents the responsible and stable black woman. She must support and suffer Mookie, her affectionately irascible brother, whom she chides for not taking care of his son. Mookie's son's mother, Tina (Rosie Perez), is the Latin firebrand who extemporizes in colorful neologism about Mookie's domestic shortcomings. And a trio of middle-aged black men, Sweet Dick Willie, ML, and Coconut Sid (Robin Harris, Paul Benjamin, and Frankie Faison), represent the often humorous folk philosophy of a generation of black males who have witnessed the opening of socioeconomic opportunity for others, but who must cope with a more limited horizon for themselves.

In one respect, Lee's use of archetypal black figures is salutary, as it expands the register of black characters in contemporary cinema. But the larger effect is harmful, and is a measure both of Hollywood's deeply entrenched racism and of the limitation of Lee's neonationalist worldview. Lee follows a tradition of sorts, as the attempt to decenter prevalent conceptions of racial behavior began in earnest in the '20s in Oscar Micheaux's films. A much later attempt to shift from stereotype to archetype in black film was crudely rendered in Melvin Van Peebles's *Sweet Sweetback's Baadasssss Song* (1971). Although Lee is light-years ahead of Van Peebles in most respects, he still adopts a crucial element of Van Peebles's work: the representative archetype.

Lee is unable to meld his two ambitions—to present the breadth of black humanity while proclaiming a black neonationalist aesthetic. His attempt to present a black universe is admirable, but that universe must be one in which people genuinely act and do not simply respond as mere archetypal constructions. Because the characters carry such weighty symbolic significance (resonant though it might be), they must act like symbols, not like humans. As a result, their story seems predetermined, a byproduct of a complicated configuration of social, personal, and political situations.

The archetypal model accounts for the manner in which Lee portrays the white characters, particularly Sal and sons. Pino is the vicious ethnic chauvinist who clings tightly to his Italian identity and heritage for fear of finding himself awash in the tide of "nigger" loving that seems to soak his other family members. Vito is the ethnic pluralist, an easygoing and impressionable young man whose main distinction is that he has no major beef with the blacks and Puerto Ricans. Only Sal, who splits the difference between his two sons, manages to rise in some complexity. He is a proud businessman whose long-standing relationship with the community has endeared him to most of the neighborhood's residents. But when provoked, he is not above hurling the incendiary racial epithet, which on one fateful occasion seals his destiny by beginning the riot that destroys his store.

This Saturday night Sal keeps the store open late to accommodate a group of neighborhood kids. That is when Radio Raheem (boom box in tow and pumping loud) and Buggin' Out shout a final request to place photos of blacks on the wall. After Radio Raheem refuses to lower the volume of his box, Sal, driven to an understandable frenzy, crushes the radio with his baseball bat. Radio Raheem also behaves understandably. He grabs Sal, pulls him over the counter, and the two men struggle from the store into the street. The police arrive and attempt to restrain Radio Raheem using the infamous New York Police "chokehold," a potentially lethal technique, especially when applied to black male necks. The police let Radio Raheem drop dead to the ground, kick him, and drag him into a police car. Meanwhile, they have handcuffed Buggin' Out and carted him away. The crowd is horror-stricken. Mookie, until now the mediator of disputes between Sal and the community, takes sides with his neighbors and throws a trash can through Sal's window, catalyzing the riot. The crowd destroys the pizzeria, overturning tables and equipment and taking money from the cash register. But it is stuttering Smiley who starts the fire. In African-American religious tradition, the Holy Spirit appears before believers in the form of fire. Smiley's torch is the articulation of his religious passion.

Lee's portrayal of police brutality, which has claimed the lives of too many black people, is disturbingly honest. The encounter between Radio Raheem and Sal is poignant and instructive. It shows that a black person's death may be provoked by incidents of racial antagonism gone amok, and that it is easy for precious young black life to be sacrificed in the gritty interstices between anger and abandonment. Thus, we can understand the neighborhood's consuming desire to destroy property—avenging the murder of a son whose punishment does not fit his crime.

It is also understandable that the crowd destroys Sal's place, the pizzeria being the nearest representative of destructive white presence, a white presence that has just denied Radio Raheem his future. But Sal certainly doesn't represent the "powers" that Public Enemy rapped about so fearlessly on Radio Raheem's box. As Lee knows, the character of racism has changed profoundly in the last few decades, and even though there are still too many ugly reassertions of overt racism, it is often the more subtle variety that needs to be identified and fought.

For instance, after viewing Lee's film many people may leave the theater smugly self-confident that they are not racists because they are not petit bourgeois Italian businessmen, because they don't call people "niggers," and because they are not policemen who chokehold black men to death. But contemporary racism is often the teacher who cannot take a black student seriously, who subtly dismisses her remarks in class because they are "not really central," or because he has presumed, often unconsciously, a limit to her abstract reasoning. (The double whammy of race and gender operates here.) Contemporary racism is often middle-class black managers hitting a career ceiling that is ostensibly due to their lack of high-level management skills, which, of course, are missing not because of lack of intelligence but because they have not acquired the right *kinds* of experience. Contemporary racism is not about being kept out of a clothes store, but rather about not being taken seriously because the store clerk presumes you won't spend your money or that you have none to spend.

To assert that racism is most virulent at Sal's level misses the complex ways in which everyday racism is structured, produced, and sustained in multifarious social practices, cultural traditions, and intellectual justifications. Sal is as much a victim of his racist worldview as he is its perpetrator. By refusing to probe the shift in the modus operandi of American racism, Lee misses the opportunity to expose what the British cultural critic Stuart Hall calls inferential racism, the "apparently naturalized representation of events and situations relating to race, whether factual or 'fictional,' which have racist premises and propositions inscribed in them as a set of unquestioned assumptions."

Those who strive to resist the new-style racism must dedicate themselves to pointing out slippery attitudes and ambiguous actions that signal the presence of racism without appearing to do so. This strategy must include drawing attention to unintended racist statements, actions, and thoughts, which nevertheless do harm. These strategies must be accompanied by sophisticated, high-powered intellectual dialogue about how the nature of particular forms of Western discourse provide the expression, reproduction, and maintenance of racist ideology and practices. People must form interracial, international lines of solidarity and develop analyses of racism in tandem with similar analyses of sexism, classism, anti-Semitism, anti-Arabism, homophobia, ecological terrorism, and a host of other progressive concerns.

Perhaps nothing does more to symbolize the shadowed brilliance of Lee's project, the troubled symbiosis of his black neonationalist vision and his desire to represent black humanity, than a scene in which Mookie is completing an argument with Jade. After they depart, the camera fixes on the graffiti on the wall: "Tawana told the truth!" It is understandable, given Lee's perspective, that he chooses to retrieve this fresh and tortured signifier from the iconographical reservoir of black neonationalists, some of whom believe Tawana transcends her infamous circumstances and embodies the reality of racial violence in our times. Racial violence on every level is vicious now, but Tawana is not its best or most powerful symbol. Lee's invocation of Tawana captures the way in which many positive aspects of neonationalist thought are damaged by close association with ideas and symbols that hurt more than help. Yes, it is important to urge racial self-esteem, a vision for racial progress, the honoring of historical figures, and the creation of powerful culture, but not if the result is a new kind of bigotry. For this reason we must criticize Lee's proximity to Louis Farrakhan's ideological stances. Real transformation of our condition will come only as we explore the resources of progressive thought, social action, and cultural expression that were provided by figures like King, X, Paul Robeson, W.E.B. Du Bois, Lorraine Hansberry, Pauli Murray, and Ida B. Wells. But we can't wallow in unimaginative mimesis. These people's crucial insights, cultural expressions, and transformative activities must inspire us to think critically and imaginatively about our condition and help us generate profound and sophisticated responses to our own crises. Only then will we be able to do the right thing.

Twenty-Four

BETWEEN APOCALYPSE AND REDEMPTION: JOHN SINGLETON'S *BOYZ N THE HOOD*

When I saw this film in the summer of 1991 with my thirteen-year-old son—and I took him to see it at least seven times—I cried each time. The film spoke to so many issues that are critical to black male life: father and son bonding, the difficulty of rearing boys in poor and working-class communities, the vicious self-hatred that threads through gang violence, the devastating costs of social policies that overlook the economic and social needs of black males, and the magical power of black love. Like the lead character Furious Styles, played with incredible sensitivity and maturity by Laurence Fishburne, I got custody of my son when he ran into trouble while living with his mother. Singleton's film gave me and my son a common point of reference in discussing important issues between black fathers and sons. In this chapter, I discuss the predicament of black American men while reflecting on Singleton's mature-beyond-his-twenty-three-years vision of the social situation of black masculinity, and the equally intelligent writing of his screenplay. I don't fail to notice the film's troubling gender politics—that only black men can rear black men, a fact rebutted by the wise, brave black women who do it every day. Still, I applaud Singleton's cautionary tale of the disappearing black father, a disappearance often supported by the culture and underwritten by the state. This film remains the high-water mark of Singleton's career.

BY NOW THE DRAMATIC DECLINE IN BLACK male life has become an unmistakable feature of our cultural landscape, although of course the causes behind the desperate condition of black men date much further back than its recent popular discovery. Every few months, new reports and conferences attempt to explain the poverty, disease, despair, and death that shove black men toward social apocalypse.

If these words appear too severe or hyperbolic, the statistics testify to the trauma. For black men between the ages of eighteen and twenty-nine, suicide is the leading cause of death. Between 1980 and 1985, the life expectancy for white males increased from 63 to 74.6 years, but only from 59 to 65 years for black males. Between 1973 and 1986, the real earnings of black males between the ages of eighteen and twenty-nine fell 31 percent, as the percentage of young black males in the workforce plummeted 20 percent. The number of black men who dropped out of the workforce altogether doubled from 13 percent to 25 percent.

By 1989, almost 32 percent of black men between sixteen and nineteen were unemployed, compared with 16 percent of white men. And while blacks constitute only 12 percent of the nation's population, they make up 48 percent of the prison population, with men accounting for 89 percent of the black prison population. Only 14 percent of the white males who live in large metropolitan areas have been arrested, but the percentage for black males is 51 percent. And while 3 percent of white men have served time in prison, 18 percent of black men have been behind bars.[1]

Most chilling, black-on-black homicide is the leading cause of death for black males between the ages of fifteen and thirty-four. Or, to put it another way, "One out of every twenty-one black American males will be murdered in their lifetime. Most will die at the hands of another black male." These words appear in stark white print on the dark screen that opens John Singleton's masterful new film, *Boyz N the Hood.* These words are both summary and opening salvo in Singleton's battle to reinterpret and redeem the black male experience. With *Boyz N the Hood* we have the most brilliantly executed and fully realized portrait of the coming-of-age odyssey that black boys must undertake in the suffocating conditions of urban decay and civic chaos.

Singleton adds color and depth to Michael Schultz's groundbreaking *Cooley High,* extends the narrative scope of the Hudlin Brothers' important and humorous *House Party,* and creates a stunning complement to Gordon Parks's pioneering *Learning Tree,* which traced the painful pilgrimage to maturity of a rural black male. Singleton's treatment of the various elements of contemporary black urban experience—gang violence, drug addiction, black male–female relationships, domestic joys and pains, friendships—is subtle and complex. He layers narrative textures over gritty and compelling visual slices of black culture that show us what it means to come to maturity, or die trying, as a black male.

Singleton's noteworthy attempt to present a richly hued, skillfully nuanced portrait of black male life is rare in the history of American film. Along with the seminal work of Spike Lee, and the recently expanded body of black film created by Charles Burnett, Robert Townsend, Keenan Wayans, Euzhan Palcy, Matty Rich, Mario Van Peebles, Ernest Dickerson, Bill Duke, Charles Lane, Reginald and Warrington Hudlin, Doug McHenry, George Jackson, and Julie Dash, Singleton symbolizes a new generation of black filmmakers whose artistic visions of African-American and American life may influence understandings of black worldviews, shape crucial perceptions of the sheer diversity of black communities, and address substantive racial, social, and political issues.

A major task, therefore, of African-American film criticism is to understand black film production in its historical, political, socioeconomic, ideological, and cultural contexts. Such critical analysis has the benefit of generating plausible explanations of how black film developed; what obstacles it has faced in becoming established as a viable and legitimate means of representing artistic, cultural, and racial perspectives on a range of personal and social issues; the ideological and social conditions which stunted its growth, shaped its emergence, and enabled its relatively recent success; and the economic and political forces which limited the material and career options of black filmmakers and constrained the opportunities for black artists to flourish and develop in a social environment hostile to black artistic production.

Another task of African-American film criticism is to provide rigorous tools of analysis, categories of judgment, and modes of evaluation that view the artistic achievements of black filmmakers in light of literary criticism, moral philosophy, feminist theory, intellectual history, cultural studies, and poststructuralist theory. African-American film criticism is not a hermetically sealed intellectual discourse that generates insight by limiting its range of intellectual reference to film theory, or to African American culture, in interpreting the themes, ideas, and currents of African-American film. Rather, African-American film criticism draws from the seminal insights of a variety of intellectual traditions in understanding and explaining the genealogy, scope, and evolution of black artistic expression. In short, black film criticism does not posit or constitute a rigidly defined sphere of academic analysis or knowledge production, but calls into question regimented conceptions of disciplinary boundaries while promoting the overlapping and interpenetration of diverse areas of intellectual inquiry.

Finally, African-American film criticism is related to the larger task of sustaining a just, enabling, but rigorous African-American cultural criticism that revels in black culture's virtues, takes pleasure in its achievements, laments its failed opportunities, and interrogates its weaknesses. African-American cultural criticism is intellectually situated to disrupt, subvert, and challenge narrow criticisms or romantic celebrations of black culture. A healthy African-American cultural criticism views black folk not as mere victims in and of history, but as its resourceful co-creators and subversive regenerators. It understands black people as agents of their own jubilation and pain. It sees them, in varying degrees and in limited manner, as crafters of their own destinies, active participants in the construction of worlds of meaning through art, thought, and sport that fend off threatening enclosure by the ever enlarging kingdom of absurdity. In this light, African-American film criticism pays attention to, and carefully evaluates, the treatment of crucial aspects of black culture in black films. Singleton's film addresses one of the most urgent and complex problems facing African-American communities: the plight of black men.

We have just begun to understand the pitfalls that attend the path of the black male. Social theory has only recently fixed its gaze on the specific predicament of black men in relation to the crisis of American capital, positing how their lives are shaped by structural changes in the political economy, for instance, rather than viewing them as the latest examples of black cultural pathology.[2] And social psychology has barely explored the deeply ingrained and culturally reinforced self-loathing and chronic lack of self-esteem that characterizes black males across age groups, income brackets, and social locations.

Even less have we understood the crisis of black males as rooted in childhood and adolescent obstacles to socioeconomic stability and moral, psychological, and emotional development. We have just begun to pay attention to specific rites of passage, stages of personality growth, and milestones of psychoemotional evolution that measure personal response to racial injustice, social disintegration, and class oppression.

James P. Comer and Alvin F. Poussaint's *Black Child Care,* Marian Wright Edelman's *Families in Peril,* and Darlene and Derek Hopson's foundational *Different and Wonderful* are among the exceptions that address the specific needs of black childhood and adolescence. Jewell Taylor-Gibbs's edited work, *Young, Black and Male in America: An Endangered Species,* has recently begun to fill a gaping void in social-scientific research on the crisis of the black male.

In the last decade alternative presses have vigorously probed the crisis of the black male. Like their black independent filmmaker peers, authors of volumes published by black independent presses often rely on lower budgets for advertising, marketing, and distribution. Nevertheless, word-of-mouth discussion of several books has sparked intense debate. Nathan and Julia Hare's *Bringing the Black Boy to Manhood: The Passage,* Jawanza Kunjufu's trilogy, *The Conspiracy to Destroy Black Boys,* Amos N. Wilson's *The Developmental Psychology of the Black Child,* Baba Zak A. Kondo's *For Homeboys Only: Arming and Strengthening Young Brothers for Black Manhood,* and Haki Madhubuti's *Black Men: Obsolete, Single, Dangerous?* have had an important impact on significant subsections of literate black culture, most of whom share an Afrocentric perspective.

Such works remind us that we have too infrequently understood the black male crisis through coming-of-age narratives and a set of shared social values that ritualize the process of the black adolescent's passage into adulthood. Such narratives and rites serve a dual function: they lend meaning to childhood experience, and they preserve and transmit black cultural values across the generations. Yet such narratives evoke a state of maturity—rooted in a vital community—that young black men are finding elusive or, all too often, impossible to reach. The conditions of extreme social neglect that besiege urban black communities—in every realm from health care to education to poverty and joblessness—make the black male's passage into adulthood treacherous at best.

One of the most tragic symptoms of the young black man's troubled path to maturity is the skewed and strained state of gender relations within the black community. With alarming frequency, black men turn to black women as scapegoats for their oppression, lashing out, often with physical violence, at those closest to them. It is the singular achievement of Singleton's film to redeem the power of the coming-of-age narrative while also adapting it to probe many of the very tensions that evade the foundations of the coming-of-age experience in the black community.

While mainstream American culture has only barely begun to register awareness of the true proportions of the crisis, young black males have responded in the last decade primarily in a rapidly flourishing independent popular culture, dominated by two genres: rap music and black film. The rap music of Run-D.M.C., Public Enemy, Boogie Down Productions, Kool Moe Dee, N.W.A., Ice Cube, and Ice-T, and the films of Spike Lee, Robert Townsend, and now Matty Rich and Mario Van Peebles have afforded young black males a medium in which to visualize and verbalize their perspectives on a range of social, personal, and cultural issues, to tell their stories about themselves and each other while the rest of America consumes and eavesdrops.

John Singleton's new film makes a powerful contribution to this enterprise. Singleton filters his brilliant insights, critical comments, and compelling portraits of young black male culture through a film that reflects the sensibilities, styles, and attitudes of rap culture.[3] Singleton's shrewd casting of rapper Ice Cube as a central character allows him to seize symbolic capital from a real-life rap icon, while tailoring the violent excesses of Ice Cube's rap persona into a jarring visual reminder of the cost paid by black males for survival in American society. Singleton skillfully integrates the suggestive fragments of critical reflections on the black male predicament in several media and presents a stunning vision of black male pain and possibility in a catastrophic environment: South Central Los Angeles.

Of course, South Central Los Angeles is an already storied geography in the American social imagination. It has been given cursory—though melodramatic—treatment by news anchor Tom Brokaw's glimpse of gangs in a highly publicized 1988 TV special, and has been mythologized in Dennis Hopper's film about gang warfare, *Colors*. Hopper, who perceptively and provocatively helped probe the rough edges of anomie and rebellion for a whole generation of outsiders in 1969's *Easy Rider,* less successfully traces the genealogy of social despair, postmodern urban absurdity, and yearning for belonging that provides the context for understanding gang violence. Singleton's task in part, therefore, is a filmic demythologization of the reigning tropes, images, and metaphors that have expressed the experience of life in South Central Los Angeles. While gangs are a central part of the urban landscape, they are not its exclusive reality. And although gang warfare occupies a looming periphery in Singleton's film, it is not the defining center.

Unquestionably, the 1991 urban rebellions in Los Angeles following the Rodney King verdict have given new poignancy to Singleton's depiction of the various personal, social, and economic forces which shape the lives of the residents of South Central L.A. His film was an incandescent and prescient portrait of the simmering stew of social angers—aimed at police brutality, steeply declining property values, poverty, and virile racism—which aggravate an already aggrieved community and which force hard social choices on neighborhoods (do we riot in our own backyards; do we maliciously target Korean businesses, especially since the case of Latasha Harlins, a black teenager murdered by a Korean grocer, who was simply given five years probation; and do we destroy community businesses and bring the charge of senseless destruction of resources in our own community when in reality, before the riots, we were already desperate, poor, and invisible, and largely unaided by the legitimate neighborhood business economy?) amounting to little more than communal triage. Singleton's film proves, in retrospect, a powerful meditation upon the blight of gang violence, hopelessness, familial deterioration, and economic desperation which conspire to undermine and slowly but surely destroy the morale and structure of many urban communities, particularly those in South Central L.A.

Boyz N the Hood is a painful and powerful look at the lives of black people, mostly male, who live in a lower-middle-class neighborhood in South Central Los Angeles. It is a story of relationships—of kin, friendship, community, love, rejection, contempt, and fear. At the story's heart are three important relationships: a triangular relationship between three boys, whose lives we track to mature adolescence; the relationship between one of the boys and his father; and the relationship between the other two boys and their mother.

Tre (Cuba Gooding Jr.) is a young boy whose mother Reva Devereaux (Angela Bassett), in an effort to impose discipline upon him, sends him to live with his father across town. Tre has run afoul of his elementary school teacher for challenging both her authority and her Eurocentric curriculum. And Tre's life in his mother's neighborhood makes it clear why he is not accommodating well to school discipline. By the age of ten, he has already witnessed the yellow police tapes that mark the scenes of crimes and has viewed the blood of a murder victim. Fortunately for Tre, his mother and father love him more than they couldn't love each other.

Doughboy (former N.W.A. rapper Ice Cube, in a brilliant cinematic debut) and Ricky (Morris Chestnut) are half-brothers who live with their mother Brenda (Tyra Ferell) across the street from Tre and his father. Brenda, as a single black mother, belongs to a much maligned group, whose members, depending on the amateurish social theory that wins the day, are vilified with charges of promiscuity, judged to be the source of all that is evil in the lives of black children, or at best stereotyped as helpless beneficiaries of the state. Singleton artfully avoids these caricatures by giving a complex portrait of Brenda, a woman who is plagued by her own set of demons, but who tries to provide the best living she can for her sons.

Even so, Brenda clearly favors Ricky over Doughboy—and this favoritism will bear fatal consequences for both boys. Indeed in Singleton's cinematic worldview both Ricky and Doughboy seem doomed to violent deaths because—unlike Tre—they have no male role models to guide them. This premise embodies one of the film's central tensions—and one of its central limitations. For even as he assigns black men a pivotal role of responsibility for the fate of black boys, Singleton also gives rather uncritical precedence to the impact of black men, even in their absence, over the efforts of present and loyal black women who more often prove to be at the head of strong black families.

While this foreshortened view of gender relations within the black community arguably distorts Singleton's cinematic vision, he is nonetheless remarkably perceptive in examining the subtle dynamics of the black family and neighborhood, tracking the differing effects that the boys' siblings, friends, and environment have on them. There is no bland nature-versus-nurture dichotomy here: Singleton is too smart to render life in terms of a Kierkegaardian either/or. His is an Afrocentric world of both/and.

This complex set of interactions—between mother and sons, between father and son, between boys who benefit from paternal wisdom or maternal ambitions, between brothers whose relationship is riven by primordial passions of envy and contempt, between environment and autonomy, between the larger social structure and the smaller but more immediate tensions of domestic life—define the central shape of *Hood*. We see a vision of black life that transcends insular preoccupations with "positive" or "negative" images and instead presents at once the limitations and virtues of black culture.

As a result, Singleton's film offers a plausible perspective on how people make the choices they do—and on how choice itself is not a property of autonomous moral agents acting in an existential vacuum, but rather something that is created and exercised within the interaction of social, psychic, political, and economic forces of everyday experience. Personal temperament, domestic discipline, parental guidance (or its absence) all help shape our understanding of our past and future, help define how we respond to challenge and crisis, and help mold how we embrace success or seem destined for failure.

Tre's developing relationship with his father, Furious Styles (Larry Fishburne), is by turns troubled and disciplined, sympathetic and compassionate—finely displaying Singleton's open-ended evocation of the meaning of social choice as well as his strong sensitivity to cultural detail. Furious Styles's moniker vibrates with double meaning, a semiotic pairing that allows Singleton to signify in speech what Furious accomplishes in action: a wonderful amalgam of old-school black consciousness, elegance, style, and wit linked to the hip-hop fetish of "dropping science" (spreading knowledge) and staying well informed about social issues.

Only seventeen years Tre's senior, Furious understands Tre's painful boyhood growth and identifies with his teen aspirations. But more than that, he possesses a sincere desire to shape Tre's life according to his own best lights. Furious is the strong presence and wise counselor who will guide Tre through the pitfalls of reaching personal maturity in the chaos of urban childhood, the very sort of presence denied to so many in *Hood,* and in countless black communities throughout the country.

Furious, in other words, embodies the promise of a different conception of black manhood. As a father he is disciplining but loving, firm but humorous, demanding but sympathetic. In him, the black male voice speaks with an authority so confidently possessed and equitably wielded that one might think it is strongly supported and valued in American culture, but of course that is not so. The black male voice is rarely heard without the inflections of race and class domination that distort its power in the home and community, mute its call for basic respect and common dignity, or amplify its ironic denial of the very principles of democracy and equality that it has publicly championed in pulpits and political organizations.

Among the most impressive achievements of Singleton's film is its portrayal of the neighborhood as a "community." In this vein Singleton implicitly sides with the communitarian critique of liberal moral autonomy and atomistic individualism.[4] In *Hood* people love and worry over one another, even if they express such sentiments roughly. For instance, when the older Tre crosses the street and sees a baby in the path of an oncoming car, he swoops her up and takes her to her crack-addicted mother. Tre gruffly reproves her for neglecting her child and insists that she change the baby's diapers before the baby smells as bad as her mother. And when Tre goes to a barbecue for Doughboy, who is fresh from a jail sentence, Brenda beseeches him to talk to Doughboy, hoping that Tre's intangible magic will "rub off on him."

But Singleton understands that communities embody resistance to the anonymity of liberal society as conceived in Aristotle via MacIntyre. His film portrays communities as more heterogeneous, complex, and diverse, however, than the ideal of consensus that grounds MacIntyre's conception of communities, which is at least partially mediated through a common moral vocabulary. Singleton's neighborhood is a community precisely because it turns on the particularity of racial identity, and the contradictions of class location, that are usually muted or eradicated in mainstream accounts of moral community. Such accounts tend to eliminate racial, sexual, gender, and class difference in positing the conditions that make community possible, and in specifying the norms, values, and mores which regulate moral discourse and that structure communal behavior. Singleton's film community is an implicit argument for the increased visibility of a politics of difference within American culture, a solemn rebuke to the Capraesque representation of a socially and economically homogeneous community.[5]

The quest for community represented in Singleton's film is related to the quest for intellectual community facilitated by certain modes of African-American cultural criticism. By taking black folk seriously, by taking just measure of their intellectual reflections, artistic perceptions, social practices, and cultural creations, the black cultural critic is seeking both to develop fair but forceful examination of black life, and to establish a community of interlocutors, ranging from high-brow intellectuals to everyday folk, whites and people of color alike, who are interested in preserving black culture's best features, ameliorating its weakest parts, and eradicating its worst traits.

Of course, specific moments of black cultural criticism also help shed light on aspects of black artistic production that may be overlooked or underestimated in much of mainstream criticism. A crucial role for African-American cultural criticism is to reveal historical connections and thematic continuities and departures between black films and issues debated over time and space in African-American society. By doing so, the black cultural critic illumines the material interests of black filmmakers, while drawing attention to the cultural situation of black film practice. Singleton's depiction of community provides a colorful lens on problems which have long plagued black neighborhoods.

Singleton understands that communities, besides embodying the virtuous ends of their morally prudent citizens, also reflect the despotic will of their fringe citizens who threaten the civic pieties by which communities are sustained. *Hood's* community is fraught with mortal danger, its cords of love and friendship under the siege of gang violence, and by what sociologist Mike Davis calls the political economy of crack.[6] Many inner-city communities live under what may be called a "juvenocracy": the economic rule and illegal tyranny exercised by young black men over significant territory in the black urban center. In the social geography of South Central L.A., neighborhoods are reconceived as spheres of expansion where urban space is carved up according to implicit agreements, explicit arrangements, or lethal conflicts between warring factions.

Thus, in addition to being isolated from the recognition and rewards of the dominant culture, inner-city communities are cut off from sources of moral authority and legitimate work, as underground political economies reward consenting children and teens with quick cash, faster cars, and sometimes, still more rapid death.[7] Along with the reterritorialization of black communal space through gentrification, the hegemony of the suburban mall over the inner-city and downtown shopping complex, and white flight and black track to the suburbs and exurbs, the inner city is continually devastated.

Such conditions rob the neighborhood of one of its basic social functions and defining characteristics: the cultivation of a self-determined privacy in which residents can establish and preserve their identities. Police helicopters constantly zoom overhead in *Hood's* community, a mobile metaphor of the ominous surveillance and scrutiny to which so much of poor black life is increasingly subjected. The helicopter also signals another tragedy, which *Hood* alludes to throughout its narrative: ghetto residents must often flip a coin to distinguish Los Angeles' police from its criminals. After all, this is Darryl Gates's L.A.P.D., and the recent Rodney King incident only underscores a long tradition of extreme measures that police have used to control crime and patrol neighborhoods.[8] As Singleton wrote after the rebellion:

> Anyone who has a moderate knowledge of African-American culture knows this was foretold in a thousand rap songs and more than a few black films. When Ice Cube was with NWA (Niggas With Attitude), he didn't write the lyrics to "Fuck tha Police" just to be cute. He was reciting a reflection of reality as well as fantasizing about what it would be like to be on the other end of the gun when it came to police relations. Most white people don't know what it is like to be stopped for a traffic violation and worry more about getting beat up or shot than paying the ticket. So imagine, if you will, growing up with this reality regardless of your social or economic status. Fantasize about what it is to be guilty of a

crime at birth. The crime? Being born black . . . . By issuing that verdict, the jury violated not only Rodney King's civil rights, not only the rights of all African-Americans, but also showed a lack of respect for every law-abiding American who believes in justice. (Singleton, 75)

Furious's efforts to raise his son in these conditions of closely surveilled social anarchy reveal the galaxy of ambivalence that surrounds a conscientious, community-minded brother who wants the best for his family, but who also understands the social realities that shape the lives of black men. Furious's urban cosmology is three-tiered: at the immediate level, the brute problems of survival are refracted through the lens of black manhood; at the abstract level, large social forces such as gentrification and the military's recruitment of black male talent undermine the black man's role in the community; at the intermediate level, police brutality contends with the ongoing terror of gang violence.

Amid these hostile conditions, Furious is still able to instruct Tre in the rules of personal conduct and to teach him respect for his community, even as he schools him in how to survive. Furious says to Tre, "I know you think I'm hard on you. I'm trying to teach you how to be responsible. Your friends across the street don't have anybody to show them how to do that. You gon' see how they end up, too." His comment, despite its implicit self-satisfaction and sexism (Ricky and Doughboy, after all, do have their mother, Brenda), is meant to reveal the privilege of a young boy learning to face life under the shadow of fatherly love and discipline.

While Tre is being instructed by Furious, Ricky and Doughboy receive varying degrees of support and affirmation from Brenda. Ricky and Doughboy have different fathers, both of whom are conspicuously absent. In Doughboy's case, however, his father is symbolically present in that peculiar way that damns the offspring for their resemblance in spirit or body to the despised, departed father. The child becomes the vicarious sacrifice for the absent father, although he can never atone for the father's sins. Doughboy learns to see himself through his mother's eyes, her words ironically re-creating Doughboy in the image of his invisible father. "You ain't shit," she says. "You just like yo' Daddy. You don't do shit, and you never gonna amount to shit."

Brenda is caught in a paradox of parenthood, made dizzy and stunned by a vicious circle of parental love reinforcing attractive qualities in the "good" and obedient child, while the frustration with the "bad" child reinforces his behavior. Brenda chooses to save one child by sacrificing the other—lending her action a Styronian tenor, Sophie's choice in the ghetto. She fusses *over* Ricky; she fusses *at* Doughboy. When a scout for USC's football team visits Ricky, Brenda can barely conceal her pride. When the scout leaves, she tells Ricky, "I always knew you would amount to something."

In light of Doughboy's later disposition toward women, we see the developing deformations of misogyny. Here Singleton is on tough and touchy ground, linking the origins of Doughboy's misogyny to maternal mistreatment and neglect.

Doughboy's misogyny is clearly the elaboration of a brooding and extended *ressentiment*, a deeply festering wound to his pride that infects his relationships with every woman he encounters.

For instance, at the party to celebrate his homecoming from his recent incarceration, Brenda announces that the food is ready. All of the males rush to the table, but immediately before they begin to eat, Tre, sensing that it will be to his advantage, reproves the guys for not acting gentlemanly and allowing the women first place in line. Doughboy chimes in, saying, "Let the ladies eat; ho's gotta eat, too," which draws laughter, both from the audience with which I viewed the film and from the backyard male crowd. The last line is a sly sample of Robert Townsend's classic comedic send-up of fast-food establishments in *Hollywood Shuffle*. When his girlfriend (Regina King) protests, saying she isn't a "ho," Doughboy responds, "Oops, I'm sorry, bitch," which draws even more laughter.

In another revealing exchange with his girlfriend, Doughboy is challenged to explain why he refers to women exclusively as "bitch, or ho, or hootchie." In trying to reply, Doughboy is reduced to the inarticulate hostility (feebly masquerading as humor) that characterizes misogyny in general: " 'Cause that's what you are."

"Bitch" and "ho," along with "skeezer" and "slut," have by now become the standard linguistic currency that young black males often use to demonstrate their authentic machismo. "Bitch" and equally offensive epithets compress womanhood into one indistinguishable whole, so that all women are the negative female, the seductress, temptress, and femme fatale all rolled into one. Hawthorne's scarlet A is demoted one letter and darkened; now an imaginary black B is emblazoned on the forehead of every female.

Though Singleton's female characters do not have center stage, by no means do they suffer male effrontery in silent complicity. When Furious and Reva meet at a trendy restaurant to discuss the possibility of Tre returning to live with his mother, Furious says, "I know you wanna play the mommy and all that, but it's time to let go." He reminds her that Tre is old enough to make his own decisions, that he is no longer a little boy because "that time has passed, sweetheart, you missed it." Furious then gets up to fetch a pack of cigarettes as if to punctuate his self-satisfied and triumphant speech, but Tre's mother demands that he sit down.

As the camera draws close to her face, she subtly choreographs a black woman's grab-you-by-the-collar-and-set-you-straight demeanor with just the right facial gestures, and completes one of the most honest, mature, and poignant exchanges between a black man and a black woman in film history.

It's my turn to talk. Of course you took in your son, my son, our son and you taught him what he needed to be a man. I'll give you that, because most men ain't man enough to do what you did. But that gives you no reason, do you hear me, no reason to tell me that I can't be a mother to my son. What you did is no different from what mothers have been doing from the beginning of time. It's just too bad more brothers won't do the same. But don't think you're special. Maybe cute, but not special. Drink your café au lait. It's on me.

Singleton says that his next film will be about black women coming of age, a subject left virtually unexplored in film. In the meantime, within its self-limited scope, *Hood* displays a diverse array of black women, taking care not to render them as either mawkish or cartoonish: a crack addict who sacrifices home, dignity, and children for her habit; a single mother struggling to raise her sons; black girlfriends hanging with the homeboys but demanding as much respect as they can get; Brandi (Nia Long), Tre's girlfriend, a Catholic who wants to hang on to her virginity until she's sure it's the right time; Tre's mother, who strikes a Solomonic compromise and gives her son up rather than see him sacrificed to the brutal conditions of his surroundings.

But while Singleton ably avoids flat stereotypical portraits of his female characters, he is less successful in challenging the logic that at least implicitly blames single black women for the plight of black children.[9] In Singleton's film vision, it is not institutions like the church that save Tre, but a heroic individual—his father Furious. But this leaves out far too much of the picture.

What about the high rates of black female joblessness, the sexist job market that continues to pay women at a rate that is 70 percent of the male wage for comparable work, the further devaluation of the "pink collar" by lower rates of medical insurance and other work-related benefits, all of which severely compromise the ability of single black mothers to effectively rear their children?[10] It is the absence of much more than a male role model and the strength he symbolizes that makes the life of a growing boy difficult and treacherous in communities such as South Central L.A.

The film's focus on Furious's heroic individualism fails, moreover, to fully account for the social and cultural forces that prevent more black men from being present in the home in the first place. Singleton's powerful message, that more black men must be responsible and present in the home to teach their sons how to become men, must not be reduced to the notion that those families devoid of black men are necessarily deficient and ineffective. Neither should Singleton's critical insights into the way that many black men are denied the privilege to rear their sons be collapsed to the idea that all black men who are present in their families will necessarily produce healthy, well-adjusted black males. So many clarifications and conditions must be added to the premise that *only* black men can rear healthy black males that it dies the death of a thousand qualifications.

In reality, Singleton's film works off the propulsive energies that fuel deep and often insufficiently understood tensions between black men and black women. A good deal of pain infuses relations between black men and women, recently dramatized with the publication of Shahrazad Ali's infamous and controversial underground bestseller, *The Blackman's Guide to Understanding the Blackwoman*. The book, which counseled black women to be submissive to black men and which endorsed black male violence toward women under specific circumstances, touched off a furious debate that drew forth the many unresolved personal, social, and domestic tensions between black men and women.[11]

This pain follows a weary pattern of gender relations that has privileged concerns defined by black men over feminist or womanist issues. Thus, during the civil rights movement, feminist and womanist questions were perennially deferred, so that precious attention would not be diverted from racial oppression and the achievement of liberation.[12] But this deference to issues of racial freedom is a permanent pattern in black male–female relations; womanist and feminist movements continue to exist on the fringe of black communities.[13] And even in the Afrocentric worldview that Singleton advocates, the role of black women is often subordinate to the black patriarch.

Equally as unfortunate, many contemporary approaches to the black male crisis have established a rank hierarchy that suggests that the plight of black men is infinitely more lethal, and hence more important, than the condition of black women. The necessary and urgent focus on the plight of black men, however, must not come at the expense of understanding its relationship to the circumstances of black women.

At places, Singleton is able to subtly embody a healthy and redemptive vision of black male–female relations. For instance, after Tre has been verbally abused and physically threatened by police brutality, he seeks sanctuary at Brandi's house, choreographing his rage at life in South Central by angrily swinging at empty space. As Tre breaks down in tears, he and Brandi finally achieve an authentic moment of spiritual and physical consummation previously denied them by the complications of peer pressure and religious restraint. After Tre is assured that Brandi is really ready, they make love, achieving a fugitive moment of true erotic and spiritual union.

Brandi is able to express an unfettered and spontaneous affection that is not a simplistic "sex-as-proof-of-love" that reigns in the thinking of many teen worldviews. Brandi's mature intimacy is both the expression of her evolving womanhood and a vindication of the wisdom of her previous restraint. Tre is able at once to act out his male rage and demonstrate his vulnerability to Brandi, thereby arguably achieving a synthesis of male and female responses and humanizing the crisis of the black male in a way that none of his other relationships—even his relationship with his father—are able to do. It is a pivotal moment in the development of a politics of alternative black masculinity that prizes the strength of surrender and cherishes the embrace of a healing tenderness.

As the boys mature into young men, their respective strengths are enhanced and their weaknesses exposed. The deepening tensions between Ricky and Doughboy break out into violence when a petty argument over who will run an errand for Ricky's girlfriend provokes a fistfight. After Tre tries unsuccessfully to stop the fight, Brenda runs out of the house, divides the two boys, slaps Doughboy in the face, and checks Ricky's condition. "What you slap me for?" Doughboy repeatedly asks her after Ricky and Tre go off to the store. She doesn't answer, but her choice, again, is clear. Its effect on Doughboy is clearer still.

Such everyday variations on the question of choice are, again, central to the world Singleton depicts in *Hood*. Singleton obviously understands that people are lodged between social structure and personal fortune, between luck and ambition. He brings a nuanced understanding of choice to each character's large and small acts of valor, courage, and integrity that reveal what contemporary moral philosophers call virtue.[14] But they often miss what Singleton understands: character is not only structured by the choices we make, but by the range of choices we have to choose from—choices for which individuals alone are not responsible.

Singleton focuses his lens on the devastating results of the choices made by *Hood*'s characters, for themselves and for others. *Hood* presents a chain of choices, a community defined in part by the labyrinthine array of choices made and the consequences borne, to which others must then choose to respond. But Singleton does not portray a blind fatalism or a mechanistic determinism; instead he displays a sturdy realism that shows how communities affect their own lives and how their lives are shaped by personal and impersonal forces.

Brenda's choice to favor Ricky may not have been completely her own—all the messages of society say that the good, obedient child, especially in the ghetto, is the one to nurture and help—but it resulted in Doughboy's envy of Ricky and contributed to Doughboy's anger, alienation, and gradual drift into gang violence. Ironically and tragically, this constellation of choices may have contributed to Ricky's violent death when he is shot by members of a rival gang as he and Tre return from the neighborhood store.

Ricky's death, in turn, sets in motion a chain of choices and consequences. Doughboy feels he has no choice but to pursue his brother's killers, becoming a more vigilant keeper to his brother in Ricky's death than he could be while Ricky lived. Tre, too, chooses to join Doughboy, thereby repudiating everything his father taught and forswearing every virtue he has been trained to observe. When he grabs his father's gun and is met at the door by Furious, the collision between training and instinct is dramatized on Tre's face, wrenched in anguish and tears.

Though Furious convinces him to relinquish the gun, Furious's victory is only temporary. The meaning of Tre's manhood is at stake; it is the most severe test he has faced, and he chooses to sneak out of the house to join Doughboy. All Furious can do is tensely exercise his hands with two silver balls, which in this context are an unavoidable metaphor for how black men view their fate through their testicles, which are constantly up for grabs, attack, or destruction. Then sometime during the night, Tre's impassioned choice finally rings false, a product of the logic of vengeance he has desperately avoided all these years; he insists that he be let out of Doughboy's car before they find Ricky's killers.

Following the code of male honor, Doughboy kills his brother's killers. But the next morning, in a conversation with Tre, he is not so sure of violence's mastering logic anymore, and says that he understands Tre's choice to forsake Doughboy's vigilante mission, even as he silently understands that he is in too deep to be able to learn any other language of survival.

Across this chasm of violence and anguish, the two surviving friends are able to extend a final gesture of understanding. As Doughboy laments the loss of his brother, Tre offers him the bittersweet consolation that "you got one more brother left." Their final embrace in the film's closing moment is a sign of a deep love that binds brothers; a love, however, that too often will not save brothers.

The film's epilogue tells us that Doughboy is murdered two weeks later, presumably to avenge the deaths of Ricky's killers. The epilogue also tells us that Tre and Brandi manage to escape South Central as Tre pursues an education at Morehouse College, with Brandi at neighboring Spelman College. It is testimony to the power of Singleton's vision that Tre's escape is no callow Hollywood paean to the triumph of the human spirit (nor is it, as some reviewers have somewhat perversely described the film, "life-affirming"). The viewer is not permitted to forget for a moment the absurd and vicious predictability of the loss of life in South Central Los Angeles, a hurt so colossal that even Doughboy must ask, "If there was a God, why he let mothefuckers get smoked every night?" Theodicy in gangface.

Singleton is not about to provide a slick or easy answer. But he does powerfully juxtapose such questions alongside the sources of hope, sustained in the heroic sacrifice of everyday people who want their children's lives to be better. The work of John Singleton embodies such hope by reminding us that South Central Los Angeles, by the sheer power of discipline and love, sends children to college, even as its self-destructive rage sends them to the grave.

Twenty-Five

GHETTOCENTRICITY AND THE
NEW BLACK CINEMA

*This reflection on the rise of a ghetto aesthetic in black cinema was first published in
the British magazine* Sight and Sound. *Later I revised it for publication in other
venues, most notably in Carol Becker's wonderful collection of essays on art and social
responsibility entitled* Subversive Imagination. *I examine a gaggle of films that
were released in the late '80s to the mid '90s. Most take their cues from hip-hop
culture and its preoccupation with masculinity as much as from earlier film culture.
Addressing the work of Lee, Singleton, Matty Rich, Ernest Dickerson, and Mario
Van Peebles, I argue that the themes, strategies, images, and symbols they employ
represent a coming of age for a generation of directors who seek to portray the
particularities of black life. At the end of this essay, I call for black male film
directors to probe female identities and the relation of black men to women with the
same insight and skill the best of them bring to masculinity, hip-hop, and the class
line. I surmised that only with the emergence of female directors would the complexity
of female identities get a full airing on film. The rise of Julie Dash, Leslie Harris,
and Euzhan Palcy pointed the way to Kasi Lemmons and Gina Prince-Bythewood
and hopefully, in the near future, to a body of criticism worthy of their talents.*

THE EXPLOSION OF CONTEMPORARY BLACK CINEMA, along with the emergence of hip-hop culture, expresses the pervasive influence of African American
styles, sensibilities, and ideas in American popular culture. The narrative strategies
that black filmmakers employ, and the images, symbols, and themes black filmmakers present, are important because they embody the coming of age of a new
generation of artists dedicated to portraying the complexities and peculiarities of
black life. Given the wretched history of often distorted, even racist, representations of black life viewed through the prism of white cultural producers, the rise of
a new black cinema promises the articulation of artistic visions of black life beyond
the troubled zone of white representational authority and mainstream interpretative dominance.

A sharp analytical understanding of the narrative strategies, themes, symbols,
and images of contemporary black filmmakers is crucial in developing a sophisticated critical vocabulary that may be employed to interrogate the cultural and

artistic practices of the new black cinema. The development of such a critical vocabulary encourages and enables the examination of the artistic perceptions and
representations of black filmmakers; a wide-ranging exploration of the material
conditions and social situations of their cultural production; an astute analysis of
the goals, aims and objectives of black film; and a rigorous engagement with the
cultural contradictions and political determinants of black film production.

A select group of new black films, in particular, investigates the politics of black
masculinity and its relationship to the ghetto culture in which ideals of masculinity are nurtured and shaped. Concepts of masculinity are central to contemporary
cultural debates within African American society, especially given the crisis of
black manhood and the widespread attention it has received in the last few years,
especially within rap music and black film. Malcolm X is the unifying cultural signifier for the powerful premise of an overhauled black masculinity within a broad
variety of contemporary black cultural expressions, the vibrant hero of a black juvenile cultural imagination seeking to contest the revived racism and increasing
social despair of American life.

The relationship between concepts of masculinity and social responsibility is
strongly implied in the life, thought, and career of Malcolm X, whose influence
on contemporary black filmmakers cannot be underestimated. In one reading,
black filmmakers can be seen as cultural interpreters of the socially responsible dimensions of black masculinity as they are taken up in the organs of American
popular culture, particularly within African American life. In another reading, the
work of black filmmakers can be read symptomatically, as examples of the failure
or success of artistic explorations of masculinity to probe the healthy and productive—or unhealthy and disenabling—consequences of black manhood within
African American life, particularly as it takes shape in the black ghetto and often
in relation to black female identity.

In this essay, I will probe the treatment of the ghetto and black manhood in several black films, examining the artistic visions of directors in relation to their responsibility in forming images of these twin subjects. In the process, I hope to illumine the ethics of representation and characterize the manner in which these
films both enable and resist helpful understandings of black masculinity, especially in connection with their views of black female subjectivity.

Matty Rich's *Straight Out of Brooklyn* is a relentlessly desolate rejection of the
logic of liberal democracy: that individuals can act to realize themselves and enhance their freedom through the organs of the community or the state. For the inhabitants of Brooklyn's Red Hook Housing Project, the possibilities of self-
realization and freedom are infinitely reduced by the menacing ubiquity of the
ghetto. The suppressed premise of Rich's film—the steely argument for its existence at all—is a deferred rebuke to all pretensions that the ghetto is not a totalizing force, that it is possible to maintain the boundaries between geography and
psychic health implied by the expression: Live in the ghetto, but don't let the
ghetto live in you. It is precisely in showing that the ghetto survives parasitically—

that its limits are as small or as large as the bodies it inhabits and destroys—that *Brooklyn* achieves for its auteur a distinct voice among black filmmakers while establishing the film's thematic continuity with black popular culture's avid exploration of black, urban (male) identities.

After disappearing for a while from the intellectual gaze of the American academy and being obscured from mainstream cultural view by the virulent narcissism of nouveau riche yuppies and the fragile gains of an increased black middle class, the ghetto has made a comeback at the scene of its defeat. The reinvention of American popular culture by young African American cultural artists is fueled by paradox: Now that they have escaped the fiercely imposed artistic ghetto that once suffocated the greatest achievements of their predecessors, black artists have reinvented the urban ghetto through a nationalist aesthetic strategy whose interpretative seam joins racial naturalism and romantic imagination. That the most recent phase of black nationalism is cultural rather than political suggests the extent to which the absorption of radical dissent into mainstream politics has been successful and expresses the hunger of black juvenile culture for the intellectual sources of its hypnotic and feral remix of pride and anger.

Mostly anger, and a little pride, stirs in the fragmented lives of teenager Dennis Brown (Lawrence Gilliard Jr.), his younger sister Carolyn (Barbara Sanon), and their parents Frankie (Ann D. Sanders) and Ray (George T. Odom). Each in his and her own way is the prisoner of an existential and ecological misery so great that its pervasive presence would suggest the impossibility of charting its affects and differentiating its impact across the spectra of gender and class within the community. In Rich's dark ghetto, it *appears* that all such difference is smothered by the lethal hopelessness spread thickly over the lives of its inhabitants in equally devastating portions.

But the exception to this apparently equally shaded misery is the extraordinarily acute misery of black men, seen first in the cinematic chiaroscuro of Ray's descent into a Dantean hell of racial agony so absurd and grotesque that its bleakness is a sadistic comfort, a last stop before absurdity turns to insanity. Ray's gradual decline is suffered stoically by Frankie, a doleful throwback to an earlier and dispiriting racial era when the black-woman-as-suffering-servant role was forced on black women by black men forced to pay obeisance to white society who, when they came home, expected to claim the rewards and privileges of masculinity denied them in the white world. The only other model lifted to black women consisted of an equally punishing (and mythic) black matriarchy that both damned and praised black women for an alleged strength of character absent in their feckless male counterparts. Thus, the logic of black communities ran: As the black man's fate goes, so goes the fate of the family.

Brooklyn's implicit narrative line ties generously into the fabric of this ideological argument, drawing its dramatic punch and denouement from the furious catastrophes that sweep down on its black male characters, the defining center of the film's raw meditation on the angst of emasculation. Ray's frequent beatings of

Frankie are rituals of self-immolation, her brutally bloodied countenance a tangential sign of his will to redefine the shape of his agony by redefining the shape of her face. Moreover, Ray's suffering-as-emasculation is further sealed by his denial of desire for white women during a Lear-like verbal jousting with an imaginary white man, a deus ex machina produced by his search for an explanation of his suffering and a dramatic ploy by Rich that ascribes black suffering to the omnipotent white bogeyman. And Dennis's out loud soliloquies in the presence of his girlfriend Shirley (Reana E. Drummond) about his quest for capital to reverse his family's collapse belies a deeper need to redeem black masculinity by displaying his virility, his goal to be the man that successfully provides for his family allied disastrously with his gratuitous desires to "get paid."

A different tack was pursued in John Singleton's *Boyz N the Hood*. Singleton's neorealist representation of the black working-class ghetto neighborhood provided a fluid background to his literate script, which condensed and recast the debates on black manhood that have filled the black American independent press for the last decade. Abjuring the heavy-handed approach of negative racial didacticism, Singleton retraced instead the lineaments of the morality play in recognizable black cultural form, richly alluding to black particularity while keeping his film focused on The Message: Black men must raise black boys if they are to become healthy black men. Thus Tre (Cuba Gooding Jr.), Ricky (Morris Chestnut), and Doughboy (Ice Cube), the three black males whose lives form the fabric of Singleton's narrative quilt, are the film's interpretative center, while Reva (Angela Bassett), Brenda Baker (Tyra Ferrell), and Brandi (Nia Long), the mothers of Tre, Ricky, and Doughboy, respectively, and Tre's girlfriend occupy its distant periphery. Singleton's film—as is the case with most cultural responses to black male crisis—is an attempt to answer Marvin Gaye's plea to save the babies, while focusing his lens specifically on the male baby that he and many others believe has been thrown out with the bath water to float up the river, like Doughboy and one out of four black men, into the waiting hands of the prison warden.

But Singleton's moral premise, like so many claims of black male suffering, rests dangerously on the shoulders of a ruinous racial triage: black male salvation at the expense of black female suffering, black male autonomy at the cost of black female subordination, black male dignity at the cost of black female infirmity. Once and for all, Singleton's film jarred into visibility the inadvertent yet unseemly alliance between black cultural nationalists and the cultured despisers of black women. His implicit swipe at black women ceded too much ideological territory and argued too little with white and black conservative social scientists who lament the demise of American culture because it is in the lethal embrace of welfare queens and promiscuous black women. The brilliant presence of Furious (the father of Tre, played by Larry Fishburne) as a redemptive and unswerving North Star, and Brenda's uncertain orbit as a dim satellite, offer the telling contrast in Singleton's cinematic world.

This premise would seem achingly anachronistic, the warmed up leftovers from black macho posturing painfully evident in '60s black nationalist discourse, were it not for its countless updates in the narrative strains of black juvenile culture, reified to patriarchal perfection in rap lyrics that denounce the racist dominance of white men while glorifying without irony black male material dominance and sexual mastery of black female life. Of course, the quest for black manhood is everywhere apparent in black culture; note its evocation as well in the upper climes of bourgeois respectability as the implicit backdrop to Clarence Thomas's claim of perfidy by Anita Hill, the innuendo of his charge only faintly arrested in the racial code of his undertone: another sister pulling a brother down. But it is with the reemergence of the ghetto in popular culture and its prominence in a revived black nationalist cultural politics, where, for better and worse, the images of black masculinity find a discursive home.

This is especially true of black film and rap music. The politics of cultural nationalism has reemerged precisely as the escalation of racist hostility has been redirected to poor black people. Given the crisis of black bourgeois political leadership, and a greater crisis of black liberal social imagination about the roots of black suffering, black nationalist politics reemerge as the logical means of remedy and resistance. Viewed against this backdrop, black film and rap music are the heightened imaginary of black popular culture, the self-announced apotheosis of a black populist aesthetic that occludes the seepage of authentic blackness into diluted cultural expression.

Rap music grew from its origins in New York's inner city over a decade ago as a musical outlet to creative cultural energies, and to contest the invisibility of the ghetto in mainstream American society. Rap remythologized New York's status as the spiritual center of black America, boldly asserting appropriation and splicing (not originality) as the artistic strategies by which the styles and sensibilities of black ghetto youth would gain popular influence. Rap developed as a relatively independent expression of black male artistic rebellion against the black bourgeois *Weltanschauung,* tapping instead into the cultural virtues and vices of the so-called underclass, romanticizing the ghetto as the fecund root of cultural identity and authenticity, the Rorschach of legitimate masculinity and racial unity.

The sensibilities afforded by the hip-hop aesthetic have found expression in many recent black films. *New Jack City,* for instance, is rife with the feral fusion of attitude and style as the replacement of substantive politics that prevails among young black males, especially those profiting from the underground political economy of crack. Similar to *Boyz N the Hood,* with Ice Cube (Doughboy) and *Juice,* with Tupac Shakur (Bishop), *New Jack City* appeals directly to the iconic surplus of hip-hop culture by drawing upon rapper Ice-T to convey the film's thinly supplied and poorly argued moral message: Crime doesn't pay.

Thus, Ice-T's "new jack cop" is an inside joke, a hip-hop reconfiguration of the tales of terror Ice-T explodes on wax as a lethal pimp, dope dealer, and bitch hater. The adoption of the interchangeable persona as the prerogative of mood and message in the culture of hip-hop is taken to its extreme with Ice-T's character: Even though he appears as a cop in *New Jack City,* his appearance on the sound track as a rapper detailing his exploits as a criminal blurs the moral distinctions between cops and robbers, criminalizes the redemptive intent of his film character (even more so retroactively in light of the recent controversy over his hit "Cop Killer" recorded with his speed metal band).

Director Mario Van Peebles's cinematic choices in *New Jack City* expose as well the vocabulary of overlarge and excessive cultural representation that characterized many ghetto films of old. Van Peebles's ghetto is a sinister and languid dungeon of human filth and greed drawn equally from cartoon and camp. The sheer artifice of *New Jack City*'s ghetto is meant to convey the inhuman consequences of living in this enclave of civic horror, but its overdrawn dimensions reveal its cinematic pedigree that can be traced more easily to '70s blaxploitation flicks than to the neorealist portrayal of carnage wreaked by the ghetto's bleak persistence presented in other recent black ghetto films.

As a black gangster film, *New Jack City* links its genre's appeal to the Cagneyization of black ghetto life, the inexorable force of women bashing and partner killing sweeping the hidden icon of the people to a visible position larger than life. Thus Nino Brown (Wesley Snipes) reigns because he tests the limits of the American Dream, a Horatio Alger in blackface who pulls himself up by forging consensus among his peers that his life is a ghetto jeremiad, a strident protest against the unjust limits imposed on black male material flourishing. As Nino intones with full awareness of the irony of his criminal vocation: "You got to rob to get rich in the Reagan era."

But it is the state of black male love that provides the story's unnarrated plot, its twisted pursuit ironically and tragically trumped by boys seeking to become men by killing each other. Thus, when a crying Nino embraces his teary-eyed closest friend and partner in crime, G-Money, on the top of the apartment building that provides the mise-en-scène for the proverbial ode to an empire gone, destroyed by the fatal winds of undisciplined ambition, Nino hugs G-Money tight, avowing his love even as he fills his belly with steel as recompense for G-Money's treacherous disloyalty. It is the tough love of the gang in action, the logic of vengeance passing as justice in gang love's final fulfillment of its unstated but agreed-upon obligations.

The mostly black and Latino gangs have also recaptured the focus of American social theory and journalism in the past decade. Urban sociologists such as New York's Terry Williams, in his important *Cocaine Kids,* and Los Angeles's Mike Davis, in *City of Quartz,* have written insightfully about the economic and social conditions that have led to the emergence of contemporary black and Latino gang culture, citing especially the yearning for love and social acceptance that animates such aggregation. And former-model-turned-journalist Leon Bing has interviewed Los Angeles gang members, who speak eloquently about their own lives in words as moving for their emotional directness as their honesty about the need for affection and comfort that drives them into mutual association. In *Straight Out of Brooklyn* and Ernest Dickerson's *Juice,* the theme of black male love in the ghetto filtered through the prism of gang or crew association looms large.

In *Brooklyn,* Rich presents a loosely associated group of three black male teens, including Dennis, Kevin (Mark Malone), and Larry (played by Rich), who are frustrated by poverty and the closure of personal and vocational horizons that lack of money has come to signify. Whereas in *Juice* the crushing consequences of capital's absence is more skillfully explored through the interactions between the characters—its damning effects as subtly evoked in the resonances of anger and gestures of surrender and regret weaved into the moral texture of the film's dialogue as they are dramatically revealed in the teens' action in the streets—in *Brooklyn,* money's power more crudely signifies in the lifeless representation of large material and sexual icons that dominate the landscape of dreams expressed by Dennis and his friends: big cars, more money, and mo' ho's.

The lifelessness of the ghetto is reified in the very textu(r)al construction through which the movie comes to us: Although it's in color, the film seems eerily black and white, its crude terms of representation established by its harsh video quality and its horizontal dialogue. Of course, the film's unavoidable amateur rawness is its premise of poignancy: After all, this is art imitating life, the searing vision of a nineteen-year-old Brooklyn youth, with little financial aid and the last-minute gift of film roll from Jonathan Demme (himself a renegade of sorts before his Hollywood breakthrough with the troubled *Silence of the Lambs),* committing his life to a film drawn partially from real-life events. This is the closest derivation in film of the guerrilla methods of hip-hop music culture, the sheer projection of will onto an artistic canvas constituted of the rudimentary elements of one's life in the guise of vision and message.

In *Brooklyn,* the triumvirate of teens is not a roving, menacing crew engaging in the business of selling crack rock and duplicating capitalism's excesses on their native terrain. Rather, they are forced by desperation to a momentary relief of their conditions by robbing a dope dealer, an impulse that is routinized and institutionalized in the crack gang, whose cannibalistic rituals of gunplay and murder feed on the lives of opponents out to seize their turf in the harrowing geopolitics of the drug economy.

The anomie and alienation produced by everyday forms of capitulation to despair, and the spiraling violence of Ray, force Dennis from his family to affectionate camaraderie with Larry and Kevin, and with Shirley. All other hints of family are absent, save Larry's barber uncle, who unwittingly provides the ill-named getaway car for their ill-fated heist. But the existential vacuum at home for Dennis is made more obvious by Ray's attempt to preserve the disappearing remnants of a "traditional" family, angrily reminding Dennis after he misses dinner that his empty plate on the table symbolizes his membership in the family. But Rich shatters this icon of familial preservation into shards of ironic judgment on the nuclear family, as Ray breaks the dishes and beats Frankie each time he becomes intoxicated.

Dennis's only relief is Shirley and his crew. When Shirley disappoints him by refusing to buy into his logic about escape from the ghetto by robbery, he turns to members of his crew, who in the final analysis leave Dennis to his own wits when they agree that they have stolen too much cash ("killing money," Kevin says) from the local dope dealer, an act whose consequences roll back on Dennis in bitter irony when the heist leads to his father's death. The film's dismal and inescapable conclusion is that black men cannot depend on each other, nor can they depend on their own dreams to find a way past their mutual destruction.

In *Juice,* the crew is more tightly organized than in *Brooklyn,* although their activity, like the teens from Red Hook, is not regularized primarily for economic profit. Their salient function is as a surrogate family, their substitute kinship formed around their protection of each other from rival gangs and the camaraderie and social support their association brings. But trouble penetrates the tightly webbed group when the gangster ambitions of Bishop threatens their equanimity. Of all the crew—leader Raheem (Khalil Kain), a teen father; Q (Omar Epps), a DJ with ambitions to refine his craft; and Steel (Jermaine Hopkins), a likable youth who is most notably "the follower"—Bishop is the one who wants to take them to the next level, to make them like the hard-core gangsters he watches on television.

Viewing Cagney's famed ending in *White Heat* and a news bulletin announcing the death of an acquaintance as he attempted armed robbery, Bishop rises to proclaim Cagney's and their friend's oneness, lauding their commendable bravado by taking their fate into their own hands and remaking the world on their own violent terms. Dickerson's aim here is transparent: to highlight the link between violence and criminality fostered in the collective American imagination by television, the consumption of images through a medium that has replaced the Constitution and the Declaration of Independence as the unifying fiction of national citizenship and identity. It is also the daily and exclusive occupation of Bishop's listless father, a reminder that television's genealogy of influence unfolds from its dulling effects in one generation to its creation of lethal desires in the next, twin strategies of destruction when applied in the black male ghetto.

Like the teens in *Brooklyn, Juice*'s crew must endure the fatal consequences of their failed attempt at getting paid and living large, two oft-repeated mantras of material abundance in the lexicon of hip-hop culture. After Bishop's determination to seize immortality by the throat leads him to kill without provocation or compunction the owner of the store they rob, the terms of his Faustian bargain are more clearly revealed when he kills Raheem, destroying all claims of brotherhood with a malicious act of willful machismo, succeeding to Raheem's throne by murderous acclamation.

Dickerson, who has beautifully photographed all of Spike Lee's films, uses darker hues than characteristic of his work with Lee, but nowhere near those of the drained colored canvas on which *Brooklyn* is drawn. Dickerson's moral strategy is to elaborate to its fatal ends the contradictory logic of the gang as a family unit, a faulty premise as far as he is concerned which overlooks the lack of moral constraints that ultimately do not work without destructive consequences. His aesthetic strategy is to move the cameras with the action from the observer's frame of reference, borrowing a few pages from Lee's book without mimicking

Lee's panache for decentering the observer through unusual angles and the fast pace of editing. Like Rich in *Brooklyn*, Dickerson wants the impact of his message to hit home, but he employs a less harsh method, a gentler but insistent drawing into his moral worldview, an invitation to view the spectacle of black male loss of love by degrees and effects.

In *Juice*, the ghetto working-class family is much more visible and vital than in *Brooklyn*. Mothers and fathers wake their children in the morning for breakfast and make certain they take their books to school. The extended family is even given a nice twist when Q fetches a gun from one of his mother's old friends, a small-time neighborhood supplier. And Dickerson draws attention subtly to the contrasts between the aesthetic and moral worldviews of the generations, and the thriving of an earlier era's values among the younger generation, at the dinner at Raheem's family's house after Raheem's funeral. As snatches of gospel music float gently through the house, Q and Steel pay their respects to Raheem's family.

When Bishop arrives, the rupture between generational values forces to the surface the grounds of choice upon which each of the remaining three crew must stand. Q and Steel are offended at Bishop's effrontery, his mean-spirited and near demented hypocrisy leading him to violate Raheem's sacred memory with this latest act born of unbridled machismo and hubris. For them, the choice is clear. The religious values signified in the quiet gospel music seem no longer foreign, gently providing a vivid counterpoint to the hip-hop aesthetic of violent metaphors in the service of greater self-expression.

Instead, the gospel music and the world of black respectability it symbolizes carry over into their grieving acknowledgment of the bonds between them and their departed friend, a sure sign of their surviving religious sensibilities bred from birth and inbred for life, no matter how distant they appear to be from its central effects. Bishop's traduction of Raheem's memory and family signify the depth of Bishop's moral failure, the unblinking abandon to which his wanton acts of violence have given portentous license. Unlike the black teens in *Brooklyn*'s ghetto, the black males can depend upon one another, but only after being forced to acknowledge their debts to the moral infrastructure given them by a predecessor racial culture, and only after discovering the limits of their freedom in destructive alliance with each other.

Unquestionably, the entire contemporary debate within black culture about black film and its relation to enabling or destructive representations of black males, and the consequences of the cinematic choices made about black females vis-à-vis these representations, started with the meteoric rise of Spike Lee, a key flashpoint in the resurgence of black nationalism in African American culture. With Lee's groundbreaking *She's Gotta Have It*, young black men laid hold of a cultural and artistic form—the Hollywood film—from which they had with rare exception been previously barred. By gaining access to film as directors, young black men began to seize interpretative and representational authority from ostensibly ignorant or insensitive cultural elites whose cinematic portrayals of blacks were contorted or hackneyed, the ridiculously bloated or painfully shriveled disfigurements of black life seen from outside of black culture. Lee's arrival promised a new day beyond stereotype.

What we get with Lee is Jungian archetype, frozen snapshots of moods in the black (male) psyche photographed to brilliant effect by Ernest Dickerson. Lee's mission to represent the variegated streams of black life denied cinematic conduits before his dramatic rise, has led him to resolve the complexity and ambiguity of black culture into rigid categories of being that hollow his characters' fierce and contradictory rumblings toward authentic humanity. And after *She's Gotta Have It*, black women became context clues to the exploration of black male rituals of social bonding *(School Daze)*, the negotiation of black male styles of social resistance *(Do the Right Thing)*, the expansion and pursuit of black male artistic ambitions *(Mo' Better Blues)*, and the resolution of black male penis politics *(Jungle Fever)*.

It was precisely Lee's cinematic representations of black male life that occasioned the sound and fury of proleptic criticism over his latest and most important project: his film biography of Malcolm X. Writer and social critic Amiri Baraka drew blood in a war of words with Lee, claiming that Lee's poor history of representing black men suggested that he would savage the memory of Malcolm X, a memory, by the way, to which Baraka presumed to have privileged access. This battle between the two diminutive firebrands, ironic for its poignant portrayal of the only logical outcome of the politics of more-black-nationalist-than-thou, a game Lee himself has played with relish on occasion, was but a foretaste of the warfare of interpretation waged in light of Lee's portrait of X.

Malcolm X is the reigning icon of black popular culture, his autobiography the Ur-text of contemporary black nationalism. His legacy is claimed by fiercely competing groups within black America, a fact certain to make Lee's film a hard sell to one faction or the other. More importantly, X's complex legacy is just now being opened to critical review and wider cultural scrutiny, and his hagiographers and haters will rush forward to have their say once again.

To many, however, Malcolm is black manhood squared, the unadulterated truth of white racism ever on his tongue, the black unity of black people ever on his agenda, the black people in ghetto pain ever on his mind. Thus, the films that represent the visual arm of black nationalism's revival bear somehow the burden of Malcolm X's implicit presence in every frame, his philosophy touching on every aspect of the issues the films frame—drugs, morality, religion, ghetto life, and especially, unrelentingly, the conditions of being a black man. For many, as for his eulogist Ossie Davis, Malcolm was the primordial, quintessential Real Man.

But, as with the films of Dickerson, Lee, Rich, Singleton, and Van Peebles, this spells real trouble for black women and for an enabling vision of black masculinity that moves beyond the worst traits of X's lethal sexism. Gestures of X's new attitude survive in the short hereafter Malcolm enjoyed upon his escape from Elijah Muhammad's ideological straitjacket. Malcolm's split from the Nation of

Islam demanded a powerful act of will and self-reinvention, an unsparing commitment to truth over habit. Lee's film reflects this Malcolm, though not in relation to his changed views about women. Although there are flashes of a subtly nuanced relationship between X and his wife Betty in Lee's film, as usual, Lee is silent on the complexities of black female identity.

Only when black films begin to be directed by black women, perhaps, will the wide range of identities that black women command be adequately represented on the large screen. Powerful gestures toward black feminist and female-centered film production exist in the work of Julie Dash in *Daughters of the Dust* and especially in Leslie Harris's *Just Another Girl on the IRT.* Less successful is John Singleton's flawed *Poetic Justice.* But until the collapse of the social, cultural, and economic barriers that prevent the flourishing of black female film, such works threaten to become exceptional, even novelty items in the black cultural imagination. In the meantime, black male directors remain preoccupied, even trapped, by the quest for an enabling conception of black male identity. But its full potential will continue to be hampered until they come to grips with the full meaning of black masculinity's relationship to, and coexistence with, black women.

PART ELEVEN

THE SOUL MUSICS OF BLACK FOLK

Black music is at the heart—some would argue, it is the heart—of black existence, providing rhythms of consolation and inspiration to the sometimes harsh, dispiriting experiences of a despised and troubled people. Gospel music expresses the spiritual genius of black survival, while soul music articulates the desire for freedom and black self-determination as the civil rights movement unfolded. Rhythm and blues has captured the gritty realities of secular black culture, while jazz music embodies the democratic yearnings and improvisational urges of black life. Hailing from Detroit, music of all sorts pulses through my blood, and I have taken special delight in writing about it as both a scholar and critic—and best of all, as a fan.

Twenty-Six

THE PROMISE AND PERILS OF CONTEMPORARY GOSPEL MUSIC

This chapter was first published in the New York Times *(1991) and probes the controversial rise of contemporary gospel music. I mention the work of the contemporary gospel groups the Winans brothers, Take Six, Commissioned, and the solo artist Tramaine Hawkins, before discussing at greater length the pioneering work of Edwin and Walter Hawkins, and the superb artistry of Be Be and Ce Ce Winans. Such controversies in the gospel music world in the late 1980s and early 1990s were glosses on earlier tensions present at the birth of gospel music when Thomas Dorsey introduced blues chords and jazz syncopations—as well as choir groups featuring women—into traditional black religious music in the 1920s. The irony is that even traditional gospel music was seen at its inception as a sacrilegious departure from the edifying quartet a capella singing of male groups. If I were to write this article today, not much would have to change, except the addition of contemporary gospel luminaries like Kirk Franklin, Donnie McClurkin, and the brightest star of all, Yolanda Adams.*

TRADITIONAL GOSPEL IS THE MUSIC OF mass choirs, ecstatic solos, and pounding, clapping rhythms. "Real gospel music is an intelligible sermon in song," says Harold Bailey, who led the Harold Bailey singers in the 1960s and 1970s. Throughout its history, this church music has influenced, and been influenced by, the popular music of its time.

Today's acts—like Be Be and Ce Ce Winans, Sounds of Blackness, Take Six, Commissioned, Tramaine Hawkins, and the Winans brothers—have added high-priced producers, up-tempo arrangements, and pop instrumentations to traditional gospel. Thus armed, they are gaining airplay on so-called contemporary urban radio, home otherwise to acts like Michael Jackson, Luther Vandross, Anita Baker, and C&C Music Factory. As gospel music gains new acceptance, it is once again moving away from its roots.

Nash Shaffer, host of a traditional gospel program on Chicago radio station WNDZ, is one of a number of gospel devotees who object to the recent popularization of the music. "The reason young people like contemporary gospel music is because of the rhythm and its secular appeal," says Shaffer, who is also the minister of music for the Vernon Park Church of God in Chicago. "The horns and the synthesizers override the message, and because of the instrumentation the message is vague and void. It gets lost in the beat and you end up having a shindig on Sunday morning."

One group Shaffer is concerned about is Be Be and Ce Ce Winans, whose phenomenal success started with a Grammy Award–winning debut album on Word Records. In 1988 they signed with a mainstream label, and their first album on the Capitol/Sparrow label, *Heaven,* was the second gospel record in history to go gold, after Aretha Franklin's success in 1972 with *Amazing Grace.* The current Winans album, *Different Lifestyles,* reached number one on the *Billboard* rhythm-and-blues charts, a first for gospel.

The new album is a curriculum of musical diversity—from rap and up-tempo rhythm-and-blues to a sample of a gospel shout. But it doesn't contain any purely traditional gospel. The single "I'll Take You There," which is at number seven on the rhythm-and-blues chart, is a remake of the Staple Singers, classic that allows the Winans to pay tribute to a seductive blend of 1970s gospel and pop. The album's first single, "Addictive Love," which went to number one on *Billboard*'s rhythm-and-blues chart, makes codependency with the divine a palatable proposition. "We were blessed with a record company that put dollars into our budget," says Ce Ce Winans, "so that we could come off sounding the way we feel gospel music should have sounded a long time ago."

The Winans help make visible the implicit sensuality of gospel music, a sometimes embarrassing gift that draws forth the repressed relationship between body and soul. The suggestive ambiguity of their art is expressed in their songs, many of which can be read as signs of romantic love and sensuous delight or as expressions of deep spiritual yearning and fulfillment. In "Depend on You," the Winans sing, "I never thought that I could ever need someone / The way that I have come to need you / Never dreamed I'd love someone / The way I've fallen in love with you."

Such lyrics are exactly the problem, according to the traditionalists. "Whereas traditional gospel music talks about the love of God," says Shaffer, "contemporary gospel music wants to make love *to* God." Lisa Collins, who writes about gospel music for *Billboard* magazine, says she receives calls from unhappy listeners when she plays a new hit by Be Be and Ce Ce Winans on *Inside Gospel,* her syndicated radio show. "We get numerous calls from listeners who think that there's not enough reference to Jesus," she says, "that their music has strayed too far from the church, that they water down the lyrics or that their music is playing to a secular crowd. But," she adds, "if you go to their concerts, there is no doubt that it is a ministry."

Ironically, traditional gospel music initially faced its own barriers within the church. It was an offspring of blues, jazz, and ragtime music born in the black Pentecostal churches at the end of the nineteenth century; early religious music consisted of barbershop quartet harmonies sung a capella by mostly male groups. A Chicago blues pianist named Thomas A. Dorsey forever changed black religious music in the 1920s by featuring women (and later men) singing in a choir tradition backed by piano accompaniments dipped in a blues base and sweetened by jazz riffs. Before the belated embrace of gospel music by mainline black churches in the 1940s, gospel thrived in mostly lower-class storefront Pentecostal churches, stigmatized as a sacrilegious mix of secular rhythms and spiritual lyrics.

Traditional gospel greats, including the late Clara Ward, Marion Williams, Roberta Martin, and Inez Andrews, took the exploration of jazz and blues further. These artists harnessed the seductive beats of jazz to gospel's vibrant harmonies and percolating rhythms, and transformed the anguished wails of the blues into holy shouts brimming with deferred joy. Performers as varied as Ray Charles, Aretha Franklin, and James Brown started out singing gospel, and the music can be said to have spawned rhythm-and-blues, soul, and funk. Gospel music gained wide popular acceptance with Clara Ward's appearance at the Newport Jazz Festival in 1957 and with the incomparable Mahalia Jackson's numerous concerts at Carnegie Hall in the late 1950s and early 1960s. (Clara Ward, in fact, was criticized in the 1960s for singing gospel music in Las Vegas.)

But gospel music's real transformation into a popular and contemporary musical art form was quietly affected by Edwin Hawkins's 1969 rhythm-and-blues-influenced arrangement of the traditional Baptist hymn, "Oh, Happy Day." The groundbreaking song was captured on a two-track recorder in the basement of a California Pentecostal church and was performed by the North California State Youth Choir, eventually selling more than 2 million copies. Edwin Hawkins's feat prepared the way for two divergent but occasionally connected developments in contemporary gospel music.

On the one hand, artists like Andrae Crouch and Hawkins's younger brother Walter experimented with gospel within the boundaries of the religious world. Their work was performed in church concerts and secular music halls to a largely religious audience. Their appeal was primarily defined by young black Christians seeking to maintain their religious identity. On the other hand, Edwin Hawkins's success also broke ground for groups like the Staple Singers, who performed primarily in secular musical arenas and whose themes and sound were adapted to popular culture sensibilities and recast as "message music." Thus, instead of the traditional gospel themes of God's love, grace, and mercy, the Staple Singers sang about redemptive community and self-respect.

On their 1971 reggae-influenced number one soul and pop song, "I'll Take You There," they claimed: "I know a place / Ain't nobody cryin' / Ain't nobody worried / Ain't no smilin' faces / Lyin' to the races / I'll take you there." And on their number two song, "Respect Yourself," from the same album, *BeAltitude: Respect Yourself,* they sang: "If you disrespect everybody that you run into / How in the world do you think anybody 'sposed to respect you? / Respect yourself." Their recordings from the 1970s showcase three crucial features of contemporary gospel: significant radio play on nonreligious formats, the broad use of pop music conventions to explore their musical ideas, and, at best, oblique references to divinity or God.

In the last few years, black gospel music also inspired a group of white religiously oriented singers like Amy Grant and Michael W. Smith, who are considered contemporary Christian musicians. (The dividing line between black gospel and contemporary Christian music is primarily racial, although black artists like Be Be and Ce Ce Winans, Take Six, and Larnelle Harris also show up on the contemporary Christian charts.) Traditional gospel music has never been completely comfortable with its parentage of black secular music. In the early parts of this century, frequenting nightclubs, blues bars, and dance halls was considered un-Christian and was forbidden. And there are still those who feel that the secular world should be kept out of the church. Harold Bailey, who is now the director of Probation Challenge, an organization that works with former prisoners in Chicago, says, "When we speak in terms of contemporary we are speaking of something temporary, of the moment, which is contrary to scripture. Those who want to rock will inevitably roll into hell."

The sound of contemporary gospel, many devotees of traditional gospel say, is indistinguishable from new jack swing or technofunk, and it thrives on postmodern instrumentation, contemporary pop grooves, and religiously ambiguous lyrics. Some contemporary gospel, in fact, is called new jack gospel: Teddy Riley, who most recently produced Michael Jackson's *Dangerous*, also helped produce the Winans brothers' album, *The Return;* and among contemporary gospel artists are rappers like Mike E.

But a gnawing skepticism about the church's ability to address contemporary cultural issues, coupled with a steep decline in church membership, may modify the hard line taken by traditional religionists. Contemporary gospel music is helping the uninitiated to discover, and the committed to remember, the church. One contemporary gospel artist, Tramaine Hawkins, who was heavily criticized when her single "Fall Down" was played in discos, says that the song "opened up some real avenues of ministry" and brought listeners to more traditional gospel artists like Shirley Caesar. "I tried contemporary gospel," confesses Caesar, "but it didn't work for me." She believes that she is part of a venerable tradition to which all gospel artists must return. "I'm part of the 'be' crowd," she explains. "I'll *be* here when they leave, and I'll *be* here when they come back."

Ce Ce Winans says that contemporary gospel brings a wider audience to the gospel message through high production values. "Being able to be played on mainstream radio without having any less quality than mainstream artists is important," she says. Without serious record company support, she says, great gospel singers of the past were deprived of a wide audience. For all its controversy, contemporary gospel music continues to evolve and inspire. Groups like Take Six, which mixes a capella jazz with gospel themes, and the Sounds of Blackness—produced by Jam and Lewis and presently touring with Luther Vandross—prove that contemporary gospel is an art form as malleable as it is durable and innovative. And as contemporary gospel music continues to provide inspiration to its religious adherents and musical delight to all appreciative listeners, it preserves and extends the classic functions of traditional gospel music.

Twenty-Seven

MARIAH CAREY AND "AUTHENTIC" BLACK MUSIC

When Mariah Carey emerged as a musical superstar in the early 1990s, a great deal of attention was paid not only to her pipes but to her genes as well. As a biracial woman, Carey evoked ancient racial tensions in a culture that embraced her music even as it struggled to reconcile her identity to her artistry. After all, our country is obsessed with racial pedigree and purity. This essay, which first appeared in the New York Times *in 1994, traces the racial tensions around Carey's racial identity, and takes the occasion of her* Music Box *album's ascent to the top of the charts to reflect on how we characterize "black" and "white" music. Interestingly, once Carey divorced husband and music mogul Tommy Mottola (who most recently gained notoriety for being called "racist and very, very, very devilish" by Michael Jackson), she became more radically identified with the black music she loves, especially the hip-hop culture from which she had been carefully steered away in her early career.*

AT ITS BEST, POP MUSIC PRESSES AN ANXIOUS ear to American society, amplifying our deepest desires and fears. At times, too, pop music almost unconsciously invites us to listen to ourselves in ways forbidden by cultural debates where complexity is sacrificed for certainty. In this vein, the re-ascent to the top of the charts of Mariah Carey's most recent album, *Music Box,* signals more than her musical dominance.

One source of Carey's significance—and undoubtedly the sharpest controversy around her—has nothing to do with the singer's gargantuan musical gifts. Instead it derives from the confusion and discomfort that her multiracial identity provokes in an American culture obsessed with race. Though she has made no secret that she is biracial (her mother is white, her father a black Venezuelan), Carey's candor evokes clashing responses from fans and critics. Some see her statement of mixed heritage as a refusal to bow to public pressure to choose whether she is black or white. But in light of the "one drop" rule—where a person is considered black by virtue of having one drop of black blood, a holdover from America's racist past—many conclude that the issue of racial identity, for Carey and other interracial people, is settled.

To make matters more complex, Carey's vocal style is firmly rooted in black culture. It features a soaring soprano and an alternately ethereal and growling melisma that pirouettes around gospel-tight harmonies. So if she's not clearly black yet sings in a black style, is she singing black music? And what difference does it make? Without even trying, Carey's music sparks reflections about how race continues to shape what we see and hear.

Partly what's at stake is the messy, sometimes arbitrary, politics of definition and categorization. What makes music "black music" and who can be said to legitimately perform it? Consider the fiery fusion of rock, soul, and blues performed by Lenny Kravitz (like Carey, the child of an interracial marriage) and Terrence Trent D'Arby, or the socially conscious hard rock of the group Living Color. Is theirs black music? Though the answer is often negative, the roots of their music can be traced to black cultural influences, from Howlin' Wolf to Jimi Hendrix. The difficulty of fixing labels on what D'Arby, Kravitz, and Living Color do highlights the racial contradictions at the center of contemporary popular music.

Behind this painful, often protracted struggle to get at the "original article" is what can only be termed the anxiety of authenticity. Such quests are more than academic for black folk because of the history of appropriation and abuse of black musical styles by white performers and producers. While black artists like King Oliver and Chuck Berry initiated musical innovations from jazz to blues–based rock and roll, the public recognition and economic benefits due them evaporated, while derivative white artists like Benny Goodman and Elvis Presley reaped huge artistic and financial rewards.

Curiously enough, the debate over authenticity lies at the heart of hip-hop, though irreverence and transgression are staples of rap culture. But authenticity, even in a genre as closely identified with black culture as rap, does not strictly follow the rules of race. For instance, while the white rapper Vanilla Ice was greeted within hip-hop with derision because he came off as a white boy trying to sound black, white rap groups like Third Bass and House of Pain have been enthusiastically embraced because of their "legitimate" sounds and themes. Conversely, black rap artists like Hammer and the Fresh Prince have been widely viewed as sellouts because of their music's pop propensities.

An even thornier issue is the belief in black communities that some artists obscure their racial roots in a natural but lamentable response to a racist environment. As a result, they benefit from being black (given the extraordinary popularity of black music) but do not identify with the black people who support them before they discover a crossover market. In the extreme, this circumstance leads to the ideal of the pan-ethnic, omni-racial artist; an exotic fantasy whose energy derives from an implicit denial of the inherent value of simply being black. While Carey has been scrupulous at award ceremonies to thank her black fans, and to mention her black father in interviews, artists like Paula Abdul (a self-described "Syrian-Brazilian-Canadian-American" who first gained public notice as a "black" cheerleader/choreographer for the Los Angeles Lakers) have increasingly underplayed their black heritage.

Still, as the old saying goes, the finger pointed at artists implies several others pointed back at ourselves. American culture is painfully redefining itself through bitter debates about "identity politics," "multiculturalism," and "universalism." Music cannot be naively expected to triumph over social differences. Because of the schmaltz that often passes for conscience in pop, the dream of transcendence—whether of race, or for that matter, of sex and class—is often hindered by sappy appeals to brotherhood and oneness. What such impulses reflect is a desire to fix what has gone wrong in a culture intolerant of difference.

The anxiety of authenticity about what and who is really black in pop music is proportional to just how increasingly difficult it is to know the answer. As multiracial unions of sex and sound proliferate, the "one drop" rule may lose its power. And, as cultural theorists are now proud to announce, race is not merely a matter of biology but an artifice of cultural convention. Such a construction is often used to establish and reinforce the power of one group over another. This view does not mean that black music is solely the product of perception. Nor does it mean that black music's power must be diluted to a generic form. What it does suggest, however, is that the meaning of race, like the art it molds, is always changing.

In the end, what Carey's career may teach us is that paranoia about purity is the real enemy of black cultural expression, which at its best is characterized by the amalgamation of radically different elements. Creolization, syncretism, and hybridization are black culture's hallmarks. It is precisely in stitching together various fabrics of human and artistic experience that black musical artists have expressed their genius.

Twenty-Eight

ARETHA FRANKLIN, VANESSA BELL ARMSTRONG, AND ME

This is my ode to two of the greatest voices of the twentieth century. As it happens, both hail from my hometown, giving them even greater resonance in my world. While Queen of Soul Aretha Franklin has rightfully been crowned a Hegelian world-historical genius of black sound, gospel great Vanessa Bell Armstrong, another Detroit sonic marvel, deserves far wider recognition. I first heard Aretha Franklin's voice as a youth who, besides reading, listened to the radio to connect me to the broader world. Since the transistor trumped the tube for me, Aretha's voice was the sound track to my burgeoning adolescence. Her wails, shrieks, moans, and piercing cries urged me to see the depth and range of female emotion— and to accept its moral authority. In this essay, I recall in detail how I first came across Vanessa Bell Armstrong's throbbing, pulsing gift, and how I treasured its regal unleashing before my very eyes and ears on foreign shores. This chapter from Why I Love Black Women *was a sheer pleasure to write. It embodies my profound appreciation for how the voices of black women have rung clearly in my head to guide my path to manhood.*

"LISTEN BROTHER, YOU'VE GOT TO COME OVER HERE RIGHT NOW," my friend and fellow church member James Pippin excitedly demanded after I answered the phone.

"What's wrong, Pip?" I anxiously replied. "You all right?"

"Man, I've got a copy of an album by a gospel singer who's gonna give Aretha a run for her money," Pippin goaded me. He knew Aretha Franklin, the Queen of Soul, was revered in my heart and that her pretty tones and thrilling shrieks often vibrated the walls of my small apartment. I didn't have to tell him that to me his egregious comparison was sacrilegious.

"Look, bro, you don't have to get all hyperbolic," I defensively responded. "If you want me to come over, man, just say so. I'll see you as soon as I can get there."

"Oh, by the way, she's from Detroit." He got in a final tease, chuckling as he clicked the receiver to its base.

Pippin was double-dipping in disaster. First, he had the nerve to challenge the Queen's throne. And if that wasn't bad enough, he attempted to exploit my native passions by pitting one homegirl against the next, and worse yet, a seasoned veteran—no, the reigning champion—against an untested newcomer. Nevertheless,

I hopped into my wife's white mustang and made my way to Pippin's house. On the long drive over, I couldn't help but think of how big a presence Aretha had been in my life, how her voice had hovered over me and marked every stage of my transition from boy to man.

To the world beyond the church, Aretha's freakish precocity seemed to emerge fully formed from obscure origins in the Detroit neighborhood where her father, C. L. Franklin, a noted preacher, brought her up. In fact, it was in Rev. Franklin's legendary rhetorical womb that Aretha gestated before hatching her monumental talent. As a bronze gospel wunderkind, Aretha's gift poured out in a theological prescience so striking that her father, a past master himself of the far-flung ecstasies and esoteric vibrations of the black voice, must have felt that a double portion of the Spirit, *his* spirit, had fallen on his woman-child. One can hear fourteen-year-old Aretha on her first gospel recording declaring with unforced believability that she was heading to a place where she would "Never Grow Old." Like all great artists, Aretha was not so much speaking to us as speaking for us, at least for the fortunate phalanx gathered at her father's New Bethel Baptist Church where the recording took place. In Aretha's mouth, the gospel standard temporarily dissolved its yearning for a distant heaven and seized her youthful form to embody its promise *right now*.

My love for Aretha was inherited from my mother, who frequented New Bethel when she arrived in Detroit from the South. Rev. C. L. Franklin was a "down-home" preacher, a lionized pulpiteer whose homilies spread over seventy-six recordings that found wide circulation in black communities throughout the nation. Ironically, I had to go all the way to the country—to the Alabama farm of my grandparents on which my mother was reared and where she picked cotton—to hear for the first time the oratorical wizardry of a Detroit icon. I listened raptly and repeatedly to Franklin's rhetorical gifts churning through my grandfather's archaic portable record player. He possessed a powerful voice with a remarkably wide range. Franklin could effortlessly ascend to his upper register to squeal and squall. He was equally capable of descending to a more moderate vocal hum and pitch, and then, at a moment's notice, he could recompose in dramatic whisper. The velocity of his speech was no less impressive, too. Franklin was the greatest exemplar of "whooping," or the "chanted sermon," where ministers coarsen their articulation, deliberately and skillfully stress their vocal cords, and transition from spoken word to melodious speech. He was the shining emblem of folk poetry shaped in the mouth of a minister whose mind was spry and keen. Franklin's style rarely undercut his substance.

Mama said that often, after Franklin finished his sermons, Aretha would rise and escalate the spirit to even more frenzied highs. Years later, after searching for a style to accommodate the magnitude of her art, Aretha would do the same in the secular realm. She carried into the universe beyond revival tents and sanctuary walls a religious passion for worldly subjects, among them the flourishing and failure of love affairs, and the pleasures of the senses. When Aretha switched from gospel to rhythm and blues, she followed a path carved by such luminaries as Ray

Charles and Sam Cooke. Because of their struggles, she didn't have to confront the same degree of reproach they had endured. But she encountered her share of resentment and anger among the faithful who believed that she had betrayed her first love and highest calling. These same folk didn't understand that when Aretha turned Otis Redding's song "Respect" into a quasi-feminist manifesto, she was, intentionally or not, signifying on the lack of regard she faced as a woman in all her homes, secular and sacred. While women largely filled its gospel choirs and sanctuary seats, the church remained, in its powers, discretions, and privileges, a man's world. Of course, so was the world outside the church, but at least women didn't lose their dignity or self-worth by being asked to believe that God made it so.

Not even Aretha's successful reentries into the gospel world of her youth, one in 1972, the other fifteen years later, have completely silenced the displeasure with her defection among those old enough to remember it. Since her departure, there has been an unspoken search for the next Aretha, for a successor who would stay the course and sing only for the Lord. Neither would her critics be mollified by C. L. Franklin's adroitly defensive claim on Aretha's 1972 gospel album, *Amazing Grace*, that his daughter "never really left the church."

I kept this debate in mind as I pulled up to Pippin's brick house. Pippin and I had weathered some hard times under the same umbrella. I had come to Knoxville in 1979 to begin my freshman year at Knoxville College, a month shy of my twenty-first birthday. As a newly minted minister, I sought out a church home where I could stimulate my faith and exercise my gifts, and I landed at the Mount Zion Baptist Church. Pippin, an older, wiser big brother, often gave me a lift to church since he worked nearby as a manager and disc jockey at a tiny radio station. He also occasionally played percussions in a local combo.

Still, we were both poor. I preached wherever and whenever I could. Pippin worked his various gigs to better financial effect, but it didn't take much to top the $50 I received on a good day for a guest sermon. We often dined at "all-you-can-eat" buffets, going in early, eating late breakfasts and early lunches, then remaining to read papers and shoot the bull until we got hungry again for supper. Pippin also shared with me promotional copies of forthcoming albums and tapes that he received at the radio station. That's how he came across this vaunted Aretha successor.

"Come on in, man," Pippin greeted me at the door. "Gerri took the baby to visit Mother Rosalyn, so we've got the house to ourselves."

Gerri was Pip's wife and a fantastic gospel singer and pianist in her own right. Before I'd gotten married for the second time, Gerri, Pip, and I hung out regularly, and she agreeably joined in many of our shenanigans.

"Now who's this singer you want me to hear?" I quizzed Pippin as I rested my coat but not my questions. "Is she Baptist or Pentecostal? What church did she attend? If she's so bad, how come I ain't never heard of her, and I'm from Detroit?"

"Take a chill pill and cool out, bro," Pippin calmly deflected my hazing. "I'm gonna play her for you right now. I guarantee you that you'll be blown away."

I suppose if Pippin's discovery had taken place in our more sophisticated technological era—a quick download and file sharing over the Internet—the mystery could have been quickly solved. Back then, in 1984, in a failed Orwellian future, we had to do it the old-fashioned way: stand before "The Stereo" and place the stylus over the rotating, compressed wax and allow the analog vibrations to brush across our soundscape and through our nearly busted woofers and tweeters.

As the familiar crackles and snaps surged through the speakers, and the needle rapidly unraveled the tightly configured lines on the album's black face—and no matter how expertly you cleaned your vinyl disc it was bound to emit faint noises from a sharp object impressing a moving, flat surface—the turntable gyrated the first few seconds of Pippin's latest find. I was unimpressed. It started with the synthesized sound of rushing wind. It was quickly followed by four strident, graduated chords hammered by a cheesy synthesizer, underwritten by a scaling piano smothered in the faux-symphonic bluster of organ and chimes. A hokey effect from an amateur outfit, I glibly, caustically concluded. I was slouched in my chair.

Then her voice broke in.

"Master," she began in an understated, clear alto declaration, delaying her next words so we could fix our minds on the meaning of her lyrics as the piano pounded out her deliberate pace. "The *temp-ehhhhhhhhhest is* ray-ging." Now I had straightened my posture and leaned in as if to grab every syllable as it spilled through the thinly wired netting of Pippin's stereo speakers. My delighted host was grinning like a Cheshire cat. The singer slid up the word "tempest" like a plane effortlessly gliding into air, except she met self-induced sonic turbulence halfway through. But she navigated her voice expertly amidst the deliberate gruffness she evoked to stress the storm she was singing about. When she phrased "tempest" as she did, she was skillfully performing what might be termed vernacular onomatopoeia. Her volcanic melisma dissolved peacefully into "raging"—an irony, to be sure, as she contrasted, even opposed, the stormy condition she described by drawing her voice back, at least for the present, into a serenely reassuring soprano. I was intrigued. After singing about the billows tossing high in a steady voice, she got guttural and let loose a minor vocal eruption as she raced up the scale in quaking glissando, telling us the sky was "oh-oh-h-hh-vershadow-w-w-w-ed with black-ness," with "black-ness" crisply and succinctly articulated.

On and on it went, as the singer unleashed growling, groaning, lacerating syllables in wild succession, occasionally stopping on a dime to accentuate the inherent drama of her subject with an equally theatrical delivery. Okay, I thought, maybe she has some Aretha-like ways, but I wasn't yet convinced she could hang with the Queen. That is, until the middle of the song. She gave voice to a series of otherworldly ejaculations that in their sheer force seemed to bend back the cast-iron sleeves on Pippin's radiator. She built slowly to a pattern of repeating, swelling crescendos that only intermittently resolved in sweetly whispered affirmations of God's peace in the midst of the storm. She rained down such ferocious assurances of divine intervention, that the storm from which she promised God's protection seemed my only refuge.

There was no room in Pippin's house to hide from her voice, no spot untouched by her vibrations, no plane unaffected by her seismic emissions, no space uninhabited by her shaking, shouting, shivering, shearing sound. She unleashed an eviscerating orchestration of notes to proclaim Jesus as "the Master, I'm talkin' 'bout the Mas-turhhh"—and mind you, she's wailing at the tip-top of her surging soprano—"of erher-herrrrrth and sky." She wasn't finished. "You see"—and in the background, the choir in staccato affirmation picks up her cue and chants "the oh-cean," before she picks back up and finishes the thought—"ohhhhhhhhohhhhhhohhh so sweet-lay, obey, they gonna obey, thy we-ee-ill." I was all but done. She had led me to the highest point of her shattering articulation and suddenly, precipitously dropped me off a cliff of cascading sound into an ocean of humming tranquility. I could only slump in my seat and let her soothing, hushing, calming benediction roll over me as she and her choir called antiphonally for "pee-e-e-eee-e-e-eee-e-e-e-uh-yeece." For the next thirty or so minutes, I was thrilled and thrashed by the merciless wave of sounds that alternately tiptoed and tore from Pippin's speakers. In that time, I met Aretha's sonic daughter, her gospel twin. It wasn't that their voices were necessarily the same in construction—although they shared similarities of tone, pitch, and style at points. But they were identical in effect, since both possessed a mesmerizing, tantalizing, enthralling gift that demanded notice.

I had no idea as I sat in Pippin's house, transfixed by a voice that I didn't believe could exist—and perhaps, didn't believe *should* exist—that six years later I would meet its owner as we journeyed together to London with Jesse Jackson. Like me, Jackson had heard that voice and was immediately smitten. He invited me into his office one day early in 1990—I was working with him on his autobiography—and he enthusiastically located a track on a gospel compact disc he had just received.

"Listen to this, Reverend, and tell me she ain't awesome," Jackson elatedly beseeched me. As soon as I heard her voice—that voice—I smiled.

"Yeah, she's incredible, amazing, Rev," I replied. "I've played all three of her albums to death."

I didn't tell him the story of how we'd met, that voice and me, years earlier in Pippin's house. But I told her when we enjoyed downtime in England. We'd gone there with Jackson—me as his shadow amanuensis, she as his soloist, as he talked and preached his way around London—to help celebrate Mandela's release from prison, and to join in his campaign to keep the pressure on South Africa to end apartheid through sanctions from the world community. Toward that end, Jackson would meet with the Mandelas at the London home of deposed African National Congress leader Oliver Tambo, attend the Wembley Stadium concert for the recently released hero, and, well, just be Jesse Jackson. And that meant that Jackson would give sermons and speeches to galvanize international support for South African freedom and black self-determination.

When Jackson preached, she sang, and amazed the folk. She belted out gospel ballads and gospel blues, reveling in contemporary and traditional, soulful and jazzy, and even hipper, up-to-date songs dipped in the aesthetic fashions of black pop music. She even wowed the rapturously raucous black crowd in Brixton, so much so that Winnie Mandela grabbed her backstage and lifted her clean off the ground, no mean feat in light of the singer's compact, substantial frame. And I remember thinking that as much as I admired Mrs. Mandela, she wasn't a woman I'd ever want to tangle with.

Back at our hotel, I regaled the singer with the story of how I'd first heard her, and how utterly powerful and riveting an occasion it had been. A wide, beautiful smile broke across her attractive brown-doll face, set off by intense button eyes, apple-red cheeks, and framed by lush, layered, reddish brown hair. She was cute as pie and twice as sweet.

I reached into my garment bag and retrieved a copy of her first album, *Peace Be Still,* the one that Pippin had snagged me with, which she happily signed for me, ending with a common valedictory that still touched me deeply, "Love, Vanessa Bell Armstrong."

Twenty-Nine

THE GREAT NEXT: JAZZ ORIGINS
AND THE ANATOMY OF IMPROVISATION

This interview, conducted by talented directors Maria Agui Carter and Calvin A. Lindsay Jr., was originally videotaped for a 1999 PBS hour-long documentary the pair directed, "The Devil's Music." Their documentary was one installment of a four-part series on transgressive art entitled Culture Shock. *"The Devil's Music" addresses the evolution of jazz in the '20s as a demonized musical genre to its worldwide celebration today as America's only genuine art form. Since I am usually asked to speak about hip-hop and rhythm and blues, it was a marvelous aesthetic departure for me. This interview permitted me to speak at length about the origins and expressions of a music I have loved for a long time. Since most of what I had to say met the cutting-room floor (how else could it be for an interview that was longer than the documentary itself?), it was a real treat when I got the chance to publish the entire interview—the equivalent of a jazz jam session between me and my interlocutors—in* Open Mike.

How did the music achieve and get assigned such lofty goals?

When you think about 1920s jazz music, you think about what led up to it. The formative period of jazz is from around 1895 till about 1905, 1910. Ragtime was big then. The music was so named because of the ragged time, the syncopated rhythmic structures, that African-inspired musicians were playing against more nonsyncopated, linear, tonal-based, harmonic European music. Musically speaking, jazz evolved out of ragtime with the assertion of the sensibilities of African communal spirits and syncopated rhythmic orders against the more regimented order of Western music. Aesthetically speaking, high society music, the music of civil and polite society performed in the chambers of the elite, was the established canon, the established norm against which all other music was judged and compared.

When ragtime came along with its raggedy, nonconventional, syncopated rhythms against the nonsyncopated, linear conceptions of music in the Western canon, it created a real rub. But I think part of the controversy erupted in response to the function of the music itself. Musicians handed out cards in New Orleans, especially in the 1920s, which had printed on them "music for all occasions." So the social contexts and geographical spaces to which the music was consigned determined its function. If you're playing in parades and picnics and funerals and Mardi Gras, the music is much more lively and syncopated and fit for those situations. But if the music is played in a limited, intimate space, the music has a different sensibility. Even the popular dances of the 1920s reflected the influence of space on aesthetics. For instance, in polite society they danced the quadrille, the mazurka, the waltz, and the polka in association with chamber music. But when there were open spaces and markedly vibrant dance halls, all characteristic of the sites of "the folk," the dances were the slow drag, the eagle rock, and the buzzard lope. All in all, the music and dance outside "official" society—and music and dance were intimately connected—reflected the infusion of African aesthetic values by means of New Orleans Creoles.

A quote: "Beware of a change to a strange form of music, taking it to be a danger to the whole, but never have the ways of music moved without the greatest political laws being moved." That's Plato's *Republic*.

Well, there's no question that the high purpose of music was captured in William Congreve's phrase: "Music hath charms to sooth a savage breast." It has been widely, and wrongly, quoted as saying "the savage beast," which appears on the surface at least to be redundant. In any case, music from either perspective is a modifying element with a modulating effect: It brings sensibility and order to chaos. Those musical forms that reflect chaos are seen to be, from a hegemonic, elite perspective, unworthy of recognition or respect. In fact, they don't count as music at all. The aesthetic value of these nonmusical, chaotic forms—the frenzy of ragtime, the frenzy of jazz—reflected in part the chaos of the social circumstances faced by its artists, including Creole musicians losing their jobs downtown, where they were playing European-inspired music in New Orleans, to go uptown, where they had interactions with these more indigenous Negro populations. That meant that there was some kind of fusion going on, and therefore the musical and aesthetic values of the musicians were being "corrupted," so that the "high" and redemptive purposes of the music—to regulate the savage—was compromised by the influence of the very forms of chaos that the music sought to relieve.

The perception of music's purpose is always indivisible, I think, from the political and social contexts through which folk, including critics, interpret the music. Remember in, I think, 1918, the *Times-Picayune*, the newspaper in the birthplace of jazz, New Orleans, the Crescent City, argued against the uncivil-like behaviors of musicians, as well as the uncivil character of the music. "This is not music that is fit for polite society," they opined, and I'm paraphrasing here. "As a result, we should suppress it." So musically speaking, the aesthetic representation of the Western conception of music, with melody and harmony and thematic resolution and tonal structure and so on, was juxtaposed in the minds of the cultural elite to musical forms that fell outside of the realm of music's purpose, or, in keeping with the Greek philosophy of your quote, its telos. The rhythmic intensity of African music, emerging from racially subordinated communities, subverted the telos, the goal of music as determined by dominant society, resulting in a huge bifurcation of musical priorities and aesthetic choices. For the dominant, elite society, music facilitated the rituals of intimate social interaction in close quarters. For the masses, music accompanied big social events that facilitated a sense of social cohesion and personal agency in chaotic and conflicted social circumstances. Now that bifurcation, like all dualities, isn't pure, since social phenomena are fluid and complex, but I think it's a functional definition of the social and aesthetic tensions that prevailed.

From a social place, what is being said?

Well, in a sense, I think we can look at what was happening in New Orleans at the time, from the late 1890s to about 1915 or 1920, as a precursor to the culture wars that are now going on as we debate the differences between Eurocentrism, Afrocentrism, multicentrism, multiculturalism, and the like. There were racial forces behind distinctions between European music and so-called non-European, or African-inspired, music. Those distinctions were really about racial caste, about keeping Negroes in their place, and about assigning less merit to African cultural products and forms of music than to European ones. The irony, of course, is that white musicians later appropriated African forms of music. The first jazz recording, which appeared in 1917 from the Original Dixieland Band, was a whitened and diluted and domesticated version of African-inspired black music. If it wasn't quite rhythmically challenged, it was certainly a watered-down version of black music rendered palatable to a wider, whiter American audience.

The racial distinction between European and African music was sometimes coded as the differentiation between what's good and bad music, what's productive and nonproductive music, and what's edifying and what's debased music. Folk were trying to figure out the place of African people in American culture, and the arguments over music were key to the process. So the aesthetics were politicized. The question of what to do with ragtime, and then blues, jazz, and gospel, was never simply a matter of taste, or should I say, that taste was never merely a matter of musical preference extracted from the prevailing racial context. Syncopation indexed race as surely as black skin. Plus, the caste question was never far away, since these ragtime musicians were not often educated musicians who had absorbed the finer points of European music. Their musical trace had to be washed away from the palette of American music, which was little more than an imitation of the so-called classical forms flowing in from Europe. The kick is that across the waters, European classical musicians and composers are digging this indigenous American music being created by mostly black musicians of an ostensibly degraded and inferior pedigree. Figures like Debussy and Stravinsky, and even Charles Ives, are being influenced by ragtime, even as the aesthetic guardians of Western culture are dissing ragtime.

Struggles over music were about social regulation because music was the front line of breaking down racial barriers. Later in the twentieth century, black musicians would play a crucial role in brokering an acceptance of African Americans, limited though it was, within the regime of American apartheid in the South, where segregation ruled. It sounds trite to say but black music, to a degree, united peoples of different races and genders and cultures in this kind of polyphonic expression of African sensibility. But they had to fight through the social stigma attached to blackness, even though, interestingly enough, in New Orleans, jazz music is also being created by Creoles. I think James Lincoln Collier, the jazz critic, has read this entirely wrong. He says because those musicians were Creoles, they weren't black, and therefore we can't claim that jazz music has black origins. But as Mike Tyson might say, that's ludicrous. Such an argument as Collier advances denies the complexity of race, how it is not simply a biological fact but a socially determined identity. The notion that jazz is not a "black" music because it was created by Creoles not only is a reflection of phenotypical literalism but ignores the politics and history of racial identity in America. A crucial feature of the American racial contract has involved the thorny question of interracial or mixed race identity, or what is anthropologically and sociologically termed miscegenation.

That debate has been renewed recently with the rise of Tiger Woods to prominence in golf. Is Tiger black or Thai, or both, and how do we talk about being both and hence not exclusively either, and how does that nuance our comprehension of racial identity? Contemporary debates about miscegenation were precipitated by the sorts of arguments around race and music that occurred in the Creole–influenced Crescent City of New Orleans back in the late 1800s and early 1900s. There was an Americanization of New Orleans after the Louisiana Purchase in the early 1800s. New Orleans, racially and ethnically speaking, was a mixture of French and Spanish and indigenous American elements. The Creole, or the light-skinned Negro, the French-inflected mulatto, was the product of a fusion of black and white. Creoles began to create ragtime and jazz music only after they had interactions with indigenous Negro or African-inflected musicians in New Orleans, a fact that causes me to be skeptical about Collier's argument that jazz is not identifiable as black music. One can hear in such denials reverberations of the stigma of blackness—of black skin and skill, of black blood, metaphorically speaking, of black styles—that was rife in American culture at the turn of the twentieth century. It's a stigma that persists to this day, even if, ironically enough, black popular culture is the idiom, is the grammar, through which America is globally articulated.

Finally, I think piano-based ragtime accentuated percussive features of black music that were later expanded in ensembles, which highlighted the shift to the multi-instrumentality of jazz music, including, say, a saxophone, a trumpet, and a drum, which facilitated the process of improvisation that was strictly forbidden in classical music, which had to be read note for note off a sheet. It was eye music versus ear music, music that had to be read versus music that had to be heard and learned by ear, the visual versus the aural, so to speak. Since there was initially little sheet music in jazz, at least not to the degree or in the manner of classical music, musicians were free to improvise, to remake the song as they played it each time. There was a structural freshness to the music's improvisational quality, allowing the musicians to enlarge or diminish themes, to rearrange musical elements, to alter tempos and tones, as the occasion or mood dictated. There's still a corpus there, a body of ideas and themes and techniques, but they are the raw material of the riffs that constitute and extend the impulse to improvisation. A huge feature of the debates over African versus European music was over what sorts of music contained our cultural and, really, our political values. If democracy is what jazz is about, glimpsed in the equal participation of varying elements in the construction of a whole, European classical music is about a kind of oligarchy of aesthetic taste; that is, there is tight control over what can be played, what can be said, what can be articulated, and who gets a chance to play it.

Talk about the imagery.

An interesting feature of African music is how it incorporates the communal basis of racial and cultural survival into its aesthetic vocabulary. That's number one. Number two, African-inflected music, at least in the case of black music in America, existed and eventually flourished in a foreign land, in a context where black folk had to struggle to create a culture of signification among each other as a survival strategy in an oppressive culture. So the double entendre, from the spirituals, blues, and so on, allowed blacks to communicate with one another in liberating fashion. When slaves sang "Green trees are bending/My soul stands a'trembling/Ain't got long to stay here," white plantation owners were being entertained while black slaves were being emancipated, since they were signaling each other about when Harriet Tubman was coming through to liberate slaves and lead them along the Underground Railroad to freedom. So the double entendre fused emancipation and entertainment in many African and African American musical forms. But black emancipation and white entertainment weren't the only functions of the double entendre.

In jazz music, the double entendre went secular as it funneled sexual play into the aesthetic creations of black folk culture. Or should I say, the aesthetic creation funnels the sexual play of certain subcultures in black life, especially among working-class black folk. But the sexual did not exhaust the double entendre in the cultural realm, since black folk through our music signified on what we understood ourselves to be and played with those images, whether of the barbarian, the savage, and so on, even as we enlarged on the narratives of complex humanity that all great art promotes. We could parody the stereotypes of black identity even as we extended our creative freedom to engage our libidos, to revel in sexual mischief, to take utter joy in what Richard Wright called the "erotic exultation" of some forms of music. He was referring primarily to gospel, but I think it can be applied equally to early ragtime and jazz as well.

Another level of double entendre reflected the utter playfulness of linguisticality and orality at the heart of black culture. Long before poststructuralists who were hooked on European traveling theories of postmodernism talked about the playfulness of culture and language, black folk comprehended *jouissance,* the sheer hedonistic pleasure and delight of experimenting and playing with black cultural forms, including music. A crucial feature of double entendres was the articulation of culturally coded messages and styles that signified on white dominant cultural structures while promoting black self-definition. Even though the dominant culture may have viewed blacks as barbarians and savages, as dumb animals incapable of abstract reasoning or "high" culture, they nevertheless reveled in the robustly playful elements of black cultural creativity. At their best, black folk refused to get stuck in narrow Victorian modes of identity where they repressed consciousness of their sexual selves while exclusively engaging their spiritual nature. They didn't buy into that bifurcation between mind and body. As critic Michael Ventura argued, African cultures often overcame the Cartesian dualism of the West because they contended that there was no such thing as being mental and spiritual over here and being physically embodied over there.

The double entendre was about black folk having their cake and eating it too, so to speak; it was about healing the rift between body and soul; it was about playfulness while contesting white power in signifying fashion; and it was about enjoying and celebrating their culture even as vicious stereotypes abounded. That was terribly liberating to black folk who had been indoctrinated with the belief that they were inferior, that they were, in the words of Margaret Walker Alexander, "black and poor and small." You must remember that at the turn of the century, black popular culture was broadly assailed in magazines and journals. A title from one magazine asked, "Did jazz put the sin in syncopation?" The *Ladies' Home Journal* argued that young people listening to jazz music would produce a holocaust of teen births. Now where have we heard that recently? There was an enormous groundswell against black and white Americans who embraced jazz music, especially as cultural guardians were attempting to control the sexual chaos and erotic frenzy of this rhythmic, syncopated music.

That's because ragtime was associated with the brothel, and jazz music in the 1920s was associated with the speakeasy. Given my earlier analysis about how the physical and social contexts in which the music was played shaped its use, the brothel and speakeasy provided a space for blacks to exult in their own bodies. The speakeasy, the brothel, and other dens of ill repute are where ragtime and jazz were regularly played. So there was an association in the public mind of morally suspicious behavior and black music. This was not strictly a contention between blacks and whites, since during the Harlem Renaissance, upper-class Negroes were inveighing against the vagaries of ghetto gutter music. When you went to the cribs of the leading lights of the Harlem Renaissance, they were playing Beethoven, Bach, and Brahms. They were not engaging the debased folk culture of the masses. Even politically progressive figures such as W.E.B. Du Bois, the young A. Phillip Randolph, and Chandler Owens spurned jazz music. At some level, there's an internalized self-abnegation, a disparagement of quotidian blackness displayed by the Negro upper crust who spurn black folk culture while uncritically deferring to European canons, codes, and norms. Thus the black cultural double entendre was directed against not only white supremacist culture but also the Negro bourgeoisie, which lacked serious appreciation for its indigenous art forms.

Was it starting to creep a little too close to home? In modern times, we see as many white as black kids buying rap music. Is that maybe an issue?

Absolutely! The degree to which ragtime and later jazz—especially through figures like Baby Dodds, Buddy Bolden, Jelly Roll Morton, and later Louis Armstrong—reached out beyond the confines of black culture certainly sparked wide cultural controversy. There's no question that when jazz penetrated the husk of white cultural circles, there was a great deal of consternation among the white artistic and political elite. Just as with hip-hop culture today, there was an enormous degree of anxiety about black art forms like jazz darkening white artistic enclaves and social settings. As a result, white elites stepped up the policing of boundaries between black and white cultures, even as jazz inspired interracial cultural exchange. The music facilitated what Jim Crow with its segregated social practices failed to prevent: different cultures connecting and interacting. Jazz helped promote the syncretic moment, the fused moment, the moment of cultural contact and cooperation between races that existed beyond the restrictions of custom, code, and law.

That's why Jelly Roll Morton, Sidney Bechet, and Louis Armstrong, who was the young cornet player in King Oliver's group, and others like them were dangerous to the white musical establishment, especially when jazz and its musicians flowed down the Mississippi, fanning out from the Crescent City to Chicago, New York, St. Louis, Kansas City, and Los Angeles. The music and its musicians were now mobile, and many critics deemed them even more harmful because they could reach a much larger audience, especially white youth. Jazz culture was seductive to white kids, and they turned from the quadrille, the mazurka, the waltz, and the polka of their parents to the slow drag and the hoochie-coochie, while reveling in the blues of the Delta filtering into New Orleans from Mississippi. This explosion of African creativity constituted a veritable Negropolis, a black cosmopolitanism whose influence sprawled beyond its original indigenous borders to capture large segments of American society.

Hence the development of the Jazz Age, which in its mainstream cultural embodiment was qualitatively different from the ragtime and jazz juke joints. But it retained enough aesthetic ferocity, in both music and fiction, to scare some and shake up many others. F. Scott Fitzgerald reflected some of the ferocious and fertile impulses of the juke joint in the linguistic creativity of his novels, where slang leapt to the foreground, and his characters were not trying to close out the body.

In certain European canonical works, the body becomes irrelevant or merely instrumental, an appendage to the mind's operations, merely instrumental. For instance, the body was good for producing wind for the brass instruments or for the muscle to stroke the string instruments in the classical orchestra. But the body itself was never as *present* in European classical music as it was in Negro hot spots, the indigenous dives of brown divas and majordomos—at least not when it was primarily interpreted by Europeans. I'm speaking here of musicians, with the singers who rose to prominence later, including folk like Caruso and Callas, being obvious exceptions. Basically, in European music, you saw the segregation of the body into measured utilities, where the hands were good but not the feet, where the lips were fine but not the eyes, and so on.

In jazz, the body was aesthetically desegregated, freed from the artificial constraints of taste, custom, and tradition. In jazz, the entire body was implicated and was truly integrated. The values of jazz include a profound vocal tonality, since the musical instruments were manipulated in varying degrees to sound like the voice. That's why we love Lester Young's and, later, John Coltrane's, sound, because the very textures they evoke on the saxophone remind us of the human voice crying, sighing, laughing, speaking and shrieking, complaining, and expressing joy. Let's move from the reeds to the brass. In a sense, the blues shouts and the field hollers get reexpressed, reemphasized, rearticulated in the longing, yearning, feral tones of the trumpet and the cornet. When you hear Louis Armstrong wailing on his trumpet and cornet, when you hear him cutting through the aesthetics of polite society with its measured, rigid, precise tonalities, lashing, as only Armstrong could, in a viciously insistent tone that suggested he was indeed "stomping the blues," you hear the quality I'm talking about. It's anger and joy, anxiety and peace in shuffling cadences that trade hope for despair as he's trading twelves in King Oliver's group and later his own.

And beyond jazz, in gospel music, for instance, when you hear the transcendent aesthetic possibilities that transmute suffering into ethical vision and religious passion, you're hearing the full-bodied character of black music. Black music, and the contexts of black experience it introduced, were just too much for an often repressed mainstream society. And you don't have to buy into stereotypes of the oppositional figures of the white savant and black savage, with the former a glutton for reason and the intellect, and the latter addicted to primal urges and nature, to get my point. The aesthetic priorities and intellectual musings of black artists (and for me, the two go hand in hand, especially when we're talking about jazz) provided white youth a different and daring prism through which to view themselves. Remember, Du Bois had written in 1903, at least that's when the essays in *Souls of Black Folk* were gathered, that it is a strange thing to see oneself, that is, the black self, through the lens of another world, a world that was in many ways a foreign, judging, hostile world. But what happens with jazz music and culture is that the prism is inverted, metaphorically speaking, so that now, in the 1920s, black culture provides the lens through which many whites begin to view and understand themselves. That was a monumental philosophical reversal achieved largely by aesthetic means.

What was it that was bringing black folks from the rural South to urban centers in the North?

Economic opportunity was one thing that drew black people from rural agrarian culture, where they were brutally segregated on post-Emancipation plantations in sharecropping arrangements. Sharecropping was little more than the evolved form of slavery. You see, after Emancipation, 90 percent of black Americans lived in the South until the early 1900s and the great black migration North, to Chicago and Detroit and other big cities, in search of greater economic opportunity. Even before the great black migration, blacks had been drawn to urban centers like New Orleans, which was steeped in racial history. Congo Square was there; it was the place where black slaves had been sold on the auction block. Congo Square prefigured the urban cultures that coalesced around New Orleans in the late 1800s and early 1900s because it was where all these Africans from every part of the world were brought, or literally *bought*, together. There's nothing like the oppressive commercialization and commodification of black culture to forge the solidarity of blackness, even if it was a defensive, protective, reflexive move, and to create modern blackness in ways it didn't exist in Africa before the coerced diaspora, the forced migration.

But this new thing, this *tertium quid*, this not-European, not-African-but-somehow-American racial reality that formed in Congo Square, was the forging of the black Atlantic, as Robert Farris Thompson, Peter Linebaugh, and much later Paul Gilroy, have described it in their work. In Congo Square, music was played outside the control of the dominant white society. Blacks reappropriated the space of domination as a source of liberating aesthetic self-expression. The drum was crucial to this process. It was the dominant symbol, the dominant metaphor, of the convergence of political meanings and aesthetic articulation. In Congo Square, the rhythm of black life, with its percussive tonalities, was literally drummed into existence. That's why the drums were outlawed: they were the language of black emancipation. The drums allowed blacks to facilitate community, to communicate valuable political messages in a percussive tongue. It was a testament to the fertility and generativity of blackness, even for those Creoles who were *passer blanc*, passing for white, although it was routinely the case that they were marked in their bodies with the outlaw(ed) meanings of blackness by the dominant society.

Still, there was something crucial about Congo Square to black identity. New Orleans provided a gumbo ya-ya of disparate black identities of African origins. People think when you say black, these identities are self-evident, but they're not. They think the same for Africa, but when you say African, what are you really saying? Are you talking about East, West, North, or South African? Are you talking about Yoruba or Hausa? And in the African diaspora, things are no different.

When you speak of African religion, for instance, are you talking about Candomble from an Afro-Brazilian experience, or are you speaking of Afro-Cuban Santeria, or perhaps a Haitian expression of Vodoun? The gumbo ya-ya of black identity evokes the African appreciation for the integrity of multiplicity, which is essentially what black urbanity is all about. The black urban experiment of the early part of the twentieth century, in its edifying moments, was about mass black exodus to cities that were ports of call for the migrations, mixtures, and mergers of all kinds of black identities, both within indigenous U.S. populations and from all over the Americas, from Caribbean cultures, and later from British cultures as well. The expansion of economic opportunity that drew blacks to big northern cities from all parts of the country, indeed the world, had a concomitant virtue: it not only eroded the vicious de jure segregation to which they had been subject in southern apartheid, but it multiplied the rambunctious collocation of ethnic, regional, religious, sexual, gendered, and class diversities within black identity.

Talk about the atmosphere of Chicago in 1919.

Chicago during that time was home to upwardly mobile blacks, relatively speaking, who had limited success in challenging the norms, the ethos, the very superior self-understanding that even average whites possessed. As a result, blacks suffered violence as reprisal for their "uppity behavior." So the de jure segregation of the South was replaced by the de facto segregation of the North. A lot of the violence blacks suffered was not simply of the top-down sort—violence regulated and mediated through political structures in an ostensibly democratic society. The violence had largely to do with the politics of resentment from white working-class folk who frowned on the even limited success of this burgeoning black working class. Tensions between the races were exacerbated when black scab workers were brought in to bust the unions, most of which barred black workers. In effect, the white power structure was playing musical chairs with nonunionized black workers and exploited white unionized workers, pitting the latter against the former. All this means that around 1919, the second great fire razed Chicago. The first fire happened in 1871, when Mrs. O'Leary's legendary cow kicked the lantern that started the fire that nearly burned down Chicago.

The second fire was more redemptive, ignited when some blacks joined the working and middle classes, turning Chicago into one of the great centers of black culture in the modern West, similar to what would happen later in Los Angeles when the booming war industry drew blacks in record numbers during World War II. In Chicago, circa 1919, the stockyards were the huge attraction that helped spark Chicago's great black migration. The stockyards and the sometimes apocryphal stories that transplanted black Southerners in Chicago sent back home that exaggerated their standard of living in the big city, as if they were, in the parlance of hip-hop, "living large." Maybe in comparison to their old southern haunts they were living large, but they were hardly living in the lap of luxury up

North; and there were virtues to the old southern geographies that formerly dominated black life. In the South, even if they were poor, they had open spaces in fields, but in the North, their enhanced economic status confined them in tenements that stretched upward several stories and choked the landscapes and skylines of ghettoes and slums.

The North had its own variety of Jim Crow, except that it was Jim Crow, Esquire, or James Crow III. Northern racism was more subtle but no less vicious. Twenty years after 1919, during the 1940s, Chicago exploded with black aesthetic creativity, with jazz, blues, gospel, and later its own variety of soul music, making it very difficult for white Americans—especially the recently arrived white ethnic immigrants, including Poles, Italians, Lithuanians, and Irish, who populated Chicago's burgeoning lumpen proletariat—to accept even marginal black mainstream success. The battle was classic: recently migrated southern blacks and recently immigrated white European ethnics—in Michael Novak's famous book title (at least during his radical phase) *The Unmeltable Ethnics*, something I'm sure he'd disavow now as a leading conservative and advocate of the melting pot. In short order, tensions mounted and eventually led to race rioting in Chicago.

Were the objections concentrated on the influx of people or was it reaction to what the people brought with them, the culture?

It was both. They were indivisible because the greatest thing the people brought was themselves and their itinerant, mobile cultural meanings. According to many conservative social scientists, the urban situation was messed up because black people reshaped industrial urbanity in the first half of the twentieth century in Chicago, Detroit, Philadelphia, New York, Los Angeles, and so on. Blacks brought their culture with them, a culture pervaded by blues and jazz and gospel music and spiritual sensibilities. They brought a particular understanding of what their place was, both geographically and racially, but they had to adjust as well, because transitioning from agrarian, rural life to urbanity's more regimented, geometric living (R. Buckminster Fuller gone ghetto, so to speak, in cloistered, crabbed cubicles, geodesic domes writ small) was very difficult. The geopolitics of industrial urban space didn't necessarily bode well for some blacks who brought cultural habits and lifestyles more suited to the South. Many blacks brought the cultural norms of creative collectivity and communal sharing with them, which were healthy and productive; black Southerners helped each other out with the meager resources they had. They also brought the habit of having a lot of family members, relatives, and friends live in one room, in the shotgun shacks that were common in parts of the South, a habit that proved to be counterproductive in some instances. Thus cultural adaptability worked for and against blacks. You usually only hear the negative side in books that detail the effect of the black migration on family structure, cultural thriving, and social cohesion and stability. But you rarely hear of the vital social and cultural habits (such as adaptable familial structures and flexible gender roles, since black women have always worked outside the home) that allowed black urbanity to flourish.

At the same time, though, the aesthetic cultures that black Southerners brought— and the joy, the frivolity, the edifying frenzy, the passionate investment in bodily expressions and syncopated rhythms and cultural significations that were important to sustaining their lives and nurturing their strong sense of self—was crucial to black survival. It also clashed with certain elements of the white mainstream, not the least of which was the perception by older whites that this black culture was ruining their children. When Louis Armstrong left New Orleans and headed to Chicago, one of his great fans was a high school–aged cat named Bix Beiderbecke. As a result, the great black migration, with its southern roots, influences the northern white populace, especially youth who are fumbling toward maturity while experiencing alienation from their parents' world. A major way many white youth articulated their alienation, and affirmed their sanity, authenticity, and legitimacy, was by latching hold of the mores mediated through the artistic values of black culture as expressed in the imaginations and visions of its great artists. What happens is predictable: Bix becomes better known than his mentor in many artistic circles and gets the opportunity to make more money than Armstrong. Or think about Benny Goodman, who reaped huge aesthetic and financial benefit from his association with (read: appropriation) and downright ripping off of black musicians. But at least Goodman had enough sense to bring Fletcher Henderson along as his musical director, even though Goodman became famous in the first place because he had purchased twenty-four of Fletcher Henderson's songs to make him the "King of Swing." Damned, Duke, my sincere apologies!

So urban migration meant much more than black bodies occupying the menial workforce. It also meant the widening influence of black cultural sensibilities, even if, as was the case with Bix and Benny, they were appropriated and diluted. Black cultural influence caused great tension in the industrialized North because it meant that blackness was just so present. Its proximity was a problem. It was one thing for whites to minstrel blackness, to appropriate it for pecuniary and performative gain. Hence you had the Cotton Club in Harlem controlled by white mobsters, catering to a white clientele in the fabled bosom of blackness with a public face that was colored by its black entertainers. But it was another thing for Negroes to show up in the North looking to benefit from their own culture. Thus the aesthetic demands of Negro art caused a quake in racial and economic relations, shifting the plates along the fault lines of race that underlay the social geography.

But what was really trying for even white liberals was the actual, embodied presence of the blacks they had spoken for by proxy. When those black folk took the boat up the Mississippi to speak for themselves, it was mutiny on the white bounty! When other folk speak for you, no matter how informed or impassioned, it's just not the same as you speaking for yourself. And part of the problem with black migration was the aesthetic encounters it forged in the public square, in the clubs and joints, and the churches and houses of worship that dotted the black urban landscape. The emotional sweep of black experience, which was largely abstract even for white sympathizers, became flesh and dwelt among the white world up North. That experience included the pain and pathos of black life; the utter despair and the defiant hopefulness of black existence; the anguished love that strode through the rhythms of black music; the sweat and strain and aspiration of black bodies in worship or erotic wooing or work or play; the murmurs, the shrieks, the barely suppressed guffaws, the edifying laughter, the comic sensibility that confronted the doom or tragedy or evil that blacks fought, elements that they refused to make their ultimate home, their ultimate reality. All of these moods and modes of blackness were indivisible from the great black migration. While the cultural rituals that mediated the normative beliefs of the black cosmos were appealing to some whites, they were to many more a source of horror, of pity, of condescending tolerance, or of grave misunderstanding, more often outright hostility, but rarely fair engagement. Often black culture alienated whites who sought to keep blacks at arm's length. White liberals didn't mind fighting for black freedom, but they didn't want blacks living next door. T.S. Eliot, the great modernist poet, said, "Between the ideal and the reality falls the shadow." This is what Chicago was grappling with, the shadow, the dark rim of black urban existence as black bodies and beliefs challenged American notions of democracy, cityhood, and industrial civilization.

Speak to the black embrace, or not, of the migration.

Black people were greatly affected by the mainstream culture's perceptions of their bodies, beliefs, value systems, and social visions: the baggage, metaphorically speaking, of migrating from South to North, as well as the virtues and vices that characterize black culture. Many black people accepted what white Americans believed about black culture: that it was barbaric and savage when it centered in jazz and blues, which meant that black culture at its best must move to embrace the transcendental traditions of spirituality that coursed through gospel music and evangelical, revivalist preaching. A huge problem occurred when Chicago-based musician Thomas Dorsey, the father of contemporary gospel music, introduced jazz and blues riffs in his music. Beyond the aesthetic dimensions of racial propriety, there were the social divisions of black society that were magnified in the great black migration. So the internal contradictions of black culture proved transportable as well. For instance, up North, blacks updated a habit they had practiced in places like New Orleans, known as the "paper bag" test—blacks who were darker than a plain paper bag were prevented by lighter blacks from participating in social clubs, civic organizations, or, informally, from marrying above their color-driven caste.

A hierarchy of sorts was generated among blacks when relocated Southerners who had been in place for even a year looked down on and teased their more recently arrived compatriots. It was pretty hilarious for barely seasoned former

Southerners to view their kindred as hicks or "Bamas"—the sometimes affectionate catchall term for a country bumpkin or hayseed that derives from a shortened
form of Alabama. Like some second-generation Mexican immigrants who were
among the most visible and articulate opponents of further immigration because
it challenged their own space and security, as well as their ability to smoothly assimilate, many black migrants expressed the most vocal outrage at newly arrived
hicks, when they were barely "unhicked" themselves. Chicago was little more
than a suburb of Mississippi, and you can trace that genealogy all the way from
blues icon Howling Wolf to the stable of stars on Chess Records and the blues
lounges along 43 Street, most famously, perhaps, the Checkerboard Lounge. So
these racial contretemps within black culture were part of the black modernist experience as blacks negotiated between the margins and the mainstream.

**Talk about the musical establishment and their criticism of this new music,
jazz.**

As already noted, the first jazz record was made in 1917 by an all-white group, the
Original Dixieland Jazz Band, led by Paul Whiteman. How suggestive can that be,
if you break down and parse Paul and white man, which is both Freudian and
Jungian, since the symbol and the archetype converge? Paul, we remember, was
the first great missionary of Christianity into the gentile world, and so Paul Whiteman as a missionary of sorts, acclaimed by whites as the first great king of jazz, is
just too much of a signification to overlook. And "white man" as the acceptable
ambassador of this music to the white world was surely glimpsed in Paul Whiteman's Aeolian Hall concert, which marked the aesthetic mediation and economic
commercialization of a black music harshly demonized by dominant society. The
first jazz record and Whiteman's Aeolian Hall concert tell us that part of the music
establishment wanted to commodify and control this music—to package, market,
and distribute jazz to consumers in the marketplace, benefiting its white distribu-
tors, appropriators, and dilutors. Even as the music was being dissed in elite white
circles, the white musical establishment still wanted to make a buck off of jazz. The
artists weren't making the biggest money; it was the producers who were cleaning
up. If you were a songwriter, you might sell your music, but you weren't going to
accumulate enough capital to really make a living from that. So the white record
producers, executives, and owners who were interested in jazz reaped enormous financial remuneration from black creativity and genius, a pattern, by the way, that
continues to this day in some artistic circles.

Still, there were huge debates about whether this was real music, in the European
sense. Moreover, conservative elements of the musical establishment railed against
jazz because they couldn't control the music. Jazz just wasn't the conservative music
establishment's ideal of good music. It was similar to what happened later on when
ASCAP got caught with its pants down, so to speak, and was unable to control
rock 'n' roll music because it was exclusively promoting the music of Tin Pan Alley,

with artists like Cole Porter and later Frank Sinatra. As a result, ASCAP missed a huge cultural moment and overwhelming financial opportunity. Since the conservative elements of the music industry hadn't anticipated the degree to which jazz would invade white youth subcultures and become influential in significant white circles, it settled on curtailing the music's circulation. Louis Armstrong made a very good living because he appealed to blacks and whites. The same was true for Duke Ellington and Count Basie and the swing movement. In one sense, mainstream white swing music was the attempt to domesticate the hot beats of ragtime in early jazz into lightly syncopated orchestral riffing. But again, it wasn't Jimmy Lunceford or Count Basie or Duke Ellington who got the biggest advantage from the swing they helped invent. Rather, it was Paul Whiteman, Guy Lombardo, Woody Herman, the Dorsey Brothers, and Gene Krupa. Harry James, who was Benny Goodman's trumpet player, was routinely favored over Louis Armstrong in jazz polls. What's up with that?

How do you reconcile a lot of the musicians feeling honored with appropriation?

I think it's the contradiction between individual artistic expression and the burden of representation. You're an individual but as a well-regarded musician, you're inevitably a race man; you're representing more than yourself.

On the individual level, I'm sure that black artists were honored that white musicians who greatly admired their music imitated what they heard and duplicated it as nearly as possible in circles that black musicians might never be allowed to darken. Some black artists took great satisfaction in the belief that America was indebted to them, even without name or attribution, for having created an art form so powerful that white musicians paid it the compliment of emulation. But we can't deny that the failure to reap recognition and reward for their achievements greatly disturbed many a black artist.

As a member of the race, as a representative of a larger agglomerative interest, there's no doubt that such appropriation was damaging. Not only were these black musicians being exploited, but there was a feeling that they should actually be grateful that white musicians were taking their music into arenas they could not enter. The coercion to black gratitude is a staple of dominant white culture in most areas of endeavor. Black students, it is felt, should be grateful for getting into good schools, despite their excellent qualifications. Black voters should be grateful for the attention from politicians that other voters take for granted. And black citizens should be grateful to live in America and hence should not criticize the nation's inequalities and injustices, especially when the nation is at war. Black jazz musicians, like any other artists, were certainly grateful in the strictly generic sense of that word, to be able to exercise their gifts. But why should they have been grateful to be exploited? Only the logic of white supremacy, with its punishing mission to make blacks actually desire their domination, could explain this phenomenon. Many of the musicians were not overtly political, even if they quietly resented the restrictions on their livelihood. Many black artists simply took things on face value, knowing what they could and could not expect. They knew they would never make it into prime time, into mainstream venues, where manifestly inferior white musicians were Pat Booneing jazz, if you will.

White appropriation of black jazz has to be placed in a social context that explains the efforts of individual white artists. What was it like to be Bix Beiderbecke, a blessed borrower, and to know that the acclaim you receive for originality of expression in fact derives from the appropriation of the artistic heritage of unheralded black artists, including a palette of aural shadings, a grammar of timber, and a tonal structure that supports their artistic endeavors. On the other hand, as a working white musician, you realize that the fate of any musician, regardless of color, is to experiment with borrowed sounds until you find your own voice. Although it was never simply a one-to-one correspondence between white appropriation and black exploitation, the larger social structure within which such dynamics take place underscores how crucial a factor race is.

Without being essentialist or romantic about these black musicians' humanity, many black artists recognized they would never get the fame or make the money they deserved, but they took solace in the fact that the aesthetic values they cherished would in some form make a contribution to the national and global cultural good. These black musicians were being called every name in the book except child of God, as they were pelted with epithets like savage and barbarian while displaying the most ennobling version of individualism, the highest vision of American idealism, and the most democratic conception of artistic creation imaginable. What purer artists can we imagine? So my hat's off to them.

What was the relationship of the mainstream white community to jazz?

From the beginning, jazz was caught in the technological forms that drove the music industry. As already noted, the first recording of black music involved its packaging, dilution, and distribution by white cultural forces. The mechanics of industrialization are coterminous with finding an available market for black music, a market that was created by the urges and desires of the masses and was shaped by the desire of white producers and record companies to make money from an art form that the doyens of American taste found morally reprehensible. On the other hand, there was the sense that the moral overtones of jazz were quite hostile to white aesthetic sensibilities and cultural authority, since blackness was perceived as polluting and contaminating white purity. To paraphrase anthropologist Mary Douglass in her classic book *Purity and Danger*, there was a sense of taboo associated with black bodies, beliefs, and behaviors.

At the same time, many whites were drawn to this allegedly polluted culture and were, in the view of their critics, fatefully sucked into the vortex of the black libido. The unlicensed and unchecked expression of sexuality, sensuality, and eroticism in jazz culture was antithetical to the repressions and virtues of Victorian culture that were selectively observed by the white elite. Unsurprisingly, the black aesthetic carried political meanings. Powerful whites sought to control the transgressive expressions of black music by suppressing its public exposure. They kept it off the radio waves, and they restricted race records for the most part to their intended black audience. When whites began to buy these records, influential whites in the recording industry began to market black music to other whites. If they couldn't whip black music into shape, they figured they'd at least benefit from the sale of this sonic pathology.

The first positive mention of jazz music in official, public white circles didn't occur until around 1933; between 1895 and 1933, jazz was evolving and undergoing tremendous transformation even as it was being demonized. In the end, to pinch the title of Robert Pattison's wonderful book, jazz proved the "triumph of vulgarity." That's not only because the music ultimately proved to be compelling to the masses and superior to its critics' aesthetic objections, but because the music, through the humanity of its greatest creators, helped America concede the vulgarity of its racism and antiblack hatred. That's not to suggest that pockets of black America weren't upset with the music as well. The vicious stereotypes of black hypersexuality made many blacks uncomfortable with openly embracing a music shot through with double entendres, sexual innuendo, erotic play, and sensual evocations. Already saddled with notions of savagery and beastlike behavior, many blacks spurned jazz as the devil's music. Many black people resented elements of jazz because they believed it compromised the complexity of black art by capitulating to white people's notion of the savage. These blacks believed that jazz culture played up the image of blacks as sensate animals and sexual predators to the exclusion of the image of the morally circumspect black. That's an argument, of course, that we hear repeated now by the black opponents of the worst elements of hard-core rap, who claim that it plays up black savagery to the pleasure and benefit of largely white producers. The only difference now, they say—a difference, by the way, that sickens the opponents of hard-core rap—is that contrary to musicians in the Jazz Age, black artists today are being paid for piping black pathology to the white world.

Then too there was a big dispute about whether black music could be said to exist at all. One of the most famous debates about this issue took place between Langston Hughes and George Schuyler. George Schuyler wrote a piece for the *Nation* called "The Negro Art Hokum," arguing that there's no such thing as black art; according to Schuyler, it's American art. Schuyler contended that there was caste art because lower-class black people produce a certain kind of cultural expression, but it's not the result of an indigenous or unique black artistic gift. Of course, other critics argued the opposite. Anthropologist Melville Herskovits in his book *The Myth of the Negro Past* writes about the "deification of Accidence" that is a defining feature of black identity. For Herskovits, black culture deifies accidental, contingent occurrences by integrating them into the vocabulary of black purposefulness.

To borrow a nonblack example (although, arguably, he embodies profound black properties and identity traits, perhaps a black aesthetic in a postmodern white face), when Pee Wee Herman falls off of his bike in his important film, *Pee Wee's Big Adventure*, he says, "I meant to do that," which captures part of what is meant in the deification of Accidence. I suppose another way of speaking about this is to call it an *improvisational intentionality*, that even when one did not intend a particular action or behavior, one incorporates it into one's grammar of activity as a willed event. It's a way, I think, of attempting to exercise control over one's environment. Herskovits's conception of deification of Accidence is an example of a historically constructed element of black consciousness and culture. In direct response to Schuyler, Langston Hughes argues that there is such a thing as black art in his influential essay, "The Negro Artist and the Racial Mountain." The racial mountain refers to the inability of black folk to affirm a splendid folk culture about which they should have no shame. Hughes argued that one day black folk would wake up and love and embrace black art and take pride in the achievements of the so-called lower castes and classes. With the worldwide veneration of jazz, Hughes has proved prophetic.

Talk about how jazz, once on the outside, is now being celebrated.

It's at once ironic and instructive. I think that jazz has traced the nearly inevitable path traveled by all sorts of music that has been stigmatized and morally outlawed. It finds its way into the vocabulary of American artistic acceptance, even veneration, and lands at the heart of American identity. What we now mean when we say American, we mean when we say jazz. It is now recognized as the singularly original American aesthetic achievement in music, which is why, I think, we've got white critics arguing that it's not really a black musical expression. You didn't get those arguments when the music was associated with the brothels and the brothers in the streets. In light of its history, I happen to believe that jazz musicians should lead the defense of contemporary black music that is demonized. I'm not suggesting that they have to like it, or even regularly listen to it, but that they should, on principle, articulate an informed aesthetic defense of the right of stigmatized black music to exist. I think that's a reasonable expectation, but one that neotraditionalists in jazz constantly forget.

I often think they need a refresher course in the history of aesthetic contusion on jazz's developing body of work in the 1920s. For all intents and purposes, bebop was hip-hop—if you don't believe me, just check out even Louis Armstrong's negative reaction to Dizzy, Bird, and company. What we have turned into nostalgia was once notorious. Bluesmen, in effect, were B-boys. Let's face it, jazz was the rap of its time. Now that jazz has been severed from its association with stigmatized blackness in the public mind, it has been elevated to an aesthetic perch from which it is favorably compared to the ostensible pathology of some contemporary black music. Of course, there are differences between jazz and, for example, elements of hip-hop, which arose under different historical and racial circumstances, but which nonetheless share a history of assault upon their early incarnations as the devil's workshop, as examples of barbarism and savagery. Of course, that's a lesson that hip-hoppers could absorb as well, a lesson, interestingly enough, which might supply rappers help in their defense of their artistic and cultural endeavors. Theirs is not the first black music to be dissed.

Speak to the irony or appropriateness of dealing with art in a congressional forum, and more specifically, jazz and hip-hop.

One can imagine a world guided by Plato's *Republic*, envisioning the philosopher-king as the arbiter of truth. Still, we don't want to concede such authority to American politicians, most of whom are neither philosophers nor kings. We don't want politicians determining and regulating "good" art or becoming arbiters of aesthetic taste. Do we really want Bob Dole telling us what films to see, or Tipper Gore, Bill Bennett, and C. Dolores Tucker telling us what music we can listen to? What these figures miss is that true art opposes such artificial restrictions and embraces individual self-expression, or collective articulation, as its raison d'être. What's intriguing, and truly sad, is that black activists from the sixties who fought the racist and fascist restriction of free speech and black cultural expression have now joined forces with white politicians and moralists, whose views on other subjects put them at tremendous odds with the liberation agenda of these activists. Plus, some of these politicians opposed the very freedom struggles black folk waged in earlier decades of the century.

Now I certainly understand, even empathize with, figures who speak against the misogyny and sexism of hip-hop culture. But it cannot be fought by legislation against the music; it's got to be fought in the trenches, in the cultural and aesthetic cul-de-sacs where music makes its mark. We've got to take the message of sexual equality and gender justice to the streets, clubs—and yes, to the schools and religious institutions—where sexism, patriarchy, and misogyny thrive and are planted deep inside the minds of our youth. That's not as sexy as sounding off before a Senate hearing, which I've certainly done, or trumpeting our views before an eager audience of journalists, something to which I'm not immune. But it's harder work, and it demands a long-term commitment to addressing the underlying causes of social injustice. But I think it's ultimately more rewarding than the simplistic pleasures of assaulting politically unprotected young blacks.

We've got to remember that all black art at one time or another has been similarly attacked, and that the effort to legislate against black music's alleged moral perversities is nothing new. Not only jazz in the early teens and 1920s, but rock-and-roll music in the 1950s—of course, it's hard to imagine that "Work With Me Annie," a hit for Hank Ballard and the Midnighters, caused consternation, but "work" was euphemistic for a sexually suggestive motion of the pelvis—and rhythm and blues in the 1970s were lambasted. The attempt to censor black music was the attempt to censor black bodies, black voices, and black identities unleashed in the naked public square. For blacks to join Senate hearings aimed at suppressing speech, policing art, and reinforcing our second-class citizenship as producers and even consumers of music, is, I think, tragically mistaken.

We need Senate hearings, instead, into the causes and conditions of economic and racial desperation that drive some of our youth to express themselves with profanity and vulgarity. Until we do that, the real vulgarity is not the curse words that pepper hip-hop lyrics, but the stigmatization and criminalization of our youth that leads to a precipitous hike in incarceration rates. The raison d'être of hip-hop's vocation of angry articulation may lie in the lyrics of one of its greatest poets, Notorious B.I.G., or Biggie Smalls, when he declares in his song "Things Done Changed": "Back in the days our parents used to take care of us, Look at them now, they're even fuckin' scared of us/Calling the city for help because they can't maintain, Damn, things done changed." That entire song to me is a translation of Weber's conception of theodicy, which, as ethicist Jon Gunneman argued, expresses the disjunction between destiny and merit, between what you get and what you think you deserve.

I think in its clever rhymes is contained a sophisticated social analysis of the conditions under which young blacks and Latinos mature in postindustrial urban spaces, especially those enclaves of civic terror called ghettos and slums. Plus, Biggie noted the shift in power from older to younger people in what I have elsewhere termed a juvenocracy, or the rule, and in some cases, tyranny of younger people over social and economic resources in domestic and public space. Many black critics in particular have wrongly concluded that black youth are in such terrible shape because they are somehow morally alienated or ethically estranged from the legacies that produced them. While there's no denying the huge generational gulf between older and younger blacks, we must, in searching for an explanation of what's gone wrong, think about the ready availability of guns, the ever growing economic and social inequality in black communities, and the political economies of drugs that prevail when aboveground economies fail. In the final analysis, we've got to help connect our youth to meaningful cultural traditions while respecting—and hence, engaging and critiquing—their own newly developing aesthetic aspirations and cultural articulations.

Comment on the likening of jazz to a boxing match.

The first thing that comes to mind is that, like a boxer, jazz music, as well as most black music at one time, has been counted down and out. For instance, some people say that the blues is down and out, complaining, "Blues culture is mostly listened to and appreciated by white Americans." Well, B.B. King thanks you, white America, and so does Bobby Blue Bland, and Denise La Salle and Koko Taylor, because they're trying to get paid and stay on the road, and they don't care who supports them, because black music fundamentally embraces whoever will listen.

But that's not to deny that blacks have not appreciated crucial elements of our culture, including urban blues, or for that matter, some agrarian forms of the blues
that have more in common with what we call country music than some music executives of Nashville might want to acknowledge. So I think black music is always
down and out, always against the rope. But like Muhammad Ali, black music
does the rope-a-dope: It just keeps on taking the punches, and when it looks as if
you're about to destroy it, it takes your worst—appropriation, commodification,
ghettoization in narrow categories on the radio—and wears you out. It turns the
energy of your opposition against you, like some aesthetic jujitsu, and strikes the
fatal blow, like Ali striking George Foreman down in that invigorating, mythological contest between black masculinities—the "appropriate" and American-flag-
bearing one (remember Foreman at the 1968 Olympics?), and the outlandish, outlawed Muslim-informed one.

Of course, in a sense, Ali was a great jazz performer, because his movements
were like extended riffs on the great themes of grace, power, and precision. But he
was also symbolically precious, and the metaphoric value of his craft was hardly
lost on his legions of followers, as he "floated like a butterfly," like a solo jazz
melody arching effortlessly above the backdrop of supporting instruments keeping
time and pace. Except, of course, Ali was a one-man combo, varying his pitch, and
punch, and the velocity and force of his delivery, "stinging like a bee," to razzle his
opponents and dazzle his fans, much like Miles Davis as he switched from *Kind of
Blue* to *Bitches Brew*. And in his flight, in his mobility, Ali also struck symbolic blows
against the demobilization of black culture and the restriction of our unique voices,
as did so many great jazz instrumentalists and vocalists, from Satchmo to Prez,
from the Duke to Bird, from Lady Day to Sassy. And this is where, perhaps, we
can see the relation between jazz and hip-hop, too, at least in Ali's artistry, because
when Ali came out with his doggerel disguised as edifying ring rhetoric—"rumble,
young man, rumble" and "I'm pretty" and "I shook up the world . . . I'm a bad
man"—his braggadocios behavior prefigured rap rhetoric.

But when you think about the metaphor of boxing and fighting as jazz, and jazz
as fighting and boxing, we've also got to focus on the serious sense of contest at
the heart of both. Not only two pugilists testing their ring generalship, but two or
three or four or more instrumentalists in the "cutting sessions" where they lift
their level of play and vision by virtue of engaging their fellow artists in friendly
competition—and maybe here is where, like all analogies, the one between boxing
and jazz breaks down, 'cause there ain't nothing friendly in boxing until the
match is over, and sometimes not even then. But if we compare jazz and boxing,
we might also compare jazz and running, since black music is truly engaged in a
race. But it's a marathon, not a sprint, since jazz and black cultural products are
about the long haul.

One of the advantages of the long view in black culture is that it allows us to
comprehend the durability and resilience of black music. Despite its appropria-
tions, imitations, dilutions, and domestications, black musical creators are peren-

nially preoccupied with the next thing. You can trace the anatomy of innovation within given genres, and in looking at how one form gives way to another. For instance, as proof of the former, think of the varieties of what we know today as jazz. To name a few changes within jazz, termed America's classical music, look at the progression. First there's blues; after blues, there's ragtime; after ragtime, there's Dixieland; after Dixieland, there's swing; after swing, there's bebop; after bebop, there's hardbop; after hardbop, there's postbop; after postbop, there's avant-garde; after avant-garde, there's fusion; after fusion, there's smooth jazz. Of course, each of these musical expressions survives, in varying degrees of intensity, but they symbolize the restless evolution of black musical forms.

And when we examine the historical development of genres of black music, we observe a constant engagement with innovation, progression, and expansion, from the spirituals, blues, ragtime, jazz, gospel, rhythm & blues, rock & roll, soul, funk, disco, hip-hop, house, go-go, new jack swing, techno-soul, acid jazz, bass and drum, and on and on. And when these forms are occasionally, almost unavoidably, appropriated, imitated, diluted, and domesticated in mainstream culture, black folk are on to something else. With black creative cultures, it's always about the great next. Indeed, the great next is the secular telos that pulls black America forward, even as we reappropriate what has been appropriated and generate the next form of creativity. The great next stands as the sign of an inexhaustible black possibility and fecundity that spawns newer forms of cultural expression.

"Next" is surely one of the key words in the vocabulary of black improvisation, related to and driven by what the French anthropologist Levi-Strauss calls bricolage, making do with what is at hand. For black culture, the great next and bricolage is about the possibilities inherent in taking the fragments, the leftovers that are both literally and symbolically at hand, and doing something imaginative and substantive with them. In one sense, black cultural creativity, the great next, is driven by what may be termed the political economy of chitlins: taking the most unsavory element of an already undesirable entity and making a living from commodifying, marketing, and consuming it. A leftover becomes a lifesaver, in the case of many blacks who had little to nurture their hunger beyond pork bellies, which later became an item sold on Wall Street. Black artistic expression often involves taking the sonic fragments and cultural leftovers of dominant culture and making a black cultural product that is desirable, even irresistible, to the margins and the mainstream. The beauty of black culture is its ability to re-create and reinvent itself as the great next thing in the long evolution of creative possibilities, at precisely the moment it's being written off.

Interview by Maria Agui Carter and Calvin A. Lindsay Jr.
New York, New York, 1999

PART TWELVE

HIP-HOP CULTURE

I have been christened "the hip-hop intellectual" in publications such as U.S. News & World Report *and* The Chronicle of Higher Education. *Although most of my scholarship has not addressed hip-hop culture—but black religion, black leadership, black moral and political thought, and various dimensions of black popular culture—I have gladly identified with the younger "hip-hop generation." I have used frequent references to hip-hop culture in my lectures, sermons, and public addresses, and I have written a book about the greatest icon in hip-hop—Tupac Shakur. I have done this in hopes of using whatever intellectual and cultural influence I possess to combat unjust appraisals of hip-hop music, and to encourage older folk to listen to the cries of hurt and desperation—and help—that ring across the culture's lyrical landscape. Furthermore, I have testified twice before Congress in the effort to forge greater awareness of the genre's brilliant social criticism and aesthetic achievements, while defending the most politically vulnerable and underrepresented group in the country—poor black and brown urban youth. Hip-hop culture is the most explosive, engaging, and controversial form of (black) American pop culture to find global circulation and acclaim in the last quarter century, and is worthy of serious critique and investigation.*

Thirty

THE CULTURE OF HIP-HOP

In 1987, as a second-year graduate student at Princeton, I published one of the first essays on rap in the academy. That essay—my first professional piece of writing—was entitled "Rap, Race, and Reality." It was written for the legendary, but now defunct, magazine of progressive Christian opinion, Christianity and Crisis, *which was founded in 1941 by the renowned theologian Reinhold Niebuhr. Two years later, I wrote "The Culture of Hip-Hop" for my monthly column in* Z Magazine. *Although the rapid proliferation of styles, themes, and trends within hip-hop threatens to make obsolete any analysis of the genre that is older than five years, this essay may be useful for the way it addresses the emergence, evolution, and redefinition of hip-hop from its humble beginnings in the Bronx to its golden age in the mid '80s to the early '90s. This essay has been widely used in college and university courses, and has appeared in several anthologies.*

FROM THE VERY BEGINNING OF ITS RECENT HISTORY, hip-hop music—or rap, as it has come to be known—has faced various obstacles. Initially, rap was deemed a passing fad, a playful and ephemeral black cultural form that steamed off the musical energies of urban black teens. As it became obvious that rap was here to stay, a permanent fixture in black ghetto youths' musical landscape, the reactions changed from dismissal to denigration, and rap music came under attack from both black and white quarters. Is rap really as dangerous as many critics argue? Or are there redeeming characteristics to rap music that warrant our critical attention? I will attempt to answer these and other questions as I explore the culture of hip-hop.

Trying to pinpoint the exact origin of rap is a tricky process that depends on when one acknowledges a particular cultural expression or product as rap. Rap can be traced back to the revolutionary verse of Gil Scott-Heron and the Last Poets, to Pigmeat Markham's "Here Come de Judge," and even to Bessie Smith's rapping to a beat in some of her blues. We can also cite ancient African oral traditions as the antecedents to various contemporary African American cultural practices. In any case, the modern history of rap probably begins in 1979 with the rap song "Rapper's Delight," by the Sugarhill Gang. Although there were other (mostly underground) examples of rap, this record is regarded as the signal barrier breaker, birthing hip-hop and consolidating the infant art form's popularity. This first stage in rap record production was characterized by rappers placing their rhythmic, repetitive speech over well-known (mostly R&B) black music hits. "Rapper's Delight" was rapped over the music to a song made by the popular '70s R&B group Chic, titled "Good Times." Although rap would later enhance its technical virtuosity through instrumentation, drum machines, and "sampling" existing records—thus making it creatively symbiotic—the first stage was benignly parasitic upon existing black music.

As rap grew, it was still limited to mostly inner-city neighborhoods and particularly its place of origin, New York City. Rap artists like Funky 4 Plus 1, Kool Moe Dee, Busy Bee, Afrika Bambaata, Cold Crush Brothers, Kurtis Blow, DJ Kool Herc, and Grandmaster Melle Mel were experimenting with this developing musical genre. As it evolved, rap began to describe and analyze the social, economic, and political factors that led to its emergence and development: drug addiction, police brutality, teen pregnancy, and various forms of material deprivation. This new development was both expressed and precipitated by Kurtis Blow's "Those Are the Breaks" and by the most influential and important rap song to emerge in rap's early history, "The Message," by Grandmaster Flash and the Furious Five. The picture this song painted of inner-city life for black Americans—the hues of dark social misery and stains of profound urban catastrophe—screeched against the canvas of most suburban sensibilities:

> You'll grow up in the ghetto living second rate / And your eyes will sing a song of deep hate / The places you play and where you stay, / Looks like one great big alleyway / You'll admire all the number book takers / Thugs, pimps, and pushers, and the big money makers / Drivin' big cars, spendin' twenties and tens, And you want to grow up to be just like them / . . . It's like a jungle sometimes / It makes me wonder how I keep from goin' under.

"The Message," along with Flash's "New York, New York," pioneered the social awakening of rap into a form combining social protest, musical creation, and cultural expression.

As its fortunes slowly grew, rap was still viewed by the music industry as an epiphenomenal cultural activity that would cease as black youth became bored and moved on to another diversion, as they did with break dancing and graffiti art. But the successes of the rap group Run-D.M.C. moved rap into a different sphere of artistic expression that signaled its increasing control of its own destiny. Run-D.M.C. is widely recognized as the progenitor of modern rap's creative integration of social commentary, diverse musical elements, and uncompromising cultural identification—an integration that pushed the music into the mainstream and secured its future as an American musical genre with an identifiable tradition. Run-D.M.C.'s stunning commercial and critical success almost single-handedly landed rap in the homes of many black and nonblack youths across America by producing the first rap album to be certified gold (500,000 copies sold), the first rap song to be featured on the twenty-four-hour music video channel MTV, and the first rap album (1987's *Raising Hell*) to go triple platinum (3 million copies sold).

On *Raising Hell,* Run-D.M.C. showcased the sophisticated technical virtuosity of its DJ Jam Master Jay—the raw shrieks, scratches, glitches, and language of the street, plus the innovative and ingenious appropriation of hard-rock guitar riffs. In doing this, Run-D.M.C. symbolically and substantively wedded two traditions—the waning subversion of rock music and the rising, incendiary aesthetic of hip-hop music—to produce a provocative musical hybrid of fiery lyricism and potent critique. *Raising Hell* ended with the rap anthem, "Proud to Be Black," intoning its unabashed racial pride:

> Ya know I'm proud to be black ya'll, And that's a fact ya'll ... Now Harriet Tubman was born a slave, She was a tiny black woman when she was raised / She was livin' to be givin', There's a lot that she gave / There's not a slave in this day and age, I'm proud to be black.

At the same time, rap, propelled by Run-D.M.C.'s epochal success, found an arena in which to concentrate its subversive cultural didacticism aimed at addressing racism, classism, social neglect, and urban pain: the rap concert, where rappers are allowed to engage in ritualistic refusals of censored speech. The rap concert also creates space for cultural resistance and personal agency, loosing the strictures of the tyrannizing surveillance and demoralizing condemnation of mainstream society and encouraging relatively autonomous, often enabling, forms of self-expression and cultural creativity.

However, Run-D.M.C.'s success, which greatly increased the visibility and commercial appeal of rap music through record sales and rap concerts, brought along another charge that has had a negative impact on rap's perception by the general public: the claim that rap expresses and causes violence. Tipper Gore has repeatedly said that rap music appeals to "angry, disillusioned, unloved kids" and that it tells them it is "okay to beat people up." Violent incidents at rap concerts in Los Angeles, Pittsburgh, Cleveland, Atlanta, Cincinnati, and New York City have only reinforced the popular perception that rap is intimately linked to violent social behavior by mostly black and Latino inner-city youth. Countless black parents, too, have had negative reactions to rap, and the black radio and media establishment, although not as vocal as Gore, have voted on her side with their allocation of much less airplay and print coverage to rap than is warranted by its impressive record sales.

Such reactions betray a shallow understanding of rap, which in many cases results from people's unwillingness to listen to rap lyrics, many of which counsel antiviolent and antidrug behavior among the youths who are their avid audience. Many rappers have spoken directly against violence, such as KRS-One in his "Stop the Violence." Another rap record produced by KRS-One in 1989, the top-selling *Self-Destruction,* insists that violence predates rap and speaks against escalating black-on-black crime, which erodes the social and communal fabric of already debased black inner cities across America:

Well, today's topic is self-destruction, It really ain't the rap audience that's buggin' / It's one or two suckers, ignorant brothers, Tryin' to rob and steal from one
another / . . . 'Cause the way we live is positive. We don't kill our relatives /
. . . Back in the sixties our brothers and sisters were hanged. How could you gang-
bang? / I never, ever ran from the Ku Klux Klan, and I shouldn't have to run from
a black man, 'Cause that's / Self-destruction, ya headed for self-destruction.

Despite such potent messages, many mainstream blacks and whites persist in
categorically negative appraisals of rap, refusing to distinguish between enabling,
productive rap messages and the social violence that exists in many inner-city
communities and that is often reflected in rap songs. Of course, it is difficult for
a culture that is serious about the maintenance of social arrangements, economic
conditions, and political choices that create and reproduce poverty, racism, sexism, classism, and violence to display a significant appreciation for musical expressions that contest the existence of such problems in black and Latino communities. Also disappointing is the continued complicity of black radio stations
in denying rap its rightful place of prominence on their playlists. The conspiracy
of silence and invisibility has affected the black print media as well. Although
rapper M. C. Shan believes that most antirap bias arises from outside the black
community, he faults black radio for depriving rap of adequate airplay and
laments the fact that "if a white rock 'n' roll magazine like *Rolling Stone* or *Spin*
can put a rapper on the cover and *Ebony* and *Jet* won't, that means there's really
something wrong."

In this regard, rap music is emblematic of the glacial shift in aesthetic sensibilities between blacks of different generations, and it draws attention to the severe
economic barriers that increasingly divide ghetto poor blacks from middle- and
upper-middle-class blacks. Rap reflects the intraracial class division that has
plagued African-American communities for the last thirty years. The increasing
social isolation, economic hardship, political demoralization, and cultural exploitation endured by most ghetto poor communities in the past few decades have
given rise to a form of musical expression that captures the terms of ghetto poor
existence. I am not suggesting that rap has been limited to the ghetto poor, but
only that its major themes and styles continue to be drawn from the conflicts and
contradictions of black urban life. One of the later trends in rap music is the development of "pop" rap by groups like JJ Fad, The Fat Boys, DJ Jazzy Jeff and
The Fresh Prince, and Tone Loc. DJ Jazzy Jeff and The Fresh Prince, for example, are two suburbanites from Southwest Philadelphia and Winfield. (For that
matter, members of the most radical rap group, Public Enemy, are suburbanites
from Long Island.) DJ Jazzy Jeff and The Fresh Prince's album, *He's the DJ, I'm the
Rapper*, sold over 3 million copies, boosted by the enormously successful single
"Parents Just Don't Understand." This record, which rapped humorously about
various crises associated with being a teen, struck a chord with teenagers across
the racial and class spectra, signaling the exploration of rap's populist terrain. The

Fresh Prince's present success as the star of his own Quincy Jones–produced television series is further testimony to his popular appeal.

Tone Loc's success also expresses rap's division between "hardcore" (social consciousness and racial pride backed by driving rhythms) and "pop" (exploration of common territory between races and classes, usually devoid of social message). This division, while expressing the commercial expansion of rap, also means that companies and willing radio executives have increasingly chosen pop rap as more acceptable than its more realistic, politically conscious counterpart. (This bias is also evident in the selection of award recipients in the newly created rap category at the annual Grammy Awards.) Tone Loc is an L.A. rapper whose first single, "Wild Thing," sold over 2 million copies, topping *Billboard*'s "Hot Singles Chart," the first rap song to achieve this height. Tone Loc's success was sparked by his video's placement in heavy rotation on MTV, which devotes an hour on Saturdays to *Yo! MTV Raps,* a show that became so popular that a daily hour segment was added.

The success of such artists as Tone Loc and DJ Jazzy Jeff and The Fresh Prince inevitably raises the specter of mainstream dilution, the threat to every emergent form of cultural production in American society, particularly the fecund musical tradition that comes from black America. For many, this means the sanitizing of rap's expression of urban realities, resulting in sterile hip-hop that, devoid of its original fire, will offend no one. This scenario, of course, is a familiar denouement to the story of most formerly subversive musical genres. Also, MTV's avid acceptance of rap and the staging of rap concerts run by white promoters willing to take a chance on rap artists add further commentary to the sad state of cultural affairs in many black communities: the continued refusal to acknowledge authentic (not to mention desirable) forms of rap artistry ensures rap's existence on the margins of many black communities.

Perhaps the example of another neglected and devalued black musical tradition, the blues, can be helpful for understanding what is occurring among rap segments of the black community and mainstream American society. The blues now has a mostly young white audience. Blacks do not largely support the blues through concert patronage or record buying, thus neglecting a musical genre that was once closely identified with devalued and despised people: poor southern agrarian blacks and the northern urban black poor, the first stratum of the developing underclass. The blues functioned for another generation of blacks much as rap functions for young blacks today: as a source of racial identity, permitting forms of boasting and asserting machismo for devalued black men suffering from social degradation, allowing commentary on social and personal conditions in uncensored language, and fostering the ability to transform hurt and anguish into art and commerce. Even in its heyday, however, the blues existed as a secular musical genre against the religious traditions that saw the blues as "devil's music" and the conservative black cultural perspectives of the blues as barbaric. These feelings, along with the direction of southern agrarian musical energies into a more accessible and populist soul music, ensured the contraction of the economic and cultural basis for expressing life experience in the blues idiom.

Robert Cray's recent success in mainstreaming the blues perhaps completes the cycle of survival for devalued forms of black music: it originates in a context of anguish and pain and joy and happiness, it expresses those emotions and ideas in a musical language and idiom peculiar to its view of life, it is altered as a result of cultural sensibilities and economic factors, and it undergoes distribution, packaging, and consumption for leisurely or cathartic pleasure through concert attendance or record buying. Also, in the process, artists are sometimes removed from the immediate context and original site of their artistic production. Moreover, besides the everyday ways in which the music is used for a variety of entertainment functions, it may occasionally be employed in contexts that undermine its critique of the status quo, and it may be used to legitimize a cultural or social setting that, in negative ways, has partially given rise to its expression. A recent example of this is the late Lee Atwater's positioning of himself as a privileged patron of the blues and soul music traditions in the 1989 Bush inauguration festivities, which was preceded by his racist use of the Willie Horton case. Atwater's use of Willie Horton viciously played on the very prejudice against black men that has often led blues musicians to express the psychic, personal, and social pain occasioned by racism in American (political) culture. Rap's visibility may alter this pattern as it continues to grow, but its self-defined and continuing challenge is to maintain its aesthetic, cultural, and political proximity to its site of original expression: the ghetto poor.

Interestingly, a new wave of rap artists may be accomplishing this goal, but with foreboding consequences. For example, N.W.A. (Niggas With Attitude) reflects the brutal circumstances that define the boundaries within which most ghetto poor black youth in Los Angeles must live. For the most part they—unlike their socially conscientious counterparts Public Enemy, Boogie Down Productions, and Stetsasonic—have no ethical remove from the violence, gang-bangin', and drugs in L.A.'s inner city. In their song "— Tha Police," N.W.A. gives a sample of their reality:

> Fuck the police, comin' straight from the underground. A young nigger got it bad 'cause I'm brown / And not the other color, so police think, / They have the authority to kill a minority / . . . Searchin' my car looking for the product, / Thinkin' every nigger is sellin' narcotic / . . . But don't let it be a black and a white one, / 'Cause they'll slam ya down to the street top, Black police showin' out for the white cop.

Such expressions of violence certainly reflect the actual life circumstances of many black and Latino youth caught in the desperate cycle of drugs and gangs involved in L.A. ghetto living. N.W.A. celebrates a lethal mix of civil terrorism and personal cynicism. Their attitude is both one answer to, and the logical outcome of, the violence, racism, and oppression in American culture. On the other hand, their vision must be criticized, for the stakes are too high for the luxury of moral neutrality. Having at least partially lived the life they rap about, N.W.A. understands the viciousness of police brutality. However, they must also be challenged to develop an ethical perspective on the drug gangs that duplicate police violence in black-on-black crime. While rappers like N.W.A. perform an invaluable service by rapping in poignant and realistic terms about urban underclass existence, they must be challenged to expand their moral vocabulary and be more sophisticated in their understanding that description alone is insufficient to address the crises of black urban life. Groups like N.W.A. should be critically aware that blacks are victims of the violence of both state repression *and* gang violence, that one form of violence is often the response to the other, and that blacks continue to be held captive to disenabling lifestyles (gang-bangin', drug dealing) that cripple the life of black communities.

Also problematic is the sexist sentiment that pervades so much of rap music. It is a rampant sexism that continues to mediate the relations within the younger black generation with lamentable intensity. While it is true that rap's sexism is indeed a barometer of the general tenor and mood that mediates black male–female relations, it is not the role of women alone to challenge it. Reproach must flow from women *and* men who are sensitive to the ongoing sexist attitudes and behavior that dominate black male–female relationships. Because women by and large do not run record companies, or even head independent labels that have their records distributed by larger corporations, it is naive to assume that protest by women alone will arrest the spread of sexism in rap. Female rappers are certainly a potential resource for challenging existing sexist attitudes, but given the sexist barriers that patrol rap's borders, male rappers must be challenged by antisexist men, especially male rappers who contest the portrayal of women in most rap music. The constant reference to women as "skeezers," "bitches," and "ho's" only reinforces the perverted expression of male dominance and patriarchy and reasserts the stereotyping of women as sexual objects intended exclusively for male pleasure.

Fortunately, many of the problems related to rap—particularly with black radio, media, and community acceptance—have only fostered a sense of camaraderie that transcends in crucial ways the fierce competitive streak in rap (which, at its best moments, urges rappers on to creative musical heights). While the "dis" rap (which humorously musicalizes "the dozens") is alive and well, the overall feeling among rap artists that rap must flourish outside the sanctions of traditional means of garnering high visibility or securing record sales has directed a communal energy into the production of their music. The current state of affairs has also precipitated cooperative entrepreneurial activity among young black persons. The rap industry has spawned a number of independent labels, providing young blacks (mostly men) with experience as heads of their own businesses and with exposure as managers of talent, positions that might otherwise be unavailable to them. Until recently, rap flourished, for the most part, outside of the tight artistic and economic constraints imposed by major music corporations. Although many independent companies have struck distribution deals with major labels—such as Atlantic, MCA, Columbia, and Warner Brothers—it has usually been the case, until the late 1980s, that the inexperience of major labels with rap, coupled with their relatively conservative musical tastes, has enabled the independent labels to control their destinies by teaching the major music corporations invaluable lessons about street sales, the necessity of having a fast rate of delivery from the production of a record to its date of distribution, and remaining close to the sensibilities of the street, while experimenting with their marketing approach in ways that reflect the diversification of styles in rap.

Rap expresses the ongoing preoccupation with literacy and orality that has characterized African-American communities since the inception of legally coerced illiteracy during slavery. Rap artists explore grammatical creativity, verbal wizardry, and linguistic innovation in refining the art of oral communication. The rap artist, as Cornel West has indicated, is a bridge figure who combines the two potent traditions in black culture: preaching and music. The rap artist appeals to the rhetorical practices eloquently honed in African-American religious experiences and the cultural potency of black singing/musical traditions to produce an engaging hybrid. They are truly urban griots dispensing social and cultural critique, verbal shamans exorcising the demons of cultural amnesia. The culture of hip-hop has generated a lexicon of life that expresses rap's B-boy/B-girl worldview, a perspective that takes delight in undermining "correct" English usage while celebrating the culturally encoded phrases that communicate in rap's idiom.

Rap has also retrieved historic black ideas, movements, and figures in combating the racial amnesia that threatens to relegate the achievements of the black past to the ash heap of dismemory. Such actions have brought a renewed sense of historical pride to young black minds that provides a solid base for racial self-esteem. Rap music has also focused renewed attention on black nationalist and black radical thought. This revival has been best symbolized by the rap group Public Enemy. Public Enemy announced its black nationalism in embryonic form on their first album, *Yo! Bum Rush the Show*, but their vision sprang forward full-blown in their important *It Takes a Nation of Millions to Hold Us Back*. The album's explicit black nationalist language and cultural sensibilities were joined with a powerful mix of music, beats, screams, noises, and rhythms from the streets. Its message is provocative, even jarring, a précis of the contained chaos and channeled rage that informs the most politically astute rappers. On the cut "Bring the Noise," they intone:

> We got to demonstrate, come on now, they're gonna have to wait / Till we get
> it right / Radio stations I question their blackness / They call themselves black,
> but we'll see if they'll play this / Turn it up! Bring the noise!

Public Enemy also speaks of the criminality of prison conditions and how dope dealers fail the black community. Their historical revivalism is noteworthy, for instance, as they rap on "Party for Your Right to Fight":

Power Equality / And we're out to get it / I know some of you ain't wit' it / This party started right in '66 / With a pro-Black radical mix / Then at the hour of twelve /. J. Edgar Hoover, and he coulda' proved to 'ya / He had King and X set up / Also the party with Newton, Cleaver, and Seale / . . . Word from the honorable Elijah Muhammad / Know who you are to be Black . . . the original Black Asiatic man.

Public Enemy troubled even more sociocultural waters with their Nation of Islam views, saying in "Don't Believe the Hype":

The follower of Farrakhan / Don't tell me that you understand / Until you hear the man.

Such rap displays the power and pitfalls associated with the revival of earlier forms of black radicalism, nationalism, and cultural expression. The salutary aspect of the historical revival is that it raises consciousness about important figures, movements, and ideas, prompting rappers to express their visions of life in American culture. This renewed historicism permits young blacks to discern links between the past and their own present circumstances, using the past as a fertile source of social reflection, cultural creation, and political resistance.

On the other hand, it has also led to perspectives that do not provide *critical* reflection on the past. Rather, many rappers attempt to duplicate the past without challenging or expanding it. Thus, their historical insight fails to illumine our current cultural problems as powerfully as it might, and the present generation of black youth fails to benefit as fully from the lessons that it so powerfully revives. This is an unfortunate result of the lack of understanding and communication among various segments of the black community, particularly along generational and class lines, problems symbolized in the black community's response to rap. Historical revival cries out for contexts that render the past understandable and usable. This cannot occur if large segments of the black community continue to be segregated from one of the most exciting cultural transformations occurring in contemporary American life: the artistic expression, cultural exploration, political activity, and historical revival of hip-hop artists.

An issue in rap that is closely related to the acknowledgment of history and sources is sampling, or the grafting of music, voices, and beats from another sonic source onto a rap record. The practice of sampling expresses the impulse to collage that characterizes the best of black musical traditions, particularly jazz and gospel. Sampling is also postmodernist activity that merges disparate musical and cultural forms to communicate an artistic message. Sampling is a transgressive activity because rappers employ it to interrupt the narrative flow and musical stability of other musical texts, producing a new and often radically different creation. But rap may potentially take back in its technical appropriation what it has given in its substantive, lyrical achievements: a recognition of history. While sampling permits a rap creator to reconfigure voices and rhythms in creating an alternate code of cultural exchange, the practice may also deprive other artists of recognition or even financial remuneration. The classic case in point is James Brown, who, along with George Clinton, is the most sampled man in rap and the primal progenitor of the beats and rhythms in hip-hop music. Although his voice, rhythms, and beats are often easily identifiable and rap's debt to him is obvious, Brown's benefit has been limited. Recent legal woes connected to the status of rap's practice of creative borrowing may hasten rap's codification of appropriate acknowledgment, particularly in an economic practice similar to the royalty that distinguishes between small bites of music and significant borrowing and quotation.

Rap is a form of profound musical, cultural, and social creativity. It expresses the desire of young black people to reclaim their history, reactivate forms of black radicalism, and contest the powers of despair and economic depression that presently besiege the black community. Besides being the most powerful form of black musical expression today, rap projects a style of self into the world that generates forms of cultural resistance and transforms the ugly terrain of ghetto existence into a searing portrait of life as it must be lived by millions of voiceless people. For that reason alone, rap deserves attention and should be taken seriously; and for its productive and healthy moments, it should be promoted as a worthy form of artistic expression and cultural projection and an enabling source of black juvenile and communal solidarity.

Thirty-One

GANGSTA RAP AND AMERICAN CULTURE

In 1994, I wrote an op-ed for the New York Times *entitled "Bum Rap," arguing that hip-hop culture was often unfairly attacked. In particular, I contended that gangsta rap was much more complex than its literal-minded opponents made it out to be. I also appeared on the* McNeil-Lehrer News Hour *to debate gangsta rap, including an exchange with political activist C. Delores Tucker, the first of our many engagements, debates, and confrontations over the years. While I am critical of many elements of gangsta rap, it is important to explore its cultural and racial roots. It is necessary as well to take stock of the moral complaint, and the venting of suffering and misery, that pour through gangsta rap's best artists. My book on Tupac Shakur,* Holler If You Hear Me, *grew in part out of my effort to understand and explore the complex genealogy of the thug in black youth pop culture. This essay is my most succinct statement of the ambitions and contradictions of gangsta rap, and its social and rhetorical uses in hip-hop and the broader culture.*

THE RECENT ATTACKS ON THE ENTERTAINMENT INDUSTRY, especially gangsta rap, by Senator Bob Dole, former Education Secretary William Bennett, and political activist C. Delores Tucker, reveal the fury that popular culture can evoke in a wide range of commentators. As a thirty-five-year-old father of a sixteen-year-old son and as a professor and ordained Baptist minister who grew up in Detroit's treacherous inner city, I too am disturbed by many elements of gangsta rap. But I'm equally anguished by the way many critics have used its artists as scapegoats. How can we avoid the pitfall of unfairly attacking black youth for problems that bewitched our culture long before they gained prominence? First, we should understand what forces drove the emergence of rap. Second, we should place the debate about gangsta rap in the context of a much older debate about "negative" and "positive" black images. Finally, we should acknowledge that gangsta rap crudely exposes harmful beliefs and practices that are often maintained with deceptive civility in much of mainstream society, including many black communities.

If the fifteen-year evolution of hip-hop teaches us anything, it's that history is made in unexpected ways by unexpected people with unexpected results. Rap is now safe from the perils of quick extinction predicted at its humble start. But its birth in the bitter belly of the '70s proved to be a Rosetta stone of black popular culture. Afros, "blunts," funk music, and carnal eruptions define a "back-in-the-day" hip-hop aesthetic. In reality, the severe '70s busted the economic boom of the '60s. The fallout was felt in restructured automobile industries and collapsed steel mills. It was extended in exported employment to foreign markets. Closer to home, there was the depletion of social services to reverse the material ruin of black life. Later, public spaces for black recreation were gutted by Reaganomics or violently transformed by lethal drug economies.

Hip-hop was born in these bleak conditions. Hip-hoppers joined pleasure and rage while turning the details of their difficult lives into craft and capital. This is the world hip-hop would come to "represent": privileged persons speaking for less visible or vocal peers. At their best, rappers shape the tortuous twists of urban fate into lyrical elegies. They represent lives swallowed by too little love or opportunity. They represent themselves and their peers with aggrandizing anthems that boast of their ingenuity and luck in surviving. The art of "representin" that is much ballyhooed in hip-hop is the witness of those left to tell the afflicted's story.

As rap expands its vision and influence, its unfavorable origins and its relentless quest to represent black youth are both a consolation and challenge to hip-hoppers. They remind rappers that history is not merely the stuff of imperial dreams from above. It isn't just the sanitizing myths of those with political power. Representing history is within reach of those who seize the opportunity to speak for themselves, to represent their own interests at all costs. Even rap's largest controversies are about representation. Hip-hop's attitudes toward women and gays continually jolt in the unvarnished malevolence they reveal. The sharp responses to rap's misogyny and homophobia signify its central role in battles over the cultural representation of other beleaguered groups. This is particularly true of gangsta rap.

While gangsta rap takes the heat for a range of social maladies from urban violence to sexual misconduct, the roots of our racial misery remain buried beneath moralizing discourse that is confused and sometimes dishonest. There's no doubt that gangsta rap is often sexist and that it reflects a vicious misogyny that has seized our nation with frightening intensity. It is doubly wounding for black women who are already beset by attacks from outside their communities to feel the thrust of musical daggers to their dignity from within. How painful it is for black women, many of whom have fought valiantly for black pride, to hear the dissonant chord of disdain carried in the angry epithet "bitch."

The link between the vulgar rhetorical traditions expressed in gangsta rap and the economic exploitation that dominates the marketplace is real. The circulation of brutal images of black men as sexual outlaws and black females as "ho's" in many gangsta rap narratives mirrors ancient stereotypes of black sexual identity. Male and female bodies are turned into commodities. Black sexual desire is stripped of redemptive uses in relationships of great affection or love.

Gangsta rappers, however, don't merely respond to the values and visions of the marketplace; they help shape them as well. The ethic of consumption that pervades our culture certainly supports the rapacious materialism shot through the narratives of gangsta rap. Such an ethic, however, does not exhaust the literal or metaphoric purposes of material wealth in gangsta culture. The imagined and real uses of money to help one's friends, family, and neighborhood occupies a prominent spot in gangsta rap lyrics and lifestyles.

Equally troubling is the glamorization of violence and the romanticization of the culture of guns that pervades gangsta rap. The recent legal troubles of Tupac Shakur, Dr. Dre, Snoop Doggy Dogg, and other gangsta rappers chastens any defense of the genre based on simplistic claims that these artists are merely performing roles that are divorced from real life. Too often for gangsta rappers, life does indeed imitate and inform art.

But gangsta rappers aren't *simply* caving in to the pressure of racial stereotyping and its economic rewards in a music industry hungry to exploit their artistic imaginations. According to this view, gangsta rappers are easily manipulated pawns in a chess game of material dominance where their consciences are sold to the highest bidder. Or else gangsta rappers are viewed as the black face of white desire to distort the beauty of black life. Some critics even suggest that white record executives discourage the production of "positive rap" and reinforce the desire for lewd expressions packaged as cultural and racial authenticity.

But such views are flawed. The street between black artists and record companies runs both ways. Even though black artists are often ripe for the picking—and thus susceptible to exploitation by white and black record labels—many of them are quite sophisticated about the politics of cultural representation. Many gangsta rappers helped to create the genre's artistic rules. Further, they have figured out how to financially exploit sincere and sensational interest in "ghetto life." Gangsta rap is no less legitimate because many "gangstas" turn out to be middle-class blacks faking homeboy roots. This fact simply focuses attention on the genre's essential constructedness, its literal artifice. Much of gangsta rap makes voyeuristic whites and naive blacks think they're getting a slice of authentic ghetto life when in reality they're being served colorful exaggerations. That doesn't mean, however, that the best of gangsta rappers don't provide compelling portraits of real social and economic suffering.

Critics of gangsta rap often ignore how hip-hop has been developed without the assistance of a majority of black communities. Even "positive" or "nation-conscious" rap was initially spurned by those now calling for its revival in the face of gangsta rap's ascendancy. Long before white record executives sought to exploit transgressive sexual behavior among blacks, many of us failed to lend support to politically motivated rap. For instance, when political rap group Public Enemy was at its artistic and popular height, most of the critics of gangsta rap didn't insist on the group's prominence in black cultural politics. Instead, Public Enemy, and other conscientious rappers, were often viewed as controversial figures whose inflammatory racial rhetoric was cause for caution or alarm. In this light, the hue and cry directed against gangsta rap by the new defenders of "legitimate" hip-hop rings false.

Also, many critics of gangsta rap seek to curtail its artistic freedom to transgress boundaries defined by racial or sexual taboo. That's because the burden of representation falls heavily on what may be termed the race artist in a far different manner than the one I've described above. The race artist stands in for black communities. She represents millions of blacks by substituting or sacrificing her desires and visions for the perceived desires and visions of the masses. Even when the race artist manages to maintain relative independence of vision, his or her work is overlaid with, and interpreted within, the social and political aspirations of blacks as a whole. Why? Because of the appalling lack of redeeming or nonstereotypical representations of black life that are permitted expression in our culture.

This situation makes it difficult for blacks to affirm the value of nontraditional or transgressive artistic expressions. Instead of viewing such cultural products through critical eyes—seeing the good and the bad, the productive and destructive aspects of such art—many blacks tend to simply dismiss such work with hypercritical disdain. A suffocating standard of "legitimate" art is thus produced by the limited public availability of complex black art. Either art is seen as redemptive because it uplifts black culture and shatters stereotypical thinking about blacks, or it is seen as bad because it reinforces negative perceptions of black culture.

That is too narrow a measure for the brilliance and variety of black art and cultural imagination. Black folk should surely pay attention to how black art is perceived in our culture. We must be mindful of the social conditions that shape perceptions of our cultural expressions and that stimulate the flourishing of one kind of art versus another. (After all, die-hard hip-hop fans have long criticized how gangsta rap is eagerly embraced by white record companies while "roots" hip-hop is grossly underfinanced.)

But black culture is too broad and intricate—its artistic manifestations too unpredictable and challenging—for us to be *obsessed* with how white folk view our culture through the lens of our art. And black life is too differentiated by class, sexual identity, gender, region, and nationality to fixate on "negative" or "positive" representations of black culture. Black culture is good and bad, uplifting and depressing, edifying and stifling. All of these features should be represented in our art, should find resonant voicing in the diverse tongues of black cultural expressions.

Gangsta rappers are not the first to face the grueling double standards imposed on black artists. Throughout African-American history, creative personalities have sought to escape or enliven the role of race artist with varying degrees of success. The sharp machismo with which many gangsta rappers reject this office grates on the nerves of many traditionalists. Many critics argue that since gangsta rap is often the only means by which many white Americans come into contact with black life, its pornographic representations and brutal stereotypes of black culture are especially harmful. The understandable but lamentable response of many critics is to condemn gangsta rap out of hand. They aim to suppress gangsta rap's troubling expressions rather than critically engage its artists and the provocative issues they address. Thus the critics of gangsta rap use it for narrow political ends that fail to enlighten or better our common moral lives.

Tossing a moralizing *j'accuse* at the entertainment industry may have boosted Bob Dole's standing in the polls over the short term. It did little, however, to clarify or correct the problems to which he has drawn dramatic attention. I'm in favor of changing the moral climate of our nation. I just don't believe that attacking movies, music, and their makers is very helpful. Besides, right-wing talk radio hosts wreak more havoc than a slew of violent films. They're the ones terrorist Timothy McVeigh was inspired by as he planned to bomb the federal building in Oklahoma City.

A far more crucial task lies in getting at what's wrong with our culture and what it needs to get right. Nailing the obvious is easy. That's why Dole, along with William Bennett and C. Delores Tucker, goes after popular culture, especially gangsta rap. And the recent attempts of figures like Tucker and Dionne Warwick, as well as national and local lawmakers, to censor gangsta rap or to outlaw its sale to minors are surely misguided. When I testified before the U.S. Senate's Subcommittee on Juvenile Justice, as well as the Pennsylvania House of Representatives, I tried to make this point while acknowledging the need to responsibly confront gangsta rap's problems. Censorship of gangsta rap cannot begin to solve the problems of poor black youth. Nor will it effectively curtail their consumption of music that is already circulated through dubbed tapes and without the benefit of significant airplay.

A crucial distinction needs to be made between censorship of gangsta rap and edifying expressions of civic responsibility and community conscientiousness. The former seeks to prevent the sale of vulgar music that offends mainstream moral sensibilities by suppressing the First Amendment. The latter, however, is a more difficult but rewarding task. It seeks to oppose the expression of misogynistic and sexist sentiments in hip-hop culture through protest and pamphleteering, through community activism, and through boycotts and consciousness raising.

What Dole, Bennett, and Tucker shrink from helping us understand—and what all effective public moralists must address—is why this issue now? Dole's answer is that the loss of family values is caused by the moral corruption of popular culture, and therefore we should hold rap artists, Hollywood moguls, and record executives responsible for our moral chaos. It's hard to argue with Dole on the surface, but a gentle scratch reveals that both his analysis and answer are flawed.

Too often, "family values" is a code for a narrow view of how families work, who gets to count as a legitimate domestic unit, and consequently, what values are crucial to their livelihood. Research has shown that nostalgia for the family of the past, when father knew best, ignores the widespread problems of those times, including child abuse and misogyny. Romantic portrayals of the family on television and the big screen, anchored by the myth of the Benevolent Patriarch, hindered our culture from coming to grips with its ugly domestic problems.

To be sure, there have been severe assaults on American families and their values, but they have not come mainly from Hollywood, but from Washington with the dismantling of the Great Society. Cruel cuts in social programs for the neediest, an upward redistribution of wealth to the rich, and an unprincipled conservative political campaign to demonize poor black mothers and their children have left latter-day D. W. Griffiths in the dust. Many of gangsta rap's most vocal black critics (such as Tucker) fail to see how the alliances they forge with conservative white politicians such as Bennett and Dole are plagued with problems. Bennett and Dole have put up roadblocks to many legislative and political measures that would enhance the fortunes of the black poor they now claim in part to speak for. Their outcry resounds as crocodile tears from the corridors of power paved by bad faith.

Moreover, many of the same conservative politicians who support the attack on gangsta rap also attack black women (from Lani Guinier to welfare mothers), affirmative action, and the redrawing of voting districts to achieve parity for black voters. The war on gangsta rap diverts attention away from the more substantive threat posed to women and blacks by many conservative politicians. Gangsta rap's critics are keenly aware of the harmful effects that genre's misogyny can have on black teens. Ironically, such critics appear oblivious to how their rhetoric of absolute opposition to gangsta rap has been used to justify political attacks on poor black teens.

That doesn't mean that gratuitous violence and virulent misogyny should not be opposed. They must be identified and destroyed. I am wholly sympathetic, for instance, to sharp criticism of gangsta rap's ruinous sexism and homophobia, though neither Dole, Bennett, nor Tucker have made much of the latter plague. "Fags" and "dykes" are prominent in the genre's vocabulary of rage. Critics' failure to make this an issue only reinforces the inferior, invisible status of gay men and lesbians in mainstream and black cultural institutions. Homophobia is a vicious emotion and practice that links mainstream middle-class and black institutions to the vulgar expressions of gangsta rap. There seems to be an implicit agreement between gangsta rappers and political elites that gays, lesbians, and bisexuals basically deserve what they get.

But before we discard the genre, we should understand that gangsta rap often reaches higher than its ugliest, lowest common denominator. Misogyny, violence, materialism, and sexual transgression are not its exclusive domain. At its best, this music draws attention to complex dimensions of ghetto life ignored by many Americans. Of all the genres of hip-hop—from socially conscious rap to black nationalist expressions, from pop to hardcore—gangsta rap has most aggressively narrated the pains and possibilities, the fantasies and fears, of poor black urban youth. Gangsta rap is situated in the violent climes of postindustrial Los Angeles and its bordering cities. It draws its metaphoric capital in part from the mix of myth and murder that gave the Western frontier a dangerous appeal a century ago.

Gangsta rap is largely an indictment of mainstream and bourgeois black institutions by young people who do not find conventional methods of addressing personal and social calamity useful. The leaders of those institutions often castigate the excessive and romanticized violence of this music without trying to understand what precipitated its rise in the first place. In so doing, they drive a greater wedge between themselves and the youth they so desperately want to help.

If Americans really want to strike at the heart of sexism and misogyny in our communities, shouldn't we take a closer look at one crucial source of these blights:

religious institutions, including the synagogue, the temple, and the church? For instance, the central institution of black culture, the black church, which has given hope and inspiration to millions of blacks, has also given us an embarrassing legacy of sexism and misogyny. Despite the great good it has achieved through a heroic tradition of emancipatory leadership, the black church continues to practice and justify *ecclesiastical apartheid.* More than 70 percent of black church members are female, yet they are generally excluded from the church's central station of power, the pulpit. And rarely are the few ordained female ministers elected pastors.

Yet black leaders, many of them ministers, excoriate rappers for their verbal sexual misconduct. It is difficult to listen to civil rights veterans deplore the hostile depiction of women in gangsta rap without mentioning the vicious sexism of the movements for racial liberation of the 1960s. And of course the problem persists in many civil rights organizations today.

Attacking figures like Snoop Doggy Dogg or Tupac Shakur–or the companies that record or distribute them–is an easy out. It allows scapegoating without sophisticated moral analysis and action. While these young black males become whipping boys for sexism and misogyny, the places in our culture where these ancient traditions are nurtured and rationalized–including religious and educational institutions and the nuclear family–remain immune to forceful and just criticism.

Corporate capitalism, mindless materialism, and pop culture have surely helped unravel the moral fabric of our society. But the moral condition of our nation is equally affected by political policies that harm the vulnerable and poor. It would behoove Senator Dole to examine the glass house of politics he abides in before he decides to throw stones again. If he really wants to do something about violence, he should change his mind about the ban on assault weapons he seeks to repeal. That may not be as sexy or self-serving as attacking pop culture, but it might help save lives.

Gangsta rap's greatest "sin" may be that it tells the truth about practices and beliefs that rappers hold in common with the mainstream and with black elites. This music has embarrassed mainstream society and black bourgeois culture. It has forced us to confront the demands of racial representation that plague and provoke black artists. It has also exposed our polite sexism and our disregard for gay men and lesbians. We should not continue to blame gangsta rap for ills that existed long before hip-hop uttered its first syllable. Indeed, gangsta rap's in-your-face style may do more to force our nation to confront crucial social problems than countless sermons or political speeches.

Thirty-Two

WE NEVER WERE WHAT WE USED TO BE:
BLACK YOUTH, POP CULTURE, AND THE
POLITICS OF NOSTALGIA

This is my representative statement on hip-hop culture. In this chapter, I range over the various genres of hip-hop in exploring its roots and ramifications in black culture and beyond. I also attempt to situate the development of hip-hop culture in reference to earlier expressions of black pop culture that endured demonization, especially jazz and blues music. I also argue that an older generation has wrongly concluded that black youth are ethically estranged from their elders; too often, older blacks assign to the unavoidable generation gap a morally perverse intent by youth that is dangerous. I argue that the moral vision of many older blacks is clouded by a nostalgic sense of the past that prevents them from identifying with the hip-hop generation—and from identifying their own lapses and failures as well. Finally, I proffer the existence of a "juvenocracy" in urban communities—urban spaces occupied and dominated by black youth under twenty-five. This demographic shift, which also represents a shift in power from older to younger blacks, has had a demonstrable, sometimes devastating, impact on black families. Only by engaging and constructively critiquing hip-hop culture—and not dismissing or denigrating it—can older blacks possibly hope to understand the most influential form of black popular culture of the last quarter century.

Our present obsession with the past has the double advantage of making new work seem raw and rough compared to the cozy patina of tradition, whilst refusing tradition its vital connection to what is happening now. By making islands of separation out of the unbreakable chain of human creativity, we are able to set up false comparisons, false expectations, all the while lamenting that the music, poetry, painting, prose, performance art of Now, fails to live up to the art of Then, which is why, we say, it does not affect us. In fact, we are no more moved by a past we are busy inventing, than by a present we are busy denying.

—JEANETTE WINTERSON
"ART OBJECTS," 1995

I WASN'T EXPECTING THE REBUFF. Its severity underscored the bitterness of the debate that has formed around urban black youth and the cultures they create.

I had just finished testifying before the United States Senate Judiciary Committee's Subcommittee on Juvenile Justice. Illinois Senator Carol Moseley-Braun, along with Maine Senator William Cohen and Wisconsin Senator and Subcommittee Chair Herbert Kohl, had called the hearing in 1994 to discuss "violent and demeaning imagery in popular music." Predictably, the hearings focused on gangsta rap. While he wasn't within barking distance, rapper Snoop Doggy Dogg was the shadow figure and rhetorical guest of dishonor at the proceedings. His body of work—like the rapper himself, slim but menacingly attractive—was relentlessly attacked by many of the hearing's witnesses. Snoop was made to appear like hip-hop's Mephistopheles, seducing black children to trade their souls for the corrupt delights of "G-funk." The latter is a jeep-rattling, bass-heavy, ripinvention (yes, a mix of ripping off and reinventing) of '70s funk. Except Snoop and G-funk impresario Dr. Dre's brand of funk is fused to the gangsterish fantasies of 1990s West Coast black youth culture. After having my say—that the music and its artists are complex, that they must be understood in both their cultural and racial setting even as we criticize their hateful sentiments—I was accosted by another witness's husband.

"Don't you have a Ph.D. from Princeton?" the tall, brown-skinned man brusquely quizzed me.

"Yes, sir, I do," I replied.

"And aren't you a Baptist preacher?" he asked, with even more scorn.

"Yes, sir, I am," I said.

"You know, for somebody who's supposed to be so smart, you sure are a dumb ass."

At that, he turned and walked off. He had the kind of self-satisfaction that only proud indignity can conjure. (To be honest, my Detroit homeboy roots nearly cracked the surface of my scholarly and preacherly gentility. But since my mama taught me to respect my elders, I kept my mouth shut.)

There were other times, too, when I caught a glimpse of the hostility between black youth culture and its older critics. Soon after my Washington witnessing, I lectured at Harvard on Malcolm X, ending with a recitation of N.W.A.'s (Niggas With Attitude) rap, "— Tha Police." After my talk, a seasoned graduate student approached me, I thought, to praise my performance.

"Your lecture was good, man," he duty noted. "But why would you end by surrendering the nobility of black folk to that barbaric nonsense?"

At still another conference, this time at Princeton, I interjected a long snatch from Snoop's syncopated soliloquy on his and Dr. Dre's rap, "Nothin' but a G Thang." A colleague later reported that a few of the Ivy League's stuffier types found my juxtaposing of Ralph Ellison and Snoop jarringly profane. And my performance led *New York Daily News* columnist Playthell Benjamin to label me a "sophist" and a "snake oil salesman." (Benjamin would later repeat these, and much stronger claims, when we went head-to-head at hearings on gangsta rap before the Pennsylvania State Legislature and on CBS radio's *Gil Gross Show*.)

Admittedly, much of the resistance I've encountered may have a lot to do with the fact that I'm a wanna-be rap star. I've even been labeled a "hip-hop intellectual." You see, even when I'm lecturing on dense theoretical issues, like, say, the relation of postmodern notions of identity to African-American culture, I've got the grating habit of dropping a line or two—okay, a few stanzas—from the latest rap release. At thirty-seven, I came along a little too late to spend my youth spinning tales about my hood in poetic meters padded by James Brown samples. It's probably pretty sad, and often maddening, for folk to see a late baby boomer like me—so late that my generation's been called "'tweeners" because we fit between real baby boomers and Generation Xers—trying to horn in on a younger age group's territory. It's probably a pre–midlife crisis, a forward-looking relapse back into a hip-hop youth that was never really mine. Or maybe in the spirit of hip-hop, I'm simply turning the tables to sample the youth of artists who sample the music of my youth.

Much of the anger I've seen directed at black youth, especially from older blacks, is tied to a belief that young blacks are very different from any other black generation. Among esteemed black intellectuals and persons on the street, there is a consensus that something has gone terribly wrong with black youth. They are disrespectful to their elders. They are obsessed with sex. They are materialistic. They are pathological. They are violent. They are nihilistic. They are ethically depraved. They are lazy. They are menaces to society.

Right away we must admit that some of these complaints form the rhetorical divide that grows between all generations. Some of these cants and carps are no more than predecessor blues. They are the laments of those who come Before judging those who come After. (Such judgments travel a two-way street. Our kids have their share of disgust about the world they've inherited.)

But many of these complaints reflect a real fear of black youth that's not confined to black communities and not explained by any "generation gap." It's hard to open a newspaper or watch television without getting an ugly reminder of the havoc our kids wreak on the streets and the terror they must confront without much sympathy or support. To be sure, the media has irresponsibly painted many of the problems of urban America black or brown. In reality, a lot of our social misery, including drugs, crime, and violence, has a decidedly whiter hue. Still, black youth are in big trouble.

For many black and white Americans, hip-hop culture crudely symbolizes the problems of urban black youth. The list of offenses associated with hip-hop culture is culled from rap lyrics and the lifestyles they promote. The list includes vulgar language, sexism, misogyny, homophobia, sexual promiscuity, domestic abuse, parental disrespect, rejection of authority, and the glorification of violence, drug use, rape, and murder. And it's true that even a casual listen to a lot of hip-hop will turn up these and other nefarious attitudes. At least if you listen to the style of hip-hop known as gangsta rap. The gangsta rap genre of hip-hop emerged in the late '80s on the West Coast as crack and gangs ruled the urban centers of Los Angeles, Long Beach, Compton, and Oakland. Since hip-hop has long turned to the black ghetto and the Latino barrio for lyrical inspiration, it was inevitable that a form of music that mimicked the violence on the streets would rise.

It was just as predictable, though not to the degree that it has happened, that a huge backlash against gangsta rap and black youth would emerge. Among the factors that made black youth culture ripe for such an attack is a general ignorance about the range and depth of hip-hop culture. Ironically, this ignorance helped make gangsta rap an economically viable music. Anti-rap crusader C. Delores Tucker can shout as loud as she wants, and she's certainly earned the right, but she was nowhere to be found when rap group Public Enemy was at its revolutionary height calling for a united black nation to fight racism and the powers that be. True, their brand of hip-hop brushed too closely to anti-Semitism and they certainly could have used a few lessons in feminist thought. But few people quit listening to Sinatra's "Fly Me to the Moon" (it was really named "In Other Words," but Sinatra's Billie Holiday–inspired phrasing was so impeccably memorable that he shifted the song's emphasis) because of his occasional racism or his denigration of women as broads.

The moral of the story is that had more support been given to so-called positive hip-hoppers and to revolutionary rappers who detested body bags and beer bottles; who encouraged black men to "be a father to your child"; who advocated love and respect for black women; who sought to build black communities; and who encouraged youth to study black history, the gangsta rap tide might have been stemmed. At the least, gangsta rappers might have been forced to take the internal criticisms of their hip-hop peers more seriously because such criticisms would have had moral and economic support. After all, it's easier to get an album made if you're "pimpin' hos," "cockin' glocks" or generally bitch-baiting your way through yet another tired tale about how terrible it was to come up in the hood without your father while blaming your mama for the sorry job she did, than if you're promoting radical black unity or the overthrow of white racism.

This is not to dis West Coast rap. They got big the old-fashioned way: they earned it. Left in the shadow of East Coast rap for years, West Coast rap reinvigorated the hip-hop game by reinventing the premise of rap: to groove the gluteus maximus. As Ralph Ellison said, geography is fate. West Coast hip-hop tailored its fat bass beats and silky melodies for jeeps that cruise the generous spaces of the West. The music appeals as well to fans in the open spaces of the Midwest and the South. The tightly drawn grooves and cerebral lyrics of the East Coast have almost become site-specific. East Coast rappers cling to beliefs in their artistic superiority and adhere to the principles of authentic hip-hop. Such beliefs give rise to poetically intense rappers like Nas or the esoteric basement hip-hoppers Wu Tang Clan. For the most part, East Coast rap lags far behind the West Coast in record sales and in popularity. Both brands of hip-hop proved too bruising for the old heads of the black bourgeoisie. The music also escaped the artistic interests of a lot of working-class black parents pulling twelve-hour shifts to keep out of the poorhouse.

But their children surely got the message. And so did the children of white suburbia. The crossover of hip-hop to white teens is certainly a driving force behind the attack on black youth. Hip-hop's appeal to white youth extends the refashioning of mainstream America by black popular culture. From sports to fashion, from music to film, innovations in American art owe a debt to the creativity of black culture. For example, twenty-five years ago, it was unimaginable that black basketball stars would make television commercials or have sneakers named after them. Teams like the New York Knickerbockers were derisively dubbed the New York "Niggerbockers" because of their share of the black talent beginning to flood the NBA. Today, the NBA is a black man's game. Michael Jordan is the most revered and perhaps the richest athlete in the world. Kids of every color lace up his shoes, sport his jersey, and want to, as the ad goes, "Be like Mike."

White kids are also adopting the dress, diction, and demeanor of urban black youth. From baggy pants to oversize shirts, the "gear" of hip-hop culture has been mass-produced and worn by youth of every ethnic and racial group. The slang of hip-hop is now widely used. "Yo" and "Whassup?" are part of our common cultural parlance. The *Arsenio Hall Show* was an extended hip-hop anthem, a limited scope of themes pegged to samples of existing material that are endlessly remixed. Perhaps that's why Hall's show lasted as long as the average rap career, proving that the genre's virtue is its vice. Even the *New York Times* regularly uses "dis" in its articles. The swagger of black youth, the sultry way they combine boasting and self-confidence, has influenced the styles of upper-middle-class white youth. For many white parents, however, such a trend is cause for concern. While white youth already face their version of the generation gap—they've been dubbed "slackers" and "Generation X"—emulating the styles, speech, and behavior of urban black youth is even more menacing.

Of course, there's nothing new about white kids imitating black kids. Neither is this the first time that white panic has followed white teens' adoration of black stars. When Sam Cooke's mellifluous voice and flawless good looks sent white girls screaming in the '50s, it caused an uproar among white adults. And now that white girls are driven crazy by Snoop Doggy Dogg's canine comeliness, especially when there's no doubt about what he wants to do in his dog pound, rap and the culture that produces it are found wanting. It wasn't until rap made a huge impact on white kids that the music was so roundly attacked. As long as the "bad" effects of rap were restricted to black kids, its menace went undetected, unprotested, or it was flat-out ignored.

Among many black adults, hip-hop culture represents a tragic rejection of the values that prevailed in black communities years ago, at least during their youthful watch on the wall of black progress. To hear legions of black adults tell it, there was a time when a black child could be disciplined by any adult in the neighborhood if he or she did wrong. Such a story is meant to show the strength, unity, and durability of black communities of the past. It is also meant to underscore the weakness, fragmentation, and collapse of black communities today.

(Once, when I visited a university to lecture, I heard this same story repeated by a black youth, all of eighteen years old, who included her generation among the duly disciplined children. Most blacks would say that her generation is unfamiliar with such an experience. That gave me a clue that such stories are, in large part, rhetorical devices that transmit folk wisdom from one generation to the next. Such stories help us define the limits of acceptable behavior.)

It's clear that the rise of hip-hop culture has provoked a deep black nostalgia for a time when black communities were quite different than they are now. When children respected their elders. When adults, not young thugs, ruled over neighborhoods. When the moral fabric of black communities was knit together by a regard for law and order. When people shared what they had, even if it was their last crust of bread or drop of soup. When families extended beyond blood or biology to take in young people in need of rearing. When communication between blacks on the street was marked by courtesy more than cursing. When black folk went to church, and even if they didn't, respected the minister as a source of moral authority. And on and on.

There's little doubt that black communities of the past were sharply different than they are now. But black communities weren't the idyllic places that nostalgic black folk make them out to be. Nostalgia is colored memory. It is romantic remembering. It re-creates as much as it recalls. The political force of black nostalgia—built on a vision of the black past as a utopian, golden age—is harmful to debates about black youth. Every culture, age, and generation has a high point whose benefits are unsurpassable. Such utopias and golden ages, and the benefits they bestow, are usually realized after the fact. Indeed, they have to be. It takes decline to highlight a pinnacle. But when blacks use nostalgia to make moral distinctions between the sort of people black communities produced Then and produce Now, we unravel the very fabric of racial memory that we claim our youth desperately need.

A cure for such nostalgia can be found in works like *Morals and Manners Among Negro Americans*, edited in 1914 by W.E.B. Du Bois and Augustus Dill. Du Bois and Dill surveyed hundreds of leading blacks about the "manners and morals" of black youth. Wouldn't you know it? Many black leaders lamented the negative impact of popular culture on black youth. One leader blamed moral decline on movies, which "have an unwholesome effect upon the young people. Roller skating, ragtime music, cabaret songs, and ugly suggestions of the big city are all pernicious. The dancing clubs in the big cities are also vicious." Another leader worried that black youth "hang around the corners in great numbers, especially the boys. Many of them are becoming gamblers and idlers." Keep in mind that these degenerate black youth make up a generation now praised for its high morals. That should stop us from writing the epitaph of what has been mislabeled a lost generation of black youth. (Even here, racial distinctions prevail. If white kids are demonized as "slackers," at least they're seen to be slacking off from a Protestant work ethic they can recover through hard work. What can you do when you're lost? Often, you get written off. That happens to too many black youth.)

The relation of nostalgic blacks to hip-hop culture can be viewed in the following way: there is a perception of *aesthetic alienation* and *moral strangeness* in black youth. Both of these perceptions, I believe, depend on a denial of crucial aspects of history and racial memory. Amnesia and anger have teamed up to rob many blacks of a balanced perspective on our kids. With such balance, we might justly criticize and appreciate hip-hop culture. Without the moderating influence of historical insight, joined to what might be called the humility of memory, we end up mirroring the outright repudiation our kids face across this country.

Since so much of the politics of nostalgia are about how things used to be, we've got to understand a bit better how things actually were. Now, I don't harbor any illusions about being able, as we used to say in my black ghetto neighborhood in Detroit, to get to "wie es eigentlich gewesen," or, "how it really was." (Me and my boys repeated that line from nineteenth-century historian Leopold von Ranke when we were frustrated in our quest for eighteenth-century philosopher Immanuel Kant's "ding an sich," or, "the thing in itself." Yeah, we had it like that back in the day. No wonder my generation wants our kids to be just like us!) But we must escape the awkward burden of remembering only what we choose to believe by getting a more insightful account of things as they happened. The past should be a fountain of wisdom and warning. It is inevitable that fictions attach to what used to be. But it is immoral to make those fictions the ground of harsh judgments of our children.

The aesthetic alienation of hip-hop has partly to do with perception. Rap is seen as wildly differing from the styles, themes, and tones of previous black music. Well, that's true and not true. Certainly the form of hip-hop is distinct. The skeletal rap crew is composed of a DJ (disc jockey), a producer, and an MC (master of ceremonies, or rapper). (Technology has enhanced, occasionally blurred, and sometimes redivided the crew's labor over the last fifteen years.) In many cases, there are at least a couple of rappers. In some cases, there are several. The DJ commands a pair of phonograph turntables. Among other functions, the DJ plays fragments of records through a technique called scratching: manually rotating a record in sharp, brief bursts of back and forth rhythmic movement over isolated portions of a song, producing a scratching sound.

The producer has several devices at her command, including a beat box and a digital sampler. The beat box, or drum machine, is an electronic instrument that simulates the sound of a drum set. A digital sampler is a synthesizer that stores in its computerized memory a variety of sounds (a James Brown scream, a TV theme song, a guitar riff, a bass line) that are reproduced when activated by the producer. The DJ and the producer work together in laying down backing tracks for the MC. The tracks consist of rhythms, scratches, beats, shrieks, noises, other sound effects, and loops, which are fragments of existing songs reworked and repeated in new musical contexts.

The MC, or rapper, recites lyrics in a rhythmic, syncopated fashion. The rapper's rhetorical quirks, vocal tics, rhyme flow, and verbal flourishes mark his or

her individual style. In the early days of rap, MCs often simulated sonic fragments with their voices, causing some rappers to be dubbed human beat boxes.
Rappers can use a variety of rhyme schemes, from couplets in tetrameter to
iambic pentameter. Their rhyme schemes can employ masculine and feminine
rhymes, assonantal and consonantal rhymes, or even internal rhymes. Rappers
may use enjambment, prosody, and sophisticated syncopations to tie their collage
of rhymes into a pleasing sonic ensemble.

But hip-hop's form joins features of black oral culture, especially toasts (long
narrative poems) and the dozens, to a variety of black musical styles. As Gil Scott-
Heron once remarked, hip-hop fuses the drum and the word. Blues music is the
style of black artistry most closely associated with hip-hop. The blues spawned
stock characters within its lyrical universe, including the hoochie-coochie man,
the mojo worker, the lover man, and the bad man bluesman. Their relation to hip-
hop's (and '70s blaxploitation flicks') macks, pimps, hustlers, and gangsters is
clear. Plus, the rhetorical marks and devices of blues culture, including vulgar language, double entendres, boasting, and liberal doses of homespun machismo, link
it to hip-hop, especially gangsta rap. And in case you're thinking, "Yeah, but the
blues and early jazz weren't nearly as nasty as rap"; think again. There are lyrics
contained in the songs of the great Jelly Roll Morton, for example, that would
make Snoop Doggy Dogg wince in embarrassment. You can read Morton's lyrics
in their most distinguished place of storage, the Library of Congress. (Does this
mean in the next century that that august institution will house the Dogg's Magnum Snoopus, "Doggystyle," for future generations to lap up or howl at?) Modern technology, together with the urban and secular emphases of black culture,
has helped expose localized traditions of vulgar black speech—including agrarian
blues, signifying, toasts, and the dozens—to a worldwide audience. And millions
of blacks are angry and ashamed.

It's clear, too, that '50s rock and roll, '60s soul music, '70s R&B, '80s new jack
swing, and '90s hip-hop soul have touched on themes that rap has addressed,
though often in a dramatically different style. Some of the most important black
music of the '60s and '70s, for instance, attempted to reconcile the political demands of a new black consciousness with the changing rules of domestic life. This
music attempted to join erotic desire to its political ambitions. Thus, Marvin Gaye
followed his 1971 masterpiece "What's Going On" with his brilliant 1973 release
"Let's Get It On," moving from the social to the sexual sphere in exploring the
complex dimensions of black culture. While hip-hop addresses these same concerns, its ideological orientation, and therefore its artistic direction, is almost re-
versed. With the increasing attacks on the black family as an unreliable space to
shape sexuality in socially acceptable forms, a lot of hip-hoppers try to join politics
to erotic desire. Many artists move from the sexual center of rap to the varieties of
political consciousness hip-hop manages to embrace along its cutting edges.

Still, there's no doubt that older styles of black music have provoked their own
controversies. But depending on which black generation you speak with, each

style represents the golden age of black music. In fact, hip-hoppers themselves have more than a little nostalgia, particularly for '70s culture and music. Their nostalgia is even more ironic, indeed laughable, because of hip-hop's grand claims to authenticity, to "keeping it real." Meaning their music won't sell out by pandering to the styles or themes of R&B. Right. Hip-hop still depends on existing black music even as it reshapes, often brilliantly, the grooves it steals. Without its creative uses of past black music, rap would be a museum of speech with little to inspire us to conserve its words, much less heed its warnings and many lessons.

The technical devices of hip-hop accent its ambiguous relation to history. Through sampling, hip-hop revives and reinvents what has been forgotten. Sampling allows hip-hop to reshape what's been neglected by removing it from the context—the actual album, the network of cultural nuances, the time period—in which it originally came to life. What hip-hop gives with one hand, it takes back with the other. While they make fresh use of a Parliament-Funkadelic beat or a Leon Haywood loop, hip-hoppers often have little awareness of the musical traditions those artists fed on. Such awareness might make rappers' creative piracy much more compelling. How? The rhetoric of rap could rework, satirize, or play off of the intellectual visions of some of the songs it lifts. What rap does so brilliantly with form it might be able to match with content.

Paying more attention to black music's intellectual traditions might keep hip-hop from completely turning its machinery of mythology on itself. Hip-hoppers get misty-eyed about the "old-school" and what happened "back in the day." There is already growing up around rap a wall of myth that excludes crucial features of hip-hop's own history. For instance, its devotees largely contend that hip-hop originated in the black (including West Indian) and Latino working-class ghetto of the South Bronx with block parties in the early '70s. But others have recently argued that hip-hop was born in the West Bronx. More significantly, hip-hop cannot be divorced from its roots in Jamaica. In the 1960s, sound system operators hauled massive speakers in wooden carts in working-class communities during backyard dances attended by "rude boys," the Caribbean counterpart to hip-hop's "b-boys." Also, the Jamaican dance hall was the site of a mixture of older and newer forms of Caribbean music, including calypso, soca, salsa, Afro-Cuban, ska, and reggae. One of the first great pioneers of hip-hop, DJ Kool Herc, was a West Indian immigrant to the West Bronx who brought with him a hunger to recreate the memories and mood of Jamaican dance hall music. Those roots nourish rap.

Hip-hoppers often forget that hip-hop was initially patronized by average working-class and middle-class kids, not gangsters or other members of the hardcore scene. Afrika Bambaataa, another old-school pioneer who created hip-hop standards like "Looking for the Perfect Beat" and "Planet Rock," also founded the Universal Zulu Nation. True enough, the organization grew out of South Bronx gang life (Bambaataa was a member of the notorious gang Black Spades). But Universal Zulu Nation was committed to peace, unity, and self-knowledge. And neither was hip-hop an exclusively black affair. African-Americans, Afro-Caribbeans,

Latinos, and progressive whites all shared in the Bronx parties where hip-hop was spawned in the States. Hip-hop's multiethnic audience helped energize its free-form expression. Old-school legends like DJ Grandmaster Flash experimented with a wide range of music, from Frank Sinatra to Thin Lizzy.

It may not be altogether unfitting that hip-hop is partially cut off from the roots of even its own history. After all, with its impulse to create sonic collages, its sampling of existing music, its disregard for musical conventions, and its irreverent pairing of the culturally sacred and profane, hip-hop is thought to be a striking instance of postmodernism. And according to critic Fredric Jameson, the lack of a sense of history rests squarely at the center, if it can be said to have one, of the postmodern moment. While it's easy to see why hip-hop is deemed a postmodern art form—quotation, pastiche, contingency, fragmentation, and the like help define its presence—it may be that its homegrown nostalgia and hunger for purity and authenticity betray modernist obsessions.

In other words, the postmodernism of hip-hop may show that we're trying to get rid of, or, at least, get over modernism too quickly. Postmodernism may turn out to be modernism in drag. At its heart, modernism looks back to move forward. Modernism is obsessed with critically reexamining the ground of its origin—which, in its advocates' minds, turns out to be our culture's origins—so that its foundations are secured. Modernist discussions are caught up in the rapture of renewal, recovery, return, and renaissance, all in the name of progress, of moving forward. The new is valuable precisely because it is formed out of reappropriating the original. The great paradox of modernism, for some critics, is that, in order to outdo it, one must hold that whatever will succeed modernism, say postmodernism, is rooted in a ground of thought that is more original than the modernist ground it criticizes. Ironically, that's a modernist move. As a result, one ends up replacing the content of modernism, but not the form of modernism itself. That's why critic Theodor Adorno said that there was no overcoming modernity.

The question of whether hip-hop is really postmodernist or modernist is, at some levels, a strictly academic affair. In other ways, the debate may help us understand the conflicts, and the hidden ties, between hip-hop and forms of black music that have modernist elements. It may shed light on the uses black folk make of their past, and the difference those uses make in how we view black youth.

If black nostalgia has distorted the relation of postmodern black youth culture to a complex black past, this is nowhere more powerfully glimpsed than in comparing hip-hop with a high point of black modernism: jazz music and culture. Critics like Stanley Crouch and musicians like Wynton Marsalis have relentlessly attacked hip-hop culture for its deficits when compared to jazz. In conversations—in truth, they were Herculean arguments between us that raged for hours at a time—neither of these gifted gentlemen has had anything good to say about hip-hop culture.

Crouch maintains that hip-hop is, in a memorable phrase comparing rap to the infamous, racist 1915 D.W Griffith film, "*Birth of a Nation* with a backbeat." Marsalis thinks rap reflects a fascism that mars humane art. Plus, rap is rooted in a banal, mindless repetition of beat, signaling a lack of musical imagination and invention. Inspired by the likes of Ralph Ellison, but especially by Albert Murray, Crouch and Marsalis argue that the artistic possibilities of jazz—its heart pumping with the blood of improvisation, its gut churning with the blues—embody the edifying quest for romantic self-expression and democratic collaboration that capture Negro music and American democracy at their best. For Crouch and Marsalis, hip-hop negates everything jazz affirms.

Many fans of black music, including stalwarts of soul and R&B, most certainly agree. They simply add their music of preference, and perhaps their own string of modifiers, to Crouch and Marsalis's list. (That's because Aretha ain't about democracy. She's about the imperious demands of gospel genius as it baptizes and is transformed by secular sentiments. I'm not so sure that Crouch and Marsalis stand ready, however, to reciprocate. Whether Aretha, Sam Cooke, Otis Redding, Marvin Gaye, Donny Hathaway, or Al Green count in their reckoning as much as, say, early Miles or middle Coltrane, Sarah Vaughan or Ella Fitzgerald, or Ellington or Armstrong, is highly doubtful.) Despite the issues that separate black musical purists of any sort, their shared disdain for hip-hop culture's claims to art unite them as citizens of the Republic of Nostalgia.

The only problem is that, like hip-hop, jazz has a history of cultural attack. That history has been buried under an avalanche of nostalgia that hides jazz's grittier roots. For instance, during the Jazz Age and the Harlem Renaissance, the response to jazz by a large segment of the black bourgeoisie, black intellectuals, and black artists anticipated the attack on rap. Such responses reflected, and were partly driven by, the negative response to jazz of large segments of white society. Jazz was viewed as a cultural and artistic form that compromised decency and morality. It was linked to licentious behavior and lewd artistic gestures. With its jungle rhythms, its blues base, its double entendre lyrics, and its sexually aggressive dancing, jazz, like hip-hop today, was the most widely reviled music of the '20s and '30s. Headlines in respectable publications asked questions like: "Did Jazz Put the Sin in Syncopation?" According to the *Ladies' Home Journal*, jazz was responsible for a "holocaust" of illegitimate births. A Cincinnati-based Catholic newspaper railed against the "sensuous" music of jazz. It said that "the embracing of partners—the female only half dressed—is absolutely indecent." Blues pioneer W.C. Handy's daughter, Lucille, was sternly admonished by the Colored Girls' Circle of an elite school for "making a fool" of herself by singing and dancing her father's blues and jazz. "It [continuing to sing and dance] will be under the peril of death and great danger to yourself," the letter concluded.

Many Harlem Renaissance intellectuals detested "gin, jazz, and sex." The publications of black organizations, from the NAACP's magazine, *Crisis*, edited by W.E.B. Du Bois, to the Socialist Party–supported magazine, *Messenger*, edited by A. Philip Randolph and Chandler Owens (with assistance from George Schuyler), expressed opposition to jazz as well. For many Harlem Renaissance intellectuals, jazz was not viewed as a serious artistic achievement on par with European classical music. The great irony of blacks worshiping European music is that European composers such as Richard Strauss were, at the same time, expressing profound admiration for jazz.

In 1926, one of the most important debates about the relation of black intellectuals to black mass culture took place in the pages of the *Nation*, between George Schuyler and Langston Hughes. In his essay, "The Negro Art Hokum," Schuyler argued that there was no such thing as a distinct Negro art apart from American art. Schuyler said that Negro art occurred in Africa, but to "suggest the possibility of any such development among the ten million colored people in this republic is self-evident foolishness." Schuyler argued that "slave songs based on Protestant hymns and biblical texts" and "secular songs of sorrow and tough luck known as the blues" were "contributions of a caste" in certain sections of America that were "foreign to Northern Negroes, West Indian Negroes, and African Negroes." For Schuyler, defining art in racial terms was "hokum."

Hughes's response, which ran a week later, became one of his signature essays. Entitled "The Negro Artist and the Racial Mountain," Hughes's essay lamented the veiled desire of some black artists to be white. Such artists feared their own racial identity. Hughes argued that the black middle class was denying a crucial part of its heritage by denying the "beauty of [its] own people" and that Negroes should stop imitating "Nordic manners, Nordic faces, Nordic air, Nordic art." In their stead, he urged Negroes to embrace "the low-down folks, the so-called common element, and they are the majority—may the Lord be praised." Hughes argued that the "common people will give to the world its truly great Negro artist, the one who is not afraid to be himself." For Hughes, the racial mountain was the inability of the black bourgeoisie to accept Negro art from the masses. Hughes exhorted his fellow Negroes to let "the blare of Negro jazz bands and the bellowing voice of Bessie Smith singing blues penetrate the closed ears of the colored near intellectuals until they listen and perhaps understand." Hughes's words are still relevant.

By rehearsing this bit of jazz history—one that is conveniently overlooked by Crouch and Marsalis as they attack rap and proclaim jazz as America's classical music—I am not arguing that we should romanticize black folk culture. Neither am I equating black folk art and pop culture. The big business of how black culture is packaged as a commodity to be bought and sold in the marketplace with billions of dollars at stake prevents such an easy equation. I'm simply arguing that all forms of black music have been attacked both within and beyond black culture. Blues and jazz, rhythm and blues, and soul have all been viewed as indecent, immoral, and corrupting of black youth. To be nostalgic for a time when black music offered a purer aesthetic or a higher moral vision is to hunger for a time in history that simply doesn't exist. (Of course, another way of stating this is to say that all black music has an aesthetic appeal, and a moral vision, that will at first be assailed, but whose loss will one day be mourned and compared favorably with the next form of hated black music to come along.) Now as Marsalis, Crouch, and other critics perched aloft the wall of high black culture throw stones at hip-hop, they forget that such stones were once thrown at their music of preference. Bebop was once hip-hop. Ragtime was once rap. Bluesmen were once b-boys. What is now noble was once notorious.

I'm not suggesting that there are no artistic differences between generations and styles of black music. Queen of Hip-Hop Soul Mary J. Blige is no Queen of Soul Aretha Franklin. (With Aretha's gifts, very few have measured up. Those who do—such figures as Vanessa Bell Armstrong, Ann Nesby, and the late Marion Williams—flourish in the gospel realm.) And neither should she be. She couldn't be even if she wanted to. Aretha's art, in large part, draws from her sheer genius. The outsized technical ambitions encouraged in her by the gospel tradition of the black church. Her apprenticeship in sanctified emotion under gospel great Clara Ward and her famous preacher father, C.L. Franklin. And a voice whose only teachers were unrelenting pathos and undaunted passion. But Aretha's greatest art has to do with a budding black feminist consciousness in the '60s and '70s. The demand for respect. The warning to men to think about their emotional intents with women. The prescription of feel-good therapies for sexual intimacy. And reckoning with the endless chain of fools produced by the quest for faithful love. In short, Aretha Franklin's greatness is a product of its times.

Mary J. Blige's art is similarly a product of its times. True enough, hip-hop soul borrows the grooves, and the rhetorical gravity, of black soul culture. But hip-hop soul's themes and rhythms occupy a distinct spiritual orbit. Blige says much of what Aretha said in the '60s and '70s, but she says it in the grittier, more explicit voice of hip-hop culture. Blige's hip-hop soul feminism seeks real love. But it remakes edifying love confessions into gut-wrenching pleas of faithfuless. It makes self-love the basis of loving others. And it bitterly, defiantly refuses to accept sexual infidelity (though Aretha hinted as much when she said if men wanted do-right women they'd have to be do-right men). Blige is full of self-enclosed hip-hop angst. She also possesses, or at least she seeks to possess, a strong degree of hip-hop self-reliance. And she has a dark, stormy, rap-inflected (or is that infected?) artistic temperament.

Blige's art reshapes the blues at the bottom of Aretha's soul feminism into a brooding female voice of resistance in an Age of Misogyny. Aretha's generation certainly faced the same forces. But '60s and '70s sexism was cloaked beneath a chivalry and condescension that even black male versions of patriarchy could express. (Let's not forget that there were plenty of brutal examples of black men mistreating black women at Aretha's artistic peak. Lyrically speaking, male rappers talk a good game of ho-smacking and bitch-beating, but the likes of James Brown, Bill Withers, David Ruffin, Marvin Gaye, and a host of other artists allegedly abused wives, girlfriends, or lovers while singing sweet, rapturous praises to the fairer sex on wax.) Aretha Franklin's and Mary J. Blige's aesthetic values reflect, in part, the cultural and musical environments that shape their art. What they respond to—norms, practices, behaviors, expectations, ideas—has as great an effect on the character of their art as their particular musical gifts. While soul and hip-hop cultures embody virtues to which each musical style responds, the cultures contain vices to which each style reacts. (Franklin and Blige, of course, embody both the good and the bad of their respective traditions in their art.) The explicitness of hip-hoppers makes their limitations more obvious. But the subtlety of soul artists doesn't make their limitations any less lethal.

The problem with nostalgic blacks is that they place more artistic stock in the aesthetic form they are familiar with. (They often have what may be termed Hegel's problem, named after the philosopher who believed that of all periods in history, the Zeitgeist, the world spirit, was best embodied in his own Prussian state during his life. For our nostalgic true believers, it translates into the notion that the best in black music happened to coincide with their own youth.) At the same time, they associate vice, or limitation, or smallness of artistic vision, with the aesthetic form most alien to them. While blues, jazz, soul, and R&B may share crucial assumptions, say, about women, the differences in their outward aesthetic forms makes us believe that one is more harmful or more foreign to black culture than the other. Thus, hip-hop's misogyny is more jolting than the antipathy toward women that came through in some R&B. But within both hip-hop and what's called urban contemporary music, there are artists who are appalled at the malevolence hurled at black women. And one need not look beyond these genres to find rich expressions of the seductive art of subtlety—as opposed to the "do me" explicitness common among current acts—practiced by artists of previous generations. Chante Moore and Tony Terry, Maxwell and Babyface, Prince Markie Dee and Heavy D are just a few.

But nostalgia can't explain every negative assessment of black pop culture. Even if it did, it wouldn't mean that such judgments are necessarily wrong, even if they're made for the wrong reasons. It may be that all the explanations about different artistic ages—and the limitations and possibilities each age presents—simply can't change the fact that Mary J. Blige isn't Aretha Franklin. Fine. But that's not an indictment of hip-hop soul per se. It's a value judgment about artists exploring similar though distinct genres at different times. I'm simply arguing that we respect the rules of each genre. We should adjust our evaluations of music based on the sorts of achievement that are possible, even desirable, in a given period. That doesn't mean we can't rank them. After all, some music is more complicated than other music. Some art forms take more mastery than others. But we should rank these different styles of music fairly. As important as it is, complexity of achievement is not the only value worth recognizing or celebrating in art. Plus, there are many kinds of artistic complexity that merit our attention.

After all, our age has seen the likes of Whitney Houston, Anita Baker, and Mariah Carey, gifted artists of a greatly changed black sound, whatever that means, whose skills of delivery and interpretation far exceed the schlock that riddles so much contemporary black pop. (Still, each has contributed her fair share of misfires, as is true, of course, of the inimitable Ms. Franklin.) Contemporary hip-hop soul has also brought forth artists like D'Angelo. His young career holds promise for melding the wispy melodies of '70s soul to hip-hop rhythms and occasionally raunchy sensibilities. And male groups Boys II Men and Jodeci, and female groups En Vogue and SWV rise above the mediocrity of their chosen idioms.

But that's just the point. Aretha outdid most of her peers whose names we have long since forgotten. Their failures, or better still, their relative successes, don't invalidate the genres of black music in which they strived to make sublime art. Soul music is judged by its brilliance, not its blight. It is measured by its supreme visions, not its short-sighted trends. Like all great music, it is measured by the size of its aspirations—which are measured by the aspirations of its greatest artists, even the unsung ones—not simply by artists who managed to make the charts or to win the awards. (Donny Hathaway was never justly recognized for his extraordinary genius as a composer, artist, and musician. And Little Willie John was one of the greatest—some argue, *the* greatest—R&B singer, but few people know his name or work, except as it's drained of its pathos by more famous but less gifted white artists.) Hip-hop is no different. It's not the mindless, numbing pornography of the notorious 2 Live Crew that is the measure of hip-hop's vitality, but the rhetorical, lyrical ingenuity of Rakim or Nas. Snoop Doggy Dogg's seductive and highly accomplished rhyme flow, and Ice Cube's narrative powers—plus Dr. Dre's pulsating, harmonically complex G-funk—define gangsta rap's metier. Not the mediocre rants of the late Eazy-E—although his brilliance as impresario and record producer, even talent scout, is undeniable. A lot of hip-hop is okay, more of it is good, and a little of it is great. Just like any other music.

(Crouch, Marsalis, and other critics have argued against hip-hop even being called serious music. Of course, these critics hold the same grudge against latter-day Coltrane, Eric Dolphy, Ornette Coleman, Cecil Taylor, Albert Ayler, Archie Shepp, Don Cherry, and almost any avant-garde jazz artist who championed unorthodox harmonies, departure from chord-based improvisations, atonal "noise," and dissonant melodies. Neither Ellington nor Armstrong, heroes for Crouch and Marsalis—and for me, too—would be today what they were when they played. To be sure, they'd still be geniuses. But the character of their genius would be greatly altered. Their relentless reach for the edge of experience pushed them to keep growing, experimenting, and improvising. Conservative advocates of jazz end up freezing the form, making jazz an endless series of explorations of already charted territory. It's a process of rediscovering what's already been discovered. Such a process led Gary Giddins to remark that the problem with so much of contemporary neotraditionalist jazz is that Thelonius Monk couldn't even win the annual contest that's sponsored in his name! The very spirit of jazz—its imperative to improvise, which can often lead into dangerous, unmapped territory—is thus sacrificed in the name of preserving the noble, heroic traditions that grow out of a specific time in jazz's history. What's really being preserved is the product, not the process, of improvisation. But that's another book.)

At base, the perception of the aesthetic alienation of hip-hop culture is linked to a perception that black youth are moral strangers. I mean by "moral strangers" that black youth are believed to be ethically estranged from the moral practices and spiritual beliefs that have seen previous black generations through harsh and dangerous times. The violence of black youth culture is pointed to as a major symptom of moral strangeness. Heartless black-on-black murder, escalating rates of rape, rising incidents of drug abuse, and the immense popularity of hip-hop culture reinforce the perception of an ethical estrangement among black youth. In arguing the moral strangeness of black youth, many critics recycle bits and pieces of old-style arguments about the pathology of black urban culture. Widely popularized in Daniel Moynihan's famous 1965 study of the black family—whose pathology was partially ascribed to a growing matriarchy in black domestic life— the notion that black culture carries the seeds of its own destruction is an old idea. The argument for black cultural pathology is really an updated version of beliefs about black moral deficiency as ancient as the black presence in the New World.

More recently, Cornel West has attempted to explain the problems of black culture by pointing to its nihilism. Since the nihilism argument has been used by many critics to prove the moral strangeness of black youth, I'll explore it in some detail before arguing for an alternate perspective.

For West, nihilism is "the profound sense of psychological depression, personal worthlessness, and social despair so widespread in black America." West wants to unblinkingly stare down the problems of black culture, and to call a spade a spade: black crime is increasing, suicide is rising, hopelessness is spreading, and ethical surrender is pandemic. Yet liberals, West argues, simply close their eyes or believe that if they say what they see they'll be thought of as cold conservatives. West also knows that mere moral corrosion, as argued by conservatives, is not large enough an explanation for what's going on in black culture. West seeks to avoid the pitfalls of both conservative behaviorists and liberal structuralists by arguing for a complex vision of black culture that takes into account the "saturation of market forces and market moralities" in black life, while highlighting the crisis of black leadership. For West, such a strategy allows us to be frank in our discussions of black moral and spiritual collapse while refusing to scapegoat those blacks who are victimized by dehumanizing forces.

West is right to grapple with issues of morality and behavior, matters that are largely taboo for the left. He's also right to zoom in on the market forces and market moralities that besiege black culture. Still, as an explanation for what ails us, nihilism has severe problems. First, nihilism is seen as a cause, not a consequence, of black suffering. The collapse of hope, the spiritual despair that floods black America, the clinical depression we suffer, are all the pernicious result of something more basic than black nihilism: white racism. (The list includes economic suffering, class inequality, and material hardship as well, but I'll get to those in a bit.) I don't mean here just the nasty things many white folk believe about black folk. I'm referring to the systematic destruction of black life, the pervasive attack on the black sense of well-being, the subversion of black self-determination, and the erasure of crucial narratives of black self-esteem that are foundational to American versions of democracy. Nihilism is certainly self-destructive. That's because black folk were taught—and have had it reinforced across time, geography, and ideology—that our black selves weren't worth loving or preserving. Nihilism is the outgrowth, not the origin, of such harsh lessons. Without the destruction of white supremacy, black nihilism will continue to grow.

Then too, nihilism shifts the burden for getting black America back on track to suffering black folk. That seems an awful tall order for a people already strapped with sparse resources and weighted down with nihilism. West argues for a politics of conversion, where a love ethic is central. As a Baptist preacher and former pastor, I am deeply sympathetic to this. The logic of such a duty, however, might be questioned. Love without resources will not ultimately solve the problems black folk face. With enough resources—employment, education, housing, food—black folk will have the luxury, the leisure, the reasonable chance to love themselves. Of course, I'm not suggesting that poor black folk without such resources don't or can't love themselves. But I am suggesting that love alone, even a complex, socially rooted understanding of love, cannot provide the material basis for the permanent high self-regard that will need to be in place for black folk to stop snuffing one another out. The presence of such resources cannot by themselves guarantee a good outcome. But we can be reasonably assured that, without such resources, a bad outcome is highly likely.

Plus, if black nihilism is really that pervasive, can nihilists resolve nihilism? Can folk for whom hope has been eclipsed really muster the moral might to throw off the psychic chains of their suffering? Conversion—which leads me to believe that this is in part a project of self-help—is a necessary, but insufficient, basis to turn back the nihilistic tide. While Martin Luther King wanted to convert white racists, he also wanted to put in place a structure of laws, duties, and obligations that had the power to change behavior. Given the choice of love and power, King took power, and let the love come later. (King said, for instance, that the law may not make whites love blacks, but it could stop them from lynching blacks. Of course, it is a dialectical process: love insists on the right laws, and the right sort of laws provide a framework for—one hopes—the eventual development of love, which could, in turn, obviate the laws. These poles are united in King's beliefs.) True enough, King's life and ministry were regulated by a love ethic. But he saw righteous power, that is, power linked to justice, as the imperfect but indispensable social translation of love.

Finally, West's theory of nihilism is driven by a nostalgic vision of black life. West says that "the genius of our black foremothers and forefathers was to create powerful buffers to ward off the nihilistic threat." West also argues that our foreparents were equipped with "cultural armor to beat back the demons of hopelessness, meaninglessness, and lovelessness." The armor included "values of service and sacrifice, love and care, discipline and excellence." Black religious and civic institutions helped black folk survive.

West is certainly right that black folk kept on keeping on, that they refused to give up. But for my money, those things haven't gone away. It's too early to tell if black folk have surrendered the fight. But I guess I just don't see where nihilism is winning, where the attempts of black folk to make a way out of no way have ceased. The black church continues to thrive against tremendous odds. Black families continue to strive to make a lie out of the vicious rumors of their inherent pathology. Poor black folk—well, it's a wonder that more haven't given up, surrendered to a life of crime and moral mischief.

The real miracle of contemporary black life is that there are still so many sane, sensible, struggling, secular, sanctified, spiritual, and spunky black folk who just said no to destruction way before Nancy Reagan figured out what crack was. In other words, those black folk of the past are us black folk of the present. Our black youth are not a different moral species than the black youth of the past. They are not moral strangers. And as the quote from Du Bois and Dill above proves, black folk are always worried about their kids. We always romanticize our past, partly as a way to jump-start our flagging efforts in the present. That's certainly okay. It's when nostalgia is used to browbeat and thrust a finger in the face of black youth in an effort to convince them that their moral makeups are grievously defective that nostalgia becomes destructive.

In the end, it may be that the concept of nihilism is symptomatic of the disease it aims to highlight. It may be that a belief in nihilism is too hopeless about the black future, too out of touch with the irreverent spirit of resistance that washes over black culture. A belief in nihilism is too, well, nihilistic. But nostalgia can do that. By viewing the black past as morally and spiritually distinct from the present, we lose sight of the resources for ethical engagement that are carried forward from the past into our own thinking, believing, hoping, praying, and doing. It would be good to remember black preacher and theologian Howard Thurman's wise words, from his book of sermons, *The Growing Edge*:

> At the time when the slaves in America were without any excuse for hope and they could see nothing before them but the long interminable cotton rows and the fierce sun and the lash of the overseer, what did they do? They declared that God was not through. They said, "We cannot be prisoners of this event. We must not scale down the horizon of our hopes and our dreams and our yearnings to the level of the event of our lives." So they lived through their tragic moment until at last they came out on the other side, saluting the fulfillment of their hopes and their faith, which had never been imprisoned by the event itself.

A belief in nihilism may make us prisoners of present events. A belief in the indomitable spirit of hope that thrives even when things are at their darkest for black folk may be the real link to a powerful black past.

Still, there's no doubt that terrible things are happening to black youth. To pretend otherwise is to ignore the obvious. Black youth are killing and being killed. Crime and violence go hand in hand. High unemployment is entrenched. Teenage pregnancy is epidemic. How can we explain these facts? I think we've got to move from a theory of moral strangeness to a theory of how power has shifted away from adults to young people in many urban homes and communities. Highlighting such a shift by no means sidesteps issues of morality, values, or responsibility. It simply gives us a handle on specific changes in black youth culture that have had a vicious effect on black life.

I think there is a *juvenocracy* operating in many urban homes and communities. For me, a juvenocracy is the domination of black and Latino domestic and urban life by mostly male figures under the age of twenty-five who wield considerable economic, social, and moral influence. A juvenocracy may consist of drug gangs, street crews, loosely organized groups, and individual youths who engage in illicit activity. They operate outside the bounds of the moral and political economies of traditional homes and neighborhoods. The rise of a juvenocracy represents a significant departure from home and neighborhood relations where adults are in charge. Three factors are at the heart of such a shift.

The first is the extraordinary violence of American life. As historian Richard Slotkin has argued, the frontier myth at the base of our country revolves around "regeneration through violence." America renews itself at the altar of devotion to violence as a rite of national identification. It is important to remember this rite as cries go up about the exceptional violence of black youth. Such violence, sadly, is quite mainstream. The prominence of hip-hop culture has provoked fresh attacks on black youth. Black youth are viewed as innately inclined to violent behavior. The lyrics and images of hip-hop are used as proof of such a claim. Well, as strong and pungent as hip-hop is, as offensive as it can be, it is still art. It isn't life, no matter what some hip-hoppers claim about its "realness." Indeed, without making too strong a point of it, hip-hop's existence may be keeping a lot of black youth away from drugs, crime, and life on the streets because they get to rap about such things in the sound booth. Thank God for what other hip-hoppers derisively refer to as "studio gangstas."

It is simply dishonest to paint black youth as the primary source of violence in America. In fact, more often than not, black youth are the victims, not the perpetrators, of violence. Although they are only 5.9 percent of the population, black males account for 40 percent of homicide victims. Black men over twenty-four are the victims of homicide at a rate of 65.7 per 100,000. For white males in that age group, the figure is 7.8 per 100,000. Youth between the ages of twelve and seventeen are the most common victims of crime in America: 1 in 3 stands a chance of being raped, robbed, or mugged. Black youth violence, especially as it is concentrated within a juvenocracy, reflects the violence directed at young black bodies.

Juvenocracies are, in part, mechanisms of defense that develop a vicious life and logic of their own. As most Americans know, it is easy to become addicted to violence. After all, the major broadcast networks average five acts of violence per hour in prime time. On Saturday mornings, networks average twenty-five acts of violence an hour. By the time kids reach elementary school, they've seen 100,000 acts of simulated violence. For poor, black children, who watch more television than most, the number is even higher. By the time kids turn eighteen, they've seen almost 18,000 acts of simulated murder on television. Add to that the profusion of gangsta rap narratives and the picture is indeed disturbing.

Since black youth are disproportionately targeted for violence, especially in their own homes, neighborhoods, and schools, the rise of a juvenocracy was predictable. Black youth hang together—in gangs, crews, groups, and so on—for affection and protection. And, yes, for destruction as well. In fact, such behavior does not show an ethical estrangement from American society, but a feverish embrace of its pragmatic principles of survival. Black youth show a frightening moral intimacy with the traditions of American violence. Appealing to a distinction that moral philosophers have made for centuries, the behavior of juvenocrats may not be *reasonable*—its effect on communities, homes, and schools is unreasonably destructive—but in light of the violence and poverty black youth face, the behavior of juvenocrats is certainly *rational.*

The second factor explaining the rise of a juvenocracy is the emergence of what Mike Davis has called the "political economy of crack" in the mid '80s until the early '90s, which shifted power to young black and Latino males in the homes and on the streets of cities ranging from Los Angeles to Chicago. The manufacturing, packaging, merchandising, and distribution of crack cocaine brought millions of dollars into the hands of formerly impoverished, grossly undereducated black and Latino youth. The postindustrial collapse of many urban areas—brought on by shifts from manufacturing to service industries (over the last twenty years, the U.S. economy lost 5 million jobs in the manufacturing sector); the decreased production of goods leading to corporate downsizing; technological change; capital flight; and the relocation of corporations to low-wage havens in bordering countries—punched a gaping hole in the legitimate economy for black youth who were already at its margins. The political economy of crack, and the goods and services it allowed black and Latino youth to provide for themselves and their families, helped shift power to young black and Latino males who became de facto heads of households and neighborhood guardians. And menaces. The number of homicides associated with the crack business soared in cities like New York, Los Angeles, and Chicago.

Finally, the rise of the culture of the gun in America drove the emergence of a juvenocracy. The American fetish for loaded weapons of destruction is numbing. In this case, statistics really do tell the story. In 1990, for instance, there were 11,730 people killed by handguns in the United States. In the UK, the figure was 22. In the US there are 201 million firearms in the hands of private citizens; 67 million of these are handguns. Every day, 65 Americans are killed by handgun fire. There are 1 million automatic or semiautomatic weapons circulating in our nation. Thus, it is twenty times more likely that a semiautomatic weapon will be used in a crime in our country than a conventional firearm. Over $1 billion is spent annually for treatment of firearm injuries.

There were 33,651 Americans killed in the Korean War. There were 47,364 Americans killed in the Vietnam War. There were 37,155 Americans killed with firearms in homicides, suicides, and accidents in 1990. In 1991, 45,536 Americans were killed in motor vehicle accidents. The same year, 38,317 Americans died from gunshot wounds. Now firearm incidents surpass motor vehicle accidents as the most likely way Americans will die. Among white Americans, 28.4 per 100,000 die from motor vehicle injuries; 15.2 per 100,000 die from firearms. For Latinos, 28.7 per 100,000 die from motor vehicle accidents; 29.6 per 100,000 die from firearms. For blacks, 23.0 per 100,000 die from motor vehicles; 70.7 per 100,000 die from firearms. In 1990, 12.9 out of 100,000 white males between 20 and 24 were killed by firearms; 140.7 out of 100,000 black males between 20 and 24 were killed by firearms in the same year. One in 28 black males born in the United States is likely to be murdered; 93 percent of black murder victims are killed by other blacks. Firearms in the hands of young black and Latino men has clearly altered the urban landscape. Firearms have given juvenocrats the ultimate weapon of death.

The American addiction to violence, the political economy of crack, and this nation's fetish for firearms account for the rise of a violent juvenocracy. Of course, there are ethical dimensions to juvenocracies as well. Are juvenocracies corrupt? Yes. Are the people who participate in juvenocracies often morally vicious? Yes. Should the destruction that juvenocracies leave in their wake, especially in black and Latino communities, be opposed? With all our might. But unlike culture of pathology arguments, or even arguments about black nihilism, my theory of juvenocracy doesn't locate the source of ethical erosion and moral corruption at the heart of black communities. Why? Because the behavior of juvenocrats can be explained by generic, or better, universal principles of human action. Murder, robbery, assault and battery, and drug dealing are not peculiar to black culture. They occur everywhere. A theory of black pathology or nihilism confuses the matter by asking us to believe that these problems are endemic to black communities. They are not.

A theory of universal human action argues that criminal behavior, and the moral corruption it implies, occur in Italian communities, too, and Korean ones. Should we have theories of Italian pathology, of Korean nihilism? Given that every ethnic and racial group has its unfair share of trouble, it makes no sense to describe such behavior with ethnic or racial modifiers. Of course, crime, pathology, and corruption come in specific shapes. It makes sense to speak openly and honestly about patterns of immoral and illegal behavior in particular communities. We can't close our eyes to the obvious. Drive-bys may be more common in black and Latino ghettos than in Lithuanian or Norwegian communities. And mob hits might be more common in Providence's Federal Hill than in Harlem's Sugar Hill. But, it should be apparent that such patterns have more to do with where criminals live—whether by choice or by circumstance—and, more important, where they do "business," than with the ethnic character of their consciences. Also, the concentration of crime in poor communities, many of these black, has more to do with economic and material suffering than ethical impoverishment. It makes no more sense to speak of the pathology of Italian communities because of the Mafia than it does to speak of the nihilism of Vietnamese communities because of the rise of gangs in such neighborhoods.

The moral viciousness of juvenocrats can be explained by their participation in illicit activities and immoral lifestyles that reinforce destructive behavior. As ethicists who study virtue have argued for centuries, moral health is encouraged by habits of thought and action that are repeatedly practiced. The same holds for vicious behavior. There's nothing endemic to black culture, versus, say, Jewish or Irish culture, that promotes vice. But there is something about the nature of a juvenocracy that encourages vicious behavior. In fact, a juvenocracy is explicitly organized around illicit, illegal, and immoral action. Its very purpose is to regularize such behavior. A juvenocracy shapes its actions so as to maximize the profits of its participants. Cutthroat, cold-hearted, vicious, and sometimes inhuman behavior—both toward other members of the juvenocracy and toward those outside its ranks—is not only common, it is crucial to the maintenance of the juvenocracy. Something like a Kantian moral imperative operates in the juvenocracy: stay safe, watch your homeboy's back, and make money at all costs. If one must make others unsafe, stab or shoot a neighbor in the back, or steal to "get paid"; so be it. That's not an example of black nihilism any more than it's an example of white nihilism. And it's not a black ethic any more than it's a white ethic. It's an all too American ethic (maybe even a universal one), one that unites a broader and deeper strand of folk than we're willing to admit. (Indeed, I've seen staggering nihilism in corporate America and in university communities, in certain businessmen for whom the buck was all, and in novelists whose narcissism and arrogance were a blight to behold.) The concepts of pathology and nihilism seem too class derived for my tastes. They stigmatize the very people who have the least resources to resist the sort of behavior for which the well-to-do are rarely held accountable.

Let me be clear. Vicious behaviors are no less vicious because they are rooted in generic factors of class, political economy, violence, and the like. But by getting a fix on how and why immoral behavior flourishes, we might have a better chance of figuring out what to do. On the one hand, if we believe the problem is cultural, we tell black folk to fix their cultures. We tell them to stop being pathological. Or if we believe they're nihilistic, we tell them to convert to love. On the other hand, if we think the problem flowers in black culture, but is rooted in complex economic, political, moral, and social factors, our answer is hugely different. A juvenocracy cannot be overcome by anything less than a radical reexamination of urban social policies, economic practices, and political measures aimed at black communities and black youth. A juvenocracy that thrives on violence, the political economy of drugs, and the culture of the gun must be viewed, in part, as a symptom of economic and racial injustice. It must also be seen as a moral surrender of black youth to the seductions of excessive material gratification. No amount of hand-wringing, navel gazing, or pulpit pounding about the good ol' black days will fix what's wrong. Black nostalgia for days when we were better simply won't do.

With that, we end up where we began: the rise of a juvenocracy has been complemented by the cultural fascination with, and revulsion to, the pop culture of black youth, especially hip-hop. For many critics, the two go hand in hand. But that's a mistaken perception. That's not to say that gangsta rappers, for instance, don't identify with real gangsters. That they don't feed off one another. That their styles and social aspirations are not easily confused. Still, most real gangsters don't listen to gangsta rap for inspiration to do what they do. They check out old-school grooves. Too many of them have said so for us to ignore it. A lot of gangsters prefer Al Green to Snoop Doggy Dogg. Too often, then, black youth are all lumped together—in the media, in discussions by black intellectuals, in the analyses of cultural critics, and in the public imagination.

Unlike Ralph Ellison's character in his famous novel, and the bulk of black folk for a long stretch of our history, black youth suffer, not from invisibility, but from *hypervisibility*. The surplus sighting, and citing, of young black bodies—in crime stories on the news, in congressional hearings about demeaning imagery in pop music, in shopping malls where they hang out, in police profiles where they are stigmatized, in suburban communities where they are surveilled—has draped paranoia and panic around their very limbs. In all the wrong ways, black youth are overexposed. (Is it any wonder, then, that they dress in oversize clothing to hide their demonized bodies, to diminish the measuring of their alleged menace?)

And unlike James Baldwin and generations of black folk, black youth don't suffer from namelessness. They suffer from *namefulness*, from too many names. The sheer nameability of black youth, the ease with which they are mislabeled, promotes among black youth a negative solidarity, a unity produced by the attacks they have in common. Like Thomas Hobbes, black youth understand that human beings wield power through calling names and avoiding names. As Hobbes knew, black youth also know that names venerate and vilify. Names influence events. Hip-hop culture has provoked the naming, really the misnaming, of black youth: sadistic, self-destructive, violent, brutal, narcissistic, nihilistic, pathological, immoral, and, for some, evil. Hip-hop has fought back. It uses strategies of naming, renaming, unnaming, and overnaming its own culture and the cultures—racist, rich, elite, bourgeois—against which it strives.

Instead of nostalgia, we need serious, rigorous analysis and critical appreciation of black youth. Instead of attacks on hip-hop culture, we need sharp, just, well-informed evaluations of its artistic statements and ethical imagination. Black nostalgia must be replaced by an even stronger force: the historic black determination to remain undefeated by pessimism from within black culture, and paranoia from beyond its borders. We must not be prisoners of our present circumstances, of current events. We must be prisoners of faith.

PART THIRTEEN

THE PREDICAMENT OF POSTMODERNITY

Postmodernism has enjoyed a thrilling if problematic run as a leading intellectual and cultural movement among some (mostly liberal or progressive) academics. Postmodernism is composed of a complex, even ambiguous, set of ideas and practices, such as blurring the boundaries between "high" and "low" culture, rejecting grand narratives—for instance, "truth" with a capital "T,"—embracing pastiche and fragmentation, and emphasizing playfulness and irony in one's intellectual exercises. A major criticism of postmodernism is that some of its advocates avoid concrete history and politics while rhapsodizing about difference, marginality, parody, and provisionality. This may account for the many American postmodernists who have overlooked the homegrown varieties of black postmodernism—and the challenges they may pose to the European imports that have colored our understanding of the concept. I have written about black postmodernism since I have been an intellectual, attempting to add nuance and complexity—and black political and rhetorical weight—to an intriguing intellectual debate.

Thirty-Three

MICHAEL JACKSON'S POSTMODERN SPIRITUALITY

Michael Jackson is unquestionably one of the greatest entertainers of the twentieth century. His most recent troubles, including allegations of child molestation, have obscured the essential fact of his career: that he has been an incredible singer, dancer, performer, and interpreter of (African) American song over the past thirty-five years. Because we were born merely two months apart in 1958—Jackson in August, me in October—I have always marveled at his prodigious output and, perhaps, identified in some small way with his struggles to artistically and personally redefine himself. From the moment Michael Jackson burst on the musical horizon in 1968, his relentless perfectionism, Herculean work ethic, and brilliant showmanship have provided a thesaurus for American musical giftedness. Only one other figure of his generation—Prince—has rivaled Jackson's genius and approached his impact on the culture. I wrote this scholarly meditation on Jackson's postmodern secular spirituality after seeing him perform in New Jersey in the late '80s. If Jackson never again reaches the artistic heights he once achieved, he will have still given the world a glimpse of a God-given talent used to uplift and thrill millions around the globe.

[Michael Jackson] will not swiftly be forgiven for having turned so many tables, for he damn sure grabbed the brass ring, and the man who broke the bank at Monte Carlo has nothing on Michael.

—JAMES BALDWIN

Sometimes when you're treated unfairly it makes you stronger and more determined. Slavery was a terrible thing, but when black people in America finally got out from under that crushing system, they were stronger. They knew what it was to have your spirit crippled by people who are controlling your life. They were never going to let that happen again. I admire that kind of strength. People who have it take a stand and put their blood and soul into what they believe.

—MICHAEL JACKSON, *MOONWALK*

MICHAEL JACKSON IS, ARGUABLY, THE GREATEST *entertainer* of the twentieth century. As an international superstar, Jackson has captured the devotion of a large segment of the world's population in a manner reserved for a select few historic personages. Jackson strikes a deep, primal chord in the human psyche, fascinating us, perhaps, because he so easily and eerily represents us, even mirrors us (all of us) at the same time. Thus, if he is not a Nietzschean *Übermensch*, he is a Promethean allperson who traverses traditional boundaries that separate, categorize, and define differences: innocent/shrewd, young/old, black/white, male/female, and religious/secular.

Perhaps this is also why he frightens us. In his cosmos, Jackson is guided by a logic of experience that flees the comfortable core of life to its often untested periphery. In some senses, Jackson celebrates the dissolution of Yeats's center and exults in the scamper for the edge. If at times his pace to the uncharted is dizzying, his achievements in the wake of his pursuit are dazzling, and at times monumental. It is the nature of these achievements that I want to examine in this essay. I understand Michael Jackson to represent a postmodern form of African-American secular spirituality that is primarily televisual and performance oriented in its medium of expression, and that wrestles in a poignant fashion with moral themes that reflect black cultural and religious consciousness.

However, to suggest that Michael Jackson's art harbors religious significance and spiritual meaning is contentious for many observers of American culture. For some, Jackson is a self-styled Peter Pan figure who is securely nestled in a fantasy world of childlike make-believe, buffered by Disney characters and exotic animals.[1] To others, Jackson is a surpassingly shrewd businessman, capable of amassing a catalogue of publishing rights to songs by such artists as Sly Stone and the Beatles.[2] To others still, Jackson is a victim of the vicious processes of commerce that commodify his image and capitalize on his persona.[3] Certainly these and many other characterizations of Jackson may ring true, but they do not reflect the central truth of his cultural significance, nor do they capture the peculiar and unique genius of his art. Above all else that he may symbolize, central to Jackson's career is an abiding spiritual and religious consciousness that is expressed in his body of work as a performer.

Admittedly, part of the difficulty in discerning the presence of positive spiritual values and redemptive religious consciousness in Jackson's art may be its nontraditional expression. In both its style and substance, Jackson's spirituality exhibits elements that may be understood as postmodern.[4] Postmodernism's broad spectrum of expression—characterized by pastiche, quotation, fragmentation, stylistic merging, transgression, and eclecticism—suggests a dismantling of the hardened distinction between high artistic expression and lowbrow, popular cultural production. These and other postmodernist practices call into question settled beliefs and rigid formulations about art and culture in American life.

For some, postmodernist culture survives, in Roland Barthes's phrase, as the "civilization of the image."[5] Jackson's spirituality exhibits a keen awareness of the important function of imagery. His spirituality is filtered through the televisual apparatus, symbolizing (and symptomatic of) the Gutenberg shift in cultural consciousness marked by the move in our society from the literate to the cinemate, and the hegemony of the visual over the verbal. True to form, Jackson's spirituality is not primarily embodied in a series of written texts, nor is it exclusively articulated in song lyrics. Jackson's postmodern spirituality surfaces in the brilliant, haunting, and sometimes disturbing images and visions portrayed in his music videos and (films of his) live performances.

For Marxist critic Fredric Jameson, postmodernism is linked to and materially precipitated by the globalization of American capital in the late 1950s, expressing the "logic of late capitalism."[6] His early analysis accentuated the negative aspects of postmodernism, with its loss of the sense of history and its exemplification of commodification. Recently, however, Jameson has at least acknowledged some positive characteristics of postmodernism, such as its stress on the wide accessibility of culture and its recuperation of the art of storytelling in literary texts.[7] Other American theorists have uncritically adopted French poststructuralist readings of postmodernism that accentuated marginality, difference, and peripheralization as articulated by figures like Derrida and Lyotard, while ignoring the development of more indigenous expressions in the United States.

Ironically, as Cornel West has noted, these theorists have sought illumination of our American postmodern contexts by borrowing from such figures while neglecting exemplary postmodern African-American cultural producers, particularly artists and musicians.[8] These artists and musicians, from Charlie Parker to Wynton Marsalis, from Romare Bearden to Betye Saar, have wrestled existentially and artistically with disenabling forms of otherness and difference. Thus their artistic production heralds unexamined but crucial resources for contesting the disempowerment that can result from political, economic, social, and cultural marginality.

As a result, these African-American artists offer the possibility of accentuating elements of postmodern cultural experience and artistic expression that are, in Hal Foster's words, "resistant" and not "reactionary."[9] This suggests that these resistant forms of postmodernist production do not simply replicate older forms of artistic production in a nostalgic sense of mimetic play, but extend in their recuperative artistic process the boundaries of cultural expression. This may be viewed in Michael Jackson, who, while drawing upon the enormously skillful performance and dancing of James Brown and the electrifying showmanship of Jackie Wilson, yet manages to insert a unique brand of spiritual consciousness into his performances, yielding powerful forms of artistic, cultural, and religious expression.

Jackson's spiritual and religious awareness can be glimpsed in his persistent preoccupation with images, symbols, and themes that are informed by his own religious background. Jackson was reared as a Jehovah's Witness by his mother, whose faith he shared and, until recently, faithfully practiced. Although the particular character of Jackson's religious reflections and moral musings were shaped by his experience as a Jehovah's Witness, his art reflects perceptions and consciousness that are easily generalizable to the larger stream of African-American spirituality. Thus we may without extensive complication, for example, draw similarities between Jackson's work and the artistic achievements of his musical comrades Stevie Wonder and Marvin Gaye.

Suffice it to say that Jackson's religious sensibilities are expressed in his wrestling with religiously informed, morally shaped, and culturally conditioned themes that include an examining of the nature of good and evil; an exploring of the potentialities for transformation of the self, human nature, and society; a probing of the true nature of manhood in American culture, as opposed to disenabling versions of machismo; a confronting of the material lures and sexual seductions of everyday life in postmodern American culture; a proclaiming of the place of peace and love in transforming the world; and a surveying of the politics of American racial identity and awareness.

These themes recur in Jackson's song lyrics and music videos, and form the basis for the articulation of his own vision of African-American secular spirituality. Jackson is acutely aware of the importance of a morally informed and spiritually grounded perspective on such themes. For instance, in speaking of his role in the "We Are the World" song-video-event that helped raise money for starving Ethiopians, Jackson, in his autobiography *Moonwalk*,[10] illumines the spiritual theme in the song's message and explains the impetus for his participation:

> In early 1985 we cut "We Are the World" at an all-night all-star recording session that was held after the ceremony for the American Music Awards. I wrote the song with Lionel Richie after seeing the appalling news footage of starving people in Ethiopia and the Sudan. . . . I think that "We Are the World" is a very spiritual song, but spiritual in a special sense. I was proud to be a part of that song and to be one of the musicians there that night. We were united by our desire to make a difference. It made the world a better place for us and it made a difference to the starving people we wanted to help. (pp. 261–262)

While Jackson does not specify the "special" nature of the song's spirituality, it is sufficiently clear that this spirituality bears social ramifications and is at minimum linked to expressing authentic and concrete concern for other human beings. In short, Jackson emphasizes the material consequences of his spiritual *Weltanschauung*, redeeming it from the possible infamy of an abstract mysticism that uncritically valorizes sentimental and emotive modes of expression. Furthermore, it is apparent elsewhere in Jackson's text that this spirituality is a gift from God and must be expressed in the particular vocational calling for which God has chosen him, namely, his music and performance:

> I've always joked that I didn't ask to sing and dance, but it's true. When I open my mouth, music comes out. I'm honored that I have this ability. I thank God for it every day. I try to cultivate what He gave me. I feel I'm compelled to do what I do. (p. 272)

In discussing the spiritual character of his gift, Jackson speaks about his mother's faith:

She instilled in me a love of Him that I will always have. She taught me that my talent for singing and dancing was as much God's work as a beautiful sunset or a storm that left snow for children to play in. Despite all the time we spent rehearsing and traveling, Mom would find time to take me to Kingdom Hall of the Jehovah's Witnesses, usually with Rebbie and LaToya. (pp. 12–13)

Moreover, Jackson is driven by a desire to enflesh this spirituality, to enable others to perceive the vision that energizes and empowers him, and in the process to transform people's lives with his art, with the stories that he sings and "tells":

I've always wanted to be able to tell stories, you know, stories that came from the soul. I'd like to sit by a fire and tell people stories—make them see pictures, make them cry and laugh, take them anywhere emotionally with something as deceptively simple as words. I'd like to tell tales to move their souls and transform them. . . . In a way, songwriting uses the same skills, creates the emotional highs and lows. . . . There are very few books written on the art of storytelling, how to grip listeners. . . . No costumes, no makeup, no nothing, just you and your voice, and your powerful ability to take them anywhere, to transform their lives, if only for minutes. (pp. 5–6)

Jackson's art, then, is intentional and goal oriented, and self-consciously related to the spiritual roots that have nourished its beginning and that continue to sustain its expanding identity.

Jackson's spirituality, though, is a secular spirituality, which may at first appear to be an oxymoronic formulation. Jackson's spirituality is secular precisely because its primary site of execution and expression is not the church sanctuary but the concert stage, and because it is not embedded in conventional ecclesiastical structures or transmitted in traditional religious linguistic or liturgical practices. Furthermore, his secular spirituality does not assume that a prior grounding in the shared language of a religious community is needed in order to grasp its basic premises.

Neither does it make identity formed in intellectual exchange or conceptual dialogue needed for comprehension or participation. Jackson articulates powerful forms of human identity in images, symbols, and language that are shaped by, but not limited to, his own religious experience. Thus, the many traditions of moral reflection and ethical analysis that derive from a common Judeo-Christian heritage in American society are consonant in many crucial respects with Jackson's own vision of peace, love, and justice. Similar to the way that devotees of African-American religion participating in the civil rights movement appealed to a language of rights, thus allowing them to express their conceptions of peace, justice, and liberation in secular terms, so does Jackson's spirituality find a "language" that is understood by members of an American culture not sharing his own religious experience.[11]

Furthermore, Jackson's spirituality is secular because it is created for, and best thrives in, the cultural, psychic, and social spaces of the concert world, and not the *ekklesia*. It is not situated in, or sustained by, conventional procedures of church participation, service, or worship. This does not mean, however, that Jackson's spirituality is devoid of religious drama involving rituals, pageantry, and spectacles.[12] On the contrary, Jackson's secular spirituality, particularly as performed on the concert stage, is replete with references to certain African-American religiocultural practices that signify in the musical arena.

For instance, Jackson's concerts thrive on call and response. Jackson's live performances mediate ritual structures of antiphonal oral and verbal exchange between artist and audience. Such antiphonal exchange permits the artist to articulate his or her vision and authorizes the audience to acknowledge its reception and even shape its meaning by responding to the emotion being expressed, refracting the message being sent, or reaffirming the idea being communicated. In this context, meaning is an open-ended process that resists premature or permanent closure. This secular koinonia of communicants (artist and audience) constitutes a text whose understanding necessitates mutual participation in order to explore and unpack its multiple meanings. In the best of the African-American religious tradition, meaning is produced by an ever evolving, perennially transforming, historically conditioned set of cultural practices, rhetorical strategies, and religious signifiers. Jackson's phenomenal and protean energies in live performance exemplify this point.

Furthermore, Jackson's performances richly fuse Bakhtinian conceptions of carnival with African-American forms of spiritual ecstasy, producing a highly animated hybrid that creates space for cultural resistance and religious agency.[13] Both carnival and African-American religious ecstatic experience have been devalued as cathartic, excessive, and celebrative of the "low" in human nature. But it is just this emphasis on the "low" religious expression of ecstasy, empathy, and subjective experientialism versus the "high" religious expression of control, stolidity, and objective experientialism that marks, in part, the subversive potentialities and powers of African-American religion.

Also, it is the "low" cultural expression of laughter, bodily pleasure, and vernacular language—versus the "high" cultural expression of solemnity, repression, and classical language—that expresses the powers of culturally degraded masses to revolt and survive. Carnival prevents rank and social hierarchy from tyrannizing social expression, much as progressive Christian conceptions of democracy allow the free social expression of equal beings.[14] Bakhtin says, "Carnival celebrated temporary liberation from the prevailing truth and from the established order: it marked the suspension of all hierarchical rank, privileges, norms and prohibitions."[15] Jackson taps into and ties these traditions together in a highly skillful and empowering fashion.

The primary form of Jackson's secular spirituality is televisual. In fact, the major moments in Jackson's vocation have been catalyzed by the visual medium, either on television or in music video. For instance, Jackson's passage from music superstar to a world historical and cultural figure was ritually enacted on May 16, 1983, with his mythic dance performance of the "moonwalk" on the *Motown 25* television special, which was beamed to almost 50 million viewers around the globe. Jackson's uncanny dexterity, disciplined grace, and explosive imagination coalesced in a series of immortal movements, which, in their turn, freeze framed the recrudescent genius of street dance, summarized the important history of Fred Astaire-like purposeful grace in executing dance steps, and extended the brilliant tradition of African-American performers like Bojangles, Sammy Davis, and Katherine Dunham surging against the odds to create vital art.

Jackson's epochal routine skyrocketed his record sales and catapulted him into the stellar reaches of fame, landing him on the cover of the *Guiness Book of World Records* for selling over 40 million copies of his album *Thriller*, the most in music history. His autobiography *Moonwalk*, edited by Jackie Onassis, was aptly named, for it captures the watershed moment in Jackson's career and symbolizes his transformation into a personality of almost universal appeal.

The televisual medium, then, is central to Jackson's expression of his musical vision of life. When he was making the album *Thriller*, Jackson writes:

> I was determined to present this music as visually as possible. At the time I would look at what people were doing with video, and I couldn't understand why so much of it seemed so primitive and weak. I saw kids watching and accepting boring videos because they had no alternatives. My goal is to do the best I can in every area, so why work hard on an album and then produce a terrible video? I wanted something that would *glue* you to the set, something you'd want to watch over and over. . . . So I wanted to be a pioneer in this relatively new medium and make the best short music movies we could make. I don't even like to call them videos. On the set I explained that we were doing a *film*, and that was how I approached it. (pp. 201–202)

Since the televisual medium is so crucial to Jackson's vision of life, it is here that I want to concentrate my analysis in examining the confluence of music, medium, and message in Jackson's art. In the remaining part of the essay, then, I will trace some of the themes that constitute Jackson's African-American secular spirituality as they are presented in a major (but not exclusive) mode of expression for him—the music video. These themes include, as stated above, the nature of good and evil; the potentialities for transformation of the self, human nature, and society; the nature of real manhood in American culture; the politics of racial identity in America; and the place of love in changing the world. In exploring these themes in Jackson's art, I will examine two representative Jackson videos, "Thriller"[16] and "Bad,"[17] and a live performance of "Man in the Mirror"[18] at the 1988 Grammy Awards.

Jackson's "Thriller" marked a revolutionary use of the music video. As Jackson indicated in the quote cited above, he intended to make a singular contribution to the field. In fact all of his videos are distinct and defy easy categorization.[19] "Thriller" (which capped Jackson's first period of music video creation) presents a fantastical, wild, even scary vision of human transformation that rests upon conventions developed in the horror film genre and utilizes the werewolf figure as a metaphor of the potential for personal transmogrification. "Thriller" employs a variety of horror film staples, such as sophisticated makeup, special effects, eerie music, and even the chillingly familiar voice of thrill master Vincent Price. It is a mark of Jackson's unique imaginative powers that he is able to explore questions of human nature and identity in this film genre.

The video begins with a written disclaimer: "Due to my strong personal convictions, I wish to stress that this film in no way endorses a belief in the occult." Jackson was then still connected to the Jehovah's Witnesses, and this statement was a concession to their concern about the possible misinterpretation of the video's content. The opening scene of "Thriller" depicts Jackson and his girlfriend, portrayed by Ola Ray, driving in a white 1950s Buick. Suddenly they are out of gas, and Jackson faces the embarrassing task of reporting this to Ray, knowing his companion will suspect a typical male ruse to initiate romantic tomfoolery. Jackson says that they are honestly out of gas, to Ray's incredulous ears. They get out of the car and begin to walk. Finally, however, Ray apologizes for her initial disbelief.

Jackson's character then begins to talk with Ray, expressing his affection for her and hoping that she will return a similar affection to him. As they embrace, Jackson asks her to be his "girl." To make it official, Jackson gives her a ring. He then tells her that he must vouchsafe a piece of important information to her, namely that he is "not like other guys." This, of course, is a statement with which Jackson observers, fans and detractors alike, would heartily agree. After Ray says she understands this, Jackson insists that she is missing his point, that he is different in a way much different than she appreciates.

Until now, the sterile placidity of the couple's nocturnal surroundings remain undisturbed, and only reinforce the engaging and affectionate emotions being mutually expressed between Jackson and Ray. But Jackson's announcement of Derridean difference shatters the unity of natural and personal calm. The pain of his self-awareness is the occasion for subsequent turmoil in Jackson and his companion. It is at the very point of Jackson's announcement that he begins to exhibit the specific and exaggerated character of his difference. The physiological structure of Jackson's countenance becomes radically altered, as he commences an ontological descent into animalistic debasement: he becomes a werewolf.

The transformation is now complete, and Jackson is the Freak, the one whose being and appearance cause utter horror and total repulsion (much like London's famed "Elephant Man," with whose remains Jackson is fascinated). He begins to chase his companion, who runs shrieking from the immense vulgarity of his transformed visage. Just as the werewolf corners her, we see a movie audience and understand that what we have just seen is a film being watched by an audience on film.

In the audience are Jackson and Ray, she horrified by what she has seen, Jackson relishing the gore of every cut, slice, and painful grimace. Ray removes herself from the audience, and Jackson, after savoring a final glimpse, follows her. After assuring Ray that "it was just a movie," the music to "Thriller" begins, with its menacing bass line foreshadowing the ominous events about to occur. Jackson sings the words to "Thriller," speaking about the evil lurking in the dark, the terror-filled night visions, and the paralysis that results from such visions. As he continues to sing, graves begin to open up, and unseemly creatures begin to emerge from long sleep, recalling some night of the living dead.

Just as the words indicate that "no mere mortal can resist the evil of thriller," Jackson is transformed into one of the creatures, growing fangs and developing dark-circled eyes. In the next scene, Jackson's face is returned to normal, as he continues to warn of the consequences of the "Thriller night." Once again, Jackson is transformed, even transmogrified, into a horrible creature, and along with other ghoulish "demons" he begins to pursue Ray. They chase her into a house, where her crying screams are met with more creatures coming out of the floorboards and through the windows. As they crowd in for the final assault, Ray offers her ultimate terror-struck shriek, and Jackson, once again changed to his normal face, greets her and asks her what is wrong. As he helps her to her feet and they leave, he turns to the camera, with fangish mouth and devilish yellow eyes.

It would be obviously stretching the truth to suggest that "Thriller" offers Jackson's self-conscious attempt to theologically thematize his conception of human nature and human identity. Also, there are troubling aspects to Jackson's adoption of the horror film genre, which has notoriously sexualized victimization by constituting women as objects of male monster violent desire. However, I believe that "Thriller" does provide a lens on aspects of Jackson's views about human nature and on problems of evil that reflect his religious and moral views.

The lyrics to "Thriller" were not written by Jackson, but by Rod Temperton, a former member of the group Heatwave, itself a product of diverse American and British cultural and musical elements in the mid-1970s. In his lyrics, Temperton represents the threat of horror approaching from the outside. The human beings (Jackson and Ray) are victimized by events external to their nature or control, and evil intent is expressed through creatures radically unlike themselves:

> It's close to midnight and something evil's lurking in the dark / Under the moonlight you see a sight that almost stops your heart / . . . You hear the door slam and realize there's nowhere left to run / You feel the cold hand and wonder if you'll ever see the sun / You close your eyes and hope that this is just imagination / But all the while you hear the creature creepin' up behind / You're out of time / . . . There ain't no second chance against this thing with forty eyes.

Jackson provides Ray protection, however, from the marauding monsters:

> Now is the time for you and I to cuddle close together / All through the night I'll save you from the terrors on the screen, I'll make you see.

The further innuendo points to Jackson's ability to romantically thrill Ray:

> . . . It's a thriller, thriller night / 'Cause I can thrill you more than any ghost would dare to try / Girl, this is thriller, thriller night / So let me hold you tight and share a killer, diller, chiller, / Thriller here tonight.

In his minimovie version of "Thriller" (which was nominated for an Oscar in the short film category), Jackson extends its range of meaning and expands its spectrum of signifiers, with the result that he expresses some of his views about human nature. First, Jackson represents the horror of evil as both an external event embodied in transhuman creatures and as an internal experience embodied in human creatures. Even more pointedly, the terrain of evil embodiment is the self, which has grave consequences for the human being, especially in altered behavior, attitudes, and physiological appearance. It is a totalizing process that affects, even infects, the whole human organism. In the movie, Jackson's turn from magnanimous protector to malicious pursuer indicates the dialectical tension of good and evil that defines the human predicament and illumines the difficult context of choice between moral opposites, particularly when they are embedded in the same human being.

For Jackson's "Thriller," human identity is an imperfect, messy amalgam of good and evil, of *humanitas* and *animalis*, of oppositional tendencies that inhabit the same psychic, spiritual, and biological space. A full comprehension of the social practices, personal habits, and cultural behavior manifested in acts of goodness must be chastened by an awareness of the potential for wrong and harm. Likewise, the judgment of the expression of evil social practices, personal habits, and cultural behavior must be tempered by the recognition of the human possibilities to do good acts and to generate productive lifestyles. In short, there are discernible traces of religious conceptions of human nature and identity in Jackson's video version of "Thriller" that acknowledge the limits of human capacities for good and also acknowledge an awareness of the human capability to do harm. It is not altogether unlike the view of human nature that informed Reinhold Niebuhr's political realism and influenced the thought of Martin Luther King Jr.[20]

Furthermore, in "Thriller" Jackson has, at least inadvertently, raised the issue of marginality, difference, and otherness in much the same way that he indirectly precipitates conversations about such topics in real life (especially because of his alleged multiple cosmetic surgeries). The werewolf signifies the Embodied Other, the spectacle of a difference so gross that it evokes responses of fear, terror, or horror in gasping onlookers. Some may view this as a proleptic revelation of Jackson's own existential grappling with his Otherness, to be subsequently revealed in the "horrifying" spectacle of Jackson's transformation of his own face.

On the matter of his plastic surgery, Jackson complains that as he went from a "cute," chubby-faced kid to a lean young man, "the press started accusing me of surgically altering my appearance, beyond the nose job I freely admitted I had" (p. 229). Jackson denies having his cheeks altered, his lips thinned, or his skin peeled. In exasperation, he asks rhetorically, "What does my face have to do with my music or my dancing?" (p. 230). Apparently Jackson fails to understand that, as a cultural icon, the seeming de-Africanization of his face and the Europeanization of his image reflect a wrestling with profound questions of identity and self-image that influence the way his artistic achievements are perceived. In any regard, the werewolf character, although a highly stylized signifier rooted in Jackson's fantasy life, communicates the aesthetic dissonance, social terror, and personal repulsion that may result from (racial, sexual) forms of otherness and difference.

That the site of otherness would be the body (versus the mind, for example, in forms of madness) speaks volumes of the African American confrontation with debilitating forms and uses of embodiment. The socially, morally, and economically repugnant uses of African-American embodiment, rooted in the commodification of the black body, began under slavocracy in American culture. The black body was articulated as the primal other, the form of difference par excellence. Such uses of the black body were repudiated in African-American religious practices, which redeemed the use of the body by employing it in rites of sanctification, rituals of purification, and acts of celebration. Jackson's expression of religious joy through his celebrative dance routines captures at least one pole of the redemptive use of the black body articulated in black religious practices.

In "Thriller" Jackson has managed, in his own peculiar and idiosyncratic manner, to encapsulate and represent certain of his views about evil and about human nature and human identity. Jackson as werewolf indicates the possibility of the radical instability of human nature and reflects the underlining of absolute distinctions between good and evil. The werewolf indicates the possibility of human beings embodying radical forms of evil and inflicting evil on other human beings, whether psychologically or in empirical events of social malevolence. The werewolf also indicates the Other, whose very embodiment occasions fear in those he or she encounters.

In his song and video "Bad," Jackson turns to more familiar cultural and social territory, as he examines the terms of existence for those who must straddle barriers between two worlds divided by race and class. Jackson searingly probes the complexities of making judgments about moral issues generated in the urban inner city. "Bad" is a takeoff on the Edmund Perry story.[21] Edmund Perry was a brilliant Harlem youth who graduated with honors from Phillips Exeter Academy, a prestigious prep school in New Hampshire, and was awarded a full scholarship to Stanford University. Ten days after his graduation, while back home in Harlem, he was killed on New York City's Upper West Side by a white policeman, Lee Van Houten, who claimed that Perry and his brother Jonah had viciously beaten him during a robbery attempt. Perry's story is told in a controversial book, *Best Intentions*, by Robert Sam Anson.[22]

"Bad" opens with a full camera view of Duxston prep school, couched in winter snow and obvious opulence, supported by ominous strains of music. As with "Thriller," the serenity and wholesome environment masks the potential for evil that lurks within, as Hitchcock's proverbial clean suburban landscape conceals the absurdity underneath. We then see the empty hallways and neat stairways of Duxston, followed by a full-face shot of Jackson slowly raising his head from a bowed position, indicating that the story and world we will see are his. The camera breaks to students running down the stairs and halls of Duxston, exulting in glee over the apparent winter break. Jackson is seen running down the hall and being stopped by a white male student who says that he wants to tell Darryl (Jackson's character) that he has done a good job this term, that he has worked hard, and that he is proud of Darryl. Darryl thanks him, after which the white student says, "High five, man. Take care." Darryl exchanges the high five gesture with the white student, and other students are shown running out of school.

The next scene switches to Jackson riding on the train, viewing the world outside his window. The camera pans back to a full view of the aisle and seats, showing Darryl talking to a white schoolmate while other white schoolmates make a mess of the train. To the left corner of the camera, and the train, sits a student of Latino descent with an open book, unsmilingly surveying the scene of recreative havoc created by the white students and glancing toward Darryl as he continues his conversation with the white student.

The scene dissolves, and Darryl and the Latino student are now the focus of the camera, with a mostly deserted background, indicating the passage of time. The Latino student begins to look at Darryl, peering at him as Darryl now sits alone. Over the loudspeaker, the announcer declares that the next station is Grand Central Terminal, the final stop of the train. The camera then pans in to a full-faced shot of the Latino student directing a piercing smirk and cutting glance at Darryl, who is foregrounded in a visually blurred manner while strains of troubling music insinuate themselves in the background. Darryl looks at the Latino student and gives a tentative smile that tests the tension of their nonverbal exchange, then looks away. The two of them, along with the few other passengers, get off the train.

The next scene shows a crowded subway, as the camera pans down a row of riding passengers: first a middle-aged black woman with her eyes closed after an apparently hard day of work; a pensive white woman; an elderly couple who look to be slightly worried; a young black woman looking down; a stern white woman blankly staring forward, the perfect exemplar of a person dulled by mind-numbing, alienated work in a Marxist vision; and finally the Latino student with Darryl next to him, both of their heads involuntarily shaking to the rhythm of the subway's movement.

The Latino student turns to Darryl, and as the camera focuses on Darryl's face, the Latino student asks him, "How many guys proud of you?" Darryl quietly counts with his lips and, without looking at the Latino student, says, "Three." With an ironic smile, the Latino student holds up four fingers and says, "Shoot, four guys proud of me!" Darryl looks at him and they smile, both recognizing that it is a source of perennial surprise to their fellow white students that they are able to excel at school. This is a subtle but powerful critique by Jackson of white liberalism, which has the power to stigmatize and punish with its often unconscious condescension even as it intends to single out and celebrate. This form of critique, of course, is linked to potent traditions of African-American religious and cultural criticism developed over centuries of protest against injustice and struggle for freedom.

As the Latino student prepares to leave his stop on the subway, he gives Darryl a soul brother handshake and says, "Be the man." Darryl responds to him, "Be the man." The significance here is that the high five of the white student earlier is juxtaposed against the soul handclasp of the Latino student. The high five, in this case, is a stylized, fashionable handshake that signifies an ephemeral, external code of relationship between Darryl and the white student. Although the white student is expressing attempted camaraderie and friendship, the high five is more a testament of the cultural distance between them than an acknowledgment of their bonds of social intimacy.

The Latino student's soul handclasp, however, is a meaningful, internal code of unspoken solidarity generated out of common circumstances of victimization and objectification. Furthermore, the Latino student's parting exhortation to Darryl to "be the man" is a culturally encoded signifier that subverts the usual semantic meaning of the term and counsels a steadfast resolve to remain strong and rooted in one's own cultural identity while achieving success at "the man's" (white man's) institution.

The next scene shows a row of dilapidated, boarded-up brownstones in Harlem and a row of men standing around twenty-gallon oil drums, warming themselves over the fires they have started within, not an inappropriate metaphor for the condition of black men in contemporary American culture. As Darryl walks down the street a black man hollers at him, "Yo. Yo, blood. Yo." When Darryl does not answer him (perhaps because he knows that what the man wants he cannot give, or that what he wants he should not have), the man shrugs him off with hand gestures that say, "Forget it."

As Darryl continues to amble down the street, three other "brothers" catch sight of him, and one of them declares, as he hugs Darryl, "The Black is back. Yo. Black is back, my man," and the other two fellows joyfully greet him. After this, Darryl goes up into his apartment telling the "fellas" that he'll be down later. After Darryl goes into his apartment and reads a note of welcome from his mother who has to work late, until seven, he finds a window and looks out over the material morass and spiritual squalor that litter his neighborhood, a Harlem gutted by social misery and urban stench. The next scene shows Darryl and his three friends in the hallways of a building engaging in harmless chitchat and ribbing, as one of his friends inquires about Darryl's major. When Darryl responds that he is in high school, which requires no major, the friend asks, "Then what's your minor?" All of them, including Darryl, have a good laugh. Not so funny later on, and indicative of the trouble to come, is when Darryl is asked if the "white boys" at his school wear "turtle shells." "That's tortoise shells," Darryl replies. There is icy silence in the room, thick with resentment over Darryl's benignly intentioned correction.

After the leader of the group indicates that it is time to "go" (i.e., engage in petty criminal behavior), the scene changes to a street corner, where a man with a cane is transacting a drug sale with another man. After the man with the cane completes the sale, Darryl and his friends are seen leaning against a car, regarding him with a cautious silence. The man pulls back his jacket to reveal a revolver and asks if they are looking for somebody. The fellas, getting the message, depart.

Later, back in a building, the leader declares to Darryl, "Hunts up. Hunts up, homeboy. There are victims out there waitin' for us." Darryl utters a defiant question–"What?"–that rebuts the leader's criminal intentions. The leader declares, "'What?' Shit! Homeboy ain't home. Naw, see he up at Dunesbury playin' tennis with his turtle shells." Thus the struggle to maintain one's integrity and to construct a stable identity as a member of the underclass in the inner-city community surfaces. Jackson's video focuses sharply on the central problems of defining identity and examining the moral character of decisions that take account of the social and economic forces that form the background against which these choices must be made. Darryl responds to the leader, "Back off." After a rough verbal encounter, the leader grabs Darryl and says, "Yo man, what's wrong? Are you bad? Or is that what they teach you up at that sissy school of yours: how to forget who your friends are? Well let me tell you somethin', I don't care what they teach you up there. You either down or you ain't down. So the question is, are you bad or what?" The basis of their past relationship is shattered, and Darryl must renegotiate the terms of his relationship to his "in-group" if any form of that relationship is to survive.

Darryl tells the leader to leave him alone, that he's tired of him "messin'" with him. Finally he takes off his gloves and jacket and says that if the leader really wants to see what is bad, then he will show him. At this point we (and Darryl) are still in a morally ambiguous position, because we cannot ascertain the particular nature of Darryl's challenge, whether it will be a show of neighborhood machismo that revels in theft and crime, or whether it will be to subvert neighborhood conceptions of what is "bad," similar to what happened between Darryl and the Latino student's subversion of the code of success in the white world. This is an implicit appeal to the culturally encoded practice that uses words like "tough" and "bad" to mean something different, often their opposite. Jackson skillfully displays the dual tensions that define Darryl's world and that, in much more detail and depth, defined Edmund Perry's world. Moral choice is seen against a background of several factors that must be considered when one judges the actions of inner-city youth who resort to a life of crime to "make it." Jackson's moral vision, unquestionably formed by his own religious views, is able to appreciate these subtleties and promotes a vision that combines compassion and criticism.

The next scene shows Darryl and the fellas at a deserted section of the subway, awaiting a lone man walking down the corridor. Darryl, under the pressure to prove his "badness," is poised to pounce and prey upon the man, but at the last moment decides to tell him to flee. The man speaks no English, reinforcing the fact that victims of ghetto machismo or criminal activity are often other underclass and struggling people. The fellas become angry with Darryl, and declare, "You aren't down with us no more," and Darryl responds, "You ain't bad, you ain't nothin.'" Here again, Jackson's own moral perspective is informed by an understanding of human nature that acknowledges that all human beings embody the potential for wrongdoing. But as is clear in his reading of the story, all human beings have the ability to contribute to their own future by the choices they make and the options they exercise. This is no static conception of human nature and identity, no social determinism that locks human beings into predestined choice. It is rather a Christian understanding of human nature that appreciates the complexity and ambiguity that surrounds our moral choices, that posits an ambivalent disposition toward the desires that occupy our social landscape, and that accentuates the historical formation of the virtues we attempt to nourish.

At this juncture, the scene, until now black and white, blooms in full color, as dancers emerge from either side of the columns in the subway, rupturing the realism that has informed the video to this point. From then on, Darryl's message is communicated in Jackson's powerful singing voice, accompanied by extraordinarily skillful dancing that choreographs his message to the fellas. Jackson reverses the power arrangement between Darryl and the fellas that has defined their relationship as he sings:

> Your butt is mine / Gonna tell you right /Just show your face / In broad daylight / I'm telling you / On how I feel / Gonna hurt your mind / Don't shoot to kill / ... I'm giving you / On count of three / To show your stuff / Or let it be ... / I'm telling you /Just watch your mouth / I know your game / What you're about / Well they say the sky's the limit / And to me that's really true / But my friend you have seen nothin' / Just wait 'til I get through ... / Because I'm bad, I'm bad—come on.

At the climax of his melodied oration, Darryl comes face to face with the leader of the fellas in a dramatic encounter reminiscent of the machismo-laden staredowns between prizefighters. Darryl scorns their wrongdoing in a fusion of speech and song that is the strongest evocation of the African-American religious rhetorical practice of "whooping," "chanting," or "tuning" since the advent of rap music. Darryl's lyrical preachment is accented by the antiphonal response of his amen chorus of backup dancer/singers, who meet his every word and gesture with a rising spiral of vocal support that crescendos with a hissing noise meant to seal their message and admonish their hearers.

At the end, Darryl and the leader lock arms and finally engage in a soul handshake, sealing the leader's respect for Darryl, as he intones, "That's the way it goes down, huh?" The soul handshake reinstitutes the possibility for personal and social solidarity between Darryl and the leader, functioning, as it did with the Latino student, to strengthen the ties of mutuality and community. As the fellas depart, one of the brothers removes his hat, acknowledging the power of Darryl's perspective, even as the scene returns to black and white and Darryl's garb returns to his jacket and street clothes.

Jackson's "Bad" video premiered on a CBS television special that aired August 31, 1987, before a national viewing audience. It conveyed a moving message about struggling with racial identity, forms of machismo, and the problems of underclass black men in a potent mix of song and dance. It also testified to the national, even worldwide, influence of Jackson's African-American secular spirituality.

Perhaps the most poignant and powerfully explicit display of Jackson's brand of secular spirituality was reserved for the 1988 *Grammy Awards Show*, beamed to millions of people around the world. As the auditorium faded to dark, a white screen was shown, silhouetting Jackson's lithe image, his head topped by a dark-brown fedora, his palm facing outward to the right on the end of his stiffened right arm, and his left leg extended, capped off by his trademark high-water pants, with a blue shirt circled at the waist by a white sash, and white socks and black shoes. As the audience screamed, strains of harmonies filled the air, and Jackson enacted ten seconds of solo dance movements, pantomiming some of his most agile poses. As the screen rose, Jackson began to sing, in an impassioned voice, a slow gospel-cadenced version of his song, "The Way You Make Me Feel." As Jackson gyrated on stage, the female dancer-actress Tatiana, famous from the video version of the song, emerged from the side of the stage. Jackson was also joined by four dancers who, with him, re-created the moves performed in the video.

Jackson then did a phenomenal foursquare version of the moonwalk, the dance that he made famous. The auditorium again faded to dark, with the spotlight on Jackson. He bowed, took the microphone handed to him, and began singing stanzas to "Man in the Mirror:"

> I'm gonna make a change, for once in my life / It's gonna feel real good, gonna make a difference / Gonna make it right . . . / As I turn up the collar on my favorite winter coat / This wind is blowin' my mind / I see the kids in the street, with not enough to eat / Who am I, to be blind? / Pretending not to see their needs / A summer's disregard, a broken bottle top / And a one man's soul / They follow each other on the wind, ya' know / 'Cause they got nowhere to go / That's why I want you to know / I'm starting with the man in the mirror / I'm asking him to change his ways / And no message could have been any clearer / If you wanna make the world a better place / Take a look at yourself, and then make a change

As he sang, the camera panned into his face as people from either side of the stage emerged from the wings. To his left were two singers, including Siedah Garrett, coauthor of "Man in The Mirror." To his right were three singers, including contemporary gospel great Andrae Crouch.

Jackson was singing, with their support, about the necessity for beginning the change in the world with one's self. As he stated in *Moonwalk:*

> "Man in the Mirror" is a great message. I love that song. If John Lennon was alive, he could really relate to that song because it says that if you want to make the world a better place, you have to work on yourself and change first. It's the same thing Kennedy was talking about when he said, "Ask not what your country can do for you; ask what you can do for your country." If you want to make the world a better place, take a look at yourself and make a change. Start with the

man in the mirror. Start with yourself. Don't be looking at all the other things. Start with you. That's the truth. That's what Martin Luther King meant and Gandhi too. That's what I believe. (pp. 267–268)

As Jackson, Crouch, Garrett, and the others continued to sing, the choir from New York's New Hope Baptist Church emerged from the back of the stage, augmenting the vocal power of Jackson's message. The religious nature of Jackson's interpretation became visually apparent, and the implicitly religious sensibilities of his performance became explicitly captured in the religious symbols surrounding Jackson. Jackson spun and fell on his knees, dramatizing his message of the dialectical relationship between personal change and social transformation. Back on his feet, Jackson pleaded once more for the world to change. Again he fell to his knees, but this time he succumbed to the spirit and passion of the moment and remained there. Jackson was spontaneously touched by what was occurring, as if he were a spectator to the event, as if he were only a vehicle, an agent of a transcendent power. Jackson was as shaken by the power of the message as if he were hearing and delivering it for the first time, a lesson that great gospel singers and preachers have mastered. Andrae Crouch then moved over from the side of the stage, as if he were in a church service where someone was "slain in the spirit," and after wiping Jackson's brow, he helped him to his feet. Jackson, with new vitality breathed into him, "got happy" again, turning several times, spinning joyously, and spontaneously jumping up and down, shaking his hands, and doing a complex walk-skip-jump movement.

Jackson's choreography of his religious joy, as he transformed the Grammy stage into a sanctuary, was infectious, and his audience, his faithful congregation, responded in the ecstatic glee of emotional abandon to his every move, groan, and gesture. Jackson exhorted them by telling them that everyone has to make a change, that the black man has to make a change, and that the white man has to make a change. As he dropped to his knees yet another time, the twenty-person choir moved ever closer to him, cutting off the stage and reducing it to a diamond, both in its shape and substance. It was priceless and invaluable because Jackson was projecting the power of African-American spirituality forward and having it rearticulated back to him in the reverberating emotion of the audience and the escalating ecstasy of his singers. Jackson went down, like a martyr figure delivering a messianic message, sinking to his knees that his audience might, as he repeatedly implored them, "stand up, stand up, stand up." Jackson then resorted to his best exhortative deep-throated vocal to release a volcanic melisma and syllabic repetition of the word you, in "you-you-you-ou-ow-ow got to make a change," catalyzing a tumultuous response in the Grammy audience.

At the consummation of his homily in song, Jackson whispered, "Make that change," and his congregation came to their feet, thundering their applauded amen at Jackson, yielding their total love and trust to his expressed desire to change the world by their changing themselves. The camera displayed a felicitous complicity in the spirit of the moment and scouted the audience for the converted and the committed, finding them scattered throughout the auditorium's scene of pandemonium.

Quincy Jones was clapping in recognition of his young charge's genius and in graceful acknowledgment of their amazingly productive and satisfying partnership over the last decade. Prince, typically unsmiling, was nonetheless on his feet, giving Jackson his due. Jody Watley was smiling broadly and clapping with joy. Behind her was Anita Baker, raising her hand in testimony to the spirit's presence and ejaculating an incendiary "yeah" in verbal testimony to her spiritual enthusiasm. There, too, was Little Richard, a cultural icon himself, whose face was brushed with a deep and clear joy, perhaps vicariously exulting in Jackson's glorious fulfillment, a fulfillment denied Little Richard, a real pillar of rock 'n' roll. (Jackson would return the joy later, as he was the first to his feet when Little Richard playfully chided the recording academy for not recognizing his original genius by awarding him a Grammy.) Finally there were the Houstons, Whitney and Cissy, exhibiting in their individual persons what Jackson combined: powerful forms of traditional, black, gospel-inflected music wed to crossover-rich, hook-laden music supported by diluted but still driving African-American beats.

Jackson's performance revealed a crucial aspect of his vocation: a theatricalization of spirituality, a festive choreography of religious reality that is often present in his live performances. The manner in which Jackson is able to evoke a virtually religious response from even secular concert attenders, a response that transcends mere emotional expression or simple cathartic release, is astonishing. He articulates a vision of the world that, although it includes idiosyncratic and fantastical elements, nonetheless communicates powerful religious truths and moral themes that are expressed in his riveting music and videos.

Michael Jackson seizes the parameters of the artistically possible and expands them to dimensions beyond most of our imaginations. He increases the influence of black religious experience and practices by articulating through televisual media his brand of African-American secular spirituality and institution-transcending piety, rife with appropriate religious and cultural imagery. He also transforms the stage into a world-extending sanctuary on which he enacts rituals of religious ecstasy, moral courage, and spiritual passion that mediate substantive concerns about love, peace, and justice, simultaneously subverting cultural consensus about what constitutes the really "bad" and the "good." He embodies a postmodern version of African-American secular spirituality that has the opportunity to spread its influence into the next century and to ensure the presence in the larger American and world culture of some of the most poignant and creative art developed from an enormously rich and resourceful tradition.

Thirty-Four

BE LIKE MIKE? MICHAEL JORDAN AND THE PEDAGOGY OF DESIRE

This chapter on Jordan was first published in 1993 for the journal Cultural Studies, *edited by renowned cultural studies scholar, and my dear friend, Lawrence Grossberg. I have written quite a bit about Jordan over the years, taking the measure of his social and political impact, as well as his athletic genius. In this chapter, I probe the racial and cultural dimensions of Jordan's achievements, placing him in the context of black athletic aspiration during the twentieth century. For much of the past century, black sports had an unavoidably symbolic and representative character; many athletes were social as well as athletic pioneers, shattering barriers for the progress of the entire race. I even take a stab at explaining Jordan's phenomenal ability in physical as well as metaphoric terms. I also specify the manner in which Jordan's is a black game—with his playing style revealing postmodern elements of black cultural creativity. Unlike many fans, I was happy to see Jordan un-retire for the second time, if for no other reason than he proved that "old" guys could still perform at unprecedented levels and show the young bucks a thing or two. I took my son to see his first "last" appearance as an All-Star in New York's Madison Square Garden, and again, in presumably his final "last" All-Star appearance in Atlanta in 2003. And later that year I watched Jordan lace up his sneakers for his final game in Philadelphia. Athletically, and culturally too, his likes will hardly be seen again. This chapter tries to capture his unique impact on his game and our world.*

MICHAEL JORDAN IS PERHAPS THE BEST, AND BEST-KNOWN, athlete in the world today. He has attained unparalleled cultural status because of his extraordinary physical gifts, his marketing as an icon of race-transcending American athletic and moral excellence, and his mastery of a sport that has become the metaphoric center of black cultural imagination. But the Olympian sum of Jordan's cultural meaning is greater than the fluent parts of his persona as athlete, family man, and marketing creation. There is hardly cultural precedence for the character of his unique fame, which has blurred the line between private and public, between personality and celebrity, and between substance and symbol. Michael Jordan stands at the breach between perception and intuition, his cultural meaning perennially deferred from closure because his career symbolizes possibility itself, gathering into its unfolding narrative the shattered remnants of previous incarnations of fame and yet transcending their reach.

Jordan has been called "the new DiMaggio" (Boers 1990, 30) and "Elvis in high-tops," indications of the Herculean cultural heroism he has come to embody. There is even a religious element to the near worship of Jordan as a cultural icon of invincibility, as he has been called a "savior of sorts," "basketball's high priest" (Bradley 1991–1992, 60), and "more popular than Jesus," except with "better endorsement deals" (Vancil 1992, 51). But the quickly developing cultural canonization of Michael Jordan provokes reflection about the contradictory uses to which Jordan's body is put as a seminal cultural text and ambiguous symbol of fantasy, and the avenues of agency and resistance available especially to black youth who make symbolic investment in Jordan's body as a means of cultural and personal possibility, creativity, and desire.

I understand Jordan in the broadest sense of the term to be a public pedagogue, a figure of estimable public moral authority whose career educates us about productive and disenabling forms of knowledge, desire, interest, consumption, and culture in three spheres: the culture of athletics that thrives on skill and performance, the specific expression of elements of African-American culture, and the market forces and processes of commodification expressed by, and produced in, advanced capitalism. By probing these dimensions of Jordan's cultural importance, we may gain a clearer understanding of his function in American society.

Athletic activity has shaped and reflected important sectors of American society. First, it produced communities of common athletic interest organized around the development of highly skilled performance. The development of norms of athletic excellence evidenced in sports activities cemented communities of participants who valorized rigorous sorts of physical discipline in preparation for athletic competition and in expressing the highest degree of athletic skill. Second, it produced potent subcultures that inculcated in their participants norms of individual and team accomplishment. Such norms tapped into the bipolar structures of competition and cooperation that pervade American culture. Third, it provided a means of reinscribing Western frontier myths of exploration and discovery-as-conquest onto a vital sphere of American culture. Sports activities can be viewed in part as the attempt to symbolically ritualize and metaphorically extend the ongoing quest for mastery of environment and vanquishing of opponents within the limits of physical contest.

Fourth, athletic activity has served to reinforce habits and virtues centered in collective pursuit of communal goals that are intimately connected to the common good, usually characterized within athletic circles as "team spirit." The culture of sport has physically captured and athletically articulated the mores, folkways, and dominant visions of American society, and at its best it has been conceived as a means of symbolically embracing and equitably pursuing the just, the good, the true, and the beautiful. And finally, the culture of athletics has provided an acceptable and widely accessible means of white male bonding. For much of its history, American sports activity has reflected white patriarchal privilege, and it has been rigidly defined and socially shaped by rules that restricted the equitable participation of women and people of color.

Black participation in sports in mainstream society, therefore, is a relatively recent phenomenon. Of course, there have existed venerable traditions of black sports, such as the Negro (baseball) Leagues, which countered the exclusion of black bodies from white sports. The prohibition of athletic activity by black men in mainstream society severely limited publicly acceptable forms of displaying black physical prowess, an issue that had been politicized during slavery and whose legacy extended into the middle of the twentieth century. Hence, the potentially superior physical prowess of black men, validated for many by the long tradition of slave labor that built American society, helped reinforce racist arguments about the racial regimentation of social space and the denigration of the black body as an inappropriate presence in traditions of American sport.

Coupled with this fear of superior black physical prowess was the notion that inferior black intelligence limited the ability of blacks to perform excellently in those sports activities that required mental concentration and agility. These two forces—the presumed lack of sophisticated black cognitive skills and the fear of superior black physical prowess—restricted black sports participation to thriving but financially handicapped subcultures of black athletic activity. Later, of course, the physical prowess of the black body would be acknowledged and exploited as a supremely fertile zone of profit as mainstream athletic society literally cashed in on the symbolic danger of black sports excellence.

Because of its marginalized status within the regime of American sports, black athletic activity often acquired a social significance that transcended the internal dimensions of game, sport, and skill. Black sport became an arena not only for testing the limits of physical endurance and forms of athletic excellence—while reproducing or repudiating ideals of American justice, goodness, truth, and beauty—but it also became a way of ritualizing racial achievement against socially imposed barriers to cultural performance.

In short, black sports activity often acquired a heroic dimension, as viewed in the careers of figures such as Joe Louis, Jackie Robinson, Althea Gibson, Wilma Rudolph, Muhammad Ali, and Arthur Ashe. Black sports heroes transcended the narrow boundaries of specific sports activities and garnered importance as icons of cultural excellence, symbolic figures who embodied social possibilities of success denied to other people of color. But they also captured and catalyzed the black cultural fetishization of sport as a means of expressing black cultural style, as a means of valorizing craft as a marker of racial and self-expression, and as a means of pursuing social and economic mobility.

It is this culture of black athletics, created against the background of social and historical forces that shaped American athletic activity, that helped produce Jordan and help explain the craft that he practices. Craft is the honing of skill by the application of discipline, time, talent, and energy toward the realization of a particular cultural or personal goal. American folk cultures are pervaded by craft, from the production of cultural artifacts that express particular ethnic histories and traditions to the development of styles of life and work that reflect and symbolize a community's values, virtues, and goals. Michael Jordan's skills within basketball are clearly phenomenal, but his game can only be sufficiently explained by understanding its link to the fusion of African-American cultural norms and practices, and the idealization of skill and performance that characterize important aspects of American sport. I will identify three defining characteristics of Jordan's game that reflect the influence of African-American culture on his style of play.

First, Jordan's style of basketball reflects the *will to spontaneity*. I mean here the way in which historical accidence is transformed into cultural advantage, and the way acts of apparently random occurrence are spontaneously and imaginatively employed by Africans and African-Americans in a variety of forms of cultural expression. When examining Jordan's game, this feature of African-American culture clearly functions in his unpredictable eruptions of basketball creativity. It was apparent, for instance, during game two of the National Basketball Association 1991 championship series between Jordan's Chicago Bulls and the Los Angeles Lakers, in a shot that even Jordan ranked in his all-time top ten (McCallum 1991, 32). Jordan made a drive toward the lane, gesturing with his hands and body that he was about to complete a patent Jordan dunk shot with his right hand. But when he spied defender Sam Perkins slipping over to oppose his shot, he switched the ball in midair to his left hand to make an underhanded scoop shot instead, which immediately became known as the "levitation" shot. Such improvisation, a staple of the will to spontaneity, allows Jordan to expand his vocabulary of athletic spectacle, which is the stimulation of a desire to bear witness to the revelation of truth and beauty compressed into acts of athletic creativity.

Second, Jordan's game reflects the *stylization of the performed self*. This is the creation and projection of a sport persona that is an identifying mark of diverse African-American creative enterprises, from the complexly layered jazz experimentation of John Coltrane, the trickstering and signifying comedic routines of Richard Pryor, and the rhetorical ripostes and oral significations of rapper Kool Moe Dee. Jordan's whole game persona is a graphic depiction of the performed self as flying acrobat, resulting in his famous moniker "Air Jordan." Jordan's performed self is rife with the language of physical expressiveness: head moving, arms extending, hands waving, tongue wagging, and legs spreading.

He has also developed a resourceful repertoire of dazzling dunk shots that further express his performed self and that have garnered him a special niche within the folklore of the game: the cradle jam, rock-a-baby, kiss the rim, lean in, and the tomahawk. In Jordan's game, the stylization of a performed self has allowed him to create a distinct sports persona that has athletic as well as economic consequences, while mastering sophisticated levels of physical expression and redefining the possibilities of athletic achievement within basketball.

Finally, there is the subversion of perceived limits through the use of *edifying deception*, which in Jordan's case centers around the space/time continuum. This moment in African-American cultural practice is the ability to flout widely understood boundaries through mesmerization and alchemy, a subversion of common perceptions of the culturally or physically possible through the creative and deceptive manipulation of appearance. Jordan is perhaps most famous for his alleged "hang time," the uncanny ability to remain suspended in midair longer than other basketball players while executing his stunning array of improvised moves. But Jordan's "hang time" is technically a misnomer and can be more accurately attributed to Jordan's skillful athletic deception, his acrobatic leaping ability, and his intellectual toughness in projecting an aura of uniqueness around his craft than to his defiance of gravity and the laws of physics.

No human being, including Michael Jordan, can successfully defy the law of gravity and achieve relatively sustained altitude without the benefit of machines. As Douglas Kirkpatrick points out, the equation for altitude is $1/2g \times t2 = VO \times t$ ("How Does Michael Fly?"). However, Jordan appears to hang by *stylistically* relativizing the fixed coordinates of space and time through the skillful management and manipulation of his body in midair. For basketball players, hang time is the velocity and speed with which a player takes off combined with the path the player's center of gravity follows on the way up. At the peak of a player's vertical jump, the velocity and speed is close to, or at, zero; hanging motionless in the air is the work of masterful skill and illusion ("How Does Michael Fly?"). Michael Jordan, through the consummate skill and style of his game, only appears to be hanging in space for more than the one second that human beings are capable of remaining airborne.

But the African-American aspects of Jordan's game are indissolubly linked to the culture of consumption and the commodification of black culture.[1] Because of Jordan's supreme mastery of basketball, his squeaky-clean image, and his youthful vigor in pursuit of the American Dream, he has become, along with Bill Cosby, the quintessential pitchman in American society. Even his highly publicized troubles with gambling, his refusal to visit the White House after the Bulls' championship season, and a book that purports to expose the underside of his heroic myth have barely tarnished his All-American image.[2] Jordan eats Wheaties, drives Chevrolet, wears Hanes, drinks Coca-Cola, consumes McDonald's, guzzles Gatorade, and, of course, wears Nikes. He successfully produced, packaged, marketed, and distributed his image and commodified his symbolic worth, transforming cultural capital into cash, influence, prestige, status, and wealth. To that degree, at least, Jordan repudiates the sorry tradition of the black athlete as the naif who loses his money to piranhalike financial wizards, investors, and hangers-on. He represents the New Age athletic entrepreneur who understands that American sport is ensconced in the cultural practices associated with business, and that it demands particular forms of intelligence, perception, and representation to prevent abuse and maximize profit.

From the very beginning of his professional career, Jordan was consciously marketed by his agency Pro-Serv as a peripatetic vehicle of American fantasies of capital accumulation and material consumption tied to Jordan's personal modesty and moral probity. In so doing, they skillfully avoided attaching to Jordan the image of questionable ethics and lethal excess that plagued inside traders and corporate raiders on Wall Street during the mid '80s, as Jordan began to emerge as a cultural icon. But Jordan is also the symbol of the spectacle-laden black athletic body as the site of commodified black cultural imagination. Ironically, the black male body, which has been historically viewed as threatening and inappropriate in American society (and remains so outside of sports and entertainment), is made an object of white desires to domesticate and dilute its more ominous and subversive uses, even symbolically reducing Jordan's body to dead meat (McDonald's McJordan hamburger), which can be consumed and expelled as waste.

Jordan's body is also the screen upon which is projected black desires to emulate his athletic excellence and replicate his entry into reaches of unimaginable wealth and fame. But there is more than vicarious substitution and the projection of fantasy onto Jordan's body that is occurring in the circulation and reproduction of black cultural desire. There is also the creative use of desire and fantasy by young blacks to counter, and capitulate to, the forces of cultural dominance that attempt to reduce the black body to a commodity and text that is employed for entertainment, titillation, or financial gain. Simply said, there is no easy correlation between the commodification of black youth culture and the evidences of a completely dominated consciousness.

Even within the dominant cultural practices that seek to turn the black body into pure profit, disruptions of capital are embodied, for instance, in messages circulated in black communities by public moralists who criticize the exploitation of black cultural creativity by casual footwear companies. In short, there are instances of both black complicity and resistance in the commodification of black cultural imagination, and the ideological criticism of exploitative cultural practices must always be linked to the language of possibility and agency in rendering a complex picture of the black cultural situation. As Henry Giroux observes:

> The power of complicity and the complicity of power are not exhausted simply by registering how people are positioned and located through the production of particular ideologies structured through particular discourses.... It is important to see that an overreliance on ideology critique has limited our ability to understand how people actively participate in the dominant culture through processes of accommodation, negotiation, and even resistance. (Giroux 1992, 194–195)

In making judgments about the various uses of the black body, especially Jordan's symbolic corporeality, we must specify how both consent and opposition to exploitation are often signaled in expressions of cultural creativity.

In examining his reactions to the racial ordering of athletic and cultural life, the ominous specificity of the black body creates anxieties for Jordan. His encounters with the limits of culturally mediated symbols of race and racial identity have occasionally mocked his desire to live beyond race, to be "neither black nor white" (Patton 1986, 52), to be "viewed as a person" (Vancil 1992, 57). While Jordan chafes under indictment by black critics who claim that he is not "black enough," he has perhaps not clearly understood the differences between enabling versions of human experience that transcend the exclusive gaze of race and disenabling visions of human community that seek race neutrality.

The former is the attempt to expand the perimeters of human experience beyond racial determinism, to nuance and deepen our understanding of the constituent elements of racial identity, and to understand how race, along with class, gender, geography, and sexual preference, shape and constrain human experience. The latter is the belief in an intangible, amorphous, nonhistorical, and raceless category of "person," existing in a zone beyond not simply the negative consequences of race, but beyond the specific patterns of cultural and racial identity that constitute and help shape human experience. Jordan's unclarity is consequential, weighing heavily on his apolitical bearing and his refusal to acknowledge the public character of his private beliefs about American society and the responsibility of his role as a public pedagogue.

Indeed it is the potency of black cultural expressions that not only have helped influence his style of play, but have also made the sneaker industry he lucratively participates in a multibillion dollar business. Michael Jordan has helped seize upon the commercial consequences of black cultural preoccupation with style and the commodification of the black juvenile imagination at the site of the sneaker. At the juncture of the sneaker, a host of cultural, political, and economic forces and meanings meet, collide, shatter, and are reassembled to symbolize the situation of contemporary black culture.

The sneaker reflects at once the projection and stylization of black urban realities linked in our contemporary historical moment to rap culture and the underground political economy of crack, and reigns as the universal icon for the culture of consumption. The sneaker symbolizes the ingenious manner in which black cultural nuances of cool, hip, and chic have influenced the broader American cultural landscape. It was black street culture that influenced sneaker companies' aggressive invasion of the black juvenile market in taking advantage of the increasing amounts of disposable income of young black men as a result of legitimate and illegitimate forms of work.

Problematically, though, the sneaker also epitomizes the worst features of the social production of desire and represents the ways in which moral energies of social conscience about material values are drained by the messages of undisciplined acquisitiveness promoted by corporate dimensions of the culture of consumption. These messages, of rapacious consumerism supported by cultural and personal narcissism, are articulated on Wall Street and are related to the expanding inner-city juvenocracy, where young black men rule over black urban space in the culture of crack and illicit criminal activity, fed by desires to "live large" and to reproduce capitalism's excesses on their own terrain. Also, sneaker companies make significant sums of money from the illicit gains of drug dealers.

Moreover, while sneaker companies have exploited black cultural expressions of cool, hip, chic, and style, they rarely benefit the people who both consume the largest quantity of products and whose culture redefined the sneaker companies' raison d'être. This situation is more severely compounded by the presence of spokespeople like Jordan, Spike Lee, and Bo Jackson, who are either ineffectual or defensive about or indifferent to the lethal consequences (especially in urban black-on-black violence over sneaker company products) of black juvenile acquisition of products that these figures have helped make culturally desirable and economically marketable.

Basketball is the metaphoric center of black juvenile culture, a major means by which even temporary forms of cultural and personal transcendence of personal limits are experienced. Michael Jordan is at the center of this black athletic culture, the supreme symbol of black cultural creativity in a society of diminishing tolerance for the black youth whose fascination with Jordan has helped sustain him. But Jordan is also the iconic fixture of broader segments of American society, who see in him the ideal figure: a black man of extraordinary genius on the court and before the cameras, who by virtue of his magical skills and godlike talents symbolizes the meaning of human possibility, while refusing to root it in the specific forms of culture and race in which it must inevitably make sense or fade to ultimate irrelevance.

Jordan also represents the contradictory impulses of the contemporary culture of consumption, where the black athletic body is deified, reified, and rearticulated within the narrow meanings of capital and commodity. But there is both resistance and consent to the exploitation of black bodies in Jordan's explicit cultural symbolism, as he provides brilliant glimpses of black culture's ingenuity of improvisation as a means of cultural expression and survival. It is also partially this element of black culture that has created in American society a desire to dream Jordan, to "be like Mike."

This pedagogy of desire that Jordan embodies, although at points immobilized by its depoliticized cultural contexts, is nevertheless a remarkable achievement in contemporary American culture: a six-foot-six American man of obvious African descent is the dominant presence and central cause of athletic fantasy in a sport that twenty years ago was denigrated as a black man's game and hence deemed unworthy of wide attention or support. Jordan is therefore the bearer of meanings about black culture larger than his individual life, the symbol of a pedagogy of style, presence, and desire that is immediately communicated by the sight of his black body before it can be contravened by reflection.

In the final analysis, his big black body—graceful and powerful, elegant and dark—symbolizes the possibilities of other black bodies to remain safe long enough to survive within the limited but significant sphere of sport, since Jordan's achievements have furthered the cultural acceptance of at least the athletic black body. In that sense, Jordan's powerful cultural capital has not been exhausted by narrow understandings of his symbolic absorption by the demands of capital and consumption. His body is still the symbolic carrier of racial and cultural desires to fly beyond limits and obstacles, a fluid metaphor of mobility and ascent to heights of excellence secured by genius and industry. It is this power to embody the often conflicting desires of so many that makes Michael Jordan a supremely instructive figure for our times.

Thirty-Five

IS POSTMODERNISM JUST MODERNISM IN DRAG?

This interview, conducted by the gifted poet, scholar, and church pianist Jonathan Smith when he was a graduate student, is one of the best I have participated in. Smith's questions are razor-sharp and knowing, smart without being smug, brilliant without being ostentatious. I had great fun in probing the complex dimensions of black culture and in exploring the modern and postmodern implications of black identity. We discuss music, literature, basketball, religion, literary and cultural theory, sexuality, slavery, boxing, masculinity, politics, television, civil rights and race, and a great deal more. It is a tribute to Smith's preparedness that the interview went so well. One can feel the electricity of the lived, dialogic moment, as his enthusiasm for the subjects we discuss contagiously passes to me, allowing me to catch fire and blaze through our exchanges. If I had to point to a single piece of writing that best expresses my ideas about black culture and identity, this would be the one.

The first thing I'd like to ask is: Who is Michael Eric Dyson? And I want you to take the liberty of answering this in a manner that is not strictly auto-biographical. One reason I ask this is because your book jacket begins describing you as "welfare father, ordained Baptist minister, Princeton Ph.D." Then in your chapter on the black public intellectual, you give yourself the shameless self-promotion award.

One of the reasons I take postmodernism so seriously, even as I refuse to make a fetish of its insights, is a notion that has been championed by its theorists, especially in cultural and literary studies: an evolving, fluid identity. What I take from the postmodern conception of identity is captured in the terms beautifully phrased in black Christian circles, namely, "I don't have to be what I once was." That Christian conception of the evolution of character highlights the variability and flexibility of human identity, even if such a view clashes profoundly with postmodern arguments against a fixed human nature on which many Christian conceptions of identity rest. But for black Christians—who are arguably situated deep inside modernism with its impulse to dynamism and disruption, as well as its unyielding quest for the new—and secular postmodernists alike, identity is a process, a continual play of existential choices over a field of unfolding possibility. The self today can be radically different from the self of yesterday.

Taking that seriously, Mike Dyson is an experiment in identity, a testament to a process of evolving self-awareness; some of the elements of my self are surely in conflict, while other fragments of my self are made coherent because they've been sewn together by the threads of history, culture, race, and memory. Who I was, say, ten years ago, was a scholar in the making, and eight or ten years before that, I was a welfare father, a hustler on Detroit's streets, a divorcing husband, a young man who was trying to figure out what to do with his life. I was twenty-one, and I hadn't gone to college or prepared myself academically to take up my vocation. So, who I am is constantly implicated in the themes I take up in my work. What does it mean to be young, black, and male in this country? What are the racial and economic forces that shape black life? How can we achieve racial justice and equality? What does it mean to be an intellectual in a world that prizes image more than substance? How should we treat the vulnerable and the destitute? How can we bridge the psychic and social gulfs between the generations? How can we speak about God in a world where religion has been hijacked by fundamentalists and fascists? How do we untangle the vicious knots of patriarchy, sexism, and misogyny in our nation? How do we affirm and protect gay, lesbian, bisexual, and transgendered people in our communities? All these questions, and many more, play out in my intellectual and political pursuits.

Who I am, then, in many senses, is a bridge builder, a bridge figure. I want to span the streets and the academy, and the sacred and the secular. I also want to bridge traditions and the transformations of those traditions, including religious belief, intellectual engagement, scholarly investigation, racial solidarity, class struggle, resistance to economic oppression, and feminist insurgence. Of course, the parts of my identity that might obviously be in tension, say the academic and the activist, suffer pressure in both directions: the academy is suspicious of the streets, and vice versa. The tension is one of proximity and distance. To the academy, there is the threat of proximity to the chaotic, propulsive, unregulated, sometimes uncivil passions of the world beyond the university. To the denizens of the streets—including its natural constituency of grassroots activists, conspiracy managers, and on-the-ground, indigenous, concrete intellectuals—there is the fear that academics will remain aloof, indifferent to their suffering, and intellectually unavailable to supply strategies to resist their oppression. I want to do the best I can to answer the threat of proximity, not by less but by more interaction between academics and activists, hoping to prove that the interactions benefit the university. And I want to help heal fears of distance by bringing the resources of intelligence and compassion to bear on the hurts of the socially vulnerable. It is that desire to bridge gulfs that unifies my disparate selves, making me much more sympathetic to the prophetic mystic Howard Thurman, who once prayed to God, "make me unanimous in myself."

I'll ask you then this question. Baldwin in _Giovanni's Room_ says: "Perhaps home is not a place but an irrevocable condition." In _South to a Very Old_

Place, **Albert Murray begins with this thought: "But then, going back home has probably always had as much if not more to do with people as with landmarks and place names and locations on maps and mileage charts anyway. Not that home is not a place, for even in its most abstract implications it is precisely the very oldest place in the world. But even so, it is somewhere you are likely to find yourself remembering your way back to far more often than it is ever possible to go by conventional transportation." Given that, in that context, where do you feel most at home?**

Yes. Yes. Good question, man. Well, as both of these writers make clear, home is about the geography of imagination. For me, it's also about the architecture of identity through aspiration and yearning, since home is carved from hope and memory. It is both forward-looking and backward leaning. And that means that home is not simply a place forever anchored by concrete foundations. It is not simply a fixed point with tangible coordinates in space and time. Home is a metaphysical possibility that seeds the ground of experience and infuses our finite encounters in local spaces with meaning. That's why Burt Bacharach's writing partner, Hal David, could pen a lyric that makes the philosophical argument that "a house is not a home," distinguishing the two by the quality of relations that turn the former into the latter. Like identity, home, to a large degree, is composed of an evolving awareness about how you can decrease the discomfort you have in the world as a result of your roots. That's why our foreparents spoke of "a house not made with hands," as it says in 1 Corinthians, casting biblical language in their own religious accents. And they suggested that this world "ain't no friend to grace," since it was alienated from God's purpose. For a people who were often homeless—rootless and adrift in a sea of chattel slavery, and later, exploitative sharecropping—home assumed a high priority. That's why many of our foreparents hoped for a day when they could, in the words of one slave, "read my title clear." Home had intense metaphoric value for our foreparents in another way: as the imagined space of unlimited access to God in heaven, a place they hoped to go after they died, signified in songwriter Charles Tindley's familiar refrain in black Christian circles, "I'll make it home, someday."

Of course, there are dangers to the notion of home in black life as well, especially when it comes to elevating one's imagined geography of spirit, one's own sense of home, as the sole source of authentic blackness. After all, roots are meant to nourish, not strangle, us. I'm thinking in particular of the vicious debates raging in many black communities about what is really black, how we define it, and how the spaces of black identity are linked increasingly to a narrow slice of black turf—the ghetto. Our kids are literally dying over a profound misunderstanding about our culture that links authenticity to geography, that makes one believe that if she is black, she must pledge ultimate allegiance to the ghetto as the sole black home of the black subject. The exclusive identification of the ghetto as the authentic black home is wholly destructive.

Out of this grows the "keep it real" trope that punishes any departure from a lethally limited vision of black life, one that trades on stereotype and separation anxiety, since there is a great fear of being severed from the fertile ground of the true black self. But to subscribe to these beliefs is to be woefully misled. Sure, the beauty of the impulse to authenticity is altogether understandable: to protect a black identity that has been assaulted by white supremacy through the assertion of a uniquely guarded and qualified black self, rooted in a similarly protected view of the authentic black home. Plus, too many blacks who "made it" have surely forgotten "where they came from." But the legitimate critique of blacks besieged by what may be termed *Aframnesia*—the almost systematic obliteration of the dangerous memory of black suffering and racial solidarity, a gesture that is usually rewarded by white elites—is different from imposing rigid views on black life of how and where blackness erupts or emerges. Thus we end up with vicious mythologies and punishing pieties: for instance, one cannot be gay and be authentically black in some circles, which means there's no home, no place of grace in many black communities for black homosexuals. Or the black male assault on black female interests is justified as the necessary subordination of gender to race in the quest for liberation. Or the only real black is in the ghetto, a ghetto that in the social imagination of its romantic advocates rarely looks like the complex, complicated, contradictory place it is. As a former resident of the ghetto, I wholeheartedly concur with the notion that we can neither forget its people nor neglect its social redemption through strategic action. Further, I think it's beautiful for folk who have survived the ghetto, who've gotten out, to carry the blessed image of its edifying dimensions in their hearts and imaginations, and to pledge to never leave the ghetto even as they travel millions of miles beyond its geographical boundaries. That means that they'll never betray the wisdom, genius, and hope that floods the ghetto in ways that those outside its bounds rarely understand. It is, after all, a portable proposition, a mobile metaphor. But we must not seize on the most limited view possible of ghetto life and sanctify it as the be-all and end-all of black existence. That leads to kids killing each other in the name of an authentic ghetto masculinity that is little more than pathological self-hatred. The black ghetto working class, the working poor, and the permanently poor have always been more complex, and more resilient, than they have ever been given credit for. We've got to avoid the trap of existential puniness and racial infantilism and see our way to a robustly mature vision that shatters the paradigm of the authentic black self and, by extension, the acceptable black home.

Given that analysis, I feel most at home in the intersection of all the energies provoked by my different roles, as preacher, teacher, public intellectual, political activist, agent provocateur, and paid pest. In one sense, I couldn't rest all of my energy in one place doing one thing; the ability to do them all gives me the vocational patience to do any of them. And I feel a sense of transgression, a sense of irreverence (and to my mind, those are good qualities) in fulfilling all these roles that gives me, oddly enough, a feeling of being at home, because I feel I'm being truest to myself when I vigorously, and critically, engage my various communities of interest or, as the anthropologists say, my multiple kinship groups. For instance, I love to preach, and whenever I get the chance, I'm in a pulpit on Sunday morning "telling the story," as black ministers elegantly phrase preaching the gospel. For all of its problems and limitations, the black pulpit, at its best, is still the freest, most powerful, most radically autonomous place on earth for black people to encourage each other in the job of critical self-reflection and the collective struggle for liberation. I think theologian Robert McAfee Brown put it best when he said the church is like Noah's ark: if it wasn't for the storm on the outside, we couldn't stand the stink on the inside.

But the stink in the black church is surely foul. There are still a lot of negative beliefs about gender and sexual orientation, and even class, that need to be addressed. There are big pockets of staunchly conservative sentiment that, I think, have to be opposed. I try not to avoid these subjects as I preach, and sometimes what I say goes over like a brick cloud! Still, I try to seduce people into seeing things differently, as I make arguments about why the opposition to gay and lesbian folk, for instance, reeks of the same biblical literalism that smashed the hopes of black slaves when white slave masters deployed it. But I try to win the folk over first, by preaching "in the tradition," so to speak, warming them up first before I lower the boom. When I was a young preacher and pastor, one of my members told me you "gain more by honey than vinegar." So I give honey before I give vinegar. I invite the folk to the progressive theological, ideological, and spiritual terrain I want them to occupy, but I try to issue that invitation in ways that won't immediately alienate them. And once they're there, they're a captive audience.

One gains his bona fides by preaching well, evoking "amens" by articulately referencing the black religious tradition, and this can be done with little fear of surrendering the politics I favor. The rhetorical forms are themselves neutral, so to speak, and thus the political uses to which they're put is something that's strictly TBD: to be determined by the rhetor, the prophet, the priest, the speaker, or the pastor. Then when I've got them where I want them, rhetorically speaking, in a velvet verbal vice, I squeeze hard, using the good feeling and theological credit I've gained from preaching well to assault the beliefs that are problematic, from homophobia, sexism, patriarchy, ageism, racism, and classism to environmental inequities. And sometimes, they're giving assent against their wills, shouting amen to ideas that they may not have otherwise supported without being pushed or prodded—or seduced. They might even muse to themselves, "Well, he's got a point," or "I disagree, but I'll at least think about it." But as much as I love the black church, and see it as my home, it's too narrow to be my only home. That's why I claim the classroom, the lectern, and the academy as my home as well, a place I love immensely, but the inbred snobbishness and well-worn elitism of elements of this home mean that I can't rest my entire self there either. I'm involved in both mainstream and radical politics, but elements of the latter are hostile to the spiritual traditions I cherish, which means my home in such circles is not one that accommodates my entire being. So I float among all of these stations of identification, so to speak. My home, while certainly not carved from a process of elimination–cutting away features I find unattractive, offensive, or burdensome in each "home"–is certainly the product of a stance of critical appreciation that allows me to derive benefit, pleasure, and sustenance from each space.

So I conceive of home as a moveable feast of identity that I'm constantly feeding on. Because of the many communities in which I'm involved, I'm constantly rethinking who I am. In a way, I'm also constantly trying to get back home to Detroit, perhaps in a more spiritual than physical manner, since I go back fairly frequently to preach and visit my mother and brothers. There's an elusive state of contentment that you nostalgically associate with home even when it was a turbulent and trying place. Detroit was, in many ways, such a place far me, but it also provided so much joy and fulfillment, and it gave me a sense of the appropriate things to grasp hold of in life, beyond the material blessings one might seek. It was a great beginning, and as I heard Toni Morrison once say, beginnings are important because they must do so much more than start. While starting is crucial, beginnings also propel us along paths of influence whose real impact we may not be able to detect for years and years to come. That's certainly the case with me.

Detroit has become for me a metaphor of the complex convergence of fate and human volition. It's a symbol for me of how destiny is at best partly determined by living one's life in a meaningful, coherent fashion. That's most acutely obvious to me in grappling with my brother's imprisonment and my quest for improvement in every sphere of my life, including my professional life, my spiritual infrastructure, and my moral landscape. Home is a complicated place for me now, which is why nostalgia is inevitable, pleasurable, even desirable–and quite problematic, perhaps dangerous at points. Nostalgia, of course, is crucial to the project of black identity, largely as a defensive move against the brutal memories of suffering we endured at the hands of those outside our communities, and from within. Nostalgia, at least in that light, is an attempt to exercise sovereignty over memory, to force it into redemptive channels away from the tributaries of trauma that flood the collective black psyche. It is the attempt to rescue ethical agency and hence manage and control the perception of suffering–from the fateful forces of racial terror. One of the most bruising racial terrors is to have the dominant culture determine what memories are most important to the dominated minority.

In that case, nostalgia is an attempt to take back the political utility of memory. After all, if you remember a horrible experience as something from which you can squeeze some good, then you've refused the hegemonic power the prerogative to define your fate. By remembering the same event with different accents, with different social purposes, through different eyes, one gives memory a racial and moral usefulness that can challenge dominant culture. I suspect that's at stake when black folk wax nostalgic about segregation and the sort of relatively self-determining culture we were able to carve out of Jim Crow apartheid. You hear it as black folk say, "When we were forced to live together under segregation, we had more unity, we lived in the same neighborhoods, we helped each other more, economically and spiritually, and we did not depend on white patronage but promoted black self-reliance. Now under desegregation we've lost the power we had. Our colleges have suffered a brain drain to elite white schools. Our black businesses that catered to black needs suffered when we were able to buy white. And our neighborhoods were turned over to the poor and destitute when 'white flight' was mimicked by 'black track' to the suburbs."

The downside of such nostalgia is that it fails to explicitly engage the radical inequality of such segregated arrangements. It also tends to exaggerate the moral differences between generations, especially as the rose-colored tint of the black past is not used to cast an eye on the present or the future, for that matter. The net result is that one's own generation is made golden, while those following are seen as tarnished by the surrender to urges, forces, and seductions that were heroically resisted in the past. Hence jazz was great and hip-hop is awful. People believe that even though earlier black generations thought jazz was terrible and preferred religious music. But there were problems there too, since many blacks felt that religious music too easily compromised its purity by integrating elements from secular blues. And it goes on and on. Then too, we've got to be careful not to ultimately justify or legitimate the oppression by nostalgically recalling its good effects. Nostalgic blacks end up reinforcing what may be termed subversive empathy from the dominant culture, which, after all, provided the conditions under which our race and culture could thrive under segregation, even if those conditions were harmful and oppressive.

Subversive empathy is similar, I suppose, to anthropologist Renato Rosaldo's notion of imperialist nostalgia, where hegemonic culture destroys an indigenous minority tradition and then has the gall to weep with those folk over the destruction of their culture. In subversive empathy, the dominant culture empathizes with our need to restore the conditions of our relative prospering under Jim Crow. While not explicitly invoking a return to the racist past, it nevertheless puts forth arguments and supports practices that have the same effect. That's why black folk have to be especially cautious about supporting Bill Bennett's partnership with C. Delores Tucker in combating hard-core hip-hop. They appeal to a golden age: nostalgic belief about the black family that is turned viciously against us in Bennett's conservative cosmology. For that matter, we ought to be careful about uncritically celebrating Bill Clinton's nostalgic appeal to black America to return to a bygone moral era. In a speech before a black religious audience in Memphis, Tennessee, Clinton invoked Martin Luther King Jr.'s memory to chide black America about pockets of immorality in our communities and pathological family structure, ignoring the harmful social impact of many of his policies on the black family. He sounds like a friend, and in many ways he is, but he is also a foe to our best political interests. His political beliefs, in many ways, are emblematic of subversive empathy.

If the impulse to nostalgia is not disciplined, it can be used to fashion moral judgments out of fantasies of the past that downplay our failures and project them more vehemently on someone, or something, else. A huge example is how older blacks nostalgically recall their idyllic lives in comparison to the ills of modern youth, assaulting their relative moral failures while extolling their own virtues.

But to sum it all up, I suppose home conjures for me that Frankie Beverly anthem, "Joy and Pain." But it remains the quintessential space of possibility, of hope, of unending yearning and unfulfilled expectation.

I guess I'd like to hear you talk about that notion in relation to this generation you belong to, "the betweeners"—very late baby boomers and very early generation x or hip-hop. This also, in the academy, seems to stand right at that modern-postmodern divide. When I hear you talk about your relationship to home, I hear an important question about history and home, time and home. I'm the minister of music at my church, so you know that when I show up with the dread thing going on and I play for the senior choir, there is this odd sense of dissonance and I feel completely at home there even though there are some looking at me as if to say "What's wrong with that brother?" But there's this odd sort of thing that goes on because where you are is always where you feel most at home. I imagine that that's what happens to you when you're in the pulpit: that it's the most natural home, but when you walk out into the classroom there is no rupture. But given our notions of race and culture and some of our stereotypes, it seems as if people would expect there to be a rupture, but there isn't.

No, no. In that sense it's seamless for me, moving from one rhetorical situation to another, from the pulpit as the axis of convergence of history, spirituality, and morality, to the classroom, where there are other axes of convergence, including inquiry, skepticism, and excavation. The orbits of these rhetorical universes might be seen to be in collision with one another. But skillful black rhetoricians, speakers, teachers, intellectuals, and orators can, by virtue of an enchanted imagination, speak worlds of discourse into existence that cross disciplinary fault lines, that move among genres, and that navigate through discursive minefields, such as the question of what constitutes "real knowledge." At its base, black culture has always been about migration and mobility. Its members, in one way or another, have been about the business of adapting ourselves to foreign spaces and creating home in the midst of them. We've constantly raised the question of Psalm 147, "How can we sing Zion's songs in a strange land?" To borrow more biblical imagery, the book of Acts contains that famous passage about Paul and his mates being shipwrecked and making it to shore "on broken pieces." Black people have always been able to take the fragments and shards of our lives, the pieces of our existence broken by oppression, and rework them into a pattern of purposeful existence. That's not simply about fragmentation as a trope of black existence in the postmodern moment. It's also about the black modernist quest for a stable identity in the midst of flux and upheaval, often articulated, ironically enough, through a premodern religious worldview.

Thus the premodern black biblical universe accommodates black modernist pursuits in postmodern conditions. "Making it in on broken pieces" has long been a rhetorical staple in the grassroots theodicies—in both the Weberian, sociological sense and in theological terms—that shape the preaching of figures from C. L. Franklin, Aretha Franklin's father, to Jesse Jackson. Add to that the fragments of European cultural influences and African cultural retentions that shape black life, and the unavoidability of black folk negotiating between disparate vocabularies, indeed, different worlds, should be dramatically apparent. I think that Levis-Strauss's notion of bricolage, of taking what's at hand, what's left over, so to speak, in the construction of culture to shape one's survival and identity, is a crucial concept as well in coming to terms with this black gift to move in and through a variety of rhetorics and discourses. In that sense, then, our identities have always been fabricated out of the content of our surroundings. Forced migration and permanent exile will make one into a sophisticated cultural polyglot and sometimes into a cosmopolitan citizen. Home was often a compromise of contexts: wherever we found ourselves, we made that home or at least we transported our home there. Home was not something we could leave and come to again, so home often had to travel with us, across turbulent waters, into hostile countries, and within resistive communities.

That's not to deny the reality of fixed points of domestic reference in time and space, and in body and memory. But the reality is that black people had to have multiple notions of home, and often multiple homes, which is why there's a thin line between coerced migration and homelessness. You've got to remember that home is a noun, verb, adjective, and adverb, and it is both a means and an end. So the lack of a sense of rupture grows from the seamless interweaving of multiple meanings articulated through a variety of rhetorical situations, whether it's preaching, teaching, writing, and so on. In my case, I can't deny that at some points all the communities I'm involved in may experience tension and conflict because I don't feel a radical rupture in moving from one vocabulary to another. But as Gerald Graff argues, we've got to teach the conflicts, and by extension we've got to illustrate the tensions. For me, that means we've got to mix rhetorical styles in edifying fashion. So when I get up in the classroom, for instance, and I really get going, talking about Foucault and Derrida, perhaps, and about Judith Butler, and about Stuart Hall and his distinction between preferred meanings versus negotiated meanings and oppositional meanings, my intellectual excitement translates to my verbal style and energizes my peculiar semantic trace. And my Baptist roots begin to nourish my oratorical engagement, and before I know it, I'm preaching postmodernism.

So here you have a professor with a staccato rhythm and a tuneful cadence who's invested in the articulation of postmodern conceptualizations of identity and power. I'm baptizing my lecture in the rhetorical waters of my religious tradition. There is no rupture, no discontinuity, nothing but seamless negotiations between diverse styles of intellectual and rhetorical engagement. There may be problems for interlocutors who believe that an etiquette of articulation should prevail, one that polices style and dictates proprietary usage. But I ain't with that, so there's no problem for me. The irony is that even in this so-called postmodernist moment, which ostensibly celebrates pastiche, fragmentation, collage, difference, irreverent fusions, and the like, black style remains problematic. When black identity marks postmodernity with its embodied articulation, there's a rupture going on in the midst of the rupturing context itself. It involves the problem that has confronted us in premodernity, modernity, and postmodernity: race, and more specifically, the issue of blackness and its unwieldy complement of transgressing expressions.

Yes. There seems always to be this move to delegitimize, to make it . . .

Literally illegal.

I remember my first semester as an undergraduate at Princeton. So, to my mind, this white guy says to me, How are you ever going to go home again? Aren't you afraid that these people won't understand?

Yes, would have to unbirth you . . .

There's some rupture. I've thought about this black Ivy League tradition that we seem to silence. Although we celebrate these people, we silence the fact that they were educated in and present at these institutions at the same time as the Eliots, Stevenses, Santayanas, and Jameses. Inhabiting the same physical space.

That's exactly right. And that's why postmodernity is so crucial, at least in theory: it helps us uncover and claim the useful legacies of modernism that were submerged in its racial silences. Of course, it could be that postmodernism is really modernism in drag. As you said, when you think of modernism, you think of Eliot and Stevens. And as you noted, you think of Santayana and James too, and we could add Royce, just to keep the Harvard modernists in line. And we could add Joyce, Pound, Frost, Crane, and a host of others. Gender got a strong foothold in the modernist canon in a way that race was never quite able to do, with figures like Marianne Moore, Virginia Woolf, Rebecca West, and Djuna Barnes. But at the same time, W.E.B. Du Bois is right in the middle of modernism, along with Countee Cullen, Langston Hughes, Zora Neale Hurston, Dorothy West, Richard Wright, Chester Himes, Ralph Ellison, James Baldwin, and many, many more. They were all thinking, writing, imagining, and populating black universes, even as many of them insisted that it was impossible to limn the American experience without viewing the nation through the eyes of blacks who were more American than African, as Ellison contended, or as they emphasized the universal moral impulse that echoes through black demands for dignity and humanity, as Baldwin argued.

The black modernists were attempting to breathe freely beyond the claustrophobic boundaries of race, trying to refigure black identity and, by extension, American identity. Yet they're always seen in these boxed, fixed, localized categories, when indeed they're trying to help us reimagine the project of America: "I, too, sing America," as Hughes sang, ringing a change, varying a theme, signifying upon and harkening metaphorically back to Walt Whitman's "I sing the body electric." Hughes and the great black modernists inserted black America into the mainstream flow and thereby proved that America must bend itself to our tune, song, riff, beat, meter, prose, rhythm, and the like in order to be truly, fully, wholly itself. For instance, Duke Ellington and Louis Armstrong swung in the mainstream and then swung the mainstream to a black rhythm, and through their music, helped America grasp the self-enlarging principle of subordinating color to culture and craft. Hughes was aggressively insinuating himself, and black folk, into the American stream of consciousness, into the American song—much like King would later do with the American dream—and thus proving that our meters hypnotically swayed the nation to our virtuosic, vernacular voices. Hughes locates the context of the development of his identity in those physical spaces in his American "home" where he is expelled to feed his growing self-awareness on the leftovers of racial exclusion.

But he flips the script. He grows strong on the negative diet of marginality that he turns into a wholesome meal of aesthetic and moral combat against white supremacy, especially its failure to recognize black beauty of every sort. So Hughes in his poem talks about being sent to the kitchen to eat, "When company comes." But he eats well, grows strong, and pledges that when company comes again, he'll be at the table and that no one will dare scold him for his presence and send him to the kitchen, because, "They'll see how beautiful I am / And be ashamed–." And then he ends by declaring, "I, too, am America." So there's a significant shift from singing America to being America, from performance to enactment. And the company, to extend my reading of modernism through Hughes's poem, is Wallace Stevens, T.S. Eliot, Hart Crane, James Joyce, Marianne Moore, and so on, grand figures whose large egos dominate the psychic rooms and intellectual tables of American modernism. At the same time, the black subject, the black ego, the black self, is shunted to the kitchen.

So what Langston Hughes does is articulate the fixed space of his own modernist identity—the kitchen, metaphorically speaking—as the locus classicus of American identity, because when you're in the kitchen, the smell of the food wafts beyond its borders. When you're in the kitchen cooking—and Hughes was cooking, really he was smoking, burning, or whatever term one might conjure from the culinary arts as a symbol of black vernacular for achieving broad excellence— the smells will pull people in to ask, "Hmm, where's that smell coming from? What's cooking in the kitchen?" If you had to be somewhere away from the dining room or living room, it was crucial to be exiled to the kitchen. This is what black folk knew, especially as they served as domestics, butlers, and cooks. Black moderns turned their limited, localized spaces into rhetorical, musical, aesthetic, political, or spiritual kitchens that emitted pleasing smells and seductive scents, so that people who picked up on them were immediately, irresistibly drawn to them. That's the language . . .

To pick up on that, even if they don't come to the kitchen, the kitchen has to come to them. They are sitting at the table waiting for the kitchen to come to them. The kitchen produces that which they consume for nourishment.

There you go, man. Metaphor is power.

I'd like to push a little away from that now and turn to something that seemed to resonate in an earlier comment you made about black rhetoricians and the premodernist Christian tradition as it relates to black resistance. The notion of speaking things that are not as though they were . . . this is not a space of acquiescence, but of resistance.

Oh, exactly right. That's very important and I'll just say something briefly about it. Too often, we read the history of black resistance, and the speech or action that supported it, through a distorted lens. Either black folk were for or against oppression, either they cooperated or resisted, and we can tell all of this in dramatically demonstrable fashion. Well, it's not quite that simple. Life has put black folk in complex, often compromising positions, especially during slavery, post-Reconstruction, and Jim Crow. Many folk were not able to outwardly resist, not simply for fear of reprisal but because to do so would have undermined their long-term plans of survival and liberation. Black folk en masse had to survive, even under conditions of harsh oppression, so that they could produce black folk who could liberate us. Their survival tactics had to be hidden, concealed to the larger white world, masked to the oppressor. These networks of hidden meanings and concealed articulations were the predicate of black survival through a signifying, symbolic culture. For instance, many of the sorrow songs of the slaves contained dual meanings. While the white masses found the songs entertaining, the slaves simultaneously signaled each other about plans for emancipation. In effect, they were, as the title of the book aptly summarizes it, *Puttin' on ol Massa*. The patterned quilts that slaves made contained crucial directions to black slaves seeking to ride the Underground Railroad to freedom. In a sense, they evoked the principle that later underlay Edgar Allen Poe's famous short story, "Purloined Letter," since the stolen missive was hidden in plain sight.

The very act of imagination was critical to strategies of resistance and proved dangerous to the hegemonic white world order. That's why the white world was so intent on controlling the black imagination, as far as such a thing was possible, by restricting its enabling mechanisms, particularly those rooted in literacy. Reading and writing were outlawed, and even earlier in slavery, blacks were divided from other blacks from the same tribe during the "seasoning" process so they couldn't effectively communicate. If blacks learned to read and write, they might grow restless with their degraded status, gaining a false and subversive sense of equality with whites. Of course, Frederick Douglass perhaps confirmed the worst fears of the white overclass when he reported in his autobiography that knowledge "unfits a child" for slavery. And if slaves spoke to each other without strict supervision, they might hatch plans to escape, so their speech and social organization were regularly policed.

But black slaves were able to carve out free spaces of intimate contact and communication that promoted racial solidarity and forms of resistance that eluded the master's ear and eye. Still, dominant whites rightly viewed the black imagination as a wedge between slaves and their oppression. The act of imagining a world of liberty was threatening. I think in this regard of a humorous statement that Muhammad Ali made about an opponent when he said, "If Sonny Liston dreams he can beat me, he better wake up and apologize." That's a brilliant gloss on the function of imagination and dreaming in black combat, and in the struggle for self-assertion and mastery of one's opponent. The attempt to regulate the black imagination is the attempt to restrict acts of black self-reinvention through dreaming of a different world where justice and freedom prevailed. That's why black folk were full of dangerous dreaming, insurrectionist imagining, and resistive revisions. The act of conceiving of an alternative world, a racial utopia, was a gesture of radical resistance that interrupted the totalizing force of white supremacy.

And a question of values, which we'll return to later. I want to push you in the direction here of talking about black bodies. Black male bodies, black women's bodies. One of the things that enters my mind here is the notion of the black masculine journey. To my mind, Morrison's *Song of Solomon* ranks right up there with Ellison's *Invisible Man* as a benchmark text for black masculinity. It's the condition our condition is in . . .

Right, it's rough all over.

To me, this statement has to do with black male bodies in everything from the Million Man March to Dennis Rodman.

Oh, no question. It's almost a cliché to say by now, but black masculinity is one of the most insightful and complex texts of American identity. For instance, millions want to, as the commercial slogan says, "Be like Mike." They're in awe of Michael Jordan, asking themselves what it is like to inhabit that pigment, that physiology, that 6'6" body whose ligaments, whose alignment of muscles determine the semblance of flight that folk around the globe vicariously identity with. Michael Jordan's head, clean shaven with those two ears poking out, at once conjures E.T.–the extraterrestrial–a sports spectacle, an incredible genius that we can scarcely imagine while also signifying the globe–round and smooth. And what can be written on its surfaces is always something that can be erased and rewritten. At the same time, that black masculine head is a signifier of the power of the black phallus. In an interesting, perhaps even subversive fashion, Michael Jordan's physical and aesthetic genius can be symbolized as a massive phallus whose seminal meanings explode on American culture, fertilizing a range of barren cultural landscapes with creative expression.

His body is a contradictory text of black masculinity. Jordan is at once embraced and fed upon as a Michael Jordan burger at McDonald's. He's being eaten by the masses, consumed, symbolically speaking. So the closest they may be able to get to Mike, besides watching him and emulating his moves on the court in their neighborhood playgrounds, sports gyms, or health clubs, is to purchase a symbolic portion of his body and consume it in market culture. It's a kind of secular Eucharist, where, at least in Protestant theology, the sacramental elements of Christ's body and blood are substituted by wafer and wine, or in Catholic theology, these elements are transubstantiated into the actual body and blood of Christ. Jordan's body is symbolically transmuted, through the material conditions of the political economy of consumption, into an edible commodity.

Or think of the symbolic and contested body of another prominent and complicated black man, the late rapper Tupac Shakur. Tupac's dead but still signifying body has the potential to become one of the first black candidates for cultural survival. I don't mean survival in the sense that he remains a vital cultural influence, like Martin Luther King Jr. I mean cultural presence beyond death through the articulation of a mythological body that defies mortality through urban legend, such as what has happened with James Dean, John F. Kennedy, Marilyn Monroe, and Elvis Presley. Particularly in the case of Elvis, there's a literal quality to his mythological persistence, since tabloid magazines claim to spot him, or JFK, on an island somewhere avoiding their fans, the media, and especially their "past" lives. I've often wondered why no one ever saw Sam Cooke, for instance, or Otis Redding, Dinah Washington, or Donny Hathaway. Tupac may be the first black figure to ascend to such heights—or depending on how one views this cultural phenomenon, to the depths—of pop memorialization.

I must confess I'm an addict, although I hope a critical one, of tabloids like the *National Enquirer* and *Star Magazine,* although since the same company that owns the *Enquirer* purchased *Star,* they often recycle the same information. Without overinterpreting or rationalizing their appeal, I think, at their best—and I place best in scare quotes—these tabloids offer counterhegemonic narratives to prevailing cultural truths. Besides that, they allow ordinary people to sound as if they're speaking the King's English to the Queen's taste. Instead of presenting an "informant" as saying, "I got afraid when I thought about that stuff later on," they sound more formal, more literate, and might be quoted as saying, "It startled me as I pondered it later."

But in the tabloids, Elvis is spotted in California somewhere, Elvis is in some secluded villa in Italy, Marilyn has joined JFK in what only appears to be a posthumous romp on the Riviera, while black icons remain sequestered in their unsexy, earthbound mortality. I think that Tupac may be the first black icon to join the pantheon of the posthumously alive, people who symbolically defeat their own death through episodic appearances in the mythological landscape. Folk are now saying that Tupac is not dead, but alive somewhere in Cuba, perhaps enjoying a stogie with Fidel. There are Web sites and chat rooms all over the Internet dedicated to debating whether Tupac is dead or is hanging out on some Caribbean retreat to escape the cruel demands of fame. His cultural survival says a great deal about how black masculinity can come to signify contested social and political meanings that erupt in popular culture.

When I think about contemporary black masculinity, I can't help reflecting on another intriguing, contradictory, infuriatingly complex figure: Dennis Rodman. In fact, he's helping redraw the boundaries of black masculinity in the most archetypically black masculine sport there is, basketball. Basketball has arguably replaced baseball as the paradigmatic expression of the highly mythologized American identity, since sport is a crucial means by which America regenerates its collective soul and reconceives its democratic ideals, to borrow Emersonian language. Basketball also has elements of spontaneity; individual genius articulated against the background of group success; and the coalescence of independent creative gestures in a collective expression of athletic aspiration. In a sense, basketball provides a canvas on which American identity can be constantly redrawn. The cultural frameworks of American identity, especially American masculinity, are being symbolically renegotiated in black masculine achievement in basketball.

Dennis Rodman has the sublime audacity to challenge the codes of masculinity at the heart of black masculine culture in the most visible art form, besides hip-hop culture, available to black men. He transgresses against heterosexist versions of machismo that dominate black sport. For instance, he wears fingernail polish and he occasionally cross-dresses in advertisements and public relations stunts, wearing a wedding gown in its white purity against that 6'9" brown body that "the Worm," as he's nicknamed, inhabits. Even his nickname signifies; it suggests the burrowing of an earth-bound insect into the hidden spaces of the soil, deep beneath the surface of things. And it's not as if Rodman were a marginal figure. He's acknowledged as the most gifted rebounder in the NBA today, and one of the greatest of all time. His specialty is unavoidably representative. He's constantly grabbing the ball off the backboard, taking shots that are left over from the failed attempt to score, enhancing the ability of the team to win. His genius on the court is, in précis, a symbolic articulation of black masculine identity; it is a major trope of black masculinity, since black men are constantly "on the rebound," and "rebounding" from some devastating ordeal. Black men are continually taking missed shots off the glass, off the backboard, and feeding them in outlet or bounce passes to some high-flying teammate who is able to score on the opposition. Ordinary and iconic black men are constantly helping American society to rebound from one catastrophe or another and to successfully overcome the opposition in scoring serious points, serious arguments, serious goals.

This is precisely why you are reviled in some circles. This reading of Dennis Rodman, with which I agree wholeheartedly. Consider me now as the organist who plays those chords behind the sermon. Dennis Rodman is terribly fascinating. I laughed uproariously to see him show up with arched eyebrows and fingernail polish in the championship series on the day after wearing a boa to his book signing. And here he is performing the dirtiest, roughest, most "masculine" aspects of the game for his team.

He's inscribing those aspects in the text of black masculinity—because 80 percent of the players in the NBA now are black, so we have to talk about it as a black man's game. Dennis Rodman's relationship to basketball is similar to disco's relationship to American music, and especially black pop music. The black gay aesthetic informed the construction of the post-R&B era before the rise of hip-hop culture. It was widely reviled, although it is now being reexcavated in popular culture for archetypal images of American identity. Disco focused on the rhythm as opposed to the substance of the words; it highlighted the rhythmic capacity of the voice against the lyrical content of what was being articulated. Disco culture was about a kind of rapturous and transgressive move against the sexual segregation of gay and lesbian bodies in social space. It was about the freedom and ecstasy of dance where clubs became sanctuaries for the secular worship of the deities of disco: rhythm, carnival, play, movement, and sexualized funk, elements that helped its adherents choreograph an aural erotopia. Those streaming, swirling globe lights that fixed on the dance floor assured that artifice was taken as the ultimate reality. I guess you could say in a sense that Sylvester got a hold of Baudrillard. The way that disco prefigures and precipitates a postmodern American sensibility often gets erased. Disco was dissed because its black gay aesthetic vogued against what was in vogue, and therefore its sexual transgression was the subtext, or what they call in philosophy the suppressed premise, of the logic of an ostensibly "straight" black pop musical culture.

Dennis Rodman's effect is comparable. He's the suppressed premise of the logic of black masculinity's prominence in basketball. So he helps to construct the public face of black masculinity along with Connie Hawkins, George Gervin, Earl "the Pearl" Monroe, Walt "Clyde" Frazier, Julius "Dr. J" Erving, Earvin "Magic" Johnson, Charles Barkley, and Michael Jordan. Through Dennis Rodman's body of work, the homoerotic moment within sport, and especially within black masculine athleticism, surfaces: Patting one another on the behind to say "good game" or "good play," hugging and kissing one another, falling into each other's sweating arms to boost camaraderie, and so on. This is a sexualized choreography of suppressed black desire and the way it is portrayed from the gridiron to the hardwood floor, pun intended! Dennis Rodman's figure invites us to see that homoeroticism has a lot to do, ironically enough, with the seminal production of black masculine athletic identities. The homoerotic and gay sensibility, contrary to popular perception, doesn't stop—and certainly in his case may even fuel—great athletic and masculine achievement. My God! The brother is an outlaw in what was formerly an outlaw and, racially speaking at least, outlawed sport.

There was a time, remember, when blacks weren't allowed to play professional basketball. When they were relatively early in their tenure in the NBA, in the early 1970s, *Ebony* magazine did an annual article that featured every black player on every team, something unimaginable today. And don't forget that the New York Knickerbockers during this time were called by racist fans the New York "Niggerbockers" because of the presence of Frazier, Monroe, Willis Reed, Dick "Fall Back Baby" Barnett, and Henry Bibby. Rodman's homoeroticized black athletic body is "outlaw(ed)" in several simultaneously signifying fashions, so to speak. The outlaw and the rebel, with apologies to Eric Hobsbawm, are countercultural figures whose lives embody the hidden and contradictory ethical aspirations of the masses, or at least some of them, even if the masses are not altogether aware of, or don't consciously identify with, the ideals the outlaw or rebel embodies. So Dennis Rodman is performing a kind of above ground "dream work" for the collective sexual unconscious of black masculinity. What Dennis Rodman's example shows is that even as black masculine culture overtly represses sexual difference and attempts to conceal or mystify homoerotic elements and behavior, it often depends on that very homoerotic dimension for athletic entertainment.

This homophobic dimension would seem to explain why most groups distance themselves from Rodman. Black people explain his absurdities by pointing to his time in Oklahoma. White people can point to his black urban ghetto origins. He thus seems to be an unusual signifier who can be whatever you need him to be. In other words, there are no false statements you can make about Dennis Rodman.

He's a successor next to Michael Jackson, in that sense. Not only is what you say about Dennis Rodman true, but what you say about Dennis Rodman is what you say about yourself. Even as you try to read Dennis Rodman, you're reading yourself. There's a relationship between ethnography and epiphany, between self-revelation and the excavation of the other.

To talk for a moment of this modern/postmodern divide about which you spoke earlier, could you talk for a moment of how your intellectual development has been affected by television and cyberspace. When I look back over Walter Benjamin's "Art in the Age of Mechanical Reproduction," I think to myself how differently he might have perceived things in the face of television.

I think immediately of what legendary singer and spoken word artist Gil Scott-Heron famously said, "The Revolution Will Not Be Televised." Well, in many ways, it has been televised, except the revolution about which he spoke has been replaced by the revolution of the medium itself. It's like Marshall McLuhan meets Barney Fife. I'm a child of television, even though my mother tells me that early on when I was mad at my family because I wanted to read a lot, I'd say, "Y'all don't read enough, you watch too much TV." I think it's God's joke on me that part of my life as a cultural critic is to be an analyst of television. Television has very deeply influenced my understanding of pop culture and my intellectual development in the sense that I take it as another very powerful text that we have to read, that we have to interpret, that we have to consume. I think that my self-understanding certainly has been to a degree both shaped by and articulated against the images, ideas, and ideologies on television, as they enable an on sight—and that's deliberately ambiguous for me, both s-i-g-h-t and s-i-t-e—negotiation of black identity. The evolution of television, along with the evolution and influence of film, sport, and music, has co-incided with the evolution of the popular conception of black people in this country.

Besides its effect on my intellectual development and the professional pleasure it has provided me in reading its various texts, television has also extended an outlet to me to advocate social change, analyze culture, and argue about ideas. I know that's not the sense you meant by your question, but it leads me to reflect on another rea-son I'm drawn to TV, I think it's a legitimate medium through which to educate the public and to disrupt, subvert, and transgress against hegemonic forces. First of all, I talk so fast, which is both a good and bad thing for television. I can get a great deal in during a five-minute span on a news or talk show, and even more when I've got more time. On the other hand, I know I should slow down sometimes, but some-times I'm really suspicious of slowing down. I sometimes prefer the machine-gun ap-proach, given the often coarse and certainly fast-paced nature of television time and rhetoric. So, on occasion, the staccato, rapid-fire rhetorical style I have is usefully un-fettered on television. I want my style to shatter that airtight medium. I want it to put a dent in television because it's an incredibly pedagogical medium.

As intellectuals, we ought to get used to the fact that television is a medium that affects people's identities and perceptions of reality, sometimes for the good. There have been studies carried out that show that people trust their local news-people more than they trust their clergy people. People still look to conventional news broadcasts on TV to get their information, even more than from written journalism or from the alternative press. So I want to bring my alternative, non-traditional, perhaps even subversive viewpoint to bear on and within this most hegemonic of mediums.

In some ways, television has proved to have ideological flexibility, especially when radicals pop up on rare occasions. At least there's the potential to shatter dominant ideological modes, if even for a brief moment. We should definitely take advantage of television's episodic fluidity. I don't see television in a snob-bish way. I've been on *Oprah* to talk about black oppression, black masculinity, and female identity. I've gone on CNN to talk about race, white supremacy, and electoral politics. I want to seize television as a pedagogical tool to help liberate or transform folk, or at least contest what Stuart Hall calls the preferred mean-ings of the dominant culture, juxtaposing them to what he terms the negotiated meanings, as I acknowledge the prevailing ideological framework while arguing for alternative structures of thought and oppositional practices. I want to use tele-vision to challenge our culture's common sense, in the way Gramsci meant it, and to help educate and occasionally uplift those who pay attention.

That does fit within the ways that I wanted to hear you talk about the medium. This also points me back to your notion of this betweener generation—people in their late thirties and very early forties. People just a few years older than the betweeners remember television in its early, formative stages, when televisions weren't ubiquitous. They remember Uncle Milty, and TV was still a novelty. But, for me, when I wake up to memory it's there and it's unremarkable. It's

on and it's unremarkable. One of my earliest TV memories, at three, almost four years old, is seeing Jack Ruby shoot Lee Harvey Oswald. That's a vivid scene I remember seeing—sitting on my mother's bed—that scene. That's one of those moments I've somehow written into my mind as an early moment. That and also realizing, somewhere around my thirtieth birthday, that from as far back as I could remember until my thirteenth birthday that the news started every day with the body count from Vietnam. That's pretty deep—to realize that there is a generation of us, eight years old in 1968, old enough to be aware of the assassinations, of the riot in Chicago, of moon landings, of Detroit and Newark, of all the stuff happening around you, seeing it come at you and no-body talks to you about it. So, in 1987 and 1988 I carried around a grudge be-cause *People, Time,* and *Newsweek* did "summer of love" and "summer of dis-content" retrospectives. So, they talked to (all) the people who were adult participants in '67 and '68. Then they talked to people who were twenty years old in '87 and '88. And I thought: "you did it again!" In 1968 no one said any-thing about this to me. Here, again, in 1998 you ask everybody but me.

You're so right. You've brought up here what is not my first memory of television, but it is my most important one. That is when I saw the newscaster interrupt the regular program to announce that MARTIN LUTHER KING JR. had been shot in Memphis, Tennessee. That is the most powerful moment of the television bonding with me, and of me bonding with the TV. I identified, almost beyond vo-lition or consciousness, with the television as a medium, as an apparatus, that brought me an ideologically contested moment in black rhetoric. That is, MAR-TIN LUTHER KING JR. speaking his last speech. They flashed an image of him as he said what would immediately become some of his most famous words, "I may not get there with you, but I want you to know tonight that we as a peo-ple will get to the Promised Land." That was a very profound and electrifying episode that shaped my life forever. I asked my mother, "Which one is he? Which one is he?" I remember distinctly, and I don't know why they showed it, Dr. King at some point reeling back on his foot. I immediately felt his power; his words were like containers brimming with the pathos of black life. Later, the newsman broke faith again with the printed program by saying, "MARTIN LUTHER KING JR. has just died at thirty-nine in Memphis, Tennessee."

And now, here I am thirty-eight, and you're thirty-seven, so we're basically the same age and almost the age at which King died. King's death was stunning to me. I had never heard of Martin Luther King Jr. before that point, and when he died in 1968—I was nine years old—it changed my life. Television literally changed my life because, after his death, I began to watch all the programs about Dr. King. I began to go to the library to read all the books I could about him that were available. I then ordered, through a telephone number I got off of the television, speeches that were available on records. I had my little record player back then, when vinyl was the medium of choice and analog was the order of the day. Then, through televi-sion, I ordered the commemorative book on Martin Luther King Jr. So, television was a very powerful medium that fused with my evolving self-consciousness as a young black person. The 1967 riots in Detroit also made me pay attention to television. It brought me scenes of social ignominy and racial deterioration right before my eyes, and made me realize that what I could see from my front porch in the streets—as people scurried up and down the pavement with money stashed in their big fros, televisions on their backs, and carrying all kinds of ill-gotten gains and goods—was refracted through the prism of a medium that made it larger than life.

Thinking back on the brothers and sisters in the streets, I'm reminded of the old joke Dick Gregory told about black people being stopped in the riots. These people were carrying a couch when the police stopped them. Dick Gregory said that when these people were stopped, they said, "Goddamn! A black psychiatrist can't even make house calls anymore!" And what else is it that they say? In a riot black people destroy everything but libraries and bookstores. Lord have mercy! Anyway, the reality is that the riots and the death of Martin Luther King Jr. point to how social catastrophe and transformation is either covered or concealed on television. These events spring from deeply embedded social processes of resolving or reinforcing conflict that are not usually explored in great depth on television, save in the rare in-depth documentary.

The contested and conflicted meanings of race in the 1960s were frequently papered over and smoothed out, resulting in the McDonaldization of Martin Luther King Jr. in a McLuhan universe where the medium was the message. It's important to me that the medium through which Dr. King was articulated for me was a televisual apparatus—since I never met him in the flesh. And the message I got from him was about social change. My early identification with TV grew from the fact that it had the radical potential to transform, not merely to anesthetize, to open up and not merely to constrain, to shatter and not merely to constitute, social reality. I saw it as an imaginative apparatus through which, ideologically, we could resist and challenge dominant racial and cultural narratives. Now, I didn't know all of this back then, but I felt a connection to King that transcended time and place and allowed me to identify with this figure whose life just revolutionized my consciousness. So, there's no question that television changed my life.

The next week in Sunday school I remember that our teacher asked us about that. That, I'm sure, was one of the very few times an adult asked about our response to current events. If I remember correctly, it was a Wednesday or Thursday evening when King was assassinated. That was when *Batman* came on. That was probably why I was hanging out in front of the tube— waiting for *Batman*.

Aww, man! Batman and Robin, brother! My boys Adam West and Burt Ward! And there was Bruce Lee as Cato on the *Green Hornet,* and I don't remember the cat who played the Green Hornet that Cato drove around in the Hornet's Lincoln Continental.

I remember that on the Sunday following my Sunday school teacher asking us how the assassination made us feel–probably the only time anyone asked us. One girl in the class said she was glad King died because some show she wanted to watch had been interrupted. There was some TV show she wanted to see, but the news preempted all that. That seems, again, to be one of the interesting ways television plays out in our culture. And occasionally I'm one of those people–I'd rather watch some sitcom than the Republican convention. I can catch what I need to later on CNN or C-SPAN. I don't have to sit there and watch it all unfold live.

These news programs are part of the option glut that television now presents. Our nation, indeed our world, has been deeply affected by the CNNing of American discourse where all information, or at least the information that is deemed worth knowing, is immediately available. Therefore, there's little psychic space for reflection, little intellectual or emotional space in which to recover what we learn or reconstitute the ideas we absorb. We have little time to figure out the meaning of what we learn. As Derrida taught us, understanding is not simply about what something means but how it signifies. However, you can't even figure that out unless you have some space, some remove, from hugely influential events. I'm not embracing the myth of news objectivity, since I think the best we can hope for is fairness, which includes placing our biases right out in the open. I'm thinking here of the need to recover the fragments of events, and to experience them as fully as possible through interpreting and articulating them.

What the immediacy of communications technology has done is to make us believe that because we've perceived something, that because we've got the raw data through our senses, we've thoroughly experienced it. But we don't know what we know until we begin to think critically about what it means, and until we intervene with a conscious, deliberate intent to classify, to categorize, and to filter our experiences. It takes much more than empirical access to information to create understanding. Without interpretation and analysis, experience remains mute and inarticulate beneath the sheer fact of its existence. The phenomenological weight of immediacy results in a distorted capacity for interpretation and analysis.

As you mention the idea of space, there is a glut of options and information such that if you know that you need space to reflect, interpret, and reinterpret, you don't have time before the next fragment hits you. This is a totally unplanned but nice little segue. There was a Jay Wright symposium here at which Harold Bloom was a speaker. Jay Wright said this in a 1983 interview: "These last two terms, explication and interpretation, should call attention to one of my basic assumptions: that naked perception (just seeing something), is misprision in the highest degree. Every perception requires explication and interpretation. Exploration means just that. A simple report of experience, if you could make such a thing, isn't good enough." Although he's talking about the art of poetry, this seems to apply to this sort of experience of information. One of the things that Harold Bloom lamented at this conference was the absence of learnedness, although he put Jay Wright on this wonderful pedestal as a learned poet in the tradition of Dante and Milton. Somehow, it occurred to me that there's something about this peculiar postmodern information glut that makes "learnedness" impossible. Bloom mentioned that earlier in his career, although it wasn't often, he would hear people referred to as a "learned" scholar.

In the light of our postmodern option glut, erudition becomes nearly obsolete and impossible to attain, at least according to a specific understanding of the concept. You can't master the discursive tongues that have proliferated via the media in our own time. In some senses, I lament the loss of such erudition because I'm a non-traditional traditionalist at that level, reared on *The Harvard Classics,* TV, and Motown. I saw no disjuncture between *Two Years Before the Mast* by Richard Dana, and William "Smokey" Robinson's "My Girl" sung by the Temptations. Although I understand and even empathize with elements of Bloom's lament, I've got disagreements with him and other critics over canon formation and related literary issues, because I think there are multiple canons and multiple forms of literacy that we ought to respect. The intellectual and rhetorical integrity of these traditions ought to be acknowledged, and not in a condescending, compensatory fashion designed to make sure that "the other" is represented, except such inclusion is usually a procedural and not a substantive engagement with a given work. We've got to take the revelations about America that "minority" authors offer as seriously as we do conventional heroes of literature. We have much to learn from black writers' engagement, for instance, with what Baraka termed "vicious modernism."

On the other hand, I think that there's a need to historicize our conceptions of erudition, too. We should constantly be reevaluating what we mean by learnedness and erudition, since those qualities were never absolutely divorced from the priorities and prisms of the dominant culture. The learned and erudite were not simply revered for their knowledge, but they reflected a hierarchy of privilege that provided some the opportunity to acquire such a status while foreclosing the possibility to others in an a priori fashion. Ironically enough, even though the possibility of a particular kind of erudition may be quickly vanishing with the proliferation of information systems, it may offer a relatively more democratic conception of literacy that invites us to acknowledge a wider range of people as legitimate bearers of "learning."

In the past, the erudite person could only be a white male whose prodigious learning was acknowledged by his peers and intellectual progeny. Now, at least, we've widened the view of what counts as erudite and learned, and in many ways that's a very good thing.

Interview by Jonathan Smith
St. Louis, Missouri, 1996

PART FOURTEEN

CODA: THE LIFE OF THE MIND

I have strived as an intellectual to enhance the public good by thinking as broadly and deeply as possible about issues of supreme importance to the nation. Although I derive immense pleasure from the sheer act of thinking, reading, and writing, I believe that those of us blessed with the leisure of such pursuits should also, if we are so inclined, and sufficiently capable, help our fellow citizens reflect on pressing social problems. In this role of engaged academic, or public intellectual, I have appeared on countless television and radio programs; written for numerous news-papers, journals, and magazines; lectured in universities, public forums, and political gatherings; and preached in pulpits around the nation, with the hope of bringing intellectual insight and moral clarity to complex matters. Public intellectuals—black ones in particular—have come in for a great deal of criticism: we are said to be more interested in fame than rigor, more moved by money than vocation, and more taken with praise than pupils. Despite the undeniable shortcomings of public intellectual life, and despite the legitimate criticism that is launched our way, I think it is honorable to serve one's society by analyzing our nation's mores, folk-ways, intellectual habits, social practices, and political behaviors.

Thirty-Six

IT'S NOT WHAT YOU KNOW, IT'S HOW YOU SHOW IT: BLACK PUBLIC INTELLECTUALS

This chapter, written for my book Race Rules: Navigating the Color Line, *was excerpted in* Emerge *magazine and extensively cited in* The Chronicle of Higher Education. *It caused quite a stir among my fellow black intellectuals, largely because of the tongue-in-cheek awards I give out at the end. This is one of the most playful pieces I've written; I poke fun at myself and my colleagues while trying to write substantively about the place black intellectuals should occupy in the culture. I found out that many intellectuals don't have a great sense of humor. Neither can many of us stand the scrutiny we routinely cast on others. Since I have received great acclaim, as well as bitter denunciation, for my role as a "public intellectual"—a loaded term that is at times a help and hindrance—I decided to speak about the blessings and burdens of my vocation. Despite the playfulness of my essay, I take my vocation—but not myself—with utter seriousness. Black intellectuals are neither above nor beneath the rest of our culture. Instead, we are agents of the critical consciousness that can spur the collective self-examination and thoughtful reflection upon which social action should rest. This is the perfect chapter to end this reader, since it captures my ambition as an intellectual to shape the culture in which I live and think. In light of the anti-intellectual environment the nation is presently living through, it is even more imperative that we explore the social benefits of the engaged intellectual.*

Distracted, instead, by false or secondary issues, yielding apparently little resistance to the sound intrusion of market imperatives on the entire intellectual object, including that of African American studies, today's creative black intellectual lends herself/himself—like candy being taken from a child—to the mighty seductions of publicity and the "Pinup" .... Might it be useful, then, to suggest that before the black creative intellectual can "heal" her people, she must consider to what extent she must "heal" herself.

—HORTENSE SPILLERS
"*THE CRISIS OF THE NEGRO INTELLECTUAL:* A POST-DATE," 1994

GENTLE READER, I BEGIN THIS CHAPTER WITH a confession and a warning. First, the warning. This is not an objective examination of the contentious debates surrounding the rise of so-called black public intellectuals. (You haven't heard of us? Well, the debates are mostly "inside baseball." To tell the truth, the debates are more like inside-the-academy bickering. Okay, you've got me: they're tempests in teapots, even though the teapots are pretty prestigious. But if it's any consolation, the debates offer the same sort of mudslinging, backbiting, gossiping, and dozens-playing you're likely to find in a supermarket tabloid.) Mine is a partisan account of how black intellectuals got into the fix of being lauded and lambasted, admired and despised, in the same breath. This is simply one black public intellectual's teeth-baring, tongue-in-cheek mea culpa and apologia rolled into one.

Now the confession: I have been chosen as one of the lucky few. I have been the recipient of great praise (and sharp criticism, but more on that later) for my writing and speaking at universities and before the general public. Along with a relatively few others—including Henry Louis Gates, Cornel West, bell hooks, Robin Kelley, Patricia Williams, and Stephen Carter—I've been dubbed a public intellectual. This designation emphasizes how our work contributes to public debate, especially about race and American society. The term public intellectual is certainly not new. It's been applied to a range of scholars and intellectuals throughout Europe and America. Other terms, like political intellectual and organic intellectual, hint at the same public function for the thinker. The term public intellectual gained fresh currency in the late '80s with the publication of Russell Jacoby's book, *The Last Intellectuals*.

But never before has such a highly educated and vastly literate group of black thinkers had access to the Public Mind of America—and acclaim or derision for managing to do so. We have been hailed and harangued by publications ranging from the *New Yorker* and the *Atlantic Monthly* to the *Village Voice*. And most of us have appeared on *Oprah Winfrey*, *Charlie Rose*, *Nightline*, and a spate of other television shows, to talk about a range of subjects, and a lot about race. So I've got no complaints about the publicity my work receives. (Well, I've got a few, but they're the carps of the privileged, so I'll spare you.) I've been very fortunate indeed.

You'd think that academics everywhere, especially black ones, would be proud that they'd see in our achievements their investments in us, and those like us, paying all sorts of dividends. Increased visibility for the profession. Heightened respect for black intellectual work. And a celebration of the unsung giants, especially the black ones, on whose shoulders we all stand. And many, many scholars and intellectuals do brim with pride and joy. But a lot don't. They simmer in resentment and prophesy trouble. Much of what makes them troubled is legitimate. Then, too, much of their resentment stems from pettiness, parochialism, and snobbishness.

In my case, as with many other black public intellectuals, there has been a strident, severe, but altogether predictable "blacklash." I've been called a "sellout." Cornel West's work has been viciously dismissed as "completely worthless." bell hooks has been assailed for being "a hustler." After my appearance on *Nightline* to talk about making the Million Man March more than a walk for testosterone or bigotry, I was accused of playing "Goebbels," the shrewd and perverted Nazi propagandist, to Farrakhan's Hitler. (Yeah, that's pretty libelous, but the guy who wrote it is named Adolf; I guess it was a case of vicarious nostalgia.) As you can tell, things have gotten nasty. What's the problem?

According to critics, there are several. First, there is the question of how the few of us who are deemed public intellectuals got anointed. Second, our work suffers from an intellectual thinness that could be remedied if only we weren't busy pontificating, prophesying, or playing pundit on television or radio. Third, the prestige, fame, and fortune bestowed on us are corrupting, making us sellouts. Fourth, we public intellectuals play an authenticity game, claiming to speak as politically rooted prophets for The Race as we peddle distorted meanings of blackness to the undiscerning white masses. Fifth, we're treated with kid gloves by colleagues and not really criticized. Finally, we all want to be HNIC (for the uninitiated, Head Negro In Charge).

Let's face it, there's some truth to some of these charges, and, depending on whom we're talking about, there's a lot of truth to many of these charges. Still, we don't have to give up on being public intellectuals. It's an honorable, even critical vocation. After all, just because counterfeit money exists, we don't have to stop spending the real thing. (Uh-oh, maybe the criticism about materialism is right; it's even seeping into my analogies!) We've just got to pay attention to fair criticisms, confess our masked and bald opportunism, admit that we're susceptible to the seductions of fame and fortune, and acknowledge that there are other equally gifted intellectuals who could do what we do, maybe even better. We've also got to face head-on the vicious personal attacks that get palmed off as brave commentary. And we've got to call a spade a spade: there's a lot of jealousy out here.

The irony of all this infighting and name-calling is that just as black intellectuals begin to receive our due—that is, a few of us, which, as you *can't* tell by the fury of the complaints, is more than received it in the past, the rule being the less there is to go around the more you fight over who gets it—we begin to knock each other off. Or others do the job for us. Hateful assaults from black and white writers often reveal their ignorance, or their distorted views, of how we got where we are. There's a difference between sharp criticism and the animus of ad hominem and ad feminem roasting. Sure, when you're the object of even the healthy kind of criticism, it can sting for days. And sometimes a literate intellectual licking leaves you feeling like you've been mugged by a metaphor. But you gird your loins to write again.

Why are so many critics hot and blathered?

The anointing of a few voices to represent The Race is an old, abiding problem. For much of our history, blacks have had to rely on spokespersons to express our views and air our grievances to a white majority that controlled access to everything from education to employment. For the most part, powerful whites only wanted to see and hear a few blacks at a time, forcing us to choose a leader—when we could. Often a leader was selected for us by white elites. Predictably, blacks often disagreed with those selections, but since the white elites had the power and resources, their opinions counted.

Such an arrangement created tensions in black communities because it reduced blackness to its lowest common denominator. Only what could be condensed into speeches, editorials, and other public declarations survived transmission to white elites. Complexity was often sacrificed for clarity. It also made the content of what was communicated about black culture conform to the spokesperson's gifts, vision, or interests. Thus, a spokesperson had a profound impact on what goods or services the rest of his or her black constituency received. The accountability of such leaders was often low.

Complicating matters further was the fact that the choice of spokespersons didn't always turn on issues that were of greatest interest or importance to blacks. Often a spokesperson was selected because his themes, style, and ideology were acceptable to the white majority. Many black leaders were viewed skeptically by their constituencies. Booker T. Washington is a prime example of this model of leadership.

Naturally, these conditions introduced considerable tension into the relationship between those who did the speaking and those who were spoken for. Black spokespersons acquired influence because they were given legitimacy by the white majority, whose power to establish such legitimacy was far greater than that of the black minority. As a result, these spokespersons used their power in black communities to reward loyal blacks and to punish dissidents. This arrangement meant that patronage more than moral principle determined the allocation of the limited resources for which the spokesperson was a funnel. As a result, few blacks benefited from the leadership that was supposed to speak for them all.

This legacy of anointment and appointment hangs like a stone cloud over the debate about black public intellectuals. Who gets to be a black public intellectual, who chooses them, and what have they done for you lately? We can answer these questions by first posing a more basic question: Why are black public intellectuals presently enjoying such prominence?

The fact that race is being bitterly debated as the national issue has a lot to do with the rise of black public intellectuals. Race has always been a deep, characteristic American problem. The refusal to face race, or our courageous confrontation with its complex meanings, defines our national identity And it goes in cycles. At some points in our nation's history—for instance, during the civil rights movement—we were forced to contend with race. At other times, such as during the erosion of racial progress in the Reaganite '80s, we believed we could just as well do without all those remedies like affirmative action, which, in any case, had been manufactured to give a leg up to undeserving blacks. Well, Edgar Allan Poe met Yogi Berra: the pendulum of race has swung back, and it's déjà vu all over again. Race is once more an inescapable force on a variety of fronts: the school yard, the job market, the justice system, politics, everywhere we look. So, living down to the crude, stereotypical version of American pragmatism, we call in the race experts to tell us what's going on.

The enhanced currency of black public intellectuals also rides the wave of popularity that sections of black life are enjoying. If there's one fact of black life in white America we can't deny, it's this: black folk go in and out of style. Most of the time our identities are exploited for white commercial ends, or ripped off to further the careers of white imitators. Blackness is today a hot commodity, but of course, it always has been: the selling of black bodies on the slave market, minstrel shows, Elvis's cloning of black gospel and blues singers all point to the fetish of black skin and skill in American popular culture. Once the barriers to black achievement were lowered, black folk ourselves got more of the fat.

Black bodies are "in" now, that is, if you don't happen to be a black man with a car, tangling with the police in Los Angeles or the white suburbs of Pittsburgh. Rodney King was the L.A. driver, and, well, you know what happened to him and to all of us because of what the police did and what the white jury didn't do. Jonny Gammage was the second driver, and he was stopped and subsequently choked to death by white police because he was wheeling his football star cousin Ray Seals's sports car in a neighborhood where everybody knows a black man shouldn't drive. You're alright if your black body shows up on professional basketball courts, where nearly 80 percent of the players are black. Or in the entertainment industry, where, despite the preponderance of decent parts doled out to whites, more blacks have slightly thicker pickin's and more leftovers to compete for than in the past. And hip-hop culture, to the chagrin of a whole lot of black folk, has literally darkened the face—some would say given it a black eye—of popular music.

Because black folk are leaving their mark all over American culture, there are renewed debates about what blackness means. Who better to call on than those blacks who spend their lives thinking, writing, and living black experience. (I can see it now: The film features our heroes being summoned to city hall to fight the slime and sludge of racism, backed by the refrain of the movie's theme song, "Who you gonna call? RACEBUSTERS! I ain't afraid of no racist.") As terrible as the fallout from all the fuss about black public intellectuals is—that is, as limited and limiting as the focus on a few elites is—at least some of us have a small say in what's done, or more modestly, in what's thought about black folk.

That's a significant improvement over the times when white critics pontificated about blackness without knowing, or in some cases, caring much about the subject. Even when white critics were righteous, when they were honest and critically sympathetic and did their homework, they were the only ones allowed to speak about black culture to the masses. If black folk weren't allowed in the front of the bus, at the top of white classes, or in the major leagues—about the only place they were invited to be first was, when they could enlist, at the war's front line—they certainly weren't going to be delivering astute analyses of their kith and kin to millions on television, radio, or in newspapers.

As usual, however, a blessing brings burdens. Some white critics have pointed out—some lamenting, others fuming—what a terrible thing it is for blacks to talk only about race, and that for them to make race their sole subject is, in the long run, harmful to the image of black intellectuals as perpetual one-noters. True enough. But a little clarification is in order. Black thinkers fought hard for Americans to take race seriously, that is, as an object of legitimate, critical examination. Early white thinkers, people like David Hume and Thomas Jefferson, resisted the process, outside of scandalously biased interpretations of black culture that masqueraded as scientific treatises on the inferiority of black culture. It was not until well into this century that white scholars began to study race for greater intellectual purposes than the proof of white superiority and the redemption, however crudely managed, of black savages. So black intellectuals paid the cost to be the boss in a realm of experience in which their thinking on the subject was usually overlooked, discounted, or berated.

Also, criticisms of the racial monomania of black intellectuals sometimes miss how black thinkers have been discouraged from making comment in public about issues other than race. The year he died, Malcolm X noted how even when whites "credit a Negro with some intelligence," they still feel the black thinker is only qualified to speak about race. "Just notice how rarely you will hear whites asking any Negroes what they think about the problem of world health or the space race to land men on the moon," Malcolm remarked in 1965.

That's still true today. Black intellectuals are rarely asked about the collapse of communism, the crisis of capitalism, whether cigarettes should be banned in public spaces, the successes and failures of feminism, the Palestinian–Israeli conflict, the state of modern Islam, the transcendentalist vision of Emerson, Walt Whitman's beliefs about erotic friendship, the impact of Heisenberg's uncertainty principle on the debate about postmodernism, Foucault's notion of power, Walt Disney's role in pop culture, fin de siècle apocalyptic thinking, Russian formalism, Murray Perahia's Beethoven concertos, and a world of things besides. We're rarely even asked about the unusual things black folk do, like scuba diving, writing histories of German warplanes, studying ancient Chinese cultures, and so on.

So before critics ascend their high horses too quickly, they should dig their intellectual spurs into the beast of history and hold on for the long, rough ride. Black intellectuals turned a deficit into a credit. They were limited to writing, or speaking in public, about race. As a result, the subject is now viewed the way black intellectuals have long viewed it, as the central problem of American society, through the eyes of thinkers who have witnessed the bitter triumphs of racism while working feverishly for its defeat. Just because the rest of the world caught on much later—and to be fair, many whites have fought side by side with blacks from the very beginning—is no reason to punish those, or at least their descendants, who got the point in the first place.

It is important to remember that contemporary black public intellectuals do have forebears. That would certainly temper whatever pride or self-satisfaction some black public intellectuals might feel about their present fortunes. They didn't fall out of the sky, fully formed and prepared to contest the demons of race. Black intellectuals learned at the knees of, and sometimes, unfortunately, at the expense of, black thinkers who blazed the paths we now travel. Too often, these pioneers were cut off from the public they coveted, their writings deprived of the close and critical readings they so richly deserved.

E. Franklin Frazier, renowned sociologist and the first black president of the American Sociological Association, was restricted within the broader, whiter world of academia in which he was trained and over which he had at least nominal influence. And W.E.B. Du Bois, the universally recognized Thomas Jefferson of black letters, the founder of black intellectual invention in the twentieth century, and the first black to earn a Ph.D. from Harvard, was prevented from sharing his genius with the institution that shaped him. As the strange career of race has evolved, the anatomy of opportunity for blacks has changed as well. The post–civil rights generation of black intellectuals has begun to get some of the benefits that even towering intellectual giants were routinely denied. For the most part, the present cadre of celebrated black intellectuals is the first generation to gain entry as students into elite white colleges and universities, later to return and find their voices and vocations within those same halls of ivy as professors.

But even that progress contains a drawback. Much of the attention has been given to those black intellectuals who have managed to find–and hog–the public spotlight. Less attention has been paid to their cohort in universities for whom the classroom and careful scholarship are enough. (Or to community college teachers whose commitment to educating black folk is undervalued.) Such scholars–shall we call them, for want of a better term, black private intellectuals?–have been, by virtue of the dramatic emphasis placed on the public intellectuals, done a grave disservice.

The cruel irony is that just as black scholars have attained legitimate standing in the academy, getting it the old-fashioned way, by earning tenure, writing scholarly monographs, and publishing learned articles, they now have to compete for attention with so-called black public intellectual superstars. Such figures are the pampered, high-profile elite who command large speaking fees; get their books reviewed in all the right, bright-light, high-gloss magazines and newspapers; appear on television to chat about their latest work; and occasionally represent the hardworking, low-wage-earning, undereducated black masses. (Sometimes these intellectuals secretly compete with the masses in their own minds, as they recall their latest critical rebuff or exaggerate their own suffering, seeing it as the moral equivalent of welfare, class warfare, and income inequality.)

In other words, not only do private black intellectuals have to put up with all the mess they take from a white academy that is often still insensitive and hostile, they now have to hear about the goings-on of black public intellectuals, who are the supposed proof that not only do black scholars have it good, they've got it better than most white academics. What a bind. (Of course, given the levels of hostility now being directed at black public intellectuals within the academy, the private intellectuals might use their status to their advantage: "Oh, no, not me. I'm not a public intellectual. I'm just a poor working stiff who grades papers, attends faculty meetings, serves on committees, writes articles and books, and, in what spare time I have, I volunteer for the neighborhood literacy project.")

As we grouch, sometimes with good reason, about the narrowness and limitations of the university, black public intellectuals should remember that it is the foothold we found inside the academy—before we "went public"—that became our launching pad for fame and fortune in the first place. The academy is still home, and our criticisms shouldn't feed into the hysterical rantings against the academy by the far right that leave our private intellectual colleagues, especially black ones, most vulnerable. Many conservatives believe the university is a den of politically correct educational thieves, robbing our kids of their moral futures with all sorts of strange theories.

Well, the university isn't all it's cracked down to be: an artificial environment removed from the lives of real people. Last time I checked at my university, there were actual bodies in the classroom, real people running the place, and life-and-death issues being fought over by people who will one day run businesses, defend clients, make millions, enrich lives, ruin government, and become politicians (sorry for the repetition) in the Real World. Be glad—okay, some of you should be sorry—that many of my colleagues get a crack at them first. Some esoteric theory, off-the-cuff comment, or chance encounter with someone completely opposite in viewpoint might make the difference, a quarter century after a student leaves a classroom, in her doing the right or wrong thing.

Sure, the alleged Unabomber went to Harvard and Michigan. But before that he lived in Chicago's white suburbs, and after he dropped out of the academy he haunted the mountains of Montana. And no one's going to argue that, based on their influence on his outlook, either place should be destroyed. (I simply can't resist noting, with all the unfairness and smallness of perspective my comment implies, that the alleged Unabomber's genius was quantitative; maybe if he'd had more humanities courses, he could have dropped rhetorical, not literal, bombs!)

Not only is the problem of the black private intellectual compelling, but, if we're honest, the current crop of black public intellectuals is selected in a way that's elitist and incestuous. Most of us went to Ivy League schools, few of the official designees teach outside of elite eastern schools, and none teach at historically black colleges and universities. I'm not aiming here at some sort of compensatory principle for the sake of including all segments of the black intellectual community. I'm simply pointing out that if the criterion for being a public intellectual is the ability to speak and write clearly and substantively about important public issues for broad audiences, then many, many more black scholars fit the bill. Black scholars like William Strickland, Jerry Ward, Gloria Wade-Gayles, Beverly Guy-Sheftall, Ethelbert Miller, and a host of others certainly qualify. And God knows that black nationalist and Afrocentric scholars like Maulana Karenga, Molefi Asante, Asa Hilliard, Ivan Van Sertima, Na'im Akbar, and LaFrances Rogers Rose were doing public intellectual work, especially among despised, invisible black communities, way before the term took hold.

Certainly that's part of the catch. Contemporary black public intellectuals are valued because we speak—by no means exclusively, and, in some cases, not even primarily, but nonetheless in important ways—to a *white* public. We are involved, however much we might not like it, with the translation, interpretation, explanation, and demystification of black culture to white masses. The temptations are readily apparent. That we become the judges of authentic blackness. That we become viewed as the most visible, and hence, the most important and informed interpreters of black culture. That we hoodwink naive white folk with a racial abracadabra whose plausibility depends upon their ignorance. That we misrepresent the cantankerous ideological and cultural differences within black life. That we come to think white folk are the only folk that count and, in trying to please them, we end up selling out black interests.

One black writer harshly reproved black public intellectuals for explaining the heart of black darkness to white folk, saying that we based our claims on being Real Blacks as we make big cash telling white folk about the ins and outs of black culture. According to him, we were conniving, careerist sellouts. He made that charge, of course, in the well-known black weekly, the *Village Voice*, gaining a reputation for tough talk, and a column in that publication to boot. Who says trashing black intellectuals for selling out to whites doesn't pay off handsomely, giving the critic, in this case a black intellectual, more visibility, a larger public voice, and more legitimacy in the white world?

Let's get real. Black folk read the papers, watch television, and consume books like everybody else. In fact, much has been made of the strong and still increasing numbers of black book buyers. Black public intellectuals are reaching broader white and black audiences through their work. Only by underestimating the intelligence of those audiences can we conclude that black public intellectuals will get away with too much rhetorical or intellectual legerdemain. Besides, most of the black public intellectuals I know make regular appearances among black folk to hash out important ideas about race, democracy, and this nation's destiny. In fact, many of the black folk who show up to see and argue with these figures read their books, saw them on television, read their articles in newspapers, or heard them on the radio.

Mass media have changed the stakes for the black intelligentsia. Even when Du Bois, Frazier, Zora Neale Hurston, or Langston Hughes held forth in black communities, they didn't have anything like the range of audience or publicity today's black scholars enjoy. Television, radio, newspapers, and now the Internet have changed all that. Now that black intellectuals regularly appear on the *Today* show and National Public Radio, and in the pages of the *New York Times*, the *New Yorker*, the *Los Angeles Times*, and the like, they have more visibility and name recognition than many of their predecessors.

It's easy to see why many critics think that's a bad thing. First, such critics play an authenticity game themselves, that follows this line of reasoning: Real scholars read, write, study, and reflect at home or in the university. The virtue of their work often rests in its ability to critically and carefully examine a subject with as much rigor and intellectual responsibility as they can muster. While their findings may apply directly to public life, their work will be read—and critics don't often say this—mainly by other academics and graduate students. Sounds good to me. I've written stuff like that, with no apologies, because as a black person, then a black scholar, I've learned that we really have little choice but to master many languages, arcane theoretical ones and eloquently lucid ones as well.

But that's not the only valid, compelling model of scholarship available. To put it simply, we need both: serious, critical reflection away from the lights, cameras, and action of the public realm; and gritty, graceful, engaged intellectual work that takes on the issues of the day with force and fire. Some of us can do both, while many of us can only master one. There's no shame either way. The elitist, snobbish attempt to say only traditional scholarly work counts is self-serving. It's also an intellectually bigoted view of the life of the mind. On the other hand, the attempt to equate fame or notoriety with intellectual achievement is vicious and small-minded.

At some point, the claim that the work of black public intellectuals is simply not rigorous enough, that its intellectual predicates are too thin, can be legitimately made about all public intellectuals. I know it's true of some of my work. (Please, don't ask what work I'm referring to; I might have to tell you which paragraph of an essay I wrote when I was twelve that I have in mind.) We all slip. And our critics should be there to catch us. But the genre of public intellectual work is not itself indictable on that charge, as some critics want us to believe. True enough, we can't equate an op-ed piece on the unfairness of sending blacks to jail in disproportionate numbers with a dense description of the ways criminality has functioned to stigmatize black folk in America. The latter will, if well done, do much to reorient thinking among scholars who influence the perception of these matters in academic circles, and, by extension, beyond the academy. The former could pull the coat of some policy wonk or congressional flunky who might pass it on to her boss. Both sorts of work are worthwhile.

What's doubly intriguing about the debate over lack of rigor, especially among black intellectuals, is that, like the mourners at a funeral, those crying the loudest are the most guilty. I've seen, heard, and participated in too many discussions with self-styled rigorous black intellectuals (shall we call them the rigorighteous?) who took special pride in the complexity, nuance, and density of their thinking—while despising the lack of same in the work of other black intellectuals—who were then denied tenure by their white colleagues for lack of substantive work, and laughed at behind their backs by those they seek to please with their displays of rigorous wizardry. There's a useful distinction to be made between rigor, which can be expressed in elegant prose or in complex theory, and wanton inaccessibility, which masquerades as cutting-edge intellectual craft when it's little more than jargon-bloated, obfuscated intellectual nonsense. Make no mistake. This is not a mini-broadside against postmodernism, poststructuralism, or any of the influential pillars, like Derrida and Foucault, of those posts. At its best, theory should help us unmask the barbarous practices associated with some traditions of eloquent expression. But like a good sermon or a well-tailored suit, theory shouldn't show its seams.

Black scholars—though this is true for other scholars as well, just not with the same implications about presence or lack of intelligence—are often put in a "damned if you do, damned if you don't" bind. On the one hand, we were told for years that our work was worthless, that it lacked the rigor and language by which serious scholarly work is known. We were subtly but insistently implored to employ the jargon of our disciplines, thereby showing our mastery of that plot of intellectual ground we were taught to plow. Then we were told that if our scholarly writings were too jargon-filled they were obtuse and meaningless. We were told that if we couldn't write in ways that made sense to a broad public our work was of no use. This is good to remember now that critics are taking black public intellectuals to task for our work. Back when scholars like Oliver Cox and W.E.B. Du Bois were doing just what it is alleged we often don't do—careful, serious, deeply thoughtful work—they were ignored or dismissed. Du Bois's monumental study, *Black Reconstruction*, sold only 376 copies in its first year of publication in 1935. The book wasn't even reviewed by the *American Historical Review*, the leading journal in the historical profession. That's a sober reminder of how black intellectuals shouldn't be too quick to surrender whatever visibility we've managed to secure in deference to a notion of scholarly propriety. We see where that got us.

It's also evident that the lure of the lights can corrupt black intellectuals by making us believe our own press. Or by making us addicted to praise and disdainful of serious criticism, which, by the way, every public intellectual lauds as a virtue, except when it's directed his or her way. Nobody hates criticism like a critic. Still, many black public intellectuals have been victims of drive-by, gangster-style criticism. In this sort of attack, one can virtually hear the machinery of jealousy working overtime to crush another black intellectual's work, to knock her reputation down a few notches to build up the critic's own. No one but the critic benefits from such hateful exercises.

Equally worrisome, too many black public intellectuals hog the ball and refuse to pass it to others on their team. Many times I've been invited on a television program, a prestigious panel, or a national radio program because a white critic or intellectual recommended me. Later I often discover that another prominent black public intellectual, when consulted, had conveniently forgotten to mention my name or that of other qualified black intellectuals. Ugly indeed.

I guess this is a way of saying that, yes, a lot of black public intellectuals, despite what we say—maybe because we say we don't—really do want to be HNIC, which, in light of the fierce and corrupting competition over the sweepstakes of visibility, also means Hottest Negro In The Country. If that's the case, it's a disgusting waste of a grand opportunity for a group of black intellectuals to make a significant impact on our nation's debates about race and blackness. By doing that well, we might open up space for black thinkers to range freely over the entire field of American interests. Black public intellectuals have a great responsibility:

to think clearly, to articulate eloquently, to criticize sharply, to behave humanely, and to raise America's and black folks' vision of what we might achieve if we do away with the self-destructive habit of racism and the vicious forces of black self-defeat taking us down from within.

Black public intellectuals are leaders of a particular kind. We stir up trouble in broad daylight so that the pieties by which we live and the principles for which we die, both as a people and a nation, are subject to critical conversation. Black public intellectuals are certainly not leaders in the sense as, say, Jesse Jackson or Louis Farrakhan, with an identifiable base in black communities from which we launch criticism or commentary that often, though not always, reflects our constituencies' beliefs. Not that black public intellectuals don't have what might be considered constituencies. There are many publics, and black public intellectuals move in and out of many of them, including the university. Sure the university is not, nor should it be, a civil rights organization, although some crotchety conservatives and miffed liberals would argue that multiculturalism, identity politics, and "PC" have made the differences between the two rather small. But the university is a public sphere, with a lot of rich people's and poor people's kids attending. And given the attention we've got, black public intellectuals have to try to help make the world smarter, safer, and saner for those, and all of America's, youth. We don't speak for The Race. We speak as representatives of the ideological strands of blackness, and for those kinships we possess outside of black communities, that we think are most healthy.

But we ain't messiahs. Nor should we have messiah complexes. We can't afford to take our world's problems lightly. But we certainly can't afford to take ourselves too seriously. In that spirit, Gentle Reader, I offer you as a send-off—perhaps even a send-up—a summary of what I think about black public intellectuals and our critics. Since we're not, for the most part, eligible for Oscars, Grammys, or Emmys, consider these the Envys, given to recipients of the First Annual Awards for Black Public Intellectuals and Their Critics.

The Cheaper By the Dozen Award. This award is given to Adolf Reed and Eric Lott, two very smart, if mean-spirited, scholars who revel in ad hominem and ad feminem arguments. Reed wrote an essay about black public intellectuals in the *Village Voice*, heaping personal attacks on me and bell hooks ("little more than hustlers"), Cornel West (whom Reed in the past called "a thousand miles wide and about two inches deep"), Robin Kelley, and Skip Gates. Reed called me and West "running dogs" for Farrakhan in another *Voice* article (but we must not be too well heeled—we still didn't get a chance to speak at the Million Man March!). Reed's bitter commentary seems based more on a writer's level of success with the public than on anyone's actual ideas, since he is so damn mad at so many different thinkers!

Lott, too, has taken to personal attacks, especially in the left journal *Social Text*, where he called West a sellout, and in the journal *Transition*, where he labeled my work "middlebrow imbecilism" (just to think, most people have to meet me twice to draw that conclusion). For both writers, we black public intellectuals just aren't radical enough. But isn't that argument worn out by now? At their worst, Reed and Lott prove that the left continues to do what it seems to do best: self-destruct! The left holds firing squads in a circle, while our real "enemies"–the radical right-wingers who detest every bone in our progressive heads (I'm sorry, I mean bodies)–get off scot-free!

The Elijah Complex Award. This award is named after the biblical figure who cried, "I, even only I, am left," proclaiming himself the only true prophet in town. It goes to the undeniably brilliant bell hooks for the numerous times she's told us, in writing, in public, or in conversation, how she's the only black intellectual to talk about class, or the only black on a panel to get the deeper dimensions of the topic of conversation, or one of the few black feminists who's a serious intellectual. Somebody tell bell that God told Elijah, "Sorry, but there are 7,000 others like you still around." Well, maybe there aren't that many black feminists and serious intellectuals who talk about class, and about race, and gender and sex, too, but there are a whole lot more than bell seems to be aware of. Please, somebody give her a list!

The Spike Lee/Terry Mcmillan Award for Shameless Self-Promotion. Okay, I'm the recipient of this award, for calling newspapers, television and radio stations, magazines, and other venues to tell them why they needed to review my book, or have me on to talk about my work. I can't believe I'm telling this. After all, I wanted people to believe my name was so hot that folk just couldn't stand to run special issues of journals, assemble conferences, or do shows on the matters that I address without me. And you thought the black public intellectual's job was easy. Listen, if there are any publishers, magazine editors, or television producers reading, I'd like to tell you about my latest book . . .

The Golda Meir "Humility Is My Strong Suit" Award. Meir once said, "Stop being humble, you're not that great." This goes to the very talented Cornel West, who genuinely is very humble, but who slipped–and don't we all–and reminded us. (My pastor once said to me, aware of my pride in my humility, "The moment you announce you're humble, you no longer are.") This award is also in honor of West's three-piece suit–a nod to W.E.B. Du Bois's Victorian duds–the armor that West slips into every day to fight the good fight. Only problem is, he made a lot of people mad when he said that, generally speaking, black intellectuals these days dress so shabbily. Since most black intellectuals can't pony up for nineteenth-century gear–or, for that matter, most twentieth-century high fashion–the only hope is for J.C. Penney to recruit West to design affordable clothes for private intellectuals. (Be careful, though, of all those low-paying sweatshops, they almost ruined TV personality Kathie Lee Gifford's clothing empire.)

The Moses "Who Me? I Can't Talk" Award. This goes to Robin D.G. Kelley, a New York University historian and cultural critic. He is, without question, one of the most gifted scholars of any generation, of any discipline, of any school, writing today. Kelley is ridiculously well rounded: a gourmet cook, an excellent father, a devoted husband, a committed mentor to graduate students, and an indefatigable researcher and writer. But he won't own up to his gift to clearly explain complex stuff in public. Given all the crap out here (uh, I wasn't referring to my crap), we need Kelley's passionately intelligent voice. To show you what a sacrificial—oops, I mean, helpful—public intellectual I can be, I once reluctantly accepted an assignment that was first offered to Kelley. The second time I appeared on the *Oprah Winfrey* show happened because Kelley turned them down and recommended me. Listen, if it had been anybody but Kelley (not me, mind you, I'm above the fray), the *Oprah* staff could have asked us to speak about birds, and we would have put on some Charlie Parker records, rented a few Tweetie and Sylvester tapes for inspiration, and become an ornithologist overnight. I've got the solution: let's introduce Kelley to R&B sensation R. Kelly. The next time we see him, he'll be known as "R.D.G., That's Kelley you see," and he'll be saying, "I don't see nothin' wrong with a little pub in *Time*."

The "I'm Not a Prophet, But I Play One on TV" Award.   This goes to Christians like West, James Cone, and myself, and to those inspired by Buddhist spirituality, like bell hooks. We all use the term "prophet" in one way or another. Although you won't catch us saying so, we sometimes mean it to apply to ourselves. Hold on. Let's be honest here. This probably applies to *all* public intellectuals, who fancy themselves prophets of a sort. We mean well, but hey, I guess we've got to realize that real prophets—of whom there are precious few—lead much more dangerous, sacrificial lives. Don't get me wrong, we've received our share of threats, nasty letters, vile communication, and hateful responses from unhappy readers, viewers, or listeners. And we are, well, deeply sacrificial, and, occasionally, prophetic. But when I think of a prophet like Martin Luther King Jr., we just don't cut it. He spent his life paying the price for the title. Plus, King made something like $200,000 a year in speaking engagements and gave nearly every penny of it to the SCLC, keeping only $4,000 to supplement his $6,000 a year salary at his church. Black public intellectuals nowadays can make anywhere from $100,000 to over $1 million a year. We say critical things in public, a lot of people hate us for it, we often act brave. But we profit while we prophet.

The Barbara Mandrell "I Was a Public Intellectual When Public Intellectuals Weren't Cool" Award.   Angela Davis wins this, hands down. A long time ago—when gangsta rappers had the bourgeois blues in their diapers while she was stepping to the revolution; when most celebrated intellectuals were eating their Wheaties, going to Jack and Jill, and courting in the front parlor while she was applying Marcuse to social misery; when more-radical-than-thou critics were enjoying the creature comforts that stoke their dizzy nostalgia for marginality while she was taking three squares in a cramped cell; and when most postfeminists were getting pedicures to put their best foot forward at the debutante while she wore jungle boots at the front line of class warfare—Angela Davis lived what we mean by black public intellectual. She continues to embody that. And she still fine!

The "Excuse the Accents But I'm a Wanna-Beatles" Award. This goes to Paul Gilroy, a black British critic who, in his book, *The Black Atlantic,* has brilliantly forced Americans to think about black identity in an international context. So what's the problem with this latest British invasion? Well, Gilroy just plain trashes most black American intellectuals, often calling us "wrong" for no compelling reason. And for a thinker who spends a lot of time talking about hybridity—meaning that black identity is complex and varied—he completely ignores black American intellectuals who talk about these issues with sophistication and skill. Plus, Gilroy pretty much disses any form of ethnic solidarity, failing to see how that solidarity has often been a means of black survival. After all, black folk weren't oppressed as individuals; we were oppressed because of our group identity.

It's painful to see Gilroy rake black folk over the coals in public lectures. He just doesn't get it. Part of the deference paid to him has to do with his ties to England, a place America still cowers before intellectually. White folk love to hear that colonial accent employed to dog black rappers, public intellectuals, and all the other Negroes who don't measure up. Gilroy may have the black Atlantic down pat; it's the black specific that he needs to bone up on.

The "Hey, Don't Compare Black Intellectuals to Jewish Intellectuals, Because They're Not That Good" Award. This award goes to critics William Phillips and Leon Wieseltier. Phillips noted in *Partisan Review* how the New York intellectuals, a large number of whom were Jewish, didn't stoop to the crass, pop cultural stuff that black intellectuals have gained notoriety for. And unlike black intellectuals, Phillips says, Jewish intellectuals weren't obsessed with (in fact, they didn't even talk about) their Jewish ethnicity or about race. And he's bragging about that?

Wieseltier is painfully transparent. His vicious attack on Cornel West in the *New Republic* is a bitter piece of calumny, a screed motivated in large part by jealousy. But Wieseltier's sledgehammer approach to West's work seems to package an even uglier view of the black–Jewish conflict: by setting West up as the premier black intellectual, and then knocking him down, Wieseltier is knocking the black intellectual enterprise in general. He does so, in part, by arguing that West's use of the Hebrew prophets is ill-fated and dim-witted; Wieseltier, in effect, is rescuing sacred Jewish texts and teachers from what he seems to think is West's inferior intelligence.

But those texts and teachers need to be rescued from Wieseltier's nasty grip. After all, the best of Jewish sacred traditions counsels wise, balanced criticism, not the sort of wholesale bludgeoning Wieseltier practices. Although we often forget it, this critical juncture of head and heart is where blacks and Jews can still embrace.

The "Do As I Say, Not As I Do" Award. This goes to talented Princeton historian Sean Wilentz, who wrote a critique of black public intellectuals in *Dissent.* Really, it was mostly about Cornel West; when he referred to me and bell hooks, it was as "another writer." That little glitch, and Wilentz's commentary, show several things. One, that white folk often choose one black to be the designated hitter, losing sight of other players, reinforcing what Zora Neale Hurston termed the "Pet Negro" system that they despise but help perpetuate. Two, by focusing on one black in what is at least a generational phenomenon, he slights the diversity of opinion, status, and style among black public intellectuals, which allows him to make generalizations that don't hold up under closer investigation.

Three, Wilentz worries that fame, fortune, and celebrity will corrupt black intellectuals. In the attempt to help black public intellectuals avoid such seductions, why wasn't Wilentz writing about black intellectual work a decade ago, before the market mandated it, before celebrity occasioned it? He would then look like a critic motivated by nothing save the best interests of black intellectual life, the academy, and so on. As it stands, he's the big winner. Since writing in *Dissent* (a public intellectual venue) about the pitfalls of too much press and exposure, he's written for the *New Yorker*, an even larger public intellectual organ, and gained more opportunity to express his views in public. I think Wilentz owes black public intellectuals some royalties!

The "Hoops At Harvard" Award.   This award goes to Henry Louis Gates Jr. Skip said he feels like the coach of the Dream Team, luring to Harvard such stars as Cornel West and William Julius Wilson to join team members like K. Anthony Appiah, Evelyn Higginbotham, and Orlando Patterson. Let's face it, a lot of people are just plain jealous of what Gates—a gifted scholar, writer, and administrator—has been able to do at Harvard: gather big names at an elite institution to think hard and long about the problems black folk face. They have the juice, and some people just can't stand it: they're smart, sharp, sophisticated scholars. They deserve to be on The Team.

The problem comes when it's said like the other places have, well, scrubs, folk that ought to think about retiring or who can only come off the bench, streak scorers who can't really start at their positions. Boy, look at how the metaphor just goes downhill, Skip. Hey, Princeton's team ain't so bad, and neither is Yale's. I hear Michigan's going to the playoffs this year, and that Emory is one of the teams to watch.

Harvard's is a great team, but maybe it's not the Dream Team. Because then Gates would have to explain why David Levering Lewis—arguably the most virtuosic contemporary black intellectual, what with his books on Africa, the Harlem Renaissance, Martin Luther King, Jr., and W.E.B. Du Bois—isn't signed. Or why Nell Painter, a formidable historian of the South, is missing. He'd have to tell us what happened to the erudite Africanist, V.Y. Mudimbe, or the learned historian of religion, Charles Long. Or why the astonishingly smart Patricia Williams isn't suited up in crimson.

Besides, if Harvard's faculty is really the Dream Team, they have an extra burden: they're expected to win the gold every time. More than that, they can't play every pick-up game (conference, television show, lecture appearance, and the like) they're offered. They can't produce sloppy, insubstantial work. They've got to generate serious, thoughtful, well-wrought books and articles.

And if, as West and Gates have repeatedly claimed, the days of HNIC are over, then both have to do a difficult thing; spread some of the influence and surrender some of the power by which they've managed to affect the careers of other black scholars. Otherwise, saying they don't desire to be HNIC becomes a cover for reinforcing their privileged status.

On the PR front, Skip, you've got to get together with Cornel so he can give you some lessons in Humility 101. (I definitely need to sit in on these as well!) First thing you learn is that from now on you say, "I'm pleased that we're assembling a marvelous collection of scholars here at Harvard. We're certainly not the only place where such good intellectual company may be found, but we're proud to be one of them." Then I'm voting you Coach of the Year. That is, if you can sign Dennis Rodman!

The problems and possibilities of black public intellectuals are huge. We've got a chance to make a difference in the world—something a lot of folk can't say, a chance a lot of scholars don't get. We shouldn't allow pettiness or jealousy to stop us. If black intellectuals keep bickering, bellyaching, and bitterly attacking one another, we'll blow it. And we shouldn't allow the forces and resources of the marketplace to set us against one another. We should be using our minds to shine a light on the real foes of black folk and democracy: poverty, capital flight, right-wing extremists, religious fundamentalists, and the politics of conservatives and neoliberals that hurt the working class and the working poor.

NOTES

CHAPTER 4. THE LIBERAL THEORY OF RACE

1. My argument here is based on the important work of Michael Omi and Howard Winant in *Racial Formation in the United States* (New York: Routledge & Kegan Paul, 1986).

2. Cornel West, "A Genealogy of Modern Racism," in *Prophesy Deliverance! An Afro-American Revolutionary Christianity* (Philadelphia: Westminster, 1982), pp. 47–68; West, *Prophetic Fragments* (Grand Rapids, Mich.: Eerdmans, 1988).

CHAPTER 8. LEONARD JEFFRIES AND THE STRUGGLE FOR THE BLACK MIND

1. Michael Bradley, *The Iceman Inheritance: Prehistoric Sources of Western Man's Racism, Sexism, and Aggression* (New York: Kayode, 1978).

2. Richard King, *African Origin of Biological Psychiatry* (Germantown, Tenn.: Seymour-Smith, 1990).

3. See Frances Cress-Welsing, "The Cress Theory of Color-Confrontation and Racism (White Supremacy)," in Cress-Welsing, *The Isis Papers: The Keys to the Colors* (Chicago: Third World Press, 1991), pp. 1–16.

4. Ibid., p. 4.

5. Ibid., p. 5.

6. Martin Bernal, *Black Athena: The Afroasiatic Roots of Classical Civilization* (New Brunswick, N.J.: Rutgers University Press, 1987).

7. Arthur Schlesinger Jr., *The Disuniting of America: Reflections on a Multicultural Society* (Knoxville, Tenn.: Whittle Communications, 1991).

CHAPTER 10. THE LABOR OF WHITENESS, THE WHITENESS OF LABOR, AND THE PERILS OF WHITEWISHING

1. There is a growing literature on the socially constructed meanings of whiteness. For some of the best of this literature, see David Roediger, *The Wages of Whiteness: Race and the Making of the American Working Class* (New York: Verso, 1991); David Roediger, *Towards the Abolition of Whiteness: Essays on Race, Politics, and Working Class History* (New York: Verso, 1994); Theodore W. Allen, *The Invention of the White Race: Volume One: Racial Oppression and Social Control* (New York: Verso, 1994); Fred Pfeil, *White Guys: Studies in Postmodern Domination and Difference* (New York: Verso, 1995); Jessie Daniels, *White Lies: Race, Class, Gender, and Sexuality in White Supremacist Discourse* (New York: Routledge, 1997); Matt Wray and Annalee Newitz, eds., *White Trash: Race and Class in America* (New York: Routledge, 1997); Michelle Fine, Lois Weis, Linda C. Powell, and L. Mun Wong, eds., *Off White: Readings on Race, Power, and Society* (New York: Routledge, 1997).

2. Renato Rosaldo, *Culture and Truth: The Remaking of Social Analysis* (Boston: Beacon, 1983, 1993), pp. 68–87.

3. For a small sample of such criticism, see Todd Gitlin, *The Twilight of Common Dreams: Why America Is Wracked by Culture Wars* (New York: Metropolitan Books, 1995); Michael Tomasky, *Left for Dead: The Life, Death, and Possible Resurrection of Progressive Politics in America*

(New York: Free Press, 1996); Arthur Schlesinger Jr., *The Disuniting of America* (Whittle Direct Books, 1991); and Richard Bernstein, *The Dictatorship of Virtue: Multiculturalism and the Battle for America's Future* (New York: Knopf, 1994).

4. See Michael Eric Dyson, *Reflecting Black: African-American Cultural Criticism* (Minneapolis: University of Minnesota Press, 1993); *Making Malcolm: The Myth and Meaning of Malcolm X* (New York: Oxford University Press, 1994); *Between God and Gangsta Rap: Bearing Witness to Black Culture* (New York: Oxford University Press, 1996); and *Race Rules: Navigating the Color Line* (New York: Addison-Wesley, 1996).

5. Tomasky, *Left for Dead*, pp. 10, 15–17.

6. Roediger, *The Wages of Whiteness* and *Towards the Abolition of Whiteness*.

CHAPTER 12. THE PLIGHT OF BLACK MEN

1. For a look at the contemporary plight of black men, especially black juvenile males, see *Young, Black, and Male in America: An Endangered Species*, ed. Jewelle Taylor Gibbs (Dover, Mass.: Auburn House, 1988).

2. See William Julius Wilson, *The Truly Disadvantaged: The Inner City, the Underclass, and Public Policy* (Chicago: University of Chicago Press, 1987).

3. See Wilson, *The Truly Disadvantaged*. For Charles Murray's views on poverty, welfare, and the ghetto underclass, see his influential book, *Losing Ground: American Social Policy, 1950–1980* (New York: Basic, 1984).

4. This section on gangs is informed by the work of Mike Davis in *City of Quartz* (New York: Verso, 1991).

CHAPTER 15. "GOD ALMIGHTY HAS SPOKEN FROM WASHINGTON, D.C.": AMERICAN SOCIETY AND CHRISTIAN FAITH

1. Stanley Hauerwas and Michael Baxter, "The Kingship of Christ: Why Freedom of Belief Is Not Enough," *DePaul Law Review* 42 (1992).

2. Ibid.

3. Ibid.

4. For a sampling of Hauerwas's criticism of Christian ethical defenses of democracy, see "A Christian Critique of Christian America," in *Community in America: The Challenge of Habits of the Heart*, eds. Charles H. Reynolds and Ralph V. Norman (Berkeley: University of California Press, 1988), pp. 250–265. See also *The Peaceable Kingdom: A Primer in Christian Ethics* (Notre Dame, Ind.: University of Notre Dame Press, 1983), pp. 12–13, 111. For claims about prophetic black Christianity's contention that democracy is a fundamental norm of prophetic black Christianity, see Cornel West, *Prophesy Deliverance! An Afro-American Revolutionary Christianity* (Philadelphia: Westminster Press, 1982), pp. 18–19.

5. George Will, "Scalia Missed Point but Made Right Argument on Separation of Religion," *Durham Morning Herald*, Apr. 22, 1990, p. 5. I am not suggesting that Hauerwas's treatment of the First Amendment is limited to this essay, or that the tension between church and state, and religion and politics, is a new subject for him, or one exclusively pursued in this essay. Anyone familiar with Hauerwas's work will know of his long-standing views on such matters. See in particular Hauerwas's books, *A Community of Character: Toward a Constructive Christian Ethic* (Notre Dame, Ind.: University of Notre Dame Press, 1981); *The Peaceable Kingdom: A Primer in Christian Ethics* (Notre Dame, Ind.: University of Notre Dame Press, 1983); *Against the Nations: War and Survival in a Liberal Society* (Minneapolis: Winston-Seabury, 1985); and *Christian Existence Today: Essays on Church, World, and Living In-Between* (Durham, N.C.: Labrinth, 1987). I am treating, however, the specific context of Hauerwas's (and Baxter's) remarks as they relate to points they make about Will's interpretation of the First Amendment.

6. Hauerwas and Baxter, "The Kingship of Christ."

7. See Walter Berns, "Religion and the Founding Principle," in *The Moral Foundations of the American Republic*, ed. Robert H. Horwitz (Charlottesville: University Press of Virginia, 1986), p. 208.

8. See Bernard Bailyn, *The Ideological Origins of the American Revolution* (Cambridge: Belknap Press of Harvard University, 1967), p. 260. Also see Martin Marty, *Pilgrims in Their Own Land: 500 Years of Religion in America* (New York: Penguin, 1984), pp. 162–163.

9. James Madison, quoted in Bailyn, *The Ideological Origins of the American Revolution*, p. 260.

10. Ibid.

11. See Berns, "Religion and the Founding Principle," p. 220.

12. Ibid.

13. Berns, "Religion and the Founding Principle," pp. 219–225. For an exposition on Locke's views of Christianity, see Michael P. Zuckert, "Locke and the Problem of Civil Religion," in *The Moral Foundations of the American Republic* (Charlottesville: University Press of Virginia, 1986), pp. 181–203.

14. For Madison on religion as opinion, see Marty, *Pilgrims in Their Own Land*, p. 163.

15. Thomas Jefferson, quoted in Hauerwas and Baxter, "The Kingship of Christ," p. 4.

16. As Robert Bellah defines it in "The Idea of Practices in Habits: A Response," in *Community in America*, eds. Reynolds and Norman, Constantinianism is the danger that "Christianity will be used instrumentally for the sake of creating political community but to the detriment of its own authenticity" (p. 277). As Hauerwas understands the term (building on the work of John Howard Yoder), which is drawn from Constantine's conversion to Christianity, it is the assumption that "Christians should or do have social and political power so they can determine the ethos of society.... Constantine is the symbol of the decisive shift in the logic of moral argument when Christians ceased being a minority and accepted Caesar as a member of the church." See Hauerwas, "A Christian Critique of Christian America," in *Community in America*, eds. Reynolds and Norman, p. 260.

17. See Hauerwas's works cited in notes 15 and 16.

18. For the pressure these groups brought to bear upon the colonies for freedom of religion, see Bailyn, *The Ideological Origins of the American Revolution*, pp. 257–258.

19. Berns, "Religion and the Founding Principle," p. 206.

20. Interestingly, Hauerwas raises the possibility of challenging the ideals that underlay the Jonestown community, but only through intellectual or religious debate or criticism of the community; even in light of the atrocities committed there, he doesn't entertain the possibility of state intervention, or active Christian intervention, to protect the exploited victims of Jim Jones's practices. He says in "On Taking Religion Seriously: The Challenge of Jonestown," in *Against the Nations: War and Survival in a Liberal Society* (San Francisco: Harper & Row, 1985), p. 103: "Our tragedy is that there was no one internal or external to that community able to challenge the false presuppositions of Jones's false ideals. Our continuing tragedy is that our reactions to and our interpretations of the deaths of Jonestown reveal accurately how we lack the convictions to counter the powers that reigned there." On the other hand, John Bennett sees Jonestown as an indication that freedom of religion is not absolute and as an example of the difficulty of determining when and if state intervention into religious practices should occur. Unlike Hauerwas, however, he concedes the possibility that state intervention is a plausible course of action under admittedly difficult-to-define circumstances. In "Church and State in the United States," in *Reformed Faith and Politics*, ed. Ronald H. Stone (Washington, D.C.: University Press of America, 1983), p. 122, Bennett says: "That ... religious freedom from any limitation by the state is not absolute is well illustrated by the terrible events in Jonestown. After those events it is easy to see there should have been protection of people against such exploitation and even lethal abuse by a religious leader, but it is not easy to say exactly at what point and by what method the state should have entered the picture."

21. This view among the Founders is characterized in Martin Marty's summary of Benjamin Franklin's views on established religion in Marty, *Pilgrims in Their Own Land*, p. 158: "Yet [Franklin] attacked churchly establishment: when a religion was good, it would support

itself. If a religion could not support itself and God did not care to come to its aid, it was a bad sign if then the members had to call on government for help."

22. Bennett, "Church and State in the United States," pp. 121–122.

23. It must be admitted that religion under the First Amendment becomes a matter of private choice versus public coercion, but that meaning of privacy is not in question here. Rather, it is whether religion under the First Amendment is rendered necessarily and exclusively private without the possibility of its public expression.

24. Of course, Hauerwas and Baxter might argue that the Founders viewed religion primarily as an aid, and not a critic, of the government. That may be the case, but as they point out in regard to the freedom of religion in their discussion of Will earlier in their essay, the intent of the Founders is not as important as what has occurred in practice. Similarly, what has occurred in practice is that persons and groups have appealed to their religious beliefs to challenge American government, ranging from the civil rights movement to antinuclear activists.

25. Marty, *Pilgrims in Their Own Land*, pp. 155–156.

26. Ibid., p. 157.

27. Ibid., p. 158.

28. George Washington, quoted in Berns, "Religion and the Founding Principle," p. 213.

29. Jefferson, quoted in Berns, "Religion and the Founding Principle," pp. 217–218.

30. Ibid., p. 213.

31. Admittedly this distinction between functional and moral subordination doesn't completely resolve the tensions created by conflicts of conscience over legally established political practices. In such cases, of course, it is clear that moral insubordination takes precedence; but the violation of the law in the name of conscience results in the Christian acknowledging the conflict created by her religious beliefs by accepting the penalty of breaking the law until the law is changed, either as a result of civil disobedience or through shifted public consensus, or reconstructed public practice, later reflected in law. The examples of Christian participation in the civil rights movement, feminist movements, and antinuclear war movements stand out.

32. For instance, Ronald Thiemann has argued that Hauerwas represents one of two unacceptable options in developing an effective public Christian response to the crises of North American civilization. In characterizing the first option, represented in the thinking of theologian Paul Lehmann, Thiemann, in *Constructing a Public Theology: The Church in a Pluralistic Culture* (Louisville, Ky.: Westminster/John Knox, 1991), summarizes Lehmann's position, expressed by Lehmann in an essay entitled "Praying and Doing Justice": "Arguing out of the Reformed tradition's close association of faith with obedience, Lehmann asserts that proper worship always has as its goal the accomplishment of justice in the world. The righteousness of faith must result in transformative justice within the public realm. Thus Christian worship is essentially political, and the *lietourgia* of the church extends naturally and directly into political action" (p. 114). The second option is represented by Hauerwas in his book, *A Community of Character*. According to Thiemann, Hauerwas contends that "by being faithful to the narratives that shape Christian character, the church will witness to a way of life that stands apart from and in criticism of our liberal secular culture. Christian worship, then, must be an end in itself directed solely toward the cultivation of those peculiar theological virtues that mark the church as a distinctive community" (p. 114). But Thiemann concludes that neither of these options "provides us with the theological resources we need to face the distinctive challenge presented to North American Christians" (p. 114). He continues: "Neither the politicization of worship nor its sectarian separation from public life will suffice in our current situation. . . . We must find a middle way between the reduction of the Christian gospel to a program of political action and the isolation of that gospel from all political engagement" (p. 114). And in an essay, "Justice as Participation: Public Moral Discourse and the U. S. Economy," in *Community in America*, in which he clarifies the position of the National Conference of Catholic Bishops in their pastoral letter on the economy, David Hollenbach juxtaposes their belief that "the church has a responsibility to help shape the life of society as a whole" to Hauerwas's position on such matters (p. 220). Hollenbach says: "Hauerwas concludes that the church should cease and de-

sist from the attempt to articulate universal moral norms persuasive to all members of a plu-ralistic society. . . . [The letter's] disagreement with Hauerwas is with his *exclusive* concern with the quality of the witness of the Christian community's own life. In the traditional categories of Ernest Troeltsch, the bishops refuse to take the 'sectarian' option of exclusive reliance on the witness of the Christian community that Hauerwas recommends" (p. 220).

33. Hauerwas and Baxter, "The Kingship of Christ," p. 11.

34. Ibid., p. 14.

35. Stanley Fish, "There's No Such Thing as Free Speech, and It's a Good Thing, Too," in *Debating P.C.*, ed. Paul Berman (New York: Dell, 1992), p. 241.

36. Ibid.

37. Ibid., pp. 241–242.

38. Quoted in Thiemann, *Constructing a Public Theology*, p. 24.

39. Fish, "There's No Such Thing as Free Speech, and It's a Good Thing, Too," p. 242.

40. Ibid.

41. Ibid.

42. Ibid., p. 243.

43. Ibid.

44. Hauerwas and Baxter, "The Kingship of Christ," p. 10.

45. Ibid., p. 17.

46. Ibid., pp. 17–18.

47. This is not to deny universal dimensions of Christian faith. It is to challenge essen-tialist notions of Christian identity fostered by references to church without spelling out the church's social location, who its members are, under what conditions they practice their be-lief, what historical factors have shaped their faith, and so on.

48. I understand "black church" as shorthand to symbolize the views of black Christianity. The black church is certainly not homogeneous, and I shall be focusing on the prophetic di-mensions of black religious faith. Hauerwas and Baxter's failure to take the black church seri-ously is part of a larger pattern that has rendered the black church invisible for most of its his-tory. Even investigations of American religion have usually, until quite recently, excluded black religion as a central force in American life. As C. Eric Lincoln, in *Race, Religion and the Continu-ing American Dilemma* (New York: Hill & Wang, 1984), says, the "religious situation is structured in such a way that any investigation of religion in America has usually meant the religion of white Americans, unless 'Negro,' 'folk,' or 'black' religion was specifically mentioned" (p. 123). And as Charles Long says in *Significations: Signs, Symbols, and Images in the Interpretation of Religion* (Philadelphia: Fortress Press, 1986): "In short, a great many of the writings and discussions on the topic of American religion have been consciously or unconsciously ideological, serving to enhance, justify, and render sacred the history of European immigrants in this land. Indeed this approach to American religion has rendered the religious reality of non-Europeans to a state of invisibility, and thus the invisibility of the non-European in America arises as a funda-mental issue of American history at this juncture" (p. 149).

49. I have in mind here the large number of black ministers among current members of Congress, continuing a tradition in this century established by leaders such as Adam Clay-ton Powell; the activity of black church leaders in the civil rights movement and the politi-cal movements it gave rise to, especially the presidential campaigns of Jesse Jackson; and the large number of black churchpersons affiliated with historically black institutions of higher education. In each area, the black church has supplied many of these persons the principles they have appealed to in making the claims of black equality, justice, and free-dom to the larger American public. For two examples, see Charles Hamilton's biography of Adam Clayton Powell, *Adam Clayton Powell Jr.: The Political Biography of an American Dilemma* (New York: Atheneum, 1991), and Roger Hatch, *Beyond Opportunity: Jesse Jackson's Vision for America* (Philadelphia: Fortress, 1988).

50. Cornel West, *Prophetic Fragments* (Grand Rapids, Mich.: Eerdmans, 1988), pp. 22–23.

51. See Mechal Sobel, *Trabelin' On: The Slave Journey to an Afro-Baptist Faith* (Princeton: Princeton University Press, 1988; original ed., 1979), and James Washington, *Frustrated Fel-lowship: The Black Baptist Quest for Social Power* (Macon, Ga.: Mercer University Press, 1986).

52. Sobel, *Trabelin' On,* p. 85.

53. Ibid., p. 85; and Bailyn, *The Ideological Origins of the American Revolution,* pp. 261–262.

54. I do not mean by any measure to romanticize the religious dissenters. Although they fought against slavery, they fought more effectively, desperately, and consistently for their own religious freedom, largely out of self-interest.

55. For instance, John Allen pointed out the hypocrisy of his fellow countrymen making claims to colonial freedom while simultaneously denying liberty to slaves, employing religious terms like "sacred," "praying," and "fasting" to drive home his point. He said: "Blush ye pretended votaries for freedom! ye trifling patriots! who are making a vain parade of being advocates for the liberties of mankind, who are thus making a mockery of your profession by trampling on the sacred natural rights and privilege of Africans; for while you are fasting, praying, nonimporting, nonexporting, remonstrating, resolving, and pleading for a restoration of your charter rights, you at the same time are continuing this lawless, cruel, inhuman, and abominable practice of enslaving your fellow creatures" (quoted in Bailyn, *The Ideological Origins of the American Revolution,* p. 240). And Isaac Backus pressed arguments for the religious dissenters to be released from the bondage of the Church of England, asserting that civil and religious liberty were one. Backus tirelessly proclaimed that the church of Massachusetts "has declared the Baptists to be irregular, therefore the secular power still *force* them to support the worship which they conscientiously dissent from," and that "many who are filling the nation with cry Of LIBERTY and against oppressors are at the same time themselves violating that dearest of all rights, LIBERTY OF CONSCIENCE" (quoted in Bailyn, *The Ideological Origins of the American Revolution,* p. 263).

56. Robert Wuthnow makes helpful distinctions between conservative and liberal versions of civil religion in *The Restructuring of American Religion* (Princeton: Princeton University Press, 1988). About conservative civil religion, Wuthnow says: "On the conservative side, America's legitimacy seems to depend heavily on a distinct 'myth of origin' that relates the nation's founding to divine purposes. According to this interpretation of American history, the American form of government enjoys lasting legitimacy because it was created by Founding Fathers who were deeply influenced by Judeo-Christian values" (pp. 244–245). Wuthnow also states that conservative civil religion "generally grants America a special place in the divine order" and that the idea of "evangelizing the world is in fact a much-emphasized theme in conservative civil religion" (p. 247). He contends that despite "formal separation between the kingdom of God and the kingdom of man, the 'two kingdoms' doctrine in conservative civil religion also confers a strong degree of divine authority on the existing mode of government" (p. 248). Conservative civil religion also grants "capitalism a high degree of legitimacy by drawing certain parallels between capitalist economic principles and biblical teachings" (p. 248).

Liberal civil religion, however, makes little "reference to the religious views of the Founding Fathers" and doesn't "suggest that America is God's chosen nation" (p. 250). Liberal civil religion "focuses less on the nation as such, and more on humanity in general" (p. 250). Wuthnow says that rather than "drawing specific attention to the distinctiveness of the Judeo-Christian tradition, liberal civil religion is much more likely to include arguments about basic human rights and common human problems" (p. 250). Liberal civil religionists also "appeal to broader values that transcend American culture and, indeed, challenge some of the nationalistic assumptions it incorporates" (p. 253). The liberal "version of American civil religion taps into a relatively deep reservoir of sentiment in the popular culture about the desirability of peace and justice" (p. 253). As a result, Wuthnow mentions, "religious leaders who champion these causes may detract from the legitimacy of the current U.S. system rather than contribute to it" (p. 254).

It would be good for Hauerwas and Baxter to keep the distinctions between the two versions of civil religion in mind when making claims about its "counterfeit" religious status. Although it probably wouldn't persuade them to change their views, it would nonetheless help them make crucial distinctions about the varying functions of civil religion as it is employed and exercised by different spheres of the citizenry, and even by different branches of Christianity.

57. Long, *Significations*, p. 152.

58. Ibid.

59. Ibid.

60. Ibid., pp. 152–153.

61. Of course, King's later beliefs about the necessity for radical social, economic, and moral transformation of American democracy presented a serious challenge to extant political arrangements. See James Cone, *Martin and Malcolm and America: A Dream or a Nightmare* (Maryknoll, N.Y.: Orbis, 1991), especially pp. 213–243.

62. Michael Eric Dyson, "Martin Luther King Jr., The Evil of Racism, and the Recovery of Moral Vision," in *Union Seminary Quarterly Review* 44 (1990): 88–91.

63. Gen. 50:20 (Revised Standard Version).

64. Quoted in Martin Luther King Jr., *Stride toward Freedom* (New York: Harper & Brothers, 1958), p. 160.

65. See William Safire's comments on the attempts by both Democrats and Republicans to use God's name "as a symbol for the other side's immorality, much as the American flag was used in previous campaigns as a symbol for the other side's lack of patriotism," in "God Bless Us," *New York Times*, Aug. 27, 1992, p. A23.

66. Fish, "There's No Such Thing as Free Speech, and It's a Good Thing, Too," p. 243.

67. See, for instance, Martin Luther King's discussion of his disappointment with the white church in *A Testament of Hope: The Essential Writings of Martin Luther King Jr.*, ed. James M. Washington (San Francisco: Harper & Row, 1986), pp. 345–346.

68. See King's response to white clergymen who deemed his actions in Birmingham, Alabama, as "unwise and untimely," in his famous "Letter from Birmingham City Jail," in *A Testament of Hope: The Essential Writings of Martin Luther King Jr.* (San Francisco: Harper & Row, 1986), pp. 289–302.

69. Ernest T. Campbell, *Locked in a Room with Open Doors*.

70. Hauerwas and Baxter, "The Kingship of Christ," p. 18.

71. Ibid., p. 19.

72. Ibid., p. 21.

73. Ibid., p. 22.

74. Denis Mack Smith, *Mussolini: A Biography* (New York: Vintage Books, 1982), p. 161.

75. James Hastings Nichols, *Democracy and the Churches* (Philadelphia: Westminster Press, 1951), p. 186.

76. Nichols, *Democracy and the Churches*, p. 182; and Smith, *Mussolini*, p. 65.

77. Nichols, *Democracy and the Churches*, p. 183.

78. Smith, *Mussolini*, pp. 159, 163.

79. Ibid., pp. 159–161.

80. Smith, *Mussolini*, p. 163; and Nichols, *Democracy and the Churches*, p. 189.

81. Smith, *Democracy and the Churches*, p. 162.

82. I have in mind here liberation theologians who link notions of Christian salvation with sharp forms of social analysis that get at the economic, political, and social forces that mask liberation in concrete form. For just one recent example, see the important work by Franz J. Hinkelammert, *The Ideological Weapons of Death: A Theological Critique of Capitalism*, trans. Phillip Berryman (Maryknoll, N.Y.: Orbis, 1986).

Also, it seems that Hauerwas's desire to make the church more socially relevant is better served by citing the work of black, feminist, and liberation theologians. Especially in regard to liberation theology, Paul Lauritzen argues that Hauerwas has a great deal in common with Latin American theologian Johannes Metz, particularly regarding each author's use of narrative in their work. In "Is 'Narrative' Really a Panacea? The Use of 'Narrative' in the Work of Metz and Hauerwas," in *Journal of Religion* (1987): 322–339, Lauritzen writes: "Although these writers represent different religious traditions, both rely in significant ways on the category of narrative in their work. . . . Both Metz and Hauerwas are concerned to revitalize Christian faith, both want to make it once again socially relevant, and both are adamant that it retain its distinctiveness. That both should also place such a heavy emphasis on the concept of narrative . . . is not coincidental" (p. 323).

83. I am not suggesting that all of Pius XI's views about the social order are captured in the "Kingship of Christ." His encyclical *Quadragesimo Anno*, issued in 1931, remains one of Catholicism's most impressive statements containing the social teachings of the church, including government's role in society and in the economy, the belief in a just wage, laborers' right to organize, and strong Christian criticism of both capitalism and socialism. But this document must be juxtaposed to Pius XI's antidemocratic actions and statements during the reign of Mussolini. Neither am I suggesting personal perfection as a criterion to determine the acceptability of an intellectual position; in that case, my example of King would be immediately nullified. I am suggesting, however, that these characteristics of Pope Pius XI that I have sketched have direct bearing on the principles and proposals under discussion; there is an organic link, I would argue, between Pope Pius XI's views and practices regarding democracy, Fascism, and the morally subordinate status of the Catholic Church and his recommendations about the Kingship of Christ. His views are suspect precisely because they have to do with his moral and theological failures in his office as pope, the official head of the Catholic Church.

CHAPTER 17. "SOMEWHERE I READ OF THE FREEDOM OF SPEECH": CONSTRUCTING A UNIQUE VOICE

The words "somewhere I read of the freedom of speech" are from King, "I See the Promised Land," in King, A Testament, p. 282.

1. Dyson, "The Cruellest," p. 33.
2. Dyson, *Race Rules*, p. 81.
3. Barth, *Christ and Adam* and *The Word* of *God and the Word of Man*.
4. Pipes, *Say Amen Brother!* Mitchell, *Black Preaching;* Davis, *I Got the Word in Me;* Pitts, *The Old Ship* of *Zion;* Boulware, *The Oratory* of *Negro Leaders;* Thomas, *They Always;* Rosenberg, *Can These Bones Live?* Raboteau, *Fire in the Bones,* pp. 141–151; Hamilton, *The Black Preacher,* Spencer, *Sacred Symphony*.
5. *Wall Street Journal,* Nov. 9, 1990, pp. A1, 6; *New York Times,* Nov. 10, 1990, p. A10; *Atlanta Journal-Constitution,* Nov. 11, 1990, p. A8; *USA Today,* Nov. 13, 1990, p. A11; *Bloomington* [Indiana] *Herald-Times,* Nov. 16, 1990, p. A6; *Chicago Tribune,* Nov. 18, 1990, p. V2; *Washington Post,* Nov. 18, 1990, p. C5; *San Jose Mercury-News,* Nov. 19, 1990, p. A1; *Newsweek,* Nov. 19, 1990, p. 61; *Chronicle* of *Higher Education,* Nov. 21, 1990, p. A8; *New York Amsterdam News,* Dec. 1, 1990, p. 24; *Time,* Dec. 3, 1990, p. 126; *Los Angeles Times,* Dec. 11, 1990, p. E1; *New Republic,* Jan. 28, 1991, pp. 9–11; *Journal* of *American History,* June 1991, pp. 11–123.
6. Higham, "Habits of the Cloth," p. 109.
7. Miller, *Voice* of *Deliverance*.
8. Ibid., esp. pp. 1–28, 41–141.
9. Ibid., esp. pp. 142–158.
10. Lischer, *The Preacher King*.
11. Ibid., esp. pp. 8, 93–118.
12. Ibid., p. 63.
13. Ibid.
14. Ibid., pp. 106–111.
15. Miller, *Voice* of *Deliverance,* pp. 67–85, 186–197.
16. Lischer, *The Preacher King,* esp. p. 14.
17. Miller, *Voice of Deliverance,* pp. 169–197. Also see Miller, "Composing Martin Luther King Jr.," pp. 70–82.
18. Lischer, *The Preacher King,* pp. 112–113.
19. The phrase is in Du Bois, *The Souls of Black Folk,* p. 45.
20. Lewis, "Failing to Know Martin Luther King Jr.," p. 82; Genovese, *The Southern Front,* p. 174.
21. Coretta King claims that her husband, in his "I Have a Dream" speech, "intended to echo some of the Lincolnian language," speaking of Abraham Lincoln's Emancipation Proclamation, to which King made early reference in his oration (C. King, *My Life,* p. 236).

The same speech famously extends Jefferson's majestic words by giving them moral immediacy in the nation's racial drama. King implored America to "live out the true meaning of
its creed, "we hold these truths to be self-evident, that all men are created equal" (King, "I
Have a Dream," in King, *A Testament*, p. 219). King claims to have been profoundly influenced by Gandhi in his beliefs about nonviolence ("Pilgrimage to Nonviolence," in Washington, ed., *A Testament*, pp. 38–39). Keith Miller, however, argues that "Gandhi exerted very
little direct influence on King," since King had "learned nonviolence almost entirely from
American sources" (Miller, *Voice of Deliverance*, p. 88). But however he got hold of Gandhi's
ideas, there is little doubt that they profoundly influenced King's beliefs and behavior. Finally, King paid homage to Du Bois's greatness, and the influence on him of some of Du
Bois's ideas, in King, "Honoring Dr. Du Bois," *Freedom Ways* 8, Spring 1968, reprinted in
W.E.B. Du Bois Speaks, Vol. 1, Speeches and Addresses, 1890–1919 (Foner, ed.).

22. Prathia Hall was the student whose prayer in Albany at a service King attended included
the phrase "I have a dream" (Lischer, *The Preacher King*, p. 93). As Lischer notes, her inspired
prayer was charged by a resonant notion in black communities of a dream or vision animating
civil rights activists. King, moved by her prayer, seized its central metaphor and enlarged its
yearning into a prophetic vision of hope for racial justice. Archibald Carey was the Chicago
preacher, jurist, banker, and politician whose speech to the Republican National Convention
gave King a galvanizing image for his "I Have a Dream" speech (Miller, *Voice of Deliverance*, p.
146). After quoting from "America the Beautiful," Carey rose to oratorical splendor: "That's exactly what we mean–from every mountain side, let freedom ring. Not only from the Green
Mountains and White Mountains of Vermont and New Hampshire; not only from the
Catskills of New York; but from the Ozarks in Arkansas, from the Stone Mountain in Georgia,
from the Blue Ridge Mountains of Virginia–let it ring not only for the minorities of the United
States, but for . . . the disinherited of all the earth–may the Republican Party, under God, from
every mountainside, LET FREEDOM RING!" (cited in Miller, *Voice of Deliverance*, p. 146).
King snatched this passage nearly word for word from Carey to cap his most famous oration.

23. Miller, *Voice of Deliverance*, pp. 192–193.

24. King, *Strength to Love*.

25. Lischer, *The Preacher King*, pp. 4–5.

26. Ibid.

27. In truth, however, the case of Milli Vanilli, the multimillion record selling pop duo who
won 1990's Grammy Award for best new artist, is not as simple as it seems. The duo, composed of black Europeans Rob and Fab, went down in infamy after it was revealed that they
hadn't sung a note on their award-winning album, and they were subsequently forced to return their Grammy. Rob and Fab were talented and handsome performers. Desperate to land
a record deal, they agreed to be the faces for a studio-produced album of songs engineered
by a manipulative white European producer. Neither the duo nor their producer had any idea
that the album would do so well and that it would garner Milli Vanilli international fame and
fortune. Disagreements between the duo and their "producer"–especially over Rob and Fab's
desire to represent their own work on wax–led to a falling out that forced the duo to confess
their mendacity publicly. Despite their extreme embarrassment and shame, Rob and Fab
eventually were able to make an album featuring their own work, proving that they had genuine talent. By then, however, their downfall had eclipsed widespread interest in their work.
Later, they split up, and in 1998, Rob committed suicide after several unsuccessful attempts.
Their story is not simply one of the massive attempt to defraud the public while capitulating
to the seductions of fame, fortune, and women. It is as well a bitter and tragic update of an
old phenomenon: a white music executive exploiting vulnerable black artists for commercial
gain. The tragedy is that Rob and Fab's authentic artistry was buried beneath the scandal of
their misdeed. See "Behind the Music," VH1, March 28, 1999.

28. Carson et al., eds., *The Papers of Martin Luther King Jr.*, Volume 1: *Called to Serve, January 1929–June 1951*, and Volume 2: *Rediscovering Precious Values, July 1951–November 1955*;
Genovese, *The Southern Front*, p. 162.

29. Branch, *Parting the Waters*, p. 66. Branch says that King borrowed his first sermon
from Harry Emerson Fosdick's "Life Is What You Make It."

30. Martin Luther King Jr., Papers Project, "The Student Papers of Martin Luther King Jr.," pp. 28–29; Lewis, _King,_ pp. 37–38; Branch, _Parting the Waters,_ pp. 72, 76; Garrow, "King's Plagiarism," p. 90.

31. Martin Luther King Jr., Papers Project; Genovese, _The Southern Front,_ p. 162.

32. Genovese, _The Southern Front,_ pp. 164–168, 173.

33. Martin Luther King Jr., Papers Project, pp. 23–31.

34. Ibid., p. 27.

35. Genovese, _The Southern Front,_ pp. 157–191, esp. p. 173; Martin Luther King Jr., Papers Project, p. 24. Also see Carson, Holloran, Luker, and Russell, "Martin Luther King Jr., as Scholar."

36. Genovese, _The Southern Front,_ p. 173. It is also interesting to note that during his second fall in Boston as a graduate student, King received a D+ on a philosophy paper, which had scribbled over it caustic comments from his professor. King subsequently earned three straight A's on papers about Descartes, William James, and Mahayana Buddhism (Branch, _Parting the Waters,_ p. 96). As with many other students, the awful embarrassment and ego deflation of a poor grade perhaps drove King to redouble his efforts, or perhaps it reinforced his habit of borrowing others' work to express his ideas.

37. Martin Luther King Jr., Papers Project, p. 29; Garrow, _Bearing the Cross,_ p. 41.

38. Pappas, ed., _Martin Luther King Plagiarism Story._

39. Lewis, "Failing to Know Martin Luther King Jr.," p. 81.

40. Ibid., p. 83.

41. Ibid., p. 85.

42. Ibid., p. 82.

43. Garrow, "King's Plagiarism," p. 86.

44. Ibid.

45. Ibid.

46. Cone, "Martin Luther King Jr., Black Theology-Black Church," pp. 409–420; Cone, "The Theology of Martin Luther King Jr.," pp. 21–39; Cone, _Martin and America_ and _Risks of Faith;_ Baldwin, "Understanding Martin Luther King Jr., Within the Context of Southern Black Religious History," pp. 1–26; Baldwin, "Martin Luther King Jr., the Black Church, and the Black Messianic Vision," _Journal of the Interdenominational Theological Center_ 12, Fall 1984–Spring 1985, pp. 93–108; Baldwin, _There Is a Balm_ and _To Make the Wounded Whole;_ Branch, _Parting the Waters,_ esp. pp. 1–26; Miller, _Voice of Deliverance,_ esp. pp. 13–40, 169–185; Lischer, _The Preacher King._

47. Lewis, "Failing to Know Martin Luther King Jr.," pp. 84–85; Genovese, _The Southern Front,_ p. 175. The second reader of King's dissertation, S. Paul Schilling, denied that there was "favoritism toward black students and therefore a lowering of standards for them," and in response to a question about whether King "was given a free ride because of reverse racism," responded "I would reject that completely" (Thelen, "Conversation Between S. Paul Schilling and David Thelen," pp. 65, 77). It may be true that King's thesis adviser, L. Harold DeWolf, was in King's case a "lax mentor who did not demand of King the analytical precision that might have prepared him for a career of scholarly writing" (Carson, Holloran, Luker, and Russel, "Martin Luther King Jr.," p. 101). But that contradicts what other students knew about DeWolf. "Once he took them under his wing . . . he really worked with them," Cornish Rogers says. "He saw to it that all of them lived up to a certain quality that he demanded. And he kept after them until they did." Furthermore, Rogers rejects the reverse racism argument, saying of DeWolf and Schilling, "I knew how tough they were on me. I had taken courses from both of them." Therefore, it would be both unfair and inaccurate to overlook _the_ plausible reason for DeWolf's strict inattention to King: DeWolf was overburdened as one of the few Boston University professors who was willing to work with black students. Rogers says that DeWolf "took on a lot of dissertations from, especially, black students or others whom other professors would not take on. If you were willing to be guided by him, he would take on students whose topics were not in his field. I got the impression that he helped a lot of folks who had difficulty getting someone to be their readers" (Thelen, "Conversation Between Cornish Rogers and David Thelen," pp. 53–55). Thus, the greater threat

to black students was not racial paternalism, as bad as that might have been, but racist neglect, a far more harmful factor in the intellectual lives of black graduate students.

48. Lischer, *The Preacher King*, p. 58.

49. Garrow, "King's Plagiarism," p. 90.

50. "Moreover, although many black scholars had passed through Boston University's doctoral program in religion, one peculiar and tragic legacy of racism involved the pernicious self-doubts that could have plagued any developing black scholar. Qualities of self-worth, competence, talent, and skill are not developed in a vacuum, but are in part socially constructed and reproduced. In the mid-fifties it is certainly conceivable that a young talented black doctoral student who was uncertain of his real worth, despite the encouragement of his professors and colleagues ... could be tempted to rely on work that had already been accepted and viewed as competent" (Dyson, *Reflecting Black*, p. 242). Also see Jerry Watt's brief but powerful discussion of the sometimes crippling self-doubt and insecurity that can smother even the most able budding scholar. Watts, *Heroism and the Black Intellectual*, p. xii.

51. Garrow, "King's Plagiarism," p. 90.

52. Hegel, *The Philosophy of History* and *Phenomenology of Spirit*. Also see King, *Stride Toward Freedom*, pp. 95, 100–101.

53. Thelen, "Conversation Between Cornish Rogers and David Thelen," p. 50.

54. Ibid.

55. Ibid., pp. 50–51.

56. John Williams captures the significance of the degree for those times when he writes: "And if a young man could take graduate studies in the white universities of the North, his status was increased manyfold. Morehouse College has sent countless numbers of its graduates north where an overwhelming majority of them have made good in professional and academic circles. The A.B. soon enough became almost nothing in terms of status; the M.A. became the target, and finally, the Ph.D. How grand to roll around on the tongue the word 'doctor'! How marvelous to be addressed as 'doctor'!" (Williams, *The King God Didn't Save*, p. 152).

57. Thelen, "Conversation Between S. Paul Schilling and David Thelen," pp. 76–77.

58. Reagon, "Nobody Knows the Trouble I See," pp. 113–117. Reagon says that in black culture, those who straddle "are born in one place, and we are sent to achieve in the larger culture, and in order to survive we work out a way to be who we are in both places or all places we move.... King was a straddler; he was who he was wherever he was—in the African-American church, on the march, in a rally, in jail, at the great and small universities, in Stockholm. We, his people, could look at him and feel him and know that he was one of us. *He succeeded in embracing the sound of our forefathers, and he never left that sound; no matter where he was, he was in the pulpit*" (Ibid., pp. 114, 116).

59. Lischer, *The Preacher King*, p. 58. Lischer says that in "the fifteen years from 1942 to 1957 only five Boston students completed doctoral dissertations on race-related topics. King was not among them."

60. Genovese, *The Southern Front*, p. 173. It should be noted that King is not now known for his facility with Plato, Hegel, formal logic, or modern philosophy—all of which proved to be in his hands little more than rhetorical fodder for Sunday sermons and inspired speeches. As David Lewis writes, King "was not an original philosopher, although, after Morehouse, it was perhaps the thing he most desired to be. There are legions of audiences that spent Sunday mornings, convocation periods, and evenings in auditoriums listening to him rhapsodically enumerate the principal ideas of Western philosophy from Thales to Miletus to Camus.... Such displays of encyclopedic knowledge sprang partly from a Baptist preacher's love of showmanship, and Mike [Martin] was a super actor. Partly, too, this was the venial intellectual arrogance of a young man who held a doctorate from one of the nation's better universities. But there was, undeniably, also an element of self-deception and self-mystification as to his philosophical acumen" (Lewis, *King*, pp. 44–45). King is known, however, for his brilliant abilities to translate the meanings of grand thinkers into the stuff of human action, thus enfleshing ideas with a genius that few others have possessed. It might have done King some good to have wrestled intellectually within the province of ideas that would motivate him to take to the streets out of disgust with merely thinking about the world. Some courses on Gandhi and race

relations might have given him even deeper insight into the nature of the beast he was to confront when he left graduate school. As Marx famously said, many philosophers have thought about the world. The point was to change it. King took that imperative seriously and thus became a derivative philosopher but a world-class activist and a pioneer in social democracy.

61. Cone, *Martin and Malcolm,* p. 30.

62. Ibid., p. 31.

63. Thelen, "Conversation Between Cornish Rogers and David Thelen," pp. 46–49. Also see Garrow, *Bearing,* p. 48; Branch, *Parting the Waters,* pp. 93–94. Apparently, however, these issues were not strongly enough debated for students like George Thomas, who was "one of a tiny minority of Negro students who lost interest in the Dialectical Society precisely because Jim Crow and other political matters were relegated to the joke period [held after the formal meeting]" (Branch, *Parting the Waters,* p. 93).

64. Cone, *Martin and Malcolm,* p. 31.

65. Thelen, "Conversation Between Cornish Rogers and David Thelen," p. 50.

66. Lewis, "Failing to Know Martin Luther King Jr.," p. 85. More exactly Lewis states of King and his professors that "neither he nor they knew who Martin Luther King was then." On that basis, it is easy enough to see that in not knowing who King was then, they had no knowledge of who he would become.

67. "Thin Ice: 'Stereotype Threat' and Black College Students," *Atlantic Monthly,* Aug. 1999, pp. 44–54.

68. Ibid., p. 44.

69. Ibid.

70. Ibid., p. 45.

71. Ibid., p. 46.

72. Oates, *Let the Trumpet Sound,* p. 24.

73. *New York Times,* Nov. 13, 1990, p. A30.

74. Lerner, ed., *Black Women in White America,* pp. 149–193; Jones, *Labor of Love, Labor of Sorrow,* p. 157; Hine, *Hine Sight,* pp. 37–47.

CHAPTER 20. X MARKS THE PLOTS: A CRITICAL READING OF MALCOLM'S READERS

1. These personal and political understandings can be described as paradigms, or theories that explain evidence or account for behavior, that shift over space and time. For a discussion about paradigm shifts in the history of science, see Thomas Kuhn, *The Structure of Scientific Revolutions,* 2d ed. (Chicago: University of Chicago Press, 1970). According to Kuhn, revolutions in science occur when a given paradigm fails to account for an increasing degree of disconfirming evidence, called anomalies. Failure of the paradigm creates a crisis, and can be resolved only with the emergence of a new scientific paradigm. For an application of Kuhn's work to moral philosophy and religious experience, see Jon Gunnemann, *The Moral Meaning of Revolution* (New Haven: Yale University Press, 1979).

2. The lack of a significant body of scholarly literature about Malcolm reveals more about the priorities, interests, and limitations of contemporary scholarship than about his importance as a revolutionary social figure. There is no dearth of interest in Malcolm, however, in the popular press, and though cultural curiosity about him is now undoubtedly at a peak, he has unfailingly provoked popular reflection about his life and career among journalists, activists, and organic intellectuals since his death in 1965. This is made abundantly clear in two book-length bibliographies on Malcolm: Lenwood G. Davis, with the assistance of Marsha L. Moore, comps., *Malcolm X: A Selected Bibliography* (Westport, Conn.: Greenwood, 1984), and Timothy V. Johnson, comp., *Malcolm X: A Comprehensive Annotated Bibliography* (New York: Garland, 1986).

3. For an illuminating discussion of the philosophical issues and problems involved in understanding and explanation in the humanities, see Charles Taylor, "Interpretation and the Sciences of Man," in *Interpretive Social Science: A Reader,* ed. Paul Rabinow and William M. Sullivan (Berkeley: University of California Press, 1979), pp. 25–71.

4. For the notion of thick description, see Clifford Geertz, "Thick Description: Toward an Interpretive Theory of Culture," in *The Interpretation of Cultures* (New York: Basic, 1973).

5. Michael Eric Dyson, "Probing a Divided Metaphor," in *Reflecting Black: African-American Cultural Criticism* (Minneapolis: University of Minnesota Press, 1993), pp. 115–128. For discussion of Malcolm's motivations for his autobiography, and Alex Haley's role in shaping the narrative of Malcolm's life, see also Arnold Rampersad, "The Color of His Eyes: Bruce Perry's *Malcolm* and Malcolm's Malcolm," and Robin D. G. Kelley, "The Riddle of the Zoot: Malcolm Little and Black Cultural Politics During World War II," both in *Malcolm X: In Our Own Image,* ed. Joe Wood (New York: St. Martin's, 1992), pp. 117–134, 155–175, respectively.

6. For more of my comment on other books about Malcolm, see Dyson, "Probing a Divided Metaphor," pp. 115–128.

7. For a good overview and discussion of these groups, see Raymond Hall, *Black Separatism in the United States* (Hanover, N.H.: University Press of New England, 1978).

8. For an excellent discussion of the links between Malcolm X and the Black Power movement, of which he was a precursor, with discussions of SNCC, CORE, and the Black Panthers, see Robert Allen, *Black Awakening in Capitalist America: An Analytic History* (Garden City, N.Y.: Doubleday, 1969), pp. 21–88. For a discussion of the economic programs and comparisons of the social visions of each group, see Hall, *Black Separatism in the United States,* especially pp. 139–196.

9. See especially John Ansbro, *Martin Luther King Jr.: The Making of a Mind* (Maryknoll, N.Y.: Orbis, 1982); Stephen B. Oates, *Let the Trumpet Sound: The Life of Martin Luther King Jr.* (New York: Harper & Row, 1982); and David Garrow, *Bearing the Cross: Martin Luther King Jr., and the Southern Christian Leadership Conference, 1955–1968* (New York: Morrow, 1986).

10. John Henrik Clarke, ed., *Malcolm X: The Man and His Times* (1969; Trenton, N.J.: Africa World Press, 1990).

11. Charles Wilson, "Leadership Triumph in Leadership Tragedy," in *Malcolm X,* ed. Clarke, pp. 36–37.

12. James Boggs, "The Influence of Malcolm X on the Political Consciousness of Black Americans," and Wyatt Tee Walker, "Nothing but a Man," in *Malcolm X,* ed. Clarke, pp. 52, 67.

13. Albert Cleage, "Myths About Malcolm X," in *Malcolm X,* ed. Clarke, p. 15.

14. Oba T'shaka, *The Political Legacy of Malcolm X* (Richmond, Calif.: Pan Afrikan, 1983); Malcolm X, *The End of White World Supremacy: Four Speeches by Malcolm X,* ed. Benjamin Karim [Goodman] (New York: Arcade, 1971).

15. T'shaka, *Political Legacy of Malcolm X,* pp. 244–245.

16. Ibid., pp. 57, 118.

17. Karim, Introduction to Malcolm X, *End of White World Supremacy,* pp. 21–22.

18. Gordon Parks, "Malcolm X: The Minutes of Our Last Meeting," in *Malcolm X,* ed. Clark, p. 120.

19. On his repudiation of the white devil theory, see Malcolm X, with the assistance of Alex Haley, *Autobiography of Malcolm X* (New York: Grove Press, 1965), pp. 362–363. For Malcolm's desire to meet Robeson a month before his death, see Martin Duberman, *Paul Robeson* (New York: Knopf, 1988), p. 528.

20. I take up this issue in "Beyond Essentialism: Expanding African-American Cultural Criticism," in *Reflecting Black,* pp. xiii–xxxiii.

21. The debate about cultural and racial authenticity as it relates to who is able to interpret Malcolm's legacy legitimately has most recently occurred in writer-activist Amiri Baraka's attacks on Spike Lee about Lee's film portrait of Malcolm X before his film appeared. Implicit in Baraka's charges that Lee would not adequately or accurately represent Malcolm is the belief that Baraka's representation of Malcolm is superior. Baraka's hagiographical recollections of Malcolm and his refusal to concede that Lee's claims and representations of him may be equally valid are a prime example of the often insular intellectual climate surrounding debates about Malcolm. The irony here, of course, is that of all current black directors, with the possible exception of John Singleton, Spike Lee appears most suitably disposed to represent a vision of Malcolm that jibes with Baraka's cultural views, given Lee's Afrocentric film and aesthetic vocabulary and his neonationalist cultural perspective.

22. Malcolm X, "Answers to Questions at the Militant Labor Forum," in *By Any Means Necessary: Speeches, Interviews, and a Letter, by Malcolm X,* ed. George Breitman (New York: Pathfinder, 1970), pp. 22–23.

23. See Henry Young's two-volume study, *Major Black Religious Leaders* (Nashville: Abingdon, 1977, 1979).

24. Louis E. Lomax, *When the Word Is Given: A Report on Elijah Muhammad, Malcolm X, and the Black Muslim World* (Cleveland: World, 1963), and *To Kill a Black Man* (Los Angeles: Holloway House, 1968); James H. Cone, *Martin and Malcolm and America: A Dream or a Nightmare?* (Maryknoll, N.Y.: Orbis, 1991); Peter Goldman, *The Death and Life of Malcolm X,* 2d ed. (1973; Urbana: University of Illinois Press, 1979). For a discussion of moral saints, see Susan Wolf, "Moral Saints," *Journal of Philosophy* 8 (1982): 419–439; and Robert Merrihew Adam's response to her essay in *The Virtue of Faith and Other Essays in Philosophical Theology* (New York: Oxford University Press, 1987), pp. 164–173.

25. Of course, the classic treatment of the Black Muslims during the leadership of Elijah Muhammad and Malcolm X is C. Eric Lincoln, *The Black Muslims in America* (Boston: Beacon, 1961, 1973). Also very helpful is E. U. Essien-Udom, *Black Nationalism: A Search for an Identity in America* (Chicago: University of Chicago Press, 1962). For a treatment of the Nation of Islam under Elijah Muhammad and Malcolm X, and it transition to orthodox Islamic practice and belief under Wallace Muhammad as the World Community of al-Islam in the West, see Clifton E. Marsh, *From Black Muslims to Muslims: The Transition from Separatism to Islam, 1930–1980* (Metuchen, N.J.: Scarecrow, 1984). For a historical and analytic treatment of the Nation of Islam, including its history under Elijah and Wallace Muhammad, and its separate revitalization as the second incarnation of the Nation of Islam under Louis Farrakhan, see Martha F. Lee, *The Nation of Islam: An American Millenarian Movement* (Lewiston, N.Y.: Edwin Mellen, 1988).

26. Lomax, *When the Word Is Given,* pp. 87, 68.

27. For an extended review of Cone's book, see my essay "Martin and Malcolm," in *Reflecting Black,* pp. 250–263.

28. Of course, Malcolm's life and thought represented and addressed various aspects of both religious and revolutionary nationalism. In this regard, see John H. Bracey Jr., August Meier, and Elliott Rudwick, eds., *Black Nationalism in America* (Indianapolis: Bobbs-Merrill, 1970), p. 505. Also see Essien-Udom, *Black Nationalism.* For a fine historical treatment of the heyday of black nationalism, see Wilson Jeremiah Moses, *The Golden Age of Black Nationalism, 1850–1925* (Hamden, Conn.: Archon, 1978).

29. Cone, *Martin and Malcolm and America,* p. 151.

30. Ibid., p. 170.

31. Other works explore the relationship between King and Malcolm, along with comparative analyses of other intellectual and religious figures, in a religious and social ethical context. For two fine examples, see Peter Paris, *Black Leaders in Conflict,* 2d ed. (Louisville: Westminster Press/John Knox Press, 1991); and Robert M. Franklin, *Liberating Visions: Human Fulfillment and Social Justice in African-American Thought* (Minneapolis: Augsburg, 1990).

32. Ralph Ellison, quoted in Robert B. Stepto and Michael S. Harper, "Study and Experience: An Interview with Ralph Ellison," in *Chant of Saints: A Gathering of Afro-American Literature, Art, and Scholarship,* ed. Stepto and Harper (Urbana: University of Illinois Press, 1979), p. 458.

33. For insightful treatments of Du Bois, see Arnold Rampersad, *The Art and Imagination of W.E.B. Du Bois* (Cambridge: Harvard University Press, 1976); Gerald Horne, *Black and Red: W.E.B. Du Bois and the Afro-American Response to the Cold War, 1944–1963* (Albany: State University of New York Press, 1986); Manning Marable, *W.E.B. Du Bois: Black Radical Democrat* (Boston: Twayne, 1986); and, of course, the definitive treatment of Du Bois to date, David Levering Lewis, *W.E.B. Du Bois: Biography of a Race, 1868–1919* (New York: Holt, 1993). For the definitive treatment of Booker T. Washington, see Louis Harlan's two volumes: *Booker T. Washington: The Making of a Black Leader, 1856–1901* (New York: Oxford University Press, 1972); and *Booker T. Washington: The Wizard of Tuskegee, 1901–1915* (New York: Oxford University Press, 1983).

34. Lomax, *To Kill a Black Man,* p. 10.

35. George Breitman, "More Than One Way 'To Kill a Black Man,'" in *The Assassination of Malcolm X,* ed. George Breitman, Herman Porter, and Baxter Smith (New York: Pathfinder, 1976), pp. 131–144.

36. Robert Franklin also makes use of Goldman's notion of public moralist in his excellent book *Liberating Vision's,* a comparative study of Booker T. Washington, W.E.B. Du Bois, Malcolm X, and Martin Luther King Jr.

37. There is a swelling literature on the possible plots and theories of how Malcolm was murdered. While the close study of this literature is beyond my purposes here, it certainly constitutes an intriguing category of debate around Malcolm. See, for example, Breitman, Porter, and Smith, eds., *Assassination of Malcolm X;* and Karl Evanzz, *The Judas Factor: The Plot to Kill Malcolm X* (New York: Thunder Mouth Press, 1992).

38. For arguments that Goldman's views about Malcolm's assassination support the official government story, and that the CIA and the Bureau of Special Services (BOSS)—the name of the New York secret police agency at the time of Malcolm's death—were implicated in his assassination, see George Breitman, "A Liberal Supports the Government Version," in *Assassination of Malcolm X,* ed. Breitman, Porter, and Smith, pp. 145–166.

39. Goldman, *Death and Life of Malcolm X,* p. 191.

40. Martin Luther King Jr., quoted in David Halberstam, "When 'Civil Rights' and 'Peace' Join Forces," in *Martin Luther King Jr.: A Profile,* ed. C. Eric Lincoln, rev. ed. (New York: Hill & Wang, 1984), p. 202.

41. Clayborne Carson, "Malcolm and the American State," in *Malcolm X: The FBI File,* ed. David Gallen (New York: Carroll Graf, 1991), p. 18.

42. Ibid.

43. See George Devereux, *Basic Problems of Ethnopsychiatry,* trans. Basia Miller Gulati and George Devereux (Chicago: University of Chicago Press, 1980); Frantz Fanon, *The Wretched of the Earth* (New York: Grove, 1966), and *Black Skin, White Masks* (New York: Grove, 1967); Erich Fromm, *Beyond the Chains of Illusion: My Encounter with Marx and Freud* (New York: Simon & Schuster, 1962); Christopher Lasch, *The Culture of Narcissism* (New York: Warner Books, 1979); Bruce Brown, *Marx, Freud, and the Critique of Everyday Life: Toward a Permanent Cultural Revolution* (New York: Monthly Review Press, 1973); Margaret MacDonald, ed., *Philosophy and Analysis* (Oxford: Blackwell, 1954); and relevant work of the Frankfurt school, including Theodor W. Adorno, Walter Benjamin, Erich Fromm, Max Horkheimer, Herbert Marcuse, and Jürgen Habermas. For a collection of essays by these authors, see Andrew Arato and Eike Gebhardt, eds., *The Essential Frankfurt School Reader* (New York: Continuum, 1982). For a treatment of their work in relation to psychoanalytic theory, see C. Fred Alford, *Narcissism: Socrates, the Frankfurt School, and Psychoanalytic Theory* (New Haven: Yale University Press, 1988).

44. Richard Lichtman, *The Production of Desire: The Integration of Psychoanalysis into Marxist Theory* (New York: Free Press, 1982), p. ix.

45. Ibid., pp. ix–x.

46. Erik H. Erikson, *Gandhi's Truth: On the Origins of Militant Nonviolence* (New York: Norton, 1969). For a more controversial psychobiographical treatment of a historical figure, see Erikson's study of Protestant reformer Martin Luther, *Young Man Luther* (New York: Norton, 1958).

47. Eugene Victor Wolfenstein, *The Victims of Democracy: Malcolm X and the Black Revolution* (1981; London: Free Association Books, 1989).

48. Ibid., pp. 1–2.

49. Ibid., p. xiii.

50. For an important historical examination of white working-class racism, see David R. Roediger, *The Wages of Whiteness: Race and the Making of the American Working Class* (London: Verso, 1991).

51. Other Marxist, socialist, and progressive approaches to race theory and racism attempt to theorize race as a socially, culturally, historically, and politically constructed category that undergoes change over space and time. See, for example, Cornel West, "Marxist Theory and the Specificity of Afro-American Oppression," in *Marxism and the Interpretation of Culture,* ed. Cary Nelson and Lawrence Grossberg (Urbana: University of Illinois Press, 1988), pp.

17–33; Lucius Outlaw, "Toward a Critical Theory of 'Race,'" in *Anatomy of Racism,* ed. David Goldberg (Minneapolis: University of Minnesota Press, 1990), pp. 58–82; Michael Eric Dyson, "The Liberal Theory of Race," and "Racism and Race Theory in the Nineties," in *Reflecting Black,* pp. 132–156; Leonard Harris, "Historical Subjects and Interests: Race, Class, and Conflict," and Lucius Outlaw, "On Race and Class, or, On the Prospects of 'Rainbow Socialism,'" both in *The Year Left 2: An American Socialist Yearbook,* ed. Mike Davis et al. (London: Verso, 1987); and Michael Omi and Howard Winant, *Racial Formation in the United States: From the 1960s to the 1980s* (London: Routledge & Regan Paul, 1986).

52. See Thomas Gossett, *Race: The History of an Idea in America* (Dallas: Southern Methodist University Press, 1965).

53. Wolfenstein, *Victims of Democracy,* p. 37.

54. Bruce Perry, *Malcolm: The Life of a Man Who Changed Black America* (Tarrytown, N.Y.: Station Hill Press, 1991).

55. Ibid., p. ix.

56. Ibid., p. x.

57. Ibid., pp. 41–42.

58. Ibid., p. 54.

59. For further discussion of this subject, see Dyson, "Beyond Essentialism," pp. xiii–xxxiii.

60. For insightful discussions of the predicament of black intellectuals, see, of course, Harold Cruse's pioneering *The Crisis of the Negro Intellectual* (New York: Morrow, 1967); Cornel West, "The Dilemma of the Black Intellectual," *Cultural Critique,* no. 1 (Fall 1985): 109–124; and Jerry Watts, "Dilemmas of Black Intellectuals," *Dissent,* (1) Fall 1989: 501–507.

61. Christian ethicist Katie Cannon writes about the "white academic community's flourishing publishing monopoly on the writing of black history, black thought, and black worldview. Black scholars did not abdicate their roles in these fields to white academicians. Blacks have written monographs, theses, conference papers, proposals, and outlines for books on various aspects of black reality since the 1700s, but white publishers did not give them serious consideration until the 1970s" ("Racism and Economics: The Perspective of Oliver C. Cox," in *The Public Vocation of Christian Ethics,* ed. Beverly W. Harrison, Robert L. Stivers, and Ronald H. Stone [New York: Pilgrim, 1986], p. 121).

62. William James, *The Varieties of Religious Experience* (1902; New York: Penguin, 1982).

63. Lomax, *To Kill a Black Man,* p. 142.

64. Goldman, *Death and Life of Malcolm X,* p. 189.

65. George Breitman, *The Last Year of Malcolm X: The Evolution of a Revolutionary* (New York: Pathfinder, 1967); Malcolm X, *Malcolm X Speaks: Selected Speeches and Statements,* ed. George Breitman (New York: Pathfinder, 1965); *By Any Means Necessary;* and *Malcolm X: The Last Speeches,* ed. Bruce Perry (New York: Pathfinder, 1989).

66. Breitman, *Last Year of Malcolm X,* p. 69.

67. Malcolm X, *By Any Means Necessary,* p. 159.

68. Breitman, *Last Year of Malcolm X,* p. 65.

69. Malcolm X, *By Any Means Necessary,* p. 159.

70. Given the variety and complexity of black nationalist thought, Malcolm could have accommodated and advocated such changes had he had sufficient time to link his broadened sense of struggle to the subsequent social and political activity he inspired. It is important, however, not to overlook the tensions between groups like SNCC and Malcolm while he lived. As Lomax says: ". . . Malcolm was never able to effect an alliance with the young black militants who were then plotting the crisis that is now upon the republic. His trip to Selma was arranged by SNCC people but no alliance resulted. The Black Power people would later raise Malcolm to sainthood but they would not work with him, nor let him work with them, in life" (*To Kill a Black Man,* pp. 157–158).

71. Breitman, *Last Year of Malcolm X,* p. 27.

72. Ibid., p. 34.

73. Malcolm X, *Malcolm X Speaks,* p. 128, quoted in Breitman, *Last Year of Malcolm X,* p. 35.

74. Malcolm X, "The Harlem 'Hate-Gang' Scare," in *Malcolm X Speaks,* p. 65.

75. Ibid., p. 69.

76. Malcolm X, *By Any Means Necessary*, pp. 159–160.

77. See Leon Trotsky, *Leon Trotsky on Black Nationalism and Self-Determination* (New York: Pathfinder, 1978).

78. C. L. R. James, interview in *Visions of History*, ed. MARHO (New York: Pantheon, 1984), p. 270.

79. I do not mean to rule out other genres in which Malcolm's life and accomplishments may be examined. For an example of a science fiction approach to his life and thought, see Kent Smith, *Future X* (Los Angeles: Holloway House, 1989), which appears to have been influenced as much by Schwarzennegger's *Terminator* films as by ideological currents in African-American culture.

CHAPTER 21. MIXED BLESSINGS: MARTIN LUTHER KING, JR., AND THE LESSONS OF AN AMBIGUOUS HEROISM

1. Gary Wills, *Cincinnatus: George Washington and the Enlightenment* (Garden City, N.Y.: Doubleday, 1984), p. 109.

2. Sidney Hook, *The Hero in History: A Study in Limitation and Possibility* (New York: John Day, 1943), p. 153.

3. Ibid., p. 154.

4. For a good social characterization of the figures who surrounded King in the civil rights movement, see Taylor Branch's commanding social history, *Parting the Waters: America in the King Years, 1955–1963* (New York: Simon & Schuster, 1989).

5. This quote is from Benjamin Mays's introduction to Lerone Bennett, *What Manner of Man: A Biography of Martin Luther King Jr.* (Chicago: Johnson, 1976), p. ii.

6. Hook, *The Hero in History*, p. 157.

7. Bennett, *What Manner of Man*, p. 131.

8. James P. Hanigan, *Martin Luther King Jr., and the Foundations of Nonviolence* (New York: University Press of America, 1984), pp. 31–32.

9. Wills, *Cincinnatus*, p. 132.

10. Conrad Cherry, *God's New Israel: Religious Interpretations of American Destiny* (Englewood Cliffs, N.J.: Prentice-Hall, 1971), p. 6.

11. Paul G. King, Kent Maynard, and David O. Woodyard, *Risking Liberation: Middle Class Powerlessness and Social Heroism* (Atlanta, Ga.: John Knox Press, 1988), p. 15.

12. Albert J. Raboteau, *Slave Religion* (New York: Oxford University Press, 1978), p. iv.

13. Martin Luther King Jr., "I Have A Dream," in *A Testament of Hope: The Essential Writings of Martin Luther King Jr.,* ed. James Melvin Washington (New York: Harper & Row, 1986), p. 219.

14. Ibid., p. 219.

15. Ibid., p. 217.

16. Cornel West, *Prophesy Deliverance! An Afro-American Revolutionary Christianity* (Philadelphia: Westminster, 1982), pp. 74–75.

17. These terms refer to the important works of James Scott. See especially *Domination and the Arts of Resistance* (New Haven: Yale University Press, 1990).

18. These Census Bureau figures are usually reported on annually by Robert Greenstein in *Christianity and Crisis*. For a good example of such reporting, see John Bickerman and Robert Greenstein, "High and Dry on the Poverty Plateau," *Christianity and Crisis*, October 28, 1985, pp. 411–412.

19. For example, the Supreme Court is now, in effect, "Reagan's Court," due to Reagan's appointees, who legally enact his conservative political agenda. For commentary on how the Supreme Court has turned back the clock on affirmative action, see my "Deaffirmation," *Nation,* July 3, 1989, pp. 4–5.

20. For a brief exploration of racism in both segments of society, see my article "The Two Racisms," *Nation,* July 3, 1989, pp. 4–5.

21. Washington, ed., *Testament of Hope*, p. 38.

22. Roger Hatch describes the relation between the perspective of the mature Martin Luther King Jr., and Jackson's vision for America, and addresses Jackson's evolution into the second phase of the civil rights movement, which concentrates on equity in every area of life (particularly economic justice), in *Beyond Opportunity: Jesse Jackson's Vision for America* (Philadelphia: Fortress Press, 1988), esp. pp. 11–23.

23. Washington, ed., *Testament of Hope,* pp. 67, 70.

CHAPTER 22. "GIVE ME A PAPER AND PEN": TUPAC'S PLACE IN HIP-HOP

1. Rose, *Black Noise;* Neal, *What the Music Said;* Boyd, *Am I Black Enough for You?* George, *Hip-Hop America.*

2. Sleeman, *Rambles and Recollection of an Indian Official,* and *Journey Through the Kingdom of Oude,* 1849–1850; Barren, *The Rastafarians;* Dyczkowski, *The Doctrine of Vibration.*

3. Hobsbawm, *Primitive Rebels* and *Bandits;* Seal, *The Outlaw Legend;* Duncan, *Romantic Outlaws, Beloved Prisons.*

4. Boccaccio, *Decameron.*

5. Davis and Troupe, *Miles: The Autobiography;* Carr, *Miles Davis: The Definitive Biography.*

6. Patillo-McCoy, *Black Picket Fences;* Massey and Demon, *American Apartheid;* Wilson, *The Truly Disadvantaged* and *When Work Disappears;* Kelley, *Yo' Mama's Disfunktional.*

7. Kasher, *The Civil Rights Movement;* Morris, *The Origins of the Civil Rights Movement;* Dittmer, *Local People;* Fairclough, *Race and Democracy;* Hine, *Hine Sight;* Giddings, *When and Where I Enter;* Garrow, *Bearing the Cross;* Carson, *In Struggle;* White, *Too Heavy a Load;* Norrell, *Reaping the Whirlwind;* Branch, *Parting the Waters* and *Pillar of Fire.*

8. Guralnick, *Sweet Soul Music;* Wolff, *You Send Me.*

CHAPTER 24. BETWEEN APOCALYPSE AND REDEMPTION: JOHN SINGLETON'S *BOYZ N THE HOOD*

1. These statistics, as well as an examination of the social, economic, political, medical, and educational conditions of young black men and public policy recommendations for the social amelioration of their desperate circumstances, are found in a collection of essays edited by Jewelle Taylor Gibbs, *Young, Black, and Male in America: An Endangered Species.*

2. William Julius Wilson has detailed the shift in the American political economy from manufacturing to service employment and its impact upon the inner city and the ghetto poor, particularly upon black males who suffer high rates of joblessness (which he sees as the source of many problems in the black family) in *The Truly Disadvantaged.* For an analysis of the specific problems of black males in relation to labor force participation, see Gerald David Jaynes and Robin M. Williams Jr., eds., *A Common Destiny,* pp. 301, 308–312.

3. I have explored the cultural expressions, material conditions, creative limits, and social problems associated with rap, in "Rap, Race and Reality," "The Culture of Hip-Hop," "2 Live Crew's Rap: Sex, Race and Class," "As Complex As They Wanna Be: 2 Live Crew," "Tapping into Rap," "Performance, Protest and Prophecy in the Culture of Hip-Hop," and in Jim Gardner, "Taking Rap Seriously: Theomusicologist Michael Eric Dyson on the New Urban Griots and Peripatetic Preachers (An Interview)" (see chap. 3, this volume).

4. I have in mind here the criticism of liberal society, and the forms of moral agency it both affords and prevents, that has been gathered under the rubric of communitarianism, ranging from MacIntyre's *After Virtue* to Bellah et al.'s *Habits of the Heart.*

5. I am indebted to Christine Stansell for this characterization of how Singleton departs from Capra's depictions of community in his films.

6. See Mike Davis and Sue Riddick's brilliant analysis of the drug culture in "Los Angeles: Civil Liberties between the Hammer and the Rock."

7. For an insightful discussion of the relationship between the underground or illegitimate economy, and people exercising agency in resisting the worse injustices and effects of the legitimate economy, see Don Nonini, "Everyday Forms of Popular Resistance."

8. For a recent exploration of the dynamics of social interaction between police as agents and symbols of mainstream communal efforts to regulate the behavior and social place of black men, and black men in a local community, see Elijah Anderson, *Streetwise*, pp. 163–206.

9. According to this logic, as expressed in a familiar saying in many black communities, black women "love their sons and raise their daughters." For a valiant, although flawed, attempt to get beyond a theoretical framework that implicitly blames black women for the condition of black men, see Clement Cottingham, "Gender Shift in Black Communities." Cottingham attempts to distance himself from arguments about a black matriarchy that stifles black male social initiative and moral responsibility. Instead he examines the gender shifts in black communities fueled by black female educational mobility and the marginalization of lower-class black males. But his attempt is weakened, ironically, by a prominently placed quotation by James Baldwin, which serves as a backdrop to his subsequent discussions of mother–son relationships, black male–female relationships, and black female assertiveness. Cottingham writes: "Drawing on Southern black folk culture, James Baldwin, in his last published work, alluded to black lower-class social patterns which, when set against the urban upheaval among the black poor from the 1960s onward, seem to encourage this gender shift. He characterizes these lower-class social patterns as 'a disease peculiar to the Black community called sorriness.' 'It is,' Baldwin observes, 'a disease that attacks black males. It is transmitted by Mama, whose instinct is to protect the Black male from the devastation that threatens him from the moment he declares himself a man.'

Apart from its protectiveness toward male children, Baldwin notes another dimension of 'sorriness.' 'Mama,' he writes, 'lays this burden on Sister from whom she expects (or indicates she expects) far more than she expects from Brother; but one of the results of this all too comprehensible dynamic is that Brother may never grow up—in which case the community has become an accomplice to the Republic.' Perceptively, Baldwin concludes that the differences in the socialization of boys and girls eventually erode the father's commitment to family life."

When such allusive but isolated ethnographic comments are not placed in an analytical framework that tracks the social, political, economic, religious, and historical forces that shape black (female) rearing practices and circumscribe black male–female relations, they are more often than not employed to blame black women for the social failure of black children, especially boys. The point here is not to suggest that black women have no responsibility for the plight of black families. But most social theory has failed to grapple with the complex set of forces that define and delimit black female existence, too easily relying upon anecdotal tales of black female behavior preventing black males from flourishing, and not examining the shifts in the political economy, the demise of low-skilled, high-waged work, the deterioration of the general moral infrastructure of many poor black communities, the ravaging of black communities by legal forces of gentrification, and illegal forces associated with crime and drugs, etc. These forces, and not black women, are the real villains.

10. For a perceptive analysis of the economic conditions that shape the lives of black women, see Julianne Malveaux, "The Political Economy of Black Women."

11. The peculiar pain that plagues the relationships between black men and black women across age, income, and communal strata was on bold and menacing display in the confrontation between Clarence Thomas and Anita Hill during Senate hearings to explore claims by Hill that Thomas sexually harassed her while she worked for him at two governmental agencies. Their confrontation was facilitated and constructed by the televisual medium, a ready metaphor for the technological intervention into contemporary relations between significant segments of the citizenry. Television also serves as the major mediator between various bodies of public officials and the increasingly narrow publics at whose behest they perform, thus blurring the distinctions between public good and private interest. The Hill-Thomas hearings also helped expose the wide degree to which the relations between black men and black women are shaped by a powerful white male gaze. In this case,

the relevant criteria for assessing the truth of claims about sexual harassment and gender oppression were determined by white senatorial surveillance.

12. Thus, it was unexceptional during the civil rights movement for strong, articulate black women to be marginalized, or excluded altogether, from the intellectual work of the struggle. Furthermore, concerns about feminist liberation were generally overlooked, and many talented, courageous women were often denied a strong or distinct institutional voice about women's liberation in the racial liberation movement. For a typical instance of such sexism within civil rights organizations, see Carson's discussion of black female dissent within SNCC, in Clayborne Carson, *In Struggle,* pp. 47–48.

13. For insightful claims and descriptions of the marginal status of black feminist and womanist concerns in black communities and for helpful explorations of the complex problems faced by black feminists and womanists, see bell hooks's *Ain't I a Woman;* Michele Wallace's *Invisibility Blues;* Audre Lorde's *Sister/Outsider;* and Alice Walker's *In Search of Our Mother's Garden.*

14. Of course, many traditional conceptions of virtue display a theoretical blindness to structural factors that circumscribe and influence the acquisition of traditional moral skills, habits, and dispositions and the development of alternative and non-mainstream moral skills. What I mean here is that the development of virtues, and the attendant skills that must be deployed in order to practice them effectively, is contingent upon several factors: where and when one is born, the conditions under which one must live, the social and communal forces that limit and define one's life, and so on. These factors color the character of moral skills that will be acquired, shape the way in which these skills will be appropriated, and even determine the list of skills required to live the good life in different communities. Furthermore, these virtues reflect the radically different norms, obligations, commitments, and socioethical visions of particular communities. For a compelling critique of MacIntyre's contextualist universalist claim for the prevalence of the virtues of justice, truthfulness, and courage in all cultures and the implications of such a critique for moral theory, see Alessandro Ferrara, "Universalisms: Procedural, Contextual, and Prudential." For an eloquent argument that calls for the authors of the communitarian social vision articulated in *Habits of the Heart* to pay attention to the life, thought, and contributions of people of color, see Vincent Harding, "Toward a Darkly Radiant Vision of America's Truth: A Letter of Concern, An Invitation to Re-Creation."

CHAPTER 33. MICHAEL JACKSON'S POSTMODERN SPIRITUALITY

1. See Larry Black, "The Man in the Mirror," *Maclean's,* May 2, 1988, p. 67; Michael Goldberg and David Handelman, "Is Michael Jackson for Real?" *Rolling Stone,* September 24, 1987, p. 55; Jay Cooks and Denise Worrell, "Bringing Back the Magic," *Time,* July 16, 1984, p. 63; and Jim Miller and Janet Huck, "The Peter Pan of Pop," *Newsweek,* January 10, 1983, pp. 52–54.

2. See Peter Petre, "The Traumas of Molding Crazes into Cash," *Fortune,* July 23, 1984, p. 48; Alex Ben Block, "Just One More Thriller," *Forbes 400,* October 1, 1984, pp. 232–234; "Michael Jackson Says 'Beat It' to Bootleggers," *Businessweek,* June 4, 1984, p. 36; and Goldberg and Handelman, "Is Michael Jackson for Real?" p. 140.

3. See, for example, "The Prisoner of Commerce," *New Republic,* April 16, 1984, p. 4.

4. For an explication of the European (especially French) contexts of postmodernism, see Jean-François Lyotard, *The Postmodern Condition: A Report on Knowledge,* trans. Geoff Bennington and Brian Massumi (Minneapolis: University of Minnesota Press, 1984); for an exploration of contemporary American postmodernism, see Hal Foster, ed., *The Anti-Aesthetic: Essays in Postmodern Culture* (Port Townsend, Wash.: Bay Press, 1983); see also Andreas Huyssen, *After the Great Divide: Modernism, Mass Culture, Postmodernism* (Bloomington: Indiana University Press, 1986); see also his essay, "Mapping the Postmodern," in *New German Critique* 33 (Fall 1984), for a historical situating of German, French, and American arguments on postmodernism. Also see the excellent collection of essays edited by Andrew Ross, *Universal Abandon? The Politics of Postmodernism* (Minneapolis: University of Minnesota Press, 1988).

5. Quoted in Richard Kearney, *The Wake of Imagination: Toward a Postmodern Culture* (Minneapolis: University of Minnesota Press, 1988).

6. Fredric Jameson, "Postmodernism or the Cultural Logic of Late Capitalism," *New Left Review*, no. 145 (1984): 53–91.

7. Anders Stephanson, "Regarding Postmodernism: A Conversation with Fredric Jameson," in *Universal Abandon? The Politics of Postmodernism*, ed. Andrew Ross (Minneapolis: University of Minnesota Press, 1988), pp. 1–12.

8. Cornel West, *Prophetic Fragments* (Trenton, N.J.: Africa World Press, 1988), pp. 168–170.

9. Hal Foster, *Postmodern Culture* (Concord, Mass.: Pluto, 1985), pp. xii–xiii.

10. Michael Jackson, *Moonwalk* (New York: Doubleday, 1988), p. 13. All future references will be cited in the text.

11. Cornel West makes this salient point about the use of a language of rights by African-American religionists involved in the civil rights movement, in West, *Prophetic Fragments*, pp. 22–24.

12. For a useful summary of the meaning of ritual in religious experience, see Leszek Kolakowski, *Religion* (New York: Oxford University Press, 1982), pp. 165–170.

13. For Bakhtin on carnival, see Mikhail Bakhtin, *Rabelais and His World* (Cambridge: Massachusetts Institute of Technology Press, 1968).

14. See Cornel West's insightful discussion of a Christian understanding of democracy in his *Prophesy Deliverance! An Afro-American Revolutionary Christianity* (Philadelphia: Westminster Press, 1982), especially the introduction and chapter 4.

15. Bakhtin, *Rabelais*, p. 10.

16. Michael Jackson, "Thriller," *Thriller*, Epic/CBS Records, 1983.

17. Michael Jackson, "Bad," *Bad*, Epic/CBS Records, 1987.

18. Michael Jackson, performer, "Man in the Mirror" (co-written by Siedah Garrett and George Ballard), *Bad*, Epic/CBS Records, 1987.

19. For a penetrating examination of rock music videos and a plausible way of categorizing MTV videos, see E. Ann Kaplan, *Rocking Around the Clock: Music Television, Postmodernism, and Consumer Culture* (New York: Methuen, 1987), esp. chap. 4. Many of Jackson's videos are more closely akin to short films, and thus demand a reading that regards them as such. Also, the religious, cultural, and racial contexts of Jackson's video films must be examined, as I attempt in my analysis of two of Jackson's video films and of a live performance on the 1988 Grammy's telecast.

20. For the effect of Niebuhr on King's thought, see his essay, "Pilgrimage to Nonviolence," in *A Testament of Hope: The Essential Writings of Martin Luther King Jr.*, ed. James M. Washington (San Francisco: Harper & Row, 1986), pp. 35–36.

21. Goldberg and Handelman, "Is Michael Jackson for Real?" p. 138.

22. Robert Sam Anson, *Best Intentions: The Education and Killing of Edmund Perry* (New York: Random House, 1987). For a hard-hitting, highly critical review essay of Anson's book, see Michael Dyson, "Edmund Perry: The Help That Hurts," *Christianity and Crisis* 48 (1988): 17–21, expanded as "The Liberal Theory of Race," chap. 9, this volume.

CHAPTER 34. BE LIKE MIKE? MICHAEL JORDAN AND THE PEDAGOGY OF DESIRE

1. I do not mean here a theory of commodification that does not accentuate the forms of agency that can function even within restrictive and hegemonic cultural practices. Rather, I think that, contrary to elitist and overly pessimistic Frankfurt School readings of the spectacle of commodity within mass cultures, common people can exercise "everyday forms of resistance" to hegemonic forms of cultural knowledge and practice. For an explication of the function of everyday forms of resistance, see Scott, *Domination and the Arts of Resistance*.

2. For a critical look at Jordan behind the myth, see Sam Smith, *The Jordan Rules* (New York: Simon & Schuster, 1992).

CREDITS

Chapter   Previous Publication

18.   **When You Divide Body and Soul, Problems Multiply: The Black Church and Sexuality.** From *Race Rules: Navigating the Color Line* (Reading, MA: Addison-Wesley, 1996), pp. 77–108.

19.   **Homotextualities.** From *Open Mike: Reflections on Philosophy, Race, Sex, Culture and Religion* (New York: Basic*Civitas*, 2003), pp. 360–384.

20.   **X Marks the Plots: A Critical Reading of Malcolm's Readers.** From *Making Malcolm: The Myth and Meaning of Malcolm X* (New York: Oxford University Press, 1995), pp. 21–76. Originally published in *Social Text* 35, Spring 1993, pp. 25–55.

21.   **Mixed Blessings: Martin Luther King, Jr., and the Lessons of an Ambiguous Heroism.** From *Reflecting Black: African-American Cultural Criticism* (Minneapolis, MN: University of Minnesota Press), pp. 221–246. Originally published in earlier form in *Union Seminary Quarterly Review*, Vol. 44, Nos. 1–2, 1990, pp. 85–99.

22.   **"Give Me a Paper and Pen": Tupac's Place in Hip-Hop.** From *Holler If You Hear Me: Searching for Tupac Shakur* (New York: Basic*Civitas*, 2001), pp. 105–139.

23.   **Spike Lee's Neonationalist Vision.** From *Reflecting Black: African-American Cultural Criticism* (Minneapolis, MN: University of Minnesota Press), pp. 23–31. Originally published in *Tikkun*, Vol. 4, No. 5, September/October 1989, pp. 75–78.

24.   **Between Apocalypse and Redemption: John Singleton's *Boyz N the Hood*.** From *Reflecting Black: African-American Cultural Criticism* (Minneapolis, MN: University of Minnesota Press), pp. 90–110. Originally published in *Film Theory Goes To The Movies*. Ed. Jim Collins et al (New York: Routledge, 1993), pp. 209–226.

25.   **Ghettocentricity and the New Black Cinema.** From *The Subversive Imagination: Artists, Society and Social Responsibility*. Ed. Carol Becker (New York: Routledge, 1994), pp. 154–167.

26.   **The Promise and Perils of Contemporary Gospel Music.** From *Reflecting Black: African-American Cultural Criticism* (Minneapolis, MN: University of Minnesota Press), pp. 322–327. Originally published in *The New York Times*, December 22, 1991, pp. 30–31.

27.   **Mariah Carey and "Authentic" Black Music.** From *Between God and Gangsta Rap: Bearing Witness to Black Culture* (New York: Oxford University Press, 1996), pp. 143–146. Originally published in *The New York Times*, February 13, 1994, Section 2 (Arts & Leisure), p. 30.

28.   **Aretha Franklin, Vanessa Bell Armstrong, and Me.** From *Why I Love Black Women* (New York: Basic*Civitas*, 2003), pp. 46–56.

29.   **The Great Next: Jazz Origins and the Anatomy of Improvisation.** From *Open Mike: Reflections on Philosophy, Race, Sex, Culture and Religion* (New York: Basic*Civitas*, 2003), pp. 179–206.

30.   **The Culture of Hip-Hop.** From *Reflecting Black: African-American Cultural Criticism* (Minneapolis, MN: University of Minnesota Press), pp. 3–15. Originally published in *Z Magazine*, June 1989.

31.   **Gangsta Rap and American Culture.** From *Between God and Gangsta Rap: Bearing Witness to Black Culture* (New York: Oxford University Press, 1996), pp. 176–186.

32.   **We Never Were What We Used to Be: Black Youth, Pop Culture, and the Politics of Nostalgia.** From *Race Rules: Navigating the Color Line* (Reading, MA: Addison-Wesley, 1996), pp. 109–149.

33.   **Michael Jackson's Postmodern Spirituality.** From *Reflecting Black: African-American Cultural Criticism* (Minneapolis, MN: University of Minnesota Press), pp. 35–60. Originally published in *Black Sacred Music: A Journal of Theomusicology*, Vol. 3, No. 2, Fall 1989, pp. 98–124.

34.   **Be Like Mike? Michael Jordan and the Pedagogy of Desire.** From *Reflecting Black: African-American Cultural Criticism* (Minneapolis, MN: University of Minnesota Press), pp. 64–75. Originally published in *Cultural Studies*, Vol. 7, No. 1, January 1993, pp. 64–72.

35.   **Is Postmodernism Just Modernism in Drag?** From *Open Mike: Reflections on Philosophy, Race, Sex, Culture and Religion* (New York: Basic*Civitas*, 2003), pp. 151–178.

36.   **It's Not What You Know, It's How You Show It: Black Public Intellectuals.** From *Race Rules: Navigating the Color Line* (Reading, MA: Addison-Wesley, 1996), pp. 47–76.

INDEX